KU-605-457

We Don't Know Ourselves

Fintan O'Toole is the author of *Heroic Failure*, *Ship of Fools*, *A Traitor's Kiss*, *White Savage* and other acclaimed books. He is a columnist for the *Irish Times* and the Milberg Professor of Irish Letters at Princeton University. He writes regularly for the *Guardian*, *New York Review of Books*, the *New York Times* and other British and American journals.

BY THE SAME AUTHOR

Meanwhile Back at the Ranch

White Savage

A Traitor's Kiss

Ship of Fools

Enough is Enough

Judging Shaw

Heroic Failure

Three Years in Hell

FINTAN O'TOOLE

We Don't Know Ourselves

A Personal History of Ireland Since 1958

An Apollo Book

First published in the UK in 2021 by Head of Zeus Ltd
An Apollo book

9 7 6 8

A catalogue record for this book is available from
the British Library.

ISBN (HB): 9781784978297
ISBN (E): 9781784978280

Typeset by Ben Cracknell Studios

Printed and bound in Great Britain by
CPI Group (UK) Ltd, Croydon CR0 4YY

Head of Zeus Ltd
First Floor East
5–8 Hardwick Street
London EC1R 4RG

WWW.HEADOFZEUS.COM

Contents

PRELUDE The Loneliest Boy in the World 1
CHAPTER 1 1958: On Noah's Ark 7
CHAPTER 2 1959: Modern Family 44
CHAPTER 3 1960: Comanche Country 53
CHAPTER 4 1961: Balubaland 64
CHAPTER 5 1962: Cathode Ní Houlihan 80
CHAPTER 6 1963: The Dreamy Movement of the Stairs 93
CHAPTER 7 1962–1999: Silence and Smoothness. 105
CHAPTER 8 1965: Our Boys 114
CHAPTER 9 1966: The GPO Trouser Suit 132
CHAPTER 10 1967: The Burial of Leopold Bloom 153
CHAPTER 11 1968: Requiem. 158
CHAPTER 12 1969: Frozen Violence 174
CHAPTER 13 1970: The Killer Chord 183
CHAPTER 14 1971: Little Plum. 196
CHAPTER 15 1972: Death of a Nationalist 216
CHAPTER 16 1973: Into Europe 235
CHAPTER 17 1976: The Walking Dead 250
CHAPTER 18 1975–1980: Class Acts 255
CHAPTER 19 1971–1983: Bungalow Bliss 262
CHAPTER 20 1979: Bona Fides. 275

CHAPTER 21 1980–1981: No Blue Hills 290
CHAPTER 22 1980–1981: A Beggar on Horseback 304
CHAPTER 23 1979–1982: The Body Politic 318
CHAPTER 24 1981–1983: Foetal Attractions 336
CHAPTER 25 1982: Wonders Taken For Signs 351
CHAPTER 26 1984–1985: Dead Babies and Living Statues 357
CHAPTER 27 1987–1991: As Oil Is to Texas. 370
CHAPTER 28 1986–1992: Internal Exiles 380
CHAPTER 29 1989: Freaks 392
CHAPTER 30 1985–1992: Conduct Unbecoming 405
CHAPTER 31 1990–1992: Mature Recollection. 416
CHAPTER 32 1992: Not So Bad Myself 431
CHAPTER 33 1992–1994: Meanwhile Back at the Ranch 440
CHAPTER 34 1993: True Confessions 451
CHAPTER 35 1993–1994: Angel Paper. 464
CHAPTER 36 1998: The Uses of Uncertainty. 476
CHAPTER 37 1990–2015: America at Home 490
CHAPTER 38 1990–2000: Unsuitables from a Distance 499
CHAPTER 39 1999: The Cruelty Man 511
CHAPTER 40 1997–2008: The Makeover 522
CHAPTER 41 2000–2008: Tropical Ireland 533
CHAPTER 42 2009–2013: Jesus Fucking Hell and God 549
CHAPTER 43 2018– : Negative Capability 560

Acknowledgements 571
Notes 572
Credits. 599
Index 600

To Kieran, Valerie and Patrick
and in memory of Mary and Colm

PRELUDE

The Loneliest Boy in the World

At Christmas 1948, ten years before my own birth, two wise men came bearing gifts for a child born in a humble cabin. Yet this child was seen as a harbinger, not of the birth of a new world, but of the death of an old one. He was called Gearóid Ó Catháin, and he was the only child left on the Blasket Islands, off the coast of Co. Kerry. The Blaskets were famous as a remnant of an old Gaelic world, a vestige of an ancient way of life. The community had a remarkable late flourishing of literary self-expression in the autobiographical books of Tomás Ó Criomhthain, Peig Sayers, Muiris Ó Súileabháin and other islanders. For Irish nationalists, it was a microcosm of the distinctive culture they had promised to revive – hardy, simple, pious, but rich in memories and dense with stories and songs in the Irish language.

Now, though, it was a microcosm of something else: the disappearance of the Irish world. The life blood of the islands was draining away westward, as the people emigrated, in particular to Springfield, Massachusetts, where they found work in the blast furnaces and cloth mills. The 'names of places spoken of by those who went and returned' were now American addresses: Van Horn Park and Chicopee, Indian Orchard and Watershops Pond.[1] This seemed to be, not just their specific fate, but that of Ireland as a whole. The writer Honor Tracy, visiting the Great Blasket round this time, called its ruined cottages 'miniatures of the ruins lying about all over Ireland'.[2]

The wise men who came with gifts for Gearóid Ó Catháin were a reporter, Liam Robinson, and a photographer from the *Irish Press*, the newspaper owned by the man who had dominated Irish politics for thirty years, Eamon de Valera, who was Taoiseach (prime minister) for most of the 1930s, 1940s and 1950s. Robinson framed his story as the swansong, not just of an offshore village, but of an epoch spanning millennia, making little Gearóid the 'heir to a civilisation and island home that is dying. He will be remembered as a last link with the Hidden Ireland.'[3] Later, as the child acquired an almost mythic status, the *Irish Press* would call him, 'the last child… on a dying island that is the last outpost of the Celtic Empire'.[4] Gearóid was the Last of the Mohicans.

On that first pre-Christmas trip, the reporter laid at his feet toys, 'bootees and things on wheels' and recorded the sounds, in his infant's Irish, that expressed his wonderment.

Robinson's story was taken up by international newspapers, often under the headline 'The Loneliest Boy in the World'. Readers moved by his plight sent gifts for Gearóid. As he told Bob Quinn in 1993, 'I got parcels from Australia and from New Zealand and from America'. In 1949 he got 'trains, cars, trucks, every sort of book… clothes and shoes. There was no stop to them. In the middle of that year my name was on everyone's lips as if I were a film star.' Patrick Fitzgerald, a rancher in Minnesota who read the story in a local paper, wrote to his parents. 'He told them he had lost two children in their tender years and that he and his wife would like to adopt Gearóid, who in time would inherit their property.'[5] When the parents declined the offer, Fitzgerald offered to take the whole family to Minnesota. The *Irish Press* reported in 1951 that 'On the wall of the cottage where he was born hangs a big framed picture of New York'. Asked in 1951 what would become of him, Gearóid replied, 'raghad go 'Merica' – I will go to America.

When the islands were finally abandoned by their dwindling population in November 1953, there were reasons to fear what their fate might portend for the wider project of Irish independence. Thirty years earlier, after a decade of turbulence and violence, the Irish Free State had emerged in twenty-six of the island's thirty-two counties, the other six north-eastern counties formed into the new entity of Northern Ireland, dominated by its Protestant majority and still part of the United Kingdom. In 1948, when Gearóid became famous, the Free State officially declared itself a republic and cut its last formal times with Britain. It was unquestionably now a sovereign state, with its destiny in its own hands.

It was ruled by two virtually identical nationalist political parties that emerged from the civil war of 1923, Fine Gael and – by far the most successful – the Fianna Fáil party of de Valera, last surviving commandant of the Easter Rising of 1916 that ignited the revolutionary movement. Both parties were fervently Catholic, deeply respectful of the right of the church hierarchy to make binding rulings on all questions of morality, especially those relating to reproduction and sexuality. Both claimed as a priority the revival of the Irish language as the vernacular of the people – and both equally did nothing to stop the death of Irish-speaking communities like that on the Blaskets. Both saw the Irish economy as essentially agrarian and Irish society as properly rural. Both insisted that partition was a great sin and that the lost six counties must be restored to make Ireland whole again. Neither did very much thinking about how this might happen.

This apparent unanimity of purpose concealed, however, a much deeper contradiction. The state was supposed to be autonomous and sharply defined and the longer it was established the more so it ought to have become. In truth, it felt ever more powerless and increasingly blurry. Ireland remained neutral in the Second World War and emerged into the world of the post-war boom as a backwater and an irrelevance. Its economic backwardness meant that it could not contain itself – its people, like those of the Blaskets, were leaving for the very thing a holy and romantic Ireland could not provide: ordinary urban, industrial modernity. Given a choice between being the Last of the Mohicans or living in Indian Orchard, Springfield, they were voting with their feet.

In 1959, the year after I was born, and the first year of a radical programme to try to save Ireland by modernizing its economy, the British astronomer Fred Hoyle published *Ossian's Ride*. The novel is a strange mixture of science fiction and John Buchan-style adventure story. In it, it is now 1970. The narrator Thomas

Sherwood, a young English mathematician, is summoned by British intelligence and sent on a mission to penetrate the headquarters of ICE, the Industrial Corporation of Éire, a fictionalized version of the actual IDA, the Industrial Development Authority which was given the task of attracting foreign investment to Ireland. The nature of ICE is explained to Sherwood: 'ICE came into being some twelve years ago. A small group of very able scientists approached the government of Éire with what seemed an entirely straightforward proposition. The proposal was to establish an industry for the extraction of a range of chemicals from the organic material in peat – turf as the Irish call it... Within a short time, ICE was producing an amazing range of valuable chemicals ostensibly from turf as raw material, although whether this was really so is open to doubt.'[6]

ICE, like the companies attracted by the real IDA, has been given a ten-year tax holiday by the Irish government. After its fourth year, however, it makes an immensely profitable breakthrough. It invents a contraceptive pill which it apparently manufactures from turf. After this ICE switches from chemistry to physics, and Ireland becomes an industrial, and potentially a military, superpower. The old world powers need to know what is going on and Sherwood is sent as a spy.

When he asks why the Catholic Church didn't stop the creation of the Pill, his handler replies, 'Ridicule, my boy. If I may parody the poet Schiller: "Against laughter even the Hierarchy fights in vain." Think of it, contraceptives from turf! For decades the church had fulminated against their use while all the time outside every cottage there'd been piled a whole mountain of the stuff.'[7]

Sherwood, on his trip to the future Ireland sees, in Dublin, a city that is being 'systematically demolished and rebuilt'. He witnesses the arrival of television and summarizes remarkably well the impact that it would actually have in Ireland a few years after Hoyle's book was published: 'It seemed as if two different worlds had come into sharp conflict.'

Sherwood discovers that ICE has sealed off the south-west corner of Ireland – Kerry, West Cork and Limerick – as its own territory. Its holy of holies, the inner sanctum where the head scientists are based and from which they have organized their futuristic enterprise to make Ireland the centre of the modern world, is the Blasket island of Inishvicillaun. In 1959, when Hoyle was writing his fantasia, it was uninhabited, but later it was occupied as a holiday home by Charles Haughey, the corrupt Taoiseach of the 1980s and early 1990s, who saw himself as the great leader of Irish industrial modernity and father of the Celtic Tiger boom that followed him.

The architects of ICE are, of course, aliens. Having taken human form, they came to the Blasket Islands from a distant imploding planet, bringing with them the knowledge accumulated by their vastly more advanced civilization. For Hoyle's original British readers there may have been a certain reassurance in knowing that the charming Irish scatterbrains Sherwood encounters couldn't really work out all that complicated mathematics and technology on their own. Yet here too there was a metaphorical ring of truth. The transformation of Ireland over the last sixty years has sometimes felt as if a new world had landed from outer space on top of an old one.

In 2004, the release of state papers from 1973 revealed that in that year an American rocket scientist, Gary Hudson, approached the Irish consul in Chicago with a detailed plan to build a space station on another of the Blaskets, Inishnabro. He intended to use it for the launching of a commercial space shuttle. He claimed to represent a group of scientists and investors, including an astronaut 'who walked on the moon' and 'British astronomer Sir Frederick Hoyle'. Civil servants in Dublin dismissed the idea as possibly 'a gigantic leg-pull'.[8] In fact Hudson was a genuine pioneer in commercial space flight. And by the time his proposal was revealed in 2004, stranger things had happened in Ireland.

1

1958: On Noah's Ark

My parents' wedding photographs always remind me of a frontier town in an old Western. To prise open the mock mother-of-pearl covers of the wedding album is to enter a world of strange contrasts. There they are, elegant and radiant, wrapped in the proud formality of the 1950s, my mother's elaborate white dress and veil, the clean lines of my father's bespoke suit. They are emblems of a great continuity, of a seriousness and respectability forged over generations of struggle against squalor and despair, against poverty and violence. Their adamant dignity sparkles like a diamond hard-won from the dirt.

What gives the pictures their air of *High Noon*, though, of a respectable wedding threatened by the dangers of a frontier town, is the setting. The Catholic church that forms the background to the photographs should be dark with gothic curves, or bright with baroque tracery, but is merely dull with the blank stare of unadorned concrete blocks. It is not really a chapel at all, but a temporary shed slapped up to serve a raw new suburb while the proper church is being built. It may have been consecrated by the wave of a bishop's hand, but it is unconsecrated by those holier things, by the skill of craftsmen or by the hopes and aspirations, the dreads and supplications, of dead generations. The place looks like what it is: transitional. It has been there for eleven years, a dreary substitute for the real thing, which was being built up the road at enormous cost, with seating for 1,700 worshippers at a time.[1]

There is no history here. Some kind of displacement is happening, but no new place has yet come into being. It is not just that those rough walls look unfinished. It is that they will never be finished. They merely await their inevitable demolition. Just as they have no past, they are not intended to have a future. They make my parents seem like settlers in an unmapped territory, their wedding staking a claim in land for which there are as yet no title deeds.

And yet the strange thing about them is that they were not emigrants, merely colonists in a new kind of Irish landscape. The temporary church was a few minutes' walk from the house on Aughavannagh Road into which my mother had moved with her family seven years previously, in 1948. It was part of the Crumlin housing estate, a big web of narrow roads, lined by largely identical two-storey working-class dwellings, spun out of the countryside south-west of Dublin city. They were not planning to live there at first. But they were also not planning to live in the place to which so many Irish people of their age were looking – elsewhere, abroad, away.

In September 1957, when my mother was four months pregnant with me, the satirical magazine *Dublin Opinion* ran a cartoon on its cover. A young woman identified as Ireland is speaking urgently to a fortune teller: 'Get to work! They're saying I've no future.'[2] The future, as it might be lived out on the island, seemed to very many people a void, a nullity. Yet, my father at twenty-five and my mother at twenty-seven, planted a foot in it by getting married. They must have been able to look into that fortune teller's crystal ball and see something worthwhile. Or maybe, as I always suspected, my mother saw it and my father, who couldn't quite believe that she was marrying him, just saw her.

My father had a job as a bus conductor, taking fares and keeping order on his routes from the southern suburbs into Dublin city. He had a dark blue uniform and a cap with an oddly boat-shaped badge in regal purple trimmed with silver that said CIE, Córas Iompair Éireann, which meant Irish Transport System in the indigenous language he did not speak and that Irish governments had been trying without success to revive as the vernacular for thirty years. But before he met my mother, he had filled out the papers for emigration to Canada. He had cousins there. Most of his brothers and sisters were in England. My mother, who worked in the Player Wills cigarette factory half a mile away from Aughavannagh Road, didn't want to leave. Except for a sister who was a nun in India, and her youngest brother, who settled in Manchester, her family tended to stay in Ireland.

So, she and my father did not emigrate. They got married. And both of these things, in the Ireland of the mid-1950s, were unusual. A few years later, my father wrote down the addresses of his siblings. Eileen and Paddy were in Dublin. The rest were – Kevin: Bicknor Road, Maidstone, Kent, England; Rita: Ruddington Way, Newtown, Birmingham, England; Jean: 'somewhere in London'; Seamus: Ossington Buildings, Mescon Street, London, England; Mary: 'somewhere in Australia!'; Carmel: Glenthorne Street, Hammersmith, London, England. He added the first cousin to whom he had been very close – Vincent: Fircroft College, Selly Oak, Birmingham, England.

As for marriage, it was more unusual in Ireland than anywhere else in the world. Ireland was one of the most Catholic countries on earth, and the church preached that the family based on marriage between a man and a woman was a sacred thing, an earthly reflection of the Holy Family. But in reality Ireland had a 'shockingly low' marriage rate – statisticians could not find a comparable country. It also had Europe's lowest proportion of women in the population, because women got out in even larger numbers than men did.[3] Census figures published two years before my parents' wedding showed that 'the percentages unmarried of all age groups were still the highest in the world'.[4]

This was just about beginning to change. On the day before my parents' wedding the front page of the *Irish Times* carried the headline: 'Slight Increase in Marriage Rates'.[5] The rate had risen from 7.4 per 1,000 people to 7.5. It was not the kind of statistical blip most people noticed. The mood was too bleak. *Dublin Opinion* had created a visual image of it on its cover in July 1956: the island with nothing on it except a sign saying 'Shortly Available: Undeveloped Country, Unrivalled Opportunities, Magnificent Views, Political and Otherwise, Owners Going Abroad'. One of those most struck by it was the recently appointed secretary of the Department of Finance, T. K. Whitaker, who began work on a document that would shape my life. He later recalled: 'As far as I remember, the immediate stimulus was seeing a cover of *Dublin Opinion*.'[6]

The image may have been powerful enough to have momentous effects, but it was wrong in one respect. It was not the owners who were going abroad. Ireland was owned very securely and very comfortably by a post-revolutionary political elite, by a well-heeled professional class, by big cattle ranchers, and above all by the hierarchy of the Catholic Church. The state founded in revolution and civil war had become remarkably stable. But it was a stability sustained by radical instability – to keep it as it was, huge parts of the population had to emigrate, for otherwise the sheer weight of their discontented numbers would drag it down.

This created a surreal disjunction. 'Ireland', as a notion, was almost suffocatingly coherent and fixed: Catholic, nationalist, rural. This was the Platonic form of the place. But Ireland as a lived experience was incoherent and unfixed. The first Ireland was bounded, protected, shielded from the unsavoury influence of the outside world. The second was unbounded, shifting, physically on the move to that outside world. In the space between these two Irelands, there was a haunted emptiness, a sense of something so unreal that it might disappear completely.

I was born on Sunday, 16 February 1958. Three events of that weekend can serve as portholes into this strangeness. Two days before I arrived, the committee of the Dublin Theatre Festival, which was due to be staged in May, decided to drop *Bloomsday*, a planned adaptation of James Joyce's *Ulysses*, from its programme. 'The board, it is understood, felt that recent "adverse publicity" which had followed the expression of disapproval by the Most Rev. Dr. McQuaid, Archbishop of Dublin, made the production of *Bloomsday* inadvisable.' McQuaid, one of the most powerful figures in Ireland, had made his displeasure known by refusing a request from the organizers to have the opening of the festival marked by the celebration of a special votive Mass.

The author of the adaptation, Alan MacClelland, was particularly disappointed because 'I had the play vetted by an authority on moral dogma and I was advised on any blasphemous passages, which I naturally agreed to cut.' Hilton Edwards, who had been due to direct the staging at the Gate Theatre, said that he was 'not surprised' because 'as always there has been a rigid censorship of plays, as of everything else'. He accepted the decision with resignation – 'All right. I am no rebel. If the people of this city think it is not for them, I am not upset.' He added that the festival would now 'end up in the kind of silly joke for the rest of the world that most things have that happened here. Everyone will feel very smug and very pure here, and they will be wrong as usual.'[7]

Sean O'Casey, whose new play *The Drums of Father Ned* had also been dropped because he refused to make alterations, had a similar response: 'The dropping of the plays will be a subject of ridicule all over the world.' (O'Casey subsequently banned the production of all of his plays in Ireland during his lifetime.) Over the weekend, Samuel Beckett withdrew three mime plays and a reading of his radio play *All That Fall* from the festival in protest at the Archbishop's interventions against O'Casey and Joyce. Within a few days, the entire festival would be 'postponed' – in effect abandoned.[8]

There was, though, one deliciously farcical little afterpiece. It emerged that the Lord Mayor of Dublin had been advised by his (Catholic) chaplain that there was nothing objectionable about staging *Ulysses*, since it was 'a story known to everybody'. This was taken to suggest that there might, after all, be some little tinge of liberalism within the church. But 'it didn't become clear until much later that he was confusing Homer's Ulysses with that of James Joyce'.[9]

While my mother was in labour, five or six masked men from the clandestine Irish Republican Army (IRA) that claimed descent from the rebels of 1916 raided a British army training camp in Blandford, Dorset, brandishing revolvers. They shot the sentry in the stomach and bound and gagged ten young soldiers, all of them raw conscripts, in the guardroom. It was very easy: the guards' rifles were not loaded. But the men then drove off in a rented Hillman Hunter without taking any weapons or doing any damage. One of the raiders muttered to a soldier he was tying up,

'This is with the compliments of the IRA'. Another was strangely dressed in an army greatcoat and blue trousers, with a red stripe down the seam, like part of an archaic dress uniform from an earlier time, as if he were playing a soldier in an old melodrama.[10]

The raid would be treated with great jollity when it was discussed in the House of Commons a few days later, with the veteran Labour politician Manny Shinwell teasing the newly appointed secretary of state for war Christopher Soames, amid general laughter, that this was 'the first battle in which he has been engaged' and asking, 'Do you regard this as a success for the War Office?'[11] But it had a haunting coda. The next day, some of his fellow soldiers at the Blandford camp teased Corporal William Courtney – 'You're Irish, better give yourself up.' Courtney, who was fifty-one and a trainer with the Corps of Royal Electrical and Mechanical Engineers, was from the Moy in Co. Tyrone. A few minutes later, Courtney was walking past his company's office when he dropped stone dead.[12] An officer remarked that 'Perhaps the excitement of the previous day affected him'.[13]

There was just one person involved in the raid whose identity was known and who could, apparently, make sense of the event. A soldier at the camp, Corporal Frank Skuse, mysteriously disappeared the night before the raid. Police launched a large-scale hunt for Skuse and described him in breathlessly admiring terms as a handsome man with 'a smart military bearing… a pleasant manner, a very clear voice, and athletic physique'.[14] They made him sound like the hero of an action movie.

He was found three months later, however, not in England, but in Ireland and not as Frank Skuse. He had been imprisoned for the unlawful possession of arms and for refusing to account for his movements, but under a different identity, that of an Irishman, Paul Murphy.[15] As the Irish newspapers would report in May, 'Red haired, six-foot tall British Army Corporal Frank Skuse, wanted by police in England since the raid on the Army camp at Blandford, Dorset, last February, has been located in the most unlikely of places – as a political prisoner in Mountjoy Jail' in Dublin.[16]

Skuse's double identity came to light when he became involved in a confrontation with prison warders while an attempt at a mass breakout by IRA prisoners was under way. 'While he was being forced to his cell, he began shouting, displaying traces of an English accent. When calm had settled once again within the prison walls the warders reported what they had heard. Inquiries were made by the authorities, thus solving the mystery of the whereabouts and the history of the man.' Yet in the descriptions of Skuse issued by the English police after the Blandford raid, it was made clear that he 'speaks with a Cork accent'.[17]

The story made no sense – was Skuse really Murphy or Murphy really Skuse and which accent, the English one or the Irish one, betrayed his real self? Intriguingly, when an attempt was made to spring Skuse/Murphy from St Bricin's Military Hospital in May, the IRA denied having any part in it and alleged that 'if such an attempt was, in fact, made, it was the work of British secret agents'.[18] But the mystery added to the surreal feeling of the event, the sense of an old history replaying itself as performance. Skuse later revealed that he had escaped from England by disguising himself in 'a conservative suit with a copy of the *Financial Times* sticking out of his pocket'.[19] Perhaps a theatre festival was not necessary after all.

While I was being born, the Irish government's leading modernizer, the minister for industry and commerce Seán Lemass, left Dublin Airport for Paris to take part in two days of discussions about whether Ireland would or could join a proposed European Free Trade Area (EFTA). The previous year, the Treaty of Rome, signed by six countries – Germany, France, Italy, Holland, Belgium and Luxembourg – had established the European Communities, also known as the Common Market. Britain had stood aside but was now pushing for the creation of a wider zone of economic co-operation between the Six and the other European countries that were outside the Soviet-dominated Warsaw Pact bloc. If EFTA were established, Ireland would have to make momentous decisions about its future: to open itself to free trade or remain as a protected but even more isolated space.

Each of these three events encapsulated one or other of the great tensions of the place I was born into. The abandoned theatre festival was supposed to be part of An Tóstal (The Gathering), a much larger series of events that had been organized at Easter each year since 1953. Its origins lay in a memorandum submitted to Lemass by the president of Pan American Airlines in 1951. He suggested that in order to boost tourism, the country should market to Irish-Americans a festival called Ireland at Home. It should include a 'world cup' of the native Irish sports, hurling and Gaelic football; a contest in Ireland and Irish-America for the perfect Irish colleen, to be judged by the Hollywood stars Maureen O'Hara and Maureen O'Sullivan (Jane to Johnny Weissmuller's Tarzan); a season of classic Irish plays at the Abbey Theatre; and the creation near Shannon Airport of a theme park to be called Valley of the Fairies or Home of the Leprechauns.[20]

Such was the strange state of Ireland that many of Pan Am's proposals were in fact adopted, albeit in toned-down versions. The Irish colleen competition became The Rose of Tralee festival. The theme park near Shannon became Bunratty folk park. The Abbey season became the Dublin Theatre Festival. There were also attractions like the Golden Golf Ball competition and a pageant characterized by the great satirist Flann O'Brien (writing in the *Irish Times* as its columnist Myles na Gopaleen) as a 'military tattoo with banshees, pookas in nightshirts, leprechauns and lady pipers'.[21]

All of this was supposed to connect Ireland with its diaspora in America, usually said to number twenty million people – and, more importantly, with its dollars. It failed: Irish-Americans did not answer the call of 'home' in significant numbers. But if Boston and New York were among Ireland's Elsewheres, there were many others. Three out of five children growing up in Ireland in the 1950s were destined to leave at some point in their lives, mostly for the shelter of the old colonial power, England. In 1957, the year before I was born, almost 60,000 people emigrated.[22] This was the latest episode in a slow, relentless demographic disaster. In 1841, the population of what became the twenty-six-county Irish state was 6.5 million. In 1961, it would hit its lowest ever total of 2.8 million. By that year, a scarcely imaginable 45 per cent of all those born in Ireland between 1931 and 1936 and 40 per cent of those born between 1936 and 1941 had left.[23]

The idea of disappearance hung over the place. A biblical image of post-war Ireland as an island submerged beneath the Atlantic occurred to very different people. John McGahern, working on a London building site, sat over lunch with a young Co. Clare man reading in his newspaper of another wet Irish summer. Prayers were being offered at Masses for the rains to cease but the young emigrant added his own supplication: 'May it never stop. May they all have to climb trees. May it rise higher than it did for fukken Noah!'[24] He was unknowingly echoing an earlier exile, Bernard Shaw, who, when the Republic of Ireland was officially inaugurated at Easter 1949, was asked by the *Irish Times* to comment on whether it was a step forward or backwards for Ireland's development. He replied: 'Ask me five years hence. If our terrible vital statistics improve to a civilized level then our steps will have been steps forward. If not, then there will be nothing for us but the ancient prescription of the submergence of the island for ten minutes in the Irish sea.'[25]

Another Nobel prize-winner, the German novelist Heinrich Böll, sat by the fire in Achill, on the outer edge of Co. Mayo, and mused that 'the Atlantic persistently carries away piece by piece the Western bastion of Europe; rocks fall into the sea, soundlessly the bog streams carry the dark European soil out into the Atlantic; over the years, gently plashing, they smuggle whole fields out to the open sea, crumb by crumb'.[26]

While Pan Am and An Tóstal were trying to attract tourists from the US, dispatches from American reporters did not make the place sound like anyone's idea of fun. Arthur Vesey of the *Chicago Tribune* conjured scenes of both rural and urban desolation for his readers: 'All is so still among the piles of stone which were once the cottages of the Irish who have gone away... Walk the back streets of Limerick, of Galway or other important centres and you see whole buildings abandoned. Some villages of the west are also half derelict.'[27] The American-based theatre critic and director Eric Bentley compared Dublin unfavourably to the bombed-out cities of post-war Europe: 'Few of the ruined cities of the Continent seem anything like as far gone as Dublin. Any who look beyond the elegant eighteenth-century squares and the lovely rural environs are bound to find it the drabbest capital in Europe.'[28]

In March 1954, small, enigmatic ads began to appear in the *Irish Times*. All they said was Coming – The Vanishing Irish.[29] These cryptic messages, like the sandwich boards of apocalyptic preachers, seemed to be a warning to the Irish to prepare to meet their doom. In fact they were trailers for the serialization of a book edited under that title by an American Catholic priest, John O'Brien. Its tenor was indicated in O'Brien's opening essay: 'If the past century's rate of decline continues, the Irish will virtually disappear as a nation, and will be found only as an enervated remnant in a land occupied by foreigners... Today Ireland is teetering perilously on the brink of near extinction...'[30]

Asked about the book by an American journalist, the Taoiseach Eamon de Valera laughed and assured him, as if he were talking about a strain of breeding cattle, that 'The Irish are not a vanishing people. There is quite good stock here who will take care of that.'[31] Nonetheless, the phrase 'The Vanishing Irish' acquired a kind of vogue. The *Sunday Independent* used it again for another series of articles in May 1957. The *Irish Times* ran an editorial in 1956, full of dark intimations that the Irish would become like other indigenous peoples who had lost out in the Darwinian struggle for survival: 'What matters is that we will disappear as a composite race. We will add our name or names to those of the races that assimilate us; but as an entity, we will cease to exist.'[32]

Around this time, Böll had a dream about a nun finding a dead American Indian in Duke Street in the centre of Dublin. She told him: 'no one ever found out where he came from, who he belonged to, no poison was found in him nor any violence on him: he was clutching his tomahawk, he was in war paint and all his war finery, and since he had to have a name... we called him "our dear red brother from the air".'[33] But in fact it is obvious enough where the dead Indian came from: the fevered images of the Irish as a moribund tribe.

There was something very Beckettian about all of this. In the wake of the controversy over O'Brien's book, the *Irish Times* published a cartoon linking it to the news that the Abbey Theatre had declined to name a winner of its competition to find a distinguished new play. It shows two bearded men in a pub, one of them reading a newspaper with the headline 'No Awards in Abbey Play Competition'. In the caption, he is telling his companion: 'I suppose my dramatization of The Vanishing Irish was considered a bit avant garde. Just a set – no actors...'[34] The cancellation of the Dublin Theatre Festival in 1958 could perhaps be seen as the real fulfilment of this avant-garde minimalism: the feast of drama with no actors, no sets, no plays and indeed no audiences.

In one of the plays that Beckett withdrew from the festival, *All That Fall*, the central character Mrs Rooney ruminates on the alternatives of staying and going: 'It is suicide to be abroad. But what is to be at home, Mr Tyler? What is to be at home? A lingering dissolution.' Flann O'Brien/Myles na Gopaleen was an embodiment of lingering dissolution, slowly drinking himself to death. Most writers lived in Ireland's intellectual and artistic capital, Elsewhere. Even the playwrights who were to be absent from the now non-existent Dublin Theatre Festival were not present anyway: Beckett was in Paris, O'Casey in Torquay, Alan MacClelland in London. Joyce had died in Zurich.

Giving one of his impromptu rhetorical performances in McDaid's pub in Dublin around this time, Brendan Behan informed his listeners that 'Ireland is a village in Trieste with James Joyce; Devon with Sean O'Casey; Paris with Sam Beckett and all tied together... to an elderly degenerate proselytising umbilical lasso known as the Archbishop of Dublin. Ireland is a figment of the Anglo-Saxon imagination, her vices extolled as virtues and her glorious memory perpetuated by Boss Croker and Tammany Hall. Ireland is a lie, a state or place non-existent...'[35]

Behan's surreal image of Archbishop John Charles McQuaid as both a lasso that captured and tied Ireland together and an umbilical cord to which it was attached had a kind of truth to it. McQuaid, a small man whose piercing eyes radiated power and perception, had been the Catholic Archbishop for eighteen years already. He embodied the authority of the church in a country in which 95 per cent of men and 94.8 per cent of women were Catholic. The nature of that authority was expressed perfectly in the Dublin

Theatre Festival fiasco. There was in fact no official censorship of plays (unlike books and films) in Ireland. But McQuaid's writ ran so strongly that it did not need mere state law to impose it.

The extent of McQuaid's obsessive monitoring of Irish cultural life for occasions of sin was as remarkable as his ability to enforce his will. Not long before I was born, the one and only national radio station, Radio Éireann, had played, on its popular and innocuous music programme, Hospitals Requests, Cole Porter's 'Always True To You':

> But I'm always true to you, darling, in my fashion
> Yes I'm always true to you, darling, in my way.

The presenter, Tom Cox, was summoned by the controller of programmes, Roibéard Ó Faracháin, a poet and playwright associated with the Abbey Theatre. He heard the most dreaded words in Ireland: 'The Palace has been on.' The Palace was McQuaid's Archbishop's mansion in Drumcondra – it is striking that the metonymy evoked a feudal aristocrat or even a monarch. Ó Faracháin told Cox that 'His Grace is concerned at the somewhat, eh, circumscribed morality of the song. Indeed he believes that it advocates the proposition that a limited form of fidelity is somehow acceptable.' The next time 'Always True To You' was requested by a listener, Cox played an instrumental version by Victor Sylvester and his Ballroom Orchestra.[36]

It was not for those listeners to understand how McQuaid's limits on what could be sung or said or written or read were enforced. O'Casey and Beckett cannot have known precisely how it worked in the case of the Dublin Theatre Festival. The church literally owned the space where Beckett's plays were to be staged, the St Francis Xavier Hall. In January, the provincial of the Jesuit order had called McQuaid to let him know that, in compliance with his wishes, he had directed that permission for the use of the hall be refused. This and the cancellation of the Mass that was meant to open the festival were sufficient to signal the unacceptability of Joyce, O'Casey and Beckett in their own native city. The lord mayor phoned McQuaid to express his loyal support. Dublin Corporation threatened to withdraw its grant for street decorations if the plays were staged. Even the secretary of the Dublin Council of Trade Unions protested to the festival's council against the 'objectionable plays'.[37]

In a neat twist, given that the purpose of the festival was supposed to be the attraction of Irish-American tourists to the ancestral homeland, two of McQuaid's fellow bishops sent a letter to the American Catholic hierarchy explaining why McQuaid had 'felt compelled' to act against Joyce and O'Casey. No such explanation was necessary in Ireland. This was real authority: McQuaid never even made a public statement, yet he effectively forced the abandonment of what was supposed to be an international showcase for Irish theatre.

Perhaps an even greater tribute to this power was the acceptance by the victims of their own impotence. It is striking that the main objection of the adaptor of *Ulysses*, MacClelland, was not that Joyce was being censored but that he himself had not been given credit for his diligent efforts to identify objectionable blasphemies which he 'naturally agreed to cut'. That 'naturally' spoke volumes. It was taken for granted that anti-Catholic sentiments should not be spoken aloud on stage. And there were no serious protests from Ireland's small core of artists and intellectuals. Indeed, perhaps the greatest writer still living in the country, Flann O'Brien, wrote in his Myles na Gopaleen persona: 'On the whole I approve of the withdrawal of these two ill-advised pieces. The total closing of all theatres for a couple of months is another notion I commend. The male actors will get healthy employment snagging turnips or footing turf, and many of the actresses would be better off down the country where they came from, making nourishing soup for their grannies in big iron skillets.'[38]

Yet McQuaid's umbilical lasso did not just capture and confine Ireland. It also held it together. Behan's flight of oratorical fancy in McDaid's suggested that Ireland was an insubstantial place, a fanciful notion upheld only by the Archbishop's iron grip, or perhaps more accurately sustained in existence only by his baleful stare. It was Ireland's greatest philosopher, George Berkeley, who suggested that 'to be is to be perceived'. McQuaid's eye was like the eye of God: all-seeing, unblinking. McQuaid had a telescope in the bell-tower of his residence – the rumour was that he used it to spy, not on the heavens, but on courting couples. He also had a magnifying glass. He once informed a director of the *Irish Press*, Eamon de Valera's son Vivion, that when he used it to scrutinize the drawings of women in ads for underwear, it was possible to see the outline of a mons veneris.[39]

This voyeurism may have been terrifying, but it was also consoling. Beckett's Vladimir in *Waiting for Godot* finds some fleeting comfort in the thought that 'At me too someone is looking'. The idea that McQuaid and his vast network of lay and clerical informants were always looking meant that Ireland had not yet succumbed to non-existence. It could not vanish so long as it was under his all-seeing eye. He fixed it with his glare – and in that minutely attentive gaze, it continued to be. Even in the emptiness of the ruins, the watchman was awake.

There was, though, a whole other level on which Ireland could be thought of as non-existent. The state that had come into being in 1922 consisted of twenty-six of Ireland's thirty-two counties. In the ideology of militant nationalists, that meant it had not come into being at all. It was illegitimate – as of course was its evil twin, the Protestant-dominated statelet of Northern Ireland. The IRA maintained as a matter of vital principle a 'refusal to recognize' the state.

That state was ambivalent about its own existence. The Taoiseach, de Valera, was the sole surviving commandant of the Republican rebels in the 1916 Rising. But he was also titular leader of the forces that opposed the creation of the southern state in 1922 in an abortive civil war. Seven members of his government were fellow veterans of this conflict. They had taken power in the 1930s, in a state whose existence they had violently opposed, with the aid of some impressive mental gymnastics.

The Constitution created by de Valera in 1937 (with help from McQuaid) distinguished between the de facto and de jure Irelands – the actual one they ruled and the one that should exist as a thirty-two-county entity. The first was explicitly temporary. It subsisted, as the Constitution had it, 'pending the reintegration of the national territory'. The main difference between the Dublin government and the IRA on this score was one of degree. For the former, the Ireland it ruled was a liminal state, hovering between the colonial past and the future of full freedom. For the latter, the existence of this ghostly entity could not be acknowledged at all.

The IRA men who raided Blandford camp on the weekend of my birth were devotees of this faith. In 1956, the IRA had begun the 'Border Campaign' of armed raids into Northern Ireland, attacking military and police installations, communications facilities and public property. The aim was to 'fight until the invader is driven from our soil and victory is ours'.[40] By February 1958, the campaign had already produced new martyrs to add to the great community of the Republican undead: Fergal O'Hanlon and Seán South (also known by the Gaelicized form he often used, Sabhat), the latter a far-right Catholic activist who wrote to the newspapers about the need to control 'bad films', asking rhetorically, 'How can this be done with Jewish and Masonic executive [sic] dictating to the Communist rank and file' in Hollywood? He suggested that the answer was to consider 'whether or not pictures should be shown at all'.[41]

In McQuaid's ideal Ireland, there would have been no plays, in South's new republic, there would have been no movies either. The IRA to which he belonged worried about emigration mainly because it exposed Irish youth to the 'irreligious completely materialistic atmosphere of England'. In a country with brutal censorship of books already in place, it had launched a campaign to 'Stop Foreign Publications', and further censor material that was 'not merely anti-Catholic or anti-Christian but definitely and deliberately Pagan'.[42]

For Seamus Heaney, a teenage boarder in St Columb's College, Derry, the impact of the IRA's new Border campaign – and specifically of a bomb attack on the courthouse in Magherafelt in his native terrain – was visceral:

Soot-streaks down the courthouse wall, a hole
Smashed in the roof, the rafters in the rain
Still smouldering: when I heard the word 'attack'...

It left me winded, left nothing between me
And the sky that moved beyond my boarder's dormer.[43]

This violence was strangely weightless. As the laughter in the House of Commons when the Blandford raid was discussed so clearly indicated, the British 'invader' was not particularly anxious about it. The Unionist government in Northern Ireland was not shaken – if anything the IRA's aggression helped to sustain its insistence that Catholics were inherently treacherous and deserved the second-class status imposed on them.

The Blandford escapade was emblematic of both the futility and the histrionic nature of the whole campaign. Nothing was actually achieved, except the shooting of one young English conscript with no bullets in his gun, who soon recovered, and perhaps the frightening to death of an unfortunate middle-aged Irish corporal. The weird way its apparent protagonist, Skuse/Murphy, hovered between existence and non-existence, captured something of the state of militant Irish nationalism. It was replaying its own history, if not quite as farce, then as surreal psychodrama.

But the psychodrama still had an audience. One thing for which the IRA had not lost its capacity was the production of martyrs, and martyrdom had a powerful emotional radiance in a culture shaped by the fusion of political myths of blood sacrifice (especially those of the 1916 Rising) with the religious drama of Christ's death and resurrection. Dying for Ireland imposed on the survivors a moral obligation to mourn. Large crowds had lined the route of Seán South's funeral cortège as it drove all the way from Monaghan near the Border to Dublin and south-west to his native Limerick, where 20,000 men, women and children, including the city's mayor, waited in pouring rain to receive his body at midnight and 50,000 accompanied it to the cemetery next day. The men who turned out in their uniforms were not just members of the IRA in black berets and armbands, but busmen and railway ticket inspectors.[44] In Dublin and in Limerick, and at various stops in between, crowds recited the Rosary, a long litany of Catholic prayers, in honour of the martyr. Hagiographic tributes hailed him as 'an exemplary and very fine type of young

Irishman' whose 'blood will fire us to a renewed enthusiasm to bring to fruition Seán's finest dream – an Ireland free and Gaelic'.[45]

But what did this mean? If South was exemplary in his religious devotion, desire to shut down cinemas and determination as one tribute put it to 'meet his death where Irish land is still held by foreign soldiery',[46] the moral duty of every young person was to engage in holy war against both the Protestants of Northern Ireland and the Masonic–Jewish–Communist forces of Hollywood. And any outsider looking at the official reactions to his death would have been sure that this was indeed what Catholic Ireland intended to do. Almost all local government councils in the twenty-six counties voted to express their profound sympathy for South. Gaelic football and hurling teams were called after him. A popular ballad, 'Seán South Of Garryowen', was composed in his honour within a week of his death, the words, tellingly, first published in the *Irish Catholic*.[47]

But all of this was steeped in an exquisitely refined ambivalence. The Catholic hierarchy declared it a mortal sin to 'co-operate with or express approval of' any organization that 'arrogates to itself the right to bear arms or to use them against its own or another state', but South and other martyrs were given huge public Catholic funerals that were attended, as well as celebrated, by the clergy.[48] The dominant political party, Fianna Fáil, and its leader de Valera, maintained that militant operations by the IRA would merely cause further suffering without weakening partition, but its representatives, including its rising star in Limerick, Donogh O'Malley, made sure to be seen among the mourners. The very appeal to the young to be fired by the blood of the martyrs with 'renewed enthusiasm' for the cause implicitly conceded that enthusiasm was waning. Militant nationalism needed regular transfusions of young blood to keep it alive, because it led a kind of vampiric half-life, imaginatively and emotionally draining but not visible in any mirror held up to contemporary Irish reality.

This was nothing as simple, or as stable, as mere hypocrisy. There were people – a small but potent minority – who fully shared the belief that the purpose of life was to free Ireland, speak

Irish and be a pious and puritanical Catholic. There were people – a larger but more tacit minority – who thought all of this to be obscurantist nonsense. But most people were capable of living simultaneously in the dreamworlds of Catholic nationalism and of modern material aspirations. It was quite possible to shed a tear for Seán South and sing the ballad of his heroic deeds in the pub on a Saturday night in London or Birmingham or Glasgow or New York. It was quite possible to think that South was a mad zealot and also that he was an exemplary Irishman.

This was another kind of performance. There was a modest surge of recruits to the IRA, whose membership reached around 1,000. Support for its political wing Sinn Féin rose to 5 per cent nationally in the general election of 1957 (an average of 11 per cent in the constituencies it contested), and it won four parliamentary seats, which it refused to occupy because, of course, it did not recognize the state. But people did not stop speaking English and start speaking Gaelic. The cinemas remained full. Young men and women continued to emigrate to English cities in search of a life better than the one they had in Catholic nationalist Ireland. In 1957 alone, an astonishing 1.8 per cent of the entire population left the country.

The same annual meetings of the Gaelic Athletic Asocation (GAA, the body that organized the native games of hurling and football) that held a minute's silence and said a decade of the Rosary for Seán South and Fergal O'Hanlon also heard reports on the 'disastrous' effects of emigration on their ability to continue to field teams of young men.[49] At the time of the Blandford raid, the Border Campaign was already faltering, and many in the IRA were beginning to feel it should be abandoned. By the middle of 1958, 500 of them were in prison or interned without trial on both sides of the Border.[50] By the end of the year, confident that the campaign was petering out, the government began releasing prisoners. While the IRA's crusade to drive out the 'invader' maintained a desultory existence, it would, in 1962, call the whole thing off and blame its failure on 'the attitude of the general public whose minds have been deliberately distracted from the supreme issue facing the Irish people – the unity and freedom of Ireland'.[51]

In this at least the IRA showed some glimmer of realism: the Irish people were indeed in a state of long-term distraction, radically uncertain about how to define themselves.

Four days before I was born, there was a public funeral in Dublin for another fallen young hero, on the same scale as Seán South's. The body of Liam Whelan, the brilliant twenty-two-year-old Manchester United inside-forward who had been killed in the Munich air disaster that took a terrible toll of the youthful side known as the Busby Babes, was flown home on an Aer Lingus freight plane and accompanied by large crowds on a five-mile route from the airport to the Church of Christ the King in Cabra, with thousands more lining the route. Traffic was repeatedly stopped along the way as 'the cortège was time and again accorded tributes from workers returning home'.[52] At the funeral, the coffin was covered with a floral arrangement sent by the club showing its Old Trafford ground and soccer pitch, complete with a ball, goals and red corner flags. The dense rows of people who stood outside the church, whose doors had to be closed to prevent overcrowding, recited the Rosary, the same litany of prayers that had been intoned for the soul of Seán South. The Mass was celebrated by Revd Charles Mulholland, a friend of Whelan's who had been due to preside at his wedding. No one seems to have taken issue with Father Mulholland's day job, which was as Catholic chaplain at the Royal Air Force base near Weston-super-Mare in Somerset.[53]

It would be easy to think that the people who said the Rosary for Liam Whelan and those who had prayed for Seán South the previous year belonged to mutually hostile and exclusive tribes: one that hankered after a pure, Gaelic and Catholic Ireland to which Whelan and his priest were traitors and another that shared at least part of its identity with working-class people in Manchester, Liverpool and Birmingham. But it is a reasonable bet that many had stood in both crowds, reciting the same litanies. Especially in urban Ireland, it was easy enough to slip between different modes of feeling, to share on Wednesday a very public mourning with the people of Manchester and on Sunday to cheer on the IRA men who raided Blandford. In the mental universe of mass migration, one could be neither here nor there, but also, sometimes, both here and there.

In the shadows of the high drama of the IRA raid and the lurid scandal of the collapse of the theatre festival, the third event on the weekend I was born – Seán Lemass's departure to Paris for talks on European free trade – was scarcely visible, a boring non-story. Lemass himself called the negotiating session 'important but of small general interest'.[54] Yet even if most people were not interested, his trip to Paris was an episode in the creation of the Ireland I would grow up in. While nationalism and religion sucked up almost all the oxygen, those dull, technical talks were exposing the existential dilemma of the project of Irish independence. What Lemass was grappling with was whether, as western Europe continued to move inexorably towards the creation of a zone of free trade, Ireland could continue to exist as an economic entity.

The question Lemass was forced to pose was whether Ireland could even be thought of as part of western Europe. It had always imagined itself to be so, to belong in some profound way, in particular to the Catholic Europe of Italy and France and Spain. But there was a rough awakening to Ireland's marginal place in Europe. In the tentative negotiations for the formation of EFTA, Ireland found itself in a group of four countries explicitly pleading that they would need very special arrangements because they were too underdeveloped to cope with the rigours of free trade. The other countries were Greece, Turkey and Iceland.[55] Irish officialdom accepted that this was indeed the constellation in which Ireland was located: 'some points of fundamental importance have emerged as common to all.' Ireland accepted its designation alongside the other three as 'less developed countries'. This was what Lemass was going to Paris to talk about – how would this strange group of four be treated in EFTA?

This cluster was not quite what Irish nationalists from Robert Emmet onwards had meant by their country 'taking its place among the nations of the earth'. Without being disrespectful to Turkey or Iceland, they were not the nations the patriots had in mind. James Dillon, a leading member of Fine Gael whose family's political roots were deep in nineteenth-century Irish nationalism, wailed in the Dáil that 'we are with the descaminados – Iceland, Turkey, Greece and Ireland, the shirt-less ones of Europe. We have elected to take our place with them. It was at our request that we were enumerated in that company, the ones who had nothing to offer anyone except outstretched hands. We do not belong in that company.'[56]

But the company of the shirtless ones was the only economic coterie in which Ireland did belong. Ireland had been an independent state for thirty-five years but it now seemed more peripheral, both literally and imaginatively, than it had ever been. It had left the British Commonwealth in 1949, cutting its formal ties to the other ex-colonies. But this departure had not ended in any arrival. Ireland was not British – but it was not really anything else either.

There is a reason why American Westerns were vastly popular in Ireland – they probably seemed like social realism. In economic terms, Ireland was a vast cattle ranch with a few cities and a lot of small provincial towns attached. When the Irish government commissioned a study on economic development from the New York consultancy firm Stacy May, its report, published in 1952, opened with the line: 'In the Irish economy, cattle is king.'[57]

Of the country's total exports of all products to all overseas markets, a scarcely credible one-third was accounted for by live cattle and almost half consisted of beef and cattle products.[58] And almost all of this went to the United Kingdom.

Even in Dublin, it was common for traffic to be held up by cattle being driven along the roads. In my childhood, it was not unusual to wake up and find a stray bullock grazing in the back garden. On the north side of the city, there was a sixty-acre cattle market on the North Circular Road that could hold six thousand beasts and was reputed to be the largest of its kind in Europe. (The beasts had religious identities: the beef farmer and cattle dealer Joe Ward recalled that 'A number of the cattle stands were owned by Protestants, who sold practically all Protestant cattle. The Catholics sold practically all Catholic cattle...')[59] From there, the drovers herded them down to the North Wall to the boats that took them to the North of England and Scotland. Sheep were also driven through the city streets. Ward remembered: 'At the end of the summer, when the lambs were being herded down to the boats, one or two of them would get underneath a tram and get entangled.'[60]

The animals may well have become entangled with the other herd making its way to the port: the trail of emigrants heading for English and Scottish cities. Often, they travelled on the very same boats as the cattle did, an image whose aptness was not lost on them. The export of live people and live animals in the same vessels epitomized the economic backwardness of the country.

In a bitter paradox, Ireland was an agrarian economy that was actually not much good at producing food. Where were the great fishing fleets of this Atlantic island? On the weekend of my birth, the minister for lands, Erskine Childers, was lamenting the fact that 'Ireland was the only maritime country in Europe without middle-water trawlers and without a substantial export trade in wet fish'. With some of the richest fishing grounds in Europe, Ireland had managed in the previous year to export a grand total of £799,000 worth of fresh fish.[61]

In spite of having huge numbers of dairy cattle, Ireland could barely make edible cheese. In 1957, Ireland had managed to sell a total of £20,000 worth of cheese abroad – Britain alone imported £25 million worth from round the world that year.[62] Food processing was entirely for the domestic market. Even commodities like biscuits, where Ireland had once had a thriving export trade, were now mostly imported. Guinness continued to be a major exporter, but Irish whiskey had lost out to Scotch and had a 'trifling' presence on world markets.[63]

Raising beef on grassland required relatively few skills, so Irish farmers were poorly educated. 'Rural science' had been taught in primary schools until 1934, but it was dropped in order to devote more time to the teaching of the Irish language. Agricultural education at second level was 'negligible': only 694 of 60,000 students took classes in the subject.[64] Even in 1964, 83 per cent of Irish farmers had received only a primary education. Of the 7,000 farmers' sons who left school every year to take up farming, only 200 received any formal instruction in agriculture. Why?

Because, in the 1930s, the Catholic bishops had rejected a proposal to establish 500 agricultural colleges. This was 'an unnecessary extension of state control into education'. And, from a moral point of view, 'there was an inherent danger in allowing boys and girls between the ages of 12 and 16 to travel unsupervised to school together'. The plan was abandoned.[65]

The US Marshall Plan had put up a million pounds to fund the creation of a National Institute of Agriculture.[66] The Catholic bishops and their lay allies opposed it on the grounds that it would not have a proper basis in religious doctrine.[67] Eight years after the Institute had been proposed and funded, it had still not been established. In May 1958, the National Farmers' Association noted that the training facilities for agricultural science were 'pathetically understaffed' and the *Irish Times* lamented the 'criminal lunacy' that the few agricultural scientists being produced in Ireland were 'being forced to emigrate in search of employment'.[68]

The result of the abject failure to develop a serious food industry was that agriculture was largely primitive and utterly colonial. A 'strong farmer' like Joe Ward stayed in the fine Gresham Hotel in Dublin whenever he was in the capital to buy and sell cattle. He had warm and trusting relationships with the English farmers and dealers he sold to, sending cattle to them in return for post-dated cheques. His family went to Harrogate to 'take the waters' and visit his business partners.[69] They remained, economically and to some degree socially, part of a British world. The young growing up in rural Ireland were destined as a consequence to be part of the British world in a more direct sense, making their lives in Manchester, Glasgow, Birmingham and London.

As for manufacturing industry, on the weekend I was born the Institute for Industrial Research and Standards, founded in the 1940s to try to encourage innovation in Ireland's small industrial sector, was complaining that Irish businesses were not particularly interested in either research or standards. The Institute itself was tiny – it had thirty-four staff, including clerks and cleaners – but, even so, it had trouble generating enough work for its specialists because of a 'surprising' reluctance of Irish industrialists to engage with its work. Part of the problem, it seemed, was 'a suspicion that the industrialist might be told to buy new machinery or change to a more expensive process if he sought scientific help'.[70]

To define the place I was born into might be to think about what subsets of countries it belonged to. One, certainly, was Dillon's descaminados with Iceland, Greece and Turkey. Another was the tiny group of European countries that experienced a fall in population during the 1950s. It was an exclusive couple: Ireland and East Germany.[71] The East German regime, in despair at the mass exodus of people to the West, would soon put up a wall to keep them in. But Ireland already had walls and they were forcing people out. These imagined walls were those of protectionism – the moral protectionism of McQuaid's repression and the economic protectionism of high tariff barriers instituted by the Fianna Fáil government when it came to power in 1932.

The architect of that policy was the very man who was now going to Paris to talk about free trade: Lemass. He had believed that 'economic self-sufficiency' and 'the preservation of our population' could be achieved only 'by a courageous application of the methods which Economic Nationalism has devised and is now being used through Europe'.[72]

Almost as soon as Fianna Fáil took office, it imposed duties of between 15 and 75 per cent on thirty-eight different kinds of imported products. By 1936, more than a thousand categories of goods were subject to tariffs of 50 to 75 per cent.[73] The holding of shares and voting rights in Irish companies by foreign nationals was severely restricted.

Protectionism was very much in fashion in the 1930s, and the idea of allowing Irish industries to establish themselves on the home market without competition from much bigger international (and especially British) firms was not innately illogical. But the Irish version of it was extreme, even by the standards of the 1930s. It was a deliberate disengagement from world trade: in the decade before the Second World War, Ireland was the most aggressively protectionist of all the small European countries. Its imports and exports fell by a combined 64 per cent.

The policy did make an emerging class of Irish businessmen rich. Between 1932 and 1948, about a hundred new industries were created and a thousand new factories were built. Eighty thousand industrial jobs were created.[74] But there were three obvious problems. First, as the complaints of the Institute of Industrial Research and Standards suggested, this was a cosy world with little incentive for innovation. Second, the idea of servicing the home market required consumers to do something they could not do: stay at home. Third, the great aim of protectionism was to break Ireland's economic dependence on the old colonial master. It failed, not just because of the dominance of the cattle trade, but because ordinary Irish people were very well aware that wages were higher in England, even in menial jobs. In 1948, girls working in Denny's bacon factory in Tralee were reportedly emigrating to England and taking jobs as domestic servants 'to better themselves'.[75]

A researcher who interviewed seven young women who were emigrating from Co. Galway discovered the uncensorable power of the simplest form of private literature: the letter home. They told him that in Ireland employers subjected them to 'long hours of duty, bad food, and, above all, lack of respect. They are treated as inferior human beings who have very few rights…' But 'in all cases, friends or sisters had written from England or talked during the holidays' of decent wages and better treatment there.[76] Rhetorically, tyranny and contempt were inflicted by the English on the Irish. In the subterranean reality of ordinary lives, England could be a place to escape tyranny and contempt in Ireland. Aodh de Blácam, a member of the official Commission on Emigration, dug deep into xenophobia and anti-Semitism to urge Irish girls to stay at home with lovely Irish Catholic families: 'Would you like to see any girl in whom you had any interest going into a Jewman's house in the English slums?'[77] The silent answer to that rhetorical question was often yes. Even low-status jobs in England were better than what Ireland had to offer people who had no property or connections and only a basic primary education.

Emigrants often left with virtually nothing. The most resonant Irish object of the time was a small, cheap brown suitcase, often battered and tied with rope to keep it shut.

Dónall MacAmhlaigh recalled the scene at the customs post

in Holyhead when he first arrived in Britain. One of his fellow emigrants put just such a case on the counter, and when asked what it contained, replied, 'Yerra, nothing at all.' The customs officer insisted nonetheless that he open it. He took out a penknife and cut the rope. 'The lid jumped up like a Jack-in-the-Box and out leapt an old pair of Wellington boots that had been twisted up inside it. Devil the thing else was in the case – not even a change of socks. A melancholy wintry little smile crossed the face of the customs officer as he motioned to your man to get along with himself.'[78]

There was another strange subset of countries to which Ireland belonged. If it was demographically twinned with East Germany, in another important respect – monetary policy – Ireland was part of a group that also included Burma, Iceland, Iraq, Jordan, Kuwait and the Persian Gulf sheikhdoms, and Libya. These were non-British Commonwealth countries that were nonetheless members of the Sterling Area. Their currencies were all pegged to the British pound. In Ireland's case, the relationship was rigid. Ireland had issued its own currency since 1927, but it was a kind of fiction: its exchange value was fixed by law at absolute parity with sterling. It was backed by reserves that (as well as some gold) consisted of sterling funds and British government securities. Behind the show of an independent currency was a very British reality.

This was one of the things we all knew and chose to ignore. We knew it in the most tangible way: British coins and notes circulated freely in Ireland. You could buy anything in the shops with them. If you had any money in your pocket, it was almost certainly a promiscuous mix of British and Irish currency.

In my earliest memories of having coins, Francis Drake's *Golden Hind* on the British halfpenny jingles along with the pig and her three little piglets on the Irish version; Britannia ruling the waves on the front of the British penny rubs against the Irish hen and her five chicks; Queen Elizabeth occupies the same obverse space as the Celtic harp with Éire stamped above it. My father would sometimes bring home older coins he had collected with the bus fares, with the profiles of Victoria and various Georges, blurred by decades of sweat and chafing, all still paying for bus rides and sweets, pints and newspapers in Dublin, as if nothing had happened since they were minted. This should have bothered a population bred on nationalism, but it didn't. It was just another example of the doubleness that characterized the culture, its permanent state of contradiction, its amphibious ability to live both on the dry land of the nation and in the aqueous fluidity of mass migration.

Already, by the end of the 1930s, Lemass was well aware that protectionism was not working. But the policy of neutrality in the Second World War actually increased Ireland's isolation. When the war was over, and the US-led reconstruction of western Europe was under way, the US authorities believed that 'Ireland's main contribution to European recovery will take place through the production of more food for export'. Ireland's future, as seen from the US, lay in helping to 'fill the tables of western Europe with eggs, milk and bacon'.[79] To get Marshall Aid, Irish governments echoed these sentiments back to the Americans. Ireland joined the Organisation for European Economic Co-operation (OEEC) that administered the aid programme. Of the $13 billion in Marshall Aid, Ireland got just $128 million (£41 million) in loans and $18 million (£6.5 million) in grants. But such crumbs from the table were still important to a country hungry for cash.[80] They represented almost half of all Irish state investment.[81] Tellingly, though, most of it was spent on agricultural projects – industrial development was not a priority.[82]

Even this minor part in the great drama of European economic recovery did not last long. In 1952, after the outbreak of the Korean War and the deepening of Cold War animosities, Ireland's refusal to join NATO, on the grounds that it could not participate in a military alliance with Britain while that country continued to 'occupy' the six counties of Northern Ireland, made it entirely irrelevant to American interests. Its ambassador to Washington was abruptly informed that 'all United States Government activities in connection with Irish economic assistance have been suspended as of January 8, 1952'.[83] Submitting his budget in April, the minister for finance Seán McEntee admonished, rather comically, that 'The fevered spending of the Marshall Aid period is over.'[84]

Two years earlier, the Irish government had put a bizarre proposal to President Harry Truman: that Ireland and the United

States would enter into a mutual defence pact. Unsurprisingly, the US did not see the advantages of Irish assistance against its enemies. The gesture, though, was indicative of an awareness that, as a state, Ireland barely registered in the world. Its neutrality in the war meant that it was of no account in the post-war settlement. It was allowed to join the United Nations only in 1955 and the World Bank and International Monetary Fund in 1957. It would not accede to the General Agreement on Tariffs and Trade (GATT) until 1967, twenty years after it was drawn up. Its refusal to join NATO made it a spectator in the Cold War – no amount of anti-communist rhetoric (and there was plenty) could convince anyone that Ireland was so much as a useful pawn in the great game of superpower rivalry.

Even when Ireland did have some kind of international presence, it tended to use it merely to lament its own post-colonial condition. The state was a member of the Council of Europe, but its delegates saw it primarily as a forum for complaints about the evils of partition in Ireland. The boredom of other members emerged when Paul-Henri Spaak, its president and a key figure in moves towards European integration, intervened in a debate to admonish the Irish minister Seán T. O'Kelly: 'We must not allow every debate to become the object of a dispute between the representatives of Ireland and Great Britain... I beg you to keep to the matter in hand.'[85]

Irish understanding of what was happening in post-war Europe was minimal. Until 1956, no officials of the Department of External Affairs were allowed to travel outside the country for meetings with their counterparts without prior and explicit approval from the Department of Finance.[86] When Ireland's parliament, the Dáil, came to debate free trade, the former Taoiseach John A. Costello suggested that 'I do not think it is a derogation of Deputies to say that there is not a handful of them who have the remotest notion as to what the difference is between a Common Market and the proposed Free Trade Area, not to talk of having an informed view on what is involved... I am sure 99 per cent of Deputies and Senators are not properly informed of the issues and arguments involved.'[87] No one objected to this assessment.

For many of those who were running the country, the dilemma created by western Europe's push towards economic integration seemed insoluble. On the one side, Ireland could stay out of the process and drift steadily out into the Atlantic, toward the middle of nowhere. As a memorandum prepared by a working group of secretaries of government departments put it in January 1957, 'If Ireland should decide to remain outside a free trade area she would be outside this mainstream of Western European development and her position in the world would become more isolated.'[88] Given how isolated Ireland already was, this was quite a prospect.

The alternative to isolation, however, seemed to be devastation. Entering a free trade area with more developed economies would mean that Irish industries, deprived of the protection of high tariffs, would disappear. As the memorandum put it, 'As regards a large section of existing industries, the Department of Industry can see no prospect of their survival even as suppliers of the home market, except with *permanent* protection.'[89] As for exports making up for the loss of domestic sales, there was 'no prospect of industrial exports from Ireland' and 'little prospect of an expansion of agricultural exports from Ireland to the continental part of the free trade area'. No prospect, no prospect, little prospect – the future was blank and bleak. As the Irish joke had it at the time, the wolf was at the door, howling to get out.

It may seem ridiculous in retrospect, but the idea of the disappearance of Ireland still haunted the official imagination. In February 1957, the Irish ambassador to France, W. P. Fay, addressed the council of the OEEC. It would be 'unthinkable', he said, to apply 'free trade as understood in the nineteenth century'. Presumably to the bemusement of many of his listeners, he said that 'The rigid application of those principles has left us terrible memories in Ireland.' Those memories were of the Great Famine of the 1840s. Fay implied that opening Ireland to free trade now without protection for its industries would have a 'catastrophic effect on our economy... probably precluding any further development'.[90]

One road led to disaster, catastrophe and the impossibility of any future development. The other led to a kind of permanent quarantine as an ever more deeply disconnected outpost, that could only, as Bernard Shaw had predicted an isolationist Ireland would, 'turn back and shrink into a little village community... and do nothing but wonder how much longer the turf will last in Donegal'.[91] It did not need to be said – because the continuing outflow of emigrants, now greater than at any time since the 1890s, was saying it all too clearly – that such a backwater would not hold on to much of its population.

The only proposal for how the state might escape from this trap was an impossible plan. This is what Lemass was laying out on his trip to Paris that weekend in February 1958. Ireland suggested to the other European states that it should be allowed to join the planned EFTA – but also to keep in place for the foreseeable future most of its tariffs to protect indigenous industry. Ireland should be allowed a 'transition period' during which it would become rich and productive enough to be able to survive without special protection. How long would this process take? Thirty years. If the EFTA came into being in 1958, Ireland would accept all of its rules by 1988.[92]

So, as a child born in 1958, I would celebrate my thirtieth birthday as Ireland was celebrating its arrival at last into economic modernity. The proposal was absurd, of course, and the other countries did not take it seriously. But the absurdity was a product of despair. Some future had to be imagined that was not either isolation or devastation. It could only be a future of very slow and careful adjustment during which Ireland was treated as a special case by its neighbours, presumably on account of the 'terrible memories' that none of them, apparently, had to endure.

The fantasy of boarding this slow boat to modernity was necessary because it was so difficult to imagine transformation. There was a kind of unspoken pact: people transformed themselves through emigration so that the state and society could stay the same. And in any case, Ireland's ludicrous demands simply irritated other European countries. Our crushing irrelevance would become even more starkly obvious when formal discussions on the establishment of EFTA began in February 1959. Apart from Britain, most of the countries invited to take part were small nations: Austria, Denmark, Norway, Portugal, Sweden and Switzerland. There was no invitation for Ireland.[93] Later that year, Greece and Turkey sought association with the Common Market. That left Ireland and Iceland alone among the seventeen European countries that had been part of the US Marshall Aid programme for post-war reconstruction who were now cut off from the move towards the economic integration of western Europe. And the Icelanders at least had fish.

This lingering dissolution could not last. The six countries that formed the Common Market had collectively grown their GNP by 42 per cent between 1949 and 1956. Britain grew by a more sluggish 21 per cent. Ireland had managed just 8 per cent.[94] If the rest of the western European economy continued to integrate while Ireland remained on the margins, it seemed inevitable, not just that the gap would continue to widen, but that Irish people would continue to flee towards the places where there was money and hope and modernity.

Already, even before 1958, almost everyone except de Valera knew that the dream of frugal self-sufficiency was over. Unless things changed, there would be no national self, sufficient or otherwise. Fianna Fáil still clung to protectionism as an ideology, but the motley collection of alternative parties that held power for two periods between 1948 and 1957 had made tentative but significant moves to attract foreign investment, notably the establishment of an Industrial Development Authority to do just that by offering 50 per cent tax relief on export earnings for five years, and of Córas Tráchtála (the Irish Export Board) to try to find new markets for Irish products. But success had been very limited. In 1958, the Fianna Fáil government expanded the remission of tax for foreign investors from 50 to 100 per cent and the tax exemption from five years to ten. But there were still few takers, especially among the American companies that Ireland had vague hopes of attracting. In 1957, the net capital inflow into Ireland was minus £2.3 million. Just twenty industries with foreign participation were established between 1955 and 1958, and just one of them was American. US companies were interested primarily in access to the European market to which Ireland did not belong.

Yet the *idea* of American investment was potent. To open the Irish economy up so that British bosses could employ Irish workers was to admit defeat. To have American firms in small Irish towns would be to embrace a thrilling modernity and simultaneously to reconnect with the great Irish-American diaspora in whom so much hope – from tourist dollars to support for the national cause of ending partition – had been invested. And within this hope there was a notion of yet another imagined place in the world. Ireland did not want to be among the shirtless ones of Turkey, Greece and Iceland or with Iraq and Burma in the Sterling Area. The place it did want to be in – western Europe – had no practical interest in including it in its plans. Where could it be instead? Of all places, Puerto Rico.

In March 1958, Myles na Gopaleen suggested in the *Irish Times* that the state should establish a new special commission: 'The objective should be to achieve federal status as the 49th state of the Union. (President Eisenhower will find our golf courses first class.) The preliminary stage will be to become an American possession ranking with Alaska, Puerto Rico and the Philippines. That will give us limited rights of US citizenship.'[95] He was being facetious but not quite absurd. Six years previously, the report on economic development commissioned by the Irish government from the US consultancy firm Stacy May had pointed to the strategy adopted by Puerto Rico – attracting light industries from the US by offering them tax incentives. The strategy had allowed the island to achieve rapid industrialization from a standing start. In 1956, the IDA reported that, on a visit to the US by its executives, they had been asked whether Ireland could offer similar incentives.[96]

It did not seem to bother anyone that Ireland, which defined itself by its independence from Britain, could take its lead from Puerto Rico, which had been a literal dependency of the US since 1898. One way out of economic protectionism might be to become, economically at least, a US protectorate. But this could not happen without radical change.

In May 1957, Ken Whitaker, a Catholic from Northern Ireland who had become secretary of the Department of Finance the previous year at the age of thirty-nine, had begun, quietly and with a small team of officials, to write a 250-page document mapping out what that change would be. Nobody asked him to do it, and he and his collaborators worked in their spare time.[97] Whitaker's motivation was existential – he believed that 'Something had to be done or the achievement of national independence would prove to have been a futility.'[98]

In December, Whitaker told the government what he was up to, and was encouraged to go ahead. By May 1958, a full draft of the document, called simply *Economic Development*, was ready and fifty copies were printed for circulation among the ruling elite. By late July, the government had adopted it as policy and authorized the drafting (by Whitaker and his allies in the civil service) of a white paper based on his analysis, the *Programme for Economic Expansion*. In November, *Economic Development* was published under Whitaker's own name, priced at seven shillings and sixpence and wrapped in a cover so bland that it became known in official circles as the 'Grey Book', even though Whitaker himself thought it was 'light green' – perhaps an unconscious reflection of its radical watering-down of nationalist ideology.[99]

Grey it certainly was not. Whitaker wrote clearly and intelligibly. His document dealt with fishmeal and jellied eels, turf, pig breeds, motels, biscuits and sweets, whiskey and gin. It had tables and statistics. It did not present itself as a revolution – Whitaker warned that there would not be 'miracles of progress in a short time'. The only stated economic target was a possible doubling 'in time' of the annual rate of growth. Considering that growth had been running at just 1 per cent, this was deliberately setting expectations very low – Whitaker felt the country was so lacking in confidence that it might have shied at a higher bar.

Lemass had a similar idea. As he later explained: 'We had apathy in mind when we set our targets. We announced that we were striving for an economic growth of two per cent. We knew we could do much better than that, but we knew, too, that public morale would suffer if we set a higher target and failed to reach it.'[100] The Irish plan for industrialization was the opposite of Stalin's Five Year Plans. Instead of setting impossible goals and urging the workers to Stakhanovite efforts to reach them, it assumed that Irish confidence was so fragile that it needed the gentle encouragement of easy wins.

But Whitaker also said things like 'It would be well to shut the door on the past'[101] – a big statement in a country still led by veterans of the 1916 Rising who maintained that the past, in the form of partition, was very much unfinished business. He described unblinkingly the 'vicious circle... of increasing migration, resulting in a small domestic market depleted of initiative and skill and a reduced incentive... to undertake and organize the productive enterprises which alone can provide increased employment opportunities'. He acknowledged, in plain terms, the sense of despair that most Irish people were feeling: 'The common talk among parents in the towns, as in rural Ireland, is of their children having to emigrate as soon as their education is completed in order to be sure of a reasonable livelihood.'

But he offered a way out: 'further industrial development must be largely on the basis of production for export markets and freer trade in Europe must be faced in due course, we can no longer rely on extensive tariff or quota protection... A readiness to welcome foreign capital is a necessary complement to secure foreign participation in industrial development.'[102]

The calm, direct language both spelled out and underplayed the nature of the transformation. A self-sufficient, protected space was going to open itself up to economic globalization. Ireland would produce things for export. It would join in with European economic integration. And it would learn to love foreigners and their 'skills, techniques and "know-how"'. The subtext was obvious enough – if Irish people were to stop leaving the island for the world, the world would have to come to the island. Irish globalization had long been about labour going to where the capital was; now it would be about capital coming to where Irish labour was.

The weird thing is that there was no discussion in the Dáil on Whitaker's paper and no attack on it by the Opposition or, more importantly, by the Catholic Church. Eamon de Valera, now seventy-six and almost blind, was still head of government and could have stopped the plan in its tracks. In the 1957 general election, the triumphant Fianna Fáil leader had pledged that economic policy would 'try to continue on the path they had trodden before' with the goal of becoming 'as self-contained as possible'.[103] (The irony of the phrase in the context of mass emigration escaped him.) Yet he chose not to oppose the momentous shift in policy. His reasons were critical to the whole nature of the revolution that followed. Meeting Whitaker at a cocktail party a few years later, de Valera complimented him on his economic plan but added, in Irish, 'ach tá rudaí eile níos tábhachtaí' – but there are more important things.[104] Economics was only about money, after all – what really mattered were the old lodestars of the nationalistic constellation: a United Ireland, the revival of the Irish language and the maintenance of Ireland's special place in the world as the exemplary Catholic nation.

De Valera dealt with the great disruption implied by Whitaker's vision by simply denying it. He did not confront the failure of his version of the Irish state. Rather brilliantly, he absorbed the shock of the new by pretending that nothing new was happening. At a government meeting shortly before Christmas, he gave his blessing to *Economic Development* but suggested that it was merely a continuation of his own long-established plans. As he told John McCarthy in 1969: 'We set out those policies in 1926 at the formation of Fianna Fáil.'[105]

De Valera's newspaper, the *Irish Press*, editorialized vapidly that *Economic Development* 'is a most useful addition to the literature on national economics' that 'should help the businessman and the student of economic affairs to acquire a reasonably comprehensive knowledge of the needs and potentialities of the Irish economy to-day'.[106] It was as if a worthy but rather dull academic book, of interest only to a small business and intellectual elite, were being reviewed. The earthquake was just a little rumble in the distance – nothing to be concerned about. The revolution would not be televised, not least because Ireland did not yet have a television station.

Absurd as this was, it hinted at a broader sense of how the future was seen by those in charge. It is apt that *Economic Development* was published at almost the same time as the great novel of conservative transformation, Giuseppe Tomasi di Lampedusa's *The Leopard*.

Tancredi, the novel's central character, famously explains to his aristocratic uncle why he is going off to fight with Garibaldi's rebels: 'If we want things to stay as they are, things will have to change.' This could have served as the hidden epigraph to Whitaker's 'Grey Book'. It was a salvage operation. Its primary aim was not to destroy the Catholic nationalist state, but to keep it afloat.

The idea of protection was crucial. What was I, as a child being born into this Ireland, to be sheltered from? At the time of my birth, there was a double layer of defence: the economic and the spiritual. I was to grow up in an economy protected from foreign competition and in a culture protected from moral danger. Nine months later, one ring of fortification against the outside world was being dismantled. The economic ramparts were declared by Whitaker, and by the government, to be no longer defensible. They had been irreparably breached from the inside by the pressure of emigrants trying to get out. But the spiritual bulwarks would, they imagined, stay in place. The 'other things' that de Valera knew to be more important than economics, would be preserved.

Thus, readers of the *Irish Press* would have seen, immediately below the editorial on *Economic Development*, the paper's daily homage to the Catholic saint whose feast it was. It happened to be St Catherine of Alexandria, Virgin and Martyr, who defeated the Roman Emperor Maximinus in a theological debate: 'Furious, the tyrant ordered her to be tortured on a spiked wheel (whence is derived the name "Catherine wheel"); but just as it would crush the Saint, it fell asunder.' Irish Catholicism would surely prove no less resistant to the temptations of economic modernity.

Whitaker specifically invoked for his work the blessing of a Catholic bishop, William Philbin, and quoted his suggestion that industry and commerce presented 'the widest and most varied field for the play of the vital force that our religion contains'. In his introduction to *Economic Development*, Whitaker wrote that 'This study is a contribution in the spirit advocated by the Bishop of Clonfert toward the working out of the national good in the economic sphere.'[107] This might be seen as a strategic appeasement of the existing gods and the religious powers that be, but there is in fact no reason to read it as anything other than wholly sincere.

Those looking for reassurance might have found it in one of the few great Irish commercial successes of 1958. A future Taoiseach, Garret FitzGerald, was working for the state-owned airline, Aer Lingus. He realized that 1958 was the centenary of the apparition of the Blessed Virgin Mary to a young girl in Lourdes in south-west France. The airline had already opened up a lucrative market in religious tourism, carrying pilgrims to Lourdes, not just from Dublin, but from Barcelona and even from Rome. Ireland had its own Marian shrine, at Knock, where Mary had appeared in 1879. But Knock was rather bleakly set in the cold and damp of Co. Mayo, whereas Lourdes was warm and sunny and exotic.

FitzGerald organized charter flights to Lourdes with two Viscount 700 aircraft from the small Aer Lingus fleet. Their success was overwhelming. Between May and October, the planes flew back and forth to Lourdes twenty hours a day, every day. For FitzGerald, who loved numbers with an obsessive passion, the operation was 'the most perfect supply-demand equation ever recorded in air transport'.[108] The episode showed both that this language of efficiency and organization could be applied to Catholic Ireland but also that piety and progress could go hand in hand. This seemed to be a harbinger of a future in which a rising Catholic middle class with money to spend and curiosity about the outside world would let its aspirations flow into approved channels of traditional devotion.

This was the great gamble of 1958: everything would change economically but everything would stay the same culturally. Suitably to a fiercely anti-communist country, the Irish future would disprove the Marxist claim that economic and technological change transforms ideologies and values. Along with 60,000 other children born in Ireland in 1958, I was to be the *tabula rasa* on which this great experiment would be conducted.

2

1959: Modern Family

My parents, Mary and Sammy, didn't want to live in Aughavannagh Road. It was my mother's family home – they wanted a home of their own. When they were married, they moved into a flat in the old part of Crumlin, near the village that had been there for centuries. They didn't like it. But after five months they escaped to a different world. They got a small flat in a handsome three-storey red-brick Victorian house in the upper middle-class suburb of Monkstown, on the south side of Dublin Bay. Like refugees, my father and his cousin Vincent loaded everything my parents owned onto a handcart. On a hot June day, they pushed it all the way from Crumlin to Monkstown, eight miles east towards the Irish Sea through the lovely, respectable roads of Rathmines, Rathgar and Donnybrook.

The flat was the basement of the house. It was dark and dank, but they loved being there. It was the place where they were happiest. It was closer to the bus garage to which my father was attached, but it was near enough to the bay that they could walk along the seafront. Soon, those walks included a baby in a pram. My brother Kieran was born four months after they moved there. Two and a half years later, I was born in that basement. My parents imagined that we would grow up there, that we would go to school around the corner, that the quiet propriety of the place would shape us. Even the address – 4A Eaton Place – mimicked London's Belgravia, retaining a flavour of colonial Ireland. The surrounding streets had names like Trafalgar Terrace and Brighton Vale. It was far above their social station, but they had impressed the landlady as clean, mannerly, decent people. Their flat Dublin accents identified their origins, and they had very little money, but in other respects they could almost pass as middle class.

This was, I suppose, their stab at emigration. They went to a foreign place, utterly different from the tight, inner-city working-class communities of City Quay and the Liberties where they had grown up, and from the unfinished housing estate where my mother had been living. And they left in the hope of becoming what Irish exiles could be in England or the United States – modern. Eaton Place may have reeked of old gentility, but the point of being there was a basic modernity. To be modern was about how you dressed and what you read, how you danced and what you thought. But it was most viscerally about something that would later come to seem old-fashioned: the nuclear family – father at work, mother at home with the children, a door that could be closed to keep the rest of the world out. If you were Irish, you could create this structure in London and Birmingham, in the Bronx or in Boston. Mary and Sammy, with their two little boys, were trying to create it in Monkstown.

And they couldn't. Their idyll lasted for three and a half years. In September 1957, while they were living there, my mother's mother Frances died. She was sixty-three. My mother's father Jack was only sixty-five and just retired from his job working machinery in Power's whiskey distillery. He was in remarkably good health, especially for a man who smoked shag tobacco and started his morning with a tumbler of his employer's product. But he couldn't be expected to live on his own – who would cook his meals and wash his clothes? Mary's newly married young brother Johnny and his new wife moved in with him for a while, but there was too much tension and they moved out again.

On their fourth wedding anniversary, 4 January 1959, Mary and Sammy and me and Kieran left Eaton Place for 93 Aughavannagh Road. My mother did it out of a sense of duty. My father, I suppose, out of a sense of duty to her.

There was nothing very dramatic about any of this, but it was, in the Ireland of 1959, the material for drama. What Mary and Sammy experienced was, in its own tiny way, a version of the conflict between ideas of tradition and duty on the one side and modernity and freedom on the other that could be staged as a family melodrama – or even as a tragedy. This is what happened that year, just as the state was launching its economic revolution. And it happened spontaneously, from below.

On St Patrick's night, 17 March 1959, there was a serious disturbance outside the Playhouse Theatre in Limerick, where a controversial new play was being staged. People familiar with the history of twentieth-century Irish theatre might assume that this was another expression of Catholic nationalist outrage at the expression of heresies, in the line stretching back to the riots that greeted John Synge's great comedy *The Playboy of the Western World* in 1907 and Sean O'Casey's great tragedy *The Plough and the Stars*, in 1926, the cradle of genius again being rocked by philistine uproar. This was, after all, Limerick, the city that had so recently embraced as its model of Irishness the censorious puritan, Seán South.

In fact, the irate mob was not trying to stop the play. It was trying to get in to see it.

Hundreds who had travelled long distances from the neighbouring counties of Kerry, Clare and Limerick found they could not get into the already packed hall and there were 'scenes of pushing and general chaos at the side entrance'. Inside, the production of a play by a young man who ran a small pub in the north Kerry town of Listowel, John B. Keane's *Sive* was drowned out, not by boos and catcalls, but by 'bursts of spontaneous applause and cheering'. Even before it began, they 'sat and stood in tense expectancy'.[1]

Keane was thirty. He had emigrated to England in 1952, but returned after two years as a navvy. His plan was to marry his girlfriend and, if they could not make a decent life, to emigrate again for good, this time to America.[2] He had hopes of opening a bookshop in Listowel, but eventually settled for a pub. In 1958, he and his wife went to see a play put on by the local amateur company, the Listowel Drama Group. That night, after his wife went to bed, he filled a pint, sat by the fire, took out a copy book and pencil and began to write. By 6.30 the following morning, he had the first act of *Sive*. A fortnight later, he had a complete first draft.

Keane sent the play to the Abbey Theatre in Dublin. After five weeks, it was returned to him 'without a word of any kind'.[3] This was not surprising. The Abbey had been run since 1941 by Ernest Blythe, another veteran of the 1916 generation and a former minister for finance infamous for taking a shilling off the old-age pension in 1924. He had been an enthusiastic supporter of fascism in the 1930s. British intelligence had feared he might be a potential 'Irish Quisling' during the Second World War, when he was a guiding spirit of a small anti-Semitic and ultra-nationalist party called Ailtirí na hAiséirgh (Architects of the Resurrection), seeking the establishment of a Gaelic and Christian totalitarian state.[4]

That Blythe continued to run Ireland's national theatre said much for the Irish state's strange detachment from the intellectual and cultural consequences of the Holocaust and the defeat of fascism. Blythe's own primary concern in running the Abbey was that the theatre should play its part in the revival of the Irish language. (Peter O'Toole, for example, was not allowed to study at the Abbey's acting school because he did not have Irish.) But he also rejected any play that disturbed his own vision of Ireland. Brendan Behan's drama about capital punishment (of which Blythe strongly approved), *The Quare Fellow*, had met that common fate in 1954. It later became an international hit.

But what happened with *Sive* was much more striking. It became the vehicle for a revolt from below. The play was put on by the local amateurs in Walsh's Ballroom in Listowel in February 1959. It was a sensation there and at the regional drama festivals around the south of Ireland. By the time it reached the All-Ireland Amateur Drama Festival in Athlone in May, 'The house was packed and there was a great babble of sound that dropped to a murmur as the lights went out, and utter stillness fell at the first quiver of the curtain.'[5]

When the production won the main prize at the festival, it was treated like a sporting, rather than a merely artistic, triumph. The *Evening Herald* reported that the award 'is being celebrated by Kerry people at home and in Dublin in a manner reminiscent of Kerry victories in All-Ireland football competitions… A contingent of 40 Listowelians who had travelled to Athlone for the final adjudication on Sunday raised a cheer which brought back memories of Croke Park in the hey-day of Kerry football. Some even waved flags... Two of the flag-wavers had set out at mid-day on Saturday to hitch-hike the 120 miles to the festival.[6]

For the rest of 1959, *Sive* was the thing that Irish people had to see. The Crumlin-based novelist Christy Brown later wrote that the play 'appeared at a time of theatrical stagnation in Ireland when... the name of the Abbey Theatre had become a dry, dusty sound in many a throat, rather like a death-rattle that refused to stop... Into this enclosed arid wilderness *Sive* roared like a strange savage incantation, a raw wind from the broader, wilder spaces of the land, with its terrible immemorial message of love sold for silver pence, the casual betrayal of principle to the blind dictates of custom.'[7]

What was being summoned up by this savage incantation was what my parents, in their own much less dramatic way, were experiencing that year: a deep anxiety about how marriage and the family were supposed to work. Keane's play is about a woman, Mena, who is in her early forties and runs a small farm with her husband. What she wants is a nuclear family. But she can't have one. Not only is she childless, but her household is occupied both by her husband's mother and by his niece, Sive, born out of wedlock and orphaned. At the prompting of a matchmaker, Mena sells Sive to a wealthy but elderly farmer. Sive runs away and is drowned. The play ends with two nomadic Travellers, the play's moral chorus, singing a dirge over her body.

The obvious thing about this plot is that it seems utterly medieval. It could be a folk tale or a ballad. The evil matchmaker who sells the young girl to the old farmer is not criticized. He is cursed. One of the Travellers, Pats Bocock, puts a hex on the grasping, cynical Thomasheen Seán Rua: 'You are the bladder of a pig, the snout of a sow; you are the leavings of a hound, the sting of a wasp. You will die roaring.'[8] The feel of the play is much more pagan than Christian – the forces of darkness and of light are at war; witches and demons are abroad.

But it is equally obvious that Irish people in 1959 did not think about *Sive* as being ancient and exotic. They responded to it as social realism. Which, albeit in an epically exaggerated way, it was. The basic story was not fanciful, even in 1950s Ireland. Keane had been inspired by an incident in his own pub. A haggard old man had ordered a drink and then announced to the company that a matchmaker had arranged a marriage for him. He asked Keane to go with him to the nearby jeweller's shop to buy the ring. But the playwright had been horrified to discover later that the bride was a young girl and that, in her grief, she had ended up in a mental hospital.[9]

Marriage, especially in rural Ireland, could still have this brutal, medieval character. In a not untypical letter to the *Sunday Independent* from these years, a 'Rathkeale reader' asks 'can the present generation be blamed if they hold on to their holdings and will not give up possession to the eldest son unless and until that eldest son will marry a girl with a worthy dowry? Let us assume that the eldest boy casts his affection on a girl possessing no visible means, would it be right to expect that his parents sacrifice the other members of the family and throw them on the road or to the emigrant ship in order that the eldest may marry? Those parents expect certain amenities from the eldest boy who succeeds them, but if he brings home a girl without means where are those amenities to come from? Why blame the in-laws for all the trouble and leave the daughters-in-law go free? I have seen cases where the daughter-in-law, after a few weeks, cleared the old couple from the kitchen into the room allotted to them under the marriage settlement.'[10]

This was not the version of marriage Irish people were seeing in the American movies to which they flocked. Modernity meant falling in love, courting, getting married and starting a household with Daddy, Mammy and the kids – not with old grandmothers and orphaned girls. What they were seeing in *Sive* was both a ferocious denunciation of the old idea of the family and a haunting demonstration that it could not be escaped.

The tension between the old and the new was even written into the Irish Constitution. In the English-language version, it referred to the 'Family' as the fundamental unit of society. But the Irish-language version (which was regarded as more authoritative) used the term 'An Teaghlach', which means 'the home' or 'the household'. It suggested, not the nuclear family but a larger group with a patriarch and a wife, children, some of their relatives and perhaps one or more servants.[11] And what was happening in the late 1950s was that Ireland was hovering, as my parents did, between these two conceptions of how one should live.

On the one hand, Irish law continued to say that every 'legitimate person' was 'liable to maintain his or her father or mother', while every 'illegitimate person' was 'liable to maintain his or her mother'. And the most recent census, taken in 1954, defined the 'family' as 'any person or group of persons living in a single household'.[12] On the other hand, one of the attractions of emigration was precisely that in London or New York one could do the modern thing: fall in love, get married and have a house without 'a group of persons' other than one's own kids. And people who stayed, like my parents, wanted this, too.

There was nothing unusual in this kind of shift. It happened in all western societies as they moved from agriculture to industry, from countryside to city. But in Ireland it was happening very quickly: 'The Irish case may well be unique in the history of family studies. Within the space of a single generation – from the 1950s to the 1980s – the patterns of the traditional extended family dissolved and were replaced by the norms of the nuclear unit.'[13] In 1959 this process was still anxious and unsettled. No one knew which set of values would ultimately become dominant.

Part of the power of *Sive* for those audiences was that it explicitly placed itself at a moment of economic change. Money dominates the action – the £200 the matchmaker promises Mena if she forces the girl to marry the farmer. And in a chorus, Pats Bocock has a vision of the coming of a commercial culture: 'There is money-making everywhere. The face of the country is changing… There will be great changes everywhere. The servant boy is wearing the collar and tie. The servant girl is painting and powdering and putting silkified stockings on her feet and wearing frilly small clothes under her dress… The servant will kick off the traces and take to the high road. Money will be in a-plenty.' His questions to the audience were about this emerging future: 'What way will he rule? What way will he hould up under the new riches?'[14]

At the same All-Ireland amateur drama festival in Athlone at which *Sive* won the big prize, the Tuam Theatre Guild submitted a manuscript by another previously unknown writer to the new play category of the competition. It won the top prize of fifteen guineas. It had been written by two young men who had been hanging around the Co. Galway town of Tuam on a Sunday morning, waiting for the pubs to open, when one, Noel O'Donoghue, asked the fateful question 'Why don't we write a play?' The other young man, who ended up writing most of *On the Outside*, was called Tom Murphy. As he later explained, he did not think there was anything odd about O'Donoghue's question: 'Everyone in the country in 1959 was writing a play.'

On the Outside is a short, brutal one-act play that centres on two young men trying to dodge their way into the dance because they can't afford tickets. It is about the class system of small-town Ireland and it is full of rage. If Sive, who is eighteen, is a body to be sold off, Frank and Joe, a few years older, see the town as a 'huge tank with walls running up, straight up. And we're at the bottom, splashing around all week in their Friday night vomit, clawing at the sides all around.'[15] It is clear at the end that they will leave for England – the last line is 'Come on out of here to hell.'

Yet while there is no future in Ireland for them, there are hints in the play of a different, emerging Irish future – an American one. There is another young man of Frank and Joe's age, Micky Ford, and he has money. He has 'an uncle in America and they get letters home from him'. He wears a 'Florida Beach tie'. He 'affects a slight American accent whenever he thinks of it'. He drives around the town 'with one arm sticking out the window' like he's seen guys do in the movies. He says 'aw' and 'gee'.[16] And the audience knows that it is Micky who will get the girl Frank was hoping to hook up with, that the family that will emerge in time from these courtship rituals will be Irish with a slight American accent.

The feeling that an old world was dying but that the new one had not yet been born was enhanced by the very sedate pace of change in political leadership. On 14 January 1959, de Valera announced that, after more than forty years as a dominant force in Irish politics, he intended to retire as Taoiseach. But he did not retire immediately and was, moreover, selected as his party's candidate for the largely ceremonial but symbolically important office of President.[17] He was going but not going. He lingered in power as a lame duck leader for a full six months before moving over to the President's residence. He was replaced as Taoiseach by Lemass, who had also been involved in Irish politics since 1916. Lemass was only sixty, and his identification with economic change added to the sense of optimism generated by Whitaker's manifesto of 1958. But it was widely remarked that he looked older than his years after so many decades in office, and that he had come too late to the top job.[18] No one was really imagining that change would happen quickly.

3

1960: Comanche Country

Crumlin was often thought of as a Wild West on the frontier of a nationalist republic. As one of its residents, Kathleen Behan, described the journey to her new house here from her inner-city home: 'I thought we were going to Siberia. Crumlin, you know, is right out of the city, on the slopes of the Dublin Mountains. It would put your heart crossways, just looking at miles and miles of new roads. No lights. It was like the Wild West.'[1] Her son Brendan, dragged out there from the tight-packed inner-city tenement he loved, described Crumlin contemptuously as the 'countryside',[2] as if it were unmapped terrain, beyond the known boundaries of Dublin.

In Holinshed's Chronicles of 1587, which Shakespeare used as a primary source for his history plays, Crumlin gets a few lines, explaining why rents there are twice as high as in the other crown manors around Dublin. It is a punishment for an assault on the seneschal by the locals: 'The lobbish and desperat clobberiousnesse, taking the matter in dudgeon, made no more words, but knockt their seneschall on the costard, and left him there spralling on the ground for dead. For which detestable murther their rent was inhansed.'[3] Lobbish is from lob, a country bumpkin or lout; a clobberiousness is an unwashed rabble.

The idea of developing Crumlin as a suburb went back to an international competition for an overall urban development plan for Dublin, launched in 1914. It was won by a Liverpool-based architect, Patrick Abercrombie, whose proposal was eventually published in 1922, dedicated to the long-departed

Lord Lieutenant and his wife, the marquis and marchioness of Aberdeen. The frontispiece of the published plan is strangely gothic, a Harry Clarke drawing, entitled 'The Last Hour of the Night', of a ghoulish spectre, one bony hand pointing towards classical Dublin landmarks, the GPO, the Custom House and the Four Courts engulfed in the flames of war, the other to a derelict Georgian slum house, through whose broken windows we can see miserable people.[4] This, presumably, is the dying city from which the poor might gain refuge in the new suburbs.

It was another ten years after the publication of Abercrombie's plan before the development of Crumlin got under way. It was the largest building project in Ireland in the 1930s and 1940s, eventually totalling 5,500 two-storey houses, most of them more or less identical.[5] The scale was such that central government became directly involved, largely to insist on lower building standards and a 'ruthless reduction of the specifications'.[6] In 1950, shortly after my mother's family moved in to Aughavannagh Road, a government pamphlet, *Ireland is Building*, boasted that Crumlin's population was 'equal to that of the City of Limerick'.[7] But if this was a new city, the order of its foundational priorities was encoded in the few public buildings: the big police station was built and opened long before any secondary school, dispensary or hospital (for the first few years, there was not even a district nurse). The purpose was obvious: 'to control the unruly crowds of workless adolescents for whom there are no factories, no technical schools, no secondary schools, no football grounds'.[8]

Just as the pioneers who drove west gave their new-found lands the names of old world places – Dublin, Ohio; Paris, Texas – in order to convince themselves that this was still the world they knew, so the planners who pushed westwards towards the Dublin Mountains named and shaped the ground in the image of that Ireland they dreamed of. The centre of the housing estate of Crumlin began to be built in 1934, two years after Dublin hosted the huge international Catholic festival, the Eucharistic Congress, and the new Irish state declared to the world its fervent allegiance to Rome. So they built it in the shape of the Eucharistic Cross badge. The badge was an exercise in branding, a logo for a specifically Irish Catholicism: the Cross of Cong, an early medieval crucifix with a chalice imprinted in the centre, on which is carved a Celtic triskel, surrounded, in the Celtic manner, by a circle. It was mass-manufactured as a badge, and heavy pressure to wear it was exerted through advertising and an instruction from on high: 'The Committee of the 31st International Eucharistic Congress suggests that a resolution to wear the official Congress Badge would fittingly inaugurate Congress Year for Catholics. It is earnestly desired that from now onwards till after the Congress the official Badge should be worn by every Catholic, young and old.'[9] Catholics obeyed – as Alice Curtayne reported in 1933, 'In Dublin, of course, the unanimity was a sort of miracle… One glimpse of this was had in the mere manner of wearing the Congress badge, which was displayed by postmen, tramwaymen, Civic Guards, jarveys, crossing sweepers, and, in short, everyone imaginable.'[10] The badges sold so well that the Dublin Jewellery Manufacturing Company warned readers of the *Irish Press* that the market was 'at present flooded with all kinds of foreign-made Souvenir Badges, and the only guarantee which people have who wish to buy an Irish article is to look for the Irish Trade Mark'.[11]

So our home terrain was a large-scale reproduction of a piece of Catholic religious merchandising. The centre of Crumlin is a geoglyph, like the Nazca Lines of Peru or the white horses and giants cut into the chalk downs of England. One axis of the cross is Bangor Road, the other Clonmacnoise Road, and they meet in an inner circle of green space. The outer circle is formed by the elegant curves of Leighlin Road and Lismore Road. This badge, this brand, is also a kind of fetish, to ward off evil and radiate outwards to the whole estate the miraculous unanimity of the Holy City, the piety shared by 'everyone imaginable'. It defined an 'imaginable' to which every one of us should subscribe.

The thing was, though, that on the ground level, where we were, you couldn't see this at all. We were too close to be able to see the intended pattern. To see the geoglyph, you had to occupy a place above it, a literally superior position. It was clear in the planners' maps, and from the air. There is a photograph called 'Crumlin from the Air', published in 1939, innocently giving a pilot's eye view in which the Celtic Cross looks like a bomber's sight locked on its target. Even without this ominous double vision, there is no doubt that the point of view implied by the way the estate is branded is that of the high-level observer, floating above our lives, somehow controlling them by the magic of Celticism and Catholicism. The caption on the photograph invites the viewer to indulge in a kind of double take in which the image looks too 'perfect' to be real: 'Not just a model at a planning exhibition, but an aerial view of one of our housing schemes at Crumlin.'[12]

Out here it was pioneer territory, a kind of Ireland, suburban and working class, not known before. It seemed to many a blank space, physically and emotionally. Behan's friend, the poet Anthony Cronin, described his plight around the time I was born there: 'He lived for the most part in his parents' house, out in the grey spaces of Crumlin, a working-class housing estate dating from the thirties, better than some of the more recent experiments in ghettoisation, but not a very cheerful place all the same.'[13]

As if to magic away the uncertainty of what might emerge from these winding rows of pebble-dashed two-up-and-two-downs, the planners gave a ready-made history to a place that had no history, gave Crumlin the shape and names of the great guarantors of Irishness: land, nationality and religion, Wicklow villages, the patriot dead, the one, holy Catholic and apostolic church. Our roads were named after the ancient dioceses of the Irish Catholic Church: Leighlin, Clonmacnoise, Ferns, Kells, Bangor, Lismore, Clogher, Saul, Kildare. When they ran out of antique monasteries and dioceses, they turned to the patriot dead, to the nineteenth-century nationalist leader Charles Stewart Parnell and his estates: Aughavannagh, Glenealy, Rathdrum, the names conjuring up not only Ireland's most benevolent landlord, but also the soft, harmless hills and glens of Wicklow.

In such a place there would be happy homes and happy families, with the huge vaulted church and the granite barracks-like police station to look down and smile. The nameless planner who named Aughavannagh Road may have thought of John M. Synge: 'Here and there in County Wicklow there are a number of little known places – places with curiously melodious names such as Aughavanna… where the people have retained a peculiar simplicity… When they meet a wanderer on foot these old people are glad to stop and talk to him for hours, telling him stories of the Rebellion, or of the fallen angels that ride across the hills.' Though perhaps he did not read on to Synge's list of the 'three shadowy countries that are never forgotten by these simple folk: America (their El Dorado), the Union and the Madhouse.'[14]

The houses themselves were, in the words of the architectural historian Ellen Rowley, 'a seemingly naïve or childlike cliché of "home" on a mind-boggling scale, consisting as it did of rectilinear terraces of cubic houses surmounted by pitched roofs of slate'.[15] Each had a single rectangular window on both levels, vertically aligned with each other, and a simple door capped with a concrete canopy. The kitchens had one sink and a single counter unit, with a tiny larder and a coal bunker. The one really nice thing in the houses was the high-quality joinery of the skirting boards, doors, architraves, floorboards, stairs and handrails.

On moving in, families found that other visions of respectability had come into play: houses specifically designed for very large families had just two small bedrooms, and yet the designers had seen fit to take up precious space with that most Victorian of bourgeois domestic ideals – a parlour. ('Somewhere', an old lady told me, 'to bring the insurance man for a chat when somebody died.') Nor could the planners bring themselves to see the houses as places of work: the kitchens were combined with the main living area, leaving the working women with no space of their own and large families under their feet. 'Somebody told me', said Dominic Behan, 'that the man responsible for their design committed suicide. I'm quite sure his death, if at all, was accidental, for no man with a mind like his could ever succeed in anything so calculated as taking a life, even his own.'[16]

In Brendan Behan's early story, 'Moving Out', a thinly described autobiographical account of the family's transplantation to Crumlin, the father wails 'what nicer am I nor an orphan, an exile with no place to lay for my head'. Behan's younger brother Brian recalled that 'We ended up in Crumlin, which was like Outer Siberia to us at that time… Da called it Barbarian Land.'

Brendan compared the estate to a Soviet prison camp ('"Kremlin's Crumlin", he called our new abode') but also 'referred to Crumlin as the Wild West'.[17] As if this encompassing of east and west was not enough, Brian himself recalled that on his first day in Crumlin, 'It was like being in a dump on the far side of nowhere. "Fuck this for a game of cowboys", Brendan said to me as he looked around him at the desolation. Maybe he should have put Indians in there as well. I felt we were in Comanche country.'

The sense of exile was potent. In 1939 Dublin Corporation's Allocations Officer, Thomas Bourke, testified that 400 of the 2,000 families placed in Crumlin by 1938 had applied to be transferred back to the city centre, but 'we did not grant any at all'. 'If we were to circularise the Crumlin tenants, and ask them how many would like to get back to the city, we would get a thousand applications... They would get the impression that they could get back, and a regular landslide would take place. For that reason, we avoid asking if they would like to get back.' The tenants 'feel out of their element, and the sooner they get back, they think, the better... we will eventually have to reach a point where we will have to force these people into these houses.'[18]

On this new planet, even the air was different. Bourke said that 'A lot of people declare that the air is so strong that the children eat them out of house and home. They cannot afford to keep the children in food. They would prefer to go back to any place out of it.' James Larkin, the legendary leader of the Dublin workers in the great Lockout of 1913, was now Chairman of the Corporation's Housing Committee. He claimed that the new inhabitants of Crumlin were put 'into areas to which they are not acclimatised. They are simply dumped down there; they don't understand their surrounds. No one ever goes near them except to collect the rent.' Larkin took up the case of a man who had tuberculosis which, he claimed, was made worse by the Crumlin air: 'The atmosphere there was such that this man with TB could not stand it.'[19]

Around the time my mother's family moved in, an American Jesuit sociologist, Alexander Humphreys, interviewed some of the inhabitants. One of the complaints he heard was not just that the terrain was strange – so were the people. Crumlin had a mix of people moved from the intensely tight inner-city slums and of migrants from rural Ireland. These rural Irish people were aliens. 'People', as one informant told Humphreys, 'have come here from the four quarters of the globe', as if Mayo and Offaly were Nigeria and China.[20]

This created a sense of unknowability. The people from the inner city were used to living in each other's shadows. The old world did not recognize privacy. In Sean O'Casey's Dublin plays, the domestic space is continually being invaded by nosy neighbours. Everything is observed; secrets are all open. But in Crumlin, there was a new idea – the notion of intrusion. One woman told Humphreys: 'If one of the neighbours on the road was having a baby, you might like to do something, but you feel you would be intruding. She would not want you walking in unless the house were in great order. She'd be embarrassed and you would feel you were just in the way, so you don't do anything.' A man summarized this shift: 'Here the people are all Sinn Feíners, all for themselves alone.'[21]

We were indeed experiencing a revolution in privacy. At its heart was an element that is abundant in Ireland but then still unusual in the form we encountered it – water, running through taps into the big Belfast sink in the kitchen, into the bath, and through the cistern of the lavatory. This, too, was the flow of modernity. It is almost impossible for a society that takes it for granted to understand what a marvel it was, and how much it changed the lives of women.

Since the 1930s, domestic modernity had been gradually working its way into the Irish countryside in the form of electricity. Rural electrification had been one of the few real innovations of the independent state – the great scheme on the River Shannon, largely built by the German company Siemens, was at the leading edge of global hydroelectric technology. It had generated, not just vast amounts of electricity, but its own heroic ballad:

If I were Homer, the ancient roamer,
I'd write a poem on a noble theme,

And I'd sing the story and praise the glory
Of that wondrous project, the Shannon Scheme.[22]

In spite of these Homeric feats, two out of three homes in Ireland still had no electricity at the end of the Second World War. Throughout the 1950s and 1960s, a million poles were shipped from Finland and erected across the Irish landscape, and 50,000 miles of wire were strung. By 1965, 80 per cent of rural Ireland would be connected to electricity. The process transformed the great indoors. The Electricity Supply Board issued detailed pamphlets on 'modernising the farm kitchen', with photographs and plans, and opened shops in small towns selling appliances.[23]

This too was, for the older people, a process of estrangement. Vona Groarke, in her poem 'The Lighthouse', contrasted the promises of modernity with the image of three elderly women suddenly thrown out of their familiar world:

In the village, a crowd of overcoated men
sent up a cheer for progress and prosperity
for all …
And in the length of time
it took to turn a switch and to make light
of their house, three women saw themselves
stranded in a room that was nothing like
their own, with pockmarked walls
and ceiling stains, its cobwebs and its grime:
their house undone and silenced
by the clamour of new light.[24]

In Crumlin, there had always been electricity. But in my great-grandmother's house in Co. Wexford, this clamour of new light was still novel and loud. She was still there like those old women, ancient and strange, so strange that the first thing I remember is being taken to see her. She was ninety-eight. She sat in a dark kitchen on a high-backed chair in black clothes, long grey hair still thick around her shoulders. My older brother Kieran took fright at the sight of her and hid behind my mother's skirts. I was too young to be scared. I gave her a daisy I had picked in the garden on the way and sat up on her lap. She pointed a bony finger at my brother: 'That fellow will come to no good', she said. 'But this – this is an elegant boy.' I was more pleased by her curse on Kieran than by her blessing on my own head.

But I remembered, too, the weirdness of the toilet, a little wooden hut out behind the henhouse. There was a smooth plank with a hole in the middle and you did your business down there. There was no flush because there was no running water. And I remembered walking with my mother for what seemed like miles, all the way from the house, up the dusty boreen to a pump where she filled two buckets before we walked all the way back. And I remembered the tin bath being filled with water that was heated in a pot in front of the fire. This was the country and in the country people did not have toilets or bathrooms or water that came out of taps.

Our houses were small but they had an indoor bathroom and toilet at the top of the stairs. People who had moved to Crumlin from the old Georgian tenements of inner-city Dublin had lived with a communal toilet at the back. One formerly grand house, 14 Henrietta Street, had ninety people living in it with three toilets. Outside the cities, sanitary facilities were often even worse.[25] The 1961 census showed that at least half of all houses outside urban areas had no fixed lavatory facilities at all, indoor or outdoor. In Longford, for example, there were 1,590 indoor toilets for the county's population of 30,000 people. In Roscommon 67 per cent of homes had no toilets of any kind.[26] Over the country as a whole, just 15 per cent of farmhouses had a flushing toilet.

The 1961 census also showed that of 374,971 dwellings in rural areas, 281,058 (almost 75 per cent) got their water from a 'well, fountain, pump' or other non-piped source.[27] Just 45,585 (12 per cent) of the homes had the use of a hot-water tap. What this meant was an immense amount of drudgery. It was children and especially women who carried the buckets up and back, up and back. Reports of women having to haul buckets of water for two miles to and from a pump or well were commonplace.[28]

This imperative governed everything, including time. A survey by the Irish Countrywomen's Association discovered that 'one-third of a woman's life was spent carrying water to her home'.[29] An advertising pamphlet issued by the state-owned Electricity Supply Board illustrated this temporal tyranny, albeit substituting a male consumer (on the assumption that the husband would control the money needed for the purchase of an electric pump) for the much more common female experience: '"With the hand pump I pump for two hours each day", said a rural consumer when he was purchasing one of our electric power pumps. He treated his water problem in terms of pumping time. We checked and verified this figure of "two hours" and, furthermore, checked the capacity of his pump. In actual fact, this consumer averaged 550 hours per annum pumping, in which time he pumped 99,000 gallons or 438 tons of water. His pumping time equalled almost eleven and a half 48-hour weeks per annum.'[30]

This sucking up of time also spoke of the wrong kind of timelessness, of a way of life that was intolerably unaltered over many centuries. But women could change it – by leaving the countryside for Dublin, for England or for the US. James Dean wrote in the *Irish Press* in 1960 that 'The womenfolk have been carrying water in pails and buckets from the well or the spring for many hundreds of years. And the net result, when we come to look at the human account sheet over the period, is that there are progressively fewer women who stay in the country. The inescapable deduction is that perhaps they don't really enjoy spending their lives being mere drawers of water and human hauliers of H_2O – when the application of a little money, intelligence and the force of gravity could put the water in a tap in their own kitchen sink.'[31]

Water was a sexual issue. It affected marriages. The bitterly ironic phrase 'Love, Honour and Carry Water', parodying the wedding vows to love, honour and obey, was used as an advertising slogan by a supplier of water pumps in the early 1960s.[32] Even late in the decade, and even close to Dublin city, it was still current: 'The waggish comment "Love, Honour and Carry Water" is frequently offered to prospective brides in the district of Donabate and Portrane, Co. Dublin. Local residents quote the line as exemplifying the constant preoccupation with water which is part of life in this section of North County Dublin. In the Donabate and

Portrane area – about 14 miles or so from the city, and growing more popular with tourists as a resort each year – there is no piped water and no general sewerage scheme.'[33]

Knowing this gave us in Crumlin a fine sense of superiority. Country people were regarded as being real in all the ways we were not – earthy, honest, close to the soil of Ireland. The old city slums were authentic in their grittiness and depth of history, while we were denizens of a no-man's-land that was barely a place at all. But we drew our water instantly from taps and made it privately in a little indoor room with the door closed. That didn't feel like Siberia, or the Wild West or Comanche country. It felt modern.

4

1961: Balubaland

On an afternoon in late September 1961, my father hopped off the back of the bus he was working on to grab a copy of a newspaper. He had seen the newsboy's poster promising the first pictures of Irish United Nations soldiers who were being held captive in the Congo. He found a picture of the men in the Hôtel de l'Europe in Jadotville, where they were being held by Katangese rebels. Their stoical commandant Pat Quinlan was at the centre and my mother's big brother Willy Heffernan was at the front, just to his left. His already thinning hair stood out on his bare head. He had a fabulous tan and a huge, warm smile on his face. A few minutes later, when the bus reached its terminus in Dublin city centre, my father told the inspector he was sick. He ran all the way back to Aughavannagh Road with the proof that Willie was alive.

A fortnight earlier, those newsboy's posters had been terrifying. On 14 September telexed messages had arrived throughout the day from agency reporters covering the war in the Congo that had broken out when the province of Katanga, rich in uranium, diamonds and other minerals, had seceded from the newly independent Belgian colony. In 1960, Katanga was supplying 10 per cent of the world's copper and 60 per cent of its cobalt.[1]

The rebellion had the clandestine backing of most of the western powers. The United Nations was committed to supporting the elected Congolese government headed by the charismatic Patrice Lumumba. Ireland, anxious to prove itself as a good member of the UN, became deeply involved. The Irish diplomat Frederick Henry Boland was elected President of the General Assembly in

1960 and Conor Cruise O'Brien became the UN representative in Katanga in 1961. During the Congo crisis a senior Irish officer, General Seán McKeown, was appointed as military commander of United Nations forces there.

As O'Brien's lover (soon to be his wife), the poet Máire Mac an tSaoi, put it, Congolese independence was intended by the Belgians to result in 'a façade of black rule, behind which white interests – economic, political and religious – would continue, as heretofore to exercise power and dictate events'.[2] In the brutal logic of the Cold War, the United States, Britain and France effectively supported the Belgians in backing the Katangese secession and overthrowing Lumumba. By becoming strongly aligned with the UN's attempts to support real independence, Ireland, in its first real intervention on the world stage, found itself arrayed against the very countries – the US and the western European powers – it was seeking to join with in its new age of industrial modernity.

This was an immediate crisis of identity. Lumumba had accepted aid from the Soviet Union and that should have been enough to make him the bad guy. But, on the other hand, he was the leader of a nation that was attempting to decolonize – Lemass and the Irish minister for external (i.e. foreign) affairs Frank Aiken had been militant revolutionaries in their youth. Moreover, Katanga – a breakaway province – could be seen as an African Ulster. These emotional connections outweighed the realpolitik of Ireland's aspirations to belong to 'the West'. In January 1961, when Lumumba was handed over to the Katangan minister for the interior Godefroid Munongo to be murdered, Aiken, in the delegates' lounge of the UN building in New York, watched him on TV being bundled down the steps of an aeroplane to be taken to his torture and death. He saw him as Jesus Christ, exclaiming: 'It's like the descent from the Cross!'[3] Aiken did not know – because it was still a closely guarded secret, that British intelligence (as well as the CIA) had been directly involved in Lumumba's murder.[4] Had he done so, his instinctive sympathies with an anti-colonial martyr would have been, if possible, deepened.

What did Irish people know about the Congo? Playing at cinemas in Ireland all through 1961 and 1962 was a French film,

Willy Rozier's *Prisonniers de la brousse*, released in France in 1960, and starring Georges Marchal and Françoise Rasquin. It was not quite arthouse. The title means 'Prisoners of the Jungle', but when it was released in English it was changed to *Prisoners of the Congo*, presumably to take advantage of interest in the crisis. It was a melodramatic adventure story of the white hero and heroine and their three companions, lost in the bush when their plane goes down and battling their way to safety against wild animals, a hostile landscape and strange tribes. The lobby poster showed a still of Marchal and the very blonde Rasquin facing off against six naked spear-toting black men, with a drawing of a bare-breasted black woman dancing ecstatically to the wild rhythm of some tom-toms. 'Awesome! Savage! Breathtaking! They dared challenge the dark hell of the Congo.'

It was into this imaginary dark hell that Willie, a gunner based in Mullingar barracks, had been sent. The Irish army was a tiny, rundown force of 7,000 men that had seen no military action since the end of the Irish Civil War in 1923. It showed. As the military historian Declan Power put it, 'Equipment was World War II vintage at best, and in many cases still World War I. Looking at the uniform and equipment of Irish troops in 1960 it would be easy to mistake them for British Tommies going to the front in 1914.'[5]

The Irish government agreed to a request from the UN to send, initially, 700 of these men to the Congo as peacekeepers. The gesture was an important statement of the existence of a new Ireland, no longer the isolated island metaphorically disappearing beneath the Atlantic, but a force for good in the big wide world. But the men carried the encrusted pre-modern past on their backs and in their hands: 'the first Irish soldiers to embark on overseas active service in Africa did so in bullswool uniforms and hob-nailed boots with bolt-action rifles'. All other national contingents in the UN force – including the Norwegians, Danes, Canadians and Swedes – arrived in tropical uniforms.

Veterans recalled the puzzlement of the American airmen who landed outside Dublin to transport them to Africa in a giant Globemaster. When they landed, perhaps because they seemed so odd and anachronistic, they were thought to be Koreans.[6] When

Willie's 35th infantry battalion arrived in Elizabethville in 1961, however, they did find that the one they were replacing had a store of 37,200 cans of Guinness.[7]

The heavy woollen uniforms seemed to be especially attractive to Congolese ants. The UN eventually issued the poor soldiers with one tropical shirt and pair of trousers each. But the Irishmen were too small and skinny for the standard fit. The official report of the division to headquarters in Dublin notes that 'our troops could be seen wearing the trousers with large waists and several turn-ups to compensate for the length of the trousers'.

They were equally unprepared linguistically and psychologically. In a Francophone country, very few of the Irish officers (let alone the men) could speak French – a deficiency blamed by the official report on 'our home educational system where the classics abound'. There was also an innocence about the Irish troops. They did not expect to be shot at. The official report complains that 'Our men were not adequately security conscious. They were not suspicious enough as sentries, on patrol or off duty. This fault prevailed right through. They are very much inclined to be "cushy" and easygoing. They trust too much in the other fellow's good intentions.'

Perhaps this is not entirely surprising – at the battle of Jadotville in which Willie took part, he was, at thirty-six, one of the oldest of the enlisted men. The average age of the Irish troops was eighteen years. Two of the 156-strong contingent were fifteen years old and twelve of them were sixteen. Ireland had sent child soldiers into a country where their use by militias would become, many decades later, an international scandal. After the battle, the Irish commandant Patrick Quinlan introduced what he called 'the baby' of his small force, Jimmy Taheney, to reporters: 'He says he's 19, but he looks more like 16 to me.'[8]

This naivety was shattered in November 1960 when a detachment of Irish troops was attacked by about a hundred warriors of the Baluba people near the small trading post of Niemba in Katanga. The Balubas had been subjected to a campaign of terror by secessionist forces led by white European mercenaries. They mistook the Irish for more such raiders and ambushed them.[9]

Nine young Irishmen were killed, mostly with arrows. The disaster seemed straight out the colonial imaginary of Darkest Africa.

At one level, Ireland knew exactly what to do with it: another huge public funeral procession, like that of Seán South or Liam Whelan. Thousands of people went to Baldonnel aerodrome and packed into the hangar where the coffins lay on top of military trucks, to pray and to leave Mass cards on a pile that 'had grown to a veritable mountain'.[10] The next day the bodies were taken into the city for a solemn Requiem Mass conducted by John Charles McQuaid, and then led in procession out to Glasnevin Cemetery. The city shut down and vast crowds lined the streets. Many people knelt on the pavement and recited the Rosary. Ageing veterans of the Old IRA marched behind the cortège with their medals pinned to their coats. In Dublin port, every ship flew the Irish tricolour at half-mast. The dead men were buried in a common grave beside that of the revolutionary hero Michael Collins, who had also died in an ambush.[11] The idea was clear: to assimilate what had happened in Congo into the tradition of Irish Catholic martyrdom.

Except that this was not so easy. The men had not died in an Irish civil war, but in a Congolese one. And their killers were Black. There was no official way to talk about this, but it hovered over the event. There is a bizarre juxtaposition of photographs in the *Irish Times*' coverage of the funeral. On the right, there is the expected image: a wide shot of the head of the cortège on O'Connell Street, with the massed ranks of mourners behind. But on the left, there is a closer shot of the crowd. It focuses on two white women with their mixed-race children, a little girl held by her mother's hand and a baby in a buggy. The caption states, laconically: 'These children were seen among the crowds'.[12] That 'were seen' is darkly resonant, suggesting almost that the children had been caught out, spotted doing – or merely being – something suspicious. The suggestion is that their presence is anomalous or discordant or ironic: Black faces watching the victims of Black violence pass by.

While the official imagery was that of Catholic and national martyrdom, Irish reporters also reached for another (by now equally familiar) trope – the Balubas as American Indians. One of the survivors described the attack in terms familiar from

Western movies: 'The air was suddenly black [with] a shower of arrows and the Balubas let out blood-curdling yells that sounded like a war-cry and rushed down the road like madmen, jumping in the air and waving their weapons... The Balubas seemed to be everywhere, crashing through bushes and giving their sort of high-pitched battle cry.'[13]

There were headlines like 'Baluba Tribes on Warpath Again',[14] 'Balubas Incited by Chief'[15] and 'Atrocities by Balubas' (uncritically citing propaganda by the secessionist government including 'photographs of whites and Africans said to have been skinned alive').[16] When the first contingent of Irish troops arrived home, they carried bows and arrows as souvenirs.[17] The caption to a photograph in the *Cork Evening Echo* in January 1961 reads: 'Cpl. Pat O'Donnell, B Co., Southern Command, looks rather fierce with his souvenir Baluba bow and arrow on arrival home at Dublin Airport.'[18]

This is weird enough, given that this was just weeks after the most shocking act of violence against their comrades. But it was as nothing compared to the bizarre disjunction between what happened and how it worked its way into life and language in Ireland. Irish people simply could not process the Niemba massacre. It could not be integrated into their sense of who they were and how they acted in the world. It belonged in movies like *Prisoners of the Congo*, not in the mental world from which the soldiers came.

What could you do with it? One possibility was to make a sick joke of it. Brendan Glackin, a young man in Ballina, wrote in his diary in 1966 about deciding to go to the library to find out who the Balubas really were: 'I bumped into Walter in Jordan's. When I mentioned my interest in finding out more about the Baluba tribe, he told me of a conversation he overheard between two of his elderly female neighbours in Bohernasup, on the day after the Congo atrocity. One of them related the news of the murder of our noble soldiers, saying they had been "strung up by the Balubas"; to which her horrified companion responded, according to Walter, that "Th-there was n-no need to be that c-cruel – could they n-not just have h-hanged them n-normally?"'[19]

Another possibility was to dress up as 'Balubas' in local fêtes and parades. In July 1961, seven months after the massacre, the local newspaper reported from the village of Stradbally, Co. Laois, that 'Balubas were a common sight parading the streets of Stradbally on Thursday, when the annual fête, sponsored by the District Nursing Association, was held'. The prize for the most topical fancy-dress display went to the children of fourth and fifth class in the convent primary school who dressed as 'Congo troops'. And the prize for the most original dress went to other children from the same classes who paraded as 'Balubas'.[20] That same month in the adult fancy-dress competition at the fête in Kinvara, Co. Galway, first prize in the 'funniest' section went to Sean Nolan as a 'Baluba warrior'. The accompanying photograph shows a white man in blackface with a leopard skin draped across his naked torso, hoisting a spear.[21]

Less than a year after the massacre, a correspondent to the *Irish Farmers Journal* complained about the fashion houses' promotion of new seasonal colours: after African Violet, she wondered whether 'the next thing we'll hear of is "Baluba Black"'.[22] This strange facetiousness deflected the shock of a home front as unprepared for its exposure to a foreign world as the Irish troops themselves had been. And of an overwhelmingly white society unprepared, too, for blackness.

Baluba Black was more than a seasonal colour. It was a void that could be filled with otherness. At its core was racism. On Leighlin Road on our estate in Crumlin, there was a beautiful black boy nine years older than me called Philip Lynott. In the Christian Brothers' primary school on Armagh Road, other kids taunted him, not just as 'Blackie', but as 'Baluba'.[23]

'Baluba' became a word in our language – a word I never remember not knowing. It was our word for savage, inferior, inhuman. Later, the lexicographer Terence Dolan, in his *Dictionary of Hiberno-English*, would define it as 'unruly or unsavoury person'. He added the derivative 'Balubaland': 'areas of Dublin reputedly frequented by such people'.[24] As late as the mid-1980s, a Fine Gael government minister, Dick Burke, would describe the Corporation estates in his own west Dublin constituency as

Balubaland.[25] But if we lived in Balubaland, were we not Balubas, too? Were the Balubas us or them?

As the word spread during the 1960s, it came to encompass not just an external, wild, Darkest African other, but a Darkest Africa within Ireland. Every kind of savagery, from street violence to political machinations to foul play on the sporting field, was Baluba. (A reader wrote to the *Southern Star* to 'condemn in the strongest possible way the "baluba tactics" which took place between Cork and Tipperary hurlers at Croke Park'.[26]) Before the end of 1961, the best-known Dublin cop, Sergeant Lugs Branigan, was telling a court in Dublin that a defendant had bitten him 'on a part of my anatomy I cannot produce in court because I am sitting on it'. He complained that 'At least the Balubas cook you first.'[27] A witness in Limerick District Court, describing the victim of an assault, said that 'He was like a man attacked by Balubas with spears'.[28]

The most popular political columnist, John Healy, used the term to condemn 'all those Balubas who were for cutting my throat on the grounds that I was biased'[29] and explained his frequent use of the word: 'for the benefit of any African readers, this is a purely technical political term, as is the frequently used "Mafia".'[30] In 1969, the minister for justice Micheál Ó Móráin, attacking protestors against bad housing conditions in Dublin, warned that 'I will see that the majority of decent people are allowed to go about their ordinary business without being held up by a lot of Balubas.'[31]

How did we know that poor and marginalized people in Ireland were human? Because they were not Balubas. Pleading for the provision of piped water to six families living outside Clonmel in Co. Tipperary, the local TD Seán Treacy insisted that 'these people are not to be thought of as outsiders – foreigners, Balubas or people from Mars. These are families prominently identified with the life of the town.'[32] A plea for decent treatment of Travellers in Mayo was predicated on the notion that 'They are not Balubas from the Bush but human beings'.[33]

But there was also the anxiety that, as the Carlow county engineer put in when complaining about vandals, 'All the Balubas aren't in Africa'.[34] The plot of James Douglas's play *The Savages*, given a reading at the Peacock in Dublin in 1968, was summed up as follows: 'a young Irish soldier… goes off to face the Balubas in the tough jungles of the Congo for the cause of world peace; but ironically he leaves behind him in Ireland a jungle in which the natives behave as savagely (in a corrupt way) as the ferocious Balubas.'[35] Could Ireland itself be Balubaland?

For those like my Uncle Willie being sent to the Congo after the massacre at Niemba, these confused reactions back home merely amplified the sense that Ireland did not really know what it was doing there. The Irish were supposed to be patrolling some kind of imaginary border between civilization and savagery, but it was shifting, porous and ambiguous – not just on the ground in Katanga, but in Ireland itself. He found himself at the centre of an event that Ireland could not officially make sense of: the battle of Jadotville.

Willie arrived with his comrades – the 156 men of A Company of the 35th infantry battalion – in the early summer of 1961 at Elizabethville, capital of the would-be breakaway Katangese state. It was also the headquarters of Conor Cruise O'Brien, the UN representative and perhaps the leading Irish intellectual of his generation. Cultured, sophisticated, cosmopolitan, witty, supremely self-confident, a brilliant critic and historian, O'Brien seemed to embody the new Ireland. The UN general-secretary, Dag Hammarskjöld, personally asked the Irish government to release him from its diplomatic service so he could serve as his plenipotentiary in Elizabethville.

The main reason for Hammarskjöld's choice was, paradoxically, the very uncertainty of Ireland's place in the world – European, but not really; anti-colonial but also anti-communist; in but not quite of the west. O'Brien astutely perceived his appointment as a result of the exclusion of almost all other possibilities: 'The system of elimination was not… altogether coercive but it did make an Irishman the best choice.'[36]

Ireland, in other words, was useful on the world stage primarily for what it was not. But this was not a particularly good basis for the exercise of power in an extremely volatile place. O'Brien heard rumours that, in the general election due in Ireland in 1961, the opposition intended to mock Lemass's incumbent administration as 'The Best Irish Government the Congo Ever Had'.[37] But the cutting joke had some reality: with the appointment of O'Brien, along with that of McKeown as UN military commander, this part of the Congo did acquire a kind of Irish government.

But it was a government with a deeply problematic mandate. On his way to Elizabethville, O'Brien could hear in his head a snatch of a music-hall song that his former boss on Ireland's delegation to the UN, Frederick Boland, liked to sing when an acquaintance was about to take a foolish risk:

It's a wonderful job for somebody –
Somebody else, not me![38]

The problem with the job was its ambiguity. The Irish soldiers thought they were in the Congo as peacekeepers and a large part of what they did was in fact pacific – guarding refugee camps and the UN mission. But the UN's role was expanded in March 1961, on foot of a Security Council resolution demanding the withdrawal of all foreign officers and mercenaries from the Congo. Since these mercenaries were the hard core of the secessionist forces in Katanga, this was an implicit mandate for conflict with them and the well-armed native militias they led. This is the conflict into which Willie and his comrades were drawn.

On 3 September 1961, his A Company, under Commandant Patrick Quinlan, was sent from Elizabethville to Jadotville, a wealthy, Belgian-controlled, mining town dominated by the giant Anglo-Belgian Union Minière du Haut-Katanga. Ostensibly, they were there to protect the white civilians against marauding Blacks – holding the thin line of civilization against barbarism. In reality, they were victims of a ruse. The Katangese mercenaries, anticipating the possibility of an attack from the UN force, had developed this story in order to draw some of its troops away from the likely action in Elizabethville. Far from seeking their protection, the local white population was extremely hostile to their presence. Later that month, Quinlan would write in his diary: 'Organised by the Belgian government we were lured to

Jadotville.'[39] Whether or not the Belgian government was involved, the men certainly were 'lured'.

They were also abandoned. Quinlan was told nothing of O'Brien's plans for Operation Morthor, a UN attack on Katangese positions in Elizabethville, whose aim was to disarm the mercenaries and arrest some of the leading secessionists, including Tshombe and Lumumba's killer Munongo. O'Brien was well aware, as he wrote in 1962, that the Katangans 'knew… what we were preparing to do'. He even anticipated that in response they would 'whip up hysteria among some of the gendarmerie'.[40] But neither he nor anyone else told Quinlan any of this.

Final plans for Operation Morthor were agreed on 12 September. The following morning at seven o'clock, A Company in Jadotville was informed about it by radio. Half an hour later, it was attacked by a force of about 3,000 Katangese gendarmerie, led by a hard core of white officers. The Katangese had surrounded the Irish on 9 September. Quinlan had been warned by two Irish engineers working for the mining company that A Company would be attacked.[41] Willie and the other men had spent the previous week digging trenches and foxholes. But they had none of the usual tools for defence: no mines, barbed wire, trip flares or heavy mortars. Even their blue UN helmets were made from fiberglass and meant for show, not for protection under fire. They were outnumbered at least twenty to one and, in terms of experience, they were hopelessly outmatched. None of them had ever fired a shot in anger. The Katangans were led by Michel de Clary, a veteran of France's colonial wars. The white mercenaries, mostly Belgian and French, had extensive experience of fighting in Europe, Asia and Africa. The Black gendarmerie was well armed and, for the most part, well trained. Against them were 156 Irish novices with no real knowledge of where they were and no clear orders as to why they were there.

What happened, though, was astonishing. Most of the Irish soldiers were at Mass when the attack came, yet they managed to scramble and fight it off. Over the next five days, they faced repeated waves of attack, heavy 81mm mortar fire and shelling from a French 75mm field gun. They were bombed by a Fouga Magister fighter jet piloted by a French mercenary. Willie manned a Vickers machine gun – the Irish also had Bren guns and field mortars. Over five days, he and his comrades killed about three hundred of the attackers. Under Quinlan's brilliant command, they lost not a single man. But attempts to reinforce them failed, and they ran out of water, food and ammunition. They surrendered and were taken into captivity at the Hôtel de l'Europe. The man who killed Lumumba, Godefroid Munongo, came to inspect them.

There's a photograph of Willy with a group of his comrades from A Company sitting around a bomb crater in front of the bus garage that was at the centre of the UN compound. The siege is just over and the men are all alive, so it's no surprise that they look happy. The crater and the holes caused by mortar and machine-gun fire seem incongruous – most of the men look like kids on a camping holiday. Willie and most of the others don't even have helmets. It seems impossible to imagine that they had just withstood six days of almost relentless violence.

But in Ireland, they were dead – or at least a third of them were. On 14 September, the newspapers had reported a steady stream of disastrous news: '20 of the encircled Irish Company at Jadotville said to have been captured and executed'; 'Five others of the 150-strong company reported killed.' In the late afternoon, the words on the agency reports arriving by telex were even starker: '57 Irish killed at Jadotville.' As the *Evening Herald* recalled on the first anniversary of the alleged disaster, 'The telephone lines in the *Evening Herald* office were jammed as people rang continuously for news. In the pubs as men downed their pints, they read the agency reports that "the chief of 1,000 fierce Bayeke warriors had declared war without quarter on the Irish troops at Jadotville." They wondered what would be the fate of the young Irishmen fighting for their lives in the middle of darkest Africa.'[42]

The BBC World Service lent its authority to these reports. So did the *Irish Times*, whose front page carried the banner headline: 'Heavy Irish Losses at Jadotville: 57 men said to have died in bitter fighting'.[43] Later that day, the Irish papers relayed claims from a clandestine radio transmitter operated by the Katanga government that 130 Irish prisoners had been taken in twenty-four hours and that 'For every single Katongese [sic] shot... 10 of the Irish soldiers will be executed.'[44]

Over that terrible weekend, it seemed clear that Willy had been either killed in the fighting or was being held hostage and at risk of being executed in reprisal for Katangese losses. My grandfather might have lost his son, my mother her big brother. In Mullingar, Willie's wife Maisie and his four children might have lost a husband and father. Hence, the picture of him that my father saw in the paper was a kind of resurrection.

The prisoners were eventually released on 25 October. Willie returned to Elizabethville with the rest of the company. He was given what was regarded as the plum job of guarding Conor Cruise O'Brien in his compound, the Villa des Roches, known locally as the Villa des Riches. As a good Catholic, he was disturbed to discover that O'Brien, who was divorced, was living in the house with Máire Mac an tSaoi, to whom he was not yet married. She later recalled in her memoir that 'no one questioned my presence there'[45] – it did not occur to her that young Irishmen from Midlands towns would certainly have questioned it if they could.

On the other hand, the great perk was that O'Brien allowed him and the other guards to use his swimming pool. Willie was a fanatical swimmer who, towards the end of his life, had to be banned from the pool in Mullingar because he kept having heart attacks while swimming. It seems likely that he was given the job out of compassion, since most of the other guards seemed to be chosen from among the boy soldiers. George Ivan Smith, a UN official who also lived in O'Brien's bungalow, claimed that the only thing that frightened him in the Congo were 'the shellshocked babies with sub-machine guns on guard duty round Conor's swimming pool'.[46] Máire Mac an tSaoi remembered that 'When Tshombe's jet-fighter flew over they trembled like aspens, and their weapons trembled too. They were awaiting repatriation, and the Villa des Roches was regarded as a benign place for them to recuperate.'[47]

This 'trembling like aspens' is the only image I have of what state Willie might have been in after Jadotville – because he didn't talk about it. The battle became another probe sent, not into Darkest

Africa, but into Darkest Ireland. As with Niemba and the Balubas, there was no collective Irish story into which the experiences of Willie and those 150 other men and boys could fit. Or perhaps it is more accurate to say that there were two stories – tradition and modernity – and they belonged in neither of them.

Objectively, what Quinlan and A Company had done at Jadotville was one of the greatest feats of arms in the history of the Irish state. It was a classic of perimeter defence. To keep 156 men alive for almost a week under the assault A Company faced was utterly remarkable. It would, and much later did, make a terrific action movie. But that was precisely the problem: nobody died. There was a traditional template: the General Post Office in Dublin in the 1916 Rising, heroic defence against overwhelming odds leading to martyrdom. The trouble with Jadotville is that it failed to produce a single martyr. There was no solemn cortège, no praying crowds on O'Connell Street, no requiem High Mass for McQuaid to perform.

When things had begun to look grim at Jadotville, the public expectation in Ireland was of a last stand by our gallant sons. The *Evening Herald*, in those days of foreboding, ran a front-page headline: 'We will hold out to the last bullet'.[48] Quinlan privately believed that his men would indeed have done so. In October, he wrote: 'They would have died to a man if I had decided to continue.'[49] And it is striking that in public Quinlan felt it necessary to suggest that this would indeed have been the right thing – if they had been fighting for Ireland, rather than for the UN. The *Irish Independent* reported just after the end of the siege that Quinlan had claimed that 'his men… would have fought to the last drop of blood – but he was not prepared to let them die… A usually reliable Informant who spoke with Commandant Quinlan at Jadotvllle told me the Irish commander said he would never have surrendered if he had been fighting for Ireland.'[50] Even this qualification was not quite enough. Quinlan recommended twenty-nine of his men for distinguished service medals and military medals for gallantry. An army board decided in 1965 that 'no medals would be awarded'.[51]

There had been no blood sacrifice and the men had surrendered.

They lived to tell the tale and yet, under a different kind of siege – a long siege of insinuations on their manhood and honour – they chose not to do so. Conor Cruise O'Brien, in his book on the Katanga affair, had little to say about Jadotville, except to suggest vaguely that A Company 'need never have surrendered had it not been for the UN's confusion of purposes'.[52] The *Irish Times* journalist Cathal O'Shannon picked up on 'a palpable sense of shame' within the rest of Irish contingent in the Congo at the outcome of Jadotville.[53] When the men returned to barracks in Ireland, there were jokes in the mess from other Congo veterans: I found your shirt in Jadotville, a white one.

Willie, even if he was traumatized, went back to the Congo in 1962. So did a lot of his comrades from A Company. There was a sense that they had to return, as one of them told Rose Doyle decades later, to redeem themselves: 'Those of us who went back... went to grind the axe, so to speak. Bury the shame we were made to feel.'[54] Nothing could have spoken more clearly of the culture of shame and silence that held such a firm grip in the country: even a heroic feat of male, military valour could be dragged down into the pit of Darkest Ireland.

But Jadotville might still have been construed differently, if only it had served internationally to prove the credentials of the new, modern Ireland as a proper western country. Unfortunately, it pitted Irish troops against the interests of the western powers, most obviously Belgium. It showed an Ireland out of kilter with its own geographic neighbours – not only too poor but too unreliable to be allowed into the EEC. Jadotville coincided with a real national humiliation: the contemptuous treatment of its application for membership of the western European club. The country had steeled itself for the full embrace of modernity through the EEC, only to have its advances dismissed.

Four countries applied to join the Common Market at broadly the same time: Ireland, Britain, Denmark and Norway. Britain applied on 10 August 1961 and negotiations were opened on 8 November. Denmark applied on the same day and negotiations were opened on 30 November. Norway applied on 30 April 1962 and negotiations opened on 12 November. Ireland actually got its application in before the others, on 31 July 1961. The Common Market never bothered to open negotiations. The *Irish Times* reported in October 1961 that the text of a formal reply from the EEC's Council of Ministers to Ireland's approach 'did not show enthusiasm for the Irish application and it is known that Holland and Germany were the only two members keen to enter preliminary talks'.[55] Belgium, France, Italy and Luxembourg 'considered that Ireland's underdeveloped economy would make it unsuitable for full membership of the E.E.C.'.

The Irish government expected the process of negotiating entry to be finished by the first half of 1963, with Ireland becoming a member on 1 January 1964. But the Common Market never got around to starting preliminary talks, even for the sake of politeness, on Ireland's accession before the whole plan for expansion of the bloc collapsed when General de Gaulle unilaterally vetoed British membership.[56] At an elite level at least, Ireland had made a huge psychological leap – it was ready to plunge into the ocean of free trade. But, as it happened, the tide was out and there was barely a splash. For a long time yet, Ireland would be stuck between a still potent idea of its past and a still elusive idea of its future.

5

1962: Cathode Ní Houlihan

It happened one time in Ireland that a boy was playing ball in front of his house when an old grey man came riding up on a white steed. The grey man challenged the boy to a game and the boy won. But the old fellow came back each evening and renewed the game until, at last, he triumphed. He then had the boy in his power and took him away to his own place. There, he set the boy a fantastical task. He took him to the bank of a river and told him that if he did not build a bridge of feathers to span it, he would cut off his head. He gave him a gun and told him to shoot birds and use their feathers to make the bridge.

The boy shot the birds and plucked them and made a huge pile of feathers. But every time he began to build with them, the wind would come and the feathers would fly. They filled the air like snowflakes in a blizzard. He chased them and caught some and tried again. The wind blew and the snowstorm of plumage swirled around him, over and over. Near nightfall, when the sun was beginning to sink, he sat down and wept, waiting for the old grey man to come and cut off his head. But instead, the grey man's beautiful dark-haired young daughter tapped him on the shoulder and asked why he was so sad. He explained his plight. She set to work and made the bridge for him.

The man telling this story was also a grey man, because he was on the black-and-white screen of the Philips television, and he looked old to me because I was not yet four. The television arrived in an RTV Rentals van on 9 January 1962. I remember the date because it was my father's birthday. My brother and I sat on the floor staring at the test card. It was a picture of a Cross of Saint Brigid, a traditional icon woven from rushes, with Telefís over one arm of the cross and Éireann under the other.

The first programme finally came on at five o'clock. It was Eamon Kelly, an actor got up in a collarless shirt, a light-coloured waistcoat and a dark suit and hat. He was sitting by a fire in an old rustic cottage, playing the part of a traditional rural storyteller, a seanchaí. I could not at the time understand how poignant this was: television re-enacting a cultural form – the long, slow, intimate, elaborate art of narration – it was about to destroy. The seanchaí by the fireside would be replaced by the box of flickering images in the corner of the room or high on the wall of the pub. In 1960, even before the TV station went on air, *Dublin Opinion* ran a cartoon of a seanchaí, dressed like Kelly, sitting by the fire in an old country cottage, beginning his story with a traditional formula 'bhí fear ann fadó agus fadó a bhí' (There was a man long ago, and a long time ago it was). But he is trailing off: 'Will ye listen to me?' The question is shouted angrily at the members of the household, from the grandmother to the baby, who are fixated by a man with a guitar on the TV on the kitchen table.[1]

Yet clearly, in 1962, it was still possible to imagine a compromise – putting the seanchaí on the TV. This, the authorities imagined, was what we would want to watch on the box: the flickering images of the old culture, magically transported from the rural west into a kitchen in suburban Dublin. Eamon Kelly looked and dressed a bit like my grandfather, but where my grandfather's voice was deep and gruff, Kelly's was high-pitched and nasal, and his Kerry accent made the story sound much more like song than speech. His tone dipped and darted like a swallow in flight. He swooped every so often from English into Irish, as if he were diving into some deeper element. The old grey man didn't say 'I will cut your head off', but 'bainfear an ceann díot'. The boy was not sad but 'go brónach'. I did not know these words, but they were not much stranger than the warbling chant of Kelly's English.

I could see him, his thick eyebrows and the scarecrow tufts of hair sticking out from the side of his hat, his gambolling eyes and wry mouth. But I could also see the blizzard of feathers in the wind, the boy slumped by the river in despair. And then the beautiful daughter making the bridge. I imagined her maybe knitting the feathers together the way my mother's fingers worked her needles with such light dexterity – if strings of wool could become a jumper, feathers could become a bridge. Kelly's pitch rose even higher as his voice made an image out of airy nothing: 'When 'twas finished, there was nothing ever seen like it within the four walls of the world. It was a pure marvel, from pier to arch and arch to parapet!'

But was it real? Or just an illusion? The boy in the story doubted his eyes. He didn't know what to think. So the girl linked his arm and led him to the bridge and they walked together over the river, across the bridge of feathers. I could nearly feel these flyaway plumes, tickly underfoot, like when my father once brushed one that had fallen from a seagull's wing gently across my sole. But I could not tell quite what was producing these mental sensations. Was it the old story and its evocation of the marvellous as it had been envisaged for thousands of years? Or was it this new thing, this television? Was it the force that could weave images that came through the air like snow into a bridge of feathers that we could cross, from where we were now to where we wanted to go?

Television had officially come to Ireland just days before we rented our set. The single national channel, Telefís Éireann, had gone on air on New Year's Eve of 1961. This was very late – Albania got its own television station before Ireland did. And Ireland was also reluctant to introduce the new medium. The spur to action was the leakage of British stations, the BBC and ITV, into the protected space of Ireland. People on the southern side of the Border could pick up signals from broadcasts in Northern Ireland. On much of the east coast, if you could afford to invest in a tall aerial, you could tune in to the airwaves drifting across the Irish Sea from Wales.

As Alan Bestic reported, 'Shrewd salesmen were quick to realize that pictures from wicked British transmitters in Wales could be picked up by Irish saints and scholars, if they planted their aerials on top of towering masts. Soon these masts were sprouting over the neat, prim semi-detacheds of suburbia and over the sprawling blocks of Dublin Corporation housing estates, like naked beanstalks, the grid on top swallowing in and spewing out the alien culture and perhaps chewing away at some of the roots of censorship too.'[2]

One anxious TD, Fintan Coogan, suggested in parliament that the state should investigate the possibility of jamming these signals from the alien world: 'There are times... when there is cause for embarrassment, particularly if children are watching the programme. In the interests of public decency, some programmes should be jammed. Certain things are censored. Why should these programmes not be prohibited entry?'[3] But the invisible airborne invaders could not be halted at the frontier and sent back to where they came from.

Shortly after TÉ opened, a government TD, Pádraig Faulkner, explained the rationale for its establishment: 'Most people were anxious that we should have a television service of our own, particularly those people who were able to get broadcasts from the different British television services. There were many reasons, national and spiritual, for this. From the national point of view, they recognized that the spate of propaganda to which we were being subjected by foreign television would undermine our whole national outlook and have a most undesirable effect on our young people in particular. From the spiritual point of view, I do not think there is any need for me to stress that there are very different standards of morality in this country as compared with those of the country from which these programmes were coming. The chief danger here lay in the manner in which matters which we consider morally wrong were being portrayed as not only not wrong but as normal codes of behaviour. For these reasons we were anxious that we should have a television service of our own.'[4]

This was the paradox: if kids like me, the children of a modernizing Ireland, were to be protected from having our national and spiritual outlook perverted by English influences beamed at us through the TV screen, we had to be exposed to a safer kind of television. The conceptual model was inoculation. Television was the vector of a virus of unIrish beliefs and codes of behaviour. The ideal defence would be a permanent quarantine behind some wall of technology that prohibited entry to the carriers of the disease. But since this was not possible, there had to be a vaccine: an Irish national station. We would get just enough television, in a carefully modified form, to stimulate our national and spiritual immune systems.

But television itself was still recognized as innately dangerous. Almost the first thing viewers heard on TÉ was an expression of fear. In his address launching the station, Eamon de Valera, now the President of Ireland, told them: 'I must admit that sometimes when I think of television and the radio, and their immense power, I feel somewhat afraid. Like atomic energy it can be used for incalculable good, but it can also do irreparable harm.'[5] His startlingly apocalyptic image of TV as an atomic bomb that might annihilate Irish culture was reinforced by a warning that bad television could 'lead through demoralization and decadence to dissolution'.

He tried to lighten the gloom by expressing his disbelief in the possibility that those who contemplated 'the grandeurs of the heavens or the wonders of life on this marvellous mysterious world in which the good God has placed us, will not find more pleasure in these than in viewing, for example, some squalid domestic brawl or a noisy street quarrel'. But his tone suggested that he was haunted by intimations that his people might actually be quite interested in watching noisy quarrels from the comfort of their own living rooms.

And, in his way, de Valera was hinting at a profound question whose answer was unknowable. He claimed to be assured that those who were running the new station 'will bear in mind that we are an old nation; that we have our own distinctive characteristics and that it is desirable that these should be preserved'. But the truth was that no one could be sure what the idea of a distinctive culture would mean in the new world Ireland was entering, what could or should be preserved, what might be lost. As the chairman of the state broadcasting authority, the Irish-born star of British light entertainment TV Eamonn Andrews, acknowledged, three days after we got our TV set, the worry was that 'Cathleen Ní Houlihan [the traditional female embodiment of nationalist Ireland]... was in danger of becoming Cathode Ní Houlihan.'[6]

Moreover, it was not just de Valera who was scared of television. The radical TD Dr Noël Browne, thirty-three years his junior, expressed similar anxieties: 'Television is… probably the most frighteningly powerful educational or propaganda media to come into the hands of man since the establishment of the printing press. Each one of us is frightened of it, whether Socialist, Liberal, Conservative, Labour, Catholic, Communist or Fascist, and rightly so.'[7]

Even on the opening night, there was a hint of one of the most subversive aspects of television: the primacy of entertainment over authority. John Charles McQuaid arrived at the studios to perform a solemn benediction of the Blessed Sacrament (perhaps, in his mind, also an exorcism), to be met by Chloe Gibson, an English theatre director who had been hired by TÉ as a senior producer. His driver, Robert, was carrying the Archbishop's fine ceremonial vestments. 'Sweetheart', said Gibson, 'you can leave the gear down here.'[8] Gibson, a devout Catholic, almost certainly meant no disrespect. But in the world of television's illusions, McQuaid's sacred vestments would be just another period costume.

McQuaid instinctively understood that this new force could not be merely bent to his will. Not that he would not try – he later approached Lemass and asked him to arrange for the removal of three senior broadcasters, Shelagh Richards and Jack White (both Protestants) and Prionsias MacAonghusa (whom he regarded as excessively liberal). Lemass refused.[9] But he also sent two smart young priests, Joe Dunn and Desmond Forristal, to New York to be trained in TV production techniques.

Just after midnight on 1 January 1962, the symbolic moment of Ireland's new Irish TV age, viewers could see on their screens His Eminence Cardinal John D'Alton, the eighty-year-old Catholic Primate of All-Ireland. He was quite clear about what should not be on television. TÉ should reflect high ideals, 'not presenting us with a caricature of Irish life such as we have had from some of our writers in recent years'.[10] Viewers would have no trouble decoding this for themselves. They would have thought of *Sive* and of Tom Murphy's *On the Outside*.

But freshest in their minds was the scandal of Edna O'Brien's

The Country Girls. O'Brien's debut novel, telling the story of two young women through adolescence and teenage years, was banned in Ireland in June 1960, almost immediately upon its publication in London. It was one of thirty-five books banned on the same day by the Censorship of Publications Board, ranging from literary novels by O'Brien, Alberto Moravia, James T. Farrell and Emigdio Alvarez Enriquez to *Diana Dors in 3D* and French cartoons, from the *Home Medical Encyclopaedia* to *What to Tell Your Children About Sex*.[11] They were all just filth.

In 1962, McQuaid sent a copy of O'Brien's follow-up to *The Country Girls*, *The Lonely Girl*, to the rising young princeling of Fianna Fáil, Lemass's son-in-law Charles Haughey, who was minister for justice, to express his alarm that 'such stuff' should be printed. Haughey went to see the Archbishop next day 'to express his disgust and revulsion'. McQuaid recorded Haughey as saying to him that 'Like so many decent Catholic men with growing families, he was just beaten by the outlook and descriptions' in O'Brien's books.[12]

O'Brien was already writing for television in Britain – her play *The Wedding Dress* was due for broadcast by Granada TV.[13] The cardinal's address on the opening night of TÉ was making it clear that she – and all the other writers who were 'caricaturing' Ireland by writing honestly about it – should not be invited to do the same for her home country's TV station. But this raised the obvious question of what *should* be on Irish television.

Seamus Dolan, a Fianna Fáil TD (Teachta Dála, member of parliament) for Cavan, mused in the Dáil that the station should make programmes about rural festivities: 'There are the mummers who go around at Christmas time. There are weddings, feiseanna, and fleadha ceoil. All these reflect life in rural Ireland.' But since Ireland was about to become modern, it should also make programmes showing how industries worked: 'Telefís Éireann could be used as a boost to our morale by showing the ability of the Irish people to manufacture and produce well designed and well finished articles.'[14]

The Galway TD Fintan Coogan suggested that the medium could be used to teach Irish dancing – for the benefit, not so much of Irish people, as for foreign tourists: 'The Irish dancing in local dance halls is not up to the proper standard. One is ashamed of it before visitors.' When the acting chairman of the Dáil asked him 'Would the Minister for Posts and Telegraphs have any responsibility for dancing?', Coogan persisted: 'I suggest he could use his good offices and ask Telefís Éireann to give a series of lessons. These dances are some of the nicest that can be seen on any dance floor. No one need suffer embarrassment before visitors from outside if Irish dancing is properly done.'[15]

When the station opened, it broadcast for forty-four hours a week. It was able to fill twenty hours with its own productions. One obvious possibility was that TÉ should fill its holes by rebroadcasting selected programmes from the BBC. This was indeed the proposal made in 1959 by the most senior civil servant involved in the process, León Ó Broin. He spoke to Seán Lemass and suggested to him that 'We were fortunately placed in close proximity to what was probably the best service in the world, the BBC, an entirely public service organisation, and I suggested that we might explore the possibility of a special arrangement for an extension of their service as a back-up to such programmes of quality as we could produce on a similar public service basis. He made no comment, but as I spoke of the BBC, I felt that the chauvinists among us would not take too well to any arrangement with the British Broadcasting Corporation.'[16]

Ó Broin's instincts were right. As one Fianna Fáil TD, Joseph Leneghan, put it, 'Steps should be taken to ensure that television does not make us more English than the English themselves.'[17] But there was an alternative: to make us more American than the Americans themselves. Just as the importation of American capital was much more acceptable than an influx of British businesses, it was decided that, if I and all the other kids of the new Ireland had to watch television, it would be much better if the images and accents we would see and hear came from a westerly direction.

On that opening night of TÉ, one of the main attractions was a film of a state visit to Ireland in June 1961 by Princess Grace of Monaco. She was Grace Kelly – beautiful, gracious, impeccably poised. She was also Irish-American and Catholic. The fairy-tale

Irish princess embodied a fantasy version of an Irish modernity in which Hollywood glamour was fused with ancestral piety. One headline from that visit summed this up perfectly: 'Princess Sits At Cottage Turf Fire'. This astounding feat was accomplished in the Widow Mulchrone's tiny two-roomed cottage 500 yards up a dusty boreen in Co. Mayo – the very place from which her grandfather had emigrated to Philadelphia. The Widow Mulchrone herself, wearing a new black dress for the occasion, welcomed the princess at the half-door: 'It is a long time since a Kelly has been here. I am honoured in welcoming one back. The key of my house is yours.'[18]

Giving the keys to the house to an American was not at all the same thing as surrendering them to the Saxon stranger. It could be construed as a return of the exile, a making whole of what had been sundered. And it hinted at a fantasy future in which we would all look as gorgeous (and be as rich) as Grace Kelly but still be as holy and Catholic as we assumed her to be. To watch this homecoming on the new medium of TV was to be reassured that aspirations to modernity could be reconciled with traditional devotion and historical continuity.

Thus, too, the appointment of Edward J. Roth as director-general of the new station. Roth was from Boston and, in his application for the job, played up his Irish Catholic roots, suggesting that growing up in Boston naturally gave him a 'considerable depth of insight to [sic] the Irish people, their likes and dislikes, their history and their culture'.[19] If an applicant had suggested that growing up Catholic in Birmingham or Glasgow had given him a special feel for Irish moods and desires, the scepticism would have been overwhelming. But Eamonn Andrews, in supporting Roth, suggested that his actual 'lack of first-hand knowledge of Ireland' could be compensated by 'his catholicity, and his Irish ancestry'.[20]

Roth quickly realized that Irish rights to the back catalogues of American film studios – produced under the Hayes Code and therefore suitably chaste – could be purchased cheaply. So could a huge range of American TV programmes – comedies, variety shows, above all Westerns.

This was the decision that was made about our dreamworld. There were Irish shows, a lovely young woman called Blaithín showing us how to draw; a slightly surreal language instruction programme in which the doll spoke in Irish and the ventriloquist replied in English; an Irish-speaking cartoon duck; Eamon Kelly telling stories. But we did not summon these shows to our minds when we were in bed between waking and sleep. We did not play them out next day among ourselves.

The dreamtime of the official culture was the pre-modern West of Ireland – the thatched cottage, the Irish-speaking children listening enraptured to the seanchaí. But somehow the powers that be had stumbled into making a whole different dreamtime for us, set in a different West, a landscape, not of shifting clouds and rolling waves and blue-tinged mountains and soft bogs, but of mesas and ravines and deserts and sharp, dry, bare escarpments. We were sucked into a world of merciless sun rather than one of relentless rain, of Appaloosa horses rather than donkeys, of dust not mist. Mayo, Kerry and Sligo had nothing on New Mexico, Colorado and Arizona.

At 5.30 p.m., the swirling strings would sound out from the box and beneath them the thunder of hooves as the Cisco Kid and Pancho came galloping over the hills and the deep male voice announced: 'Here's adventure, here's romance, here's O. Henry's famous Robin Hood of the Old West – the Cisco Kid!' Every night, the duo would help somebody out of trouble or foil an evil plot, not because it was their job but just because they were boundlessly benign. Cisco was handsome and had a shirt with lacy filigrees that were kind of girly but okay because he also had a gun. Pancho was his comic sidekick. He was fat and mangled English so he was hard to understand. But his language was as richly exotic as Eamon Kelly's Irish – desperado, compañero, chili, frijoles, arroyo.

Sometimes, when we could stay up late, there was Bat Masterson, who was a sheriff and a gambler and so handsome that there were always lingering shots of women making eyes at him that were a bit boring. But he was great because he had a silver-topped cane he always carried, which meant that when you were playing him you could have a stick in one hand and a gun in the other. I used to sing the theme song to myself:

Back when the West was very young
There lived a man named Masterson
He wore a cane and derby hat
They called him Bat, Bat Masterson.

Roth, the director-general, was a particular fan of *Have Gun – Will Travel*, which ran for half an hour before the nine o'clock news on Wednesdays. The first episode, broadcast a fortnight after TÉ went on air, opens, before the title, with a close-up of a holster with a design of a chess knight on the front. A hand reaches down, takes out the gun, pulls back the trigger and points the barrel straight at the viewer. The voiceover begins: 'I'd like you to take a look at his gun. The balance is excellent. This trigger responds to a pressure of one ounce. This gun was handcrafted to my specifications and I rarely draw it unless I mean to use it.' Every episode would begin with the same film sequence but a different voiceover. 'I've seen you lie, cheat, steal and try murder. You've tried everything but begging. Now get down on your knees and beg.' 'There's an irritating roughness about the way you people speak. Makes me obstinate. If you want me to leave, you're gonna have to make me.' 'I read your name on a wall somewhere along with a lot of other names of dirty little men. But wherever you are, I'll dig you out.' 'Sit down gentlemen and sit still. I've come to order a coffin for the first one of you that makes a move.'

There was something mesmerizing about this sequence. It was not like anything else. Westerns had been embedded in Irish popular culture for decades, through films, and novels and comic books. But this was not Roy Rogers or Audie Murphy. There was no face. The only flesh was the gnarled hand that reached down from out of shot to grip the gun and turn it right into our faces, so that we, for that moment, were the dirty little men who would have to beg for mercy. The voice was disembodied, mysterious but unquestionable in its authority, like the voice of God. The light on the gun was pure and stark and beautiful, making the thing it illuminated a sacred object, at least as holy as the chalice the priest held up to be adored at Mass. It left no doubt that the hero was not even the darkly enigmatic Paladin who rode through the succeeding stories. It was the gun itself. The series was self-consciously based on medieval romances of the knight errant, except that there was a twist. The Holy Grail was not being sought. It was there already, in that hand, pointing at us. The gun was the Holy Grail.

At the time, of course, I did not know how to think any of this. I just knew that I loved this image, that it was more powerful than any other. What is strange is that, when everyone was afraid of television and sure that exposure to the BBC would have 'a most undesirable effect on our young people', no one seems to have thought about its effects. The IRA's Border campaign had not yet formally ended – it was abandoned a month later. There was, in Seán South and Fergal O'Hanlon, a recently renewed tradition of male heroism based on the supreme authority of the gun. Nothing glamorized that authority more seductively than that repeated opening sequence of *Have Gun – Will Travel.*

The only politician who seemed concerned was Noël Browne. In the Dáil in April 1962, he raised the question of the imagery of the Westerns: 'It is undesirable in so far as it does create in the minds of young people the belief that violence is permissible and acceptable, that violence is the correct solution for a physical dilemma, that when you do not like somebody or when you do not agree with somebody, it is permissible or acceptable—"Adults do it; why cannot we?" I would condemn all portrayals of violence and brutality, for instance, as in Westerns.'

Browne accurately noticed what all the boys on my street and around Ireland were wearing. 'Nearly 60 per cent of the children in most towns and villages in Ireland do not wear their own clothes. They are all dressed up in cowboy outfits, wear cowboy hats and carry guns.'[21] But the only reply to Browne's concerns came from an Independent TD, Frank Sherwin, who could not see what the problem was: 'My children love pictures featuring violence. If there is a peaceful, easy-going picture being televised they turn it off because they are not interested. For the Minister's information, cowboys are very popular with children…'

Sherwin was right. We loved 'pictures featuring violence'. Even out in the Comanche country of Crumlin, we knew we were the cowboys. One of the big boys, Paddy Murtagh, got hold of a rope. He made it into a lasso and practised all the moves he had seen on TV. Finally, he put them into action. A little girl was passing on her kid's bike. With exquisite skill and timing, he threw the rope so that the loop dipped gracefully over her head, down over her arms and round her waist. He pulled the rope so that the lasso tightened around her and, in the same movement, jerked her off the bike. She squealed in fright and pain but when she stood up and saw the rope so perfectly coiled around her body, even she gave him a look of wonder and admiration.

Almost nobody seemed to worry about our imitative obsession with these images of violence. They were American and therefore exempted from vigilance. They came as part of a package that included American investment and the embrace of consumerism. In 1967, Merritt E. Freeman, director of the American Fortnight that was opening at one of Dublin's high-end department stores, Arnotts, told the US Chamber of Commerce in Ireland that 'All international trade, and particularly that which involves consumer merchandise, encourages people and governments to greater understanding.' He announced that, as a token of this understanding, the centrepiece of American Fortnight would be 'real cowboys and Red Indians flown in from America'.[22]

A decade after Heinrich Böll had dreamed about a dead Indian in Duke Street as an image of the ebbing away of Ireland, the five living Indians – Chief Woolfe Robe, Ho-Ga-Na-She, Mi-Tsi-Ga, Blue Sky Eagle and Was-Be-Was-Ska-Ka – danced on the street a few yards away. The 'real' cowboys (actually a cowboy and cowgirl, Sam and Hendy) did tricks with ropes and whips. The *Irish Times* reported that 'the conflict between cowboys and Indians... emphasized dramatically on television' was now being 'nicely remedied' in the name of commerce.[23] Arnotts advertised the daily 'cowboy and Indian parade' as an added attraction to 'the greatest, most exclusive collection of made-in-USA top quality goods (from fashions to furniture) ever to come to Ireland.'

6

1963: The Dreamy Movement of the Stairs

After Mass in Saint Bernadette's on Sundays we would cross the road to Jim O'Keeffe's shop to buy sweets. Mr O'Keeffe was a monument to good feeding: broad-beamed, moon-faced, double-chinned, glowing red with humour and self-satisfaction. He was called Jim by the adults and Mr O'Keeffe by us, but in public life he was J. J. O'Keeffe, a stalwart of the conservative Fine Gael party on Dublin Corporation. In 1963, he was elected Lord Mayor of Dublin and got to do two very exciting things. The one that interested me most was that on 25 March 1963 he 'inaugurated', in Roches department store on Henry Street, the first escalator in Ireland, imported from Germany.[1] 'The Lord Mayor cut the ribbon', the *Evening Herald* reported, 'silent motors began to purr somewhere, and the dreamy movement of the stairs began.'[2] The *Irish Press* referred to our own portly Mr O'Keeffe as 'the first man to make the ascent', as if he were Edmund Hillary and Roches Stores was Everest.[3]

I remember it because, like every other kid in Dublin, we went into Roches Stores to try it out. There were actually two escalators, one from the basement to the ground floor and the other from there to the first floor. They were magic carpets of modernity. Even the word was new and shiny: we had never imagined a need for such a verb, for such a motion: to escalate. We levitated like fakirs. The effortlessness had the thrill of sin. Everything had to be worked for. Duty was all. But this was a free ride. You just did nothing. You glided upwards like a gull catching a thermal. I had seen images on the TV of astronauts floating around in zero gravity and this is what it felt like – weightless and out of this world.

The second most exhilarating moment in Mr O'Keeffe's year was that a short while after he had made that glorious first ascent, he was in the Oval Office with John Fitzgerald Kennedy. There he is on 2 May, his big bum perched on the side of a sofa in his old-fashioned black three-piece suit, his big hands on his big knees, beaming jovially at the young man in the rocking chair on his left. JFK might be from a different century. His suit is two-piece, sable grey, slim cut. His shirt is a cool, pale blue, his tie narrow and divided by diagonals of gold and blue and scarlet, his cufflinks shooting out perfectly from his jacket sleeve. The two men are like illustrative figures from a cartoon: old world and new, dullness and glamour.

But the thing is, their gazes are locked in mutual enjoyment. The president's eyes are half-closed in laughter and his dazzling white teeth are reflecting their radiance onto Mr O'Keeffe's big red face. His pleasure must have been genuine: he gave our shopkeeper half an hour on a day when he was receiving reports of the abuse of civil rights protestors by police in Birmingham, Alabama. The newspapers reported that the two men 'exchanged jocular remarks about election procedures during their thirty-minute talk'.[4] In Crumlin, it became a matter of fact that President Kennedy and Jim O'Keeffe had struck it off mightily and were now bosom buddies. It was thought to be very unjust that the lord mayor's term of office would run out just before JFK was due to arrive in the city on 24 June. There was talk that his replacement, Seán Moore of Fianna Fáil, would delay taking up office so that the two old friends – as they were now known with absolute certainty to be – could greet each in their official capacities. (Moore declined the opportunity for such a courtly gesture.)

After the torch had been passed to a new generation, after his son had been sworn in as the 35th President of the United States, old Joe Kennedy went to the celebration lunch for his family which he had arranged at the Mayflower Hotel in Washington. He found a huge table in the buffet room, and hundreds of people milling around it. He had never seen most of them in his life before, and he was mightily annoyed. 'Who are these people?', he asked the social secretary who had organized the lunch. 'Your family, Mr Ambassador.' 'They are not. Just who are these freeloaders?' Old Joe grabbed the nearest half-dozen guests and demanded to know their names. Sure enough, they were Kennedys and Kennedy in-laws and Fitzgeralds. 'They are all family', Old Joe admitted, 'and it's the last time we get them all together too, if I have anything to say about it.'[5] Meanwhile, down on the old stone quay in New Ross, they were lighting bonfires and brushing up on family connections.

When John F. Kennedy arrived at Dublin Airport on the evening of 26 June 1963, he conjured up an image of a broken and scattered family being reunited. He stood on the tarmac, tanned and gleaming, and told us that 'No country in the world, in the history of the world, has endured the haemorrhage which this island endured over a period of a few years, for so many of its sons and daughters. These sons and daughters are scattered throughout the world, and they give this small island a family of millions upon millions who are all over the globe.' In his words, in his presence, was the tacit promise that all of these sons and daughters and in-laws would be brought together again at the buffet table of the post-war world. But we still feared that when we arrived for the feast, we would be confronted by a sour old man muttering 'just who are these freeloaders?' and demanding our names.

At the time, the *Observer* described the four days of Kennedy's state visit in June 1963 as Ireland's 'first wholly satisfactory act of nationhood'[6] and this was not wrong. But in retrospect, the ambivalence of that moment of arrival is striking. Even the image of family that was trotted out with such apparent comfort is disturbingly paradoxical. Eamon de Valera, President of Ireland, went to greet Kennedy at the airport, and it was as if, here as well as in Washington, the torch was being passed to a new generation. In de Valera's eyes, the young man who had come down from the sky was a fulfilment of a millennium of Irish historical oppression. Bizarrely, he evoked an image of JFK as an ancestral avenger, summoned from the deep past to smash the foreigner.

He hailed him as a representative of 'the great Kennedy clans of the Dal gChais, who under the mighty King Brian nine-and-a-half centuries ago, not far from the spot on which we are standing, smashed the invader and broke the Norse power forever'.[7]

In this squaring of the circle, the idea of foreignness itself melted away. An Irish president born in Brooklyn came to do homage to an American president 'from' New Ross. And to this strange symmetry was added the aura of a ritual succession of kingship, for these two men could have been father and son, and we were swopping the monkish, puritanical image of Ireland which de Valera embodied for the smooth, sexy, urbane Kennedy. The disturbing question, though, was who was the father and who the son? President de Valera addressed President Kennedy now as a proud father, now as a humble and grateful child. In his address of welcome, he spoke to Kennedy like a beaming daddy who has called his boy into the study to congratulate him on his exam results. He called him 'a distinguished son of our race' and told him frankly, 'We are proud of you, Mr President.'

Yet, at other times, he spoke like an awed child, or like the chief of a remote tribe who has just been presented with a looking-glass and a necklace of cheap beads by a captain of the Royal Navy who is all the while eyeing his island for signs of removable wealth. He greeted Kennedy, not as President of America, but as 'the first citizen of the great republic of the west, upon whose enlightened, wise and firm leadership hangs the hope of the world'.[8]

This ambivalence, this strange mixture of homage and absurdity, continued whenever Kennedy mentioned de Valera. He conjured alternative histories and parallel universes. In his address to the Oireachtas, for instance, he said that 'If this nation had achieved its present political and economic stature a century ago, my great-grandfather might never have left New Ross, and I might, if fortunate, have been sitting down there among you. Of course, if your own President had never left Brooklyn, he might be standing up here instead of me.'[9]

The words were funny and ingratiating, and were obviously meant courteously, but the images they suggested must, even then, have been comic and mocking: John F. Kennedy as parliamentary secretary to the minister for local government answering questions about the state of the road between Ballina and Belmullet. Eamon de Valera and his lovely wife Jackie and their children Mick, Tadhg, Carmel and Concepta, having a quiet evening at the White House with their friends Marilyn Monroe and Frank Sinatra. It was a very big 'if', so big as to remind us all the more forcefully of what we were not.

The same 'if' was on Kennedy's lips when he spoke on New Ross quay about his great-grandfather. 'If he hadn't left, I'd be working over at the Albatross Company, or maybe for John V. Kelly.' The Albatross Company was a fertilizer plant that employed half the town. John V. Kelly was an auctioneer who, that same week, advertised an 'Important Sale of Tractors, Farm Implements, Household Furniture & Effects', presumably from abandoned or bankrupt farms.[10] The double-edge was cutting. On one hand, every factory worker in New Ross could imagine himself, for an instant, as this tanned gorgeous man, radiating power and sex, and the thought, however instantaneous, could not be anything but pleasant. On the other hand, the instant after, the meaning of that sentence would clarify itself in the mind: 'If we Kennedys hadn't got the hell out of here, even I'd be a no-good schmuck like you.'[11]

He went on, standing there on that quay, to tell a joke. It was the story of the New Ross man who emigrated to the States. He was doing all right, but not as well as émigrés have to pretend to be doing to the folks back home. So he went on a trip to Washington, and stood in front of the White House, and got a passer-by to take a picture of him. He sent the photograph to his family in Ireland, and written on the back were the words: 'This is our summer house. Come and see it.'

Did he know what he was doing, telling this story to us? Did he know that that was what all those photographs of his own visit would be, a message to ourselves back home in our dreary lives, to pretend to ourselves that we were doing well? Did he know that the unwritten words on the backs of those photographs of our faces in the crowds, beaming at him in beatific bliss, pressing towards him as towards a messiah, were 'This is my cousin. He came to see me'?

Was he savouring the secret triumph of his power, that he was inside the White House, while we, poor Paddies, were standing outside the railings concocting false images to hide our failures?

He was a star performer. He knew tricks that we were too naive, too excited, too grateful, to see through. There was one particular stunt that he pulled again and again on his Irish visit, and that we fell for every time, like the suckers we so badly wanted to be. He did it first in Cork, while he was accepting the freedom of the city. He stopped in the middle of his speech, looked out into the crowd, and said, 'I would like to ask how many people here have relatives in the United States. Perhaps they could hold up their hands?' And a forest of hands arose on the spot, hands reaching out towards him, waving at him, wanting to be seen by him. Whether you had a relative in the States or not, you put up your hand, for how else could you identify yourself to him? And he smiled and said, 'Well, I want to tell you they're doing well.'

He did it again in Galway and in Limerick. Again the hands went up and again we claimed the honour of having scattered our families. And again we were rewarded with that blinding Kennedy smile: 'No wonder there's so many of them over there.' For decades, the people in those crowds had listened to politicians and churchmen talking about the shame of mass emigration. Yet here, on the streets of our cities, at the prompting of this showman's ploy, we were holding our hands up to claim it, to wave it before the world. So desperate were we to respond to the first citizen of the great republic of the west, that we could not be restrained from claiming our own disgrace. And in that, perhaps, for all the neurosis of the event, there was some kind of healthy acknowledgement, some form of truth. In the unseemly rush to claim Kennedy, we also had to claim all those scattered families of ours, inglorious and unglamorous as they were. Those arms that reached out to him also grasped a painful history.

And, performer though he was, there is no reason to think that he was not also sincere in many ways, that he was not also looking for something from us. Our hunger for his glamour, for his success, for his ease with the world and the flesh, was open, palpable, sometimes pathetic. But he, too, may have had both personal and political desires which only we could fulfil.

At a political level, the agenda of his speeches was so clear that only our euphoria could stop it from being heard. He harped continually on the war against communism, on 'the most difficult and dangerous struggle in the history of the world', and there was nothing secretive about his desire for Ireland to play its part in that struggle by joining NATO. Even the sentimental versions of Irish history that he repeated were carefully pointed in this direction: 'Ireland is still old Ireland, but it has found a new mission in the 1960s, and that is to lead the free world, to join with other countries in the free world, to do in the 1960s what Ireland did in the early part of that century.'

But even in this there was an unmistakable sense of a man trying to convince himself, as well as his listeners, of something. By the time he came to Ireland, Kennedy had committed over 12,000 American 'advisers' to Vietnam, and he felt, contemplating this anti-communist crusade, like an alcoholic contemplating the bottle. He had told Arthur Schlesinger what would happen in Vietnam: 'The troops will march in... then we will be told we have to send in more troops. It's like taking a drink, the effect wears off and you have to have another.'

For a man slipping into disaster, and pulling his country with him, Ireland usefully blurred the issues. In Wexford town, he warned communist oppressors everywhere that they would 'do well to remember Ireland' and its long and ultimately successful fight against 'foreign domination'. In this rhetoric, he could, for a while, talk as the representative of a small, oppressed nation rather than of a new imperial power asserting its control over Indochina. He could be Ho Chi Minh as well as John F. Kennedy, the plucky little guy standing up to the foreign bullies, as well as the imperial overlord sliding into a terrible war. No wonder he seemed to be enjoying himself.

This, too, may explain the odd clash of expectations in which Kennedy's visit was entangled. He may have represented modernity and glamour and sophistication, but in fact his rhetoric about Ireland was of a sort that even de Valera could no longer get away with using. He talked about this 'green and misty isle', a phrase he had honed on the Irish-American circuit in the 1950s. He talked about loyalty to faith and fatherland. He talked about endurance and fortitude. He talked to us as if we were plucky little South Vietnam, a God-fearing peasant people who would always be loyal and always endure.

He didn't seem to know that what we wanted was to drive cars like his, to wear dark glasses like his, to be beautiful like him and Jackie, to be rich and happy, to shop in malls and bowl in alleys. He didn't seem to know that when he came the First Programme for Economic Expansion had just delivered increases of 20 per cent in purchasing power and wages. He didn't seem to know that in five years the rate of unemployment had dropped by 30 per cent and that in ten years the number of cars on the road had doubled. He didn't seem to know that while he was looking for a past, we were looking to him as an image of the future, that the confidence he would give us would be the confidence to outgrow our desperate need of him.

There was a hint of this clash in Limerick when Frances Condell, the mayor, welcomed him by reminding him that 'we have seen the introduction to Ireland of a new type of American who is taking his place in our civic and social life, and who is bringing to our people the skills and techniques of industry', and asking please could we have some more of them in Limerick. In reply, Kennedy merely did his hands-up trick and quoted the words of 'Come back to Erin, mavourneen, mavourneen…' It was a silent movie and he was Valentino. We adored him, but there was no dialogue. If he had listened to the bells of St Nicholas Collegiate Church playing 'The Star-Spangled Banner' as he drove through Galway he might have understood better what faith and fatherland really meant to us.

In this confusion of desires, Kennedy created strange hybrid images of the Irish situation that mingled economic jargon and personal grief. He told us that 'most countries send out oil, iron, steel or gold, some others crops, but Ireland has only one export and that is people'. Later he told us that 'other nations of the world, in whom Ireland has long invested her people, are now investing their capital as well as their vacations here in Ireland'. In these images of Irish people as raw materials for export, as investments in foreign economies, of tourism as a fitting return for lost families, he spoke, without meaning to, a truth no Irish leader would have dared to utter. In these brutal words, intended to be flattering, he revealed the nature of the exchange Ireland was involved in.

Kennedy's allure was universal, but in Ireland he was both a disguise and a mirror. The huge banners and American flags that covered buildings in the centre of Dublin were strategically placed to camouflage the tawdriness of a city that was literally falling down. After a Siberian winter and monsoon-like rains, old tenement buildings had begun to crack and collapse. When Kennedy's press secretary Pierre Salinger and an advance guard of US reporters arrived in Dublin on 14 June, the local newspapers were still dominated by the deaths of two eight-year-old girls, Marie Vardy and Linda Byrne, two days earlier. They had been on their way home from a sweet shop when two houses on Fenian Street fell down and they were crushed under tons of rubble. People who lived in all the old parts of the inner city were terrified that their homes might implode on them. The authorities were terrified of something worse: that the Americans might notice. 'It was hoped that no curious visiting reporters would poke around in the tenement streets, tempted to do a side story on the city.'[12] Dublin Corporation evacuated 485 families from 147 dangerous tenements. Some of them were left on the side of the road, living in primitive tents or shelters made from canvas, cardboard and plywood.

But Kennedy was also a particular kind of mirror, one in which a raw, uncertain society saw a fantastical reflection of itself that could be at once flattering and maddening. On the one hand, as Garda Séamus McPhillips, one of the thousands of policemen on duty as Kennedy's motorcade went through the city, put it: 'My attitude, and the attitude of a lot of my countrymen, was "That guy is 'us'... from us, we are of him! There's the success!" You could feel it.'[13] If that guy was us, we were grand. It was not that simple, though. Kennedy was also way above us, and in this gap there was room for hysteria.

For the most part, the crowds on the streets and the dignitaries at receptions were able to carry the whole thing off, to maintain their poise, to hold a line between enthusiasm and dignity. But then came the bourgeois riot, the establishment melee, a breakdown of order that showed the path to modernization was not like a ride on Roches Stores escalator, weightless and serene. There were a lot of people, it turned out, who literally did not know how to behave. And they were not from Balubaland or Comanche country. They were within the elite.

For those who were not going to be at the official functions, the social highlight of the visit was the garden party at de Valera's official residence, Áras an Uachtaráin, the former Viceregal Lodge in Phoenix Park. The 1,500 guests were 'several heads of corporations and State bodies, members of the judiciary and assorted government types, along with their wives'.[14] The men had to wear top hats, but the women had no such limitations.

The day before the garden party, Ida Grehan reported in the *Irish Times* that 'a leading Dublin milliner told me she hasn't a hat left. She brought back a big collection from London… and everything from thirty shillings to thirty guineas had walked out the door! Hats as flamboyant as umbrellas; tiny as schoolboys' caps; hats like silk scarves and hats like souffles of silk chiffon; hats of elegant straw and flower petal berets in a riot of colour will emblazon the lawns of Áras an Uachtaráin.'[15] The leading Dublin-based couturier Ib Jorgensen and his team has been 'working round the clock', while Miss Doran's salon on Dawson Street which had 'been dressing the best people for quite a number of decades; wives of Government Ministers and wives of members of the Opposition; the Diplomatic Corps and the hierarchy of medicine, the law, commerce, the Turf, maybe even the Fourth Estate' had 'scoured the salons of London, Paris, Nice, Switzerland'.

By the end of the garden party, much of this lavish millinery was in disarray. The weather did not collude in the pretence that Dublin was Paris. The lawn was 'miserably wet and stiletto heels sank deep'. The 'constant echoing refrain from women all around was on the lines of "I could sit down and cry"'. Bare arms were covered in goose pimples from the chilly breeze.[16] Perhaps this anguish contributed to what happened when Kennedy and de

Valera emerged from the house, 'something near to mob hysteria… suggestive of the adulation of the film or pop star'.[17]

The *Irish Times* reporter Tom McCaughren witnessed the scene: 'There was pandemonium on the lawns… as a crushing, pushing crowd of guests literally mobbed President Kennedy… In the middle of the melee an obviously distraught Mr de Valera motioned the crowd back with his hand and appealed, "Move back, move back, please!"'[18] 'His appeal to the crowd to keep back fell on deaf ears.'

The police commissioner Daniel Costigan and members of the Special Branch and of Kennedy's bodyguard tried to push people back but they were overwhelmed. 'Toes were trampled on, high heels sank into the lawn, shoes were lost, beautiful hats were crumpled, guests fell over chairs… One woman roared "Jack, Jack, shake my hand". When he did, she turned away and adjusted her hat, and expressed her utter satisfaction to her friends and to others on whom she had trampled.'

In this moment, the deference that had been so deeply ingrained in Irish society collapsed under the weight of the need to touch JFK. It was bad that de Valera, the frail but revered embodiment of the state, was jostled and that his distraught pleas for order were ignored. But, as McCaughren reported: 'One man, determined to get out of the surging, swaying crowd, found his shoulder caught under the scarlet cape of a bishop. But too late. The bishop was almost pulled to the ground and his cape was ripped.' That tear in the bishop's scarlet cape was a rent in the fabric of Irish society. A rising middle class, not knowing what to do with itself, was a force beyond control.

The debacle of the garden party raised again the old spectres – were we civilized at all? An anonymous report in the *Sligo Champion* a few days later said the garden party had 'turned into a demonstration of uncouth bad manners, ignorance and bad breeding… men in the top hats and the swallow-tailed coats and their women in their expensive finery pushed, scrambled and actually came to blows in their efforts to mob the guest of the nation as if they were a collection of aborigines… the élite of Ireland's Society behaved like a collection of ignorant Hottentots'.[19]

Aborigines, Hottentots – the reporter did not say Balubas, but might as well have thrown in that other racist slur. But this racism was inwardly directed – the ignoble savages were our own elite.

All of these complexities and anxieties were beautifully simplified for us five months later in Dallas. The grief of Kennedy's assassination was profound, but it also brought relief. Grief was the emotion we could best handle. Martyrdom was familiar. My grandfather put a picture of JFK on the wall of his bedroom, next to one of Pope John XXIII, who had also died that year. The ground was firm again. 'Our consolation', de Valera told the nation in an address after the murder, 'is that he died in a noble cause', a formulation that made no sense but that linked him to Ireland's patriot dead.[20] The following day, the State Department in Washington passed on a personal request from Jackie Kennedy that Irish army cadets perform at his burial a drill they had done for her husband and that he had spoken about with great admiration. Twenty-six young Irish army cadets, some of them still teenagers, waited for three hours at Kennedy's open grave in Arlington Cemetery for his funeral procession to arrive. JFK had watched them perform when they did the drill at the graves of the executed leaders of the 1916 Rising in Arbour Hill in Dublin. It was a strange moment of world history: an American president buried with the honours of a foreign country's patriot dead, a thing that had never happened before and hasn't happened since.

I saw them on television. They were immaculate, poised, balletic. The only sound was of the orders being given in Irish. The cadets moved their rifles as if in slow motion, turning them in perfect synchronicity so that they faced the ground. They shot out their right arms, then the left ones, and brought them both back to rest on the butt of their reversed guns. They bowed their heads, kept them down, then raised them again. Each movement was controlled, contained, precise. We were experts at obsequies. We knew, in this if not in much else, exactly where we stood.

7

1962–1999: Silence and Smoothness

The man sipped, replaced his pint on the bar counter and glanced through the haze of cigarette smoke at the television screen. The shot on the screen moved from a close-up of Gay Byrne's face to a wide view of the studio audience. The man froze for a moment, grabbed his coat and pushed furiously through the doors onto the street leaving his half-finished pint on the counter. Back in the pub Gay Byrne's voice continued to mingle with the Saturday night chinwag, with the passion and the trivia, with the vital questions of the day and the chitchat that would not outlive the night – the usual mix of *The Late Late Show*.

A short while later in Montrose, on the south side of Dublin, where the TV and radio studios were located, the *Late Late Show* audience was streaming out into the pouring rain. Many were sheltering under the colonnade in front of the studio when they heard the screams. The security staff heard them, too, and rushed to Montrose House, just across the grounds from the studio entrance. There, on the steps of the old house, they found the man from the pub brandishing a knife at another man while a woman screamed. The man with the knife had seen something he did not expect to see on *The Late Late Show*: his wife in the audience with another man. He had suffered a more extreme version of the things that had outraged, delighted, entertained and disturbed Irish people since Gay Byrne began to present *The Late Late Show*: the revelation of intimacies in the glare of the studio lights, the disclosure in public of things that had never been disclosed in private.

It began life in July 1962, as a cheap, thirteen-week filler. The listings described it as 'a programme for late viewing' in which the twenty-six-year-old host 'in lighthearted fashion sets the ball of conversation rolling'.[1] It sounded innocuous and in truth it often was. That was what made it so dangerous. Nothing that did not seem harmless could have been so insidious. Nothing that seemed insidious could have burrowed its way into a conservative and controlled culture so gently that by the time anyone really noticed, it was already too far under the skin to be excised.

The Late Late Show was the thing you watched for two hours on Saturday (later Friday) night so that you could talk about it on Monday morning at school or at work or in the shops. A lot of the time, what you talked about on Monday morning was how dull it was, how really it had gone on too long and needed to be put out of its misery. And then you watched it again the following weekend because you couldn't afford to miss the thing that happened, whatever it was – a lesbian nun, or a pompous politician making an eejit of himself or a man, apparently the only such man in Ireland, talking about what it was like to be homosexual, or Spike Milligan jumping up out of the audience wearing a German army helmet and shouting, 'Adolf Hitler is alive and well and living in Maynooth College', which was the headquarters of the Catholic hierarchy.

Gay Byrne's extraordinarily central place in Irish life was due, not to his own obvious skills – the flow of language, the plausibility, the urbanity – but to their opposite, to the culture of silence which surrounded them. 'I have never', the letters he read out on his daily radio show would begin, 'told this to anyone in my life.' 'I feel very depressed at times and wish I could reveal my secret to somebody…' Or: 'That was ten years ago and since then my mother and I have never mentioned this. Please don't use my name or address as I couldn't stand it if the neighbours knew.'[2]

It was the silences that made Gay Byrne what he became in Ireland: the silences of the breakfast table, the silences around the fireside, the silences on the pillow. Without them he would have been what he so patently was – a superbly professional broadcaster, confident, adaptable, quick thinking and fast talking – but nothing more. With them, he was something else altogether: the voice in which the unspoken could be articulated, the man who gave permission for certain subjects to be discussed. His was the tone – calm, seductive and passionless – in which things that were otherwise unbearable could be listened to.

Things like this letter which he read on the radio in February 1984: 'When I learned that the thing that happens between men and women, as it was locally known, had happened to me, I slowly realized that I might also be going to have a baby. In terror and panic, I tried to find out from newspapers any snippets of information. I learned that babies like the one I might have are usually placed in brown paper bags and left in a toilet and I resolved to do this. For that reason, I started to carry around the one penny I would need to get into the toilet to have the baby. I kept the brown paper bag in my schoolbag and kept the bag under my bed at night. Since I spent most of my time in chapel praying, the nuns told me I had a vocation.'

Surrounded by that silence, we wanted, in the 1960s, to hear ourselves speak in a charming, sophisticated and worldly-wise voice. And here was a man who had made it in England with Granada TV and the BBC but still wanted to come home, a man who could talk on equal terms with suave foreigners yet still be one of our own, who could mention sex and nighties and contraceptives and still be a good Catholic. It was always important that Byrne was not a rebel, that he made clear his great admiration for John Charles McQuaid, for Seán Lemass and later for the man to whom he remained personally loyal, Charles Haughey. The problem with him, for the existing system of authority, was that the even greater object of his devotion was entertainment, a more merciless god than any other.

It was significant that the thing most frequently said about Gay Byrne's broadcasting style by himself and by others was that he asked the questions that the audience at home would want to ask but wouldn't dare. His achievement was founded on Irish people's inarticulacy, embarrassment and evasiveness, on speaking for us because we were afraid to speak for ourselves. If we were too embarrassed to have a national debate about contraceptives, *The Late Late Show* would do it for us. If we were too shy to harass the fellow who sold us a dud washing machine, the Gay Byrne radio show would pester him for us. If we were too ashamed to tell our friends that our husbands hadn't spoken to us for twenty years, Gay Byrne would tell the nation for us. And however much pain might go into such letters, just hearing them read aloud with his perfect enunciation already transformed the agony into something cool and clean and modern, into another masterly performance. We were literally making a show of ourselves, with Gay Byrne as the cast of thousands.

By the mid-1960s, his presence was so all-pervasive that it was easy to forget that the first star of *The Late Late Show* was not Gay Byrne, but television itself. Byrne later explained that the initial idea for the show was that its ambiance would be that of an evening around an Irish country fireside with the young master entertaining his guests. The image was one out of de Valera's Ireland. But he didn't present *The Late Late Show* as a cosy fireside chat. On the contrary, and long before it became the fashion in television elsewhere, it went out of its way to make television itself a star, showing the wires, the lights, the monitors, the cameras, the technicians and, of course, the hero of the hour, the audience. Byrne's one real catchphrase was 'Roll it, there, Colette', an on-screen instruction to play in some recorded material, usually a clip from a movie whose star was on promotional duty. It celebrated television as the very image of modernity, of technology, of all the things that we were trying desperately to become.

It modelled itself, not on Irish fireside conversation, but on American television, specifically on *The Tonight Show*, hosted by Jack Parr and then by Johnny Carson. The first producer, Tom McGrath, had worked in Canada; the first director, Burt Budin, was from the Bronx. And it gradually filled up with the very 'squalid domestic brawls' that de Valera had warned against on the opening night of Irish television, presenting the good, the true and the beautiful only insofar as they added to the mix, kept the audience amused and the ratings up.

But if the Gay Byrne who was doing this had not existed, he would most emphatically not have been invented. For *The Late Late Show* was doing precisely what those in authority thought television should not do. What those in authority did not understand, and what Byrne lived for, was the logic of a good show, the fact that fireside chats and high-minded discussions put the plain people of Ireland to sleep, while brawls and revelations kept them up and watching.

The authorities – the bishops, politicians, county councillors, GAA officials, Vocational Education Committees – realized very quickly what was afoot but had great difficulty doing anything about it. Of all the avalanche of protests that began in 1966 when a hapless woman called Eileen Fox revealed on the show that she had worn nothing on the night of her honeymoon and continued when a student radical, Brian Trevaskis, called the Bishop of Galway a moron, very little was directed at Byrne personally. The object of attack was television in general and *The Late Late Show* format in particular.

The show could be described by Loughrea town commissioners as 'a dirty programme that should be abolished altogether' or criticized by Meath VEC for its 'mediocrity, anti-national tone and recently low moral tone', but objectors knew better than to accuse Byrne himself of being dirty or morally low and were thus left flailing at abstractions. Byrne's own personality was crucial in that he became an Irish everyman, spanning the past and the present, tradition and modernity. Neat, sober and kind to old ladies, he was the son every Irish mammy would like to have. Suave, confident and upwardly mobile, he was the man every mother's son, dragging himself up by his bootstraps, would like to be.

Only two aspects of Byrne's personality (as opposed to his professional skills) were important to his broadcasting achievement, but both were essential to the survival of his shows. The first is that his own life represented in microcosm much of what happened in Ireland over thirty years. Brought up in a sheltered, frugal and conservative family environment. Inculcated by the Christian Brothers, the order of lay celibate men that ran the biggest number of schools for Catholic boys, with the values of piety, hard work and patriotism. Emigrating to England along with everyone else in the 1950s. Coming back along with everyone else in the 1960s. Getting richer as the country gets richer. Suffering financial calamity in the 1980s and contemplating emigration again.

His personal odyssey, then, followed the same course as the national epic, the same serpentine currents of hope and despair, of excitement and boredom. Because he had been shaped by those conflicting currents, he could be compared by one person to the leader of godless communism, by another to a Christian Brother. Senator J. B. Quigley saw him as Stalin: 'like Khrushchev I'm all against the cults of personality.'[3] June Levine, who worked for him, saw him as often 'like a Christian Brother of the nasty type Irish men have described to me, merciless, unreasonable, relentless in his attack on anyone who fell short'.[4]

What he was most like, though, was contemporary Ireland: fluid, contradictory, elusive, a country in which the terms either/or were replaced by both/and. Byrne, like his country, was both traditional and modern, both conservative and liberal, Catholic and materialist. The relative emptiness of his public persona was his greatest strength, preventing him from freezing into any set of unified attitudes, keeping him close to the irregular pulse of Irish life. The other aspect of his personality that was important is related to this emptiness: the fact that he was at heart an actor. From a very early age he wanted to act, and it was in the drama academies and the Dublin Shakespeare Society that he created himself as a performer. It is very doubtful that he would have had the emotional commitment or the imaginative sympathy to be a really good actor, but it was the playing of roles that kept him alive on screen. On the one hand there were the funny voices, the prancing around the studio with the contraceptive cap on his head, the willingness to have darts thrown at him or to have a melon on his chest chopped in half with a samurai sword. This aspect of his showing off made his programmes a form of light entertainment, making the more serious and unpalatable parts of them just a part of the package, in which the man with AIDS would be followed by a song and dance after the commercial break.

The other side of the acting was the detachment, the coldness. He could ask the hurtful, nasty, embarrassing questions because it's in the script, because it is the part he's playing, because the interviewee is playing a part, too, and is not to be thought of as a bundle of real fears and emotions. How, the victims asked, can he be so nice one moment and so nasty the next? The answer was that neither the niceness nor the nastiness were anything personal, just a change of roles.

It was the slippery quality, this refusal to be fish or flesh, one thing or the other, that his enemies had always recognized as Byrne's most dangerous quality. His one consistent credo, the one thing in his public persona that could be described as a principle rather than an attitude, was that it is in the nature of television to throw everything in together, to refuse to recognize the distinctions between entertainment and seriousness, and that the medium, rather than any set of rules, had to be respected. They all came under that most subversive heading, what he called 'things which affected people in real life rather than the imaginary things that affected imaginary people'. The imaginary things that affected imaginary people were the materials from which church and state constructed their version of Irish reality.

This tendency to see television as a force that made up its own laws as it went along had been resisted from the start. The most consistent line of attack of those who found Gay Byrne uncomfortable was to demand, not that he be removed, but that he be defined: serious or entertaining? 'Telefís [Éireann]', wrote the TV critic of the *Irish Catholic* in 1966, 'has a responsibility to define which programmes are suitable for responsible expressions of views of important controversial content and which programs by their nature are unsuitable for this… if *The Late Late Show* is to become a place for expression of views in which selected guests can say what they like, then it must be acknowledged and prepared as a serious discussion programme… there would have to be a chairman who preserves a balance rather than throwing innocuous comments or asides which amount to an uneasy handwashing… If on the other hand it is not intended to be such but to be merely a form of entertainment then it must be controlled so that nobody uses it, no matter how sincerely, for soapbox oratory.'[5]

Sixteen years later, almost exactly the same argument was being made by Fred O'Donovan, then chairman of the RTÉ Authority, when he banned a *Late Late Show* discussion on abortion. 'Because of the emotional situation with cameras, people say things they wouldn't normally say. This is too important a subject to be treated trivially.' The same thing had happened before, in 1968, when the show was prevented from discussing a biography of Eamon de Valera, on the grounds that it would be inappropriate in the context of *The Late Late Show*, and again Byrne was prevented from broadcasting a programme on the defeat of the government in a referendum on changes to the electoral system. The implicit message was always the same: if serious things were to be discussed, they should be discussed on serious and predictable programmes, where the ground rules had been worked out in advance. Byrne's openness and unpredictability were dangerous because people might say things they wouldn't normally say.

Government ministers, particularly Fianna Fáil ministers, were reluctant to be interviewed by Byrne not so much because they were afraid he would make them say things they'd rather not have said, but because his whole style refused to recognize them as fundamentally different from the knife thrower or the film star. To submit to Byrne was to submit to being treated as entertainment, to being stripped of office, record, power, everything except your ability to hold an audience's attention for five minutes or fifteen minutes. Pan Collins, a former *Late Late Show* researcher, once wrote that her job was to produce a list of possible guests under six different headings: 'an intellectual, a glamour personality, a VIP, a cynic, a comic and a cookie character'.

But in Byrne's hands, the borderlines between those categories fell away. The intellectual of one shot could be made the cookie character of the next. The cynic who performs well can become a glamour personality in the space of a few minutes. The VIP who is too pompous ends up as the unintentional comic. Where a current affairs programme treated people according to the category it finds them in – expert, economist, political leader, victim – *The*

Late Late made and unmade the categories as it went along, treating people by their performance, not their credentials. Byrne, who made his way up in Irish society solely through his ability to entertain, always presented entertainment as uncomfortably egalitarian. Anyone can speak so long as they speak engagingly enough and anything can be said so long as it's gripping enough.

McQuaid's successor, Archbishop Kevin McNamara, probably had *The Late Late Show* and the Gay Byrne radio show in mind when he bemoaned the loss of traditional authority in our society in 1985: '[There are] certain topics which have exercised the greatest minds for centuries and on which a fund of traditional wisdom has been built up slowly and with difficulty over the years. These today are regarded as suitable topics for chat shows on radio and TV and speakers of little or no qualifications parade with confidence the most varying and contradictory opinions.' He was, of course, right to be concerned, for in Gay Byrne's pluralist republic of entertainment, the Archbishop would come to owe his authority, not to traditional wisdom, but to his ability to sing an old song and the politician's power could be diminished by his inability to tell a good yarn.

8

1965: Our Boys

Two boys are standing at a bus stop. They wear the same school uniform, they are the same height, but they do not stand the same way. One has his hands in his pockets, his shoulder propped against the pole, his body slouched like a flag on an airless day. His hair is as tossed as a night on the Atlantic in a force ten gale and his school cap is perched on top of it like a small craft about to go under. His school tie dangles from his grubby neck like a miscreant left hanging on the gibbet as a warning to others. His schoolbag, feral and untamed, crouches at his feet, ready to attack passing old ladies or members of the clergy.

The other boy's left arm is straight down by his side, his right tucking his schoolbag snugly into his chaste body. He stands as straight as an exclamation mark and what he proclaims is the honour of his school, his family, his country and the Christian Brothers. His cap sits on his head with the obedience and poise of a well-trained lapdog. His clothes are as unruffled as his smoothly boyish face, whose lustre of serene self-satisfaction sets up a pleasing symmetry with the shine on his shoes. His tie is as straight as a plumbline, pointing to the centre of his moral gravity – his unbreakable, unquestioning faith. He is a good boy. He is the boy I wanted to be.

I remember these drawings from *Courtesy for Boys and Girls*, written and published by the Christian Brothers and used as the basis for a class called Civics, more clearly than anything from any other book I read in childhood.

Civics, in theory, was about society and how it worked but, in practice, about good behaviour, decorum, the way you comported yourself. You understood, implicitly, that these two things were one and the same, that a society full of good boys standing up straight at the bus stop would be a good society, that this drawing was a sort of political vision, a large-scale map of Utopia. Us Crumlin kids were the first boy. Through work and prayer and hard discipline, we might become the second.

Why is a man like a tack? I read this riddle in *Our Boys*. Under duress, for we would rather have spent what little money we had on English comics like the *Beano* or the *Dandy* or on American superheroes like *The X-Men*, we bought *Our Boys* at school for sixpence a month. It was a tradition. It had been going since 1914, when it was established by the Christian Brothers to 'interest, instruct and inspire the boys of our Catholic schools, to create in them a taste for clean literature, to continue the character-forming lessons of their school days, to fire their enthusiasm for what is noble and good, to inflame their love of country and to help in preserving them as devoted children of Our Holy Mother the Church.'[1] Its masthead carried, under the title, the words 'To God and Eire True' and 'Purity in our Hearts, Truth on Our Lips, Strength in Our Arms'.

For many years, it was edited by the militantly nationalist Brother Canice Craven, who had inspired Patrick Pearse when he taught him at CBS Westland Row, and who was famous for having beaten off with his umbrella an assault by three drunken British soldiers.[2] Craven's favourite rebuke to a naughty pupil was to tell him that he 'would never die for Ireland'. He liked to publish stories about English Protestants persecuting Irish Catholics: 'No mercy for the Papist dogs! Ho, ho, you rotten Papist!' Not to buy *Our Boys* was to side with those who kicked Papist dogs, to be the boy who slouched against the bus stop, a disgrace not just to your school, but to your country – Catholic Ireland.

I wanted to be a good boy so I coughed up my sixpence and pondered the similarities between man and a tack: 'Man is like a tack because he must be pointed in the right direction, driven hard and then he will go as far as his head will let him.' This piece of wisdom might well have replaced *Farere et Docere* (To Do and To Teach) as the motto of the Christian Brothers. It summed up more precisely what they stood for: the right direction, hard driving, going far. Or, translated into Irish, Catholic faith, strict discipline, social mobility. Out of these three things, they made not just an educational system, but an Ireland. They shaped, not just a notion of a country, but many of the conditions in which that country had come into existence.

Another riddle: who made the world? It was the first question in the Catechism and the answer, of course, was 'God made the world'. But there were times when it seemed that the Christian Brothers had been his main subcontractors. On the back of all my brick-coloured and red-margined copybooks, full of compound interest, irregular verbs and days at the seaside, was a map of the world. At the centre of this world was Ireland, and arcing out of Ireland like shooting stars were lines leading to Australia, North America, Argentina, Africa – the contours of a spiritual conquest that had begun in 1802 when Edmund Ignatius Rice founded the Christian Brothers in Waterford. Shining over it all was the five-pointed radiant star of the Brothers' logo. It was our Empire, our answer to the British maps of the world in which its colonial possessions glowed scarlet in every continent, while the rest skulked in dull and watery hues. Even when I scratched NFFC (for Nottingham Forest Football Club, which I started to follow because its manager, Johnny Carey, was from Dublin and because I loved Robin Hood) into the red-brick paper with the sharp end of my compass, I knew it was their world I was defacing. They had given us our map of the world by giving us our map of Ireland.

'Ireland', said Eamon de Valera in 1944, 'owes more than it will probably ever realise to the Christian Brothers. I am an individual who owes practically everything to the Christian Brothers.'[3] In his memoirs, Todd Andrews, a leading technocrat in the creation of the state, explained their centrality: 'Without the groundwork of the Christian Brothers' schooling, it is improbable there would have been a 1916 Rising and certain that the subsequent fight for Independence would not have been successfully carried through. The leadership of the IRA came largely from those who got their education from the Brothers, and got it free.'

If this claim seems far-fetched, the figures largely bear

it out. The extent to which, in the Easter Rising, Christian Brothers boys elbowed aside the Jesuit-educated upper middle-class boys who had imagined themselves as a ruling class in waiting, can be gauged by comparing two nearby schools on the north side of Dublin. The Jesuit Belvedere College supplied five ex-pupils to the ranks of the rebels; the Christian Brothers' O'Connell Schools supplied 125. Seven of the fourteen men executed as leaders of the Rising were Christian Brothers boys. Three of the five members of the IRA executive elected in 1917, including the chief of staff, Cathal Brugha, were in the same category. Of the seven-man cabinet appointed by the Dáil in 1921, five – Kevin O'Higgins, Austin Stack and Arthur Griffith, as well as de Valera and Brugha – had spent their schooldays praying, as we still did, for the beatification of Edmund Rice.

Throughout the years in which an independent Ireland was formed, other CBS boys were to the forefront of militant nationalism: Tomás MacCurtain, Liam Lynch, Liam Mellowes, Ernie O'Malley, Seán Treacy, Harry Boland, Seán Lemass. The impact of the Brothers on the minds that formed the state cannot be overstated. It was not just in what they taught but in the way they taught it. They stressed that the function of education was to turn raw boys into manly patriots: 'Ireland looks to them, when grown to man's estate, to act the part of true men in furthering the sacred cause of nationhood.' It was not even that they invented and gave currency to a narrative of 800 years of exceptional oppression that fused Ireland's suffering with Christ's: 'In the martyrology of history, among crucified nations', said the Brothers' *Catechism of the History of Ireland*, 'Ireland occupies the foremost place. The duration of her torture, and the ferocity of her executioner, are as revolting as the power of the victim is astonishing.'[4] It was also, more subtly, but no less importantly, that they channelled this victimhood into social mobility. The underlying idea of their schools was that, if driven hard and pointed in the right direction, their pupils could rise as Ireland itself was rising.

Social mobility and nationalism went hand in hand, and the Brothers dealt in both currencies. Having moulded young men who were fit and eager for power, it was almost as if a place in which that power could be taken had to be invented. That place was an independent but implicitly Catholic Ireland. Take up any Christian Brothers' school yearbook from the decades after Independence and you can almost touch the sense of triumph, the naked delight that Our Boys are taking over the state that *Our Boys* had made for them. The CBS Synge Street yearbook for 1946–7, for instance, opens with a message from an old boy, now a TD and lord mayor of Dublin, praising the 'good Brothers who taught me to love God, His Holy Mother and Ireland'.

There is a spread on 'Our New Attorney General', a young man called Cearbhall Ó Dálaigh, later to become chief justice and president, in which the word 'our' has a special emphasis: 'resurgent Ireland is coming into its own'. There is another feature on 'men on the Air', with pictures of five Synge Street boys who have become announcers on Radio Éireann, among them Eamonn Andrews. And the seizure of power is only beginning: 'The boys who did the Leaving Certificate in 1945 have gone down to the sea of their dreams in ships with sails courageously unfurled which even now point to many and diverse ways dream-charted by their youthful pilots...'

Todd Andrews, the ex-Synge Street, ex-IRA man, then managing director of the state turf company Bórd na Mona, is, in an obituary tribute to the school's recently deceased head Brother, most explicit about what is going on: 'Boys attending Synge Street came from modest homes. They had no influence, no contacts, no background, the auspices were not favourable for their advancement in fields of professional endeavour. Brother Roche foresaw the changing times and the shift of power from the alien to the native... he applied his vitality to equip his pupils to take their part in forming the new regime.'

Contacts, influence, advancement – the CIA of the new Catholic middle-class. This was the secret code of the state I was growing up in. It permeated, not just the political class, but the civil service. A study in 1963 found not only that 60 per cent of senior civil servants had gone into the administration straight from secondary school, but that 'three-quarters of the administrative, executive and clerical classes received their secondary education from the Christian Brothers'.[5] In 1972, the political scientist Basil Chubb described the higher officials of that era as 'Christian Brothers school stereotypes... intellectually able and hard-working but rather narrowly practical in their approach and inclined to be concerned with the short-term objective'.[6] The poet Sean Dunne described the ideal product of the Brothers as 'a top Irish-speaking civil servant and hurler'.[7]

Yet the idea that Edmund Rice, who founded the order to educate the children of the very poor, or indeed the martyrs who died for Ireland inspired by the Brothers' fervent nationalism, might have intended to signify something more profound than equipping the children of the lower middle class for cushy jobs in a claustrophobic society could not be banished entirely. Was Ireland's uniquely terrible place in the martyrology of history a mere prelude to Synge Street boys becoming announcers on Radio Éireann – especially when the most famous of them, Eamonn Andrews, had then gone on to become a suave star of British television, disconcertingly at home with the ways of the alien oppressor? Did the men of 1916 die so that good CBS boys could aspire to be principal officers in the Department of Posts and Telegraphs?

There was a gap somewhere, a lacuna that could only widen into a dangerous fissure in the apparently stable surface of the monolith the Brothers had done so much to construct. One of those tensions was about class. My primary school, Scoil Íosagáin, was actually on our road. It was part of the estate and had been built to cater for its boys. Synge Street was just fifteen minutes' walk away, but it was on the other side of the canal, much closer to the city and in a much older middle-class district. It was much more respectable. And, crucially, it had a secondary school attached. Secondary schools charged fees – this was the great divide. Social mobility had its limits. It was, in the world of the Christian Brothers, about rising from the lower middle to the upper middle class. It was not supposed to be about us – but then, suddenly, it was.

When T. K. Whitaker published *Economic Development* in 1958, there was one remarkable gap in his thinking about how Ireland could become part of the modern world: education. It was not discussed at all. And yet one of the most obvious ways in which Ireland was backward was that it had failed to keep up with the great expansion of schooling in post-war democracies, and in particular the extension of free tuition to second level. When I started school in 1962, the church-dominated school system had left the Irish among the worst-educated people in the western world.

In the mid-1950s, there were 476,000 pupils in the primary education system, but just 83,000 in secondary and vocational schools, suggesting that more than 80 per cent dropped out of formal education at fourteen, the legal school leaving age. The reason was simple: secondary schools, overwhelmingly owned and run by the church, were private institutions and charged fees that most families could not afford. About 5 per cent of secondary students had publicly financed scholarships – a mark of the state's commitment to educational equality was that the level of the scholarship was set in the 1920s and not increased, so that its real value was eroded by inflation.

Even the primary system was abysmally underfunded. Twenty-two per cent of primary school buildings were officially classified as 'obsolete' by the Office of Public Works and 40 per cent were either in this category or were more than eighty years old. As late as 1964, a survey of primary schools revealed that 53 per cent had no drinking water in the school or even on the site. Only 48 per cent had either a flush or a chemical toilet. Sixty-three per cent were heated by open fires.[8]

There were technical schools in which post-primary students could study practical skills, usually for two years, but their number was small – Ireland had 'possibly the most underdeveloped vocational education system in western Europe'.[9] In the brutal class system that Ireland pretended it did not have, these schools were for what one vocational teacher called 'dead-end kids'.[10]

Nor, when I was born, was there much prospect of radical change. A Council of Education had been established in 1954 to consider the possible reforms of second-level education, but it sat so long that its members began to die off before it could issue a report.[11] When it finally did report in 1960 (the report was not published until 1962), it remarked contentedly of secondary schools that 'The dominant purpose of their existence is the inculcation of religious ideals and values. This central influence, which gives unity and harmony to all the subjects of the curriculum, is outside the purview of the State…'[12] The report therefore recommended no real change.

In the meantime, the state's education budget for 1958, the year I was born, was cut for the second year in a row.[13] The standard of discussion on the subject in parliament was such that in 1959, the Opposition spokesman and former minister for education Richard Mulcahy despairingly asked, 'What is the use of asking the Dáil to talk about education policy? The ordinary deputy cannot talk with any more information than the people in the streets…'[14]

Most civil servants had completed their education at sixteen and were recruited directly from school, a system, 'reminiscent of… Tsarist Russia where those who ran the empire were recruited at 14 and kept well away from awful places like universities'.[15] T. K. Whitaker's immediate predecessor as secretary of the Department of Finance, Owen Redmond, who retired in 1956, had entered the public service in 1906 as a fifteen-year-old clerk in the Office of Public Works.[16]

Even for those who did get to secondary school, the curriculum was dominated by a narrow range of subjects. Half of all teachers of science had no science degree.[17] Astonishingly, a second-level school could be deemed to operate a full curriculum even if it did not teach science at all.[18] Thus, as late as 1963, only 30 per cent of boys and 14 per cent of girls took the Leaving Certificate science exams.

The small minority who managed to complete secondary schools were not encouraged to learn contemporary European languages. The main 'foreign' languages were Latin and Ancient Greek: 90 per cent of males sitting the Leaving Certificate took the Latin exam; just 9 per cent took French, 2 per cent German, while Spanish and Italian attracted negligible numbers. (In 1955, a grand total of two students sat the Spanish exam, and both failed.[19]) The teaching of Irish was prioritized at both primary and secondary levels, but the attempts to revive it as the national vernacular had failed so badly that the self-mocking joke was that most Irish people were illiterate in two languages.

All of this reeked of complacency – privilege was a relatively closed world and competition for the most desirable professions was limited to men and to those with access to educational capital that was carefully rationed. In August 1965, when I graduated from convent school into the care of the Brothers at Scoil Íosagáin, it was understood that we were a layer below the Synge Street boys. Most of us would leave school at fourteen and go to work in factories or, if we were more ambitious, to the tech to learn a trade. Alan Bestic noted in 1969 that 'An effective and unspoken apartheid operated. Children from the secondary schools regarded those from the primary schools as "no class at all". They spoke of them as "gutties", an attenuation which made the implication of the word "guttersnipe" even more objectionable.'[20]

When the government did establish a steering committee to produce a landmark report on investment in education, one of its internal debates was about the suggestion that free transport to secondary schools be provided for pupils in rural areas. A member of the committee, Father Jeremiah Newman (later the Catholic bishop of Limerick) 'objected on the basis that the Catholic Church would never agree to teenage boys and girls travelling together on school buses'. There was a serious proposal about how to overcome the problem: 'the buses would have a door on each side with a vertical partition down the middle of the bus – one side of the bus would be for girls and the other side would be for boys.'[21] The partition would be vertical rather than horizontal to avoid comparisons with the race-based system that operated on buses in the American Deep South.

But in September 1966, the most glamourous and charismatic of the new generation of Fianna Fáil politicians, the minister for education Donogh O'Malley, suddenly announced that he was going to introduce free secondary education for all students the following year. He did not consult the minister for finance, Jack Lynch, in advance. More daringly, he did not consult the Catholic bishops. He calculated, rightly, that the measure would be so popular that both the state and the church would have to fall in line with his demarche. (He also told primary school managers to go ahead and arrange for 'adequate sanitation and heating' and send the bill to his department.[22])

This decision was, for me, much more revolutionary than any Rising. It influenced my life more than any other political act. O'Malley's announcement was dramatic in its content, but also in its blunt expression of anger at the class system underpinned by educational apartheid. He spoke of the one-third of children emerging from primary school who got no further education, training or opportunity for 'cultural development': 'This is a dark stain on the national conscience. For it means that one-third of our people have been condemned – the great majority through no fault of their own – to be part-educated unskilled labour, always the weaker who go to the wall of unemployment and emigration.'[23]

He was talking about us. My father was an unskilled manual worker, and so, when she returned to paid employment later, was my mother. So were the parents of most of my classmates. And until O'Malley made his speech, the chances were that their children would be little different. This is what made the announcement of free secondary education so exciting and, to some, so disturbing: it altered a future that had been, at our level of society, grimly predictable. It shunted us onto a different track.

But could the Christian Brothers be the engine, as they had been for the rising Catholic middle class in the late nineteenth and early twentieth centuries, of this revolution in social mobility? They knew they had to be – or else someone else might move in and control the process. Very soon after O'Malley's announcement, they were planning to build a secondary school on the land around their monastery just next to Scoil Íosagáin. Two years later, it was open.

I remember a class on chemistry conducted by a Brother there. He cleared the desks from the middle of the room and lined us up on either side. 'Ye are all molecules. Ye boys on the right are molecules of sodium. Ye boys on the left are molecules of chlorine.' We shrank into ourselves, divesting ourselves of everything in our make-up except the elements he had enunciated. 'When I raise my hand, I am applying the heat. Ye will start to shake and shudder.' At his command, a quake ran through us and we started to tremble in unison. 'Then ye will begin to bounce off each other, one from either side, until a reaction takes place.' We threw ourselves blindly forward, crashing into each other with painless violence, anaesthetized by the knowledge that we were insensate molecules obeying the laws of nature.

Even then, I was dimly aware of the metaphoric significance of what we were doing. We were molecules, they were Bunsen burners. Our given stuff was combined into new compounds of their invention. Our characters were formed according to laws as definite as the laws of chemistry. The purpose of the Brothers was to provide a passage from one state to another. Their problem was that they could not imagine anything outside the inherited categories of the unruly bad boys and the angelic good boys. And their notions of what it was to be respectable persons in the future to which we heading were still utterly Victorian.

They were stuck in the colonial antithesis of wild natives and civilized denizens of the mother country, an antithesis they had merely internalized, imagining themselves as missionaries from a mother country that was also Mother Church. They could not allow for the possibility of profound change in the way people might behave or in the make-up of social hierarchies. They could not envisage the way a society like the one that was being formed in my childhood – shaped above all by the demotics of American popular culture – might work.

They had no hold on urban life, on television, or on pop music, no way of coping with the forces that were seeping ineluctably into our souls. Indeed, they could not even cope with Independent Ireland. Instead of trying to come up with some Catholic X-Men, the *Our Boys* that I was reading in the late 1960s and early 1970s was still full of second-hand versions of English *Boy's Own* stories of the 1920s, sometimes with Irish names superimposed on the characters, sometimes not. The schools in the stories were English public schools where boys strolled across the quad and had fights with fellows called 'Greene of Middle School', while uttering expletives like 'great pip!' and giving 'a first-class ribbing' to 'this chump' or 'that rotter!' At best, the boy delivering the ribbing was called Murphy rather than Bunter or Brown.

Sometimes, in the adventure stories in *Our Boys*, Irish names were scattered among exotic American landscapes and inserted into Western stories: 'Corporal Sean Dowling of the Canadian Mounted Police sighed contentedly' or 'The Lazy L ranch was shorthanded just now and O'Leary would be very glad to have an active young Irishman on his payroll'. But just as often, no attempt was made to evade the irony that in 1960s Ireland, half a century after the Easter Rising they had helped to inspire, the Brothers were still peddling stories about firm-jawed Englishmen facing up to shifty Arabs or squaring off against the natives of Darkest Africa. 'And many a time had Derek heard the tale of how his uncle stole the amulet from the arm of the Great One Amen-Atop, in that temple half-buried by the sand, away out in the desert beyond Cairo. His uncle Jack, then a youngster in the fifth Northshires – part of the force stationed in Egypt in those far-off days before people like Nasser were ever heard of – had all the average youngster's hair-brained passion for adventure, and the more risky the better.'

The only version of Ireland, the only language not imbued with rotters and boys called Kennedy Minor, was that of stories narrated by an ancient crone called, for reasons I never understood, Kitty the Hare. To me, that language was even more incomprehensible: 'Musha, I'm thinking that he'd just as soon not have her brother Jeremiah coming to the house at all at all. You see Jeremiah never pulled well with Paddy, Kitty, and, as Father Malachy told us, when he got the letter from Boston, Jeremiah is just as hard on Paddy as he ever was. God help us! So 'tis no wonder Paddy wouldn't be very eager to see Jeremiah again!' This stuff was even more alien than that of English public school stories, which I knew from Biggles, Enid Blyton and Billy Bunter books I borrowed from the library. It could not be construed.

While the students of Paris were on the barricades and my father and the other busmen of Dublin were on strike, I was reading in *Our Boys* about Maurice, who got a nice girl, joined the Saint Vincent de Paul Society, and became a good boy: 'he was getting on better with his boss. Before, he had always been pushing for more pay, or looking for easier work, or something. But now he didn't mind getting the toughest job – and the dirtiest – and he was always willing to change his shift to suit someone else.'

While the world was mourning the death of Martin Luther King, I was reading in *Our Boys* the story 'Murphy and the Boy from Africa': '"Meet Zaka the Zulu", grinned Curtis. "Exa balla murullo!" said Zaka, or words to that effect, bowing low instead of taking the proffered hand. "Eh?" "Samaruddy jara waramacky!", said the boy from Africa amiably. "A nigger from Africa is expected at Saint Michael's", said Murphy his eyes gleaming. "All right, a nigger will turn up, only it won't be the genuine article. It'll be little me."'

In the gap between the reality and the image, there was a fearful darkness. The only aspect of the *Our Boys* stories that made real sense to me was the constant violence of boys being 'spiflicated': '"Yarooh!", howled Murphy. Whack! "Yow-ow-ow!" Each whack wrung an anguished yell from Murphy and there were smothered chuckles from the black-robed figures standing around.' Cries of pain and black-robed figures belonged together. Violence and twisted sexuality were the expressions of troubled confusion on the part of the Brothers – not because they had a monopoly on any of these things in a society where violence against children and sexual repression were the norm, but because they were themselves secretly and institutionally haunted by their failure to control them. Corporal punishment, delivered mostly with a short, very thick strap called 'the leather', whose blows stung and reddened our tender palms, and administered as often by the lay teachers as by the Brothers themselves, was so inescapable a part of a Christian Brothers education that we completely accepted it.

When I was eighteen and in my first year at university, I was still living on Aughavannagh Road. Because I was so close, the head Brother in Scoil Íosagain would occasionally send for me in the morning to fill in for a teacher who had failed to turn up. The first day, I was given my own leather. It smelled of sweat and fear. I could hardly bear to touch it. Thrown in with forty-five eight-year-old boys, I introduced myself and immediately told them that we were all going to behave ourselves and that I would not hit them. They looked at me, not with relief or gratitude, but with a disconcerted puzzlement. As the day wore on, it turned to pity. When it was clear that I would not inflict physical pain, it also seemed obvious to them that there could be no other form of authority. I was lost. In the end, a boy sitting at the front put up his hand and spoke to me in the tone of sorrowful condescension teachers used with pupils: 'Ah, sir', he said. 'You have to hit us.'

When I was their age, the leather was the civilized, routine, impersonal instrument of punishment. It was the baseline of fear. But the real terror was more intimate. It was the child's dread of an adult out of control. This was the paradox: we were punished for perceived transgression, but the punishment itself could be wildly transgressive. It was orgiastic. When I was ten and in third class, we had a teacher we called Hoppy because he had a limp. His head was bald and seemed to throb red with rage. It could take almost nothing for the lava to overflow. One morning, when his mood was especially volatile, he was writing something on the blackboard and had his back turned to us. With other teachers, that would be a signal for some whispering among us, but we were so scared of him that there was complete silence. It was only because of this silence that, when I dropped my pencil on the floor, the sound hung in the air. Hoppy spun around: 'The next boy who drops a pencil will get the bata.' The bata was his bamboo cane. It whistled like a dive bomber and struck like a whip.

The moment stiffened into a pure petrified dread. There was a hush, not of calm, but of stifled, strangulated panic. The fear was kinetic. The boy to my left had placed his pencil stub in the shallow indentation carved at the top of the desk to hold it. It began to roll down the desk in slow motion, and fell to floor with a tiny slap. The noise, inaudible in ordinary air, was, in that echo chamber of apprehension, earsplitting. Hoppy grabbed the boy by the scruff of his neck and dragged him out to the front of the classroom. He started to lash at him with the bata, dancing lopsidedly around him, flailing indiscriminately at his head, his arms, his legs, his backside. The kid began to scream and fell to the floor, curling up into a foetal position. Hoppy just kept flogging him. His face was purple and there was spittle on his lips. Even under the squawks and whimpers coming from the heap on the floor, I could hear his low grunts but could not tell if they expressed effort or pleasure.

Eventually, the door opened. I could not see who was outside and no one came in. I presume it was the head Brother, since, when Hoppy walked out, it was he who appeared a minute later and took over our class for the rest of the day. The jabbering boy was told to collect his bag and sent home. Hoppy was back next day. So was the boy. So was the terror. Nobody said anything. Nothing had happened.

But something had happened to me. The whole thing had been my fault, because I had dropped my pencil first. I was the one who should have been lashed. But I knew why he didn't do it to me. Hoppy was the first person ever to praise me for writing. He had given us what was called a 'composition', an exercise in exploring a subject on paper. The subject was Birds. I wrote a piece called Waxwings. These pinkish-brown migrants had hit Dublin in unusual numbers that autumn. I went out on the bus with my father to a road of grand townhouses near the American embassy in Ballsbridge. The waxwings were feasting on the berries of the rowan trees that lined the footpath, feeding in such numbers that the tree itself seemed animated by their movements. I took delight in them, but even more in my father's delight.

I wrote this down because it was the easiest way to do the exercise – just describe the experience. Hoppy beamed at me when he handed back my copy book next day. He said it was terrific. He made me read it out in front of the class. And then he carefully detached the page from the copybook and put it up on the wall. My fear of him melted. The heat of his rage became, for me alone, a glow of approval. That was why he savaged the other boy, not me. Even as I was watching that assault and listening to the screams and grunts, I knew that the waxwings had saved me. I knew that I was glad it wasn't me being beaten and made to whimper like a baby or a pup. I knew that this knowledge was terrible, that I could never articulate it.

And the next time I wrote something for Hoppy's approval and he told me to stand up and read it aloud to the class, I couldn't do it. I started to stammer: wu-wu-wu, re-re-re, meh-meh-meh. He scowled at me. I was letting him down. That made it worse. I somehow gathered myself and started to breathe and I could say the words again. But the stammer came back and got worse. It was as if my fluency with words had become my enemy. It was punishing me for my sin.

The violence of Christian Brothers schools was itself inarticulable. Everybody knew about it, but almost no one could utter it without the stammers of euphemism and evasion. Recalling his schooldays, Charles Haughey, a CBS boy who had become a defining figure in the state, said that 'Basically what the Brothers do is lay foundations for practically every aspect of one's life. They equip the individual to achieve any level of learning he has the wish and capacity to aspire to… To love one's country and work for it was another fundamental part of the groundwork laid.' He added: 'There may well have been intellectual and social refinements to which we had not access…'[24] – a lovely way of saying that they were a rough crowd.

In the same hagiographic feature in the *Sunday Independent* in 1974, the most popular Irish sports commentator, Micheál Ó hEithir, said of his CBS schooldays, 'There was always discipline, but it wasn't overdone by any means.' John Marrinan, head of the police union, recalled that 'I thought the Brothers severe. But in retrospect I realize that they played a major part – only slightly less than my parents – in the formation of my character.' Gay Byrne was more subtly ambiguous about his time in Synge Street: 'It was a rough school and a tough school and we were beaten each day – on principle. I understand that is changed, and I wouldn't like sons of my own to experience it, but in my final years any bad impression I had was eradicated by a splendid teacher.'

Yet, fifteen years later, in his autobiography, Byrne wrote a concentrated description of what reads like torture: 'They beat the tar out of us… We were beaten with straps, sticks, even the leg of a chair. We were beaten for failure at lessons and simply, it seemed to me, on principle. They were careful not to leave marks. They generally struck on the hands, the legs, the buttocks and around the body. If they were thumping, they would thump on the body where it would not show. They never hit us on the jaw but across the side of the head…'[25]

In 1975, Byrne had an item on his *Late Late Show* about the Christian Brothers and their hopes that their founder Edmund Rice would be beatified by the pope. I was at that time involved with the Irish Union of School Students. One of the producers arranged for me to be in the audience and told me that at some point Gay would come to us for our opinions and he would point to me to let me say something about corporal punishment. I realized that this meant that he was not going to talk about it himself. When he came to the audience, I had my hand up. His eye caught mine for a second and then he turned away. He had clearly decided that it would not be right to spoil the evening. As he put it some years later: 'I am not a critic of the Brothers… I have been in the forefront of defending them from attack.'[26]

I did learn one thing from Gay Byrne. Hoppy had a special torture. He would stand a boy in front of him and take hold of the wisps of hair beside the ears on both sides of his head. Then he would slowly lift the boy off the floor by these strands of hair. It was horrifically painful. No other teacher did this and we thought it was a signature of his own. But Byrne, too, recalled in his autobiography how Brothers 'lifted us bodily by the side-hair at our temples'. So Hoppy hadn't invented it. Perhaps he had learned it from colleagues. Perhaps it had been done to him when he was in school.

The Brothers themselves had always understood that this intimate violence, and the absolute power over the bodies of children that made it possible, easily shaded into sexual abuse. As early as 1920, the order's Superior, Brother Patrick Hennessy, listed 'the fondling of boys' alongside such abuses as 'peering into tramcars' that ought to be avoided: 'The fondling of boys, the laying of hands upon them, in any way, is contrary to the rules of modesty, and is decidedly dangerous.' An internal guidebook for Brothers, *The Soul of Our Vocation*, in use in the 1960s and 1970s, advised them that 'all excessively sentimental friendships must be avoided, particularly with the young who are placed in our charge'. But it also counselled Brothers not to be dismayed when they learned of failures to follow this advice: 'It must needs scandals come.'[27] They would not come for a very long time.

9

1966: The GPO Trouser Suit

My mother had premonitions. She would start running up the stairs and a moment later one of us would fall out of the bed and start crying. She would dream that a cousin from the country was going to call to us that morning and he would turn up unannounced. At 1.31 on the morning of 8 March 1966, she elbowed my sleeping father and said, 'God, what was that?' She had given birth in that bed to her sixth and last child the previous day and he lay now in his cot at its foot. My father thought she was just having an uneasy dream and told her there was nothing to worry about. He turned over to go back to sleep and, a moment later, he heard the dull thud of a distant explosion.

The bomb had cut cleanly through the great Doric column of what everyone in Dublin called simply the Pillar, cutting off the plinth, with its viewing platform and the statue of the English naval hero Admiral Horatio Lord Nelson. It was not the only grand monument to the hero of Trafalgar in what was then the United Kingdom, but it was the most ostentatious and prominent, presumably because, in 1808 when it was erected, Dublin had most to prove in terms of loyalty.

The Pillar was the axis round which the city revolved. There had long been talk of replacing Nelson at the top, but no agreement on who should occupy so pivotal and lofty a place. Patrick Pearse and James Connolly, leaders of the 1916 Rising, had been proposed. But the suggestion that had provoked most interest in the immediate period before 1966 was that Nelson should make way for the slain John F. Kennedy. The most interesting objection came from Thomas Doyle of Dorset Street, writing to the *Evening Herald* in December 1963, who feared that this would in fact be to consign JFK to oblivion: 'Let us not put the proposed statue of John F. Kennedy on Nelson Pillar. Let us not put him way up there in seclusion where, like Nelson, he will be forgotten in a few years. How many of us know what Nelson looks like? I don't know, although I was born and bred in Dublin. John F. Kennedy's statue is deserving of a better site than that. This man I saw; I knew the warmth of his smile. Put his statue on the ground, so that when I pass I may see again the smile and feel the warmth that I knew. This man I know; for he honoured us all – our culture, our race, our nation. This was a man.'[1] JFK was too intimately known to be consigned to a lonely, pillar-top seclusion.

Later, after the bomb, a correspondent describing himself as 'an Englishman' argued that if only JFK had been installed, all would have been well. 'Much hurt could have been averted had your Government accepted the Irish offer abroad [sic] of erecting a statue of Kennedy where Nelson was. The Pillar could have remained, and violence would have been averted.'[2] The odd thing is that this was certainly true. An American president was now a far more acceptable image of Irishness than an English admiral.

In peculiarly admiring tones, reporters speculated that, in order to achieve the effects they did, the explosives must have been hung like a necklace or a garland around the neck of the column. In fact there was no such delicacy. Huge chunks of Wicklow granite showered down, one boulder hitting a passing taxi but leaving the driver safe. Some plate-glass windows shattered and a ten-foot neon sign crashed down from one of the shops on the eastern side of O'Connell Street.

A dance was still in progress in the Metropole Ballroom on the other side. It was due to finish half an hour later, sending a crowd out towards the site of the explosion, but it was not clear if the bombers knew or cared about them. What mattered to them was the gesture. The fiftieth anniversary of the Easter Rising was due to be celebrated in April. The Pillar towered forty-one metres over the General Post Office, the headquarters of the rebels, and members of an offshoot faction of the rump IRA had decided that this reminder of Ireland's former place within the British Empire literally could not be allowed to stand.

That night, twenty young people were injured and taken to hospital. But not in the explosion. They were at Dublin Airport, in a mob of teenagers, many of them from around Crumlin, that had gathered to welcome home from Luxembourg Dickie Rock, who had finished joint fourth in the Eurovision Song Contest with 'Come Back To Stay'. This may not seem like much of a triumph, but the British had finished ninth, and Ireland was still desperate for any kind of vindication in the eyes of the outside world. And Dickie was a big star, the Irish equivalent of Elvis Presley or Cliff Richard.

Perhaps there was an unintended poignancy in the title of the song. It was a standard, soupy love ballad but staying and coming back were notions that touched other nerves in the Ireland of 1966. The great national hope was that teenagers and young adults like these fans would indeed stay in Ireland and not emigrate – and that families who had emigrated would even come back home to a place with new prospects for them.

But that same day of Dickie Rock's return, the Organisation for Economic Co-operation and Development (OECD) published its annual survey of the Irish economy. It noted that while the population had a natural annual increase of an average of 30,000 since 1962, the actual increase was only 10,000 a year. The rest emigrated. The Programme for Economic Expansion was not going well: 'employment remained virtually static during the first half of the 1960s, whereas the Programme envisaged an increase of 7 to 8 per cent over the decade. The expected declines in emigration and unemployment have therefore not been achieved.'[3] Dickie Rock's emotional plea:

> Please, come back to stay
> Oh darling, please come back to stay

had an added piquancy in a society pining for, but as yet unable to reach, a state of equilibrium in which staying in Ireland could be regarded as a normal thing to do.

The scenes at the airport were terrifying. Policemen linked arms in front of both the arrival and departure terminals to prevent about a thousand fans from smashing through the glass doors. Young boys and girls carrying placards declaring We Want Dickie, We Love Dickie, Welcome Back, Dickie and Come Back To Stay, shouted and screamed, hammered on the airport windows, and rocked parked cars. They lined the terminal balconies and pressed five and six deep against barriers.

As Dickie Rock stepped down onto the tarmac, the Ballyfermot Boys' Band, conducted by Brother Cyprian, struck up 'Come Back To Stay'. Immediately, hundreds of teenagers crowding the balcony waved their banners and screamed: We Want Dickie. When Dickie looked up and waved, the crowd on the balconies pushed forwards and the kids at the front were crushed.[4]

These were different kinds of violence, to the participants mutually incomprehensible. The fans on the one side and the fanatics on the other were animated by different notions of freedom. For the teenage Dickiemaniacs, their passion and obsession was an expression of a new freedom from restraint, the stirrings of a rising consumer culture in which you could do what you desired. They were driven by youth and sex and the money in your pocket from a job in a factory or a shop. The energy of this pursuit of personal freedom was borderless. The airport was a good place to unleash it because the force was not specific to Ireland. It was moving through the western world. Its pulse was novelty.

But to the men who blew up Nelson's column, Liam Sutcliffe and the Christle brothers, Mick and Joe, freedom was very much specific to Ireland. It was about the Border. The IRA, from which they had formed their own splinter group, had tried in the previous years to wage its Border Campaign, attacking installations along the frontier between the Republic of Ireland and Northern Ireland. Freedom for them was not new – it was eternal, the old, endlessly recurring cause of removing all British power from the whole island.

When Liam Sutcliffe initially went to place the bomb, made from gelignite and ammonal, on the viewing platform at the top of the Pillar, he took his three-year-old son with him to allay suspicion.[5] The bomb didn't go off the first time. He went back to collect it, adjusted the timer and returned a week later. The sequence of events suggests it was pure luck that there were not mass casualties.

My father got us up early that morning and we took the bus in to see the wreck of Nelson. He said it was a big thing, an event we should remember. He took us right up close to the base where huge lumps of stone were scattered randomly like pebbles. Nobody stopped us. My father picked up a small piece of the granite, its outside worn grimy by the murk of the city, its inside glistening with newly revealed speckles of quartz, a secret self, hidden within the monument until the shock of the explosion so violently brought it to life. He put it in his pocket, a fragment of history, a shard of time, a petrified moment that had come in the night and would not be repeated. This, it seemed, was what history was: strange and unusual events that just detonated without warning, leaving mute, jagged traces.

But for me this was also the first time I was conscious of pure memory, of the idea that something you had in your head was now gone forever. I remembered just the previous summer, when my father's cousin Vincent was home from England. They took me and my older brother into the city centre and decided that we would climb the Pillar. We paid at a little turnstile and began the slog up the 168 steps of the stairway that wound its way through the hollow interior of the column. It was dark and strange and then, when you emerged at the top, bright and strange, the restored light illuminating the streets and cars, the church spires in every direction below and the low hills in the distance, even beyond our house in Crumlin. I felt that I was suddenly out of the city, floating over it, coolly detached from everything, even myself.

Stranger still was that, before we went up, Vincent bought half a dozen plums in a fruit shop. At the top he opened the brown paper bag and gave us one each. He and my father were laughing about spitting the stones down on the people below. I found this deeply unsettling because I did not know my father could be like that, that he could joke about something that would get you in big trouble. I also did not know until much later that their adult joke was that in James Joyce's *Ulysses* two old ladies do exactly that, that as well as history and memory there was a third thing, a layer of fiction that clung to buildings in Dublin like the residues of coal smoke and petrol fumes that coated and blackened their surfaces.

When I saw the ruin of the Pillar that morning in March 1966, I was disappointed by it. It was curiously unsatisfying. I had expected obliteration, annihilation. Instead, the bulk of the column was still standing, like a tree whose upper branches had been crudely lopped off, but whose trunk remained, intact but forlorn, or like a great sign pointing nowhere. And the violence seemed random, almost aimless. The big steel door through which we had passed when we paid to climb the steps was viciously twisted. But just a few feet in front of it, the flimsy wooden hut that served as the bus company's information desk (the Pillar was the terminus of most routes) was serenely unharmed. The thing was both gone and still there. Which was much more apt than I could possibly have understood at the time.

And the public response to the event was odd, too. There seemed to be a determination not to take it seriously as an act of violence that might portend worse. President de Valera, in an unprecedented indulgence in levity, reputedly called the *Irish Press* newspaper, owned by his own family, to suggest the headline: 'British Admiral Leaves Dublin By Air'.[6] Ten days after the bombing, a group of art students stole Nelson's head from a municipal storage yard and made drinking money by hiring it out to the folk groups The Dubliners and The Clancy Brothers to display at their concerts. Seven of the students posed with the head for a photograph for the *Evening Press*. In it, they are wearing balaclavas and hoods over their heads, creating an image that would later come to seem chillingly emblematic of terrorism but that then still seemed like a joke.

There was soon a surreal proliferation of Nelson heads. I saw the head myself that morning, lying amid the rubble at the foot of the column, the nose severed, the blind right eye now looking as if it has been gouged out entirely. But in April, a London antiques dealer, Bennie Grey, had the head on display in his shop in

Marylebone. An expert at Christie's attested that it was 'consistent with a statue more than 100 years old'. Grey said he was sure it was the genuine Dublin article and that 'Since he had brought it to London it had been kept in car boots and garages.' However, Butty Sugrue, who ran the Admiral Nelson public house in the heavily Irish London district of Kilburn, claimed that he had bought the authentic head for £550 and was having it brought from Dublin to be unveiled in his saloon.[7] Asked whether it was possible that his Nelson head had actually been stolen in Dublin and sold on to Bennie Grey, Sugrue said, 'Impossible. I saw it myself only two days ago. Nobody would dare steal my head.'[8]

Nelson may have famously lacked an arm and an eye in real life but in his symbolic death he became Hydra-headed. What was meant to be a story ending – the metaphorical conclusion of British Ireland – was merely the unspooling of other yarns.

In April, for a while, we stopped playing cowboys and Indians. The ambushes from behind the garden wall, the shots fired from the safety of the stone lamp posts, gave way to barricades, house-to-house fighting and the grim heroism of the lone sniper pinning down the alien advance. It being 1966, and the fiftieth anniversary of the Easter Rising, we watched Hugh Leonard's *Insurrection* on television every night. It went out at 9.15, usually past my bedtime, but there was no question of not being allowed to stay up for it. This was epic stuff: the most ambitious project yet undertaken by the national broadcaster, a recreation night-by-night of the events of the Rising, with ninety-three speaking parts and crowd scenes filled by 300 members of the Irish army and 200 civilian extras.

It was overwhelmingly male: very little attention was paid to the prominent role of women in the real events, with only Constance Markievicz featured. It was also constrained by the instruction from the RTÉ Authority that the whole episode must be presented as 'a nationalist and not a socialist rising'.[9]

In particular, the state was determined that the public would not see by far the greatest artistic depiction of the Rising, *The Plough and the Stars* by the unmistakably socialist Sean O'Casey, which had provoked riots in 1926 by challenging the founding myth of blood sacrifice. The official orders issued to the Abbey

Theatre were that there should be no O'Casey plays staged during Easter Week because it 'would not be in keeping with the spirit of the occasion'.[10] The Taoiseach, Seán Lemass, personally extended this instruction to RTÉ. In July 1965, he told the minister in charge of broadcasting to check on what programmes were being prepared: 'to ensure that these programmes will be suitable. (This means in particular no O'Casey).'[11]

Yet *Insurrection* was jarring in its own way. The director, Louis Lentin, complained of the twin phenomena that cursed his filming of street scenes in the city. On the one hand, there was Dublin's characteristic fusion of memory, history and fable. While filming, he was constantly interrupted by older citizens 'all well-meaning, who were certain it didn't happen like that at all, and said so'. On the other, this was already a media-saturated world, whose totems of modernity were visible markers of the present: 'if only there weren't so many television aerials.'[12] The year 1966 was the first one in which a majority of Irish homes had a TV set.

The format for the eight half-hour episodes reflected this double vision. The films were presented, not as reconstructions of history but as live news reports. Ray McAnally played the news anchor in the studio. He interviewed actors playing the roles of participants, including the British commander General Lowe:

R. McA: But the battle has been raging for hours in Northumberland Road.

Lowe: I shouldn't call it a battle exactly. More of an extended incident.

The anchor would cut to 'live' footage from inside the GPO and other sites, where reporters in 1960s suits spoke into the camera as rebels in 1916 uniforms rushed around behind them.

This structure was full of tensions. On the one hand, it seemed to do exactly what the state did not want: to suggest that the Rising was not safely in the past. It was *now*. We were vicarious participants in a drama that unfolded day by day whose ending, in the willing suspension of our disbelief, was still unknown. Why did the authorities allow this? Because, on the other hand, the format was ostentatiously modern. It imagined Ireland, not just as a place in which the rebels were fighting the British, but as a country that had progressed far enough to have television and know how its genres worked.

Above all, the format of *Insurrection* was American. It was an Irish version of a US original: the long-running series *You Are There*, in which Walter Cronkite in the studio anchored 'live' coverage of the battle of Hastings or Joan of Arc, the death of Socrates or the capture of Jesse James. All history could be assimilated to the present, controlled by the authoritative figure of the host at his desk, literally anchored in the assumptions of the confidently contemporary present. It was time travel without tears.

The bet with *Insurrection* was that, filtered through this American technological modernity, the vivid immediacy of the recreated Rising would not encourage us to think about the unfinished business of the past, but, rather, take pride in the transformed Ireland in which we were growing up.

I was more interested in the action scenes, the shooting and banging, than in this complex framework, but these were essentially American, too. The genre was another staple of American TV: the Western. When an edited version was reshown in 1968, the *Irish Times* TV critic Ken Grey noted 'moments when it seemed likely to turn into a cowboy and Indian epic with a Dublin setting'.[13] Twenty-five years after the original screening, the historical consultant for *Insurrection*, Professor Kevin B. Nowlan, said ruefully that the presentation of the fighting in 1916 was 'a cowboy and Indian arrangement, the pursuer and the pursued'.[14]

We didn't need to be told that. It helped that on the television the rebels wore hats that were like Stetsons with one side of the brim turned up, but even without this cue we knew how to insert our usual games into the scenarios we saw acted out each night. Next day, we played out the manoeuvres, blocking the stairs with mattresses and chairs, ducking below the window of the front bedroom to reload and fire again on the British cavalry prancing arrogantly up O'Connell Street. Sometimes, one of us would forget and swoop at a barricade with a plastic tomahawk, hand to mouth in a fearsome whoop, and would be resisted by another with a plastic 1916–66 badge – green shamrock on a white background with orange lettering – fixed to his cowboy hat.

At Scoil Íosagáin Christian Brothers primary school, a framed copy of the Proclamation of the Irish Republic, read out in front of the General Post Office by Patrick Pearse in 1916, appeared on the wall. But for quite a while I confused the Seven Leaders with the Magnificent Seven. In the same school hall where we recited Pearse's 'The Mother', the Brothers, for some reason, gave us a showing of *The Magnificent Seven*. We crunched our crisps in time to the gunfire and, when the good guys fell in the dust, brushed away incipient tears with toffee-apple fingers. The number seven, the nineteenth-century rifles, the barricades, the cowboy hats that the rebels wore, above all the quiet, dark leader, pure and brave, willing to sacrifice himself for the humble, cowering peasants, all contributed to the intermingling of images. Yul Pearse and Patrick Brynner became one.

There were, however, two disquieting elements in the parallel. One was that in the movie, one of the Seven made a speech to a little boy, telling him that heroism was not the preserve of gunmen, that courage was more manifest in the daily struggle to survive and raise children than it was in showy violence. That disturbed me. And the other was that *The Magnificent Seven* won. They were not led away by the bandits to be executed. And that made the story much better than the heroic failure of the rebels. I liked the happy ending.

The annual school concert, staged in the same hall, was to be a celebration of the glorious anniversary. We were kept in after school time to learn the songs and rehearse the actions, the Brother's pounding on the piano mingling in a muffled echo with the tramp of marching feet on the bare floor of the hall. I had a sweet, pure voice so I was chosen to sing solo, a sentimental ballad of martyrdom to a mournful waltz tune, called 'The Black And Tan Gun'.

The song was a minor hit in the Irish charts that year, though RTÉ banned the playing of 'rebel songs' during the fiftieth-anniversary celebrations.[15] There was still an official unease about these ballads glorifying the tradition of republican violence. Yet this number must have seemed harmlessly anodyne. It had, however, a hidden complexity. The lyrics (uncredited to any writer) were standard Irish nationalist martyrology:

It was down in the town of old Bantry
Where most of the fighting was done.
It was there that a young Irish soldier
Was shot by a Black and Tan gun.

It sounds like a shard of folk memory from the Irish war of independence, when the IRA fought the crown forces, including the notorious Black and Tan irregulars.

But if you look closely at the record label, the song is credited as 'The Black And Tan Gun (Nobody's Darling But Mine)'. It is in fact a version of a classic American country-and-western song, written by Jimmie Davis, later governor of Louisiana, in 1934, and recorded as the B-side of 'When It's Round-Up Time In Heaven'. It was released in 1966, moreover, by a showband called Sean Dunphy and The Hoedowners.

Dunphy was the co-host of a country music show called *Hoedown* on RTÉ. It was ersatz Americana. There was a dance group of pretty girls in gingham dresses called the Larri-ettes, the name taken from a high school troupe in Laredo, Texas. It was immensely popular – by 1969, Dunphy and The Hoedowners would be the most successful act in the Irish charts (The Beatles were third). Around the time of our concert, the Irish newspapers advertised the dates of The Hoedowners' upcoming tour. Sunday: Royal Ballroom, Castletown; Monday: Brandon Ballroom, Tralee; Tuesday: Toomevara Carnival; Wednesday: Portumna Carnival; Thursday: Depart Shannon for New York; Friday: Jaeger House Ballroom, New York; Saturday: Jaeger House Ballroom, New York; Sunday: Jaeger House Ballroom, New York.[16]

Jaeger House was a dance hall at 85th Street and Lexington Avenue in Manhattan, one of a constellation of venues – the Caravan, the Tuxedo, City Center, the Leitrim House – where Irish exiles and Irish-Americans danced and drank and paired off on the weekends. It was part of the Irish world: Toomevara, Portumna, the Upper East Side. Presumably, Dunphy sang 'The Black And Tan Gun' there that weekend. Did it seem at all strange to them: Irish nationalist martyrdom filtered through second-hand American country kitsch and re-exported to Irish immigrants in

America? Or did that very oddness make a kind of sense of their own condition, half there, half here, suspended between versions of the past that functioned on either side of the Atlantic?

All of this was beyond me then, but the song with which I was to make my first starring appearance was weirdly resonant of that moment. It was not just the way it fused the Irish Troubles with notions of America. It was that the very fact that this could be done spoke of a sense that the Troubles were in fact over. When the Black and Tans could be assimilated into old-timey country music, they had become harmless. This past was now fully sentimentalized. It was a free-floating, imaginary world to which you could take a day trip and then leave behind, knowing that it had no purchase on mundane reality.

Indeed, the song was quite explicit in its sense of an ending. The young Irish soldier is shot by the Black and Tan gun. As he expires, he leans up on his elbow and tells his comrades his dying wish:

> Won't you bury me out on the mountains,
> So that I can see where the battle was won…

As I practised the song over and over, I grasped the shape of this drama, that this was the whole point. We won. I could wring all the pathos out of his death and then bring the audience back to the comforting conclusion:

> And now we are back in old Dublin, our victory over and won,
> We think of our comrades we buried under God's rising sun.

We're back in Dublin. It's all over. I liked that – no more Troubles. I could make them feel sad and then happy. I could see them brushing away a tear and allowing themselves a gentle smile.

At a very late stage in the rehearsals, the Brother decided to expand this little drama by making the number an 'action song' with the story of the murder of the Irish hero being shot by a Black and Tan played out in dumb show across the stage while I sang from a position over near the side. A very large eight-year-old misnamed Fred Tidy was assigned the martyr's part, dressed in a trench coat with the sleeves rolled up to fit his short arms. A mean, ferret-faced boy was to play the Black and Tan, his evil bearing emphasized by a black beret that slouched ominously over his brow. Two weedy, scrawny kids were chosen as pall-bearers and instructed to drape Fred with the Irish tricolour as the last verse of the song got into its stride, salute solemnly, lift Fred on their shoulders and carry him offstage.

I stood at the side of the stage in starched white shirt, tricoloured tie, green short trousers and green socks with golden stripes at the top, watched for the signal from the Brother and began, as the assembled parents quietened to a hush:

> It was down in the town of old Bantry,
> Where most of the fighting was done.

I could see nothing of the tableaux behind me.

> It was there that a young Irish soldier
> Was shot by a Black and Tan gun.

There was a bang, a thud and a titter as Fred crashed to the stage, mortally wounded. I heard the pall-bearers march on as the last verse waltzed its way towards the emotional climax:

> As the blood from his wounds ran red
> He turned to his comrades beside him
> And these are the words that he said…

Ripples of adult laughter gathered themselves in the body of the hall, restraint giving way to raucousness. I could feel it pulsing towards me, drowning out my high, light voice. I looked down quickly: my fly was closed. I battled on mechanically:

> So they hurried him out on the mountains
> Neath a cross that stood facing the sun…

The laughter had become helpless, wild and hysterical. I had to look. I turned my head to see what was going on behind me. The puny pall-bearers, having apparently failed at several attempts to lift Fred, had taken him by the heels and were dragging him slowly by his feet, the tricolour bunching around his neck and face, his head bumping off the rough boards, to the side of the stage.

The state's own big show had its moments, too. Aiséirí: Glóir Réim na Cásca (Resurrection: the Easter Pageant), the official jubilee pageant written and directed by Tomás MacAnna of the Abbey Theatre, was staged in the headquarters of the Gaelic Athletic Association, Croke Park. The religious title was typical of the unselfconscious association of the Rising, and thus of the jubilee, with Catholicism. At the opening of the official memorial, the Garden of Remembrance, the Church of Ireland Archbishop and the representatives of the general assembly of the Presbyterian Church found themselves locked out while the Catholic primate John Charles McQuaid performed the blessing.[17] This was said not to be deliberate – but it was, at best, an eloquent oversight.

Aiséirí 'traced the story of the Irish Republic from the American War of Independence to the execution of Roger Casement in August 1916, with a brief coda that referred to Irish neutrality during World War II'[18] – a rather telling starting point. It was intended in part to instil patriotic fervour in Irish youth. For the final performance 20,000 schoolchildren 'assembled under marshals provided by the National Organisation of Ex-Servicemen in the city centre, and marched to Croke Park, preceded by a colour party'.[19] The militarism provoked no comment or criticism.

Ironically, the pageant required the use of the Union Jack in a recreation of the battle of Ballinahinch in 1798 and, as the *Evening Herald* noted, this was 'the first time the British flag made its appearance on that jealously guarded sod' of Croke Park, which had always been a bastion of Irish cultural nationalism. The sequences were linked by a narrator whose lyrical manner of speaking, in both English and Gaelic, was held up to us as the acme of Irish elocution: 'Through it all is heard the voice of History (Micheál MacLiammóir) speaking in clear, measured, sonorous and authoritative tones.'[20] Most adults in the audience probably knew that the voice of History was flamboyantly gay, a fact that was as obvious as it was rigorously unacknowledged. Most probably did not know his real dark secret, revealed after his death: that he was in fact an Englishman called Michael Wilmore who had entirely invented his Irish identity.

There were other tensions, too, for 1966 was a year of bitter industrial conflict as workers found reality falling short of their expectations of a better life. Bernadine Trudden, a visitor from Boston, recorded in her diary the enthusiasm of the pageant crowd for the scene dealing with the huge Dublin labour dispute of 1913, generally seen as the crucible from which the Irish trade union movement emerged: 'the greatest cheers came not for any of the marching men but for the strikers of 1913, when they burst onto the field with their placards. And the loudest boos were not for the redcoats, with their muskets and their canons, but for the baton charge by the police that helped break the strike.'[21]

Heroic failure dogged the pageant. The weather was so bad that the Friday night had to be cancelled.[22] The director's eleven-year-old son Ferdia was given a role as a letter-carrier, one of four children whose signs would spell out ÉIRE, the official name of Ireland. 'My job was to walk on at the end holding a massive plastic letter E. This formed the final letter of the word Éire, the visual centrepiece of the closing celebrations… On the third night, the wind snapped off the bottom half of my letter. From the stands, it appeared that the glorious, heroic blood sacrifice of 1916 had culminated in the birth of the Republic of EIRF.'[23]

Somewhere in all of this was the notion that History, now speaking in MacLiammoir's lush tones, had become meta-history. It could be performed, enacted, even sold.

The state imagined the commemoration might attract visitors from America. A 'colourful brochure featuring the Rock of Cashel with a party of huntsmen (in hunting pink) and hounds at the base of the rock' was used to market 'The Easter Rebellion Anniversary Tour' to 'visit the birthplace of the great Irish martyrs and to Dublin to take part in all the religious, civic and military pageants and ceremonies.'[24] Meanwhile, in New York there was an Irish fashion show at the Waldorf Astoria, organized by Anna Livia

Boutique of Dawson Street, Dublin. There was 'a disc jockey... reading Yeats'.[25] Models, including one wearing 'the GPO trouser suit', strutted on the catwalk to the music from the execution scene from the documentary film *Mise Éire*.

Conor Cruise O'Brien and his now wife, Máire Mac an tSaoi, daughter of a veteran of the Rising, walked out in protest.[26] But the GPO trouser suit was not entirely out of keeping with the national moment. In the GAA's own pageant, *Seachtar Fear, Seacht Lá* (Seven Men, Seven Days), also staged at Croke Park, James Connolly was surrounded by working men in 'new dungarees... white coats... welding visors'. Seán McDermott, another of seven executed leaders, came on stage accompanied by 'Irish sailors, Irish airmen and air hostesses, and Irish transport workers in uniform'.[27] This was the same kind of wilful anachronism that shaped the style of *Insurrection*. Yeats had asked:

What stood in the Post Office
With Pearse and Connolly?

and answered himself that it was the spirit of the ancient Irish hero Cúchulain. But what stood beside them in these fiftieth-anniversary imaginings were not legendary warriors but skilled workmen in visors, Aer Lingus hostesses in uniform and sharp-suited TV reporters. The message was that what Pearse and Connolly and McDermott had really died for was the brave new Ireland of the 1960s that would have such people in it. That Ireland was not up in arms to reclaim the Fourth Green Field of Ulster, but revelling in the wonder that it had its own engineering works, its own airline, its own TV station.

There were those who were uneasy about this. Scarcely noticed by most of the public, twelve men and one girl staged a hunger strike in Dublin throughout the week, to protest about 'the death of the Gaeltacht, economic dependence on Britain, partition and emigration'.[28] They stopped eating at noon on Monday, when the Rising began, and at 3.45 p.m. on Saturday, corresponding to the time of the rebels' surrender – they 'went to the Gresham Hotel where they sipped soup'.[29] In between they paraded in front of Leinster House, the GPO and the newly opened Garden of Remembrance. It was a strange kind of ritual, deeply rooted in Irish history, but also lacking the drama of a real hunger strike: the idea of death as a possible outcome. The climax was not martyrdom but soup in the Gresham. A narrative of agonized self-sacrifice was evoked, only to be defused.

Thomas Kinsella, the leading voice among the young poets emerging in the Republic, had also protested the transformation of the Rising's romantic ideals into validation for a commercial and capitalist culture. In 'A Country Walk', he wrote, in relation to the martyrs of 1916, of encountering a shop and a hotel:

> That bear their names: MacDonagh and McBride,
> Merchants, Connolly's Commercial Arms...[30]

Tom MacIntyre, another young writer, went further in his story 'An Aspect of the Rising'. The narrator picks up a prostitute in Dublin and they go Phoenix Park, to a spot opposite Áras an Uachtaráin, the official residence of the head of state and sole surviving commandant from the Rising, President Eamon de Valera. She excites herself with a diatribe against the occupant of the Áras: 'You crawthumpin' get of a Spaniard that never was seen... with your long features and your long memory and your two-and-twenty strings to your bow, what crooked eggs without yolks are you hatching between Rosaries tonight... She left nothing out, there was nothing she didn't fit in: The treaty, the Civil War, the Oath, the hangings of the 'forties, Emigration, Inflation, Taxation, the Language, the lot. His Excellency heard not a word but, chosen by the gods, I heard...'

Yet the most forlorn protestor of all was de Valera himself. His note of dissonance was discreet and somewhat mournful: a simple reiteration of his own ideas of what 1916 meant and what aspirations the jubilee should inspire. In his official anniversary address, de Valera expressed the hope that Ireland would 'become again, as it was for centuries in the past, a great intellectual and missionary centre from which would go forth the satisfying saving truths of Divine Revelation...' He expressed the fear, on the other hand, that Ireland might 'sink into an amorphous cosmopolitanism – without a past or a distinguishable future'.

This rhetoric was increasingly anachronistic. No one much believed in it. On 1 June, with the ceremonials and pageants and dramas fresh in their minds, voters went to the polls in a presidential election in which de Valera was seeking a second seven-year term. Even with Fianna Fáil's young princeling, Lemass's son-in-law Charles Haughey as his campaign manager, Dev scraped home with a majority of just over 10,000 votes, 1 per cent of the total. He lost in every one of Dublin's eight constituencies.[31] It was as if George Washington had almost been humiliated in an election on the fiftieth anniversary of 1776.

But de Valera was nonetheless touching, in that expression of unease, on something real: not Ireland's part in the unfolding of Divine Revelation, but the anxiety about the meaning of history. If men in visors and air hostesses were the contemporary avatars of the martyrs of 1916, what past could have led towards their existence? And what future could lead from them that would still be 'distinguishable' from that of any other country or culture?

That year, Ireland got its first American-style shopping mall, the Stillorgan Shopping Centre, with fifty shops and parking for 600 cars, which was opened in south Dublin in December by Seán Lemass. By then, he had already stepped down as Taoiseach, explicitly linking his resignation to the idea that the time had come for the revolutionary generation to which he belonged to leave the stage: 'The 1916 celebrations marked the ending of a chapter in our history... As one of the 1916 generation, this marked the end of the road for me also.' Opening the shopping centre, after a blessing by the local parish priest, Lemass said that 'in recent years, considerable changes had been taking place in all spheres of business. Traditional practices were dying out and were being replaced by more up-to-date skills and techniques of business management... The opening of the new shopping centre in Stillorgan marked a further step forward in the continuously changing process of economic development.'[32]

That 'traditional practices... dying out' was, in his eyes and presumably in those of most of his listeners, a good thing could be taken for granted. But where would that leave church and state, whose authority rested on traditions of religious faith and of national identity? What would newness look like? Like Ireland's first high-rise system-built housing development, Ballymun, on the north side of Dublin, 'far less remote from the city centre', as the *Irish Press* pointed out, 'than... parts of Crumlin'.[33] Neil Blaney, another of the new generation of Fianna Fáil politicians, launched the scheme for 2,569 flats, in 1965, not merely as a quick fix for Dublin's housing crisis, but, rather, as a statement that 'would stand as a model for Ireland and other countries'.[34]

In 1963, the architect Robin Walker said that 'Dublin must be reconstituted to become more a part of the urban conglomeration that stretches from here to the Ruhr'.[35]

It was important that the scheme not be understood as British. W. A. Newman, a columnist in the *Irish Press*, de Valera's family newspaper, described it in 1965 as 'the most exciting development in this city of Dublin for many a long year' and noted in particular that its inspiration did not come from the new towns, constructed in Britain after the Second World War: 'for a closer parallel to Ballymun... you have to look at America... And not merely the basic concept, but the design. The American planners, like ours, propose to mix the housing styles...'[36]

This was not true: the precast concrete system used in Ballymun was French and Sir William Holford, widely regarded as the leading technocrat of town planning in post-war Britain, and the father of the modern industrial estate, was associated with the project in an overall consultancy capacity. But to think of this strange new place as American was much better than to admit that the new Ireland was going to look rather like much of urban Britain.

One of the few sceptics expressed precisely this fear. In one of his last Cruiskeen Lawn columns for the *Irish Times*, Myles na Gopaleen (aka Flann O'Brien/Brian O'Nolan) made a grim prophecy: 'Another spasm of "planning" has taken possession of the notorious Department of Local Government Board. Again faithfully following British improvisation, a "new town" is going to be run up in a jiffy in the Ballymun area, and thousands of indigent town dwellers, who have harmed nobody, permanently exiled there. It will inevitably and quickly become a new concrete slum, like Crumlin and Ballyfermot, and workers drafted there can face a lifetime of poverty by having a substantial slice of their earnings earmarked for extortionate bus fares. Scarcity and malnutrition will be the lot of their families.'[37]

Neil Blaney, who launched the scheme in 1965, suggested that, when completed, it should be called Árd Glas, from the Gaelic words for high and green, conjuring images of sylvan bliss and grand elevation. But in the enthusiasm of the following year's jubilee, it was decided instead that the seven fifteen-storey tower blocks should be named after the seven martyred leaders of the Rising. And so, the great monument to the state's founding fathers turned out to be a row of grey slabs that loomed over the city like giant tombstones, making the new town a necropolis of modern aspirations.

The families who moved out to Ballymun from the inner city dreamed of light and cleanliness and rational order, of a different kind of place in which their own histories could begin anew. But the promise was no sooner made than broken. When the flats were handed over by the builders in 1969, it quickly became clear that the landscaping was never finished, that the lifts kept breaking down, the heating system was unreliable. The town centre was unbuilt, so there were few shops. The schools and sporting facilities were not there. David Dickson, the historian of Dublin, pronounced the harshest possible judgement on the experiment: 'worse than the Crumlin story of three decades before.'[38]

By the mid-1980s, traditional families were already reluctant to settle in Ballymun and the tower blocks were disproportionately occupied by single mothers and their children, by single men (many recently moved from institutional care) and by people who had been homeless. Few of them had access to the income, jobs, services and supports they needed. And because they were often politically disempowered the authorities did not feel pressure to maintain the blocks to a decent standard. Ballymun recreated in a new form the old slums it was meant to replace. History did not begin anew – it repeated itself.

Like Nelson, these monuments eventually came down. One by one they fell: Patrick Pearse in 2004, Thomas MacDonagh, Seán McDermott and Éamonn Ceannt in 2005, James Connolly in 2007, Thomas Clarke in 2008. For seven more years, an increasingly forlorn reminder of lost dreams, Joseph Plunkett Tower stood alone, a metre higher than Nelson Pillar used to be, until it, too, was brought down in 2015.

For the implosion of MacDonagh Tower on 5 June 2005, the minister of state Noel Ahern, brother of the then Taoiseach, was joined for the detonation by Muriel McAuley, grand-daughter of Thomas MacDonagh, and her eight-year-old grandson Oscar McAuley. There was a thirty-minute delay to the implosion because somebody said they thought they had seen a shadowy figure flitting around the exclusion zone around the tower, some spectre perhaps. Then, at 11.30, Oscar pressed the button and his great-grandfather's monument collapsed in on itself. There were cheers from the crowd, even as a cloud of fine grey dust plumed out towards them and covered their clothes in the ghostly remains of another obliterated history. The dull thud of the explosives lingered in the air after the cheering had died down.

10

1967: The Burial of Leopold Bloom

The end of our garden was a grey pebble-dashed wall about fifteen feet high. It was the boundary of Dolphin's Barn Jewish Cemetery. From my grandfather's bedroom, which became mine after he died, you could look over almost the whole cemetery. It was also the view from the upper floor of the primary school at the end of the road and, when the secondary school was built in 1969, from those classrooms, too.

Half of it, the part next to my primary school, was densely packed with gravestones, some standing upright in what we regarded as the proper Christian manner, but most set out in symmetrical rows of stone memorial slabs, laid flat and level, so that the dead seemed to repose all the more serenely. The other half was empty, just well-cut grass and a line of half a dozen neatly trimmed cedar trees, its unused expanse indicating a community too small to fill its own resting place.

The cemetery hovered, literally and imaginatively, in my peripheral vision. It was the most interesting space in the vicinity. Everywhere else, the eye fell merely on the identical rows of identical houses. The tenants were not allowed to paint the front doors – every few years, men from the Corporation would come and apply a new coat of light-brown varnish to maintain (or if necessary restore) the required uniformity. But the Jewish cemetery expressed difference, otherness. It was the most outside part of the outside world. The back wall of our garden was a line between the familiar and the strange.

We passed the cemetery gate half a dozen times a day, going to and from school or walking down to the canal to play. It was always shut. In the house beside it lived the caretakers, a middle-aged country couple with one daughter. They were odd, ill at ease in the city. They did not mix much, but my parents were nice to them. They asked me to help the girl, who was slow, with her homework. Once, when I was passing the gate, it was open, and the caretaker asked me if I wanted to look in. I walked up the entrance lane to the Tahara house where the dead were prepared for burial, an elegant little curved structure with a Star of David over the door. On the nearest headstones there was writing in a strange alphabet. I was overcome with the feeling that I should not be there. I ran back down the laneway and out again into mundane existence.

Something in this disjunction between the proximity of the place and its foreignness generated an uncertainty about the real and the unreal. A boy in my class told me that the reason the cemetery was half empty was that the Jews buried the dead standing up to save space. I knew this was not true. We all did – we could see with our own eyes that the graves were the same size as the ones in any other cemetery. But I believed it nonetheless. The evidence of my own eyes was easily routed by an inherited idea of Jewish meanness.

Five minutes' walk from our house, across the canal bridge that marked the entrance to our estate, was the United Hebrew Congregation synagogue on South Circular Road, a dull blocky building with a neoclassical façade, complete with faux Ionic pillars, that clothed its religious difference in discreet respectability. Even its name, Greenville Hall, seemed like a disguise. It showed no sign of the bomb damage it had suffered in a German air raid in January 1941. My mother told me about the raid and marvelled that the Nazis had been able, even in an attack on neutral Ireland that was supposed to have been an accident, to pinpoint the holy place of the Jews.

This can hardly have been true – the Germans had hit the nearby Presbyterian church, too. But people believed it, and so did

I. It was the first image I had in my head of Nazi persecution of the Jews, this notion that less than twenty years before I was born, Hitler had sent his big bombers into the sleepy Dublin night just to get at these strange people who lived on the margins of my own little world.

Looking now at the contemporary newspaper reports from 1941, I find that a German government spokesman in Berlin claimed that 'Those bombs are English or they are imaginary. Our fliers have not been over Ireland.'[1] The imaginary bombs had done real damage. They had also created a story that while untrue – the Dorniers or Heinkels had not picked out the synagogue – also encoded a truth: they would have done it if they could.

At some time in my childhood, Asher Benson, one of the repositories of the memories of Dublin's Jewish community, went into the Bleeding Horse pub on Camden Street for a quiet drink. He was confronted by a man called Sniffer Cohen, 'a barrow-pushing petty dealer in manufacturer's offcuts, so named for his quivering proboscis'.[2] Four pints later, Sniffer became maudlin. 'If only Leopold Bloom was here', he snuffled. 'There was a man who knew how to down a pint!' Bloom is the central character of James Joyce's *Ulysses* and not exactly real. But Cohen told Benson that, in 1942, he had been summoned urgently to a fourth-floor attic room of a tenement in Bishop Street and enjoined to bring a jug of porter.

There, lying on a rusted rickety iron bed was his childhood friend, Leopold Bloom, who, 'since the publication of *Ulysses* in 1922, had sensibly chosen to keep a low profile'. His thin shoulders were draped in a faded prayer shawl with 'Property of Greenville Hall synagogue' written on it. He had a grease-stained skull cap embroidered with the word 'Jerusalem' on his wizened head and a tattered Hebrew prayer book upside down on his lap. 'I'm dying', he announced, 'and this is the last jug I'll ever down.'

'Promise me', he entreated Cohen, 'to bury me in the Jewish cemetery in Dolphin's Barn.' Bloom then took the jug of porter, blew off the froth, drank the contents in one uninterrupted swallow and expired, cursing James Joyce and saying he would 'settle with Jimmy in Hell'.

The committee of the Jewish Holy Burial Society turned down Bloom's request to be buried in Dolphin's Barn Cemetery on the grounds that he was 'a confirmed apostate, an eater of forbidden non-kosher food, and had married out'. But Cohen had an idea: Aughavannagh Road, which is on the perimeter of the cemetery, was then being built. That night, with the assistance of three cronies, Sniffer put Bloom's corpse on his barrow and they wheeled it over Sally's Bridge, along the canal path, stopping occasionally to refresh themselves from bottles of stout concealed under the dead man's armpits.

When they reached the half-built Aughavannagh Road, they went into one of the back gardens and started digging under the cemetery wall, undisturbed by a dozy night watchman, until they were alarmed by a sudden eruption of howls from the neighbourhood dogs. 'Bloom's sextons just about managed to get his head under the wall; from shoulder downwards he remained in Aughavannagh Road, where his attendants hurriedly covered him with building rubble.'

After another two pints in the Bleeding Horse, Sniffer agreed to accompany Benson to the cemetery to show him the place in the wall under which they had pushed Bloom's head. 'In the thick undergrowth inside the cemetery I discovered the wooden marker they threw over the wall on the following day, and which is now in my possession. Through the woodwormed surface, the inscription is just visible: "Leopold Bloom, 16th June 1942. His head was Jewish even if the rest of him wasn't. May he rest in pieces."'[3] Given the small number of houses that might have matched the location, there is a strong chance that Bloom's fictional torso was in our actual back garden.

On feast days and anniversaries, our road, which usually had only three or four cars parked along it, filled with those of visitors to the cemetery. One of the kids on the street told me that what you did on these occasions was accost the people going to visit the graves and say, 'I'll mind your car for sixpence.' I went up to a well-dressed middle-aged couple and said the words. The man looked at me sourly, then dug in his pocket and gave me sixpence. I sat watching his car but after an hour realized that I was the only kid doing this. It dawned on me that we were involved in a protection racket, that the threat implied in the words was that, if the owner did not pay up, something nasty would happen to the car. I felt ashamed and uneasy, conscious that we were menacing people that the Germans had tried to bomb. The words were a fiction that blurred into some kind of dark reality.

One day, my cousin Barry, a year younger than me, was playing in the back garden with us. He asked my brother and me what was on the other side of the wall. My brother told him it was a graveyard and I could sense that he was suddenly scared. I was delighted. 'And every night at six o'clock', I added, 'the ghosts come over the wall.' I forgot I had said it and we played away for hours until we went in for tea. Someone asked the time and my mother said, 'It's six o'clock.' Barry looked out of the window and saw the ghosts coming over the wall. He turned deathly pale and began to scream: 'They're coming! They're coming!' He became hysterical. I pretended not to know what he was seeing.

I did not know then that the ghosts were real. A large proportion of the people buried there came from a town called Akmijan (Akmiyan in Yiddish) in the Kovno district of Lithuania. The older tombstones carried inscriptions like 'Hannah Jackson, a Good Woman of Akmijan'.[4] They had fled Tzarist persecution in the 1880s. When they got to Dublin, even the small, established Jewish community looked on them as outsiders, referring to them as 'Russians' and 'foreigners'.[5] They had initially scraped a living as 'peddlers, sellers of religious pictures, petty moneylenders, musicians'. But the name of their home place, the name on their tombstones, Akmijan, was by the time of my childhood, already a ghost. All traces of the Jews who lived there were systematically erased in pogroms and then in the Holocaust. The last of them were murdered in August 1941. The place is now called only by its Lithuanian name Akmene. Akmijan has vanished. Its spectral citizens lived over our back wall.

11

1968: Requiem

On a cold, bright Friday morning in the middle of January 1968, I was walking up Clogher Road to Saint Bernadette's, the vast and imposing church that had replaced the temporary structure where my parents had been married. It was still early, perhaps around eight o'clock. Almost no one was around. Just before the church, walled off behind high trees, was the handsome house of the parish priest. Parked outside it on the road was a grand Humber Pullman limousine, its stately curves thrusting out like the prow of an ocean liner in front of the high cab that recalled the elegant coach of a nineteenth-century aristocrat. The metal body shone so brightly it seemed to be generating its own luminosity from some secret source of power.

As I approached the Humber, I could see a man in a grey uniform kneeling on the cold footpath and leaning in towards its interior. I thought he must be fixing something that had broken. But when I was almost at the car, I could see that two dainty feet were poking out from the side of the passenger compartment. The chauffeur was polishing the shoes that encased them with a brush. The man wearing them was the Archbishop of Dublin, John Charles McQuaid. I hugged the inside of the footpath and walked quickly and quietly on. I did not think either of them had seen me. I scurried on to the church to get ready for the performance of my lifetime: serving a high, solemn requiem Latin Mass for the man who was the voice of God in Dublin. But I could not quite shake the thought that I had seen something I should not, the guilt of the accidental voyeur.

By that time I was nearly ten, and a veteran. I had been an altar boy at Saint Bernadette's for three years. I started out as an awkward and inattentive novice. At my first Mass, I was unprepared for the weight of the heavy liturgical book as I moved it from one side of the altar to the other, and I dropped it. Shortly afterwards, I got bored during the sermon and started to play with the screw that held together the three bells that I was to ring during the consecration. The screw came off the top and the three bells clattered one by one down the high, red-carpeted steps of the pre-Vatican II altar, tolling out my impious carelessness for all to hear.

But I became adept, and I felt like an initiate. I often heard my oldest relatives whisper to each other: 'Wouldn't he make a lovely priest?' I was already a little of the way across the divide between the profane and sacred worlds. While the civilians entered the church through the huge public doors, I went round the back, up the steps to the special entrance that led to the sacristy. Like those who work backstage at the theatre, I knew the mechanics behind the magic. I lit the candles on the altar before the punters gathered for Mass. I knew how to load the thurible with charcoal in the bottom part and incense in the top, so that clouds of mystical, heavy-scented smoke would drift over the altar, catching the light that flooded in from the big cruciform windows on even the dullest days.

I knew the sweet smell from the mundane bottles of altar wine, like sherry brought out for ancient aunties at Christmas. And I saw the priests arrive for seven o'clock Mass, having tumbled out of bed, their hair askew, their eyes heavy with sleep, and throw on the sacred vestments, transforming themselves from flawed mortals to messengers of the divine. Perhaps, in retrospect, this familiarity ought to have made the priesthood seem less glamorous. Instead, it made it seem like the kind of job that you could imagine yourself doing. And it seemed, in the Ireland of the mid-1960s, a pretty decent job, too. Not all of my attraction to the idea of the priesthood was mercenary. But a lot of it was.

While we slept five-to-a-room, priests had nice, spacious houses. The parish priest's was by far the grandest on the estate.

Even better, groups of curates lived together in what seemed to a ten-year-old boy the perfect circle of male pals. Priests had housekeepers to look after them – like having a mammy who was not the boss of you. They had cars – very rare in Crumlin. And they had prestige – people looked up to them and they could wander into any house at will for a cup of tea or a plate of rashers and eggs.

The non-mercenary part of the attraction of being, as an altar boy, a kind of mini-priest, was not exactly religious, but it was to do with ritual – the sonorous secret language of call-and-response Latin formulae; the candles and incense; the luscious whiff of the altar wine; the dazzling white of the sacred host, transformed from sticky unleavened bread into the Body and Blood of Our Lord Jesus Christ. There were also crumbs from the table of power. I got to officiate at weddings, to be vicariously a part of other people's happiness. Even amid the adult grief of funerals, holding the holy water for the priest to sprinkle over the coffin made me feel serious and important – rare feelings for a child in those days.

This sense of importance was not confined within the church. Its writ ran in school, too. One morning, our teacher was absent and we were messing and talking loudly in the classroom. The head Brother burst in, dark-browed and furious and roared at us. As we sat terrified, he asked: 'Do any of any of ye even know what saint's day it is today?' While the others cowered, I put up my hand: 'Saints Zachary and Elizabeth, father and mother of John the Baptist.' 'Stand up', he said, and as he came towards me I thought for a moment that I had said something wrong and he was going to hit me. He put out his hand and shook mine, as though I were not a boy but a friend. 'Now this is a true Christian. The rest of ye are pig-ignorant heathens.'

Because I was an altar boy, I was also prefect of the Sodality, which we all had to attend after school on the first Friday of every month for prayers and a sermon. I sat at the edge of the long pew and marked off each boy as he went past me in a little ledger I was given. On Monday, any boy who had not been marked present would be questioned roughly in front of the class. Once, there was a boy called Fagan who was not ticked off on my list. He was told off. But far worse, in the schoolyard at break, we invented a spontaneous chant. We surrounded him and bellowed it over and over:

Fagan the pagan
You'll never get to Heaven.

I could see his distress and I knew I had colluded in causing it. But I felt a tug of power, the pleasure of cruelty made even more heady by the odour of sanctity that permeated it.

Once a year, in June, that sanctity was paraded through the streets of the estate. The Corpus Christi procession was by far the biggest annual event in the parish. The Blessed Sacrament was taken from the tabernacle, placed in the gold monstrance with the transparent ring in the middle of a sunburst of projecting spikes. It was held under a white silk canopy embroidered with gold thread and carried through the streets. The priests had pride of place, but this was also a display of state authority, an emphatic statement that ours was a Catholic country. The policemen from Crumlin Garda station formed a guard of honour as the monstrance was carried out of the church and then walked along either side of the procession, not so much to keep order as to show their own devotion.

Even better, a platoon of soldiers from the nearest barracks, led by a captain in dress uniform with gorgeous leather boots and a sword that caught the sun, followed behind the canopy. Behind them, more prosaically, came the Legion of Mary, the Catholic Boy Scouts, the Children of Mary, the Irish Red Cross and the men's and women's sodalities. Thousands of people lined the streets, kneeling as the Blessed Sacrament passed, then turning to follow it towards the green on Bangor Road for the open-air benediction.

But in front of all of them, leading the priests and the soldiers, leading God himself, was me. My brother and I, in our altar boys' black soutanes and white surplices, were chosen one year to walk at the head of the procession, scattering rose petals from big wicker baskets, so that the priest carrying the monstrance would walk over them. It was a flood of sensations: the sun melting the tar on the road, the familiar streets transformed by the reverent crowds, the murmur of prayers, the bunting in the papal colours of yellow and white flying from the houses, the velvety feel of the rose petals like puppies' ears, the scent like when my mother was dressed up, above all the thrill of being seen at the head of it all.

I did not think there could be another such moment, until the parish priest died. Father Joseph O'Connor was a stocky, grumpy, thick-browed Corkman. He seemed ancient, though he was only seventy. He was cantankerous: he threw a girl I knew out of Confession because she had come from another diocese and they said the Act of Contrition slightly differently there. We stayed out of his way as much as we could. We were not sorry he died. But John Charles McQuaid was – O'Connor was an old friend of his. The news that he was coming to celebrate the Requiem Mass was, to us, exactly like hearing that a king is to visit his remote subjects.

I was called out of school early on the Thursday to go to the church for rehearsals. I had done lots of funerals before, but the solemn requiem Latin Mass was rare and special. It could not have occurred to me at the time, but one reason why McQuaid, who was now seventy-two, may have been glad to come to Crumlin to celebrate it is that it was a rite undisturbed by all the changes that had been roiling the church since the reforming Second Vatican Council of 1962. McQuaid had arrived back from a session of the Council in 1965 and announced to the faithful: 'Allow me to reassure you. No change will worry the tranquillity of your Christian lives...'[1]

Among those changes were a shift in the language of the liturgy away from Latin and towards the local vernacular, and a reversal of the physical relationship of the priest to the congregation, moving the altar forward and having the Mass conducted from behind it, so that the celebrant was facing the people. Neither of these attempts to make the ritual less mysterious had been implemented at Saint Bernadette's under O'Connor, which may have been one of the reasons McQuaid liked him. The solemn Requiem Mass, moreover, was more of everything – more traditional, more Latinate, more theatrical, more defiantly insistent on the power of the priest and the passive observance of the people. Perhaps for

McQuaid, this funeral was also a kind of exorcism, a momentary banishing of the evil spirits of liberalism that has possessed the body of Mother Church.

Saint Bernadette's, when I arrived for rehearsals, was like the backstage of an opera house. Beautiful black vestments, with a sheen like the carapace of a beetle, had appeared and the young priests were trying them on. Four huge candelabras had been fetched from somewhere and placed along the back of the altar, and the sacristan was painstakingly placing a tall white wax candle in each slot. Up in the loft a choir (not our own local singers) was practising the 'Dies irae':

Dies irae, dies illa
Solvet saeclum in favilla

The day of wrath, that day will dissolve the world in ashes.

The next day, the day of wrath, the world did not dissolve into ashes. It lit up into drama and excitement and an odd kind of glamour that I would not then have known to call high camp. I remember lighting those stepped rows of tall white candles on the altar with a taper attached to a brass fitting on the end of a long wooden shaft, touching them one by one into life until forty-eight of them danced gently in the incense-heavy air, occasionally sending a little puff of smoke like a soul ascending. I remember the white gloves we were given to wear especially for the occasion. I remember the solemn ranks of clergy on the altar to concelebrate the Mass and the guard of honour provided by the army.

I remember above all John Charles's regal bearing, his unforced assumption that he was in control of all he surveyed. Being in his presence was like being a page at the palace of a great potentate, suddenly called into the presence of power. I had never seen before, and have never seen since, a man so utterly in command. He seemed to glide across the altar, so much so that I managed to forget during the Mass those dainty feet and polished shoes.

When the Mass was over, we went back into our room in the sacristy. We were glowing and buzzing like actors after a triumphant performance. Then we fell silent as John Charles came in. He had changed out of his black vestments and was wearing instead a red-trimmed black cassock with a scarlet pellegrina over his shoulders and breast. He was a small man, and his ears stuck out under his biretta, but his monarchical presence was undiminished. He raised his right arm gently to the height of his own waist, palm down, so that I could see the amethyst in the Borgia ring presented to him on his elevation to the episcopacy by the Irish medical profession and said to have been worn by medieval popes.[2]

I genuflected as we had been taught to do, my right knee on the floor, the left heel tilted slightly forward, and brushed the precious stone with my lips. When I stood up again, he put his hand on my cheek. His touch felt soft, like a girl's. His eyes were deep and dark and they were lit with flickers of interest and curiosity. His smile made the worry lines under them crinkle and seemed to indicate something much more than graciousness – a familial intimacy. As he patted my hair, I felt thoroughly known, not just because the most important man in the public world was asking me my name and how good I was at school, but because he seemed somehow not to have to ask.

I felt, at that moment, the intense pleasure of certainty. It was the assurance of an external form that stretched in space from Crumlin to Rome and in time from now to eternity. The Requiem Mass had been solemn but it did not make me feel sad – on the contrary, there was an exhilaration in being up there just in front of the altar, centre stage in a drama that always had, and always would, play its way out word for word, gesture for gesture, in saecula saeculorum. I had touched the infinite.

I felt encompassed. I never felt this before or since.

But there was also a more intimate kind of certainty now in the sacristy with McQuaid's sprightly eyes on my face and his hand on my cheek. It felt as though he knew everything about me and that this was a wonderful thing because what he could see when he looked into my soul was goodness. I was a good boy and now the man who, for me, embodied God on earth, was letting me know that a perpetual light was shining on this truth. I need have no anxiety about falling way from this state of grace – McQuaid's brown eyes had fixed it forever in their warm and intense gaze.

Perhaps for him, too, these were moments out of time and history, of freedom from the anxieties of his vigilance against the constant threats of pollution and degradation that he had to ward off. I was innocent and pure and if he could see that in me, he could also see in me an image of an Irish future that was not debased by modernity. Perhaps that was why he lingered so long in our room. I could see through the open door the priests waiting for him, but he stayed with us altar boys, touching our cheeks, patting our hair, asking us about school and our families.

If this was the illusion he was indulging as he allowed himself this luxury of staying with us, he knew very well that it was a trick of the mind, a lie he himself was living. He knew, for example, that the chaplain of Our Lady's Children's Hospital in Crumlin, a short walk from Saint Bernadette's, Father Paul McGennis, was a paedophile who assaulted patients aged between eight and eleven. Almost eight years earlier, in August 1960, McQuaid was informed that a security officer at a photographic film developer in England had referred colour film to Scotland Yard. Scotland Yard had passed it on to the Commissioner of the Garda Síochána (the Irish police force, generally known for short as the Garda) in Dublin.

In a manifestation of McQuaid's power, the police in Ireland did not launch a criminal investigation. Instead, the Garda Commissioner Daniel Costigan asked for a private meeting with McQuaid at which, according to the Archbishop's own note, he informed him that the photographic company had 'handed to Scotland Yard a colour film with label Rev. McGennis, Children's Hospital, Crumlin, Dublin, of which 26 transparencies were of the private parts of two small girls, aged 10 or 11 years'.[3]

The Commissioner asked McQuaid 'to take over the case'. Though it is not recorded, he presumably gave him the roll of film. McQuaid did record his interview with McGennis the next day and his own response to it: 'The children were playing about, lifting their clothes. He rebuked them. Seeing this was a chance of discovering what the genitals were like, he pretended there was no film in the camera he was carrying and photographed them in sexual postures, alone and seated together, chiefly in a way or posture that opened up the parts. He declared that he had done so, as one would take an art photo, seeing no grave sin at all and suffering no physical disturbance in himself. He was puzzled, though he had seen line drawings, as to structure and functions of female. [sic] In questioning, I discovered that he had been reared with brothers, had never moved about socially with girls and tended to avoid them as in the hospital with the nurses. I suggested I would get [a doctor] a good Catholic to instruct him and thus end his wonderment.'

McGennis continued to abuse children until he was finally convicted in 1997. McQuaid made no effort to find the children or to warn the hospital. In February 1968, a month after I served Mass for him, he appointed Father Ivan Payne as chaplain to the Children's Hospital in Crumlin. Over the next six years, Payne abused at least sixteen children there, almost all of them boys.[4]

Saint Bernadette's was one of two Catholic parishes that covered the Crumlin estate. The other was Saint Agnes's. Around the same time that McQuaid was saying the Requiem Mass in Saint Bernadette's, he appointed a new curate to Saint Agnes's. He already knew that Father James McNamee was a child abuser. The priest had been active in one of Dublin's best schoolboy soccer clubs, Stella Maris. He had been seen swimming naked with boys and this had given rise to complaints to the Archbishop. McQuaid told McNamee 'to forget about it' and noted his conviction 'that the man was quite without blame'.[5] In 1968 he sent him to Crumlin, where he later became parish priest.

In the 1970s, the kids in Crumlin called McNamee 'Father Smack My Gee' – gee being Dublin slang for vulva, though it was also 'noted that he had a total aversion and hostility towards all women'. Everybody knew that he would turn up at breaktime in Saint Agnes's primary school on Armagh Road to hold little boys by the hand and ask them to come for a spin in his car, a green Lancia Delta. In 1969, he built a swimming pool in the back garden of his house. He made it clear that only little boys were allowed to come in and use the pool.

What is so striking about all of this is how open it was. A private swimming pool was unheard of in Crumlin – the very fact that McNamee had one was sensational, all the more so when he added a second pool indoors. Some children did revolt, calling him names and even throwing stones at his car. Yet he was promoted to parish priest and carried on in Crumlin for ten years, until a private complaint from a mother to a nun prompted the archdiocese to send in a senior priest to investigate. He reported back that 'a possibly explosive situation exists locally' and that there was a danger of 'a real scandal in Crumlin'.[6]

But was there really? For there to be a real scandal, there would have to be open revelation. This would require four huge things to happen. A child would have to tell a parent – what language would any child have to speak of this? The parent would have to make a formal complaint to the police – what parent would call down such shame on the family? The Gardaí would have to actually investigate the crime – was it not better to inform the Archbishop and let him 'take over the case'? The state would have to launch a prosecution – and the state believed, as the church did, that such a thing would cause too much distress to the population at large. Meeting even one of these tests was unlikely; passing all four close to impossible.

It all depended on who could say what they saw, who could give meaning to experience. And McQuaid had created in Dublin a world in which he and the church held a near monopoly on those capacities. The authority that so enthralled me that day in 1968 was not just his personal charisma. It had been implanted in the minds of the faithful, subsumed fully into their own consciousness. In the 1970s, McQuaid's successor, Dermot Ryan, would note privately of his dealings with the parents of children as young as six who had been raped by a priest: 'In several cases, they were quite apologetic about having to discuss the matter and were as much concerned for the priest's welfare as for their child and other children.'[7]

This was the church's great achievement in Ireland. It had so successfully disabled a society's capacity to think for itself about right and wrong that it was the parents of an abused child, not the bishop who enabled that abuse, who were 'quite apologetic'. It had managed to create a flock who, in the face of an outrageous violation of trust, would be concerned as much about the abuser as about those he had abused and might abuse in the future. It had inserted its system of control and power so deeply into the minds of the faithful that they could scarcely even feel angry about the perpetration of disgusting crimes on their own children.

McNamee's career in Crumlin was a window into the single most important aspect of Irish culture in these decades: the unknown known. Ours was a society that had developed an extraordinary capacity for cognitive disjunction, a genius for knowing and not knowing at the same time. McNamee understood it perfectly. His grooming of boys in the schoolyard, his cruising for victims in his green Lancia, his openly proclaimed rules for entry to his swimming pool, were all common knowledge. But it was knowledge of a very specific kind. He knew that awareness is not acceptance, that seeing is not believing, that the obvious can remain obscure.

But the unknown known operated at many different levels, and it could also be turned the other way, against the church. An area in which it functioned was one that would certainly have been on McQuaid's mind in early 1968. At the time of the Requiem Mass, he, like most of the world's Catholics, was awaiting a momentous ruling from Pope Paul VI. There had been widespread speculation, amounting among liberal Catholics to an expectation, that the pope would announce the end of the church's ban on 'artificial' contraception. This was, in Ireland, a matter for the state as well: the importation and advertising of contraceptives were banned by law. For McQuaid, the hope was that these expectations would founder, that the liberals would be vanquished and a line drawn under the period of disturbance and change. To his delight, the papal encyclical *Humanae Vitae*, published in July 1968, reinforced the most hardline version of the doctrine.

One senior Irish theologian, Revd James Good, described the encyclical as a 'major tragedy'. He was immediately suspended from his priestly functions – a disgrace that had not been visited on any clerical child abusers.[8] Open clerical dissent was crushed. The message was implacable and clear: no condoms, no Pill.

But many Irish Catholic women had already found a special way of not knowing and not sinning: the cycle regulator. From 1963 onwards, the Pill was imported into Ireland to keep menstrual anarchy at bay. Particularly in the middle-class, urban milieu, a woman could learn from her friends that a certain doctor was sympathetic and would prescribe the Pill, not of course as a contraceptive, but for menstrual problems. It turned out that Irish women were unique in the world in their inability to put some discipline on their periods without chemical help. The leading obstetrician Professor John Bonner noted that 'Ireland would [appear to] have the highest incidence of irregular cycles in women in the history of the human race'.[9]

In 1968, the journalist Alan Bestic reported on an interview he conducted in Dublin: 'Dr Raymond Cross, a well-known and brilliant Dublin gynaecologist, stated with a hint of satire, I suspect: "If a woman has heavy or irregular periods, or painful periods, or sometimes none, or if she has pre-menstrual tension or endometriosis, bleeding between periods, excessive hairiness or pimples (caused by an excess of androgenic hormones) or is excessively fat or is approaching the change of life, her doctor is morally justified in prescribing any treatment he likes." His colleagues pointed out that his list was sufficiently comprehensive to cover half the women in the world.'[10]

More to the point, of course, it covered half the good Catholic women in Ireland. It was a manoeuvre in the tradition that might be called Connie dodging. Connie was McQuaid's friend and ally, the Bishop of Cork, Cornelius Lucey. He insisted on the very strict regime of Lenten fasting in his diocese: the faithful could eat one meal and two 'collations' each day during the forty days before Easter. A collation was something like a biscuit taken with a cup of tea. Moyra Riordan, who ran the Greendoor coffee shop on Patrick Street in Cork, invented a huge biscuit, and most of the other bakers in the city copied it. The biscuits were known as Connie Dodgers. The law of God was not defied. It was dodged. And so it was with the Pill. By 1968, it was reckoned that five Irish women in every hundred were using the Pill compared with ten in Britain. Immediately after *Humanae Vitae*, 'sales went down all over Ireland by twenty-five per cent. Then gradually, as the debate died, they began to rise again…'[11]

This involved lying on a heroic scale. The journalist John Healy later confessed that 'There isn't a manjack of us in my generation who'd admit to favouring contraception when the matter became one of public morality – but it didn't stop us from laying our hands on them all the same.'[12] In Anne Enright's novel, *The Gathering*, the narrator recalls having Durex: 'Apart from anything else they were illegal. Everyone had them. Whether we needed them or not.'[13]

Everybody knew that some women were using the Pill as a contraceptive. On 9 April 1970, for example, the legal affairs correspondent of the *Irish Times* wrote that 'the pill is not described as a contraceptive in presentation by manufacturers for import to Ireland. It is imported under the title of "Cycle regulator". It is supposedly being used for "medical purposes" other than contraception. But it can safely be said that the vast majority of women using the pill do so for contraception and that this is their doctor's intention.'

And this wasn't just the lying Jezebels of the prosperous south Dublin suburbs. The practice of this deceit was a national sport, rivalling camogie as the distinctively Irish game for women. In a letter to the *Irish Times* of 2 March 1972 the Westmeath and Longford county obstetrician Michael Twomey wrote that he and his colleagues were prescribing the Pill as a cycle regulator 'in large quantities', knowing full well that this was a lie: 'We are not allowed to be honest and give it its correct description.' In 1973, 38,000 women were being prescribed 'cycle regulators' every month. By 1978, this had risen to 48,000.

But just because everybody knew the lie for what it was, this did not mean that the sham did not have to be maintained. An importer who described the contraceptive pill as a contraceptive pill would have the cargo seized by customs.

A doctor who prescribed it as a contraceptive was breaking the law. And many pharmacists policed the fiction. At the congress in October 1976 of the Irish Pharmaceutical Union, Noel McManus, a Dublin pharmacist, explained that he was completely opposed to artificial contraceptives but sold the Pill because 'You never know if it is being prescribed therapeutically as a cycle regulator or for contraceptive purposes. In cases where I thought it was [the latter]

I have come out from behind the counter and said "if this is for that purpose I will not give it to you".'[14]

Behind the absurd comedy, there were consequences for women. The high-dose oestrogen Pill was not suitable for some women but they used it because it was the only form of contraception they could get. At the Irish Medical Association conference in 1978, Dr Mary Henry warned: 'because of this hypocrisy, women had suffered: too many unsuitable women were put on the pill in the past and were still on it today and Dr Henry saw them when they developed clots in the deep veins of their legs as a result.'[15] The tacit arrangement also left women dependent on the goodwill of doctors, most of whom were male and Catholic. Control of their own fertility was a favour to be bestowed on women, not a right to be asserted. It was an intimate lie that required an authority figure to suspend disbelief. Women had no power , except that of playing up to the sexist stereotype of feminine duplicity.

The Catholic Church itself was silently complicit with this duplicity – Catholic schools and hospitals would have ceased to function if teachers and nurses were not having awful trouble with their periods. It was only in the week after I was born that the government announced that it was lifting a ban on married women serving as teachers. But when *Humanae Vitae* was published in 1968, the country was also beginning its belated but radical expansion of secondary education. The new convent schools could not be staffed entirely by nuns – more and more young lay women would have to be recruited. Most of them were, or would be, married and if they obeyed church teaching and had a baby every year, the system would soon collapse. The cycle regulator saved the day.

This was a way of functioning – through silence, evasion, creative ambiguity – that could be normal only in a society in which power seems permanent while ordinary life is changing. If it appears that the structures of authority are so deeply rooted that they will not alter even as the society is being transformed, the vast majority of people will not confront that authority directly. They will navigate their way around it, tacking and jibing to avoid the reefs of public antagonism and shame.

Irish people in this era – and perhaps in the long colonial period before it – were masters of ingenious hypocrisy. John McGahern was asked by a friend and neighbour in rural Co. Leitrim why he didn't go to Mass. He said he'd like to but he'd feel a hypocrite because he did not believe. 'But sure none of us believe.' 'Why do *you* go then?' 'We go for the old performance. To see the girls, to see the whole show... We go to see all the other hypocrites!'[16]

Hypocrisy was the tribute realism paid to piety. It was not a threat to church and state but a homage to their stability and durability. But it had one rule: the duplicity, the slipperiness, the dodging, were supposed to be for the laity. There had to be a fixed point to weave around, a node of assurance in all this endless equivocation. If the people were to keep making the considerable mental effort to deal with great changes in their lives without challenging the moral monopoly of the church, the church for its part must be its predictable, straightforward self. To know how they themselves should dance, the people had to know where the church stood. This was the seed of destruction that was already present in 1968: the church was not the counterweight to our hypocrisy. It was the greatest hypocrite of all.

None of this was evident then, but two strange things happened in Saint Bernadette's that year. One miserable weekday morning that winter, I was serving eight o'clock Mass for Father Seery, a tall, rather grand man with an intellectual mien. The church was empty except for the regular gathering of daily communicants, mostly older women, who sat in the front rows. Seery, about to start his sermon, looked down on them and then bellowed: 'To Hell with God!' He paused for a moment, then gathered himself again: 'To Hell with the Pope!' I was sitting at the side of the altar, facing out into the congregation so I could see the women jump in fright at Seery's first shout and freeze in horror at the second. The world was coming to an end. The nice, somewhat posh, priest had revealed himself as the Antichrist.

I looked across at Father Seery. His tall, slightly stooped form and thin, bony face had their usual ascetic, almost unworldly, demeanour. He seemed calm and in control. He paused again to register the shock and savour the unusually full attention of his normally torpid early morning congregation. And then he breathed, in a soft, melancholy tone: 'That, my dear people, is what is being heard increasingly in the faithless world beyond our shores.' His face remained completely straight and I was not close enough to see whether a little smile of mischief was playing around his lips.

I don't know what this did to the old women, but I was electrified. It was the funniest thing I had ever seen, though so utterly surprising that I only started laughing half an hour later as I was walking to school. I kept repeating it to myself in that plummy voice: 'To Hell with Gaawd!' But over the coming days I tried to disentangle the ways it made me feel. On the one hand, I was in awe of Seery. He had, in his paradoxical way, demonstrated the majesty of the church – only a priest could get away with what he had done. On the other hand, he had spoken those words and they were out there, still quivering in my mind as they had vibrated on the air inside Saint Bernadette's.

Later that year, one of the priests dropped into the old concrete shed where my parents had been married. It was now serving as a youth club and there was a dance for teenagers in progress. It was a slow set and the lights had been dimmed. The priest turned up the lights, broke up the dance and sent everyone home. This was a familiar episode – priests breaking up dances and hunting courting couples out of ditches with blackthorn sticks were standard characters in the soap opera of Irish sexuality.

But the next Sunday, an astounding thing happened. Two groups of teenage boys and girls arrived early for eleven o'clock Mass – a remarkable occurrence in itself but a mere prelude to the drama. They occupied the front two rows of pews, right in front of the altar. They behaved impeccably through the first part of the liturgy, until the priest climbed up into the pulpit to begin his sermon. Then they stood up as one and turned their backs on him. They filed out into the central aisle and walked slowly down towards the vestibule and out of the church. The silence in which they moved was not the old taciturnity of strategic evasion. It was a hush in which you could hear the sound of thunder approaching from a distance.

12

1969: Frozen Violence

I owe my existence to a pair of British army gloves. My mother was engaged to be married to a man called Francis Foley, but she was having her doubts because she thought he would always be dominated by his mother. She went dancing one night in the Metropole Ballroom on O'Connell Street. She and her friends watched the young men coming in. They had a rule of thumb: look at the gloves. Almost every fella had one good suit, made by a local tailor. All the suits were pretty much alike. But if a fella had woollen gloves, it meant he was almost certainly unemployed. If he had good leather gloves, he had a job and was worth a dance.

I actually remember the gloves because my father still had them when I was a kid. The soft, worn brown leather was beautiful to touch. But they were also unusual. The palm was a lighter coloured mesh, almost whitish, made for gripping. My father got them from his big brother Kevin, who was eight years older. Kevin got them from the British army. The story was that he had worn them at the battle of El Alamein in 1942, the first significant military defeat the Nazis suffered in the West in the Second World War.

In July 1969, my father took my brother and myself to England for ten days. We sailed over on the boat from Dublin to Liverpool, then took a bus through the English Midlands, a foreign landscape of motorways and service stations and giant power plants, to London. My father's first cousin Vincent met us at the terminus and we took another bus across to the East End, where we'd be staying with my mother's sister Brigid. Brigid was a nun, so we were actually going to be staying in a Catholic convent. Between the heat and the prospect of three days behind convent walls, my dad decided he could do with a pint. So my brother and myself were left sitting on a low wall with bottles of Fanta, while Vincent and my father disappeared into the pub.

I remember sitting on that wall and sucking on the straw to try to suppress a rising panic. We were alone in England, abandoned in an alien place. England, as an idea, terrified me. I knew from history lessons in school that the English only ever did bad things to Irish people. And I knew that the heart of that badness was Protestant. There was one true faith, which was, of course, Catholic, so England by its very nature was deviant. You wouldn't know what to expect of such people – except that it would not be nice. My older brother was playing it cool. I was sweating with heat and inherited anxiety.

Then, along the road, came an enormous man in flowing white robes, his height accentuated by a tall leopard-skin hat. He had an entourage of five or six men, also dressed in white but far less flamboyant. He was surely some kind of dignitary, a minor king perhaps or a tribal chief. I couldn't help staring at him. He held my gaze and his face lit up with a huge smile. He patted me on the head in a gesture of blessing and benevolence and said something to his sidekicks in a language I did not recognize. He looked down at me and asked, 'Are you enjoying your pop?' Pop wasn't a word we used in Ireland for sugary drinks, but I knew what it meant. I knew from the English comics we devoured, the *Beano* and the *Dandy*, that it was something English kids said. And it struck me that he thought my brother and myself were natives, that we were English. I was quite indignant. I wanted to explain to him that he had it all wrong, that we were visitors at least as foreign as himself. But I was too awestruck to say anything and in any case he was sailing majestically onwards down the street, trailed by the brilliant white wake of his entourage.

After that, it was quite a relief to be in Brigid's convent, Saint Margaret's in Canning Town. A lot of the nuns were Irish. They doted on us, feeding us heaped plates of rashers and sausages and eggs. And they asked us as a special favour if we would serve Mass in the chapel on Sunday morning. We graciously agreed to come out of retirement for a command performance. The chapel was small and intimate but richly ornate with pillars of brown and white marble and with enough capacity for the nuns and some local worshippers. Kieran and I were star attractions – genuine Irish altar boys. We moved daintily, gave the responses clearly and confidently and radiated piety. After Mass, the nuns flocked around us like stage-door Johnnies. I took the adulation as our due: it was natural that we should be more radiantly holy than any English kid they might be used to. Were there even such things as proper English Catholics?

We luxuriated in the safety and comfort of the convent, a protected space in this outlandish environment, so much that we were quite disturbed when my father came up with a suggestion. Brian Jones had died and The Rolling Stones were playing a free concert in Hyde Park in his memory. Would we like to go? It would have been the coolest thing to be able to say when I went back to school the following month: I was there. Kieran and I discussed it, but there wasn't really much to discuss. Of course we didn't want to go. The place, we said, would be full of weirdos and hippies and drug addicts. We stayed with the nuns that day. I remember sitting in the parlour, while one of them put on her favourite record, Jim Reeves's 'Forty Shades Of Green'. While Mick Jagger was snaking his hips and performing an eighteen-minute-long version of 'Sympathy For The Devil', I was quite happy in the bosom of the Lord.

We left London and went to stay for a few days in Maidstone in Kent with Kevin, his wife May and our cousins. Kevin was a court clerk. He voted Conservative. He beckoned me and my brother into his bedroom and slid a heavy metal box out from under the bed. He unlocked it and took out a sub-machine gun. He had somehow managed to keep it from his days as a quartermaster sergeant. He would use it, he told us proudly, to fight the communists if they invaded England. It was the most exciting object I had ever seen. It belonged to the world of comics and war films, but it was real. It did not strike me as especially mad that he kept it under his bed, though that night as I was going to sleep I could hear raised voices from downstairs as Kevin and my dad, who was a thoroughgoing socialist, argued politics.

Next day, my father's other older brother, Paddy, arrived from Dublin to join us. I picked up that this was some kind of reconciliation, that the three brothers had not been together for a very long time and that my father had planned this trip to make something right. Paddy and Kevin looked very alike, with the same square bodies, round faces and curly heads gone bald. But their personalities were opposites. Kevin was straight, respectable, conformist, settled. Paddy, six years younger, was a sailor, a rogue, a dodger, a drinker, a joker. His eyes blazed with mischief.

I learned the story of their epic falling-out. Kevin had fought his way through the war in North Africa and Italy and ended up in bombed-out Berlin in 1945. He was trusted by the top brass and set to work getting the railway system running again. Paddy joined up towards the end of the war. By that stage, not only was Kevin in the army, but my father's big sister Rita had joined the Women's Royal Air Force, so even though Ireland was neutral, my father had three siblings at war. Paddy saw little, if any, fighting but by 1946, he too was stationed in the British zone in Berlin.

Then he went missing. Kevin started to look for him and discovered that, not only was he absent without leave, but he was living with a German woman and they were selling cigarettes and other goods from British army stores. Wartime regulations were still in force – both going AWOL and working the black market were technically capital offences. Kevin came to a decision: if he could capture his brother and bring him into barracks before he was arrested, he could claim that Paddy had surrendered voluntarily and plead for leniency. He spent nights tracking him through the ruined city and eventually caught him coming out of a shebeen. He knocked him down, tied him up and threw him into the back of a jeep. Paddy fucked and blinded and cursed his brother for betraying him. But the plan worked: Paddy was imprisoned under military custody but when most of the army was being demobbed, he was given a dishonourable discharge and sent home to Dublin.

I loved this story. It was like something out of a film. Together with Kevin's sub-machine gun, it opened up a different history – not the endless, dreary tale of Ireland's oppression and martyrdom, but one that was both vast and intimate. It was European, English, German. But it was also familial. There was a moment in those days in Maidstone when I was walking behind the three brothers and I realized that they looked identical from the back. I couldn't tell which was which. I wished my father had been there in Berlin, too. Later, it struck me that if he had been older or the war had gone on longer, he would indeed have joined the British army and I would eventually come to understand why.

When I got back to Dublin, I immediately started borrowing books about the Second World War from the library: D-Day, Hitler, Stalingrad. It felt like one of those scenes in the Westerns where the wagon train finally makes it to the top of the Rockies and the people look down on the limitless terrain spread out ahead of them. And it was just as exhilarating. I was not in 1916 anymore. This astonishing upheaval lay between me and the Irish past as it was packaged for us in school: 800 years of oppression, keeping the faith through the trials of religious persecution, heroic risings that always ended in failure, the winning of our freedom – except, of course, for the unfinished business of the Fourth Green Field. Wallowing in this sense of release from Irish history, I was barely aware that that unfinished business was becoming, again, insistent.

The night we got back from England, a sixty-seven-year-old man, Francis McCloskey, was found lying on the roadside in Dungiven. He had been struck by a police baton. He died next day. Two days after that, Samuel Devenney died in hospital in Derry city. On 19 April, eight policemen from the Royal Ulster Constabulary who were pursuing fleeing rioters smashed their way into a small house on William Street in the Catholic Bogside area. Four of them surrounded Devenney, a forty-two-year-old taxi driver, and kicked him and battered him with their batons. His daughter Anne, who was eighteen, threw herself across his body but the policemen grabbed her by her dress and threw her off so they could keep beating him. When she again lay across him, they grabbed her by the hair and pushed her against the fireplace. He suffered severe internal injuries and died of a heart attack on 17 July. Half an hour before the police burst in, he had been watching an opera on television.[1] The inquest later returned a verdict of death by natural causes.[2]

McCloskey and Devenney were the first two fatalities of what was not yet called the Troubles – a euphemism that still applied to the revolutionary period between 1916 and 1924. Before Devenney's funeral, his widow Phyllis, mother of their nine children, pleaded for an end to violence: 'Sammy was a peaceful man. All his life he hated violence and would have been appalled at the thought of any violence now committed in his name.'[3] Even at this point, her wish did not seem like a fantasy.

The eruption of Northern Ireland was both sudden and slow. On the one hand, very few people expected it. By 1965, when Lemass and Whitaker crossed the Border to meet with Northern Ireland's prime minister Terence O'Neill, the future seemed to lie in a gradual rapprochement between the two parts of Ireland and moves towards practical co-operation in areas like energy and tourism. This was part of what modernity would mean, the arrival of a new set of values in which old animosities would matter much less than practicality and prosperity. After the collapse of the Border campaign, and its formal end in February 1962, the IRA's business of making martyrs seemed bankrupt. Even some hardline IRA families in Belfast had given up the ghost. One later IRA activist, Gerry Bradley, would recall that he did not even know that his father had been sentenced to ten years in prison for planting bombs in England in 1939: 'the IRA and republicans in general were discredited and shunned… In this atmosphere of defeat and depression, Bradley's mother had not tried to inculcate any republicanism in him or his brother. It seemed there was no future in it. It was over.'[4]

On the other hand, there was the slow burn of what twenty-one-year-old Bernadette Devlin, elected to the House of Commons in London for Mid-Ulster in April 1969, summarized in her maiden speech as 'fifty years of neglect, apathy and misunderstanding'. After the establishment of Northern Ireland in 1921, the British government had left its inbuilt Protestant and Unionist majority to its own devices: systematic discrimination against Catholics in employment and housing and the gerrymandering of local government electoral districts to ensure that, for example, the Catholic-majority city of Derry had a solidly Unionist majority on its council.

While we in Dublin were calling people Balubas, the revolt of Catholics and their allies among liberal Protestants and left-wingers was arguably the first white rebellion to be directly and explicitly inspired by a Black movement. The Northern Ireland Civil Rights Association, formed in 1967, was another example of the Americanization of Ireland. But the defining influence was not the America of capital and commodities and Westerns. It was the America of Rosa Parks and Martin Luther King. 'We plagiarised an entire movement', acknowledged the manager of the Derry museum, Adrian Kerr. 'We even went as far as stealing the song.'[5] The song was the civil rights anthem, 'We Shall Overcome', adopted almost immediately by NICRA.

One of the key turning points in the emergence of the struggle in Northern Ireland as an international story was consciously modelled on a similar moment in US history. In January 1969, a march for civil rights, from Belfast to Derry, was organized by the student-led People's Democracy group. When it came to Burntollet Bridge, the marchers were viciously attacked by a loyalist mob that included off-duty members of the notoriously sectarian auxiliary police force, the B-Specials. Some of the RUC members on duty tried to protect the marchers, but most stood by while they were assaulted with iron bars, bottles, and cudgels studded with nails. Burntollet Bridge was a knowing simulacrum of Edmund Pettus Bridge in Selma, Alabama. The main organizer of the march, Michael Farrell, wrote that 'The march was modelled on the Selma–Montgomery march in Alabama in 1966, which had exposed the racist thuggery of America's deep South and forced the US government into major reforms.'[6]

If the aim was to expose the thuggish sectarianism that was woven into the bland respectability of the Northern Ireland state, Burntollet was a horrifying success. But the analogy on which it was based was problematic. Northern Ireland was not the Deep South. Organized discrimination against Catholics was outrageous, humiliating and deeply corrupt. It locked in generational poverty and undermined the pretence of equal citizenship in the United Kingdom. But its scale and depth were nothing like the legacy of slavery and the Jim Crow laws. The self-conscious claim that Catholics 'viewed ourselves as Ulster's white negroes'[7] was an appropriation of the pain of others. While for most civil rights activists such an identification was meant to imply solidarity in an international struggle for justice, it could also fuse uncomfortably with the old Christian Brothers claim that 'In the martyrology of history, among crucified nations Ireland occupies the foremost place'.[8] Solidarity could shade into exceptionalism.

Nor was the strategy of revolt nearly as clear. If Selma and the rest of the civil rights struggle forced the US government into major reforms, the parallel ambition was to force the British government in London to pay attention to the conditions it had allowed to fester in Northern Ireland and enact an equally momentous series of reforms. The problem was that, while this was indeed the goal of NICRA, it was not the only agenda. Farrell suggested that the goal of his Irish Selma was also to reopen 'the whole Irish question for the first time in 50 years' – in other words, to revisit the partition of 1921 and move towards a United Ireland.

Which was the aim – to reform Northern Ireland or to wipe it off the map? The hesitation between these two purposes would prove to be fatal. Unionist reactionaries could claim, in self-justification, that the true purpose of the civil rights movement was not to end discrimination but to destroy the state and force them against their will into a Catholic-controlled thirty-two-county Ireland in which the boot of repression would merely be placed on the other foot. Nationalists could conclude that Northern Ireland was unreformable and that indeed there could be no justice without the demolition of the existing state. These were existential questions and such questions tend to be answered by violence.

In October 1968, the foremost Irish intellectual Conor Cruise O'Brien wrote that 'The conditions of Derry may be thought of as one of frozen violence: any attempt to thaw it out will liberate violence which is at present static.'[9] Even a year earlier the image of a thaw in Northern Ireland would have been a hopeful one.

The improvement in relations with the Republic of Ireland was matched by a rise in the number of 'mixed' marriages between Protestants and Catholics, itself in part a product of the flowering of a youth culture that transcended sectarianism. In the Catholic diocese of Down and Connor (which includes Belfast) the proportion grew during the late 1960s and early 1970s, reaching 25 per cent of marriages by 1971.[10] Something was indeed unfreezing.

O'Brien's experiences in the Congo had made him a political pessimist, but his image of 'frozen violence' was all too accurate. The violence, however, was two-sided. There was the violence of a Protestant sectarian bigotry that need little excuse to assert itself. And there was the side that O'Brien most feared – the long history of armed, conspiratorial, revolutionary nationalism. In organizational terms, it had withered into irrelevance. A meeting of the IRA leadership at a farmhouse in Co. Tipperary in August 1967 was given the grim news that the secret army had 217 active members, a bank balance of £770, and 'enough ammo for one good job'.[11] But what that leadership did not know then was that Northern Ireland was about to implode with extraordinary rapidity.

There is a photograph of a group of fifteen members of the Belfast branch of Fianna Éireann, a Boy Scout movement that was essentially the IRA's youth wing, on a camp in Drumshanbo, Co. Leitrim, in the summer of 1968. They are children. Some of them look younger than ten – but they wear uniforms of white shirts and dark ties topped with black berets. Watching over them are two adults. One is an older man called Brendan Kielty, who had volunteered in 1936 to go to Spain – not in the International Brigades formed to support the democratically elected government, but with an Irish Brigade formed by the would-be Irish fascist caudillo Eoin O'Duffy, to fight for Franco. The other is a nineteen-year-old wearing a uniform and beret. His name is Gerry Adams.[12] There is a past in this picture – but there is also a future.

13

1970: The Killer Chord

It was me that let the pigs out. There were about eight of them in a sty to the left of the farmhouse. It was the first day of the month I had to stay there to learn Irish from the native speakers. It was about halfway between the small village of Baile Mhúirne and the even smaller village of Cúil Aodha. The area was still Irish speaking because it was remote and the land was relatively poor. There was a bog-brown river, the Sullane, at the back of the house with quick-moving trout and slow, fierce pike in it. There were dark green hills, the Boggeraghs, to the north and the Shehies to the south, low against the horizon. The road in front of the house was narrow and rough, with small thickets and patches of scrub on either side.

Someone said one of the pigs had given birth and I went to look at the bonhams. The mother squealed and bared her teeth at me. I didn't know pigs could be so scary. I ran back to the house and lay on the bunk bed in the room where six of us, kids from different parts of the country slept. There was an angry shout from the bean an tí (woman of the house), Bean Uí Shúilleabháin, a big, warm, motherly woman who, as I would find, never shouted and was never angry.

Everybody rushed out to see what was going on. Half a dozen pigs were waddling happily up the road towards Baile Mhúirne. I remembered that I hadn't shut the gate to the sty when I fled, but I said nothing. I chased after the pigs, making sure not to catch them. Coming westwards along the road was a fine car, a Jaguar I think. It stopped in front of the pigs. A man got out. He had thinning, light-coloured combed-back hair and dark quizzical eyes. A thick moustache flourished under his nose. He was wearing a tweed suit, the bottom half of which was a pair of plus-fours. I had never seen the like anywhere but in an English comic book.

He took a walking stick from the car seat and began to wave it majestically at the pigs. His movements were calm, graceful, utterly assured. His stick was a conductor's baton, or a magician's wand. The pigs were spellbound. He waved them back toward the farmyard. They turned obediently and trotted homeward. He followed them unhurriedly until they were all in the sty. He closed the gate I had left open, raised his stick in greeting to the woman of the house, walked back to his car and drove off towards Cúil Aodha.

I was both awestruck and mystified by this man. I had recently read *The Odyssey* and as I was lying in bed that night, between waking and sleep, his image somehow blended with that of Circe the sorceress, the pigs with the creatures into which she turned Odysseus's men. But the moustache and the plus-fours also seemed faintly ridiculous, as if he had stuck one on his face as a disguise and was wearing the other for a laugh, as if he had been going to a fancy-dress party. I was desperate to ask the bean an tí about him. But that would raise the uncomfortable subject of how the pigs got out on the road in the first place. Curiosity struggled with guilt and guilt won. I avoided the subject but privately wondered if I would ever see the man again.

The next morning was a Sunday and we were all herded up to the little church in Cúil Aodha for Mass. It was grey, pebble-dashed, with no steeple, more like a hall than a chapel. Someone said the church was called Saint Gobnait's and I sniggered at this with a boy from my class in Crumlin. It was such a stupid redneck name. You just had to say it to know that there was something backward about these country people – gub, nit. We were marched up to a low balcony at the back of the church. I was literally looking down on the country people on their wooden benches, across at the plain painted walls, up at the unadorned wooden ceiling. White light came in through the rows of narrow, oblong windows on both sides.

There was a small organ and two or three rows of stalls, which

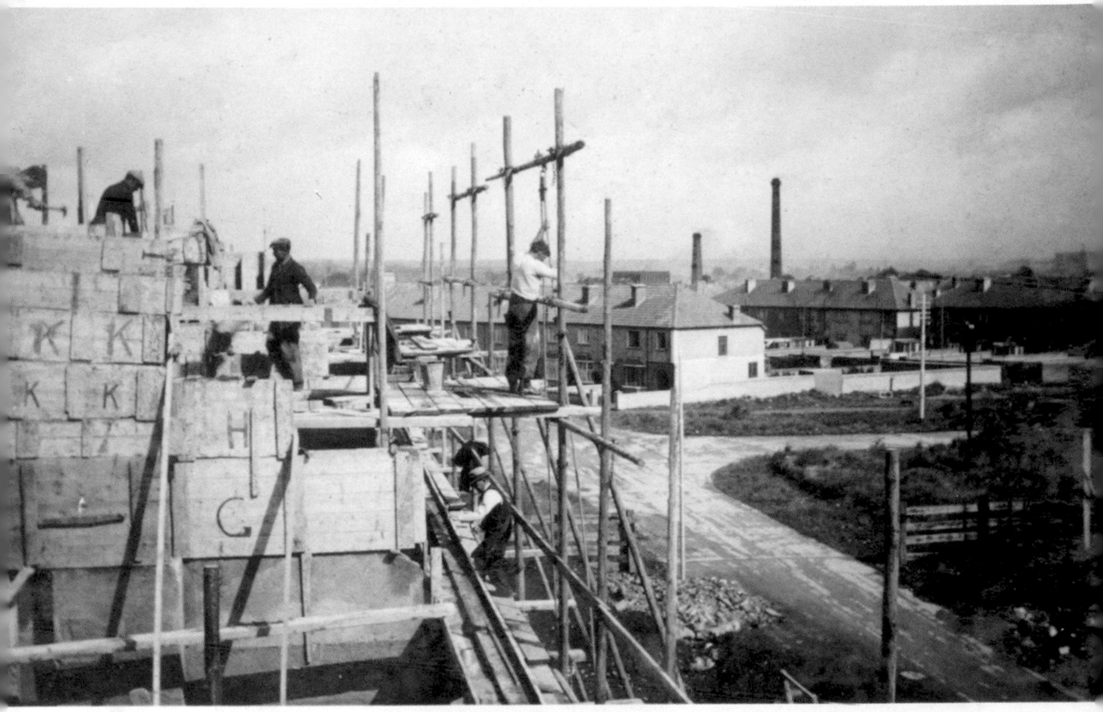

1. The housing estate of Crumlin under construction in 1936.

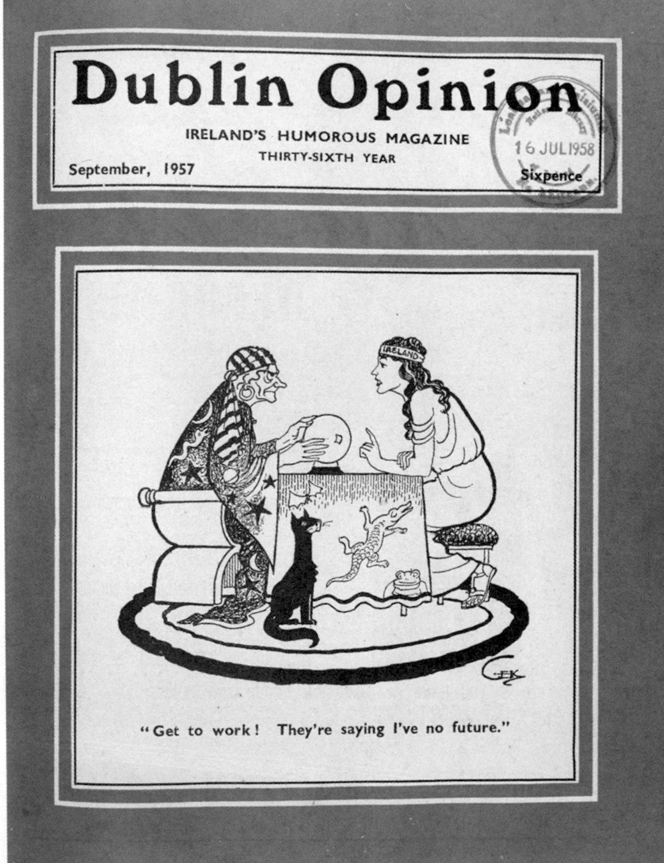

Dublin Opinion
IRELAND'S HUMOROUS MAGAZINE
THIRTY-SIXTH YEAR
September, 1957
Sixpence
16 JUL 1958
IRELAND
"Get to work! They're saying I've no future."

2. 'They're saying I've no future.' The cartoon that sparked a revolution.

Most Holy Father
Samuel O'Toole
and
Mary Heffernan
humbly prostrate before Your Holiness, beg the Apostolic Blessing on the occasion of their marriage 4th January 1955.

Almus Dominus benigne annuit precibus
Ex Aedibus Vaticanis die 22 nov. 1954

3. The Pope's blessing on my parents' marriage.

4. Eamon de Valera kissing the ring of the Archbishop of Dublin, John Charles McQuaid.

5. Irish United Nations soldiers at the siege of Jadotville, 1961.

6. President John F. Kennedy with Lord Mayor of Dublin, James O'Keefe (centre) and the Irish ambassador, Thomas J. Kiernan, May 1963.

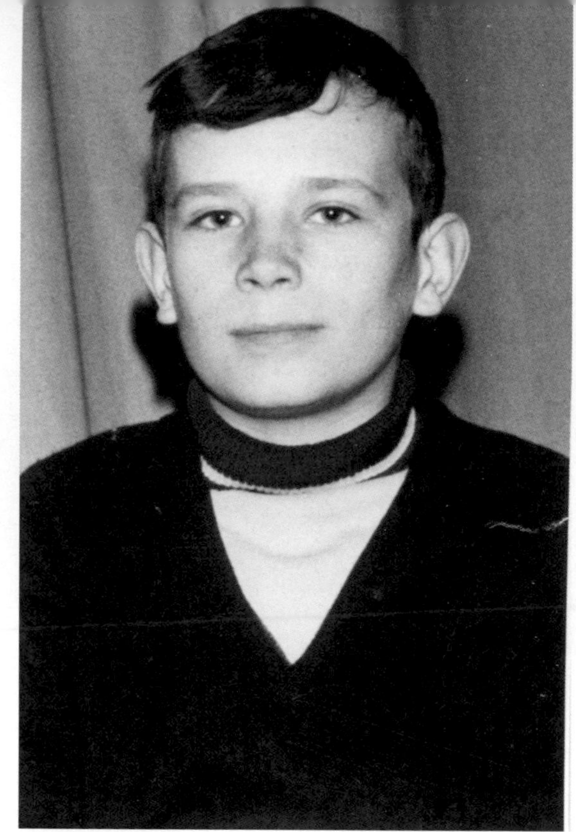

7. A good boy: me aged 10, 1968.

8. Gay Byrne, star of Irish television and radio.

9. Artane industrial school, Dublin.

10. Nelson Pillar, Dublin, after it was blown up by an IRA faction, 1966.

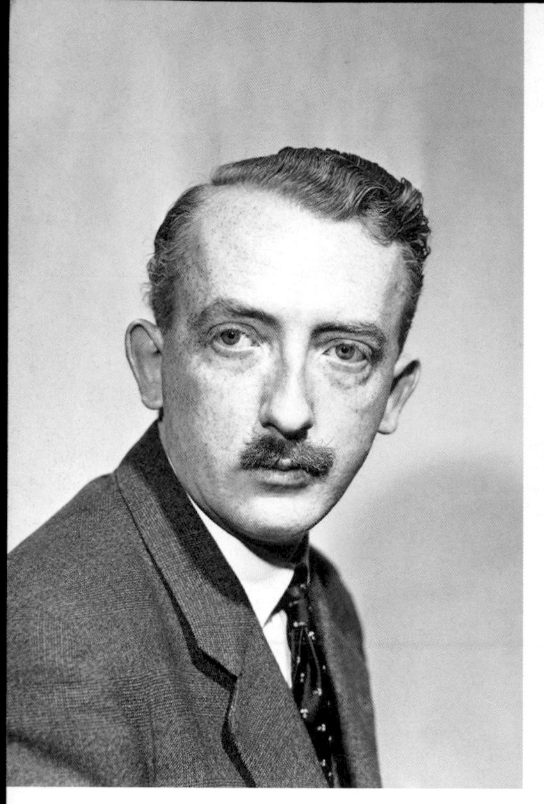

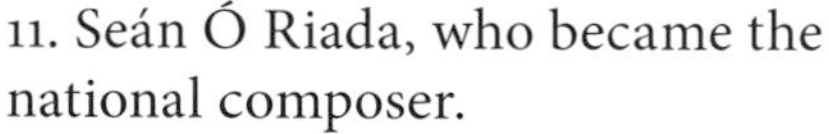

11. Seán Ó Riada, who became the national composer.

12. Charles Haughey, the most controversial figure in Irish politics between the 1960s and the 1990s.

13. Charles de Gaulle departing for Dublin Airport, June 1969.

14. Muhammad Ali before his fight with Al 'Blue' Lewis in Dublin, July 1972.

15. Women on the platform in Dublin before boarding the 'contraceptive train' to Belfast.

16. Bloody Sunday, 1972, when the British Army's Parachute Regiment killed fourteen unarmed civilians.

17. Repatriation of the body of Frank Stagg at Shannon Airport from Wakefield Prison in Britain, where he died on hunger strike in February 1976. Stagg's funeral became a surreal Gothic drama.

filled up with men and boys. They all wore white shirts and black trousers that made them seem, in that time of male flamboyance, austere, even ascetic. A man sat down at the organ. It was him. He kept one hand on the keyboard and with the other, the hand that had cast his spell over the pigs, began to conduct the choir. I knew enough Irish to know that the words were merely those of the Our Father, words flattened by repetition into meaninglessness. But the melody was like a meandering river, slow and serene yet utterly implacable.

The man at the organ was the composer Seán Ó Riada and the choir was singing the Mass he had written for them after he moved to Cúil Aodha in 1963, using the traditional airs of the locality. It was not like any music I had ever heard, mostly because it seemed not to be trying to do anything at all. Pop songs or classical symphonies or the folk ballads of the cities were out to capture your attention, to stir your emotions, to tell you a story, to make you laugh, to honour the martyrs. This music had no interest in staking any claims. It just enfolded you within itself. That gave it an immense dignity.

I couldn't place it. The choir was all male, but it did not sound masculine: the voices were nasal and high-pitched but restrained, declining to strain for effect. The melodies were long and linear and seemed, because they were sung in unison, utterly simple. But as you listened, they released themselves into gentle, unshowy ornamentations and then curved back into line. The Irish words were at once guttural and baroque. It was all as plain as the church itself, but it also had the assurance of high art.

I had, at that time, become deeply bored by Mass. I had long given up my career as an altar boy. Perhaps after the heights of being a performer on the altar, the status of mere member of the congregation watching from the pews was too much of a come-down. I had not yet found the courage to stop going on Sundays, though I knew I would if I could. But as that sound washed over me and pulled me into itself, I felt that there was something supernatural at work. I wasn't sure if it was God as I knew him, but then maybe this was what God might be: this music, these country people, the chant of their responses in Irish, the light falling on the white walls. Up on the balcony, I felt like I was no longer looking down on it all, but that it was rising towards me.

On the way out after Mass, I noticed that over the door of the church was written in old Irish script Tá an Maistir Annso – the Master is Here. I knew what was meant by it, but it also seemed to me that it referred to Ó Riada, and that in any case there was not much of a distinction between these masters. I later heard people say that when he had first written his Mass and performed it with the choir, some of the congregation were not happy. Not because it was not beautiful but because it was so beautiful that it distracted them from their devotions.

Ó Riada's presence in Cúil Aodha was exotic. He hunted and fished. He wore those suits and drove that car. He had a genuine Irish wolfhound. But in his own eyes, he was going native. He had been a European art composer called John Reidy. As a student, he played jazz piano for fun and began to write music in the manner, first of Debussy, then of Stravinsky, Schoenberg, Webern and Berg. He had no interest in traditional Irish music. He adored James Joyce, smoked French cigars and wore a beret. He wrote a setting of Ezra Pound's *Lustra*. After graduation, he performed his solo piano pieces on RDF, the French national radio station.

It was only in the late 1950s that he became fascinated by Irish music, and in particular by the unaccompanied sean nós (old style) singing that he heard in the Kerry Gaeltacht. In 1959, he composed the music, based on traditional airs but scored for classical orchestra, for a documentary film telling – from a nationalist perspective – the story of Ireland's fight for freedom, *Mise Éire*. Although I had no idea he had written it, I already knew some of this music – its big, swelling theme, 'Róisín Dubh', was part of the soundtrack of my childhood. He also created a group, Ceoltóirí Cualann, to play traditional Irish dance tunes and laments as if they were chamber music. It later evolved into The Chieftains.

As Seán Ó Riada, John Reidy was now the national composer. He was even commissioned by RTÉ to write two works which were intended to be used on the death of Eamon de Valera.[1] But being the national composer meant turning away from his roots in European art music. He formalized this breach when he moved from Dublin to Cúil Aodha in 1963 – he would speak Irish and work in an Irish idiom. According to his friend and biographer Tomás Ó Cannain, by the late 1960s 'Seán said that he was finished with European music and in future would only be concerned with Irish music'.

This turning inwards was one answer to the problem of Irish modernity. Ó Riada, like many young artists and intellectuals, did not see the opening up of the economy as a liberation from repression and stasis but, rather, as the country and its traditions being sold out. Shortly before he moved to Cúil Aodha, he wrote angrily in the *Irish Times*: 'The country that was won by such costly sacrifice, that was bought with the blood of good men, is being sold, physically, spiritually with its people, by its people, for the customary thirty pieces of electro-plated nickel silver. This is more than a scandal, more than a disgrace. It is the betrayal of every man who through the centuries took up arms for this country's freedom.'[2]

He began to evoke *An Naisiún Gaelach*, the Gaelic Nation, a revitalized version of the early twentieth-century nationalist ideology in which Ireland must be, in the words of Patrick Pearse, not merely free but Gaelic as well. It would not have bothered him that this nation could not include Protestants in Northern Ireland. According to Ó Cannain, 'Seán had strong opinions on the North and what should be done to solve its problems. His solution was generally one of force. His opinions were not only simplistic, but dangerous and reckless – those of a person who had never lived in the North and who had not experienced its problems at first hand.' Ó Riada's wife Ruth 'had difficulty restraining him in 1969 when the Northern troubles broke out in earnest, as he very much wanted to take his gun and fight for his own Gaelic nation on the barricades of Belfast.'

But Ó Riada, also like many Irish intellectuals and artists, wanted both to reject commercial modernity and enjoy its fruits. He fantasized about building a large hotel on the banks of the Sullane, with an airport beside it to bring tourists into the area to hunt and fish – and listen to his music and that of the local singers.[3] That, presumably, would also have 'sold' the old Ireland he loved. The easy opposition of good tradition to bad modernity was a refuge from reality, not a way of living.

Neither, though, was Ó Riada a phoney. His respect for the oral and musical cultures of rural Ireland was genuinely deep and, as I experienced that morning, he gave that culture a moving sense of its own dignity. But he was trying somehow to answer a question that was at the heart of the dilemma of modernity: did Ireland have to be destroyed in order to be saved? Whitaker and Lemass had set out to shake the country out of its isolation and self-regard. But was it merely going to end up as an Americanized, homogenized dependency, stripped of its cultural distinctiveness and national independence?

In his 1969 play *The Mundy Scheme*, Brian Friel asked, 'What happens to an emerging country after it has emerged?' In the play, which ran at the Olympia in Dublin, having been rejected by the Abbey, the minister for finance discovers that the country has run out of money and is 'on the point of national death'. The bankrupt government comes up with a scheme to sell the West of Ireland to a New York property developer as a giant graveyard ('the world's resting place'). The satire was heavy-handed, but Friel was returning to the sense of morbidity that had forced Whitaker and Lemass into action in 1958. For them, the impending death was demographic. For many of the artists and intellectuals a decade later, it was cultural. The avoidance of one form of extinction had, they thought, created another.

Ó Riada, for all his creative genius, was haunted by the idea of death. He imagined himself writing a musical horror film to be called *The Killer Chord*. The protagonist, a famous composer, would experiment with the ever more 'lethal possibilities of music'.[4] He eventually devises 'a chord which, by its particular combination of pitches, harmonies, tone colour, volume and duration, should kill the listener'. At the end of a big, nationally broadcast concert of his new work, he stuffs his ears with impenetrable plugs and then plays the chord. 'The orchestra and audience collapse dead, people slump by their firesides all over the country and cars with radios slaughter hundreds as they career out of control. The composer, calmly removing his earplugs, has survived.' At the heart of this fantasy was despair at the possibility of reaching any kind of acceptable compromise between authentic Irish art and the new Ireland: one of them would have to go.

In June 1974, from the stage of the Peacock Theatre in Dublin, Michael Hartnett, perhaps the finest poet of his generation in the Republic, announced his intention to stop writing poetry in English and to find his voice instead in Irish. He, like Ó Riada, left Dublin and went to live in rural Ireland, in his case in West Limerick. These flights were driven by a deep pessimism: there was no authentic way of being Irish in the cities, in the English language, in a European modernist tradition. The only future lay in the past, in a reconnection with the real people, the more rural the better.

And yet, in the same year that I was encountering Ó Riada's almost mystical power in Cúil Aodha, a census was taken. Published the following year, it revealed two epoch-making facts. One was that for the first time in Irish history, a majority (52 per cent) of the population was living in towns and cities. The other was that almost half of the population was under the age of twenty-five. Ireland was an urban country and a very young country. Since, as a city boy, I belonged to both of these categories, was I not as authentically Irish as an elderly grandmother living in a cottage up a mountain?

We had an equal and opposite prejudice. In the city, the rural world was obviously inferior. We all watched – because there was nothing else to watch – RTÉ's rural soap opera, *The Riordans*, set on a farm. It was actually a brilliant and pioneering series, but the main point of it for us kids in Crumlin was to mock the rural accents. The son was called Benjy – the worst insult we traded with each other was to say to another kid: 'Will you get up the yard, there's a smell of Benjy off ya.' We made up funny sentences: 'Julie Riordan, where do be she?'

Beyond that, the underworld of ancient, Pagan belief that persisted in Ireland before television, had become an absurdist joke. Shortly after eleven o'clock on the night of 8 December 1962, about sixty young men and women crushed around the door of the police station on College Street in the centre of Dublin city. Many of them pushed inside and 'began a systematic search under the tables, chairs and benches'. They claimed there were leprechauns in the station and 'they just had to find them'. They had been convinced of their existence by a French hypnotist, Paul Goldin, whose show was playing at the nearby Olympia Theatre.[5] 'The grand climax to his arduous performance came when he seemingly convinced his "pupils" that they had each just lost a leprechaun and as the curtain came down a group of docile young folk suddenly erupted into a wild scramble around the theatre searching for their lost leprechauns.'

This was what the desire to reconnect with a Gaelic past could look like if you were an urban Irish kid: a hypnotized search for lost leprechauns. I think one of the reasons the experience of encountering Ó Riada in the church that morning was so overwhelming for me was that, as well as making the Mass seem beautiful again, it showed that there was something more to it than that. The desire for connection was given meaning by the reality that there was still something to connect to, traditions of music and singing and storytelling and language that had their own highly distinctive texture.

The odd thing is that, for a large part of that half of the population that was under twenty-five, the dilemma of whether to try to relate to these indigenous traditions or embrace international modernity was partly solved by an unlikely cultural force: the rise of the hippy. Hippies didn't look like Ó Riada in his tweeds, but they were in fact following the same compulsion – the desire to escape urban modernity, the allure of indigenous wisdom, the dream of getting back to the garden, the return to a primal innocence before the corruptions of capitalism.

I first heard the word 'hippy' when I was ten and was taken to a pantomime in Dublin. For some reason, Cinderella's Ugly Sisters at one point dressed in beads and bangles and skipped around the stage singing

Everybody's going to be a hippy some day,
A hippy some day, a hippy some day
Everybody's going to be a hippy some day
And run around the garden.

I thought it was hilarious and for a long time afterwards I would sing it to myself. But it was also somewhat prophetic. In the summer of 1972, I got my first job, working in Dunnes Stores. I saved up my own money and, for the first time, I was able to buy some clothes for myself. I chose a pair of luscious purple seersucker trousers with thirty-two-inch flares, an orange shirt with huge white flowers blossoming all over it and a lurid green tie that was almost as wide as the flares. I couldn't get over how beautiful I looked. I was not the child who had refused to go to The Rolling Stones in Hyde Park two years earlier. I was a child of the universe.

It is hard to fathom that for us the big conflict was not the emerging disaster north of the Border. It was hair. The idea of letting it grow contained within it every possible kind of growth, from darkness towards enlightenment, from square to hip, from childhood to adulthood, from dependence to independence. Its importance was total. The proudest moment of my life to date was that summer, when instead of going to the barber in Crumlin, I climbed up the stairs over the China Showrooms in Grafton Street to Herman's Klipjoint, Ireland's first unisex hair salon, opened by a Dutchman, Herman Koster. There were chocolate-brown walls and orange chairs. 'Brown Sugar' was blaring from the stereo. The cutters were all girls and they wore blue jeans and kaftans. It was heaven.

It was also trouble. The Christian Brothers declared war on long hair. In September 1970, fifteen pupils at the De La Salle secondary school in Skerries were sent home because of the length of their hair. Then 120 students were turned away from St Joseph's CBS in Marino and, ominously, from Synge Street, down the road from us, for the same reason. The manager of Synge Street, Brother S. B. Donovan, explained that parents had agreed unanimously that the boys attending his school should have a presentable appearance and that the parents left it up to him to turn away any boy whose appearance was not up to the required standard. 'Apart from the traditional standard of personal neatness maintained by C.B.S. schools and accepted by parents, it is of great importance that the boys be of good appearance, as from time to time, prospective employers visit the school with a view to employing many of the boys.'[6] Some of the boys told reporters that under no circumstances would they have their hair cut: 'Most say they would prefer to look for jobs than cut their locks.'

What the Brothers could not grasp was that the desire to be hippyish was actually encouraging us to take an interest in the very thing they supposedly wanted to promote: the idea of a distinctive Irish culture. This paradox was beyond them but, for us, it was potent. What made it so was the notion of the Celtic. One of the odder effects of the explosion of youth culture in the 1960s and early 1970s was what might be called a second Celtic Revival in Ireland. In the search for an alternative, anti-establishment aesthetic, the notion of a pre-Christian 'Celtic' world promised a kind of authenticity that dovetailed with the international counterculture. It manifested itself in everything from jewellery, to the invention of 'Celtic rock', to the graphic art of Jim Fitzpatrick.

Fitzpatrick inserted himself into a million bedsits when he created one of the most reproduced global images of the 1960s and 1970s, the dramatic red and black screen-print of Che Guevara that was blazoned on T-shirts, badges and posters, and borne aloft in student riots in Paris in 1968, anti-war protests on American campuses and peace marches in Northern Ireland. But Fitzpatrick also developed a visual language that combined psychedelia with a comic book Celticism, to create calendars, cards, posters, place mats of mythic Irish figures reimagined as Marvel superheroes. It was, for us, a perfect reconciliation.

Not long after I got back from Cúil Aodha, one of the regular passengers on my father's bus route, Lily Shanley, who was front-of-house manager at the Abbey Theatre, gave him tickets for a production of *Macbeth* with Ray McAnally and Angela Newman. It was the first time I had ever seen a play and I was enthralled by it. The visual trademark of the production was that it was a Celtic *Macbeth*. The men were got up as Celtic warriors. The designs were full of Celtic spirals and triskels.

With all of this swirling around, I went to the library and borrowed a copy of Augusta Gregory's *Cuchulain of Muirthemne*, a

1902 retelling of the *Táin Bó Cúailnge* (The Cattle Raid of Cooley) cycle of legends, describing the mythic conflict that erupts when Queen Medb of Connacht invades Ulster to capture its most prized treasure, a great brown bull. Ulster is defended by its youthful champion, Cúchulainn. This stuff from the first Celtic Revival now seemed exciting again. It belonged to us, it was ancient and indigenous, but it also sat very comfortably with what Phil Lynott's Thin Lizzy were doing in *Vagabonds of the Western World*, an album whose cover was designed by Fitzpatrick, and indeed with the hippy mysticism of Led Zeppelin's 'Stairway to Heaven'.

The most electrifying invention was the Celtic Rock band Horslips. It was somehow perfectly representative of where we were. On one level it was entirely ersatz. It was formed in 1970 by an advertising agency in Dublin that needed a 'rock band' for a TV commercial. Three of its own staff played band members. But they needed a keyboard player and somebody knew Jim Lockhart, who was an accomplished multi-instrumentalist with a strong interest in both classical and Irish traditional music. Lockhart in turn was a follower of Séan Ó Riada, with ambitions to synthesize these two forms. When they decided to form a real band, they brought in Johnny Fean, who grew up playing banjo and mandolin in traditional music sessions in Co. Clare before falling under the spell of Jimi Hendrix. It all came together in a line-up kitted out in glam rock gear playing loud electric versions of Irish and Scottish dance tunes alongside their own riff-heavy compositions.

It couldn't have been more phoney and it couldn't have been more real. How could this strange brew make any sense? All I knew is that it made more sense to me than anything else did. I saw Horslips play at a concert in Baldoyle racecourse in May 1972, after a charity walk led by Jimmy Savile. This latter fact should itself give some idea of how bizarre the time was. First, Savile was English, a DJ and TV personality for the BBC. The Troubles were raging in the North and we were supposed to be against the English. But no one seemed to think his controlling presence was strange – even Charles Haughey, who as I remember it, waved us all off as we began the ten-mile walk from the city centre. The *Evening Herald*, which organized the walk, even hailed Savile's dominion over 'his loyal Irish subjects. The Danes made no greater conquest than this. Neither did the Normans.'[7] And second, Savile himself was a weirdo. We did not know then that he was one of the most prolific child rapists in British history, but it would not have come entirely as a shock if someone told us.

So weirdness was very much a relative concept, and when Horslips started playing, they sounded to me, not just normal, but a revelation of my own normality. Their yoking together of American rock and roll and Irish traditional music expressed exactly the way so many of us were living. And it was not a cacophony. It worked. They were able to hold it all together, to keep it going, to make it hum with energy. I loved them for this, absolutely and unconditionally. I got a Horslips poster and put it up over my bed. I went to as many of their concerts as I could afford. When they did their concept album version of the *Táin*, I was there for its first live performance. Afterwards, I bought a copy, not just of the album, but of the 1969 translation of the original myth by the poet Thomas Kinsella, wonderfully illustrated with abstract blot drawings by the painter Louis le Brocquy.

This was cultural escapology. You didn't have to choose. Not between modes – high or low, kitsch or serious, contemporary or ancient. But more importantly not between here and there, Ireland and the world, tradition and modernity. The great sin, cultural as well as religious, was impurity. But impure seemed just fine in both dimensions. That was not how it seemed to Ó Riada or Hartnett or to those who felt that salvation lay in the search for a lost authenticity without which Irish lives would be valueless.

In October 1971, I heard the news on the radio that Seán Ó Riada was dead. It did not say that his death certificate named the cause of death as 'cirrhosis of the liver, caused by alcohol'. He was two months past his fortieth birthday. Hundreds of cars followed the hearse from Cork to Cúil Aodha. All the shops were shut along the road and all the children came out from every school to stand and see him pass. His body lay in the little church where I had watched him conduct his Mass. Charles Haughey and other prominent figures travelled to the funeral. His choir sang a Requiem Mass of his own composition, with his sixteen-year-old son Peadair taking his father's place at the organ. Giving the oration, the poet Seán Ó Riordáin said that Ó Riada had connected people to 'an rud a aontoinn sinn leis an dream a tá curtha I gcre na cille seo agus i gcre gach cille in Eirinn',[8] the thing that unites us to those who are laid in the clay of this churchyard and in every churchyard in Ireland. I didn't really think so. I thought he had connected me to something that was very much alive.

14

1971: Little Plum

We called him Little Plum because somebody had once decided that he looked like a Native American character in the British comic the *Beano*: small, round-faced, goggle-eyed, snub-nosed. He was the Christian Brother in charge of the new classes coming into Coláiste Caoimhín, the fine new secondary school that had been built just around the corner from Aughavannagh Road to deal with all the boys who were now entitled to free education. It was an amazing place, reeking of modernity, with a swimming pool, a language laboratory, a science lab. It was a future that had arrived. But it still contained Brother Plum.

He taught Latin, but he also seemed to have been given this special job of supervising the first years. What made this interesting was that this suited him best. The younger boys were less likely to know what to do when he started fondling them.

He was right about that. Like all the Brothers, he wore a black cassock, but unlike most of them, he was constantly feeling himself under it. He rubbed himself up against the school desks. He sat down beside boys and put his hand on their legs, working it steadily upwards. If he got a boy to stand beside him, his hand would sneak around behind him and land on the boy's arse. He did all of this openly, constantly, shamelessly.

Once, after a few months of this, my friend David Crowe, who was much braver than me, suddenly stood up and started roaring at Plum, using the only language we had: 'You're a queer. You're a homo. You're bent.' Plum just kept looking at him calmly, steadily, silently. He simply refused to react and told us to turn to another page in the Latin grammar. David was defeated. He just sat down again and everything went on as if his accusations had never been voiced.

Here it was again: the open secret, the thing that everybody knew and nobody grasped, the truth that could be seen but never identified. We were adepts at epistemology. Most of us could walk like circus performers across tightropes that were strung between private knowledge and public acknowledgement. The only ones who ever looked down were those who were badly abused, and they became even better at suppressing reality.

I colluded in it all. I knew instinctively that Plum wouldn't do much more than feel my leg. He wouldn't go too far because we were known to be a strong family, respectable and well-minded, and because my father was tough and could be fierce. Something actually came back to me, a memory from a few years before. When I was eight or nine a new, young Christian Brother, Brother Cahill, had come to the primary school. He was gentle and sweet-natured. He didn't hit us if he could help it.

I attached myself to him. I would walk up and down the yard with him at breaktime, talking ninety to the dozen. And obviously I must have talked a lot about him at home. One day, I was jabbering on 'Brother Cahill this', 'Brother Cahill that'. My father became angry and stern: 'Don't get close to those Brothers, it's not healthy.' I was hurt and mystified. But why? My father didn't want to say why. He just repeated that it wasn't healthy.

When I encountered Plum, I knew why. But the realization also gave me an appreciation of the complex ways in which this whole business worked, the many layers of silence just beneath its surface. So my father knew that there was something wrong, something dangerous, about the way these men might treat a boy. But he did not, could not, do anything with that awareness. And somehow, they in turn had intimations of his vigilance. And that protected me. Plum would sense out the vulnerable boy, the kid who got into trouble, the kid whose father had died. The evil thing would be deflected away from me. I was grateful for that, so I said nothing either.

At the time, I did not realize that this complex life form had evolved over decades, maybe centuries. It was like the way children's street games and rhymes passed down from generation to generation even though adults ignored them. Many years later, when I had written something about the Brothers, I got a letter from an anonymous man:

'I went to Synge St. first in '36 or '37 and finished in '41. I am 65 now and can't remember precisely. That's not important what is important is the dread and terror that abounded there. Thank God it's being exposed at last.

'The years I spent there made my childhood the most miserable one. It wasn't though just the beatings from sadists and the humiliation. I recall once, I think I was 9 or 10, being brought up to a little back room and the Brother after remonstrating with me over my crime (I was caught mitching [i.e. not attending school]) told me to take off my trousers and after several slaps on my backside started fondling my penis. It didn't go further than that. I started to cry. But I'll never forget the trauma of that event. Believe it or not you are the first and last person I ever related that incident to. Funnily enough the thing that I remember most vividly about that room and lying across the Brother's knee is a blue and white statue of the Virgin on a table close by.

'I admit I was forever mitching. The Brothers hammered me. My poor father hammered me. He thought I just didn't want to go to school never realizing poor man his son was too frightened to go. The really crazy thing is that it was all part of everyday life.'

'You are the first and last person I ever related that incident to' – not a lover, or a wife or a husband, or a friend. This was a phrase most Irish journalists would hear at some point.

All through the early years of my childhood in the 1960s, a peculiarly Irish sex pest was at work. He would call young married women, mostly middle class and suburban, on the phone when their husbands were at work. He would introduce himself very politely as Father Malachy, a Franciscan priest who was working on a book about Irish marriage. Would they mind answering a few questions? The questions began innocuously but gradually became more intimate. Eventually, he would ask what sexual positions they preferred and the women would realize that he was a pervert. He had tricked them into talking about things that no one would talk about.

The story, which ran for years, took an even stranger turn when the Franciscans felt compelled to make a public statement to the effect that there was no Father Malachy among their congregation. But in the course of this denial, they added that one of their priests, the Revd Lucius McClean, actually was in the process of writing a book on marriage. (Father McClean wrote the problem page in the *Sunday Independent*.) The suggestion seemed to be that a priest calling women to ask about their intimate lives might be entirely legitimate – the big problem with Father Malachy was that he was not a priest. The church, especially through the confessional, had natural ownership of Ireland's sexual secrets. Which meant, of course, that it also had complete possession of its own. The priests asked the questions. They did not answer them.

Outside of the confession box, there was endless prurience. When I started secondary school, one of the first short stories we read in English class was Seán Ó Faoláin's 'The Trout'. It is about a twelve-year-old girl who finds a fish trapped in a rock pool 'panting in his tiny prison'. She gets up one night and goes, with a ewer of water, to find the trout and release it into the river: 'Her pyjamas were very short, so that when she splashed water, it wet her ankles. She peered into the tunnel… Kneeling down in the dark, she put her hand into the slimy hole. When the body lashed, they were both mad with fright. But she gripped him, and shoved him into the ewer.'[1]

Thirteen-year-old boys read everything sexually, sniggering over the faintest whiff of a double entendre. Yet none of us could find anything titillating in this passage. However, Oliver J. Flanagan, a veteran Fine Gael TD, who would go on to serve in cabinet as minister for defence, read it out in the Dáil. He claimed that it was 'most suggestive. It is a paragraph which should not be put in any short story which is read in the schools… I know there are parents who view this book with the gravest concern because of the language contained in it.'

The brilliant minister for education, Donogh O'Malley, had to point out to Flanagan that 'this young girl is going into the tunnel to catch a trout and not to catch anything else'. Other implications existed only in Flanagan's 'own vivid and excitable imagination'.[2] But the vividness and excitability of the TD's imagination were beyond even our feverish dirty-mindedness. They have a heroic quality. Panting, short pyjamas, tunnel, slimy hole, gripped, shoved – mere words could become, for a middle-aged Catholic politician, tumescent.

There was, in this mentality, no room for innocence. The paradox of this paranoid style was that, when sex was not open to discussion or acknowledgement, everything was hyper-sexualized. There was no proper arena for sex, no place in which to contain it. So it could bleed out in everything. It lurked everywhere. It was encoded in stories about twelve-year-old girls and fish. Precisely because of its own success in keeping sex out of the public arena, Irish Catholic conservatism was forced to become deeply Freudian, to read everything as an expression of hidden libidinal desire. Flanagan, looking around him in 1971, saw that 'the country was reeking with drink, drugs and sex'.[3] Mary Kenny, the women's editor of the *Irish Press*, joked that he had been put up to this claim by the Irish tourist board, Bord Fáilte, 'in order to add a bit of much-needed fleshpots-of-sin glamour to the auld sod's hick image abroad'.[4]

Flanagan claimed in 1966 that 'Sex never came to Ireland until Telefís Éireann went on the air', a statement that became proverbial as 'there was no sex in Ireland before television'.[5] The claim was widely ridiculed, but it was not entirely foolish. It was on television, and particularly on Gay Byrne's *Late Late Show*, that sex became an idea rather than a regrettable fact. It was not stupid to think, moreover, that this idea was imported, that it had been brought in with all of the other innovations of the 1960s. As Flanagan put it in 1971, 'It is popular in Ireland and in Europe, to speak on sex, divorce and drugs. These things are foreign to Ireland and we want them kept that way.'[6] The Fianna Fáil TD Frank Carter said at around the same time that 'there is nothing wrong with sex in the right place'.[7] Very large numbers of Irish people would have agreed that the right place for sex as an activity was in the marriage bed and, for sex as a subject for discussion, it was in the confession box.

There had been those who would have liked even private discussions to be monitored and controlled. The TD Frank Sherwin complained in the Dáil in 1962 that 'From time to time most obscene and profane language is used on the telephone... Is there any way by which these people can be detected? From what I have seen in the cinema, it is possible to identify immediately the phone from which a call is made. I do not know whether that is peculiar to films. There ought to be an occasional prosecution to stop the use of obscenity on the telephone.'[8]

There were also fears that American films could be shown on television without being subjected to the strict censorship that applied in the cinema. Brendan Corish, leader of the Labour Party, was especially anxious that it 'is not the method by which sex education should be given to the Irish people—through the medium of these American films'.[9] Responding to a motion at the Fianna Fáil Árd Fheis (annual conference) in 1959, suggesting that films should be graded rather than banned outright, Seán Lemass had been unequivocal in his opposition: 'We regard these regulations as being in exactly the same category as other regulations which prevent the sale of putrid meat or contaminated milk.'[10]

Ireland, in this analogy, was a naturally healthy body. Films might contain toxins that would make it sick. Censorship was a health and safety issue. But for much of the population, hungry for knowledge, these movies, might, on the contrary, be vital sustenance. For if American films were a form of sex education for the Irish, it might at least be said for them that no nation needed it so much.

On the one hand, the revolution of the 1960s led to more frequent marriages among partners who were getting younger. The 1971 census recorded the number of families up by 48,000 since 1961, compared with a rise of only 11,000 in the previous fifteen years. The number of marriages was up from 14,700 in 1957 to 22,000 in 1971. And the mean age at marriage for men fell from 30.6 to 27.2 years; for women it fell from 26.9 to 24.8 years.[11] The population was recovering, too – it had risen over the course of the 1960s from 2.82 million to 2.98 million. In itself, this was hardly a demographic miracle, but the reversal of what had seemed an inevitable decline had great psychological significance. We were no longer vanishing. Sex was fulfilling its crude demographic function.

On the other hand, there was a gap between reproduction and relationships, between the peopling of the country and the pleasures it entailed. The American Jesuit sociologist Alexander Humphreys reported in the mid-1960s on the sexual experiences of married couples in Crumlin. One woman told him that, when she was first married, 'it never occurred to me that children or the purpose of marriage had anything to do with sex'. Her husband confessed to being equally ignorant: 'People just spoke about sex in whispers.' Another man told him that 'there is something repulsive about it and nothing will ever get that out of my system'. A third said: 'Back of everybody's mind is the notion that there is something wrong with it, something bad. It is deeply ingrained in us. I know that is true of myself and of most people I know.'[12]

Even younger working-class married women often had very little understanding of contraception, except that the Pill and condoms were banned by the church. One anonymous Catholic doctor told Humphreys that ignorance of sex 'still exists to a greater extent among the younger women. They come to me and ask me about limiting the family by rhythm because I am a Catholic doctor... Well, one thing leads to another, and it is surprising how little these women know about the matter.'[13]

It is a startling fact that, up until the reform of the second-level curriculum shortly before I started in Coláiste Caoimhín, the only biological subject to be studied in most Irish schools was botany. In 1966, the Revd Seán Ó Catháin told a public meeting on the poverty of biological education that one 'reason why we kept away from the biological sciences in our schools was that they could be a bit troublesome – all that stuff about pollination, and so on'.[14]

This wall of ignorance may have been slowly crumbling by the late 1960s and early 1970s, but much more so in middle-class and urban areas than in rural and working-class ones. Nell McCafferty reported in 1971 that she had 'spent 27 years on Irish soil without so much as a hint of sex education' and that she was 'once told that menstruation was a gift from Our Lady'.[15] What Mary Holland had called in 1966 'the darting furtive guilt about sex which begins at our first convent kindergarten and maims too many of us for too many years afterwards' left a very long trail of shame. Edna O'Brien, in the same year said that 'I don't think I have any pleasure in any part of my body, because my first and initial body thoughts were blackened by the fear of sin: and therefore I think of my body as a sort of vehicle for sin, a sort of tabernacle of sin.'[16]

Kate O'Brien, the novelist who had also been banned for her relative frankness, was against sex education in schools: 'I am against this forcing of sexual knowledge on children... It is wrong, I believe, to expose innocents to the insolence of the school blackboard and the "educative" sex film.' Her recommendation for children was that 'we must leave them alone', with the added bonus for most in Ireland that 'There is for the Catholic child the simple practice of Confession.'[17]

For me and my friends the overwhelming reality was one of sexual segregation. The Catholic Church's policy remained that laid down by Pope Pius XI in 1929: that co-education was 'a confusion of mind which cannot distinguish between a legitimate association of human beings and a promiscuous herding together of males and females on a completely equal footing'.[18] We longed for some promiscuous herding together, but the church insisted otherwise. An American woman living in Dublin remarked in the late 1960s that 'Adolescence lasts longer in Ireland, I think, than it does in any other country because the sexes are segregated so rigidly.'[19]

Ignorance was reinforced by fear. Ireland in the 1960s had one of the lowest rates of children born out of wedlock in Europe. But like so much else about the country, this was deceptive. Young women who were unmarried and pregnant took the boat to England. As early as 1955, London County Council had so many Irish babies left in its care that a dedicated children's officer was appointed to spend six months each year in Ireland to try to find homes for them.[20] Alan Bestic reported in 1969 that 'So many girls who find they are going to have a baby go to England that social workers and almoners automatically jot down on their papers: "P.F.I." It signifies "Pregnant From Ireland".'[21]

These women were not tourists or emigrants. They were refugees. They fled in terror. A Catholic social worker in England described it: 'The fear in these girls has to be seen to be believed. It is only by endless gentleness that we can persuade them that going back [to Ireland] to have their baby wouldn't be so awful. What sort of society do you have in Ireland that puts the girls into this state?'[22]

The answer is one in which girls and young women could be incarcerated, potentially for the rest of their lives, for the mere perception of possible or actual moral deviancy. As the report of the Kilkenny Social Services Conference of 1970 put it, 'these women are regarded and treated as second-class citizens and very often their misfortune is interpreted as being of their own devising'.[23] Second-class citizen is a term that was widely used by Catholics in Northern Ireland to describe their status. It applied even more forcefully to women in Catholic Ireland who were judged to be on the wrong side of its sexual boundaries. Their legal rights could be suspended indefinitely.

It is striking that the *Irish Times* journalist Michael Viney used the term 'on the run' in 1964 in relation to Irish women who were pregnant and unmarried.[24] In the Irish context, the phrase usually referred to the IRA. It evoked the image of the guerrilla flitting unseen through the landscape, appearing and disappearing, a liminal, ghostly, hovering presence. But while the man on the run was a glamorous figure, imbued with the romance of mystery, the woman on the run was impregnated with shame.

In the archipelago of coercive confinement in Ireland, there were two great islands dedicated to the punishment and control of 'fallen women'. One was the system of mother-and-baby homes. This was yet another sophisticated structure of unknowing. Viney called it Ireland's secret service: 'The mothers in these homes are protected by a benevolent conspiracy of unexpected thoroughness and ingenuity. If they resist all persuasion to tell their parents what is happening, then no device is spared to keep their secret.' If a young woman told her parents she was in England, her correspondence with home was routed through an accommodation address there. If she claimed to have gone on pilgrimage to the Marian shrine in Fatima, she was given Fatima medals and souvenirs to 'substantiate her alibi'. Like spies, 'each girl in these homes is given a code name, by which the nuns and her fellow-patients address her and which appears on the card at the foot of her baby's cot'.

The unwritten part of this secret code was that those babies would be given up for adoption – either legally or illegally. After 1952, it was against the law for any adoption to be arranged without a court order. But the system was above the law. For the right clients, documents could be faked to show the adoptive mother as the birth mother, erasing the latter entirely. One of those involved in arranging this service was the son and namesake of the national patriarch, Professor Éamon de Valera, a leading Dublin gynaecologist, who organized it in a number of cases during the 1960s. In a letter of July 1982, responding to a query by the adoptive family of a child about his medical history he wrote, 'I am aware of the boy you have noted in your letter. I can confirm no adoption certificate was necessary at the time because there was to be no further communication between the boy and his biological mother. An arrangement was made for a birth certificate in the late 1960s for his new family. Given his illegitimate background, we felt it best the child was placed with a good family as a matter of urgency.'[25] It was an eloquent phrase – 'an arrangement was made'. The lives of aberrant women and children were things to be arranged for the benefit of good families and the good Catholic society.

The strangest part of this arrangement was that it included a form of literal Americanization. Catholic Americans could effectively buy babies from Irish mother-and-baby homes. This practice was coming towards its end in 1971, but it had gone on for a long time, especially in the decades after the Second World War. It was organized under McQuaid, but facilitated by the state. Official figures suggest that, between July 1949 and the end of 1973, around 2,100 babies were exported to the US.[26] The real figures may be very much higher: the *Irish Times* reported in 1951 that 'almost 500 babies were flown from Shannon for adoption last year' alone. The attraction was obvious: Irish babies, unlike those available for adoption in the US, were almost all white. As an Irish nun put it, 'Irish children are pure-blooded'.[27]

The market in Irish babies briefly attracted international attention in that same year when the Hollywood star Jane Russell announced her intention to 'fly to Dublin this week to pick out a child and make all the arrangements for bringing him to America'. In fact, an Irish couple, the Kavanaghs, offered Russell their fifteen-month-old son Tommy. The Irish authorities colluded with the fiction that she was taking him for 'a three-month holiday'. He never came back, and ended up as a rock star in California.[28]

The story brought unwelcome attention to what was going on, and there was a belief that the whole business would end. It didn't. Young women who had given birth in mother-and-baby homes continued to be informed peremptorily that their babies were being taken away for adoption. They continued to catch last glimpses of them as they were driven away.

One of the reasons for this torment was that it remained lucrative. Sister Hildegarde McNulty, superioress of the largest of the homes, Sean Ross Abbey in Co. Tipperary, from which at least 438 babies were exported to the US, admitted shortly before her death in 1995 that 'donations coming back from American adopters had constituted the largest single source of income' for the institution.[29] She also admitted to removing and destroying the documents relating to these payments.

The second, even more fearful, form of incarceration was the network of Magdalene asylums where women were held, forced to work without pay in the attached laundries, and often institutionalized for the rest of their lives. The system, which was not particular to Ireland, dated back to the eighteenth century. What is remarkable is that it was not just allowed to continue in Ireland until 1996, but that it was actively renewed in 1960, just as the country was supposedly modernizing. The country may have been opening up, but women were still to be locked up.

In 1960, when he was introducing the Criminal Justice Bill to update the penal system, Fianna Fáil's minister for justice Oscar Traynor, a veteran of the 1916 Rising, briefly mentioned that, in relation to young female offenders, the law was being amended to 'give discretion to the district justice to send her wherever he wishes'. That could include a prison, a convent or a third option:

'I acknowledge, with grateful thanks, the assistance of His Grace the Archbishop of Dublin who has made arrangements that St. Mary Magdalen's Asylum, Seán MacDermott Street, Dublin, will accept Catholic girls who may be remanded in custody.'[30] This gave rise to a short discussion of which of these options was least shameful for the girl involved. The Fine Gael leader John Dillon pointed out, apparently to general agreement, that 'if she goes to Mountjoy [prison] there may be a reflection on her reputation as a law-abiding citizen in regard to other matters, but no suggestion of sexual immorality... I can understand a girl remanded on a shoplifting charge or on a variety of other charges we can imagine, being a simple person and feeling that remand to a Magdalen home may hereafter be upcast to her as evidence that she was guilty of unchaste conduct in the past.' The implication was clear – an ordinary decent female criminal would be shamed by being placed on remand in St Mary Magdalene's Asylum alongside those who were obviously guilty of sexual immorality. The stigma of being regarded as impure was much worse than the disgrace of prison.

St Mary Magdalene's Asylum was (and is – the main building still exists) five minutes' walk from the principle thoroughfare of the nation's capital, O'Connell Street. It is not hidden away. It fronts right onto the street, a long, imposing three-storey brick façade suggestive of solidity, permanence, normality. It was there – but its residents were not there. They had disappeared into an abyss of memory, dignity, belonging, citizenship, human rights, personhood. They were beyond the reach of the law. Many of the inmates were children unlawfully transferred from industrial schools, a vast network of institutions, also under the control of religious orders, in which children whose parents were deemed incapable of caring for them, were incarcerated – trafficked is probably the right word. Labour laws governing wages and conditions were entirely flouted – slavery is certainly the right word. In Dublin, as in Cork and Galway, these black holes were not at the edge of the ordinary cosmos. They existed side by side with the shops and the offices and the cafés and the pubs, just as the culture of hypervigilance that created them existed side by side with a profound instinct for when to look the other way.

How could thousands of girls and women be made to vanish in such plain sight? Sex. The widespread belief – largely false – was that the girls and women who were unseen inside the Magdalene institutions had been prostitutes or, at the very least, loose women. This belief sexualized them, and once that reek of sex had been sniffed in the air, further discussion was unnecessary. What Dillon called 'the suggestion of sexual immorality' was a forcefield that repelled all inquiry. The suggestion was always enough.

But when sexual immorality is such an unexamined concept, so is sexual morality. When all sex is wrong, no kind of sex can be more wrong than any other. Everything is beyond the pale of discourse. Everything is out of bounds – so therefore there are no boundaries. Everything is unspeakable, so nothing is speakable. This is part of what created a perpetual open season for sexual predation on children.

To the church in particular, child sexual abuse by priests and brothers was sinful and regrettable but indistinguishably so from all other lapses from the vows of chastity. There was no difference between consensual and non-consensual sex. It's all sex. For me, at thirteen, what Brother Plum did in class was sexual and therefore no more suitable for discussion with adults than my own discovery of masturbation or sneaking into adult films.

But then, a group of women began to talk about, as one of them, June Levine, put it 'how men make sex dirty and blame women for it'.[31] This, too, was another form of Americanization. Second-wave feminism, like civil rights, was an idea that could open up the closed worlds of Ireland. One of the prime movers was a brilliant Chicago-born Irish-American journalist, Mary Maher, who worked for the increasingly radical women's page of the *Irish Times*. Maher and Margaret Gaj, Máirín Johnston, Máire Woods and Máirín de Burca began to meet in Bewley's café on Westmoreland Street in Dublin. Through the early months of 1971, the group expanded to include Mary McCutchan, Mary Anderson, Nuala Fennell, Nell McCafferty, Eavan Boland, Emer Philbin Bowman, the Sweetman sisters, Rosita and Inez, and the flamboyant *Irish Press* journalist Mary Kenny. The Irish Women's Liberation Movement was formed and produced a manifesto, printed on a borrowed photocopier, called *Chains or Change*.

In 1971, a woman in Ireland could not, in effect, sit on a jury – that privilege belonged to registered property owners who were almost exclusively male. She could not, if she was a civil servant or worked in a bank, keep her job when she got married. She could not buy contraceptives (unless the Pill was misprescribed as a 'cycle regulator'). She could not buy a pint of Guinness in a pub – some pubs refused to allow women to enter at all (my grandfather's local on Leonard's Corner was colloquially known as The Man's House); some allowed a woman in if, and only if, she was accompanied by a man; and many refused to serve women pints of beer. (Even in 1978, in a popular pub in central Dublin, a barman accidentally sold me a pint of Guinness for my girlfriend. He could not take it back, since I had paid for it, but insisted on pouring it into two half-pint glasses instead.)

A woman could not, as of right, collect the state allowance paid to help her raise her children – the legislation specified that it be paid to the father, who might, or not might not, mandate her to collect it. She could not get a barring order in court against a violent husband. She could not, if she was married, live securely in her own home – even if she paid for the house, her husband could sell it at any time without her consent. She could not refuse to have sex with her husband – the concept of marital rape was regarded as a contradiction in terms. She could not choose her own legal domicile – if her husband moved to Australia but she stayed in Ireland, she was legally domiciled in Australia. She could not get the same rate for a job as a man. She could not get a divorce under any circumstances.

Over the course of the 1970s, most of these legal disabilities (divorce very much not included) would be dismantled or ameliorated. Some of this change came from the top: Ireland's desire to join the European Economic Community meant that it had to be seen to fall into line with western European standards. The establishment by the Fianna Fáil government of a Commission on the Status of Women in 1970 gave official sanction to the imperative for change. But even the woman who chaired the commission later admitted that she herself did not realize how bad things were.

Thekla Beere was a remarkable pioneer, who had become secretary of the Department of Transport and Power in 1959 (it would be thirty-six years before another woman was appointed to such a position). But she came from a privileged upper middle-class background. She acknowledged that she was taken aback by the realities she had to think about as chair of the commission: 'A lot of us were absolutely amazed at the things that we found… appalled because they didn't affect many people but they affected people who had no means of communicating with the press… People like me – we hadn't realised – I don't think there [on the commission] did know a lot of these things.'[32]

This same cloud of unknowing had engulfed another female member of the commission, Kathleen Delap, who had attended the same privileged school in Dublin that Beere did: 'She and I were both at Alexandra College which was very much ahead of other women's colleges and schools at the time, and I mean the whole world was open to us – you went into the university if you wanted and took up a profession and so on. So again, I was brought down to earth when I came into the commission because I definitely had not realised all the discriminations that were there – just, we didn't come up against them.'[33] The Irish class system had made it possible even for brilliant and self-confident women not to know how systematically misogynistic their own state really was.

The women who formed the IWLM didn't just come up against the multiple discriminations, they were determined to confront them. In 1971, Anderson and de Burca were arrested while protesting against a new law aimed at homeless families who were squatting in vacant houses. They were to be called before an irascible District Court judge, so they decided to opt for trial by jury instead. It struck de Burca what this meant: that two women protesting against the way property rights were being imposed by the law would be tried by twelve male property owners.[34] She and Anderson launched a constitutional challenge, claiming that they were being denied the right to trial by a jury of their peers.

They lost the case in the High Court but eventually won it in the Supreme Court.

This whole idea of taking constitutional challenges was also very American. The young lawyer who initially advised de Burca and Anderson, and then acted as junior counsel in their case, was Mary Robinson. Robinson, in turn, had returned from postgraduate studies at Harvard Law School and had been profoundly influenced by the protests against the Vietnam War, the civil rights and women's movements, the assassinations of Martin Luther King and Robert Kennedy and by the possibilities of using a written constitution to seek vindication for the rights of oppressed groups.

Robinson, like Beere, was a product of comfortable middle-class privilege. There was also something she did not know: how much a woman who stepped out of line could be hated. She was elected as a member of the Senate, representing the graduates of Trinity College Dublin, where she had become Reid Professor of Law. In early 1971, she introduced, with the support of John Horgan and Trevor West, a bill to amend the law prohibiting the sale, supply and distribution of contraceptives in Ireland. It was a simple, technical bill, a few lines on one page, repealing the prohibition contained in the 1935 Criminal Law (Amendment) Act.

She was not surprised that the bill was strongly opposed by the Catholic hierarchy. McQuaid told his flock in his Lenten pastoral that contraception is evil 'and there cannot be, on the part of any person, a right to do what is evil'.[35] He required his priests to read at Mass on 28 March a statement that Robinson's bill would be a 'curse upon the country' and that contraception was 'a right that cannot even exist'. (Many of the IWLM women attended Mass for the sole purpose of walking out, Mary Kenny shouting 'This is a wicked pastoral… This is church dictatorship' as she did so.[36] On the night before the protest, June Levine had a nightmare in which McQuaid was speaking from the pulpit 'and suddenly spied me kneeling behind a pillar. He just shook his head sadly.')

But what Robinson was not prepared for was how personal the assault would be. Knowing that her mother and father, devout Catholics, were present, the bishop, Thomas McDonnell, denounced her directly from the pulpit of the cathedral in her home town of Ballina. Her parents 'left the cathedral in terrible distress'.[37] Robinson was deluged with hate mail: 'You must be the Devil incarnate to do this!' 'May you burn in Hell, from a Catholic Priest.' Someone sent her crude imitation condoms made from the cut-up fingers of garden gloves. A false rumour circulated – and was widely believed – that her husband Nick (a Protestant) was one of the Robinsons of the successful chain of pharmacies, Hayes, Conyngham & Robinson, and that she would be paid a penny for every Pill and condom that it sold.

The telling thing is that she did not know any of this would happen: 'It affected me very much. I was used to being admired and supported and it was a whole new experience for me, not only to be criticised but to be actually hated by people, strangers.'[38] Liberals, who thought that the new Ireland could be more like the US or Britain in such matters, did not understand the deep, visceral loathing that they evoked among those who felt that, precisely because Ireland was changing, Catholic morality was a vital redoubt of continuity and distinctiveness. They did not realize that Mother Church, to which most of them still belonged, could fight dirty. Or that the state was still prepared to dismiss them with contempt: Robinson's bill was not even granted the technical first reading that would allow it to be printed. 'God', as Robinson later reflected, 'I was so naive.'[39]

To me, though, this hardly mattered. That summer, contraception was the word of the season. It was on the news. And it was about sex. Sex was on the news. This became an even more thrilling reality on 22 May, when the IWLM organized a group of women to do an extraordinary thing: get the train from Dublin to Belfast, buy contraceptives, declare them to the customs authorities when they arrived back in Dublin, and see what would happen.

The most dizzying aspect of this stunt was that it messed with the other big story of the moment: the Troubles in the North. They were getting worse, much worse than anyone had imagined possible. In 1970, twenty-nine people were killed and that seemed terrible. In 1971, the number would be 180. Most of the escalation in violence happened after 9 August, when the British government agreed to a request from Brian Faulkner's Unionist government in Belfast to introduce the internment without trial of suspected paramilitaries. Internment was arguably the greatest public policy disaster of the Troubles. Of the 342 people seized and locked up, every single one was described as a suspected Republican. Not one Loyalist was initially interned. Very many of those interned, moreover, were not members of the IRA at all – and those who were belonged largely to the more political Official wing. (The IRA and Sinn Féin had split in 1970, with the majority favouring a policy of contesting elections and taking seats in Dublin, Belfast and London; the minority, which formed the Provisional Army Council, was more militarist, more sectarian and much less interested in electoral politics.) The introduction of internment – and the use by the British army of torture-like techniques against arrested men (hooding detainees, forcing them to stand for long periods with their arms against walls, subjecting them to white noise, depriving them of sleep and food) turned Northern Catholics as a whole into a suspect community and made the army, which had initially been regarded as a peacekeeping force, seem much more like an invader.

This escalation had not yet happened in May, when the IWLM launched what became known as the contraceptive train. But things were already bad enough. Sectarian rioting was becoming ever more serious. The first British soldier to be killed in the conflict, Robert Curtis, was shot by an IRA sniper in February. He was twenty – the same age as his pregnant wife. On 9 March, three young Scottish soldiers were lured from a pub where they had been drinking and shot in the head on a mountain road overlooking Belfast. The fact that two of them, Joseph and John McCaig, were brothers and were, respectively, eighteen and seventeen, made the killings especially inflammatory.

All of this was part of a narrative that most people in the Republic accepted in one form or another. We believed that the South was free, the North unfree. Many of the women involved in the contraceptive train stunt would themselves have accepted this. The idea for the performance, indeed, seems to have come from an incident the previous year during a cross-Border march by the student-led People's Democracy group from Belfast to Dublin. It had been stopped at the Border and the marchers had their bags searched. A customs man held up two objects, saying: 'This is Edna O'Brien's *Country Girl*, which has been banned, and this is a Durex and it's not allowed in the South.'[40]

But the confrontation they were staging in 1971 actually reversed the whole story of Irish nationalism. It was meant to demonstrate that, for women, the North was in fact a lot more free than the South. The point was that they could buy in Belfast the means to control their fertility that were denied them in Dublin. It drew on a very different idea of freedom.

The women who got off the train first in Belfast went to the chemist shop opposite the Europa Hotel near the station. But even many of these bold women were also naive, ignorant, unknowing. June Levine, who was Jewish, divorced, and more worldly wise, recalled that, once they got to the pharmacy, 'there now followed an amazing display of ignorance of the facts of life... I was pressed with questions such as "What does gossamer mean?", "What do you do with this jelly stuff?"! and, from one woman, "Would I take the same size Dutch cap as you, d'you think?"... I had been impressed by the "newness" of some of these young women of the seventies. Now I saw them as their mothers' daughters, women who knew little about their own bodies, who had never been free to feel responsible for their own fertility and felt awkward about it. They handled the condoms as if they were packages of sins, hooted at sight of a diaphragm. Such shopping was foreign to them and a hint of hysteria made them vulgar.'

When they got back to Dublin, the boldest of the women declared to the customs officers that they were carrying packages of contraceptives pills and that they were refusing to surrender them. What followed was a wonderful game of charades. The customs men simply pretended that all of this was not happening: 'The men dropped their eyes, silent and fussed, as a group of us who had decided to declare and not surrender waved our purchases at the customs men, who ignored us and passed us through.'[41]

But there was in fact a dark secret. The main purpose of the provocation was to illegally import the Pill. In fact, when they got to Belfast, the women realized that they could not purchase the Pill without prescriptions, which they did not have. The solution, as Nell McCafferty later revealed, was that 'We bought aspirin instead, to declare to the customs officers in Dublin, on the reasonable assumption that those men in uniform would not be able to tell the difference, never having themselves seen a contraceptive pill.'[42] This was also, somehow, perfectly attuned to the state of Ireland. The state, in the form of the customs men, pretended not to see non-existent sexual contraband. The women pretended to have broken laws when in fact they had been horribly law-abiding all along. Something big was simultaneously both happening and not happening.

All I 'knew' was that these fabulous, scandalous, mischief-making women had defied everybody and somehow managed to get away with it. Like the customs men and many of the women themselves, I would not have known a condom or a Pill if I saw one. But they had created a suspension of disbelief – this aspirin is really the Pill – that was also the beginning of a suspension of belief. They made the church and the state look powerless. This was still very much a theatrical illusion. But for me, too, it was an act of liberation.

15

1972: Death of a Nationalist

I had no idea I was going to shout 'Up the IRA' at the Taoiseach, Jack Lynch. It was a Sunday in March 1972 in Croke Park, the stadium of the Gaelic Athletic Association. A big charity walk had terminated there, with around 20,000 people, most of them kids like me, watching a concert. I was wearing a Red Cross uniform with a fetching black beret. I had put a few plasters on a few sore feet. I was allowed to wander around between the stand and the platform, as if I had some kind of official status.

The master of ceremonies was Father Michael Cleary. He was wearing a long black leather coat, belted across the middle with a big metal buckle, that, with his slightly scruffy beard and tousled hair, made him look like a roadie for a particularly debauched rock band. Dickie Rock and The Miami Showband played a few songs, but I wasn't interested. Then there was a huge German brass band, maybe 120 of them, in lederhosen and feathered hats.

I was waiting for Crumlin's own stars, Phil Lynott and Thin Lizzy. Brian Downey played the drums like tom-toms and Philo chanted Buffalo Buffalo Buffalo Buffalo Buffalo Buffalo Gal. It was a world away from anywhere we were, somewhere out on the Great Plains. The band passed me as they made their way back across the pitch. I shouted, 'Hi, Philo' and he waved at me. It was still in my head: Buffalo Buffalo Buffalo Buffalo.

I was going to wander off, but then Cleary announced the ballad group The Wolfe Tones. They were four big hairy men with big round badges on their jackets that said Up the IRA. They already occupied a lucrative niche market in recreational republicanism, belting out the sentiments that could not be spoken on the radio but could be sung. (Charles Haughey would say, in 1984, that 'they're a bit of the ould rabble-rousin', but sure they're alright!'[1])

They sang 'Seán South Of Garryowen'. They sang 'The Men Behind The Wire', a big hit in the Irish charts, about the men who were interned without trial by the Unionist regime in Belfast:

Armoured cars and tanks and guns
Came to take away our sons
But every man will stand behind
The men behind the wire.

In the schoolyard, we had our version, a paean to masturbation:

Every man will stand behind
The man who pulls his wire.

But the way they sang it, with a thunderous, implacable force, left no room for sniggering. They were like armoured cars themselves. They crashed into 'Come Out Ye Black and Tans' and battered on into 'A Nation Once Again':

Freedom comes from God's right hand,
And needs a Godly train;
And righteous men must make our land
A Nation once again!

They roared to an end, clenching their fists and waving them in the air. They shouted Up the IRA! and stalked off holding their instruments as if they were heading straight for the barricades. I wasn't on the Great Plains anymore.

What happened next was also politics, but only if that word were translated into a completely different language. There was a Gaelic football match between Dáil deputies and senators from both Fianna Fáil and Fine Gael, supposedly representing the four green fields of a United Ireland, Munster–Leinster versus Connacht–Ulster. There were actually no Ulster politicians on the team.[2] Ulster politicians were otherwise engaged. Father Michael Cleary took off his big leather coat and refereed the game. Middle-aged men chased around after the ball but mostly seemed interested in barging and pushing each other. Half the time, there were bodies sprawled around the pitch.

Weirdly, there were some striking-looking young Black men on both teams. They were cadets from Zambia, who were training with the Irish army. They had been brought along for the event and, when various politicians failed to turn up, persuaded to make up the numbers. They clearly had no idea how to play the game, but they loped around with a speed and grace that made the red-faced TDs seem even more pitiful. The surrealism deepened at half-time when one of the politicians circled the field in a bedstead that had a bicycle built into it. The game resumed for a while, until Cleary, either on a whim or because he was afraid that some of the fat men would have heart attacks, peremptorily declared it over.

It was at this point that Jack Lynch left the stand and came down onto the pitch to present a trophy to the captain of whichever team of politicians had just been declared the victors. I was lurking on the sideline, near the entrance to the tunnel. I wasn't expecting him. I moved out of his way and he strode onto the pitch, a place he had graced many times as an All-Ireland winning hurler. When he had passed about two yards ahead of me, I heard myself shouting at him: Up the IRA! He didn't turn around. Somebody else shouted out, 'Give him a kiss, Jack' when Lynch presented the cup to the winning captain, but he ignored the joke with the same studied insouciance with which he disregarded my catcall.

I looked around to see if anyone was coming to get me, but it seemed no one had noticed. I slinked away. I didn't know what had come over me. It was something about the passion of those Wolfe Tones songs being followed by the farce of the politicians' football game. The disjunction had opened up a black hole and I had been sucked into it for a moment. All I knew about how I really felt was that I did not know how to feel about what Irish politics meant at that moment.

Two months earlier, we were having our dinner (in the middle of the day as everyone did then) in Aughavannagh Road. My father arrived back on his break from work. Usually, when he was with us for the meal, we would chat about school or sport or funny passengers he had on the bus that morning. But this day he was white-faced and solemn. He asked us all to be quiet and then he spoke to my mother: 'Mary, we have to face it. Me and the boys are going to be up in the North, fighting. It's coming. There's no choice now. It's just the way it's going to be. It'll be them or us. We have to be ready for it.' I don't think any of us said anything at all. We just finished our dinner in silence and then went back to school. I was stunned, terrified, but also excited. It was a big thing to think about, this civil war that was going to shape our destinies.

My father was not given to such gestures. He had always been sceptical of Irish nationalism. His own family connections to England, and indeed to the British army, made him acutely aware of the complications that Anglophobia elided. His childhood left him with a horror of violence, at least outside the boxing ring. He wasn't relishing the imminence of all-out war on the island. He was simply accepting its inevitability and warning us that, when it did come, complicated feelings would not matter. In the end, the Catholics of Derry and Belfast were our people and we would have to take up arms to defend them. Choices and ambiguities would evaporate.

Two days earlier, the British army's Parachute Regiment had opened fire on the streets of Derry, after an illegal but essentially peaceful civil rights march against internment. They killed thirteen unarmed people, fatally wounded another and wounded seventeen others. It was, as the Derry coroner Major Hubert O'Neill put it, 'sheer unadulterated murder'. We could see it on television. We could hear the local priest, Father Edward Daly, describe how he was fleeing from the shooting when he saw a kid called Jackie Duddy laughing at the undignified sight of a clergyman running. 'The next thing he suddenly gasped and threw his hands up in the air and fell on his face. He asked me: "Am I going to die?" and I said no, but I administered the last rites. I can remember him holding my hand and squeezing it.' Duddy was seventeen, but as Daly said, 'he only looked about 12'.[3]

RTÉ was running footage of the massacre and interviews with eyewitnesses, all of whom said that the people who were killed were running away and that the British army had not been fired on. The very fact that thirty-one civilians had been shot while no soldiers had come to any harm underlined the plausibility of these accounts. But the army claimed that they were responding to attacks from snipers and nail bombers, that over 200 shots had been fired at them, and that at least four of those killed were wanted terrorists. (They were not.) It was this attempt to create an alternative reality that gave the event its apocalyptic quality. It was not just that innocent people had been so openly murdered by the British state. It was that an official fiction was being woven in real time, right in front of our eyes. The dead would not even be truly remembered – they would be buried in lies.

In our world, on the other hand, the Derry dead were immediately subsumed into history. The events of 30 January 1972 were coupled with those of 21 November 1920, when British soldiers opened fire indiscriminately on players and spectators in Croke Park. The same number of people – fourteen – had been killed. So the same name was given to the day: Bloody Sunday. Even though the victims of this second Bloody Sunday were emphatically not members of the IRA or part of any armed insurrection, this act of naming brought them into the capacious company of the martyred dead and defined the Derry massacre as another chapter in the long narrative of Ireland's fight for freedom.

Within the British and Unionist worlds, it could be imagined that telling lies about what happened would diminish it. Within the Irish nationalist world, it magnified it. If the official version – soon formalized as a state cover-up by an 'inquiry' headed by Lord Widgery – was so much at odds with the facts, maybe the facts themselves were not even the whole horror. In the Dáil, Des Foley, a TD for a breakaway hardline faction of Fianna Fáil around Neil Blaney, claimed, 'There were more than 13 people shot last Sunday. People were taken away and shot and are now in the [River] Foyle; no one knows where they will re-appear. People were taken away who have not turned up.'[4] It was easy, in the circumstances, to believe this, to believe, indeed, anything.

I remember, around this time, a party down in the flats where my father had grown up. His mother had died and his half-sister

Mary, who had been in the British forces, was home and living there. There was, as always, a sing-song. When it was my turn, I sang Dominic Behan's ballad about Fergal O'Hanlon, the kid who had been killed alongside Seán South in 1957. It is in O'Hanlon's voice:

This island of ours has for long been half free,
Six counties are under John Bull's tyranny.
And most of our leaders are greatly to blame
For shirking their part in the patriot game.

I could sense as I sang it the rapt attention in the room. I was undoing the debacle of 'The Black And Tan Gun' in 1966 – the first time as farce, the second time as nationalist tragedy. I closed my eyes and felt my way into that darkness. I was the dying O'Hanlon.

And now I am dying, my body's all holes.
I think of the traitors who've bargained and sold.
I'm sorry my rifle has not done the same
To the quislings who sold out the patriot game.

There was complete silence for a moment, then shouts of 'Good man!' and long applause. People clapped me on the back. Mary said, 'You sang that with such passion. You're going to carry the torch.' Nobody seemed at all bothered that Mary had been in the British army. I know I wasn't. The incongruity was scarcely worth noticing. Ambiguities were being swept away.

The day after the Bloody Sunday massacre, Bernadette Devlin attempted to interrupt the Home Secretary Reginald Maudling in the House of Commons, after he claimed that the army had 'returned fire' against those who were 'attacking them with firearms and with bombs'. When the Speaker prevented her from doing so, she ran down the gangway shouting, 'If I am not allowed to inform the House of what I know, I'll inform Mr Maudling of what I feel.' She launched herself at him and hit him three times in the face.[5] The moment was eloquent: if what was known could not be said, what was felt could be expressed only in violence.

There was a spontaneous demonstration in Cork of about 10,000 people, some of whom burned a Union Jack. The lord mayor of Cork, T. J. O'Sullivan, told protestors that 'If they want murder, they'll have murder – one of theirs will go for each of ours.'[6] O'Sullivan did not represent the IRA, Sinn Féin or even Fianna Fáil. He was solid Fine Gael stock. On 1 February, members of the Provisional IRA threw a bomb made of twenty pounds of gelignite at the British embassy on Merrion Square in Dublin, while a crowd of some 7,000 sang 'A Nation Once Again'. Women who were about to give birth, or had just done so, stuck their heads out of the windows of Holles Street maternity hospital across the road and joined in the singing.[7]

Two days later, the crowd outside the embassy had grown to about 35,000. The entire membership of Fianna Fáil's student branch at University College Dublin marched to the embassy.[8] At one point, the telephonists from a nearby exchange arrived and began to recite the Rosary. Most of the crowd joined in, and so did the policemen guarding the building. Some protestors started to throw bottles and rocks. Then a young man was seen swinging from a second-storey balcony seven houses down from the embassy. He made his way along from balcony to balcony. When he got to the front of the embassy, he unfurled an Irish tricolour and ran it up the flagstaff. Two other men made their way to him by the same route. They produced a hammer and a hatchet, smashed through the reinforced windows and kicked in the wooden shutters. Another man joined them. He poured petrol inside the building. He called out to the crowd and someone threw him up a box of matches.

As the flames took hold inside, there was an apparently co-ordinated fusillade of petrol bombs from the crowd. As the building began to be engulfed, a woman called out, 'Will you join me in saying the Rosary? The Rosary has saved Ireland in the past and it will save it again now.'[9] But this time, nobody was interested. The conflagration was much more satisfying. It was also, in its way, more modern, more American. As the flames rose, the crowd, instead of saying its prayers, chanted 'Burn, Baby, Burn' – a slogan learned from the Watts riots in Los Angeles in 1965.

The police did not try to arrest anyone and the fire brigade could not get through to the front of the building. Cynics pointed out that, had the east side of the Georgian square been consumed, as it might well have been, a nice block of historic central Dublin would have opened up for lucrative redevelopment. A more plausible motive for letting the embassy burn was the sense that, as Foley suggested in the Dáil, if the crowd's anger was not consumed in those flames, they might have marched the very short distance away to Leinster House. The IRA and their supporters had characterized Lynch as a quisling whose government was failing to protect the beleaguered Catholics of the North. It was not impolitic to let the immediate rage burn itself out against British, rather than domestic, targets.

This was the moment, nonetheless, when Catholics in the Republic might have been fused with their Northern brethren in a single nationalist revolt. A woman standing at a bus queue in Dublin a few days after the embassy attack captured the way in which indifference was shading into engagement: 'Well I was never up there, and I'm inclined to think of them as different people, with the accent and all, but when I saw their photographs in the paper and thought they could be our men complaining or making a protest about something down here, and to have them all gunned down, it would be terrible, and I felt outraged that the British should do this and I felt that whatever the rights and wrongs, they would know how we felt when we burned down their embassy.'[10]

This was what my father was telling us that day at dinner. 'How we felt' was fully aligned with Bernadette Devlin's 'what I feel'. And it was what I felt, too. The massacre had made it all too easy to conclude that there would have to be a reckoning and that the Unionists, the Protestants, the British, could be reckoned with only by violence. If they want murder, they'll have murder. And if murder is to be the point from now on, then the IRA was the way to do it. There was something almost comforting in this grim clarity.

But then murder came too close. A fortnight after Bloody Sunday, a kid visited his mother, who lived on Sperrin Road, just off the Crumlin Road, and about a mile and a half from our house. Tommy McCann was eighteen. He had joined the British army when he was fifteen, following his older brother Daniel, who was stationed in Cornwall. He had asked to be transferred to a barracks in Northern Ireland because he missed his widowed mother Kathleen and wanted to be able to visit her. Somebody spotted him in a pub in the city centre. When he left, he was bundled into a car. His body was found the next day at Newtownbutler just across the Border in Co. Fermanagh. His hands were tied behind his back. He had been gagged, hooded, shot in the back of the head and dumped in a field.[11]

At school, we whispered about this, but the adults didn't want to say much. The IRA, unusually, did not claim responsibility, though the word was that the Officials had done it. The murder of a working-class kid from Dublin didn't quite fit the story of heroic resistance to oppression in the North. But the British didn't acknowledge it either. When he was buried in Mount Jerome Cemetery, it was without military honours. There were no representatives from the British army or embassy. Daniel McCann, on official advice, did not travel home for his brother's funeral. Regimental emblems and messages were removed from the wreaths. Only a handful of his friends and family members followed his coffin.

The problem was that Tommy McCann was us, too. We all knew kids who joined the British army or had fathers who had served in it. The same men who came for him could have come for my uncles or my aunts decades earlier but in the same cause. Even for my schoolfriends who did not have these familial connections, the brutality of his murder, the dumping of his body like a carcass, the pitiful funeral, the inability of his mother to grieve in public, left a profound unease. Is this what the fight against British imperialism was going to look like, hooded kids, crying for their mothers, being shot in the back of the neck?

The IRA had split in December 1969 (with Sinn Féin doing so a month later). The Officials, increasingly influenced by Marxist ideology, wanted to pursue a more social class-based political strategy and in particular to allow Sinn Féin members to contest elections for the Dublin, Belfast and London parliaments and take their seats if successful. Their leadership worried about the likelihood that conflict on the streets of Northern Ireland would descend into a sectarian bloodbath. The Provisionals (known as the Provos) had no such qualms and were committed to a much narrower, purely military, struggle for a United Ireland. In 1972, both were happy to shoot at the British army. Both were illegal in the UK and Ireland, but some streams of public and political opionion in the Republic were still sympathetic to the Provos, who were seen as less of a threat to the established order south of the Border.

Neither wing of the IRA really had a clue what to do with all the emotion Bloody Sunday had unleashed. The Officials' response to the massacre of civilians was a massacre of civilians. They smuggled a huge car bomb into the Parachute Regiment's headquarters in Aldershot – an apparent military coup. But it killed no soldiers, just the Catholic chaplain, a gardener and five female cleaners, Jill Mansfield, Margaret Grant, Thelma Bosley, Cherie Munton and Joan Lunn. I remember feeling a sense of elation at the first reports that the bomb had gone off, the delicious savour of revenge. The Officials claimed at first that they had killed at least twelve British officers, a number that roughly matched the Derry dead.[12] Justice had been served and the world had been put to rights. And then, as the names and occupations of the real victims emerged, I felt dizzy with nausea. My own mother worked as a cleaner. I could imagine those women and the children they left behind.

Less than two weeks later, the Provisional IRA planted a bomb in a restaurant, the Abercorn, in the middle of Belfast's shopping district at 4.30 on a Saturday afternoon. The place was well known as a favourite resort of women who would go for coffee and cake after buying clothes. The two bombers did not stand out because they were teenage girls, not unlike many of the seventy people they killed or mutilated. The two who died – Ann Owens and Janet Bereen – were twenty-two and twenty-one respectively. Both, as it happened, were Catholics. Janet's father, an anaesthetist at Royal Victoria Hospital, took part in emergency operations on the victims, unaware that his daughter was among them. But the image that stuck in my mind was that of two sisters who had been shopping for a wedding dress. One lost both legs, an arm and an eye. The other lost both legs.

Because the Abercorn was Catholic-owned and the dead and mutilated were Catholics, we thought at first that this must be the work of Loyalist paramilitaries. This was easy enough – it was an absolute outrage, savage, indefensible. When it became clear that the IRA had done it, it just seemed incomprehensible. How did maiming random young women balance the moral scales against Bloody Sunday? Since I had already decided, when I thought it must be the act of the other side, that this was monstrous, it was impossible to change my mind now.

And yet, just a fortnight after that I was in Croke Park, shouting Up the IRA! at Jack Lynch. It was not, I think, just the force of The Wolfe Tones or the absurdity of the politicians' football match. It was also that, at that moment, I thought that the war was over and that the IRA had won. Just three days earlier, the British prime minister Edward Heath, announced the suspension of the government of Northern Ireland and the transfer of its powers to London. The hated Unionist regime at Stormont had fallen and there would be direct rule from Westminster pending a new settlement. The parliament of Northern Ireland, established at the time of partition in 1921, held its last ever meeting on 28 March 1972. The Orange State was no more.

Half a century of history was over. The Provisional IRA seemed to declare victory, claiming that the end of Stormont 'places us in a somewhat similar position to that prior to the setting up of partition and the two statelets'.[13] Thus, that weekend, it was possible to forget Tommy McCann and the women shopping for the wedding dress who had their legs blown off. Horrible things had happened but, after all, they had served a purpose.

While I was in Croke Park, in the Bogside in Derry, a young IRA man discussed the problem of his forthcoming redundancy with Nell McCafferty. What was he going to do with himself? 'I'm wheeling myself around like a spare tyre', he complained. 'People don't realise that I just cannot go down town and have a cup of tea like everyone else. I can't go and collect the dole and I can't look for a job, even if there is one going.'[14] McCafferty witnessed a British army officer addressing a crowd of young stone-throwers in the Bogside: 'Look here, chaps, you did get direct rule. What more do you want?' A local activist listed some political demands – the release of prisoners and the withdrawal of the army and police from the Bogside – and then added his own: 'I want more trees in Shipquay Street and then they've got to bring back the Chinese restaurants.'

The mother of Martin McGuinness, the twenty-one-year-old leader of the IRA in Derry, who had been systematically destroying the centre of the city, until, as the local left-wing activist Eamonn McCann, put it, 'it looked like it had been hit from the air', worried about what her son would do now: 'His trade's been interrupted. His father is a welder, his brothers bricklayers and carpenters, but what will become of Martin? That's why they'll have to get an amnesty, so's he can get back to work and not always be on the run.'[15]

There was even a wistful realization that people might miss the excitement of the violence. A local woman, contemplating the probability of a return to dull normalcy, asked rhetorically, 'What in God's name will we talk about now?' The man who wanted the Chinese restaurants back reflected that in October 1968, he had been 'nothing'. 'Now I'm king of all I survey… I was somebody for a while. I've been on television, on radio, in the newspapers… I was a star, me that was only on the dole. I even gave an interview to an Egyptian newspaper and I drank vodka with the Russians.'

Now that the violence was over, the world's media would move on and Derrymen on the dole would no longer be stars. Local newspapers worried about how they would fill their pages and sustain their readership. Malachi O'Doherty, a young reporter for the Belfast *Sunday News* recalled that the staff 'agonised over how to retain its high circulation and hold the public interest when the violence had stopped'.[16] I had no such worries. My father my brother and I would not be going up North with guns. My Up the IRA! was a valedictory salute, but also a cry of relief. A foreordained future had been averted. Any number of new ones were possible – for me and for the island.

But the Provos also had something new: the car bomb. It was, for them, the perfect weapon: it could be deployed to cause immense destruction at little risk to its own members. In March, their propaganda paper *Republican News* was astonishingly frank in pointing this out. Previously, it said, 'four or five armed men placed low-powered bombs which only destroyed a single shop or building. Quite obviously, the chances of being caught by the enemy were great.' In city centres, 'men on foot doing this type of job would have no chance of escape'. But, while it was not sure whether the first car bomb had been used earlier that month in Lisburn or on Shipquay Street in Derry, 'The Lisburn bomb destroyed eighty shops and the Derry bomb destroyed an entire street.'[17]

There was no mention at all of the risk to innocent civilians. What mattered was the diminished chances of the IRA's volunteers being confronted by, and therefore having to engage with, the army or the armed police. This is a reality that the Provos would later try, with great success, to hide under heroic images of brave volunteers shooting it out with heavily armed Brits. Their war was driven as much by technology as by ideology. The car bomb revolutionized the mathematics of urban conflict. It was not just that it multiplied the destructiveness of a single operation. Much more tellingly, it changed the location of risk, diminishing it for the perpetrators at the expense of civilians. (Henceforth, the biggest dangers to IRA members would be from accidental explosions of its own bombs and from being killed by their own side in internecine feuds.)

But the car bomb also diminished blame. Both a literal and a moral distance were created between the act and its consequences. A mode of operation was created: leave the bomb in a high street, walk calmly away, have someone call in a 'warning' a few minutes before the car was timed to explode, not so that lives could be saved (it was usually too late for that) but so that the IRA could say it was all the fault of the authorities for not reacting quickly enough. Sometimes, as with a 100-pound car bomb the Provos left on Donegall Street in Belfast on 20 March 1972, killing six people and injuring more than a hundred, the call gave false information that deliberately directed shoppers towards the bomb.

These new economies of risk and blame made it highly attractive for the Provos to carry on. The Official IRA effectively called off its campaign on 29 May, after hostile public reaction to its murder of a nineteen-year-old local boy, William Best, a member of the British army's Royal Irish Rangers, home on leave in the Catholic Creggan area. The Provisionals then followed suit, announcing a ceasefire on 22 June. Both the new Secretary of State for Northern Ireland William Whitelaw and the leader of the Labour Opposition Harold Wilson separately met an IRA delegation, including its rising stars Gerry Adams and Martin McGuinness, in London. (Adams had told a British intermediary, P. J. Woodfield, just before the ceasefire that he planned to go to university when it was all over.[18]) But the Provos resumed their violence on 13 July.

It was through the power of the car bomb that they declared their intentions. On 21 July, they set off more than twenty bombs in just over an hour in Belfast city centre, including the bus and rail stations, a motorway bridge, a hotel, a bar and a taxi office. They killed nine people and injured 130. Seventy-seven of the victims were women and children. The horror was compounded by the panic of crowds rushing from one explosion into the path of the next. Parts of human bodies were scattered all over city streets. The image I remembered from the TV was policemen with shovels scooping remains into black plastic bags. The day soon acquired its own name, one that was not part of the Irish nationalist lexicon: Bloody Friday.

The mentality of the people who inflicted this suffering was another example of the unknown known. Brendan Hughes, a close ally of Gerry Adams, organized the Bloody Friday massacre. He later explained his thinking: 'I sort of knew that there were going to be casualties, either the Brits could not handle so many bombs or they would allow some to go off because it suited them to have casualties… It was a major, major operation but we never intended to kill people. I feel a bit guilty about it because as I say there was no intention to kill anyone that day… I don't hold myself personally responsible for all that took place there… but certainly I take some of the responsibility.'[19] I knew there were going to be casualties but I never intended to kill anyone – this unknown known would allow two generations of ordinary young men and women to see themselves as curiously passive creatures, their actions almost as impersonal to them as their victims were.

On the other hand Loyalist murders, perpetrated by the Ulster Volunteer Force (UVF) and the Ulster Defence Association (UDA), were becoming more personal. On the evening after Bloody Friday, a gang of Loyalist paramilitaries kidnapped a random Catholic man called Francis Arthurs. They beat and tortured him before shooting him seven times. One of the gang was Lenny Murphy, who was twenty. This is believed to have been the first killing of at least eighteen he was directly involved in. He became the leader of the Shankill Butchers, the most sadistic outfit of the Troubles, named for its use of butcher's knives. Loyalists used car bombs for mass killings, too, but this style of intimate murder, revelling in extreme and individualised cruelty, was distinctive. Ten days before Bloody Friday, four young men, who had connections to both the UVF and the UDA, broke into a house in North Belfast occupied by a Catholic widow and her three children. Two of them sexually assaulted the mother. They then brought her fourteen-year-old son, David McClenaghan, into the room. He was mentally disabled. Mrs McClenaghan 'pleaded with the gunman not to touch the boy as he was retarded and he looked so afraid'. He shot the boy dead anyway and when his mother tried to shield him shot her, too, leaving her with permanent injuries.[20] Later in the year, a UDA gang tortured to death another mentally disabled Catholic, Patrick Benstead, and burned a cross into his back.[21]

There would be too many killings to apply a neat taxonomy, but a rough pattern was emerging. Loyalist murders were often intended to be luridly gruesome. The purpose was to terrify the Catholic population into submission – for that purpose, the more hideous the better. IRA murders were intended to create a more general sense of anarchy, to make it clear that Northern Ireland was ungovernable under British rule. For that purpose, the more impersonal, the more distanced the perpetrator was from the victim, the better. The people who died in car bombs did not matter – they were not chosen or singled out. They were killed to make a point about mayhem – any mangled body would do.

Another distinction was that while Loyalists were happy for the mutilated bodies of their victims to be found and seen, the Belfast IRA, in 1972, instituted a new policy: disappearance. Most of the IRA's killings were meant to demonstrate the inherent instability of Northern Ireland. But there was a subcategory: those that were about the IRA's own government of Catholic communities. The killing of 'touts' (those who gave information to the authorities or those who were accused of doing so because they had somehow stepped out of line) was its internal policing operation. Because the victims were members of its own community, it was not convenient to claim their murders. They were instead buried in secret graves, precisely so that their fates would be unknown. This strategy of disappearance began in the summer of 1972, its most notorious victim, Jean McConville, the widowed mother of ten children, who was killed and buried in December.

The IRA unit that carried out these disappearances was literally called the Unknowns.[22] The purpose of their operations was to create a zone of radical uncertainty, in which some of the victims were undead, condemned to hover like ghosts between existence and oblivion. This was a special kind of torment in a Catholic culture, the endless torment of the unquiet grave whose occupant can neither rest nor depart, of the bereaved who cannot grieve.

One of the dead of Bloody Friday, Stephen Parker, was a fourteen-year-old Protestant boy who played French horn in the Ulster Youth Orchestra. Another, Rose McCartney, a twenty-seven-year-old Catholic, was a well-known singer of traditional Irish folk songs. The new style of armed struggle did not lend itself to heroic ballads. In late 1972, the great American anthropologist Henry Glassie was observing a night of drinking and singing in the village of Swadlinbar. The village is on the Cavan side of the border with Fermanagh and thus on the southern side of the contested divide between Northern Ireland and the Republic of Ireland. It was common on 'a Sunday for south Fermanagh men to cross the Border past the blasted Customs hut for a drink in Swad. They came out of the cold, bursting through the frigid doorway to pack along the counter and around the shop, muffled in warm clothes. Huddles of men traded cigarettes and sent emissaries to the bar... Heat and patternless sound increased until the right request met the right mood within the men obliged to entertain.'[23]

As the sing-song proceeds, 'the topic becomes Irish heroes, Irish martyrs'. The Border country is strongly nationalist and the violent conflict in Northern Ireland is at its height. Dead members of the IRA from previous eras are hymned in ballads. 'Owney McBrien sings *Seán South*. Hugh Collins sings *Kevin Barry*. Feelings tighten, heighten, expand.' The song ends and the drinkers begin to chat again, until a young man 'trembling with excitement' steps up to address them: 'There's only one or two words I can say to you tonight... The people of Swadlinbar is enjoyin' themselves and *Seán Mac Stiofáin is dying in a hunger strike*.' He calls for a 'good clap' for the hunger striker.

Mac Stiofáin is a martyr in the making. He was a key figure in the foundation of the Provisional IRA, and had become its chief-of-staff. He was sentenced to six months in prison in the Republic for membership of the IRA but had already begun a hunger strike, which he continued for fifty-seven days. The connection the excited young man is making is an obvious one: like Kevin Barry, Seán South and Fergal O'Hanlon, Mac Stiofáin is in the process of dying for Ireland.

But there is no clap for Mac Stiofáin. It is not, Glassie believes, that the drinkers are out of sympathy with his impending martyrdom or the IRA. It is rather that they are discomfited by the sudden irruption of the present into the past, of a barbed and living history into the heroic version of the 'struggle' encoded in the songs. 'The speaker's words were too direct. The way to discuss the present aloud in the pub is to offer images from the past and to offer them in a way at once patriotic and entertaining. Public words should be referential and complex. More cannot be done; more contention would make life impossible.'

The young man had disrupted an unspoken code of manners. Inferences about the present may be drawn from the past, but they must remain at the level of inference. Emotions that may be enjoyed when they are formalized in a ballad are not enjoyable when they are spoken in a political rallying cry. The passage of time has filtered out all the ambivalence and unease about acts of violence, so that when they have been enshrined in song they are pure and simple. But the violence of the present has not yet been processed in this way. By introducing current conflict into the celebration of dead martyrs, the young man has gauchely contaminated the purity of the past. In Irish memory, 'There's a great gap', as John Synge's Pegeen Mike says in *The Playboy of the Western World*, 'between a gallous story and a dirty deed.'

In 1972, 1,853 bombs were planted. Four hundred and ninety-seven people were killed. Just seventy-four of them were members of either wing of the IRA, and many of those had been killed by their own bombs. Just eleven were Loyalist paramilitaries. Most of the dead – 259 – were civilians. They were not martyrs. They had not sacrificed themselves – they had been sacrificed. There was nothing, in our tradition, to sing about. I never sang 'The Patriot Game' at parties again.

But the poet James Simmons took up the challenge of making ballads about the unmartyred dead. Ten days after Bloody Friday, the IRA systematically car-bombed the peaceful and religiously mixed village of Claudy in Co. Derry, setting three devices, so that people fleeing from one explosion would move towards the next. Intelligence at the time suggested that the attack had been directed by a Catholic priest, James Chesney, who was believed to be quartermaster of the South Derry IRA.[24] Nine ordinary civilians were massacred, including nine-year-old Kathryn Eakin, who was cleaning the front windows of her parents' shop.

Simmons wrote and sang 'The Ballad Of Claudy':

For an old lady's legs are ripped off, and the head
of a man's hanging open, and still he's not dead.
He is screaming for mercy, and his son stands and stares
and stares, and then suddenly, quick, disappears.
And Christ, little Katherine Aiken is dead,
and Mrs McLaughlin is pierced through the head.
Meanwhile to Dungiven the killers have gone,
and they're finding it hard to get through on the phone.

We didn't have a phone in Aughavannagh Road – very few working-class people did in 1972. On 1 December, my father was still at work when we were watching the nine o'clock news. Two bombs had just gone off in Dublin. The first was at Liberty Hall. Twenty minutes later, there was an explosion on Sackville Place, a side street that ran off the city's main drag, O'Connell Street. When we heard the newsreader say Sackville Place we all just sat there, numbed. That was where the canteen for the bus workers was. We'd often gone in there with my father, for chips and a glass of milk. When word came through that two men were thought to have been killed there, it was obvious to us that they were probably busmen. We just sat there for an hour, my grandfather, my mother and me. Nobody knew what to say – even to articulate what we were thinking might somehow make it real. I had no idea how much time had passed until we heard the key in the door. My father hadn't been in the canteen – he had just finished his shift and come home.

It was two other bus conductors, George Bradshaw and Thomas Duffy, both fathers of little children, who had been blown to bits. But I knew I was never again going to feel that such people were somebody else.

16

1973: Into Europe

In July 1972, my father was working on an early morning bus that went out on the quiet roads into the foothills of the Dublin Mountains. It was trundling along outside Enniskerry when he saw a very unusual sight for those times in Ireland: a group of men running along the side of the road in tracksuits. They were big men. They were also Black men. One of them was the person my father most adored in the whole world. The bus pulled up ahead of the group and my father jumped off to say hello to Muhammad Ali. He was in Dublin for a fight in Croke Park against Al 'Blue' Lewis, promoted by the same Butty Sugrue who had once claimed to have Admiral Nelson's head.

My father asked him if he would like a lift. Ali joked that he had left his wallet in his hotel and couldn't pay the fare. My father said he would make an exception for Ali and his entourage. They got on the bus and Ali said good morning to the few sleepy passengers, then got off and continued his training run. When he was telling us about this magical encounter, my father kept using the word 'beautiful' about Ali – the first time I had ever heard a man use it about another man.

This was the most exotic thing that had ever happened to any of us. But for the Americans who came with the boxers, Ireland was disappointingly unexotic. Diane Lewis, the girlfriend of 'Blue' Lewis's trainer Don Elbaum, and a professional dancer in Las Vegas, explained that prior to her arrival in Dublin, she had imagined Ireland to be full of cottages surrounded by fields. 'I was absolutely amazed at your hotels. I never dreamt you would have lifts; in fact, I was quite disappointed when I discovered I would not have to ascend long wooden staircases leading on to some rafter-type apartments. I reckoned on hotels being similar to enlarged farmhouses, with not another building in sight.'[1] She was more pleased with the Dublin night clubs that had 'floor shows and go-go girls... that American counterparts could hardly match.'

Ali himself, however, had a more serious interest in Ireland. He made it clear that, apart from winning the fight, his main ambition was 'to meet Miss Bernadette Devlin': 'Ali wants to have a long talk with the Mid-Ulster M.P., and hopes to put a series of penetrating questions to her about her role in politics, her philosophy, and the things she is trying to achieve in public life... He admires her very much.'[2] Devlin did in fact visit Ali's camp and had dinner with him. She would later recall that, even in the middle of a violent conflict, this fact was much more important to her constituents than anything else she had done: 'None of the other famous people I met impressed my constituents at all but they were all nearly shaking my hand after that – not because I had gone through hell for them – but because mine was the hand that had shaken the hand of Muhammad Ali.'[3] She would also confess late in life that she could recall relatively little about hitting Reginald Maudling in the House of Commons, 'but Ali I remember vividly'.

My father had also shaken the hand of the great man and, even vicariously, the idea of being associated with him was thrilling. So Ireland as a whole decided to take possession of him. During that visit, it was revealed that Ali's maternal great-grandfather, Abe Grady, was an O'Grady from Co. Clare. The *Limerick Leader* reported that 'To-day there's many an O'Grady from Clare, who regard Muhammad Ali as one of their own.' It also reminded its readers of equally famous members of the clan: 'Stanislaus O'Grady was the founder and first master of the Clare Hunt; Sean O'Grady, in the forties, was prominent in Government circles and a Parliamentary Secretary. And, of course, O'Grady the poet was renowned during the era of the famed bardic school in the Burren.'[4]

Placing Muhammad Ali on the same familial roll of honour as O'Grady the Fianna Fáil TD was, at one level, just the usual Irish impulse of elevation by association, not fundamentally different from the absorption of JFK as 'one of our own'. Except, of course, that Ali had changed his name precisely to reject the history of slavery encoded within it. For Ali, this was a sore subject. He was acutely aware of the racist narrative in which his 'white blood' could be used to explain away his greatness. He also presumed that this part of his ancestry was rooted in coercion. He told Cathal O'Shannon in an interview for RTÉ that the Irish 'have names like O'Connor and Grady and Kennedy. Africans have names like Lumumba, Nkrumah... We have names like Grady and Clay and Hawkins and Smith and Jones and Johnson but we're black.'[5]

The Grady part of his heritage in fact contained a more complex history than he knew at the time. Abe Grady was not a slave owner. He had married an emancipated African-American woman in Kentucky. And, while the insistence of journalists on asking him questions about his Irish roots threatened to ignite Ali's anger, he defused a possible row with a graceful dismissal: 'You can never tell. There was a lot of sneakin' around in them days.' There was no better way to shut down a controversy in Ireland than by hinting that, if you really wanted to talk about it, you would have to talk about sex.

For Ali, the connection was political, not genealogical. His desire to meet Bernadette Devlin reciprocated the identification of the civil rights movement in Northern Ireland with that in the US. He presumably saw his own persecution for his opposition to the Vietnam War mirrored in Devlin's imprisonment for four months in 1970. But in Ireland the attempt to possess Ali as a child of the Irish diaspora raised questions that were still unanswerable. Did this make Ali Irish-American, like JFK or Grace Kelly? How did being Black cohere with Irishness?

It was still impossible to imagine that this might ever become a question of the implications, not of emigration, but of immigration. When the Irish government published its white paper on its renewed attempt to join the European Economic Community in April 1970, it stated laconically that 'It was not considered likely that the treaty requirements for free movement of workers would have any significant effect on the Irish labour market.'[6] It was not a controversial claim. Nobody thought 'free movement' of people would mean an influx of white Europeans, never mind of people of African or Asian ethnicity.

I remember finding the notion of Ali's Irishness amusing and absurd. I said to a friend: 'If Muhammad Ali and General de Gaulle are Irish, maybe everybody in the world is.' For I had also been tickled pink in 1969 when Charles de Gaulle, having shocked France by stepping down as president, suddenly turned up in the tiny village of Sneem, Co. Kerry. The *Irish Times*, in an editorial, captured the surprise: 'The presence of General de Gaulle in Sneem, Co. Kerry, is almost as bizarre, in its first impact, as would be the announcement that Chairman Mao had arrived in Bangor, Co. Down to enjoy the amenities of Pickie Pool.'

De Gaulle stayed for six weeks. His only explanation for his presence was: 'I feel, perhaps because of the Irish blood running in my veins, that it is an instinct which attracted me towards Ireland at this time. One returns to the place of one's origins.'[7] De Gaulle's mother, it turned out, was descended from Patrick McCartan, an Irish Jacobite who fled to France in 1689. While in Ireland, Madame de Gaulle visited an old lady, Philomena O'Hara, in St Joseph's Rehabilitation Centre in Dublin, who was one of her distant McCartan relatives.

But the truth of de Gaulle's Irish sojourn was more prosaic and less flattering to our sense of global destiny. He wanted to be out of France while his successor was being chosen and to avoid all comment on the election. If he had gone to any of the neighbouring countries, his presence would have been taken as a matter of some political or historic significance. He chose Ireland precisely because it meant nothing. Jean Guéguinou, the diplomat who was dispatched from Paris to help de Gaulle with his arrangements, later explained that 'Ireland was a neutral country. It was a place without political significance for him at the time.'[8]

The irony was that it was de Gaulle himself who had done much to ensure that Ireland's political significance was so minimal. It was his veto on Britain's membership of the EEC that had ensured that Ireland's attempts to join had barely been considered. Even while the Irish were being flattered by his long stay and his

'Irish blood', the very reason for his visit – his resignation and replacement – had a much greater import. His absence was far more meaningful for Irish history than his presence. Without de Gaulle, the prospects of Britain and therefore Ireland being admitted to the European club were suddenly much brighter.

When I was twelve or thirteen, in the very early 1970s, a new phrase came into our language: we're into Europe. '*How are things?*' you'd ask, and the reply would be '*Ah sure, we're into Europe.*' Or, '*Isn't it a grand day?*', someone would say, and you'd answer '*Oh, it is, sure we're into Europe.*' We picked it up from a TV series called *Into Europe* that ran on RTÉ, presented by the suave and brilliant Justin Keating. For a year or two either side of Ireland's entry into what was then the EEC, the phrase lingered in our speech. It was a substitute for the usual expressions of contentment: grand, fine, terrific, couldn't be better, doin' mighty. Like so many Irish phrases, it was half ironic, half serious, tossed out with a rueful grin but containing some kind of truth.

The biggest thing that happened to Ireland since Independence was its formal entry into the EEC on 1 January 1973. It was the moment at which Ireland became officially a western country, fixed in space at last as part of the developed and democratic world. This was all the more important because, unofficially, it was not quite either of those things. It was not economically developed in the sense that its new partners like France or Germany were. And its democracy, though institutionally very well established, was not as certain as it looked. It had within it two great subversive forces – its own traditions of violence and martyrdom; and the continuing confusion of citizenship with Catholicism.

Thus, Ireland's entry into the EEC was not quite make-believe, more the other way around. It was an assertion of belief, an act of faith, that in turn would gradually make a reality. It said: this is who we are. And, slowly and often painfully, that is who we became.

Being European was the ultimate way of not being British. Lemass had set the tone in 1962 in an address to the EEC heads of state in Brussels: 'Ireland belongs to Europe by history, tradition and sentiment no less than by geography. Our destiny is bound up with that of Europe... Our people have always tended to look to Europe for inspiration, guidance and encouragement.'[9] This overlooked, as his listeners were surely aware, the small matter of the Second World War, when Ireland had abdicated from Europe's destiny. But it was also suitably humble: guidance and encouragement are what a good child expects from a parent. They were words Lemass could never have used about Britain.

An example of how this might work in daily life was the German manufacturer of mechanical handling equipment Steinbock of Moosburg, that opened a 60,000-square-foot plant in Galway in 1961, employing 240 men. The site had the remains of 'a regional sanitorium and rolling acres of grass and grey rock walls'. The transformation of a sanitorium into a factory for German-engineered machinery was emblematic of the sudden and radical change ushered in by the revolution of 1958. By way of reassurance, Steinbock's managing director, Dr Shattenhemel, presented the Bishop of Galway Michael Browne, a domineering ally of John Charles McQuaid known locally as Cross Michael, with a wood carving of the Madonna from Oberammergau and, more importantly, a cheque for the fund to build the gigantic new cathedral he was planning.[10] (Browne's monstrosity would include, when it was finished, an icon of JFK among the other saints and martyrs.)

Forty students from local technical schools were sent to Moosburg, outside Munich, to be trained, but the rest of the workforce was made up largely of local farm boys. Five German foremen were employed to control them. One of them, Joe Hoerhammer, later described the problems and how he dealt with them: 'We had very young men – fourteen, fifteen, sixteen, years of age. They did not understand about time at first. I had a whistle. Every morning I used to blow it, call them all together and count them before they settled down to work. Then in the evening I would blow my whistle again and count them again before they left work.'

The joint managing director, Sona Sevcik, recalled that more drastic methods were sometimes necessary to force the young men to understand that industrial work was not like farming.

'When it was haymaking time, they stayed away from work... The fellows just didn't turn up.' How did his foremen react? 'Normally enough. They beat their heads against the wall and yelled and told the boys they would be fired and so on. It was difficult, really, because they spoke hardly any English, but I think they made themselves clear.'[11]

Imagine if these were English foremen blowing whistles at Irish workers, yelling at them and banging their heads off the wall. This would have been a great scandal, an intolerable new chapter in the long history of oppression and domination. The IRA would certainly have got involved. Death threats would have been issued. Or imagine that this was not Ireland but any of the European countries that had been occupied by Nazis just twenty years earlier. That would not have ended well either. But Ireland had not been occupied by Nazis and the German foremen in Galway had the inestimable virtue of not being English.

In a talk he gave in 1977, Ken Whitaker recalled how, when he visited the shrines of Irish saints in churches in St Gallen and Salzburg, local Germanic saints shared the honours on the altars: 'I suppose Irish initiative and devotion needed eventually to be underpinned by German organisation and method!'[12] The image is interesting for its Catholicism – one of the most reassuring things about the EEC from an Irish perspective (and one of the least reassuring from a British) was that it was largely a Catholic project. But it also suggests a willingness to accept tough love if it came from the Continent and not from Britain. 'German organisation and method' would not be easily adapted to, but there was a broad sense among the managerial and political classes in Ireland that the rigour of EEC membership would be a necessary ordeal. And – crucially – that it would 'underpin' Irish 'devotion', that this bracing immersion in industrial modernity would buttress, not threaten, the Catholic hegemony.

The great contradiction in all of this was that this hope of escaping British domination was utterly dependent on what would happen to Britain. One thing almost no one really thought about was the possibility that Ireland would find itself committed to joining while the UK remained outside. The real, more plausible, fear was that things would work the other way around: the French, now that de Gaulle had departed, would allow the British to join, but not anyone else. In 1969, the Department of Foreign Affairs in Dublin was deeply concerned about rumours coming from Paris that the new president Georges Pompidou had been persuaded by Valéry Giscard d'Estaing that, while Britain should be admitted, the other applicant countries, Denmark, Norway and Ireland, should be offered merely some kind of associate status.[13]

The Action Committee for the United States of Europe, chaired by the EEC's founding father, Jean Monnet, expressed warm support for British membership but did not mention Ireland. Monnet himself suggested that opening negotiations with four states at the same time would mean 'certain failure'. Talks with the UK would be 'difficult enough' – 'Meanwhile certain relations can be maintained with the others.'[14] The Taoiseach Jack Lynch told Monnet that 'such a move would be disastrous for the Irish economy'. This was not an exaggeration. Ireland would lose its preferential status in the British market without having enhanced access to European ones.

Nor was it at all obvious that the British would be helpful in allowing the Irish to follow in their wake. When, in August 1970, the Irish diplomat Kevin Rush called to see Geoffrey Rippon, the Conservative minister who was going to lead the British side in negotiations on entry, he found that Rippon was 'going through the motions' of a routine courtesy call and 'clearly couldn't get rid of me quickly enough, or care less what I had to say'.[15]

The truth was that Ireland in the early 1970s wasn't much of a catch for the EEC. As de Gaulle's sojourn and the phenomenal popularity of Heinrich Böll's *Irish Journal* in Germany suggested, the country had a certain sentimental appeal. But much of that was tied up with the very things that so many Irish people – and particularly Irish women – were trying to get away from. Böll, in a postscript to a new edition of his book, written in 1967, lamented what was passing: 'nuns have practically disappeared from the newspapers; other things have disappeared too: the safety pins and the smells.' Worst of all, 'something has made its way to Ireland, that ominous something known as The Pill – and this something absolutely paralyzes me: the prospect that fewer children might be born in Ireland fills me with dismay.' He imagined the Pill 'not only approaching the incomparable beaches of green Erin, but reaching the last cottage in the bog, far away in the west, where Connaught begins, where the donkeys, consumed with love, bray goodnight to one another'.[16]

If Ireland was valued for its difference, its backwardness, its smells and safety pins and teeming children, its religiosity, why spoil it by making it just like the rest of the western world? And, in any event, as Whitaker wryly put it, 'No one so loves us as to want us in the EEC on our own terms'.[17]

Ireland was tiny – its population in 1971 was still a shade under three million, not much more than that of Paris. Even after a decade of modernization, it was still both relatively poor and highly dependent on the British economy. In 1973, Ireland's GDP per capita was still less than two-thirds (64.2 per cent) of the EEC average.[18] Ireland's total exports were worth little more than €1 billion, and the economy had a balance of trade of minus €340 million. Moreover, 55 per cent of the total value of exports went to Great Britain or Northern Ireland. Food, drink and tobacco products accounted for over 43 per cent of total exports. Women made up just 27 per cent of the total employed workforce. The amount of new foreign direct investment in Ireland in 1972, the year before the country went into Europe, was the equivalent of €16 million euro. (Thirty-five years later, it was €30 billion.)

Nor was Ireland going to be a significant contributor to the EEC's budget. Its contribution would be notionally in line with Ireland's share of the Community's total GNP, which was 0.6 per cent. But since it was agreed that less than half of this should be paid during a period of adjustment, Ireland's actual share in 1973 was to be, at most, 0.27 per cent.[19] On top of that, there was the small matter of an incipient civil war. Ireland made much – not without justification – of its standing as a stable democracy. But there was no telling where the increasingly vicious Troubles of the North might lead.

The EEC formally opened negotiations with Ireland on 30 July 1970. Less than three months earlier, on 6 May, the Taoiseach

Jack Lynch had issued a dramatic statement at three o'clock in the morning: he had requested the resignations of two of his most senior ministers, Neil Blaney and Charles Haughey, because they 'do not subscribe fully to the Government policy in relation to the present situation' in Northern Ireland. A third senior minister, Kevin Boland, resigned in support of Blaney and Haughey. The story as it unfolded was breathtaking: Haughey, as minister for finance, had used money voted for the 'relief of distress' in the North to support a plan to import arms from the Continent and smuggle them to the then embryonic Provisional IRA in Belfast. The plan had been thwarted by the Special Branch of the Irish police. Haughey, along with three others – a Belgian businessman, Albert Luykx (who had been a Nazi collaborator during the Second World War), an Irish army officer, Captain James Kelly, and a Belfast IRA activist, John Kelly – was charged with conspiring to import arms illegally.

All of them were acquitted. Haughey declared to his ecstatic supporters that the whole affair had been 'a political trial'.[20] The successful defence was immensely damaging to the Irish state – that the attempt to import the arms was not illegal because it was an official government action, known about in advance by Lynch. (Haughey also contended that he did not know that the consignment in question consisted of weapons but added that it would have made no difference had he done so.) Lynch and his supporters vehemently denied that he knew anything about the plot or that his government had ever authorized it. These opposing positions would continue to be maintained for the following decades.

The Arms Trial affair had thus become another great node of uncertainty. It presented two possibilities, each scarcely credible. One was that Lynch had smeared his own ministers, Haughey and Blaney, to consolidate his political position. The other was that Haughey, the most senior minister in the cabinet of a democratic republic, had used official funds to help create a private army across the Border. Neither, it seemed, could possibly be true – but one of them had to be. Or perhaps the truth was that there was no fixed truth, that this whole thing had happened because the state itself, in these early years of the Troubles, simply did not know what it was supposed to feel or think or do. Caught between the mythology of Catholic martyrdom with which I had grown up and the reality of what a private Catholic army would mean, it inhabited a swampy terrain where there was no firm footing. Maybe Lynch both knew and did not know.

Lynch, in any case, was able to re-establish his control over Fianna Fáil and the government. Haughey, for the moment, was marginalized. I have often wondered what would have happened if Haughey had managed at that moment to take power. For these were also the months in which the EEC was considering Ireland's membership. Would the place have seemed, not just too poor and underdeveloped to join the club, but too volatile, too unpredictable, too likely to be drawn into direct conflict with the most important of the other applicant states, Britain?

It was a great achievement of Irish diplomacy, in these strange circumstances, to present the country as normal enough to be let in. What remained, though, was to convince the Irish electorate in the referendum that was held on 10 May 1972. Fianna Fáil and Fine Gael strongly urged approval. The Labour Party and both wings of Sinn Féin were against. But so, remarkably, was much of the intellectual and cultural nexus of Irish left-liberalism. Justin Keating, who had given us our 'into Europe' catchphrase, had become a Labour Party TD and party spokesman on the EEC. Perhaps to overcompensate for his cosmopolitanism, he adopted a hysterical anti-German rhetoric: 'the origin of the EEC lies in Hitler's New Order. There is no difference in the basic outlook, the morality, the social system between the Germany of 1914, the Germany of 1939 and the EEC of 1972.'[21]

The Common Market Defence Campaign, formed to campaign for a No vote, had an impressive line-up of artists and intellectuals among its patrons: the great essayist Hubert Butler, the poet Austin Clarke, the 1916 Rising veteran and activist Máire Comerford, the playwright John B. Keane, the novelist Monk Gibbon, the actor Siobhán McKenna, the lawyer and anti-apartheid campaigner Kadar Asmal, the novelist and editor Peadar O'Donnell, my favourite singer Luke Kelly of The Dubliners and the academic sociologist and future president Michael D. Higgins.

Its declaration was a return to the apocalyptic pessimism of the mid-1950s: EEC membership would result in 'the depopulation of Ireland, the decline of our industry, the decimation of our farming population' and 'the eventual destruction of the Irish people as a viable distinct national community'.[22] It was The Vanishing Irish again, but this time the disappearance was going to result, not from the underdevelopment that led to mass emigration, but from the kind of development that the EEC would bring.

The gloom was rooted in a paradoxical lack of confidence in the existential condition of Ireland. Even after a decade of growth, it expressed a belief that everything – even the population – was still so fragile that it could be swept away at any moment. In the 1950s, this pessimism derived from a feeling of stasis: nothing was changing. Now, it expressed a fear of too much change, a sense that, in a world where Muhammad Ali and Charles de Gaulle were Irish, the term had no secure meaning.

Yet this intellectual and cultural angst turned out to be of almost no interest to most Irish people. Of the three applicant countries that held referendums (Britain did not do so until 1975), the Irish were by far the most fervently in favour of joining the EEC. In Ireland 83 per cent voted Yes; in Denmark it was 64 per cent; and the Norwegians rejected membership by 53 per cent to 47 per cent. (Norway's defection had the vast consequence for Ireland of increasing its notional share of the EEC budget from 0.6 per cent to 0.61 per cent.[23]) Getting 83 per cent of Irish people to agree on anything was remarkable – that they consented to such a huge change requires explanation.

It was not very surprising that urban Ireland voted for entry. The really significant fact – and the one that best captures the nature of the place in the early 1970s – is that rural Ireland was even more enthusiastic. The most conservative parts of the country – the ones most devoted to orthodox Catholicism and to traditional ways of life – were most determined to embrace this transformative moment. Indeed, voting for the EEC could be seen as a revolt against the urban radicals. The divide over Europe could be presented to farmers as a split between their honest, hard-working selves and pinkish, effete city types. The influential

Irish Farmers Journal asked its readers to note that: 'Most of the voices on the radio and TV against entry you'll notice have Dublin accents... Do you find any one among them who earns his living the hard way?'[24]

How was this possible? The simple answer is the primacy of economic discourse. For socialists and Republicans and artists and intellectuals, the Irish people were supposed to have their minds on higher things – the national struggle against the Brits, the threat to Ireland's cultural distinctiveness, the need to remain outside of the bourgeois world of businessmen and their narrow values. But the overwhelming interest of the public was in the economics of membership. In a Eurobarometer poll taken in the autumn of 1974, 82 per cent of Irish people said that the most important aspect of the EEC was economic.[25]

Economically speaking, people like us in Crumlin were not the issue. Irish politics and public discourse were still heavily dominated by agricultural interests. The overwhelming question about joining the EEC was: will it be good for farmers? Their position had become precarious. Half of what they produced was surplus to the requirements of the domestic market, so it had to be sold abroad. But international food markets were essentially a dumping ground for everybody's excess production, so prices were low. Irish farmers had some preferential deals in the British market, for cattle and sheep, and to a lesser extent for processed food like butter, cheese and bacon, but they could be lost if Britain joined the EEC and Ireland didn't.

On the other hand, the official estimate was that, under the EEC's common agricultural policy, Irish farmers could expect an increase of 50 per cent on what they had been getting for cattle and milk.[26] The reality would turn out to be less spectacular (the increase was about half what was expected), but it is not surprising that rural Ireland voted overwhelmingly in favour of EEC membership, given that the official white paper estimated that per capita incomes in farming would increase by over 150 per cent by 1978. (They actually rose by 112 per cent.)

In the cities, the promise was not so obvious. Being in the EEC would mean a speeding up of what had been happening since 1958.

Tariffs on manufactured goods would be reduced by 20 per cent a year, so that they would be eliminated by July 1977. Exporters to the UK would lose the preferential treatment they had enjoyed under previous arrangements and would have to compete more directly with other European firms. Nobody really knew how Irish industries, mostly small-scale and used to being protected, would manage. The official claim was that manufacturing industry would gain 38,000 jobs by 1977. Trade union estimates were that it would in fact shed 30,000–35,000 jobs.[27] (In the event, the truth was precisely in the middle, which is to say that there was very little immediate change. In 1972, there were 197,000 people working in manufacturing industry. In 1977, there were 202,000 and by 1982, the numbers were pretty much back to what they were in 1972.) But a lot of the jobs around us were particularly vulnerable. If you worked in clothing or textile-based industries, as a lot of people in Crumlin did, the years after Ireland joined the EEC were bad – most of these small factories closed.

But the emphasis on the coming bonanza for farmers was actually crucial to shaping the way Irish modernity would work. It lured the core of conservative Ireland into a radically modernizing project under the guise of a great scheme to increase farm incomes. Consequently, the Catholic Church was also convinced that EEC membership would stabilize rather than undermine rural Ireland.

It was not that the opposite possibility was not mooted. In 1970, the editor of the *Irish Independent*, Aidan Pender, suggested that among the concerns of his readers about EEC membership might be: 'is there a danger of importation of foreign ideologies? Can the church survive this situation?'[28] The Common Market Defence Committee (in spite of its radical leadership) sent out a circular to priests and nuns warning that a consequence of membership of the EEC 'would be an irreparable damage to the fabric of our socio-cultural identity as a Christian people with a unique ethos' and that 'the same forces which have done so much to weaken Christianity on the continent would be given full play here with undoubtedly the same consequences'.[29]

There was, on the other side, what the radical Catholic theologian Father James Good called a 'spiritual arrogance' in 'the concept of Ireland as an island of saints and scholars poised for missionary conquest in the EEC'.[30] The idea, alluded to by Whitaker and Lemass and paid homage to by de Gaulle when he was in Ireland, that Ireland was spiritually at the heart of western Europe and umbilically tied to Rome, certainly helped to fend off the fear that its Christian identity would be annihilated by membership of the EEC. But none of this was nearly as important as the money. Irish farmers wanted to be exactly the same as French farmers, not because they shared a faith or a destiny, but because the French got much better prices for their sheep and cattle. The Irish were fed up with being poor and colourful and different. European normality looked pretty good.

John Charles McQuaid died on 7 April. He had submitted his resignation as a matter of form on reaching his seventy-fifth birthday in 1971, and was shocked when Pope Paul VI accepted it. By the time of his death he was, according to Father Joe Dunn, 'powerless, unemployed and semi-ostracised'.[31] Yet, in death, he was still a prince. The Confederation of Irish Industry postponed the start of its annual general meeting to facilitate those who wished to attend his funeral.[32] Virtually the entire political class, the diplomatic corps and the judiciary were at the ceremony. The police provided a motorcycle escort for the cortège. All the schools closed for the day. It was entirely like the obsequies of a head of state. Charles Haughey, just as he had done at the funeral of Seán Ó Riada, managed to make himself especially prominent. When McQuaid's body was lying in state in the pro-cathedral, Haughey 'stood in the guard of honour during the day'.[33]

But in his sermon at McQuaid's funeral, his successor as Archbishop, Dermot Ryan, acknowledged that perhaps 'his statements of doctrine seemed insufficiently nuanced to rest easily on the consciences of his hearers'.[34] He defended this inflexibility as a consequence of McQuaid's saintly devotion to 'absolutes'. Watching a very feeble, blind Eamon de Valera, still president, arrive at the cathedral for the Mass, I realized that the era of absolutes was fading.

17

1976: The Walking Dead

Hunger strikes were not particularly Irish. The suffragists had pioneered their use as a political weapon in Britain. In India, Mahatma Gandhi repeatedly used them to exert pressure on the British. But Irish republicans had deployed hunger strikes specifically as a form of unarmed struggle that prisoners could engage in. They could produce spectacular outpourings of public grief, as in 1920, when Terence MacSwiney, lord mayor of Cork and IRA commander, died after seventy-four days without food. MacSwiney had predicted in his inaugural speech as lord mayor that 'It is not those who can inflict the most, but those who can suffer the most who will conquer.'

I knew about this from the history books but in February 1976, it ceased to be history and became part of the surreal present. An IRA prisoner, Frank Stagg, died after sixty-four days on hunger strike in Wandsworth prison in England. Stagg had been on a previous hunger strike in 1974 with another prisoner, Michael Gaughan, who died after sixty-four days. Gaughan had been brought back to his native Ballina in Co. Mayo and buried in the Republican plot in Leigue Cemetery there. His coffin was draped in the same flag that had covered MacSwiney's fifty-four years earlier. When Stagg died after sixty-two days of another hunger strike in 1976, his body weighed four stone and he was blind. Since he was also from Ballina, the IRA planned to bury him in the Republican plot beside Gaughan. The Irish government determined that it would not allow this to happen. Stagg's shrunken body became a battlefield.

Stagg was actually one of the vast number of Irish people, like most of my father's family, who emigrated to England in the 1950s. He worked as a bus driver in Coventry.

Stagg's widow Bridie wanted a private funeral. According to Garret FitzGerald, who was then the Irish minister for foreign affairs in a coalition government headed by Fine Gael's Liam Cosgrave, she was 'threatened by the IRA with being shot through the head if she pressed her view'.[1] The Irish government discovered that the British authorities had refused to give her police protection because they saw Stagg's body as a useful bargaining chip with the IRA: they would hand his body over to the IRA if it would agree to confine any public demonstrations of mourning to the island of Ireland.[2]

In the week leading up to his death, Stagg was enfolded by the IRA into the afterlife, not just of Republican, but of Catholic martyrdom. Like Patrick Pearse and MacSwiney and Seán South, he would be an avatar of Jesus Christ. Addressing a rally in Belfast, Sinn Féin's vice-president Máire Drumm said that Stagg would take his example of how to die from 'the greatest of them all, great Christ, who died for us on Calvary'.[3] Stagg's sister Monica lived in Coventry and denounced this rhetoric: 'We have to live here and a lot of Irish people, particularly in Coventry, are really frightened by this kind of talk.'[4] This was, in essence, the great tension in Irish Catholic identity: on the one side, the mythic imperative of heroic death; on the other – we have to live here, here being the ambiguous space of real lives lived between competing contexts.

The Provos planned to parade Stagg's corpse from coast to coast in 'a "military" funeral from Dublin to Co. Mayo'.[5] To prevent this, the Irish government arranged for the plane bringing it back to Ireland to be diverted from Dublin to Shannon. Bridie Stagg, who had flown to Dublin, had her hotel room invaded for three hours during the night by men seeking to 'persuade' her to hand the remains over to the IRA, but she refused.[6] Next day the body was flown by Air Corps helicopter from Shannon to a field next to the Church of Our Lady of Sorrows in Ballina. The coffin was carried, not by Stagg's family members, but by four detectives from the Special Branch. Children in the primary school nearby were ordered to stay indoors. The church gates were locked. The only mourners allowed in for the reception of the body were a small number of policemen. One elderly local man doffed his cap and knelt on the gravel on the road outside the church.

Stagg's body, even under these controlled conditions, would not be buried in the Republican plot. This was, allegedly, because there was no room left, a claim that encouraged intrepid reporters to establish that in fact 'several more bodies can be accommodated there'.[7] Speculation at the time suggested that this was because 'some persons now in authority have recent ancestors buried there who might resent the newcomer'.[8] More credibly, Stagg's brother Emmet claimed that he had agreed, as a compromise, that the body could be buried in the plot with IRA honours, but that the IRA, deprived of its planned cross-country parade of the corpse, had refused to accept this.[9]

The burial became one of the most concentrated security operations in the history of the state, with Gardaí, troops in riot gear and even the Air Corps controlling the town as the body was taken from the church to the cemetery. On a headstone hear the entrance to the graveyard, someone had daubed 'Shame on Cosgrave's body-snatchers'.[10]

Stagg's widow, brother Emmet (later a junior minister in the Irish government) and sister Monica attended this burial, but his mother and most of the rest of his family attended a ghostly funeral without a body organized by the IRA next day, featuring a bizarre 'colour party' of ten pre-pubescent girls dressed in black skirts, white shirts, black ties, black berets and dark glasses. Stagg's other brother Joe told the crowd that 'People are saying of my mother that there is no sorrow equal to her sorrow. But I say there is no pride equal to her pride.' This was a conscious echo of the language used by Patrick Pearse about his own mother shortly before his execution in 1916.

The IRA leader Joe Cahill vowed at this demonstration, attended by about 7,000 people, that Stagg's body would be moved to lie beside Gaughan in the Republican plot. Addressing the dead man, he said, 'I pledge that we will assemble here again in the near future when we have taken your body from where it lies.

Let there be no mistake about it, we will take it, Frank, and we will leave it resting side by side with your great comrade, Michael Gaughan.'[11] As the *Mayo News* noted, 'it is by no means certain that Stagg has found his final resting place... It seems we can't even bury our dead.'[12] The story became even more morbid when Stagg's brother George, part of the side of the family that wanted an IRA funeral for him, claimed that Frank's body had been 'the subject of experiments and parts of it taken from the coffin and not returned'.[13]

Police were left to guard the grave 'because of fears the remains might be interfered with'. They were still there in early August, keeping a 'round-the-clock vigil' when the state, presumably concluding that this could not go on, had the full length of the grave 'filled with reinforced concrete'.[14] The government would later say this was to 'prevent desecration'[15] but it was obviously to stop the IRA from digging up Frank Stagg.

It didn't work. In November 1977, ten members of the IRA, in the middle of (of course) a dark, wet and squally night, dug up Stagg's body. They removed it by digging a tunnel from a nearby grave and burrowing their way under the concrete shield. They carried it to the Republican plot and, with the help of a Catholic priest, reburied it beside Gaughan's grave. It was like a daring prison break, except for a corpse.[16]

In the end, just as there had been three heads of Admiral Nelson, there were three different headstones for Frank Stagg in the same cemetery. One was over the original grave, erected by his wife and one side of his family. The second was in an empty plot next to it bought by George Stagg so that it could be used as the base from which to start the tunnel. The third was over the new grave in the Republican plot.[17]

We were living inside a gothic horror story that was also like an even more grotesque version of the greatest Irish comedy, John Synge's *The Playboy of the Western World*. I am pretty sure that the phrase 'the walking dead' was invented by Synge in that play, where he uses it twice. In it, the allegedly dead body of the father, Old Mahon, keeps walking in on the action, refusing to lie down. But the image was not funny anymore.

This drama of unquiet graves and mobile corpses suggested that something was breaking down. We had a way of doing these things, which was to keep the world in which we really lived separate from the world of martyrdom and blood sacrifice. It had functioned well enough ever since I was born – honour the martyrs but do not follow them. Pray for them and sing about them but close your ears to their siren call. Bury them with honour but bury them deep. Leave them to their underground afterlife. But this wasn't working anymore. The dead did not want to be prayed for or sung about. They wanted to be avenged, and everyone knew what that meant. It meant doing what the IRA had done after Stagg and Gaughan's hunger strike in 1974, which was to massacre over two dozen ordinary working-class people in a series of bomb attacks on packed pubs in Guildford, London and Birmingham. Dead bodies wanted company, craved multiplication.

It was no longer possible, then, for most of the Irish public to remain amphibious, to live mostly on the dry land of the everyday, while dipping occasionally into the dark ocean of deathly romance. The dead were abroad in daylight and demanding their due. They had to be either appeased or shunned.

18

1975–1980: Class Acts

On my first day in University College Dublin in the autumn of 1975, we were told to introduce ourselves randomly to our new classmates. I was waiting outside the big lecture theatre in the brutalist Arts Block of the unfinished Belfield campus, when I offered my hand and name to a young man who was standing beside me. He took it and reciprocated. Where do you come from, I asked. 'Foxrock' – one of the wealthiest of Dublin's southern suburbs – he said, 'and where do you come from?' 'Crumlin.' 'Oh, do you go home at the weekends?' I thought he was joking, but realized that he wasn't trying to be smart or facetious. He had genuinely never heard of Crumlin and assumed it must be some place down the country. It came home to me that moving between social classes was still not so easy in Ireland.

This was a country in the middle of a social revolution, a time when fluidity should be the norm. I was myself a prime example of it. Hardly anyone in my extended family had ever gone beyond a primary education. Almost everyone, as a result, worked in manual or low-skilled jobs or as homemakers. By far the best form of social mobility was emigration – if you went to England, your kids would get a secondary education and could reasonably aspire to go further. Yet I got to secondary school and was accepted without question at UCD because I got enough points in the state exams.

It was an odd place. The English department, where I studied, was dynamic and exciting, with big figures like the commanding Denis Donoghue and the intense, intellectually fiery poet and critic Seamus Deane. But the philosophy department, where I also studied, was like a thinly disguised seminary. My professor, Desmond Connell, was a priest whose doctoral thesis had been on Malebranche and the thought processes of angels. His idea of fun was to write a mock treatise in Latin on why women should not be allowed to drive. He believed, and taught, that scholasticism, as practised by Thomas Aquinas, had the standing of science and that most of what came after was merely and obviously erroneous. Most of his lecturers were also priests, hired for their orthodoxy rather than their brilliance. And this clerical domination extended, not just into logic and ethics as subjects, but into departments like sociology and psychology. The institution was, in theory, secular, but in these respects it was still obviously the successor to the Catholic University of Ireland founded in 1854 by John Henry Newman.

I did not, however, really know how odd this was. I had no idea of what a university was meant to be like. The fact that I was there at all was, for me, an adequately radical idea. This perhaps also explained my own general doziness about a career. I had a vague idea of what I did not want to be – a lawyer or an accountant or a civil servant or a diplomat or a teacher or a doctor. It was an amply sufficient wonder that I could feel this way, that not being any of those things was a matter of choice for me, whereas for everyone who had come before me it was a tyranny of fact.

My only real thought was that I would somehow make a living from writing, and, since I didn't write fiction, this must have meant some kind of journalism. My mother worked as a cleaner in one of the main newspapers, the *Irish Press*. She mentioned my proclivities to Vincent Jennings who edited the *Sunday Press*, and he offered to see me. He was very nice and, as my mother and I sat across from him at his desk, he asked me some questions about what I wrote. He looked at me sadly and said, 'I'm afraid it's too late.' To my mother he said 'He'll be too old by the time he leaves UCD.' He said I should have gone to the College of Commerce where there was a course for basic journalistic skills like shorthand and typing. That was where solid professional reporters – almost all male – were made. It was obvious that he thought I had already acquired too many notions to ever be any good. I remember he used the word 'wordsmith', which I had never heard before, to suggest what he thought I thought I was. I mumbled something that might have sounded like agreement. He stood up and shook my hand and wished me luck in the future.

I could tell that my mother was worried and disappointed, though she was too gentle to say so. But I was entirely undaunted. I'd have been worried if he'd told me that, as soon as I graduated, there was a job waiting for me on de Valera's newspapers, that they couldn't wait to put me to work in the newsroom. I went back to being happily clueless about a career. I now suppose this was possible because all around me the middle class was expanding rapidly and though I would angrily have denied being part of it, I knew that, having made it to UCD, I would join it in one way or another. Even if I struggled to make a living, that living, however meagre, would come from the manipulation of symbols, not from cleaning offices or keeping order on buses or any of the things my family had done through the ages.

This realization that you could work in a whole new kind of job was shared by more and more people in the Ireland of the 1970s. By the time I graduated, after three years at UCD, the World Bank had, in 1978, recognized Ireland as one of the eighteen industrial market economies in the world. This did not mean that Ireland was particularly rich. By 1980, per capita income in Ireland was still the third lowest in the European Union, ahead only of Portugal and Greece. It was $3,027, compared to $6,656 in the US, $5,516 in Germany and $4,500 in the UK. But just being in this league at all was an amazing transformation. In twenty years, Ireland had gone from being an agrarian economy where cattle was king to one that could be understood as part of the international capitalist industrial order.

Yet this was a remarkably conservative revolution. It was not just that the Catholic Church and Fianna Fáil were still the great bastions of permanent power. It was that the society as a whole was proving to be very adept at navigating the turbulent waters of transformation and yet, in respect of its class system, landing back on very familiar terrain. It is hard to understand why, with the

Troubles at their most vicious and huge changes in everyday life, the Republic was so stable in the 1970s, how it managed to largely ignore the first and control the tensions created by the second. A big part of the answer lay in the operation of social class and in the paradox of everything moving and everything staying more or less where it was.

'There are no classes in Ireland', the economist Roy Geary wryly remarked, 'because we're all descended from the High Kings of Tara.'[1] This was not entirely a joke. As early as 1965, Myles na Gopaleen noted that Charles Haughey, a lower-middle-class upstart, was 'publicly boasting that he was descended from the High Kings of Ireland'.[2] The illusion of classlessness was one of the great strengths of the Irish class system. It had specific historic roots. Irish nationalism defined itself in opposition to England, and one of the things it most disliked about England was its class-ridden nature. Class in Ireland could be associated with snobbery and deference, with the image of an England divided between chinless aristocrats and firm-jawed miners, bowler hats and cloth caps. Since the only remnant of that kind of upper class in Ireland was the vestiges of the old Protestant Ascendancy of landowning grandees that had lost its power in the late nineteenth and early twentieth centuries, it followed that, having largely marginalized that class, Ireland was a classless society. The relative intimacy of Irish life made display of class pretension difficult (although by no means impossible). The values of old-fashioned civic republicanism made notions of class superiority highly unpopular. Many powerful institutions, from the big political parties, to the Catholic Church, to the GAA, emphasized their classlessness and brought people of all classes physically together. The political system itself was not class-based.

In some ways, the situation in Independent Ireland was not unlike that among the nomenklatura of the communist bloc. Because those with power had acquired it out of the dispossession of an old establishment, they were able to see power and privilege as something that by definition belonged to the old enemy and to remain blind to their own position as the new establishment in Ireland. The revolutionary movement slowly worked its way into the nooks and crannies of embedded advantage, but retained the sense of itself as representative of the victimized and the oppressed and therefore as being itself still excluded by 'the establishment'. Underneath the carapace of egalitarianism, Irish society was rigorous in its policing of the boundaries between farmers and farm labourers, between 'gutties' and 'good families'. Judges, for example, openly remitted sentences for criminals who had committed serious crimes on the grounds that the miscreant came from a 'good family'.

Ostensibly, this system ought to have been threatened by economic transformation. What was happening in Ireland was what always follows from industrialization: a shift in the nature of what it means to be well off. Salaries were replacing property as the main source of income. Wealth based on the ownership of land was being exchanged for wealth based on professional positions. The farmer's son (and, more problematically, daughter) was becoming a manager, an engineer, a lawyer, a senior civil servant, a journalist. All of this was happening very quickly. There was, in the 1970s, a huge shake-up in the Irish class system and it created a sense of opportunity and mobility. Young people like me were moving up from manual backgrounds into white-collar jobs, especially in the expanding public sector.

But there was also a great continuity – in this radical and rapid transformation, the distribution of privilege was not really altered. Old money turned itself into new money; old poverty tended to persist. The cards were being shuffled, but the winners of the game were not all that different. By 1980, Ireland still had a greater degree of income inequality than most western European countries.

In the twenty-five years between 1971 and 1995, the proportion of the Irish labour force that was making its living from agriculture halved. This also meant that the number of employers and self-employed people making their income from the ownership of property fell from 40 per cent in 1961 to 22 per cent in 1991.[3] Conversely, between 1961 and 1991, the proportion of upper-middle-class employees – professionals, managers, technocrats – more than doubled from 10 to 22 per cent. Meanwhile, the number of women at work outside the home rose by 46 per cent in that period. Women in particular were moving into the rapidly growing education and health systems and also getting more jobs as clerical and service workers. Equally, though, the proportion of semi-skilled and unskilled manual jobs was shrinking all the time. If you were not able to get on the escalator of education, you were stuck in an old economy – sewing factories or docking, for example – that was disappearing.

In other words, desirable positions were up for grabs in Irish society. The new jobs were in areas where it didn't matter whether or not you had inherited land. Education was the new currency. A lot of people like me were acquiring it, people who, twenty years previously, would have had no hope. But the deeper story was the remarkable success of the propertied class in turning itself into the educated class, in parlaying the privilege of the strong farmer in one generation into the privilege of the managerial and professional class in the next. Some of this happened, of course, in most societies. But in Ireland this translation of advantage into a new language was exceptionally fluent.

As one of the very few studies of the subject put it in 1990: 'It is rare to find a society that so stoutly maintained the basic distinctions among families in terms of advantaged and disadvantaged in the face of sudden and successful economic development. The "empty places" changed, as did the mechanisms for allocating individuals to those places, yet the families that enjoyed privileged positions in the old class structure secured comparable positions in the new one. Those families at the bottom of the old class hierarchy have, if anything, drifted downward into a new underclass dependent on State income maintenance for their livelihood.'[4]

This is why the economic revolution did not immediately become a revolution in ideology or identity. There was no need for the rapidly emerging new middle class to attack the legitimacy of the old order. Indeed, there was a very good reason for it not to do so – the new middle class was largely made up of the children of that old order. It might, because it was urbanized and better educated, be more liberal. It might chafe at some of the absurdities of the Catholic hegemony. It might even be embarrassed at some of the anomalies of Irish laws on, say, contraception and divorce. But Whitaker and Lemass's ambition to create economic change and opportunity without upending the governing orthodoxies was, it seemed, working out just fine.

19

1971–1983: Bungalow Bliss

'For the first four years of my life I lived in a two-roomed thatched cottage rented by my father at two shillings per week. The floor area was about 300 square feet. The furniture consisted of a settle bed full of rubbish and rats, a table, iron bed and a few chairs. It had a front door and two tiny windows. Built in a hole on the side of a hill, if you can imagine such a situation, it blended into the landscape, surrounded by privet hedges, white-thorn bushes and trees. I have still nostalgic memories of the cricket in the hearth and the high, thatched, smoke blackened ceiling. But animals now would not be housed in such conditions.'[1] The words are those of Jack Fitzsimons, author of a book of standard plans for people who wanted to build their own houses in the Irish countryside. It was called *Bungalow Bliss*. It went into nine editions between 1971 and 1990, sold 150,000 copies and helped to change the face of the Irish countryside.[2] Fitzsimons, who lived in Kells, was so famous, and his designs so deeply imprinted on the Irish psyche, that a letter addressed simply to 'The Author of the Book of Kells' reached him safely and promptly.[3]

In the 1970s and 1980s, the despised thatched cabins of Jack Fitzsimons' boyhood, picturesque, at ease with the soft Irish landscape, were swept away in a fervour of house building. No more rat-infested settle beds; no more tiny windows; no more blending into the landscape. The bliss of the new bungalow was its ostentation. For all the admonitions of architects and planners, it sat on the landscape like a beached whale, puffing and blowing to assert its presence. The modern Irish country house displayed its assorted ornamentations, gathered from a bewildering variety of sources, as if they were peacock's feathers. It was not just a place to live – it was a direct expression of the dreams and aspiration of its owners, who were, usually with the help of Fitzsimons's book, also the designers.

The abandoned cottages that littered the Irish landscape had been the most heart-rending reminder of the pain of mass emigration. I remember, even in the 1970s, occasionally coming across one. You could look through the grimed-up window and see cups and dishes still on the kitchen table, ghostly fragments of vanished lives. But with the new rural prosperity, which came with Ireland's entry to the EEC in 1973, the building boom gathered momentum. By 1976, 5,500 new private bungalows were being built every year in the countryside. By 1981 the figure had doubled to 11,517. In 1982 and 1983 country bungalows were the biggest category of new housing, surpassing even the sprawling urban estates and accounting for 40 per cent of the houses built in Ireland. Only 11 per cent of the new country houses were designed by an architect. When the money came in, the ground was levelled. Young couples talked into the night of the lovely arches they had seen in a magazine, of the picture window from that house on the television. They went on reconnaissance missions around the countryside, spotting a nice coloured brick here, a sunburst doorway there, a wrought-iron porch on the doctor's house and a plaster dog on the ballroom owner's gatepost.

'A young fella building a house now', Pat O'Grady, one of the biggest builders in the Galway area, told me in 1984, 'he wants to do it in his own way. Fellas go around with cameras and take photos of houses they like around the place and they'll ask you to put in this or that feature. You even get people bringing back photos from their holidays on the Continent and maybe it's something they've seen in a magazine or on the television. Very few have money upfront so they build the house in stages as the money comes in and they get ideas as they go along.'

At Knocknacarragh, on the road to Barna, was a house that Pat O'Grady built. Michael Paul, a very successful hairdresser, returned from America in the mid-seventies with the plans for his dream home in his pocket. It stood now at the gateway to Connemara, a huge monument to success in modern Ireland. It had all the features of the native version of the American dream home: white mock-adobe walls, a huge sun veranda beneath the grey Galway sky, a sweeping Spanish arch, wrought iron and coloured stone. It was, said Pat O'Grady, the most popular house he had ever built. It was the symbol of aspiration and the source of inspiration.

Bungalow Bliss was the great leveller of Irish rural society, a bible of social mobility. For £100, a young couple could buy a basic house plan and a schedule of building materials. With a free site from one of their parents and tax-free local labour, they could build a bungalow thousands of pounds cheaper than they could ever buy on the open market. And they were free to take whatever images of success they most desired and use them in their own house. The new bungalows were the perfect compromise between consumerist individualism and the desire to stay put in your own place, between the new values and the old.

Reflecting Fitzsimons's belief that 'I do not think... close proximity of families in a rural setting fits in well with the Irish temperament',[4] they strung themselves along the roads, instead of clustering into villages. 'A young fella will gravitate towards his own townland where he grew up', said Pat O'Grady, 'and often would be willing to travel twenty-five miles to work. He has his contacts at home and doesn't want to be institutionalized.'

Traditionally, when houses were built in the Irish countryside, they were assembled from the few materials available locally: slate or thatched roofs and walls of stone or brick, either whitewashed or left to weather naturally. The uniformity of the houses reflected the poverty and the relative social homogeneity of the society. Nobody had much more than anyone else, so there was no need to compete. Because it reflected its society so well in its simplicity and humility, the traditional thatched cottage became more than just a house: it became the home of a myth, a symbol of pure Irishness. The athletic youths and comely maidens of Eamon de Valera's dream lived in the countryside 'bright with cosy homesteads'.[5]

But having become a symbol of stability for one generation,

the old cottage was a natural symbol of stagnation and decay for the next. It summed up all that was abhorrent to a new generation infinitely more conscious of class and status: it was low, mean, dingy, poky, above all uniform and classless. The new houses of the 1970s and 1980s on the other hand, were bright, open, ostentatious and fiercely competitive.

When people build their own houses, they are expressing their own sense of themselves. And what the great hacienda baroque villas of modernizing Ireland expressed was a mixture of confidence and insecurity: confidence in the ostentation, without thought to the surrounding landscape, insecurity in the obvious delight in going one better than the neighbours, the obvious terror of being left behind. The belief that our houses in some way reflect our moral worth is a deeply rooted one. In a foreword to *Bungalow Bliss*, Fitzsimons wrote: 'I always believed when growing up that people who live in big houses and look out through big windows must have a superior outlook, a desirable dimension to their character, that is denied to those who are brought up in poky rooms with puny windows – that they must have a deeper perception and broader outlook.'[6]

The dream that architectural features could somehow increase the status of a homeowner had a real effect. Windows in Irish houses in those years went from being traditionally vertical to being predominantly horizontal. Horizontal picture windows look brighter from the outside but in the Irish climate they in fact let in a good deal less light and are much less effective for ventilation. Yet they became standard. The dream had overtaken the reality.

Because they were the products of dreams and aspirations as much as practical realities, the bungalows often stood in stark opposition to their surroundings. Picture windows that might have looked happily out on Californian sunshine were filled with the dull reflection of the bogs of Ireland. Spanish arches looked like raised eyebrows, astonished to find themselves in the wetlands of Leitrim. A riot of different stones and bricks burst forth, clashing wildly with each other and with the colours around. Multicoloured split concrete joined white adobe and red roof tiles and coloured plaster and dark wood – sometimes all on the same house. In the imitation stone facings, the regularity of the 'irregularities' in the cast stone moulds showed that something was not quite as it should be.

What did the new bungalows aspire to? Self-expression, the proud independence of the hacienda owner Big John in *The High Chaparral* shooting bandits and Indians from the dazzling white patio. The greatest store of imagery for the new country houses was the Wild West. Many of the biggest new houses in places like Leitrim, Roscommon and Mayo belonged to cattle dealers, and the mythology of the American rancher was strong. The cattle dealers built houses like one actually called 'The High Chaparral' in Co. Mayo, with picket fences and Mexican verandas and wagon-train cartwheels decorating the walls, and a horned bull's skull over the driveway entrance, houses that can only have been conceived in the midst of a cowboy fantasy.

In the 1970s, country and western had become the staple music of rural Ireland. In 1971, on their first night home from Las Vegas, where they played the Stardust Lounge on the Strip of Broken Dreams (three shows a night and every one packed out), the glamorous Irish showband The Big 8 were mobbed in Mayo. Two thousand people packed the dance hall, another thousand outside smashing the glass door trying to get in. Brendan Bowyer, Tom Dunphy, Paddy Cole and Twink were pushed through the crowd by big country policemen, eventually getting to the stage by a disused fire escape.

The Big 8 was a slick, smooth showband, versatile, professional and sophisticated. But what mattered was that they had conquered America; they had the queues leading halfway down the empty Strip while the English crooner Engelbert Humperdinck was playing to half-empty houses in the same town. They signed a deal for a residency at the Stardust 'worth two million dollars'.[7] They were hailed as heroes and became the biggest draw in the dance halls of Ireland. 'Here we were all the way from Vegas, coming down to the arsehole of Mayo', Twink (her real name is Adele King) told me years later. 'They thought we had landed from Mars.'

But when they returned to Ireland three years later, in 1974, The Big 8 were trying to catch up. It no longer mattered that they went down big in America. America had been absorbed into the dance halls of Ireland. Merged with the native product, country and western was becoming the staple dance music. The band played half the year in Vegas, the other half in Ireland. To stay ahead of the pack in Ireland they had to stay in touch with the mood at home. 'The Big 8 was very much a pop band, and we were very popular, but things were changing. One thing about the dance halls is that crowds follow crowds. More than they follow a band, they follow a band that attracts a big crowd, because that's the way you're sure of meeting a girl or a fella. In Las Vegas, Brendan Bowyer and the others started to notice that there were a lot of bands coming up that people had never heard of, that were beginning to attract crowds. They realized that it was what they were playing rather than the stars in the band that was pulling the crowds. We used to rehearse our coming-home programme about a month before we left Vegas and as the years crept by, from 1970 to 1974, our manager would always slip home and come back with a suitcase full of records for us to rehearse. And I noticed the influences were getting more country and western.'

Twink had started at the age of thirteen, in the early 1960s, when the ballrooms of the West of Ireland were in their heyday. The music then was pop, jive, big band jazz – a smooth transatlantic vibe. America was always the source of the ballroom sound, copied directly from the movies and the records, with little local variation. Typically, the ballrooms were owned and managed by a local man, a large farmer who owned the grocery shop and the petrol pump, a man of substance who cared about money. 'Those guys were up at six in the morning, out in the fields, giving the foxes lessons in cuteness. Money – lots of money, but the sort you wouldn't think had an arse in his trousers to look at him. They'd be always whinging and they always – to a man almost – always hated paying you. There were times when you couldn't get an extra body in the hall short of having your granny hanging out of the chandelier. The owner would still come in and say, "It's a bit down, the crowd tonight. It wasn't as good as we thought it would be."'

Tony Loughman was the kingpin of Irish country music and his Top Rank organization made Castleblayney, Co. Monaghan, into Ireland's Nashville. In the seventies he controlled the scene from his base in the Three Star Inn, named after his three biggest acts: Big Tom, Philomena Begley and Susan McCann. When I met him in 1986, he was still managing Susan McCann. Like her, he came up the hard way and rode the great country and western boom for all it was worth. For years he worked in a quarry outside Castleblayney, and in the mid-1960s, as prosperity began to worm its way into the countryside, he started to run dances in marquees during the summer.

When Loughman was working in the quarry, Susan McCann was growing up 'on bacon and cabbage and hard work' on a small farm in South Armagh. 'We were very rural and very poor', she remembered. Their farm was too small to support the family and her father worked 'like a slave' in the fields of the bigger, more prosperous farmers around him. She remembered getting on her bike to bring him his lunch to the neighbour's farm where he worked. 'They were so mean and they cared so little about a low farm labourer that they wouldn't give him his dinner in the house.'

There was always music in the McCann house. Her father played traditional music on the accordion when Susan sang as a girl, and the songs were generally traditional Irish ones. She told me that when she relaxed with friends, they would often go to the local Comhaltas Ceoltóiri Éireann gatherings of traditional musicians and occasionally she would sing a folk song for them. Her husband, Denis Heaney, whom she met through singing in local semi-professional bands, also played the accordion and was Comhaltas Ulster champion accordion player at the age of fourteen. By the 1980s, he was playing electronic keyboards in The Storytellers, his wife's backing group. 'Times change and he had to change with them', said Susan.

The changing times brought a new music. From the early 1960s the big showbands like The Capitol began to include a few country numbers in their set. In 1964 Jim Reeves came to tour Ireland and popularized the country sound as no one had before. There were immediate echoes of the music in Ireland. Country had its roots in the Irish and Scottish music brought to Appalachia by emigrants. (When Susan McCann played in Texas, her backing band started a traditional session in the dressing rooms backstage which ended with forty-five American country musicians joining in.) And the simple stories the country songs told were greatly to the Irish taste. ('The songs are about basic things like people dyin' and people gettin' jilted', Paddy Cole, who had played ballrooms and cabaret rooms of Ireland for almost a quarter of a century, told me, 'and we have plenty of both in Ireland.' 'Irish people love tears and blood', said Susan McCann, 'and that's what they get in country songs.')

But such echoes do not create an industry. For the ballroom owners and the promoters of the circuit, country was a godsend. It was the ballroom owners who decided the musical taste of country people. 'Most of the smaller bands', said Twink, 'had some kind of pride and they wanted to play what they wanted to play. The owners would come up to them and say, "That kind of rubbish doesn't go down well here at all now. You'll not get another booking here playing that kind of crap. Play something that people want to hear." They would come up to you in the middle of the night, in the break between sets and say, "You have to change your programme." The ballroom owner decided what the punters wanted to hear in their area.'

And all over rural Ireland, that was country and western. This was, in its way, a revolt, a reaction against the big thing that was happening in Ireland as a result of the modernizing programme: urbanization. Until the mid-1960s, the rural punters had accepted mainstream commercial music, the same smooth rhythms that had them swaying in Dublin and London and downtown Boston. It was an American sound. But as the focus of popular music shifted from America to the hard, fast, urban sound of Merseybeat, a slow rebellion began to shape itself; an insurrection against this new commercial mainstream. 'What got their backs up', recalled Twink, 'was when the pop music began to take a very English influence, with it coming across from nearer shores. "The Beat's changed", they'd tell you. And they didn't like this change of beat. I think they looked for an option. I think it was looking back to further shores.' Hank Williams and Hank Snow, Tom T. Hall and Jim Reeves were played on the radio and now a group called The Smokey Mountain Ramblers started to play bluegrass country music round the halls. 'Suddenly you noticed that the record sales were very American-biased rather than British. And of course the demise of the old showbands like The Dixies and The Capitol saw the upsurge of a new type of band, which was now beginning to adopt the American suits. The mohair ones of the showband era were turning more into the cowboy look with the stencil tie and the Cuban heel boots.'

Paddy Cole played with the elite of the showbands, The Capitol, and he remembers ballroom managers complaining to him that The Capitol were setting too high a standard. The slick, sophisticated, highly polished sounds of the best showbands were difficult to emulate. Bands of that quality were in short supply and were therefore in a position to make strong demands on ballroom owners.

But country music was simple and almost anyone could play it. All you needed was a rhythm section and a singer, instead of a showband frontline of trumpet, trombone and sax. 'Country music became a fad overnight', says Paddy Cole. 'There were hundreds of bands joining in the boom. It was better music for the ballroom owners because more people could play it'. ('Even if some of the country singers can't sing very well', one promoter told me, 'that's no great harm – it gives the ordinary fella looking on the feeling that he's not too far behind the stardom himself.')

By the mid-sixties there were almost 700 professional bands making a living out of the ballroom circuit in Ireland. And it wasn't just the ballroom owners who benefited. 'It was a hell of an industry in the 1960s', says Paddy Cole. 'When there was a dance in Castleblayney practically the whole town was making money out of it: the hotels, the pubs, the hairdressers, the garages, the boutiques – we called them clothes shops then – they were all turning over a tidy few shillings. It was a big part of the economy.'

Albert Reynolds's rise as a political figure was rooted in the chain of ballrooms he and his brother Jim built to take advantage of the 1960s boom: Cloudland in Rooskey in 1959, then Roseland in Moate, Fairyland in Roscommon, Dreamland in Athy, Lakeland in Mullingar, Jetland in Limerick, Barrowland in New Ross, Rockland in Borris-in-Ossory, Borderland in Clones, Moyland in Ballina.[8] They rose from nowhere, each built in fourteen weeks. 'There were four walls and a stage and a thing the size of a telephone box which was called a dressing room for the band', remembers Paddy Cole of these ballrooms. 'There was a lot of infighting between chains and a lot of efforts to monopolize the circuit. Bands were told, "You play for the right price or you don't get any dates in maybe a dozen venues."' Suddenly the bands needed protection. 'Most of the showbands had someone in the band who would do their bookings for them', says Paddy Cole, 'but when the boom came the professional managers came into their own.' Petty corruption was endemic. 'The bands had to pay someone to watch at the door and check on the number of people going in, because they were paid on a percentage of the takings. There was a famous story of T. J. Byrne when he was manager of The Big 8 taking a stroll out from the ballroom when a dance was beginning and finding the ballroom owner out on the road half a mile away from the hall with a bus conductor's bag over his shoulder selling tickets for the dance.'

To break it big, a band needed the muscle of a manager like Tony Loughman. 'The ballroom owners', he told me, 'were mostly farmers or shopkeepers and a lot of them made big money and got out fast. Even big bands were often very badly paid. It was a screw job. Promoters screwed the bands. And it's still the same. If you have what they want you screw them, if you haven't they screw you. And if you're stuck you might have to take it because you have to pay the wages at the end of the week.' But it wasn't only the bands and the promoters who were getting screwed.

Behind all the deals and all the music was the real business of the ballroom: the promise of sex. 'I know girls used to tell me', said Twink, 'that you could be lambasted from the pulpit if you were seen carrying on disgracefully after a dance. Those country parish priests would read you the hell-and-high-water book. And therefore the girls tried to keep the image as, "Oh sure I wouldn't do that at all, Michael. You're a terrible man." But it was very pretentious. The devilment that went on in the streets afterwards was nothing ordinary. There's always a chip wagon outside the dance hall and that was a great meeting place. After the dance, if you'd half scored at all, it would be "I'll meet you down by the chip wagon." Our van would inevitably be parked somewhere round the chip wagon because it was inevitably in the most convenient place and you could watch what was going on. God, I was astonished! They were so outrageous in their conduct. It must have been like the fox and the grapes: the harder it was to get, the sweeter a bit of juice was. The one thing that astonished me was the amount of groupies that there were around the country. Nice respectable country girls, and they hung around our boys in the band. There was no shortage of takers after the dance for the wagon or the dressing room, or the back of the ballroom. I remember waiting around on my own in the car park on freezing cold nights, until eventually I'd have to go to the van and demand that they get out.'

Into this world came Susan McCann. She sang at dances and carnivals within a fifty-mile radius of her home in the Border counties of Down, Armagh, Monaghan and Louth, a couple of nights a week from the time she was sixteen. One of the promoters she played for was Tony Loughman. After a few years she and Denis decided to settle down and give up the dance-hall business. She took up hairdressing, he did accountancy. In 1977 she met Tony Loughman again and he persuaded her to go back to the business.

Loughman was very clear about the kind of music he liked. 'Country music', he told me, 'is popular with rural people. I don't like "progressive" country and I can't stand this heavy stuff. I like commercial pop and most of all I like middle-of-the-road country.' Susan McCann didn't talk much about her own tastes. It's what the punters want that matters. 'I read my audience fairly quickly by the applause I'm getting and I'll change the music to suit. Most audiences like to have their hankies wet now and then. The older audiences love the "poor mammy" type of songs. I sing to suit the crowd, not myself. I have to please everybody, not just a small few.'

On stage she managed to be perfectly ambiguous, combining glamour with homeliness, a whiff of illicit sex with a cosy reaffirmation of traditional values. She looked good in ball gowns or satin trousers, but never unapproachable. She sang of adultery and infidelity ('There's as much of that going on over here as there is in America, even though it's not supposed to, so people can still relate to those songs') and sex ('I think that I saw Heaven / While I was making love to you'). But in the middle of a song about a married woman running away from home with another man she would go over to her husband Denis at the keyboard and put her arms around him. The audience loved it.

The new bungalows were the petrified spirit of Irish country and western. Like the music, the bungalows were democratic – almost anyone can sing country and western; almost anyone could build a bungalow with *Bungalow Bliss*. Defying the exhortations of aesthetes was, in both cases, part of the pleasure. Fitzsimons mocked the idea of congruity: 'Has anyone ever seen an old thatched hovel... that was incongruous in its setting?'[9] The urge to build and to build where people can see you, touched a deeper nerve in rural Ireland than ideals of respect for landscape. For all that they were unattractive and sometimes absurd, the bungalows were an expression of faith in the future by a generation only a few years away from mass emigration. Their irony was that they were at the same time a product of discontinuity, and of a faith in continuity, of the possibility of a future. That future may have been founded on new insecurities taking the place of the old ones, but the intention was clearly to stay put. The new generation in the countryside would rather own an American homestead in Ireland than pine for an Irish homestead in America.

Fianna Fáil, party of traditional values, fully embraced *Bungalow Bliss* and country and western culture. Jack Fitzsimons was elected to the Senate in 1983 and Charles Haughey appointed him as the party's spokesman on the environment in the upper house. Irish country music had its own moment of bliss in March 1982 when the former ballroom owner Albert Reynolds, now minister for posts and telegraphs charged with modernizing the ramshackle phone system, appeared on RTÉ's programme *The Live Mike* wearing cowboy boots and hat and a check shirt and singing Jim Reeves's 'Put Your Sweet Lips A Little Closer To The Phone'. A decade later, when he moved against Haughey in the eternal struggle for power, his faction was known, truthfully enough, as the Country and Western Alliance.

20

1979: Bona Fides

The severed head of Saint Oliver Plunkett is displayed in a glass box surmounted by a bejewelled golden turret in St Peter's church in Drogheda. The Irish Catholic archbishop was hanged, drawn and quartered on trumped-up charges of high treason, in London in 1681. His head was thrown on a fire, but rescued by sympathizers. There are marks of burning on the left cheek and the skin, preserved by creosote, is like dark leather. But it has an eerie, undead quality. The veins still bulge beneath the skin. Little pockmarks fleck the forehead and the outlines of the eyebrows are still clear. The eyes are closed, but the mouth is half open, the lips curled into what 'might be construed as a grimace, a snarl or even a twisted smile'.[1] It hovers between life and death, between anguish and ecstasy, between the horror of unspeakable torment and the joy of martyrdom, between past and present.

Shortly after noon on 29 September 1979, the parish priest of St Peter's, Monsignor James Lennon, lifted Oliver Plunkett's head from the shrine and passed it to two men, members of the all-male right-wing Catholic fraternity, the Knights of Columbanus, who carried it down the aisle. Twenty-five more Knights formed a guard of honour for the head as it passed out of the church. The priest carefully placed the head on a velvet-draped and flower-strewn army jeep manned by Corporal James Shields and Private Terence Reilly of the 27th battalion of the Irish army. They drove slowly through the town, accompanied by the members of Drogheda Corporation dressed in their official robes, brass bands, the Boy Scouts and the Girl Guides.

As the procession came towards its end point at the huge field outside the town where Pope John Paul II was preparing to say Mass for about 200,000 people, there was another guard of honour, this time formed by a thousand nurses in their dazzling white hospital uniforms, members of the Catholic Nurses' Guild.[2] John Paul knelt in silent prayer before Oliver Plunkett's head. It was then placed on the altar while he said Mass, so that its sightless eyes could witness this ultimate moment of vindication, a church once persecuted now utterly victorious, a reviled criminal elevated to sanctity, a traitor triumphant. Plunkett's presence proclaimed the power of martyrdom and the resurrection of the dead.

Nobody thought any of this at all strange. Not the procession through the town of a 300-year-old severed head. Not the Knights of Columbanus or the avalanche of white-clad nurses. Not the participation of a supposedly secular state, through its army, in a religious ritual. And not the feeling this all conveyed that this might be the 1930s, that whatever outward changes had happened since 1958, power still lay where it had before. The values and emotions of Catholic Ireland were not merely unadulterated. They were stronger than ever.

In the Catholic calendar, 29 September is the feast day of the archangels Michael, Gabriel and Raphael, who protect us against temptation, carry messages from on high and guard us on our travels. Earlier that morning, the people gathered in Phoenix Park in Dublin were waiting for an angel. The low morning sun gave the gathering pilgrims long shadows, like second incorporeal selves. The bravest were perched high up in trees, as if they themselves had just sprung up from the ground. In a few hours, Pope John Paul II would swoop in over their heads in a big red helicopter. About 1.3 million heads would turn to watch it arc gently downwards behind a vast stage. When the pope emerges onto it, there will be a sound not heard before in such a vast throng: utter silence. The crowd will hang on every word, as if hearing a message from the divine.

And the message they will hear is also one of anticipation. John Paul is indeed angelic: commanding, charismatic, radiating authority and spiritual power. He does not shy away from announcing his own presence here as a fitting reward for centuries of Irish devotion. 'One of my closest friends', he tells the crowd, 'a famous professor of history in Cracow, having learned of my intention to visit Ireland, said: "What a blessing that the pope goes to Ireland. This country deserves it in a special way." I, too, have always thought like this.' Yet, behind this magisterial gesture – you deserve my presence – there is a remarkable level of anxiety about what is to come.

This apprehension was not so obvious at the time. On that morning, and over the three days of his visit, this seemed a moment of pure triumph. Around two-thirds of the entire population would attend one or other of the pope's outdoor Masses. The gathering in Phoenix Park was reported to be the largest crowd of people to come together anywhere in Europe since the end of the Second World War. The tone almost everywhere – on the streets, in the media – was one of utter reverence. Catholic Ireland seemed invulnerable, impervious to change or challenge. Only in retrospect did I pick out the bass note of foreboding in John Paul's booming addresses to the faithful.

What he was afraid of was money and modernity. The pope did not say directly that Ireland's faithfulness was linked to its relative poverty, that the country was much more religious than the rest of western Europe because it was less developed economically. But he strongly implied it in his warnings about the coming times.

There is oddly little joy in his sermons – the focus is firmly on the looming threats he sees on the horizon, threats that are encoded in visual representations: 'The very capability of mass media to bring the whole world into your homes produces a new kind of confrontation with values and trends that up until now have been alien to Irish society', he warns the faithful in Phoenix Park. 'The most sacred principles, which were the sure guides for the behaviour of individuals and society, are being hollowed out by false pretences concerning freedom, the sacredness of life, the indissolubility of marriage, the true sense of human sexuality, the right attitude towards the material goods that progress has to offer. Many people now are tempted to self-indulgence and consumerism...'

Speaking in Galway at a Mass for 250,000 young people the next day, he cautioned that 'the lure of pleasure, to be had whenever and wherever it can be found, will be strong and it may be presented to you as part of progress towards greater autonomy and freedom from rules'. In Limerick, he conjured up the Devil himself, plotting to ensnare Ireland in his trap of material prosperity: 'Satan, the tempter, the adversary of Christ, will use all his might and all his deceptions to win Ireland for the way of the world. What a victory he would gain, what a blow he would inflict on the Body of Christ in the world, if he could seduce Irish men and women away from Christ. Now is the time of testing for Ireland.'

His sense of foreboding is remarkable, for nothing he saw in those days could have generated such anxiety. The country seemed almost freakishly unified in its adoration of the pope. It was not just the overwhelming size of the crowds that gathered for his outdoor Masses. It was the sense that there was hardly any critical space outside of this suffocating consensus. I remember, for example, that the Abbey Theatre had on display in its foyer the gifts that the artistic community were planning to present to John Paul: 'Celebration: A Salute to a Visiting Artist', a vellum-bound book of poems by eighteen writers including Seamus Heaney, Brendan Kennelly, John Montague, John Jordan, Eavan Boland, Pearse Hutchinson, John Hewitt, Richard Murphy and Michael Longley; a solid silver medallion made by students from Dún Laoghaire College of Art; a banner of Madonna and Child by the artist Patrick Pye; a sculpture in bronze, *St Francis and the Birds*, by John Behan.

As it happened, I shared John Paul's apprehension about the future, but for precisely the opposite reason. He worried that Ireland, its most faithful child, might be lost to the church. I feared that it wouldn't. The church had played its trump card: not just the first ever visit to Ireland by a reigning pope, but the arrival of a pope whose conservatism was almost irresistibly radiant. If John F. Kennedy had arrived sixteen years earlier as a herald of transformation, John Paul came as a harbinger of reaction. His message was plain. Things have gone far enough. One more step on this road of pleasure and they will have gone too far.

It was impossible, at that moment, to doubt the unassailable force of his admonitions. It seemed like we were living again through the 1932 Eucharistic Congress. Donal Foley, reporting on John Paul's Phoenix Park sermon for the *Irish Times*, noted the retro theme: 'I heard it myself almost word for word, from the parish priest in Ferrybank, Canon Brennan, when I was a boy.'[3] This message, moreover, was not passively received. The pope's schedule was repeatedly thrown off course because those who drew it up had not left enough time for the waves of applause and roars of approval that greeted his pronouncements.

The distinction between church and state was abolished: Dublin Airport was closed to all planes except the pope's. All traffic, including public transport, was banned from the city centre. Seven thousand members of the 10,000-strong police force were deployed on papal duties. A planned debate on contraception on *The Late Late Show* that weekend was cancelled. On Seán McDermott Street, just yards from the Magdalene Laundry, a big banner was draped across the flats: John Paul Rules OK. It really felt like he did – okay or not. And, though this would take some time to become obvious, this was a problem – even for the church.

Two months before John Paul's arrival, Charles Haughey, now back in government as minister for health, had engineered an apparent solution to one of the great problems of conservative Ireland. In 1973, the Supreme Court had ruled that the seizure by the customs of spermicidal jelly belonging to Mary McGee, a married mother of four children, had infringed her constitutional right to privacy within her marriage. The blanket ban on the importation of contraceptives could not continue. But to legislate for a general freedom to buy contraceptives would bring down the wrath of the Catholic Church and its lay organizations like the Knights of Columbanus. The narrow path towards an acceptable form of change lay through the marriage test – married couples could not be prevented from using contraceptives but the rest of us could.

Within the mainstream political system, this was controversial only in the sense that there were deep anxieties that even allowing married couples this freedom of choice would open the floodgates of promiscuity. In 1974, when the first attempt to reform the law was made, the attorney general Declan Costello, a highly influential figure on the left of the Fine Gael party, had actually suggested that it should contain a provision allowing any member of the Garda who had 'reasonable grounds for suspecting that a person who is in possession of a contraceptive has committed or is committing an offence under this Act, may require the person to state if he is married [and]... the place where and the date on which the marriage took place'.[4] This was deemed not to be practical, though its comic potential would surely have compensated for any difficulty. (One can but regret the absence of courtroom cross-examinations in which hapless policemen tried to explain how they came to the reasonable suspicion that a woman had taken the Pill or, indeed, had a coil fitted.)

By 1979 there was no evidence that public opinion had become much more liberal. In a 1977 poll for *Magill* magazine, 43 per cent supported access to contraceptives for marrieds only, and fully a third continued to oppose any legalization at all.[5] But, crucially, in March 1978, the Catholic hierarchy had signalled its tolerance for a conservative compromise. It acknowledged that 'the present legal situation is unsatisfactory' and that 'minimum amending legislation was required'.[6] In discussions with Haughey, the bishops made it clear that they would not go to war provided the legislation expressed support for the 'natural' methods of contraception sanctioned by the church, that there be no public family planning service, that intrauterine devices would not be available and that both the advertising of contraceptives and the availability of sterilization would be strictly controlled.

Haughey complied with all of these conditions. The bishops also wanted a specific restriction of contraceptives to married couples, but this presented the same legal difficulties as Costello's proposals in 1974. The formula Haughey used instead was 'bona fide' couples, pursuing 'bona fide family planning purposes'. They would be allowed to purchase condoms, but only if a doctor, satisfied as to their bona fides, issued a prescription. Ireland became the first and only country in the world to make a condom a medicine. As the Irish Medical Association dryly noted, 'the prescription or authorization of condoms is not a medical function'. Nonetheless, the legislation passed in July 1979 and came into effect in November 1980.

This might be seen as a victory, albeit a very small one, for liberalism. It seemed to me to be precisely the opposite. It was a great victory for the status quo, not in spite of its absurdity, but because of it. Nothing in it was going to change the ambition of me or my friends or of most young people in Ireland, which was to have as much sex as possible without getting either pregnant or married. But that was not really the point. The point was that this was, as Haughey called it, 'an Irish solution to an Irish problem', adding: 'I have not regarded it as necessary that we should conform to the position obtaining in any other country.'[7]

This begged the question: what was the Irish problem? It was not sex or pregnancy, which were known to be issues of some relevance to foreigners, too. It was the maintenance of an acceptable gap between what we knew and what we acknowledged. Everybody knew that fornication would continue to be recreational as well as procreational. The problem was how to legislate for this activity without being seen to give any form of official recognition to its inevitability.

It was entirely understood that the solution was ridiculous – why else would it not apply in 'any other country'? Nobody else would have doctors writing prescriptions for condoms because it was mad. But this was a good thing. It meant that we were preserving our unique way of life – the way of ambiguity and unknowing, of dodging and weaving around reality. Even that weird term 'bona fide' (good faith) had a peculiarly Irish history that reeked of evasion. Until 1963, there was a notorious loophole in the pub licensing laws: a 'bona fide' traveller (defined in Dublin as anyone five miles outside the city) could be served a drink outside of normal licensed hours. 'Bona fide' was a part of the everyday lexicon of Irish drinkers. Haughey's legislation transplanted it into the language of Irish lovers. The idea was precisely the same – the law was to be rigorously applied except when it wasn't.

Another way of understanding these subtleties would be to recall the deft way in which a landmark moment in Irish broadcasting was allowed to happen. On Wednesday 4 April 1979, six months before John Paul's visit, RTÉ broadcast a sober, sensitive but in its own way revolutionary radio documentary made by Marian Finucane. It was called simply *Abortion*. It was a straight, non-judgemental account of a young woman's journey to England to have an abortion. But the very subject created alarm. The station's editorial committee instructed the head of features, Michael Littleton, to determine 'the suitability of this item before it is transmitted'.

Littleton, a fine and supportive editor, asked Finucane for the tapes and told her: 'I want to listen to that to see if it is suitable for transmission.' As Finucane later recalled, 'He came back, and he came over to me and said, "That's OK: the sound quality is excellent". He never said another word to me about it. And it went out.' She was somewhat taken aback by the brevity of his response and the absence of any real reaction to the content of a groundbreaking documentary. 'In retrospect', she later reflected, 'I think he was making another point altogether.'[8]

This is the way things worked. Littleton did not defy the instruction from the editorial committee. He pretended to think that the order to check its suitability for transmission related to technical sound quality. He did not commit himself to any praise for Finucane's work – he just engaged in the evasive manoeuvre necessary to ensure that it could be broadcast. If there had been an inquiry, the editorial committee could say that it had issued an instruction and Littleton could say that he had done as he was told.

This was, in its way, a highly sophisticated culture. It depended on a phrase that Brian Friel fashioned in this same year of 1979 in the play he was writing, *Translations*. In an Irish-speaking community, old schoolmaster Hugh agrees to teach Máire English: 'I will provide you with the available words and the available grammar. But will that help you to interpret between privacies?'[9] In its public self, Ireland had available words and an available grammar of law and religious orthodoxy. And underneath them, it had the silences and evasions with which it interpreted between privacies.

The society was fluent in this shadow language. And like any language, it was highly collusive. It demanded that, on the one side, the system did not really, seriously, believe that it was going to push too far into people's lives, that, for example, young people would be frisked for condoms at discos and prosecuted if they could not produce a marriage certificate. But it also depended on most people not flaunting their defiance of the law or pushing too hard against the boundaries of what was acceptable. Sure, why would you not just go to a sympathetic doctor and say your periods needed to be regulated or that you were a bona fide family planner?

But the pope's visit threatened to upset this delicate balance. It was too successful, too startlingly triumphant. The Popemobile in which John Paul moved through the immense crowds was a steamroller that seemed to flatten out the entire society, crushing into a false uniformity its fragile nexus of nods and winks. John Paul was a great necromancer who summoned from the dead a monolithic Ireland that no longer existed. By sheer force of will and personality, he made it walk the land again. But that did not mean that it knew where it was going.

This sense that time was reversing itself was especially powerful because the present was unravelling. The year 1979 was the one in which the promise of the economic revolution began to seem hollow. There had been ups and downs, but broadly, since 1958, the trajectory had been upwards. In 1978, Ireland seemed to be doing well. House prices rose by over 30 per cent that year and personal borrowing from banks rose by 45 per cent. At the end of the year, unemployment dropped below 100,000 for the first time since January 1976. Farm incomes rose by 20 per cent. 'If', wrote the economics correspondent of the *Irish Times*, 'you've ever wondered what an economic boom felt like, then 1978 was the year to experience it'.[10] There was also a huge shift in Ireland's alignment with the international economy – the country joined the European Monetary System, ending the parity of the Irish pound with sterling, involving, as the same writer put it, 'an effective switch of economic matters from Britain to Germany'.

But in 1979 the boom evaporated. The global oil crisis triggered by the Iranian revolution hit car-dependent Ireland very hard, driving up inflation. Workers responded with wage demands and strikes. In March, around 200,000 people – me among them – marched in support of union demands for reform of a tax system that placed almost all the burden on ordinary employees, with farmers and business owners paying little or nothing. The transition period that followed Ireland's entry in the EEC had ended and increased competition and lower farm prices added to the gloom. It suddenly felt that Ireland's progress was being thrown into reverse.

There was also a sense of despair about the Troubles. There was no change and no hope. The conflict had settled down into a pattern of intimate obscenity. Any movement forward quickly dissolved into the familiar horrors. There was no imaginable future that did not look like the past, no present misery that did not seem to stretch endlessly into the future.

A month before the pope's visit, on 7 August 1979, the IRA had what it would always regard as its best day. At Mullaghmore, on the Sligo coast, it murdered a seventy-nine-year-old man, a fourteen-year-old schoolboy, a fifteen-year-old schoolboy and an eighty-three-year-old woman. The ground for these executions (the word the IRA itself used) was that the old man, Louis Mountbatten, was a cousin of Queen Elizabeth. Later that day, at Warrenpoint, the IRA set off two massive 800-pound bombs, the first killing six British soldiers, the second killing a dozen more. Most of the dead were from the hated Parachute Regiment, which had inflicted the equally murderous violence of Bloody Sunday in Derry. The graffiti declared the triumph of revenge: 'Thirteen dead but not forgotten / We got 18 and Mountbatten.' They did not mention the schoolboys or the old woman.

John Paul's Mass outside Drogheda was in reality a substitute. It had become clear that he could not, as he had hoped, visit Armagh, the ancient capital of the Irish Church, because it was in Northern Ireland and the occasion might be incendiary. Drogheda was as near as he could get, and Catholics from the North came in huge numbers to be part of the celebration of their religious identity. This, too, created an illusion of unity – all Irish Catholics together. Contemporary reports brushed over the trouble on the night before the papal Mass. Gardaí had to threaten force to remove 'Northerners' from the site of the planned event. The pilgrims from over the Border managed to get caravans onto the papal site and park in the aisles leading to the altar. Extra Gardaí had to be called in to deal with the situation, which 'became ugly at times when the Northerners refused to move. But after some persuasion, including threatened use of batons, the Gardaí succeeded in clearing the site with the help of some tow trucks'.[11]

In his homily the next day, John Paul made a dramatic intervention in the Troubles, effectively using all of his authority and charisma to try to get the IRA to stop its campaign of violence. He denounced its efforts to 'push the young generations into the pit of fratricide' and 'the absurdity of war as a means to resolve differences'. He preached 'that violence is evil, that violence is unacceptable as a solution to problems, that violence is unworthy of man. Violence is a lie, for it goes against the truth of our faith, the truth of our humanity. Violence destroys what it claims to defend: the dignity, the life, the freedom of human beings. Violence is a crime against humanity, for it destroys the very fabric of society.'

Using all his dramatic skills, John Paul turned from magisterial preacher to abject supplicant: 'Now I wish to speak to all men and women engaged in violence. I appeal to you, in language of passionate pleading. On my knees I beg you to turn away from the paths of violence and to return to the ways of peace… Further violence in Ireland will only drag down to ruin the land you claim to love and the values you claim to cherish. In the name of God I beg you: return to Christ, who died so that men might live in forgiveness and peace.'[12]

It was a heart-stopping moment. Watching it, I thought: this is history. The pope is metaphorically on his knees begging the IRA to stop the killing. Something big has to come from this. The news agency United Press International issued a report quoting an unnamed 'high-ranking Provisional IRA officer as saying that active service units had been affected by the pope's plea for peace'. Gerry Fitt, leader of the mainstream nationalist Social Democratic and Labour Party (SDLP), said that 'the Pope's words would have direct bearing on people engaged in violence. There would certainly be less people who had been involved in violence who would wish to continue'.[13] The murderous Loyalist paramilitary gang the UVF said it would 'stand down' if the IRA declared an unconditional ceasefire in response to John Paul's plea.

Sinn Féin's ard comhairle (national executive) met on 1 October to consider its response to John Paul's plea and 'consultations and soundings' were reported to be taking place 'at many levels of the movement'.[14] The following day, the IRA issued a statement: 'In all conscience we believe that force is by far the only [sic] means of removing the evil of the British presence in Ireland.' It claimed that its 'prospects of victory' were high because of the 'widespread support we know we command'.[15]

Even the IRA knew this last part to be untrue. Tommy McKearney, a senior member of the Provisionals, later wrote that the IRA at this time found it 'virtually impossible' to maintain the level of action it had achieved in the 27 August massacres and that 'there appeared little prospect for immediate advancement'.[16] The IRA 'had the ability to disrupt almost any political settlement designed to address the Northern Ireland Troubles' but remained 'unable to impose their own will on the area'. A key reason for this inbuilt strategic failure was, as McKearney realized, that 'the IRA was finding it more difficult to win supporters in the Republic of Ireland… Southern Ireland wanted the IRA war to end rather than the IRA to win'. The movement, as he saw it, 'risked the danger of finding itself politically isolated within a gradually diminishing archipelago of Provo strongholds in the Six Counties'.[17]

This sense of futility ought, logically, to have given even greater force to the pope's plea. It surely offered a way of saving face: we have not been defeated, but we are responding to a passionate entreaty from the spiritual leader of the community we claim to represent. Yet it is striking that, in his history of the IRA from the inside, McKearney refers to the Drogheda homily of 'Pope John Paul VI', a Freudian slip if ever there was one.[18] The IRA was incapable of responding to John Paul II, paradoxically, because of its strategic weakness. It lacked a large political base on the island as a whole. It had no realistic or realizable political objectives, just the fantasy of a British capitulation. Its only power, as McKearney acknowledged, was negative: it could prevent anyone else from reaching a solution. And in order to do that, it needed to keep digging 'the pit of fratricide'. In this nihilistic mindset, atrocity was its own end.

Ironically, however, even while the IRA's own strategists were coming to terms with their failure to win support in the Republic, a broader nationalist appeal could still be politically potent there. Jack Lynch's leadership of Fianna Fáil, and his hold on governmental power, was coming under pressure from the economic recession and social unrest. Charles Haughey saw his opportunity. One of his supporters, Síle de Valera, began to attack Lynch for the alleged weakness of his Northern policy. As Lynch's press secretary Frank Dunlop recalled, 'The symbolism of the granddaughter of the founder of the party criticizing its current leader over his handling of the Northern situation was not lost on anybody.'[19]

Haughey followed up with a fiery speech, praising, on the centenary of his birth, the legacy of Patrick Pearse and asserting that Ireland was 'spiritually, emotionally, intellectually and politically one indissoluble nation'.[20] Lynch, who was on an official visit to the US, issued a statement to the effect that Haughey's sentiments were not a reflection of government policy. When Dunlop called Haughey to inform him of the contents of Lynch's statement, Haughey replied: 'Fuck him, Frank, he's finished. Tell him to come home and see for himself the mess he's left the party in.'[21] He was indeed finished. Lynch resigned and, on 7 December, Fianna Fáil elected its new leader. The general assumption – shared not least by himself – was that the continuity candidate George Colley would win. Haughey, who had prepared the ground meticulously, won by forty-four votes to thirty-eight.

In the renewed atmosphere of piety generated by John Paul, people couldn't wait to have babies. One 'North of Ireland woman' actually went into labour during the pope's Mass in Galway (where his warm-up men were Father Michael Cleary and Bishop Eamonn Casey), and had to be rushed to the Regional Hospital to give birth.[22] One in ten baby boys born in Ireland in 1980 was named John Paul. It seemed that the papal visit had not merely revived the past – it had captured the Irish future. At that Mass for youth in Galway, when John Paul announced, 'Young people of Ireland, I love you', a thunderous wave of noise rolled around the racecourse, echoing from one side to the other and gathering force as it went. He raised his hands like a rock star to acknowledge the cheering and with every gesture, it intensified. After a minute, it seemed to be ebbing, but as he waved again, apparently to mark the end of the moment, it crested again. It fed off itself. He scratched his face with his left hand and it was as if he were inadvertently turning a dial to increase the intensity and volume. He was trapped in a feedback loop of adoration where every movement he made to signal that he was about to continue his sermon was received as if he were conducting the crowd. They started singing a hymn, then applauded its ending, then got back to roaring out their love for him. This went on for fourteen minutes, until Father Michael Cleary intervened to say, 'The Holy Father has not finished his sermon.'

At the time, it seemed to me that this adulation was definitive. These young people were, give or take a few years, all my age. They had all grown up after television and the arrival of sex, after industrialization and Gay Byrne. Yet here they were entirely in thrall to a conservative vision of who they were and how they should live their lives. It was only looking again at the film of those fourteen minutes that I grasped what was going on. That unstoppable noise, that torrent of sound, was entirely of their own devising. The pope was helpless, powerless. He had lost control. He had been rendered speechless. This deluge of noise was filling the space where his stern sermon was supposed to be. He was like a man shouting into the face of the Niagara Falls. He was being drowned out. Because he was adept enough as a performer not to show a flicker of annoyance or anxiety, because the sound that was reverberating around the racecourse was filled with ecstasy and exaltation, it seemed like this was a religious reverence that would reanimate Catholic Ireland for a whole new generation. In fact, it was outrageously irreverent. This crowd was not revelling in piety. It was revelling in itself, in its own youth and energy and unbounded vigour. It was taking over, inserting itself into the event, insisting on its own anarchic presence. It did not know or care about what it was actually doing: shutting the pope up.

21

1980–1981: No Blue Hills

In May 1960, an eight-year-old boy told a policeman on London Bridge that he was lost. This might be the beginning of one those gentle English TV dramas about kindly policemen and the benign workings of law and order. It is actually the beginning of a story about how heroin came to Ireland twenty years later.

The kid was called Henry Dunne. He lived on our estate in Crumlin, a few minutes' walk from us, in a house on Rutland Avenue that was almost exactly the same as ours on Aughavannagh Road. His twelve-year-old brother Larry went to my primary school, Scoil Íosagáin. When the policeman questioned Henry further, he discovered that he and Larry had been living for five days in an unlit cellar beneath a greengrocer's shop on the street level of a block of flats in Paddington.

Their disappearance had been a big deal on our estate and around Dublin. The police searched the whole area. Their mother Helen (sometimes called Ellen) Dunne gave interviews to the papers about her fears for them. There was a beautiful picture of Henry on the front page of the *Evening Herald* in a well-made jacket and open-necked shirt, his big eyes shining with innocence and only the stray licks of hair on his forehead hinting at any roguishness.[1]

Larry and Henry told the other kids they met in Paddington that they had 'sneaked over' on the boat from Dublin. They somehow made their way to the flat where their aunt lived with her seven children. They had tea with their aunt but told her that they were in London with their mother and were going back to her after the visit. Instead, they hid in the cellar. Their cousins would bring them food by heaping their own plates at dinner and pretending they were going outside to dump the leftovers. During the day, they would emerge to play with the local kids, then go back into the cellar for the night.

The picture of Henry was published in the London papers and their aunt saw it and alerted the police. But no one knew where the boys were. They had six Irish pound notes, two of which they managed to change in a shop. At one point, they went out to buy candles and then went to play in Hyde Park. Henry, for some reason, got the bus on his own to London Bridge, where the policeman found him. But Larry was still missing. A photograph of him was published, too. He has his head tilted to the left and a quizzical expression on his face. He is strumming a guitar.[2]

Eventually, the boys' father, Christy, who was working in a steel plant in London, got the news that Larry had been found as well and there was great relief in Crumlin. The whole thing was reported as an 'adventure'. The lovable scoundrels had gone for a wander, they were safe, no harm had been done to anyone and now they were back home in the bosom of their family.

Except it wasn't like that. There were eleven Dunne boys (and they had five sisters) – eight of them were incarcerated as children in the industrial school system. The eldest, Christy junior, had been sent to Carriglea in Dún Laoghaire when he was eleven. He recalled that it was 'a brutal place': 'I actually seen children eating their own woollen socks, it was so bad.'[3] Hubert drowned in a swimming accident while he was in Upton in Co. Cork. Another of the brothers, Johnny, was there with him and later said that he knew what happened but would never tell.[4] Christy later claimed that 'There was an incident and he saved eight kids from drowning, and was then kicked back in by the Brothers to save more kids – and died.'[5] Hubert, Robert, Vianney and Gerard all spent time in industrial schools, too.

And what happened to Larry and Henry when they got back from London wasn't the happy ending to an adventure. Larry was sent to one hellhole, Daingean, and later to another, Letterfrack; Henry, shortly after his ninth birthday, was sent to Upton and later to Artane.[6] I'm not sure whether Larry had already been in Daingean, but the boys' trip to London looks much more like a flight than a fling, more escape than escapade. Children don't hide on their own in dark cellars unless they are afraid of being in some darker place.

In 1990, Henry recalled his time in the industrial school system: 'They beat and abused us so much, they made animals of us. When we came out of there all we wanted to do was hit back at society. We were angry and warped, with no loyalty to anyone except our own. They savaged us even when we played by the rules. After that we felt what's the fucking point?'[7]

The thing about the Dunnes when I was growing up in Crumlin was that everybody knew they were a criminal family but nobody was really afraid of them. The boys graduated up the scale of robbery, from housebreaking to bank jobs. But they didn't steal from the neighbours. And they were not known to be violent – Christy senior, known as Bronco, was said to have decreed that his sons could make their living from crime so long as they didn't kill anybody. Henry, when he became a big-time criminal, could still produce as a character witness the prominent Jesuit Father Michael Sweetman, who called him 'a friend and someone with great sensitivity' and even 'a philosopher'.

Christy junior, the eldest boy, had given up crime in the early 1960s and was, remarkably, heavily involved in the local branch of the ultra-respectable Fine Gael party. He had a flatbed truck and he drove it round for the candidates to make speeches from. I remember Jim O'Keeffe, the mayor of Dublin who got on so well with John F. Kennedy in the White House, and the Fine Gael presidential candidate Tom O'Higgins speaking from the back of Christy's truck outside Saint Bernadette's after Mass one Sunday during the 1966 presidential election. O'Higgins later became chief justice.

I did not know it then, of course, but Christy's main political aim was to expose the industrial school system. He had written a book about it, called *Wildfire*, based on his own experiences and those of his brothers. Nobody would publish it. Over those years, Christy met senior Fine Gael politicians Liam Cosgrave, Richie

Ryan and Declan Costello and was on particularly good terms with Patrick Cooney.[8] He must have spoken to them about what had happened to himself and his brothers, but none of them made any effort to put it into the public domain.

By the mid-1970s, around Crumlin and in the big nearby flat complexes of Dolphin House, St Teresa's Gardens and Fatima Mansions, it was known that if you wanted to buy hash, some of the Dunne brothers were dealing. And then, in 1979, they suddenly had a new product. If you went to buy some hash, they gave you a free sample of heroin as well. Larry in particular had realized that, because the drug was addictive, it generated its own demand. It was much easier than robbing banks and the returns were fabulous. He and his brothers became the first heroin dealers in Ireland.

Nobody was ready for this. It was assumed that 'hard drugs', like every other form of moral threat, were associated with foreigners. In 1968, for example, the minister for justice Micheál Ó Moráin could list, in the Dáil, all the people who were caught using heroin in Ireland: 'The people who have been charged are outside offenders… The one that got most publicity in recent times was the case of a gentleman who told the court here he was just experimenting with the drugs when, in fact, he had been convicted in London for illegal possession of drugs. Another case was that of an American girl who was just here for a short time. In the few cases we have had where hard drugs were involved our evidence was that the people involved were from the other side.'[9]

The Dunnes were not from 'the other side'. They were intimately local. I remember walking past their house on Rutland Avenue, now occupied by Henry and his family. You could see through the front window that they had installed a spiral staircase. The word was that they had extended the house out the back to include a sauna and a bar. But the façade was still the same. My mother told me that Henry had bought miniature motorbikes for his two sons, aged seven and four, and that they had frightened the neighbours by riding them up and down the footpath. The neighbours complained and Henry and his wife apologized. The motorbikes didn't appear on the footpath again. Everything was normal; nothing was really happening.

Intimacy was intertwined with innocence. In 1985, the then Taoiseach Garret FitzGerald would admit that 'As a result of complacency and the misplaced belief that we were somehow sheltered from the world outside, the drugs problem had got out of control to a degree that was shattering and horrifying.'[10] This was a telling admission. FitzGerald was a cosmopolitan. His father, a member of the evolutionary elite, was an Imagist poet and friend of Ezra Pound. His mother was Bernard Shaw's secretary. He was also personally democratic. Even when he was Taoiseach, I sometimes met him on the streets near Government buildings. I was nobody but he would stop and talk, full of curiosity. Yet even he could imagine that Ireland was somehow sheltered from the outside world and could remain happily unaware of what was happening around him.

He was a skilled and popular politician and he established himself as the anti-Haughey, decent and open instead of lurid and devious. But he was also the most absent-minded person I ever met. Once, after he had retired from active politics, he and I shared a flight from Dublin to Donegal on a small commuter plane. Between the gate and the door of the plane, he managed to lose his boarding pass. The steward, who was English and did not recognize him, wouldn't let him in. I shouted down to the passengers who were already seated: "Can you tell her who this man is." Everybody roared delightedly: "It's Garret, Garret FitzGerald!" She checked her manifest and reluctantly relented.

This absent-mindedness was more than a personal quirk. It was embedded within government. The official mind went entirely absent from what was happening in working-class communities. A culture obsessed with danger and purity turned out to be completely unguarded. The Dunnes found it astonishingly easy to create a market for heroin, first in St Teresa's Gardens, where Mickey Dunne used a flat he was squatting in as a distribution centre, then from Crumlin through all the flat complexes in the south and north inner city, then into the southern coastal suburbs where Larry established himself. Their targets were teenagers and young adults. They were clueless.

For many of those kids, this is what globalization looked like. The heroin that ended up in their veins had flooded into western Europe through networks established after the Iranian revolution and the Soviet invasion of Afghanistan. World events crystallized themselves into a white powder burning on a spoon. Here was proof that Ireland was now truly connected, fully integrated into global trading networks.

In a mocking irony, this niche triumph of economic globalization was happening just as the bigger project was falling apart. Since the beginning of the 1960s, the Irish economy had grown steadily, though not spectacularly. In the period between 1960 and the first oil crisis of 1973, real GDP grew by 4 per cent a year. This was lower than in other relatively poor western European countries like Portugal, Spain and Greece, which grew by 7 per cent a year.[11] But it was still real progress, particularly since the growth was creating manufacturing jobs in urban areas. Between Whitaker's revolution of 1958 and 1973, the annual average rate of growth in manufacturing employment was 2.4 per cent.

But the growth started to slow down – and then it went into reverse. Between 1973 and 1979, manufacturing jobs increased by a mere 0.8 per cent a year. This was not enough to mop up the traditionally high levels of unemployment in old working-class areas of the cities, especially in Dublin. The growth of new jobs could not keep pace with the loss of traditional employment in, for example, docking or clothing factories. In fact, modernization did not create more factory jobs for ordinary workers in Dublin at all – manufacturing employment in the city actually fell by 10 per cent between 1961 and 1981.[12]

Disappointment became catastrophe after the oil crisis of 1979. Manufacturing employment fell for eight consecutive years until 1987.[13] This was a disaster for the working-class kids born in the mid-1960s. The jobs that were supposed to have been there for them were not merely not being created. They were disappearing.

What was going on? Essentially the failure of the native Irish business class. Business owners and employers had been broadly enthusiastic about the opening up of the economy in the 1960s and about membership of the European Community. The story of the future was to be that, while Irish firms would face increased competition as protectionism was dismantled, they would be more than compensated for any losses in the home market by their ability to export into Europe and beyond. The first part came true. The second didn't. Bluntly, Irish business as a whole was not up to it. It turned out that 'into Europe' wasn't so great a blessing after all. There was no great cohort of young, thrusting Irish entrepreneurs ready to take on the world.

This failure had two huge consequences. The first was the social calamity of mass unemployment in working-class areas. Between 1980 and 1987, there was a 27 per cent reduction in employment in indigenous Irish firms. This meant that, by 1985, the level of employment in Irish companies was lower than at any time since the 1940s.[14] In this part of the economy, it was as if the whole Whitaker/Lemass revolution had never happened.

The other big consequence was that Irish economic development was becoming increasingly dependent, not just on foreign investment, but on a small cohort of high-tech firms. The hope that animated the revolution of 1958 was that foreign firms would come in, help to stop emigration, raise spirits and encourage native enterprise. What was actually happening was that, because of the failure of the native business class, the Irish economy was becoming more and more dependent on a relatively small number of US-owned multinationals who had set up in Ireland to take advantage of low wages, virtually non-existent corporate taxes and tariff-free access to western European markets.

From the beginning of the 1980s, many of the first wave of relatively low-tech foreign companies that had been attracted in during the early 1960s were themselves shrinking or closing down. Employment in foreign-owned firms established before 1969 fell by 12 per cent between 1973 and 1980. To compensate for this, Ireland needed to attract newer investment. It did so reasonably successfully in the 1970s, with some more highly skilled jobs being created in pharmaceuticals, medical instruments and electronics. But American investment in Europe began to slow down after 1979, and this new wave of good jobs was not strong enough to counteract the receding tide of employment in Ireland.

The upshot was that Ireland was becoming more heavily reliant on American investment even at a time when American multinationals were becoming more reluctant to invest. Thus, by 1988, foreign firms accounted for 44 per cent of total manufacturing employment, 55 per cent of manufacturing output and 75 per cent of manufactured exports. But actual employment in these firms, even though it was declining less rapidly than in indigenous companies, had fallen from 88,400 in 1980 to 78,700 in 1987.

What was emerging was a deep sense of disconnection. Some of what was happening in the world being shaped by the multinationals was fabulous. My older brother got a job in the mid-1970s in Galway. This in itself would have been strange – in previous decades, the last place you would migrate to looking for work was the West of Ireland. But Kieran's job was with the American minicomputer giant Digital Equipment Corporation (DEC), which set up a plant on the Mervue Industrial Estate in 1971. By 1973, the *Irish Independent* was reporting breathlessly on the ways in which it was altering the identity of the city, changing its whole sense of space: 'It's quite an experience to go from the "old" city of the quaint, narrow streets and the many links with the past to the big industrial estate out Mervue way… Here, far removed from the old, leisurely, "romantic" days of the Claddagh, is the Galway of the seventies. There is a sense of purpose that is almost tangible, a spirit of adventure in the air, a widening of horizons so that Europe is seen as almost on Galway's doorstep.' The sense of newness was reflected in the ages of the 300 DEC workers: at that point, the vast majority were under twenty-five.[15]

Ten years later, DEC was employing 1,300 people in Ireland. Its success had helped to attract other computer manufacturers: Analog Devices and Wang Laboratories in Limerick, Bell and Howell, Sord Computers, Technicon and Dataproducts in north Dublin – 200 electronics companies in all. In 1972, Ireland had exported just £35 million worth of electronics; by 1982, the figure was almost a billion pounds.[16] If, like my brother, you could get a job in one of these companies, you were entering America without leaving Ireland: 'The Irish electronics industry is something of an industrial sub-culture of its own in Ireland. With so many U.S.

firms involved in the industry here, many of the plants are run on lines similar to what might be expected across the Atlantic.'[17] For the vast majority of those who worked in these plants, it was a wonder.

But by the early 1980s this dislocation was economic as well as cultural. As a headline in the *Irish Independent* put it, 'Micro chip is our brightest star on the so gloomy industrial front'. As the rest of the economy imploded, this American enclave seemed increasingly, not just a bright star in a gloomy sky, but a parallel universe. Most of the multinationals imported their components into Ireland and then exported almost all of their profits. About 40 per cent of what they did (paying wages and buying local products or services) was 'Irish'. The rest was not. And this began to play tricks with the very idea of Irish reality. For most of the 1980s, while the actual Irish economy was in dire straits, Ireland had, officially, the highest rate of growth in industrial output in the developed world.[18] But almost all the growth was in pharmaceuticals, office and data processing machinery, electrical engineering and instrument engineering – in other words in the American-dominated multinationals. All other sectors combined had no growth at all. There were statistical lenses through which you could look at Ireland and see a shining star. There were real experiences through which you could look at it and see a dump.

The Dunnes were successful native entrepreneurs, arguably the most influential Irish business people of the early 1980s. But while this idea of indigenous innovation in the marketplace was supposed to be the coming thing, their product was the elimination of the future. In communities where the promise of the 1960s and 1970s was drying up, where jobs were actually scarcer than in the 1950s, belief in the better life to come had become a mockery. It was a noise in the head and heroin could drown it out.

The heroin epidemic was like a slaughter of the innocents. It went after children and young adults. It was also a repetition of an American nightmare. While the civil rights movement in Northern Ireland had been inspired by the struggle of Black people in the American South, what was happening in Dublin in the early 1980s was a replay of the devastation by heroin of Black communities in urban America a decade earlier.

In the north inner city of Dublin, one in ten of all young people aged between fifteen and twenty-four was using heroin. Among girls aged between fifteen and nineteen, the figure was higher than one in eight.[19] The south inner city, which included the flat complexes next to the Crumlin estate on which I grew up were reckoned to be even worse. One teacher in the north inner city reported coming across four boys aged between ten and twelve who said that all of them had skin-popped heroin on at least four occasions, had distributed or sold heroin for older people, knew lots of abusers, thought that everyone 'did it', saw no danger in their activities and were approaching teenagers in order to buy heroin.

John Bradshaw, an English expert who was commissioned (reluctantly and under pressure) by the government to try to get a handle on what was happening in Dublin, compared it directly to the situation in the New York districts of Bay Ridge, Bedford-Stuyvesant and Fort Greene in 1970 as the first flush of heroin washed through from the Vietnam War. He found Dublin's north inner city to be similar to the mostly Black area of Bed-Stuy a decade earlier, though actually much worse in terms of the addiction rates for teenage girls. If there was one American 'sub-culture' thriving in the form of high-tech plants, it had an evil twin in the mirroring of an American disaster.

But the authorities didn't want to know. The not-knowing was literal. While Bradshaw managed to study the north inner city, he concluded of the huge housing estate of Ballyfermot that 'one visit to the area and a discussion with two local priests was sufficient to establish that there was no group of people knowledgeable about the area'. In Dún Laoghaire and its vicinity, where Larry Dunne had established a lucrative operation, Bradshaw managed to talk to one heroin user who 'named correctly the family he believed to be supplying heroin to the area. (My confirmation came from the Gardaí.)' This undoubtedly referred to Dunne. But that was as much information as Bradshaw could get and he abandoned his study of the situation there.

Most strikingly, even though the flat complexes near Crumlin, St Teresa's Gardens and Fatima Mansions, were known by police and healthcare authorities to be ground zero of the epidemic, Bradshaw also struggled to get enough reliable information to conduct a rigorous survey and gave up trying. This meant that the state, which commissioned his report, was leaving itself in wilful ignorance of what was happening. Even as a problem of law enforcement, heroin was largely ignored. Bradshaw reported that 'among concerned and well-meaning middle-aged lay people in the Dublin North Central area, there is doubt about the earnestness of the Gardaí in relation to drug offences, and even a belief that the motivation of the Gardaí in this field is suspect.'

The city had one 'grossly overloaded' drug treatment clinic, a prefab shack attached to the crumbling Jervis Street Hospital, swamped, as its director put it, by 'a motley crew of schoolchildren, hardened addicts and criminals coming through the waiting room'.[20] The entire country had one residential addiction centre, the Coolmine Community, which was not specifically geared to dealing with heroin. Bradshaw found only a sense of despair: 'Neither the law enforcement agencies nor the Jervis St clinic personnel nor the Coolmine Community director nor those involved in various local initiatives were, on the whole, anything but pessimistic about a possible further increase in heroin abuse and about their own efforts at treatment, rehabilitation, education, and elimination of the supply and distribution of heroin; and their pessimism seemed justified.'

It was indeed. The official response to the Bradshaw report was the establishment, in April 1983, of the impressively named Special Government Task Force on Drug Abuse. It resulted in a few small improvements in law enforcement and treatment facilities. A key recommendation – the provision of a budget of a million pounds a year for youth and community development in the most affected areas – was rejected by the cabinet. A National Coordinating Committee on Drug Abuse was established. It was supposed to make specific recommendations to government ministers and to publish an annual report. It was convened in 1985, with no independent secretariat or other staff. Bizarrely, faced with

Bradshaw's finding that 10 per cent of young people in the north inner city were using heroin, the main follow-up was not to find out whether this figure was replicated in other working-class areas. It was to launch a study of the other 90 per cent, 'aimed at establishing the distinguishing features between the 90 per cent of those in the 15 to 24 age group, living in a north central Dublin area, who do not abuse hard drugs and the 10 per cent who decide to abuse hard drugs'.[21]

The official mind could not process what was happening. In part, this was because of social class – most of the early heroin users were poor and badly educated (a significant minority of them could not read or write), their lives marked by what Bradshaw called 'squalor, illiteracy, anomie, and unemployment'. They were too sharp a reminder of a shameful, unfinished past. James Dillon's wail in 1957 about Ireland's place in the world – 'we are with the descaminados... the shirt-less ones of Europe' – had been silenced by the achievement of European modernity. The shirt-less ones of Ireland were ghosts at the feast. But there was also a cultural problem: how did these doomed children fit into any inherited idea of Irishness? Bradshaw, in trying to place them, struggled to articulate the notion that these kids could not even be said to have lost a traditional Irishness because they never had it in the first place. They had 'no blue hills to remember, no spires, no farms, no happy highways; no Connemaras, no Books of Kells. What they have lost instead is simply all of real value on the temporal plane they ever truly possessed – their youth.'[22]

What he seemed to be trying to say was that, if only these teenagers came from the land of legend, they could get back to it. They could be rescued from a modernity that had turned to nightmare and returned to the blue hills of the West, to faith and farmland. But they were not even amnesiacs, because they never had any properly Irish memories to lose. The one official document that tried to chart the crisis seemed haunted by the notion that the walking dead of the heroin-infested flatlands had never really been alive in Irish culture.

Bradshaw, in that report, reached for the only idea of salvation that was available in Irish political culture: religious redemption.

He suggested that deliverance, if it would come at all, would be brought, not by the state but by the church: 'The one source of some deeper philosophy of life than to live from hand to mouth, evading reality with drugs and crime and drinks, is the Catholic Church… It seems to the present writer that the Catholic Church could well play a unique part in relation to the containment of drug misuse in Ireland, and perhaps to its diminishment'.

He suggested that the heroin users were the new pariahs of Irish society and that it had always been the church's business to rescue such people. The drug abuser was 'par excellence a candidate for the exhibition of the charity… that has in the past enabled Christians to tend the leprous, the grossly handicapped, the lunatic, when others looked away'. The best hope therefore was that 'the Jesuits, Franciscans, and Cistercians' could establish retreats in the countryside for the male addicts, while 'orders of nuns could similarly cater for the girl abusers'.[23]

Which meant, of course, that the kids hadn't a prayer. The idea was, in one sense, perfectly logical. This was what Irish society had done with its social lepers. It was the church that had operated the system of social hygiene, tidying away the problem people in the industrial schools, the Magdalene Laundries and the Mother and Baby Homes. Why should it not do for the heroin addicts what it had done for the fallen and the deviant throughout the previous century? But the world in which the church had this institutional power was itself passing away. What Bradshaw's desperation really pointed to was the reality that nothing was taking its place. Ireland had one way of dealing with unwanted people. When it was no longer available, it had no way at all. There was no Letterfrack or Artane to which to send the children who had become the ideal customers of the kids who, in the previous generation, had grown up in such places.

The only thing the state could think to do was to go after the Dunnes, who had become too open, too notorious. In a way, they were as innocent as their victims – they did not know how to use their new wealth to insulate themselves from their crimes. In 1982, Charles Haughey, as Taoiseach, demanded that Garda commissioner Patrick McLaughlin have the Dunnes in prison within twelve months. In the following fifteen months, eleven members of the family were either convicted or arrested.[24] Larry managed to escape while on trial. He hid out in Crumlin and dyed his hair before absconding to Spain. In 1985, he was arrested and extradited to face a fourteen-year sentence. As he departed to prison, he told reporters: 'If you think we're bad, wait till you see what's coming after us.'

22

1980–1981: A Beggar on Horseback

In May 1981, I went to the first political press conference I ever attended. Charles Haughey had called an election and Fianna Fáil was launching its manifesto. I wanted to take the opportunity to ask him a fairly innocuous question about arts policy for the little magazine I wrote for, *In Dublin*. It was all dull stuff until Vincent Browne, editor of *Magill* magazine, stood up at the back and asked Haughey: 'Where did you get your money?' Haughey grunted and literally waved the question away with a grand gesture of contempt. He had probably expected it: Browne had asked the same question at Haughey's first press conference as Taoiseach in 1979. As editor of the magazine, as I discovered a few years later, he would give every young journalist looking for work a list of projects. At the top was 'Charlie Haughey's finances'.

Browne asked the question again, and this time Haughey said something about how he was not going to respond to ridiculous trivia when there were such serious issues facing the country. Browne asked again: where did you get your money? And then the most interesting thing happened. I could sense that almost every other journalist in the room was becoming intensely irritated, not with Haughey's refusal to answer the question but with Browne's persistence. There were sighs of weariness and impatience. Somebody grumbled, 'Shut up, Vincent.' Vincent asked the question again, but he was drowned out in the general hubbub. Only one journalist, the RTÉ broadcaster John Bowman, spoke up, addressing Haughey directly: 'You called a press conference. You should answer the questions.' But everybody moved on. There were important stories to write.

These were all good, professional journalists. But Haughey's money was not really a journalistic question. It was, like child abuse or abortion or Magdalene Laundries, one of those things that was both known and unknowable. On the one hand, it was entirely obvious that the country was now in the hands of a man who had been a professional politician since the year before I was born, yet who had a mansion, a stud farm, a yacht, even a private island. On the other, there was nothing about this that could be properly comprehended. It could not be assimilated into public consciousness, so it floated there in the peripheral vision of Irish politics. Like the sun, its light was everywhere, but you could not look at it directly. Browne's question was unanswerable which made it, for working journalists with deadlines to meet, also unaskable.

Running things for his boss that day was Haughey's press secretary, Frank Dunlop. He would later recall the nature of the epistemic vacuum. He recollected that, although Irish reporters other than Browne did not raise the issue of Haughey's money, they would often prompt visiting foreign journalists to do so – itself an indication of the roundabout approach to the question. But 'Charlie never commented on the stories and I never asked him to. While people might say to me that they "heard" something, nobody ever asked me directly to check out any facts, so I had no reason to bring up his finances with him.'[1]

This was, in political life, the parallel to the church's open secrets. It had its own genealogy, one that was intimately connected to the modernizing project of the 1960s.

In April 1963, the upmarket Irish women's magazine *Creation* ran a feature on the latest ideas for dinner parties. This was a time when a new Irish middle class was inventing itself. The First Programme for Economic Expansion was well under way. American money was coming in. John F. Kennedy was due to drop from the sky soon. Fridges and televisions were filling the forlorn alcoves of kitchens and sitting rooms.

Large chunks of dirty old Georgian Dublin were being pulverized by Haughey's friends and replaced with such hideous second-hand imitations of the international modernist style as Hawkins House, O'Connell Bridge House and Liberty Hall. The ESB was planning to demolish much of the grand Georgian terrace on Fitzwilliam Street and replace it with a graceless building by the up-and-coming architect Sam Stephenson, a man who later told me, with no sense of irony, that one of his professional inspirations was Albert Speer. There were plans to fill in the manky, old-fashioned Grand Canal with cement.

But dinner parties were, for many, still an astonishing notion. Mostly, men met their mates in the pub and women had a cup of tea and a chat. If you had visitors to the house, they were entertained with beer and whiskey and tea and sandwiches and apple tart and a sing-song. So what were you supposed to do at a dinner party? In the interests of its readers, *Creation* went to the experts. The new minister for justice, Charles Haughey and his lovely wife Maureen, daughter of the Taoiseach, Seán Lemass, explained what would happen at a typical dinner party for six to eight people chez Haughey.

The glamorous couple would offer you, *Creation* informed the women of Ireland, 'their special favourite, Steak Fondue. Small cubes of very tender raw steak, well-seasoned, are placed on a platter. Then each guest, using a special two-pronged fork, selects his pieces of steak and cooks them at the table exactly to his taste, in hot melted butter in the chafing dish. A variety of sauces and a tossed salad complement the dish.' The lucky guests, added the magazine, 'find Steak Fondue a very amusing novelty'.

The average Fianna Fáil voter, who still ate dinner in the middle of the day, probably wasn't reading *Creation* in 1963. Or if she was, she was reading it for a glimpse of an exotic new world, way out on the horizon of aspiration. The amusing novelties of our very own nouveaux riches were still far beyond the reach of most people, especially in Fianna Fáil's heartland of small farms and working-class housing estates. When, later in 1963, the Haugheys advertised for a nanny (the pay was £5 a week), they stressed that their house had both television and central heating, luxuries that were obviously not to be taken for granted.[2]

The problem was that, as the new middle class expanded, the cost of social distinction rose. Within a few years, producing a fondue set at a middle-class dinner party would be an appalling lapse of taste, like having flying ducks or *The Crying Boy* on your wall or Mantovani on your new stereo. People like the Haugheys would be mortified if you produced a copy of *Creation* from April 1963.

Before the 1970s, you needed relatively little money to be a cut above the social norm. Because the plebs didn't have much, it didn't take much more to be better than them. Simple things like having dinner parties, knowing a bit about food, drinking half-decent wine, qualified you as a member of a social elite. If you were a government minister, you could afford mohair suits rather than shiny nylon, tender steak instead of hairy bacon, melted butter rather than Stork margarine. You could send your kids to the Jesuits and the Sacred Heart sisters, with their much more onerous school fees. You could maintain a status higher than what you came from. But as more money came into the state and the middle class got larger, a ministerial salary, though enough for a comfortable life, was not enough to place you at the top of the social hierarchy. The magazines no longer gushed about your fondues.

If you were a normal, well-adjusted person, this hardly mattered. You could get over it. You could get your kicks from the power and prestige of office. You could even flatter your own ego by believing some of your own rhetoric about public service and patriotism and the Irish language and the importance of fostering the national ideal.

But if you were shallow and insecure enough to measure your worth by the enormity of your expenditure and the conspicuousness of your consumption, you had a real problem. You had to go higher. And the only real notion of what an upper class might look like was the memory of the very class that de Valera and Lemass and all the other revolutionaries had destroyed, the old Protestant landowning Ascendancy. It is a great historical joke that just as

Catholic nationalist Ireland is coming into its own, it is haunted by Haughey's attempts to become an Ascendancy squire. It is the revenge of the landlord class. They lost their power. They lost the land. The IRA burned them out. But they left behind a particular image of wealth. The Big House. The horses. The exotic holiday home in the rugged West. How amusing it would have seemed to them that one day the Catholic state would be run primarily for the purpose of allowing its Taoiseach to ape the old gentry by becoming, literally, a beggar on horseback.

What is interesting about this is the political style. The preferred Irish mode was the modesty of the self-sacrificing revolutionary. Eamon de Valera projected a positively austere image. Lemass lived plainly and patently within his means. Yet Haughey, even early on, was willing to hint at wealth, at his enjoyment of a lifestyle that was a cut above that of his own constituents in working-class and lower-middle-class north Dublin. Once he had decided to do this, he upped the ante and entered the horsey world that had defined the old elite. (Brendan Behan had quipped that an Anglo-Irishman was simply a Protestant on a horse.)

In March 1962, Haughey's purchase of a racehorse, Miss Cossie (by Le Lavandou, out of Monkey Puzzle), was widely reported.[3] When Princess Grace Kelly made a visit to Ireland in 1963, she was seen chatting to Haughey at the Curragh racecourse before placing a one-pound bet, assumed to be on his horse. 'If so, she was disappointed, for Miss Cossie finished well down the field and certainly the Princess did not return to collect' any winnings.[4] She would not be the last to find the results of backing Haughey disappointing, but the reporting on such incidents still made a point: this man is rich enough to own a racehorse. And he seemed to want to move even further up the social scale, to project the image, not of being nouveau riche, but of old money. Even as the young pretender of de Valera's nationalist party, he began to project himself as an Anglo-Irish gentleman. The image generated inevitable unease.

In 1964, the *Sunday Times Magazine* in Britain had a section called 'Images of Ireland'. At the bottom was a photograph of a group of Travelling people plodding along a lonely road across a misty mountain, all their possessions apparently loaded on two carts pulled by donkeys. Above it was a group portrait of five men in riding coats mounted on fine horses. Four of them were wearing top hats; the fifth a bowler. The man in the bowler was Haughey. Commenting on the picture, the journalist Prionsias MacAonghusa wondered 'if this is the new image of Fianna Fáil. Gone are the days when Fianna Fáil was the people's party which cared for ordinary people and shunned the rich and the mighty. The aim now is to hobnob with the remains of the Ascendancy and their native imitators.'[5]

Yet Haughey understood that, in the shifting psychological terrain of 1960s Ireland, there were more complex possibilities than this apparently obvious contradiction between populism and aristocracy. He was an outsider, a lower-middle-class Christian Brothers boy from Donnycarney, a northside Dublin suburb that was just a cut above Crumlin, more settled, more respectable, but no more fashionable. His father was an army officer who had retired early because of ill health – the family of nine survived on his small military pension. Haughey was brilliant, hard-working and fiercely ambitious. He won first place in Dublin Corporation's scholarship examinations. It was public money that got him into UCD and allowed him to become an accountant. It was also at UCD that he met his wife, Lemass's daughter Maureen. He was not part of the hereditary revolutionary elite, but he married into it.

That revolutionary generation was, however, on its way out – very slowly but inevitably. When Lemass retired in 1966, Haughey thought he had a good shot at being the first Fianna Fáil leader and Taoiseach who was not involved in the 1916 Rising. He was beaten to it by the emollient Jack Lynch, but even so he had already implicitly answered the question that arose in this time of transition: what should a 'modern' Irish ruling class look like? The painful contrast between JFK and de Valera in 1963 had raised this question, not as an abstract topic for discussion, but as a drama of embodiment. Dev, long and lean and old and dour, embodied Irish freedom. JFK, glowing and tanned and young and glamorous, embodied the dream of what that freedom might be for.

There was no going back to de Valera, but there was also no way forward to JFK either. The Kennedy style depended on inherited wealth – JFK never had to worry about money – and Hollywood charisma. Haughey, a lower-middle-class kid and a monotonous public speaker – had neither the ease nor the sparkle of JFK. So he created something else. It was, in retrospect, an astonishingly bold gambit. If he could not skip forward a generation towards American allure, he would skip back a generation to aristocratic Ascendancy. Instead of being post-revolutionary, he would look pre-revolutionary. To pull this off he would have to navigate a very Irish ambivalence.

In his *Begrudger's Guide to Irish Politics*, Breandán Ó hEithir told the story of a parish priest in West Cork talking to Con the blacksmith on the morning after the signing of the Anglo-Irish treaty of 1921. The priest hails a 'great day for Ireland', but the blacksmith is gloomy because his trade depends on the horsey ruling class: 'It was the gentry kept me going and what's left of them are going to leave the country now. Ireland may be free but I'm ruined.' The priest is reassuring: 'Now Con, my dear man, will you listen to your parish priest. Everything will be all right. We're going to have our own gentry now. Believe you me.' As the priest saunters off to his breakfast, Con mutters, in a mordant undertone, 'Our own gentry? We will in our arse have our own gentry.'[6]

The point of this story is its contrariness. We need a ruling class; we will in our arse have a ruling class. This, perhaps, is what you get with the implicit ambiguity of a conservative revolution: an uncertain, vacillating attraction to and repulsion by the idea of a new elite. Haughey crystallized and embodied this indeterminacy. He embraced the idea of 'our own gentry' while also reshaping it as a patriotic ideal. He gave equal weight to the first and second parts of the phrase, making himself, in his own eyes and those of his patrons and supporters, the people's aristocrat.

He even had a racehorse called Aristocracy.[7] Being a horseman was so central to his self-invention as a natural denizen of the upper class that he had a life-size portrait of himself in full hunting regalia hung in the main hall of his mansion, Abbeville. But it mattered, too, that he was a Gaelic equestrian, that his horsiness was a genetic marker of indigenous Irish nobility. In the biography of Haughey at the front of his collected speeches, *The Spirit of the Nation*, it is stressed that '[His] descent can be traced to the Uí Neill, Kings of Ulster. Haughey in Irish means a horseman or knight as the Irish version Eochaidh is derived from the word "Each" meaning a steed. The numerous O hEochaidh clan inhabited a wide area of mid-Ulster and were kings of Ulidia up to the end of the 12th century. One of the O hEochaidh kings fought and fell with Brian Boru at Clontarf. Haughey's Fort is part of the Emhain Macha (Navan Fort) site near Armagh.'[8]

To understand how this preposterous fusion of Gaelic kingship and Anglo-Irish style could possibly work, it is necessary to identify the very specific class that made it possible: the same gang of property speculators that was systematically destroying Dublin. Haughey was funded in particular by John Byrne and Matt Gallagher. They made their fortunes by knocking down Georgian houses. They also, to reverse Oscar Wilde, loved the thing they were killing. They demolished the houses of the old aristocracy, then filled their own homes with antiques and artefacts they had salvaged from those eighteenth-century buildings. They were abolishing the pre-revolutionary past but also rather liked the elitism of the *ancien régime*. What they saw in Haughey was the possibility, not as his critics believed, of aping the Ascendancy but of occupying its space, both literally and metaphorically. Through him, they would not be, in MacAonghusa's mocking phrase, 'native imitators' of the Anglo-Irish gentry. They would be native replacements for them.

This is not a speculative interpretation. In 1998, Patrick Gallagher, who took over from his father as Haughey's primary patron, explained to Frank Connolly that 'his father and his business friends agreed to bankroll Haughey in the 1960s so the politician could pursue his political career and concentrate on "building the nation". He said the Fianna Fáil politician was "financed in order to create the environment which the Anglo-Irish had enjoyed and that we as a people could never aspire to".'[9] He added that 'Somebody had to live in the big house.'

The first wave of revolutionaries had burned the Big Houses of the gentry. The cadres of the new revolution of the 1960s hovered between two options. They could demolish the Big Houses and build lucrative housing estates on their lands. And they could, vicariously through their chosen darling, live in them. The egalitarianism of the revolution was always more rhetorical than real, but even so it did not sit well with the buccaneering spirit of the 1960s, in which a select few (like Gallagher and Byrne) could rise up from small farms in the West to become fabulously rich. It was much better to recreate an eighteenth-century hierarchy, except this time with good Catholics in the place of the Protestant Ascendancy.

This was, moreover, a patriotic cause. 'We as a people' could now aspire to be lords of the manor, not literally, of course, but at one remove, through the leader who embodied the popular destiny. Charles Haughey's grand Georgian existence would not be, in this mentality, an affront to the people. It would be a compliment to them, a signifier of their elevation. This may seem to be something of a stretch, but it should be borne in mind that the idea of reflected glory, or drawing pride from identification with 'one of our own', had been at the heart of JFK's Irish visit and the claiming of Muhammad Ali.

There was something deliberately provocative in Haughey's flaunting of his wealth, but also fiendishly clever. His money became a question of form (the way he spent it), not of substance (the way he got it). Haughey had set up a small accountancy practice in 1950, but he had ostensibly retired from it in 1960, when Lemass appointed him as parliamentary secretary (junior minister) for justice. His income was supposedly that of a full-time politician. Yet by 1968 he owned a grand Georgian house on forty-five acres in north Dublin, Grangemore, and a 157-acre stud farm in Co. Meath. The following year, he sold Grangemore for the then enormous sum of £204,000 and bought Abbeville, one of the finest private houses in Ireland, a twelve-bedroom eighteenth-century house on 250 acres of lush north Dublin farmland, partially designed by the great architect of Georgian Dublin, James Gandon. Haughey's salary was £3,500 a year. The wage bill for the staff at Abbeville alone was £30,000 a year. The stud farm he established there made no profits – Haughey described himself on official documents as a 'gentleman farmer'.[10] He had no visible means of support.

But he needed this form of ascendency. It was ruinously expensive, but the point of ascending is to float above the normal. The normal instinct of a corrupt politician in a democracy would be to conceal his unexplained wealth. Haughey's great aptitude, on the other hand, was for the unknown known. By acting the aristocrat, he magnified his money, made it grand, elevated it beyond the mundane, beyond the rational, beyond scrutiny. The church kept its open secrets on the plane of willed ignorance through the force of its spiritual power. Haughey kept his money outside the realm of acceptable discourse by making it so obvious that it became a feature of the Irish landscape, like the River Shannon or the Cliffs of Moher. The trick of aristocracy is to make great wealth seem natural. Haughey, at least for most of the people, most of the time, pulled it off.

To call Haughey a hypocrite would be like calling Rembrandt a portraitist or Mozart a piano player. His mastery of hypocrisy was mesmerizing, exquisite, magisterial. And it operated not just with money but with the only other thing that had the same ambiguous fascination in modernizing Ireland: sex. Sexual hypocrisy was never Haughey's weakness. It was a great part of his strength.

In Irish culture, there were two co-existent attitudes to the sex lives of great men. There was, of course, the official Catholic morality that demanded monogamous heterosexual marriage and the production of faithful Catholic children. But there was also a much older folkloric expectation of the hero (including in the popular imagination idols as diverse as Jonathan Swift and Daniel O'Connell) as a figure of fabulous and unbounded sexual potency. Haughey, the great rider, managed to be both.

I remember the first time I became truly aware of Charlie Haughey. It was through that most entrancing medium for a twelve-year-old, the whispers of adults. It was 1970, in fact just before the Arms Crisis broke. Haughey was minister for finance and he was just about to deliver the annual set-piece Budget, a matter of supreme indifference to me. But instead of Haughey, it was the Taoiseach Jack Lynch who stood up in the Dáil to give the speech. He explained that 'Before leaving his home this morning, the Minister for Finance met with an accident which resulted in concussion.' Maureen Haughey told the press that her husband had gone for a walk around the outside of the mansion when he was 'hit on the head and knocked unconscious by a large piece of gutter pipe which fell from the roof of the house'.[11]

But like every story in Ireland, this one forked off in different directions. Maureen explained that 'He was just out getting a breath of fresh air. He was on his own at the time.' Her husband told journalists that in fact he had been on his horse and had tried to dismount on his way back into the stable by grabbing hold of a gutter, which then broke off and fell on top of him.[12] Fianna Fáil's semi-official newspaper the *Irish Press* elaborated on this version. It said that Haughey 'fell off his horse' when the gutter gave way and he 'struck his head and shoulders when he fell heavily on the tarmacadam yard'.[13] His walk was now a ride; the gutter fell, not from the roof but from a stable wall.

Except, as I heard it, it was none of the above. My mother's brother Johnny was a salesman for a large bakery and he picked up all the gossip as he went around the shops. He was telling my father and mother in low tones the 'real' story: Charlie had been beaten up by an outraged husband who had caught him in bed with his wife. The man had left him for dead and, sure, who could blame him? It was a wonder he was alive at all. And poor Maureen – a lovely woman, God bless her – maybe she knows the truth or maybe he has her fooled up to the two eyeballs. But he got his just deserts anyhow.

So far as I could gather, this was what 'everybody knew'. It was almost certainly nonsense but it was a way of filling another lacuna. Haughey was a womanizer. He was a conservative Catholic husband and father. The story of the outraged husband meting out violent retribution brought these two realities into contact within an acceptable frame of sin and punishment.

Haughey himself had created the imaginative vacuum into which such stories could be sucked. As a politician, he was not just a conservative Catholic but a reactionary one. His vigil at the lying-in-state of John Charles McQuaid was a public statement of his identification with the old Grand Inquisitor. In 1964, for example, Haughey, as minister for justice, was in charge of Ireland's ludicrously severe film censorship regime. (This was a system in which Irish people saw a version of *Casablanca* that cut out all the references to Rick and Ilsa's passionate love affair in Paris, leaving their motivations entirely mysterious.[14]) Haughey refused all efforts to have a classification system introduced as an alternative to banning or savagely cutting movies. He also appointed as film censor his own Fianna Fáil constituency running mate, who admitted that he 'knew nothing about film' except that it should have a moral and didactic purpose.[15]

In 1983, four years after he had become Taoiseach, Joe Joyce and Peter Murtagh included, in their book *The Boss*, what I think was the first public reference to Haughey's mistress: 'In political circles and at some levels of Dublin society, his lengthy liaison with a married woman was widely discussed.'[16] This phrase was itself altered from the original version: 'His interest in the sexual exploits of others was matched by gossip about his own sexual activities. In political circles, and at some levels of Dublin society, his lengthy liaison with the wife of a judge was widely discussed.'[17] Certainly by 1979, but I think before then, everyone I knew could identify exactly who this was: Terry Keane, fashion editor of the *Sunday Press*, wife of the High Court judge Ronan Keane, and Haughey's lover since 1972.

Later, I could have said how I knew this: I knew people who knew her and she never made any secret of it. But at the time, being far removed from 'Dublin society', I did not know how I knew. It was another of those facts that drifted on the breeze, always in the air but never settling on firm ground.

There was a way of reading, a subtle textual analysis that applied, not to the news pages but to the gossip columns. For example, in 1981, the *Evening Herald*'s John Feeney wrote about an opulent lunch in the Mirabeau restaurant in Sandycove to decide on Ireland's best-dressed men and women. One of the jurors, he said, mounted a 'last minute lobby for ex-Taoiseach Haughey'. He did not name the juror, but followed this immediately with: 'Just as all started voting, a huge birthday cake arrived in Sandycove by taxi – for Terry Keane, well-known wife of Judge Keane… It was her birthday and she cut the cake amid loud jokes from the other judges.'

There were two ways of reading this. One was that it was almost pure nonsense. What does 'well-known wife' mean and why were there raucous jokes and who can afford to send a birthday cake by taxi to a restaurant on the far side of Dublin Bay? The other was to insert 'mistress' for wife and get a titillating story about Keane lobbying for her lover and Charlie sending her a birthday cake in a taxi. The pleasure of the second reading was that you were 'in'. But what no one could quite tell was how many people were 'in' – even though it seemed to be almost everyone. There was a kind of doubleness in this, too: pretty much everybody knew but almost all of them got the thrill of feeling that they were in the elite company of a select few initiates.

This doubleness suited the times and enriched Haughey's claim to be the great representative of the people. In a way, he was. Mores and morals were uncertain: Catholic conservatism was increasingly impossible to live with in private life but not yet dispensable as a marker of public identity. Haughey's sexual hypocrisy – the way his private life contradicted his political stance as defender of faith and morals – made him emblematic of the state of the place. Many years later, Terry Keane, asked by Gay Byrne when Maureen Haughey knew about the relationship, replied indignantly that 'We never talked about each other's spouses. Charlie is an old-fashioned sort of man. That would really be beyond the bounds of decency.'[18] There is no reason to believe that this, at least, was untrue.

But the bounds of decency were much wider when it came to money. Haughey's fall from power in the arms crisis of 1970 meant that his patrons lost their enthusiasm for funding his extravagance. Haughey did not stop spending. His overdraft with Allied Irish Bank continued to mount up, but the bankers knew, because he told them so, that if they moved against him, he could be 'a very troublesome adversary'.[19] He taunted them by flying to London or Paris with Keane, drinking Château Petrus and Dom

Perignon and eating at the most expensive possible restaurants. In 1973, he sold some land to Cement Roadstone, chaired by his personal bagman Des Traynor, for £140,000 but in 1974, he bought one of the Blasket islands, Inishvicillaun for £25,000 – five times his official salary, and had the materials for a stone house flown over by helicopter. As of December 1979, when Jack Lynch resigned, Haughey had a debt of £1.1 million with AIB.

But as Haughey moved back towards power, the money began to flow again. Five days after he became Taoiseach, Patrick Gallagher alone stumped up £350,000. Within weeks of taking charge of the state, Haughey was able to pay £750,000 to AIB, which then wrote off the rest – effectively a gift of £260,000. On 9 January, he went on television to announce in grim tones that the nation was broke: 'As a community we are living away [sic] beyond our means… we have been borrowing enormous amounts of money, borrowing at a rate which just cannot continue… We will have to continue to cut down on government spending… so that we can only undertake the things which we can afford.'[20]

23

1979–1982: The Body Politic

Bodies had always been the ultimate currency of the Troubles – bodies shattered, torn apart, broken, beaten, tortured, displayed, disappeared. But, from the point of view of the members of the IRA, the bodies in question were other people's. They belonged to the people they killed. As the surreal saga of Frank Stagg's corpse had shown, however, there was also a tradition of using the Republican body itself as a weapon of war. That saga had also reminded the authorities south of the Border just how dangerous this kind of war could be, how the dead or dying body could take a fierce grip on the living. The British government, though, never really understood this. It allowed itself to be dragged into a conflict it could win physically but would always lose imaginatively – a fight, quite literally, to the death in the H-Block prison complex at Long Kesh, nine miles southwest of Belfast.

The eight single-storey buildings known from their shape as the H-Blocks were, ironically, at the centre of 'the most up-to-date and luxurious prison in Europe'. The complex had sophisticated training workshops and classrooms, a fine indoor sports hall, two all-weather sports pitches, a hospital and a dental clinic. As David Beresford put it in his sympathetic account of the hunger strikes mounted there by Republican prisoners, 'Imprisonment in the H-Blocks was a status tens of thousands of prisoners around the world would have envied.'[1]

Up to 1975, political prisoners in Northern Ireland had been recognized as such and given 'Special category' status. This system allowed them to wear their own clothes, move freely around the compounds outside the H-Blocks in which most of them were housed, and maintain quasi-military structures, with their own commanders. But, after it ended internment, the British government announced that those convicted of terrorist offences committed after 1 March 1976 would be treated as ordinary criminals and subjected to ordinary prison rules. Brendan Hughes, the IRA commander in the H-Blocks, recalled the 'shock to the system' – 'Here I was that morning being called "Mr Hughes" or "O/C" [officer in command], now being called "704 Hughes" and dumped in a cell.'[2]

What followed was a process of acceleration that no one really planned. Hughes described it as 'like getting on a bike at the top of a hill… it gained its own momentum'.[3] It started in September 1976 when one newly arrived prisoner, Ciaran Nugent, asked what size uniform he would take, replied, 'You must be joking me.' He was placed in a cell with just a blanket to cover him. Other new prisoners followed his example. This meant that they were not allowed to leave their cells and lost almost all privileges, including remission of sentences. After furniture in one wing was broken in a confrontation between prisoners and warders, all cell furniture was removed.

In 1978, Hughes decided to escalate the protest. Prisoners going to have their weekly shower were subjected to jeering from warders because they were covered only in a towel. They demanded two towels. When that was refused, Hughes ordered the prisoners to stop taking showers. He also ordered his men 'to smash the basins' that were supplied by the prison authorities and 'stop washing altogether'. But, as he explained, 'by not going out to take showers, that meant you did not get out to go to the toilet. So the wastage, the excreta and the urine built up in the small chamber pots that everyone had.' Hughes then ordered that the prisoners must not co-operate with the collection of this waste from their cells. The only alternative was for the prisoners to smear their waste on the cell walls.[4] By late 1980, 341 of the 837 Republican prisoners in Long Kesh were on what was now called the dirty protest.[5]

This was both deliberate and unplanned. Hughes had a general strategy, which was to set up a spiral of conflict within the H-Blocks 'as a tool to help the leadership on the outside – specifically Gerry [Adams] – to build up a propaganda machine'. But 'we had no idea where it was going to finish'.[6] No one, including Hughes and Adams, ever imagined that the abyss at the bottom of the hill down which they were freewheeling was prisoners wrapped only in blankets, filthy and unshorn, lying amid the maggots and stench of bare, excrement-lined cells. The most luxurious prison in Europe was turned, by its own inmates, into a hellhole.

Another unintended consequence was to make the warders, many of them already violent, more brutal. The IRA began a campaign of murdering prison officers in or around their homes. Between early 1978 and December 1980, it killed thirteen of them, including the governor, Albert Miles. The knowledge that Hughes and other IRA leaders inside the prison were sending messages as to which of the officers was to be targeted generated even more personal hatred than already existed. As Hughes acknowledged, after the killings began, 'the half-decent prison officers [were] pulled out of the blocks and you… were left with the hard core of bigots and the Catholic and Republican haters… The tactic of shooting the screws did not work.'[7]

I found the images of these prisoners unfathomable. This flaunting of filthiness went against every instinct of the modernity and respectability for which we as Irish Catholics had been striving. Dirt was poverty and shame. The kids who smelled of piss and sweat, who had black stuff under their fingernails and dark rings around their necks, were the kids you did not want to be. This was personal, but it was also collective – being dirty was a slur on the nature of the Irish. To look and smell foul was to be inferior. We also internalized the Victorian truth that cleanliness was next to godliness. Physical and moral hygiene went together – to be spotless was to be free of pollution and defilement.

The prisoners' self-abasement drew us back into the nightmares of being unEuropean, uncivilized, unmodern. In their nakedness, they were the ultimate descaminados. In August 1978, when the head of the Irish Catholic Church Archbishop (later Cardinal) Tomas Ó Fiaich visited the H-Blocks, he excavated from his sense memory the only comparable experience: 'The nearest to it that I have seen was the spectacle of hundreds of homeless people living in sewer-pipes in the slums of Calcutta. The stench and the filth in some of the cells with the remains of rotten food and human excreta scattered around the walls, was almost unbearable. In two of them, I was unable to speak for fear of vomiting.'[8]

My mother's sister Bridget had been a missionary nun in Madras (Chennai) for thirteen years. When I read Ó Fiaich's statement, I remembered the horror with which she spoke of the conditions endured by the homeless street people of India. It gave us a sensation of revulsion tempered by superiority. We were not like that – and if we had been so in the past it was the fault of the English who had made us poor. We had raised ourselves up under the guidance of the church. Now, in Ó Fiaich's image, the slums of Madras and Calcutta had been transplanted into contemporary Irish politics.

And yet, even this abjection could be given both aesthetic and religious meaning, especially for those who didn't have to face the stench. The smearing of excrement on the walls could be seen as a form of artistic expression. Ó Fiaich, a distinguished scholar of the Irish language, was moved by the fact that the prisoners were teaching each other Irish and by 'Irish words, phrases and songs being shouted from cell to cell and then written on each cell wall with the remnants of toothpaste tubes'.[9] The Tate Gallery in London acquired a diptych by the English painter and pioneer of Pop Art, Richard Hamilton, of one of the dirty protestors, Hugh Rooney, set next to a panel of abstract brown shit marks which Hamilton compared to 'the megalithic spirals of Newgrange' and the 'Gaelic convolutions of the Book of Kells'.[10] But Hamilton also hinted at the most visceral visual connection. Rooney, barefoot and draped in a rather fetching blanket, is darkly beautiful, his naked and hairless chest and stomach marked by improbably well-defined muscles. He looks remarkably clean. And with his long hair and beard and his unflinching gaze, he is also the Jesus of countless icons. This was not just Hamilton's fantasy. As the H-Block conflict escalated towards its ultimate destination – death by hunger strike – the religious meaning of the events would become increasingly conflated with the political.

This was a meta-conflict – a war to determine the nature of the war. At its heart was the question of knowledge. We understand the world by organizing it into categories. A 'Special category' prisoner was, from the point of view of the British, an unacceptable anomaly, a failure of classification. It was all a matter of taxonomy. The British government wanted to define the prisoners as ordinary criminals and therefore to name their actions as species of legal delinquency (murder, assault, robbery, kidnap, hijacking) and the IRA itself as a terror gang or mafia racket. Once these definitions were accepted, even tacitly, the prisoners could enjoy one of the most pleasant prison regimes in the world. There was no need to sign up to any statement of submission to these designations, any renunciation of the claim to be patriotic warriors for Ireland. All that was necessary was sullen conformity – a condition that is inscribed in the standard contract of all prison life.

This logic of giving things their proper names was not just British scientific rationalism. It was also what John Paul II tried to do in his sermon in Drogheda in 1979. At its heart was his decree, delivered with the full of authority of Christ's representative of Earth, 'that nobody may ever call murder by any other name than murder'.[11] Essentially, the pope tried in that sermon to do exactly what the British were attempting in the H-Blocks: to fix once and for all the relationship between the signifier and the signified. The name for shooting someone in the head is murder and, once the act is so named, it is heinous. The British defined that heinousness as crime, the pope as mortal sin. The effect was the same: the meaning of the act is objective.

This was, however, precisely why the IRA could not respond to the pope's plea. Its system of classification was not objective but subjective. In their different ways, the British and the pope used a taxonomy based on action – what was the deed that had been done and how did it fit into the legal codes or the Ten Commandments? The IRA arranged its world according to motivation – why was the deed done? It agreed with Hamlet: 'there is nothing either good or bad, but thinking makes it so.' Thinking and feeling – the whole structure of sacrifice and martyrdom that gave meaning to violent Irish nationalism – could transform the nature of any action, from smuggling fuel across the Border to make a fortune, to robbing a bank, to maiming a child by shooting off his kneecaps, to putting a bomb in a crowded pub. Outside of the code of meanings that the IRA applied to itself, these actions would be, indeed, despicable. Within that code, they were not merely honourable but heroic.

The problem for the IRA and its supporters, however, was that this same claim could then be made by the Loyalists and indeed by the British themselves. The sectarian gangs who tortured and murdered Catholics would not be murderers because their deeds had a political and ideological motivation. The British soldiers who murdered Catholics on the streets of Belfast and Derry did so, unquestionably, for political reasons. This is the innate difficulty of subjective meanings – everybody has their own subjectivity.

The IRA had therefore become mired in a swampy linguistic terrain. The slipperiest word was 'war': 'the war goes on. When Britain goes, so goes the war.' It's war when you kill 'inevitable casualties' or make mistakes. It's war when you shrug your shoulders and shake your head and say that, yes, such things are regrettable, but that's what war is like. It's war when you kill building workers or census collectors for 'collaboration', the analogy being with the French Resistance and the Nazis. It's war when you want your prisoners to be treated as POWs.

But it's not war when you demand that those same prisoners be granted full remission of their sentences – how many belligerent countries release enemy POWs while the war is still going on because they have been of good behaviour? It's not war when you want a fair trial before being held captive or the right to appear on your enemy's state television to make the case for your armed struggle. It's not war when you complain of dirty tricks by British intelligence and shoot-to-kill policies by the British army against IRA members. It's not war when the enemy starts to behave as you do and to shrug its shoulders at the inevitable casualties. It's not war when you are outraged by failures to adhere to due legal process after you've been caught with Semtex in your car, but it is war when you drag sixteen-year-olds out of flats in impoverished Catholic ghettoes and maim them for life because 'everyone knows they are guilty' of anti-social behaviour.

The other big problem of definition for the IRA was that of 'legitimate targets'. The IRA's self-image, expressed in the manual for members known as the Green Book produced in 1979 was that it was the army of a legitimate, democratically elected parliament: 'the direct representative of the 1918 Dáil Éireann parliament and that as such they are the legal and lawful representative of the Irish Republic... The Irish Republican Army, as the legal representatives of the Irish people, are morally justified in carrying out a campaign of resistance against foreign occupation forces and domestic collaborators.'[12]

So the IRA itself evoked the idea of legality and projected itself as the lawful army of a state, albeit one that had only a shadow existence. But states are not free, even in waging war, to do whatever they like. They are bound by international law. They can't target civilians, non-combatants or off-duty soldiers. The IRA did this all the time. 'Domestic collaborators' was a floating signifier, one that absorbed meaning rather than transmitting it. It could mean Irish policemen, builders or catering staff who worked in a police station or an army barracks, census collectors, a kid working on a boat owned by Earl Mountbatten, business executives like Jeffrey Agate, managing director of Du Pont in Derry, whose crime was attempting to 'stabilise the economy', and long-retired Unionist politicians like Sir Norman Stronge, killed by the IRA in 1981. He was eighty-six years old and had withdrawn from public life in 1969 but he was, said the IRA, a 'symbol of hated unionism'.[13] So, domestic collaboration could be metaphorical and still merit death. Or it could just mean Protestants in general.

The power of hunger striking lay in its potential to cut through these problems of definition and to draw new lines of victimhood and oppression, of nobility and cruelty. It does not seem accidental that the senior IRA prisoners in the H-Blocks began to discuss a hunger strike in 1978 after one of the most horrific examples of the consequences of their movement's elastic and expanding definitions of domestic collaboration. The IRA attacked the annual dinner dance of the Irish Collie Club. Collie breeders on the island of Ireland had split after partition – the Irish Collie Club was the Northern Ireland branch and therefore its members could be assumed to be Protestant owners of Protestant dogs.

On the evening of February 1978, the IRA hung a firebomb on the grille of a window of the La Mon, a country hotel east of Belfast. The device was specifically constructed to create a firestorm, with cans of petrol attached to the explosive. The effect was like napalm, the victims showered with burning petrol that clung to their skin. Bodies were found, charred beyond recognition, huddled against a brick wall opposite the window. People with their clothes and flesh and hair on fire ran out of the building. Twelve victims, seven of them women, all of them Protestants, died. Thirty others were injured, many of them horribly. The IRA claimed that it was all a mistake and that it had given an 'inadequate' warning, but the nature of the bomb strongly suggested that it was designed to do what it did, incinerate Protestant civilians. The IRA insisted that no one except the immediate relatives of the dead or its own supporters had any right to complain about this.

If this was war, these were war crimes. Atrocities like these created an increasingly unavoidable imperative – to prove that this was not criminality, the prisoners had to cease to be perpetrators and become victims. They could do this only by showing that they could suffer even more pain than they inflicted: you might burn quickly in our firestorm; we will die slowly in the agony of hunger. You are an unfortunate casualty. We sacrifice ourselves. By doing so we show that life itself – including your life – is not the ultimate value.

It is striking that this gesture had to be male. There is nothing innately masculine about hunger striking. The suffragists had pioneered it as a modern political weapon in Britain. The Price sisters, Marian and Dolours, arrested during an IRA bombing campaign in London in 1973, had endured a horrifically long hunger strike, kept alive by the brutal practice of forced feeding.

Female IRA prisoners were being held in Armagh jail. They were allowed to wear their own clothes. Until February 1980, they supported the H-Block protests by refusing to do prison work. This led to a withdrawal of privileges, petty harassment and a build-up of tension that resulted in the decision by thirty-two women to emulate the dirty protest. This was experienced by them as perhaps an even greater trial than it was for the men. As one of the protestors recalled, 'It was completely alien to all of us to have to be unclean as far as our bodies were concerned.'[14]

This bodily war had a new element – menstrual blood. Many of the women, because of the stress, had more frequent periods. The prison authorities rationed sanitary towels. 'The women still had to make do with the quota of sanitary towels allocated to them. The fact that they had to sit in their own menstrual blood amidst excreta and urine did not concern the prison authorities. It was a particularly humiliating form of punishment.'[15]

Yet this extra layer of suffering did not really belong in the story. The menstrual blood on the walls of Armagh jail was not compared to Newgrange or the Book of Kells. The women's suffering was not Christlike. In May 1981, the *Donegal Democrat* could note that the Armagh women 'have received little attention'.[16] This was not entirely true, but much of the comment on it was an argument within feminism, with, for example, Nell McCafferty supporting the women and Máirín de Burca refusing to do so.[17] But it was certainly the case that the Armagh protest never acquired the status or potency of that in Long Kesh.

Some of this was squeamishness about female bodily functions. Some of it reflected very different ideas of dirt and cleanliness when it came to women. One sympathetic account in 1984 pointed out that 'Even between men and women political prisoners, the sexual "double standard" can still apply.' It was regarded as normal, even obligatory, for young women in Republican areas to write to and visit male prisoners in Long Kesh. But this sympathy did not apply to a female Republican prisoner in Armagh. 'Before her imprisonment, she had been promiscuous. Now, when she sent out requests for visits, man after man chose to ignore her. As one ex-lover complained… "Christ I'm not going to see her – people might think I actually *like* that slut."'[18]

In any event, the women were ordered off their dirty protest in January 1981 in order to 'focus the full spotlight of world attention on the… hunger strike taking place in Long Kesh'.[19] This was in fact the second strike. The first began in October 1979, after the prisoners rejected an offer from the authorities that they would be allowed to wear 'civilian-style' clothes. The struggle was coming down to such fine sartorial distinctions. Seven H-Block prisoners, including Hughes as their leader, began a hunger strike on the same day, 27 October 1979, one from each of the six counties of Northern Ireland plus one member of the smaller faction, the Irish National Liberation Army, but the number also echoing the martyred seven signatories of the proclamation of the Republic at Easter 1916. Twenty-three more joined on 15 December; another seven the following day. But two days later, after Ó Fiaich called on the men 'in the name of God' to end the protest, and with one of the original seven, Seán McKenna, on the brink of death, the hunger strike was called off.

It collapsed after fifty-three days because the prisoners had not been ready to die. As the original seven entered the killing zone, they realized there was another 'shock to the system' – a realization that this was not, in the end, a symbolic act. The figurative mimicking of Christ's crucifixion and of the martyrs of 1916 could sustain the drama through weeks of torment. But in the last act, there was only a terrible reality. Faced with making the direct decision after McKenna had gone into a coma, Hughes shouted out, 'Feed him'.[20] Hughes knew that many of the other men were waiting for McKenna to die in the hope that the hunger strike would then be called off and they would not have to.

The thing that everyone needed at that point was obfuscation. After the first strike was called off, the British produced a vague document that in effect conceded no more than the 'civilian-style' clothing that had already been offered. Sinn Féin declared victory and called for a celebratory parade in West Belfast. Everyone knew this was a fiction – so few people turned up that the event was 'an embarrassment'. But, in essence, declaring victory was the only way out for them. And it could really have been a way out if the British had understood the fertility of ambivalence, the possibility of allowing this gap between what Sinn Féin and the IRA wanted to claim (that the prisoners had won) and what 'everybody knew' (that they had lost) to remain open.

The Irish authorities, unlike their British counterparts, knew how to avoid the murderous logic of certainty. Both the British and the Provos were looking for hard and fast distinctions, clean lines of separation between criminality and legitimacy. Both ended up in a binary mindset, a zero-sum game. In this war of signifiers, everything had to mean, in the end, one thing or the other. But the Irish government, which was every bit as hostile to the Provos as the British were, had the advantage of the Irish culture of ambiguity. There were threatened and indeed actual hunger strikes in Portlaoise prison, where the IRA and INLA prisoners were held in the Republic. But they were not allowed to reach the point of irreconcilable difference. The political status of the prisoners was allowed to become yet another unknown known. It existed in effect but not in principle. The prisoners wore their own clothes and were allowed some element of free association, prison work was construed in the broadest possible terms to include cultural and educational activities and the military command structures of the groups were recognized implicitly but not explicitly.

Everyone within Irish Catholic culture knew how to do this. For all the profound antagonism between democratic politicians and the IRA, there was a mutual interest in avoiding deaths on hunger strike. The IRA in Long Kesh would have accepted what Hughes and the rest of the leadership called a 'Portlaoise-type settlement'.[21] It kept everyone alive. Irish governments knew how incendiary the culture of martyrdom could be and how important it was to damp down that fire before it could take hold. The fire extinguisher was ambiguity.

The great problem was that neither the British prime minister Margaret Thatcher nor Hughes's successor as commanding officer of the IRA prisoners, Bobby Sands, wished to wield it. Both were wedded to implacability, adamant for clarity. The authorities in Long Kesh had begun to grasp the need for mutually accommodating fictions. The governor, Stanley Hilditch, seemed to be ready to implement a perfectly orchestrated exercise in deliberate indefinition. The prisoners would be issued simultaneously with their own clothes, to be supplied by their families, and with prison-issue 'civilian-style' clothes.[22] They would be at once criminal and not criminal.

At this point, in effect, the IRA in the prisons had been defeated. Brendan Hughes, knowing after the first hunger strike that he had failed, was suicidal. He tried to tense up his body so much that his heart would stop beating. He had a 'constant clear image of just having a gun and blowing my head off'.[23] Men were steadily drifting away from the dirty protest and conforming to prison rules. Prisoners were co-operating with the deep-cleaning of their cells. Their sense of gloom was heightened when their most charismatic voice on the outside, Bernadette Devlin McAliskey, was attacked in her home by three UDA gunmen. One of them shot her husband Michael four times. The other two shot her seven times. Astonishingly, both of them recovered. Devlin was the sixth campaigner on behalf of the H-Block protestors to be shot by Loyalists in six months.

There is little doubt that had the British simply embraced Hilditch's plan of giving the prisoners both their own clothes and some prison-issue clothing, everything that happened next, and all the deaths it entailed, could have been avoided. Instead, on 23 January 1981, the prison authorities refused to issue their own clothes to the prisoners who had been co-operating with them. Those prisoners, who were now in clean cells, smashed up the new furniture they had been given. The cycle of violence within the prison began again, with the more brutal warders beating prisoners in retaliation.

On 5 February the prisoners announced their intention to begin a second hunger strike, this time to achieve the maximalist demand of prisoner of war status. It was unachievable under any circumstances, but that was the point. After the failure of the first hunger strike, the instinct of the leader of the second one, Bobby Sands, was that only absolute defiance, with the absolute consequence of death, would suffice. As he wrote to the IRA's governing Army Council, 'We accept the tragic consequences that most certainly await us and the overshadowing fact that death may not secure a principled settlement.'[24]

This is worth dwelling on. What Sands was saying was not just that he would die. It was that he would probably die in vain. This was a process of purification. Death itself would be cleansed of any instrumental adulterations. It would be refined into its purest state. It would be its own statement, its own purpose, its own meaning. What Sands was embarking on was an act of unalloyed will. This required an almost superhuman level of trust in his own resolve. He would repay his own confidence.

Sands was a bomber. He had, in his own words, been caught in 1976 in a car containing 'four ticking bombs'[25] though in fact the bombs had been planted in a furniture showroom and he was trying to drive away when he was arrested. This was 'war' at its most unheroic. It did not have the romance of the IRA's self-image of 'taking on the Brits'. Blowing up furniture for Ireland did not exactly equate to the deeds of James Connolly and Patrick Pearse. Perhaps this was part of Sands's extraordinary implacability – he had something to prove and only one way to prove it.

Sands was also steeped in romantic Irish nationalism. He wrote poetry in the nineteenth-century vein of Speranza (Lady Jane Wilde, the mother of Oscar) and Pearse. He took notes on revolutionary theory from Frantz Fanon and Che Guevara. And he also fully understood the religious dimension of what he was undertaking. As he told the campaigning Catholic priest Father Denis Faul, 'Greater love hath no man than that he lay down his life for his friend.'[26] It was not accidental that he and the other prisoners became more fervently Catholic after the second hunger strike began on 1 March, saying the Rosary twice a day.

The new hunger strike was also structured so as to ensure both the maximum dramatic effect and the maximum pressure on those who came after Sands to continue it. It was a cascade of death. With prisoners joining the strike at regular intervals, the likelihood was that Sands's death would be followed by that of Francis Hughes, who started to refuse food two weeks later, and by Raymond McCreesh and Patsy O'Hara, who joined a further week on – and so on. This would escalate public tension, but it would also place the burden of the previous deaths on the next man entering the killing zone – and just as importantly on his family. To pull back as the abyss approached would be to betray those who had already made the sacrifice. In this way, the logic set in motion by Sands would continue to work its way long after his own death.

There was something both very cold and deeply emotional at work. Brendan Hughes, after his own ordeal in the previous strike, reflected that 'the body is a fantastic machine – it'll eat off all the fat tissue first and then it starts eating away at the muscle to keep your brain alive. When that goes, all that's left is your brain and it starts to go as well.'[27] The hunger strike itself was a fantastic machine, though one paradoxically fuelled by starvation. It consumed deaths to keep itself alive – not just within the prison, but on the streets outside. Yet it also had a ferocious psychic power. It unleashed passions and sympathies in ways no other gesture could match. All the things the Irish government had tried to seal in when Frank Stagg's grave was covered in concrete would now emerge from it.

What Irish governments had always been determined to avoid was the fusion of nationalist with Catholic martyrdom. They understood, simply because they were steeped in the history of blood sacrifice from Easter 1916 onwards, that when these two currents met, there would be an explosion. This is exactly what happened as Sands's hunger strike proceeded. H-Block support rallies segued seamlessly into prayer meetings as denunciations of the British led into chanting of the Rosary.[28] The murals on the walls of Catholic areas in Belfast became ever more explicit in their identification of Sands with Christ: a dying hunger striker holding up his Rosary beads with the Virgin Mary watching over him, captioned, 'Blessed are those who hunger for justice'; an emaciated hunger striker attached to a crucifix formed from the H of H-Block; Jesus himself, with his Sacred Heart on display in his chest, looming over a kneeling blanketman. In perhaps the most telling image, an angel spreads its golden wings over both a prostrate, naked hunger striker and a kneeling uniformed IRA volunteer whose Armalite points heavenwards.[29] The sanction of heaven itself is conveyed, not just to the hunger strike, but to the IRA's armed struggle.

This was exactly what anyone with an understanding of Catholic nationalist mythology would have anticipated. To me, it was both repellent and utterly inevitable. On the one hand, there was no doubt that, as the mural so vividly illustrated, the ultimate point of the hunger strikes was to strengthen the IRA's campaign. It was dying in the cause of killing. On the other, the sheer agony of this slow self-sacrifice could not be gainsaid. This pain was a language of which I was, like it or not, a native speaker. I did not like what was being said, but I knew the grammar inside out.

It had the structure of art. Just as a drama works by distilling the great world down into a small cast of characters, the hunger strike did precisely what the executions of the leaders of the 1916 Rising had done before it. The complex events and many deaths of Easter 1916 were sublimated into the heroic tragedy of the seven signatories of the Proclamation of the Irish Republic and their executions. (Seven other executed leaders of the Rising were largely forgotten.) Now the complexities of the Troubles and its thousands of dead were boiled down to ten men who would die on the hunger strike. And not even that – it did not take very long for most of the ten to fade from memory and the entire drama to be concentrated into the body of Bobby Sands. History was shrunk down to the passing of time. The drama of the deathwatch played out day by day, then hour by hour. It crowded out the larger conflict that was being reignited on the streets.

Yet it was also altering, in ways not yet visible to the IRA, the terms of that conflict. Sands was showing, in the most visceral ways, the truth of his predecessor Terence MacSwiney's insistence that it was those who could suffer the most, not those who could inflict the most, who would win. The deep sympathy he evoked produced an early victory – not in the arena of armed violence but in a field he himself disdained – that of electoral politics. When Frank Maguire, the independent nationalist MP for Fermanagh-South Tyrone in the Westminster parliament, died, the obvious nationalist candidates for the by-election were his brother Noel or Bernadette Devlin McAliskey, who publicly declared her interest in standing. She made it clear, however, that she would stand down in favour of one of the H-Block prisoners. Somewhat reluctantly, the Sinn Féin leadership agreed that Bobby Sands himself should stand.

The sheer weight of his Christlike suffering forced the main nationalist party, John Hume's SDLP, to withdraw its nomination of one of the founding figures of the civil rights movement, Austin Currie. For many Northern Catholics, the point now was to save Sands's life and the belief was that if he won the election, Margaret Thatcher would have to back down and the pall of the hunger strikes would be lifted. Most of them were not willing to vote for the IRA; but most of them were willing to use their votes to stop several IRA men from dying. This was an ambivalence the British did not understand.

The clearest evidence that the IRA did not really understand it either came on 7 April, just two days before the election, when it killed Joanne Mathers for the crime of distributing census forms. She was twenty-nine, married and had a little child. A star graduate of Queen's University Belfast, she was helping a resident of Anderson Crescent, a Catholic enclave within the largely Protestant Waterside area of Derry, to fill in a form, when the IRA shot her in the head at point-blank range. Even for purely cynical reasons, this made no sense. Shooting a defenceless young woman in cold blood reminded everyone that the IRA was not primarily in the business of enduring suffering – it was no whit less committed to inflicting it.

Sands nonetheless won the election by a very narrow margin. His victory in fact changed nothing in relation to the H-Block conflict. There was no transformation of Thatcher's attitude. What had changed was something, ironically, that Sands himself would not have wanted. It was that there was now the possibility that candidates associated with the IRA and Sinn Féin could win elections. The hidden clause was that if they wanted to do this in the Republic, they would have to stop the killing.

After the death of the fifth hunger striker, Joe McDonnell, on 8 July, the Taoiseach Garret FitzGerald warned Thatcher that 'a rising tide of sympathy for the hunger strikers was threatening the stability of the Republic'.[30] But this was not quite true. There were large demonstrations in favour of the hunger strikers all over the Republic. It was easy to see, if you were my age, that a lot of young people who had previously been uninterested in 'the North' were being drawn into the ambit of militant nationalism by their compassion for Sands and his fellow prisoners. Most saw themselves as part of a broad human rights campaign. Few understood that, as the IRA prisoner and thinker Tommy McKearney later acknowledged, 'the IRA briefed its members and trusted supporters to make sure that the Anti H-Block committees being set up throughout Ireland were firmly, if discreetly, kept in Provo hands'.[31]

Sands died on 5 May 1981, after sixty-six days without food. There was again a great Republican funeral, attended in Belfast by at least 100,000 people. The coffin was carried to the grave by six men in camouflage jackets and black berets, their faces hidden by balaclavas. What was not hidden was that the meaning of his death was also 'in Provo hands', that it was inextricable from the IRA's armed struggle. This, though, was double-edged. If Sands's martyrdom sanctioned the IRA's killing, did sympathy for him and admiration for his courage necessarily translate into an acceptance of the cruel deaths of others at the hands of his comrades? For most Irish Catholics, it did not.

On 10 June there was a general election in the Republic. Two H-Block prisoners, Kieran Doherty and Paddy Agnew, won seats in the Dáil, both in Border counties. This was a very notable achievement. The director of their electoral campaign, Sinn Féin's Dáithí Ó Conaill, hailed it as a transformative moment in Irish history on a par with the change in mood in 1917 that led Sinn Féin to victory in the elections of 1918. Just as that triumph had sprung from the blood of the martyrs of 1916, the country was now 'witnessing a 1917 situation when people came around to a different way of thinking after the execution of the 1916 martyrs'.[32]

This was a massive overstatement. There were nine H-Blocks candidates; two got elected, the rest polled respectably. But considering the emotional stakes the hunger strikes had placed on the table, these were modest winnings. They showed that a politicized Sinn Féin that was not asking directly for a mandate for the IRA's violence could make serious inroads in the Republic. This was, though, no revolutionary moment. Inside the H-Block, Tommy McKearney, who had taken part in the 1980 hunger strike, grasped what was for him this harsh reality. The fact that, as he put it, 'only two IRA candidates had been elected to the Republic's parliament' dispelled 'any lingering doubt about the southerners' views... After ten years of bitter conflict in the North, Southern Ireland wanted the IRA war to end rather than the IRA to win.'[33]

This meant, in the end, that the hunger strikers could not win either. Even the great energy generated by their suffering and by what most Irish Catholics saw as Thatcher's unfeeling intransigence was not enough to turn sympathy for prisoners into mass support for killers. After the tenth hunger striker, Michael Devine, died on 20 August, the family of the man next in line, Pat McGeown, authorized medical treatment to save his life. Three other families followed their example in September. On 3 October, the five remaining strikers ended their protest. Three days later, the British government announced that the prisoners would be allowed to wear their own clothes after all. Had it done so a year earlier, dozens of people, inside and outside the prison, would not have died.

The essential power of the hunger strikers was their willingness to see things through until the end. They compressed history into the fifty or sixty days it took a body to ingest itself. They created a tragic drama that seemed to move inevitably towards its unbearable climax. But after that climax, the tragedy is supposed to be resolved. The much more profound tragedy was that nothing was resolved and nothing was over. This history refused to be measured out in days – it could, and would, drag on for years. It refused to be reduced to a few bodies and continued to consume many more. Ten men achieved a terrible finality, but outside the prison, nothing was concluded. If anything, these deaths gave new life to the Troubles. Bobby Sands had set an undeniable example of absolute implacability. To be unyielding was also to be relentless.

24

1981–1983: Foetal Attractions

Three days before Bobby Sands died in May 1981, an Irish-Australian former Trappist monk, Lawrence James Downey, hijacked an Aer Lingus Boeing 737 jet on route from Dublin to London and demanded to be flown to Iran. A few years earlier, Downey had seen himself as an apostle of Irish modernity. He had arrived in Shannon in 1978 with a proposal to create a major international language school. He was also going to build a £10 million multipurpose sports stadium that would hold 20,000 spectators.[1] None of his hopes were realized. There was something emblematic in Downey's downward slide. Dreams of economic triumph were evaporating all over the country. The OECD forecast that among its twenty-four member countries, 'Ireland would have the lowest rate of growth in 1982, the fourth highest rate of unemployment, the second highest rate of inflation, the worst balance of payments deficit, and the highest level of debt repayment.'[2]

The number of unemployed people had doubled over the course of the 1970s. Mass emigration was back. There was a balance of payments crisis and government debt was out of control. The H-Block horror movie was playing on a loop. The whole project of making Ireland a normal western European country was in deep trouble. A nervous breakdown, a diverted flight from reality, was a reasonable recourse.

Early in 1981, when the hunger strikes were under way, Downey contacted the *Irish Times*, wanting the paper to report on his scheme for solving the problem. He would, he said, take the prisoners from the H-Blocks and form them into a volunteer army for the tiny Central American state of Belize that was just about to become independent from Britain. Citing the example of the film *The Dirty Dozen*, he suggested that the new army of men who had been on the dirty protest could be called the Filthy Five Hundred.

Downey also took flight into religious mania. When his schemes came to nothing, he wrote a book called *The Christian Manifesto*, showing how the Devil was in league with communism and how between them they had led even the pope astray. On the weekend when Bobby Sands lapsed into a coma and while everyone was waiting for him to die, Downey entered the cockpit of the Aer Lingus plane, smelling of petrol and with a vial of what he claimed was cyanide around his neck. As well as being flown to Tehran, Downey's main demand was the publication in the *Irish Independent* of a nine-page-long statement about 'the third secret of Fatima'. This was a message passed by the Blessed Virgin Mary to the Portuguese children to whom she appeared in 1917, with instructions that it be revealed only to Pope Benedict XV. Downey wanted to know what was *really* going on.

So did we all. The implosion of the modernizing project seemed to confuse even the most basic categories of knowledge and understanding. The big world of history collapsed down into the little world of the body. Public discourse became excremental in the H-Blocks and gynaecological in the Republic. The body wars of the 1980s dissolved the distinction between public and private, between inside and outside, the epic and the intimate. In Long Kesh, the private and internal parts of men's and women's bodies became a primary medium of communication. Messages etched in tiny writing on cigarette papers and wrapped in cling film were carried into the visiting area secreted in prisoners' mouths, rectums or foreskins. (One prisoner was reputed to have managed forty messages at one time in his foreskin.) Female visitors carried them out of the prison in their bras, panties, sanitary napkins or inside their vaginas.[3]

The language of politics south of the Border went further inside – all the way into the womb. Running parallel to the dirty protests and the hunger strikes was the emergence in the Republic of the Pro-Life Amendment Campaign (PLAC) demanding a referendum to amend the Irish constitution to outlaw abortion. The practice was already illegal in Ireland, under the Offences Against the Persons Act of 1861. It prescribed a penalty of 'penal servitude for life' for the woman who had an abortion and also criminalized anyone who helped her. It would be hard to imagine a more repressive legal regime. No political party with any power was suggesting any change to this law. In 1974, one of the few liberal public intellectuals in parliament, the Labour Party's David Thornley, told the Dáil that 'There are absolutely no circumstances in which I would vote for abortion. I regard it as murder...'[4]

Yet here, too, there was the Irish solution to an Irish problem: distance and silence. The unspoken and unspeakable compact was that Irish women would have their abortions elsewhere, mostly in England. And, when they came back, they would not talk about it. This had obviously gone on for a long time. The opening sentence of Brendan Behan's (aptly aborted) novel, *The Catacombs*, written in the 1950s, is 'There was a party in the Catacombs to celebrate Deirdre's return from her abortion in Bristol'[5] but the point of this is to be utterly outrageous. Abortion in England, yes, but party in Dublin, never. And, of course, this novel was not completed, much less published.

After abortion became legal in Britain in 1968, hundreds of Irish women began to travel to terminate their pregnancies. In 1970, 261 women gave addresses in Ireland to abortion clinics in England and Wales. By the early 1980s, the annual numbers were at or above 4,000 – and many Irish women gave addresses of friends in England and so did not feature in these statistics. In all, from 1970 to 2019, when abortion was finally legalized in Ireland, at least a quarter of a million Irish women crossed the Irish Sea for a termination. The number who spoke about it in public was vanishingly small; in private not much greater.

In its way, this was a perfect system. It did what Catholic Ireland always wanted to do – to construct two parallel universes, two truths. It could be said, with reasonable accuracy, that there was no abortion in Ireland, unlike, of course, in godless England. But Irish women, provided they could afford to travel, could have abortions and be grateful for England's godlessness. Don't ask, don't tell, don't bring these two worlds into contact with each other, and the system can carry on for a very long time to come.

I got a sense of this when I was eighteen. I knew nothing about anything and even less about abortion. I had never really thought about it. I suppose I had a vague feeling that it was a bad thing, to be contemplated only in extreme circumstances. And then in summer 1976 I had to discover what I felt about abortion. It took me all of thirty seconds.

Very few people in my part of the world went to university. I was a student in UCD. This lent me an aura of sophistication and knowingness that was laughably distant from the truth. But because of it, a male friend my own age called in and asked me to go with him to his house. His mother and father were in the sitting room with his sister who was, I think, sixteen. She was pregnant and she had made up her mind that she did not want to have the baby. Did I know how to go about arranging to have an abortion in England?

What was I supposed to do? Get up and storm out in a show of moral outrage? Or sit there and squirm and stammer out the quite truthful answer that I knew sweet damn all about any of this stuff? Or try somehow to be of use, to help the girl get this thing done so that after the school holidays, she could just turn up in class like everyone else, study for her Leaving Cert and get on with her life?

It's at moments like this, when you find yourself under pressure to make a choice you are not prepared for, that your hidden instincts reveal themselves. Sitting on the couch looking at that girl, two things were immediately obvious. One was that this was not about me or my feelings at all – it was about her. And the other was that the part of her that was most important here was not really her body. It was her mind, her free will, her right to make the decision she had come to. I just knew that I'd be a pompous little prig if I walked out. And I just knew that I'd be a miserable little coward if I hid behind my ignorance.

I didn't have the information she wanted but I was in a position to get it, to find people who could talk to her and help her get to a clinic in England. I knew absolutely that if I did this, it would make me morally complicit in the arrangement of an abortion. A small part in the facilitation of a murder makes you a murderer. If this was a baby killing, and if I helped even a little bit, I would be, then and now and forever, a baby killer.

This was not, moreover, what anti-abortion people like to call a hard case. There was no suggestion that the girl had been raped. She was in the bloom of youthful good health and there was no reason to think that she could not have a glowing pregnancy and a happy delivery. There was not even a melodramatic scenario where shamed and scandalized parents were about to fling her out on the road and warn her never to darken their doorsteps again. Her parents were good people – they loved her and respected her and would have supported her in any decision she made. If she had wanted to have a baby and keep it, I had no doubt they would help her and welcome her child.

But she didn't. This was the simple, salient fact in that sitting room at that moment. She wasn't weeping or pleading. She was calm, controlled, determined. She had a mind and she had made it up. She needed help, not to make her decision, but to carry it through. And it actually did not occur to me for one instant that it was my business to do anything except try to make a difficult situation for her a little easier if I could. Why? Because the alternative was unthinkable: that this girl be forced against her will to go through a pregnancy she did not want.

I told the family I would be back the next day with the phone numbers they needed. I went in to UCD next morning and got the numbers and went back to the house. Her father answered the door and I gave him a piece of paper with the information on it. I never talked to the family again about what happened. I just know that the girl was not pregnant that summer, that she was back in school in the autumn, that she got her Leaving Cert and went on to have a good life. That was the way things were done.

On the face of it, Ireland in 1981 was still outstandingly religious, in practice as well as in theory. The vast bulk of the population was Catholic and 88 per cent of Catholics went to Mass at least once a week. Nearly a third actually went more than once a week.[6] This wasn't just a throwback. In my own age group, those aged between eighteen and twenty-six, 79 per cent went to Mass once a week. Ninety-five per cent of Irish people believed in God, 76 per cent in life after death, 55 per cent in the reality of Hell and 58 per cent in the Devil as a real person.[7] Nearly half of Irish people, compared to just a quarter of Europeans generally, accepted the proposition that 'there is only one true religion'.[8] Seventy-eight per cent expressed either a 'great deal' or 'quite a lot' of confidence in the church as an institution.

There was very little public tolerance for abortion. On a scale of one (never justified) to ten (always justified), abortion ranked at 1.7 for Irish people. (In all of western Europe, it scored four.)[9] To put this in context, this meant that Irish people on the whole rated abortion as being only slightly less reprehensible than having sex with a minor or political assassination (1.4). A woman terminating her pregnancy was almost as much a moral wretch as a priest raping a child or the IRA man who blew up Mountbatten, the two boys and the old lady.

So why, of all countries, did Ireland need a specific anti-abortion clause in its Constitution? Deep down, this was about the future. Back in the 1950s, there was no future. The whole point of the great economic revolution had been to create one. But now, the future that had emerged – Ireland as a normal, prosperous western European country – was slipping away. The future was again a dark place. In Europe as a whole in 1981, 49 per cent of people agreed that 'the future is uncertain; we must live from day to day'. Fully 67 per cent of Irish people agreed.[10]

What the idea of an anti-abortion amendment offered was an illusion of control over the future. Legalized abortion in Ireland did not exist as a present-day concern. But by making it a constitutional impossibility, it would seem like something that could never happen. And if it could not happen, then Ireland could never be the kind of society in which such a thing was thinkable. The amendment would itself abort an impermissible Irish future.

Significantly, at a time when Ireland's American dream was becoming increasingly problematic, the thing that would not happen was what had happened in the US.

The spectre of America haunted these activists. The Irish

Supreme Court ruling in favour of Mrs McGee's right to access contraception had been based on the idea of a right to marital privacy that in turn drew on a 1965 US ruling that formulated that right. The legal adviser to the Pro-Life Amendment Campaign, William Binchy, argued that 'the right to marital privacy in the United States had become a right to procreative privacy entitling a woman to have what, in effect, amounts to "abortion on demand"'.[11] The 1973 *Roe* v. *Wade* ruling by the US Supreme Court was thus a precedent that, in the minds of the anti-abortionists, loomed over Ireland. This was one way in which Ireland must not be allowed to become Americanized.

The harbinger of this potential doom was announced in the *Evening Herald* in November 1973: 'An American priest, Father Paul Marx, arrived at Dublin Airport today. In his hand luggage were three bottles – each one containing the foetus of an aborted baby... The little bodies in Father Marx's bag were aged between 10 and 16 weeks. All were perfectly formed human shapes.'[12] By accident or design, he landed in Dublin on the same day that Mary McGee was beginning her Supreme Court challenge to the state's seizure of the contraceptive jelly she had attempted to import the previous year. Marx toured Ireland twice in 1973, and again in 1976, and was allowed by the Conference of Major Religious Superiors to tour its schools – especially Catholic girls' schools – displaying garish colour slides of what he claimed was an abortion, as well as his aborted foetuses in bottles.[13]

The film critic Ciaran Carty noted in 1973 that Marx's slide show was almost certainly illegal, since it had not been submitted to the film censor or granted a certificate. A cinema in the Midlands had recently been prosecuted for admitting a twelve-year-old girl, accompanied by a parent, to the film *Wuthering Heights*, which was deemed suitable for over-sixteens only, even though the novel was actually on the school curriculum. A documentary on childbirth, *Helga*, was restricted to over-eighteens.[14] But even so, a section dealing with abortion had been cut out entirely. Another German sex education film, *The Cure of Patty Switl*, had its references to abortion cut and its name changed, tellingly, to *The Shame of Patty Switl*.[15]

In 1976, Marx had replaced the slides with a film – not submitted to the censor either and therefore certainly illegal. 'The film he showed on abortion showed an actual abortion with the sucking out of the uterus. What was taken from it was poured through a sieve and then the camera zoomed in on decapitated [sic] limbs.'[16] But the church and the state seemed to have no problem with Marx's visual terrorism or his insistence that 'it was impossible to get through to people unless you shocked them'.[17] The shock was certainly delivered. At a Marx show in the Mercy convent in Galway, for example, 'a number of people became ill'. The head nun acknowledged that the film was 'gruesome' but insisted that the showing was still 'worthwhile' as a warning to the girls of the 'danger and challenges' that faced them 'in an increasingly promiscuous society'.[18] No doubt many Irish teenage girls saw Marx's abortion freak show in their convent schools before they had even knew fully how conception, pregnancy and birth worked. Those 'little bodies' in bottles were their introduction to reproduction.

This very need to terrorize the young hinted, however, at the pessimism about the Irish future that made the idea of banning abortion forever and ever seem attractive. It fused neatly with the predictions of a coming decade of poverty and stagnation.

There has long been in Irish Catholicism an ideology of compensation – if Ireland was poor and static, that made it all the holier. Its very dreariness could be a spiritual beacon, lighting up the fallen world. This desperate resort had apparently had its day in the 1950s. But now it was a place to visit again. Michael Woods, the Fianna Fáil minister for health who first introduced legislation for the anti-abortion referendum, asked the Dáil to note that 'The experience in America is particularly relevant. There are those who say that there has been an American holocaust.' He more or less suggested that Ireland could help to save America from damnation: 'If we as a people mark our respect for the life and dignity of the unborn, who knows what ripples may flow throughout the world which has lost its reverence for life in the womb'.[19]

The first time I really became aware of the strength of the gathering campaign for an abortion referendum was in the middle of 1981. I was living in the south Dublin suburb of Blackrock. Notices appeared on the lamp posts and in the local shop advertising a public meeting on the subject. I went to it with my girlfriend. It was in a beautiful Georgian house on its own grounds called Temple Hill. It had a two-storey modern annex that could house up to a hundred babies. I thought it was a small hospital for infants. But it wasn't a hospital at all. It was a kind of holding pen for babies whose mothers had signed away their parental rights. The infants were kept there while they waited for adoption. The place was another centre of the Irish secret service.

Temple Hill was run by nuns from the Sisters of Charity. When we went into the room where the meeting was held, the superior nun, Sister Frances, was at the top table and there was a row of young nurses in high-necked, starched white uniforms with pointy white headdresses. After the speakers warned of the moral danger Ireland was in and of the urgency of forcing the political system to respond immediately to the demand for a 'pro-life' referendum, someone from the campaign asked for volunteers. There was a moment's silence and then the head nun began to point to individual young nurses and started volunteering them. None of them spoke or was asked to speak. They just signed the sheet.

I didn't know it then, but one of Temple Hill's customers was the best-known priest in Ireland, Michael Cleary. He had been in Crumlin for a while when I was a kid and he had become famous as the Singing Priest, performing shows all over Ireland. He had officiated at that concert in Croke Park in 1972 when I shouted Up the IRA! at Jack Lynch. He had also been the warm-up man for Pope John Paul II at his big youth Mass in Galway in 1979.

Cleary had impregnated his twenty-year-old lover Phyllis Hamilton. After she gave birth to their son Michael Ivor in 1970, Cleary christened him and then a friend of his drove mother and child to Temple Hill. According to Hamilton, 'I felt powerless to protest; I had no control over what was happening.' She handed the baby over to a nun 'like I was handing over my soul'. Three weeks later, when she had not yet signed adoption papers, she wanted her baby back. She called Temple Hill to explain this. The woman who answered the phone (almost certainly a nun) told her: 'You selfish little bitch. That baby has gone to a very good home and you should be very grateful.'[20] When she told Cleary she wanted to keep the baby, he 'went into a rage… and told me how immature I was.' She signed the adoption papers.

One of the nurses in Temple Hill who may have been present that night of the anti-abortion meeting was Jennifer Sadurski. She later recalled for Caelainn Hogan one prematurely born little baby who was delivered from the Coombe maternity hospital in the city. 'When the trainee nurses went to wash her, they discovered that her name and date of birth had been scrawled in red ink on her back.'[21] This image of a branded baby haunted her. It was a token of the wider branding of babies as 'illegitimate', a practice that continued in Ireland, even on official documentation, until 1988.

Did babies have souls? The passionate belief that they did was at the heart of the horror of abortion. The year after that meeting in Temple Hill, I talked to one of the most vocal campaigners for the amendment, Father Simon O'Byrne. He explained to me: 'Some people have this idea that a little child has a child's soul. The soul does not occupy space; the soul is spiritual whether the person is ninety years of age or ninety seconds, the soul, when it leaves the body, is a full mature soul knowing all the mysteries and all the things that we don't know. The soul is created at the instant of conception. That is the teaching of the Church.'

But the church didn't really believe that a foetus was a person with a soul in the same sense that a ninety-year-old woman might be. If it did, how could Father Marx carry around and display the 'little bodies' in glass bottles? Should they not be buried in a churchyard with a headstone and prayers and solemn ceremony? The truth was that babies were disposable, not just before they were born, but afterwards as well.

Temple Hill was part of the system that included the Mother and Baby Homes. Many of those homes did not even bother to record the burials of the huge numbers of babies who died in their care. This was, according to the church's own canon law, perfectly fine. Of the Bessborough home in Cork, the commission of investigation into Mother and Baby Homes noted in 2019 that 'More than 900 children died in Bessborough or in hospital after being transferred from Bessborough. Despite very extensive inquiries and searches, the Commission has been able to establish the burial place of only 64 children. The Congregation of the Sacred Hearts of Jesus and Mary who owned and ran Bessborough do not know where the other children are buried.'[22]

In the Tuam Children's Home, run by the Sisters of Bon Secours (Good Help), around 800 children were buried in a structure 'built within the decommissioned large sewage tank'. Between January 1920 and October 1977, the bodies of more than 950 children, almost all of them 'illegitimate', were sent to the medical schools at University College Dublin, Trinity College Dublin and the Royal College of Surgeons in Ireland for the purpose of anatomical studies. Church-run institutions were among the main suppliers. Some of these babies were never buried. The commission noted tersely that 'It may be that stillborn infants were preserved as "wet specimens" for display purposes in medical schools.'

By the time of the abortion referendum campaign, there was significant public knowledge of the church's habit of dumping the bodies of babies in unrecorded mass graves. The minutes of a Galway County Council meeting of 17 December 1979, just six weeks after the pope's Mass in Galway, record a motion proposed by a council member for development of a playground on the site of the Tuam home '... having regard to the existence of... a children's Burial Ground'. The council approved £2,000 to 'Provide playing equipment on children's burial ground'. There was no comment on this, no questioning of how the nuns had buried these children. Nobody wanted to know. It had been common in Britain and Ireland after the First World War to mark the graves of unidentifiable soldiers who died in battle as 'A soldier of the Great War known unto God'. The church was happy enough to bury babies as known not even unto God.

None of this interfered in any way with the demand that the Irish Constitution should recognize the full personhood of a foetus 'from the moment of conception'. On 30 April 1981, five days before Bobby Sands died, a delegation from PLAC, led by the prominent Catholic gynaecologist Dr Julia Vaughan, met with both the Taoiseach, Charles Haughey, and the leader of the Opposition, Garret FitzGerald. FitzGerald, who many looked to as the leader of liberal Ireland, immediately agreed to their demands for an anti-abortion amendment and pledged the full support of his Fine Gael party. FitzGerald, 'influenced by my personal antipathy to abortion', completely accepted the idea that Ireland must be protected from any possibility that its Supreme Court would follow the American precedent.[23] Haughey told the delegation that he fully accepted the principle of the amendment but asked for more time to consider its practical implications. A fortnight later, he wrote to PLAC to 'convey… on behalf of the Government, a solemn assurance that an appropriate constitutional amendment' would be forthcoming.[24]

I subsequently spoke, in June 1982, to two members of that small PLAC delegation that had met Haughey and FitzGerald and found them so astonishingly agreeable to a proposition that had been formulated only months before those meetings. Julia Vaughan was obsessed with the US precedent. 'We have a constitution', she told me, 'and they have one in the United States. It is worth remembering that the right to life in the US was destroyed by a court judgement in 1973.' She also told me that the life of the foetus is sacred from the moment of conception and that both the IUD and the morning-after pill are abortifacients. It was clear that she hoped that the amendment would end up banning at least some forms of contraception.

I went to hear another member of the delegation, Loretto Browne, one of the founders of the Society for the Protection of Unborn Children (SPUC) speak on a harsh rainy night on the Curragh, in Co. Kildare, as seventy-five people sat transfixed in the ballroom of Lumville House. All, apart from two boys who had come in the hope of seeing some pictures of female genitalia, were quiet and serious. 'You don't have to look if you don't want to', she told them. On the screen there was an image of primeval chaos; from the audience there were low groans. A tiny arm, a twisted half-formed leg, an umbilicus, another hand or foot, all strewn about the clumps of glistening raspberry-coloured blood and flesh. 'This', Browne said, 'is the remains of a baby sucked out of the womb at ten weeks.'

As the slides flashed up on the screen, culminating with a black rubbish bag full of foetuses, everyone, including the boys who were just hoping to see some genitalia, was reeling from the shock and the terror. 'Now you can make up your own minds', says Browne, but her speech was just beginning. It is all about the foreignness of this threat. 'Agents of change are being imported to foist abortion on the Irish people', she said. The pro-abortion Women's Right to Choose campaign, she alleged, 'is a small group and a very pathetic group. Most of them have had abortions, and, were it not for the fact that they have each other for support, many of them would go to make up the statistics which show the high incidence of suicides among women who have had abortions.'

She went quickly on to the subject of the US-based International Planned Parenthood, an organization that most of her audience has probably never heard of before. She outlined a conspiracy theory of its strategy: first, limited contraceptives are introduced, then there is pressure for free access to contraception. This is coupled with sex education that teaches young people about the use of contraceptives. 'If you vote for free access to contraception', she told the audience, 'your kids will get them and use them even more because of no-holds-barred sex education. The more that use them, the better for International Planned Parenthood. No contraceptive is one hundred per cent safe, so there are more unwanted pregnancies, then the pressure is on for abortion.'

When I asked her later whether she really believed in this conspiracy, Browne produced proof: 'Margaret Sanger, the woman who started the International Planned Parenthood, had a friend, Dr Havelock Ellis.' Ellis, she says 'was a bit of an oddball'. 'He intimated that all sexual relations, provided that they were not physically harmful, were quite acceptable, and that included sexual relations between people of the same sex.' Browne recalled being at a meeting in Trinity College in October 1980 when a gay rights group offered support to the Women's Right to Choose Group. She knew, she told me, that all the people in Ireland who said they are gay could not really be so. 'Let's say that in the last couple of years in this country we have seen an unprecedented rise in the number of people who call themselves gay. By natural law we couldn't have so many misfits in society. And I don't mean misfits psychologically. They are – there's something wrong with people who think they are gay if they are not actually physically deformed. There couldn't be that many physically deformed people in society.'

On the platform, Browne had talked about something that was almost never discussed in public in Ireland: rape. One of the ways the abortion lobby works, she explained, is to argue on the basis of 'soft cases'. 'Rape is very horrible, but most women who are raped don't conceive.' She added that 'men who go in for rape are not very fertile, they tend to be impotent'. Even if a rape victim does become pregnant, it is no excuse for abortion… A woman who has been raped can have a washout. It may not be very successful but it can be tried.' She looked around the room. 'How many people here know how they were conceived? Do they know that they weren't conceived as a result of rape? That's worth pondering.'

On the table at the back of the hall there was a free newsletter from another of the groups that formed PLAC, the Responsible Society. It attacked suggestions that the status of 'illegitimacy' for children should be ended: 'the removal of the so-called status of illegitimacy is an empty public relations gesture which does little of any value for the illegitimate child and at the same time serves to weaken the family unit founded on marriage, which is the cornerstone of Society'. It also boasted of the partial success of its campaign to stop state funding for the Dublin Rape Crisis Centre.

Two things seemed to be completely clear. One was that the people pushing for the amendment were motivated by a deep belief that Ireland was being infiltrated from without by foreign forces who, as the pope had warned in 1979, saw the corruption of its innocence as a great prize. Abortion was a cipher for the nexus of evils that included contraception, homosexuality and extra-marital sex. The other was that this paranoid vision, based on a denial of the realities of the way Irish people were actually living their lives, would undoubtedly triumph. It offered a refuge from the psychic disturbance of the apparent failure of the modernizing project. Most Irish people wanted to book their place on that flight. The referendum, when it was held on 7 September 1983, was a triumph for those who had conjured it out of nowhere three years previously: 67 per cent voted in favour. The future was now safe. The rot had been stopped. The line had been drawn. The Ireland that was to come would always be the same as the Ireland that had already been: holy, Catholic and a beacon to the world.

25

1982: Wonders Taken For Signs

On the last weekend in July 1982, I went into the local shop just beside where I was living in the coastal Dublin suburb of Blackrock. One of the sisters who ran it was reading the paper. She looked up at me and her eyes widened in fright. Then she did a kind of double take. She knew me as a regular customer. I asked her for some eggs and the *Irish Times* and she handed them over. She looked at me oddly again, as if she was scrutinizing my face for some surreptitious mark of guilt. I thanked her but she said nothing at all to me. I didn't know what to make of this peculiar behaviour. The poor woman seemed a bit mad.

Back home over breakfast, I opened the paper. The big story was about two murders that may or may not have been connected. Bridie Gargan, a twenty-nine-year-old nurse, had stopped her car to sunbathe on a beautiful afternoon beside the entrance to the American ambassador's residence in Phoenix Park. A man ordered her into her car and told her to lie on the back seat. He then bludgeoned her with a hammer. A young farmer, Donal Dunne, had been found dead on a bog in Co. Offaly, killed by a shotgun blast.

The Garda said they were looking for a thin man who was around twenty-five years old, five feet ten inches in height, with wavy, dark brown hair. There were two very telling details: he sometimes wore a fisherman's tweed hat and he had a neatly trimmed beard. I was thin. I was twenty-four. I am five feet ten inches tall. I had curly dark brown hair. I sometimes wore a tweed hat exactly like the one the killer had been seen in. And I had just trimmed my beard.

There was another clue: a Blackrock connection. After hitting the nurse with a hammer, the man had driven off with her and even been escorted by an ambulance driver who thought he was trying to take the injured woman to hospital. When he abandoned the car, with the fatally injured woman inside, he went into a travel agency and asked the staff to call him a taxi to Blackrock. I felt dizzy. My doppelganger was out there, randomly murdering young people. The headlines said he might strike again.

I waited for the police to come to the door. It was impossible that the woman in the shop had not called them to say that she had seen Ireland's most wanted man. I started to prepare my alibi. I was thinking about the fact that I could not drive and so could not have killed the poor nurse or, surely, driven to the bog and shot the young farmer. But how do you prove you can't drive? They could check that I had no licence, but that was hardly conclusive. Where had I been on that lovely afternoon when she went sunbathing in the park? Just with my girlfriend at home. I wondered whether I should go to the police station down the road and identify myself. Or would that be just the sort of devious thing a psychopath would do?

That same weekend, the word was that the attorney general, Patrick Connolly, was struggling to come up with a wording for the proposed constitutional amendment banning abortion. He was a nice man who had built up a very lucrative practice at the Bar, representing insurance companies in personal injury cases. He liked opera and reading James Joyce. He was not seen as particularly political, but he knew Charles Haughey because he had been one of his junior counsel at the arms trial in 1970. It was nonetheless a bit of a surprise when he was appointed as attorney general by Haughey on his return to power in March 1982. One of the trials of the job was that he was now responsible for wording a brief amendment that would define the beginnings of life and confer full citizenship on a foetus. Even for a man whose colleagues would give him a first edition of *Finnegans Wake* to mark his fifty years at the Bar, this was a conundrum.

In the first weeks of August, while I was waiting for a tap on the shoulder from the police and they were searching for my evil twin who was still out there somewhere, reports were suggesting that Connolly had given up and that another outsider lawyer was being employed to try to find a wording.[1] Other reports suggested that Connolly 'had been working on the wording and had produced several preliminary drafts, but had not reached any firm conclusions on the matter'.[2] Small wonder the man needed a holiday. He booked himself a flight to New York for 14 August and then planned to go on to New Orleans, Phoenix, Salt Lake City and Washington.[3] It is easy to imagine him daydreaming of new cities, with the whole Atlantic Ocean and the whole American continent between him and the impossible words for whatever it was Ireland wanted to say about itself through the medium of abortion.

Ten days before this blessed relief, Connolly was in his flat in a modern apartment complex called Pilot View, overlooking the harbour at Dalkey, just down the coast from where I lived in Blackrock, when Malcolm Macarthur arrived. The attorney general had generously offered Macarthur his spare bedroom for a short stay. He knew the younger man (who was thirty-four, not twenty-five) as the partner of a friend of his, Brenda Little. Macarthur had explained on the phone that he was in Dublin for a short stay to sort out some financial matters. That Sunday, Macarthur was driven to Croke Park with Connolly in the latter's state car, for the All-Ireland hurling semi-final. The driver was a Garda sergeant. Over the following week, Macarthur rode with Connolly and the Garda driver several times into the city.

On the evening before he was due to leave for his American holiday, Connolly arrived home in Dalkey to find three detectives waiting for him outside. They told him that his guest was wanted on suspicion of conducting an armed robbery. When Macarthur opened the door and the detectives rushed in and pinioned him, the attorney general said, 'I don't know what this is about, Malcolm, but whatever it is you are on your own.'[4] What it was about was not just the robbery, but the murders of Gargan and Dunne. The police found the shotgun that had been used to kill Dunne in the flat. When Macarthur was charged with these crimes, he gave his address as that of the attorney general. But Connolly flew out nevertheless. He landed at JFK to be besieged by reporters before taking refuge in the Roosevelt Hotel on Madison Avenue. The *New York Post* led with the story: IRISH BIGGIE FLEES HERE AFTER SLAY SCANDAL.

These events generated a great mist of gossip and guesswork. When Macarthur was arrested, Haughey was on his island, Inishvicillaun off the coast of Kerry. The telephone line was bad and no one could get hold of him.[5] When he got the news, he phoned Connolly and asked him to postpone his holiday, but the attorney general left anyway. It was only the following day that Haughey ordered him to come home immediately. He was collected from Concorde at London Heathrow by the Irish Air Corps, flown to the military airfield in Dublin and then driven straight to Haughey's mansion and instructed to resign in view of 'the embarrassment which, however unwittingly, must inevitably be caused to the government'.[6]

I was glad to be off the hook, but the whole affair was dizzying. It just couldn't all be coincidence. Murderers don't just accidentally end up living with the state's most senior law officer and being chauffeured around by police sergeants in state cars. Why had Connolly apparently fled the country, then returned and gone straight to Haughey's private house? What had they discussed? What was the deal? Why did Haughey, in his press conference to announce Connolly's resignation, praise the police for 'putting the whole thing together and eventually finding the right man'. Was this not a deliberate gaffe that would make it impossible now for Macarthur to get a fair trial? And if there was no trial, what would be kept out of the public domain? Irish journalists, more responsible than the Taoiseach, did not repeat his remark in their news stories, but they did report that he made a highly prejudicial comment, so that everyone knew that something weird had been spoken but only those in media and political circles knew what it was. That week, for the country as a whole, was peak paranoia. Conor Cruise O'Brien captured the moment by reassembling four words Haughey used in the press conference – grotesque, unbelievable, bizarre and unprecedented – to forge the deathless acronym GUBU.

It was all too Haugheyesque. Macarthur's idea of hiding in plain sight had been, after all, his very own modus operandi. And Haughey had generated a sense that nothing was ever quite what it seemed, that Irish reality had layers within layers. Only a fool could believe that there was in fact nothing much to see here. By far the strangest thing was that there really wasn't. Connolly had indeed been innocently caught up in a horrible co-incidence. The phrase Haughey himself actually used – 'grotesque and almost unbelievable mischance' – was, for once, truthful.[7] But what was most unbelievable was that it actually was all mischance. He had himself helped to create the cognitive slippage in which the line between the believable and the unbelievable was never quite clear. Now that the implausible and the actual had come into random collision, it was impossible to tell them apart.

In the Macarthur episode, the truth itself lacked credibility. How could there be so much noise but no signal? It was absurd that the connections between a double murder, the state's chief law officer and Haughey were genuinely random, that there was no deep meaning behind these sensational developments, that the Irish Biggie and the Slay Scandal had been thrown into conjunction merely as an illustration of chaos theory. A squall in the brain of a psychopath had produced a tornado in Irish politics that sucked the wildest imaginings high into its atmospehere.

The irony was that there was also actual chaos. That year, Haughey's new minister for justice, Seán Doherty, was running amok. An assault charge against his brother-in-law, Tom Nangle, a Garda, was dismissed when a key prosecution witness was detained across the Border by the RUC while he was due in court. A Garda sergeant in Doherty's constituency alleged that Doherty tried to have him transferred when he refused to fix cases or drop charges for favoured voters or supporters. Responding to Haughey's increasing paranoia about leaks from government and party meetings, Doherty authorized the illegal tapping of the phones of political journalists Geraldine Kennedy, Bruce Arnold and Vincent Browne. In the case of Arnold, who was born in England, the alleged 'justification' carried more than a hint of treason: 'Mr Arnold was anti-national in his outlook and might be obtaining information from sources of a similar disposition.'[8]

The factional manoeuvring in Fianna Fáil was byzantine. There was, according to one veteran party figure and government minister, Pádraig Faulkner, 'a reluctance, almost a fear, to talk to more than a few trusted colleagues. A climate existed in which any open and frank debate on issues was viewed as being disloyal to the leader.'[9] The minister for finance, Ray MacSharry, was a supporter of Haughey but the anti-Haugheyites believed that he was remaining loyal only because he had money problems. The word went out from one of Haughey's most determined opponents, Martin O'Donoghue, that £100,000 could be made available to MacSharry if he changed sides. MacSharry then set up a meeting with O'Donoghue, planning to tape him making an offer he regarded as potentially treasonous. He asked Doherty for help. The minister for justice then got the deputy commissioner of the Garda, Joe Ainsworth, to deliver to MacSharry a special device for secretive recording. O'Donoghue did not in fact take MacSharry's bait and offer a bribe, but he did say, 'There is a lot of money around all right but not for C. J. [Haughey], not for him to stay.'[10] MacSharry gave the tape to Doherty, who in turn gave it to Ainsworth, who had it transcribed.

All of this became public at the end of 1982 and in early 1983. It added to the feeling that the state, under Haughey, had gone out of control and become prey to obsessions and suspicions, plots and counterplots. Nothing was incredible, nothing was neatly contained within the bounds of likelihood. The unbelievable was entirely possible; the real was hard to believe. Events that looked like conspiracies might turn out to be mere accidents, while surface normalities might conceal the most convoluted political machinations. When the state was enveloped in this cloud of unknowing, it was not surprising that society at large was struggling not to lose its reason. It became easier to accept fantastical explanations than to settle for plain facts. In this state of mind, wonders could be mistaken for signs.

26

1984–1985: Dead Babies and Living Statues

The revelations that week were disturbing. Sergeant Patrick Reidy told a public tribunal of inquiry in Tralee of how he had been called to see the body of an infant on the rocks at White Strand, near the west Kerry village of Caherciveen. On the evening of 14 April 1984, a local farmer, John Griffin, had been jogging on the strand when he climbed across the rocks on the southern end to check on some cattle he kept there. He saw what he thought might be a doll, but there was something about the hair that didn't seem right. When he looked more closely, he realized that it was the body of a newborn baby boy. When Reidy and another Garda got there, they dislodged the body from the rocks and brought it to the local undertakers. The next day the state pathologist determined that the baby had been stabbed twenty-eight times, including four times in the heart.

Later that week at the inquiry Superintendent John Sullivan, outlined the course of his investigation into the death of this infant. It was a cross-section through the secret lives of the place. The guards had, he said, checked into cases of incest, of married men known to have been associating with single girls, of a woman who was pregnant and went to England but might have returned. The parents of a fifteen-year-old girl whose diary contained references to rape were interviewed. There were checks on 'tinkers and hippies'. The residents of a Mother and Baby Home were considered. There was the possibility that 'strangers' might have come to the strand by boat and inquiries were made about a small plane that had been spotted over the area. There was 'the case of one girl in a certain Kerry town who might be pregnant'.

His description of the investigation became steadily more gothic. Since there was, he said, a possibility that the mother might come to the grave in Caherciveen where the baby's body had been placed under a little plastic sign that said 'In memory of me, The Kerry Baby', the gravedigger had been asked to keep watch. Somebody, he said, had even suggested that there might be 'a possible link with black magic – that was some information somebody had suggested'.[1] The *Irish Examiner* duly carried the headline 'Black Magic Ruled Out'.[2]

Forty kilometres away from Tralee, at twenty past twelve on Thursday, 14 February 1985, the day that Superintendent Sullivan was giving this evidence to the tribunal of inquiry, Elizabeth Flynn entered the little church of St Mary which is next door to her school in Asdee.

I went to Asdee a few weeks later. It was no more than a dip in the road from Ballybunion to Ballylongford, a tiny line of buildings of which the church, the school, two pubs and the shop-cum-petrol pump were the most notable. From down in the centre of the village's one street there was nothing to be seen but the straggling, sparsely populated dairying land around. From the brow of the hill where the village starts, however, the winking towers of industrial Ireland, the power stations of Moneypoint and Tarbert, loomed up from the Shannon estuary. And in the estuary the long, dark bulk of a 140,000-tonne coal carrier, the biggest ship ever to dock in an Irish port, lay at Moneypoint.

Elizabeth was seven and went to the church every day at lunchtime. She was due to make her First Communion. Mrs Eileen Moriarty, the principal teacher in the school, was a devout elderly women and she encouraged all her pupils to go next door at lunchtime to 'give two or three minutes to Jesus and the church'. Elizabeth told me, in a story that was already so well-rehearsed that her voice seemed almost bored, that she prayed to the two statues, painted plaster images of the Blessed Virgin and the Sacred Heart which stand in the alcove at the back of the church on the left-hand side, separated by a brass trolley, surmounted with votive candles and a small, round stained-glass porthole which lets in a dim, diffuse light. Then she saw the Sacred Heart crook his finger and beckon her over to him. When she looked again, Our Lady's mouth was open.

Martin Fitzgerald, who was ten and one of the altar boys in the church, told me he was playing 'hunting' out at the back of the school when Elizabeth Ryan and other 'young ones' came up to him. They told him that the statues were moving. He went in with a large group of other children and looked at the statues for a while. He saw the head and eyes of one of the statues move. Some of the other children who were there at the same time saw nothing. Gradually all of the children gathered into the church to look. Over the coming weeks thirty-six of them altogether would say that they saw the statues move in various ways. Some, like Blanaid Quane, had more than one vision, seeing the statues move on different occasions. A few of their parents said they, too, had seen movements in the statues.

When the children of Asdee told their parents what they had seen in the church, some of them thought of the terrible things that were being dragged to light at the Kerry Babies inquiry in Tralee. 'There was all that Kerry Babies business', one father told me, 'and there have been other things, too. There've been two murders in the Listowel area and over in Tarbert there was the case of a man who was having sex with his two nieces and got one of them pregnant. That's why some of the people here think that what's happened is a sign. There's a message there and it's to do with all the bad things that have been happening.'

By the beginning of March, up to 6,000 people were turning up at the church on Sundays. A barrier had to be built around the statues to stop people scratching off fragments as relics.[3] Within weeks, statues were moving all over the country. From Asdee, the phenomenon spread to Ballydesmond, near the Cork border, and then to Ballinspittle, where, by late July, the statue of the Virgin in the grotto was moving so spectacularly that CIE was laying on special bus services for the huge crowds (an average of 10,000 a night – twice that on some occasions) that flocked to see her.

('The litter from half a dozen burger and chip vans', reported one witness, 'is something to behold.'[4]) Some 80 per cent of those visiting the grotto – most of them respectable middle-class people – reported seeing the statue move, and 30 per cent said they had 'seen the face of Our Lord appear'.[5] The visions even travelled on the airwaves – dozens of people wrote to the Mike Murphy radio show claiming that they had seen the face of Christ on screen while the nine o'clock news was showing a report on Ballinspittle.

In Dublin, people joked about seeing the statue of the Labour leader Jim Larkin on O'Connell Street wave his arms or the statue of Daniel O'Connell himself levitating over McDonald's. Likewise, a man in Cork, seeking directions to Ballinspittle, was told 'just follow the star'.[6] The surrealism reached a point of absolute absurdity in October 1988, when there were mildly violent clashes outside a screening in the Cork Opera House of Martin Scorsese's *The Last Temptation of Christ*. The scuffles were between a group wielding Rosary beads and denouncing 'blasphemy' and a second group of white-clad women describing themselves as 'handmaidens of Ballinspittle' and 'keepers of the third secret of Fatima'. The first group thought the second was making a mockery of them, but the handmaidens insisted that they were serious. One of them, who had her placard torn by the first group, was outraged when asked if her white robe was a spoof: 'What about the moving statue? Have you ever heard of the third secret?'[7]

The government was embarrassed by all of this. The government press secretary, Peter Prendergast, told the *Wall Street Journal* in August 1985 that 'three-quarters of the country is laughing heartily'.[8] But the truth was that it wasn't just gullible or desperate people who were seeing things that did not exist. It was the state itself. The spectacle of the moving statues began with the sense of psychic disturbance that radiated out from the story of the Kerry Babies. And that was a story created, not by children in a church, but by policemen in a Garda station.

Having eliminated 'tinkers and hippies' and practitioners of black magic from their inquiries, the Gardaí investigating the killing of the baby found on White Strand in April 1984 discovered that a twenty-five-year-old woman called Joanne Hayes, who lived with her mother, brothers and aunt on a farm in Abbeydorney, had been admitted to the hospital in nearby Tralee. She said she had had a miscarriage, but a scan indicated that she had given birth to a full-term baby. But there was no baby now and there was no report of a stillbirth. Not unreasonably, Hayes was suspected of being the mother of the White Strand infant and of having killed it.

Hayes was the sort of woman who, in the previous generation, would probably have been locked away in a Magdalene asylum. She was involved with a married man, Jeremiah Locke, who worked with her in the sports centre in Tralee. She had a daughter, Yvonne, with Locke in 1983. So Hayes and Locke were taken in for questioning by the state's crack murder squad at Tralee Garda station. Over the course of 1 May 1984 the squad interrogated Hayes and Locke, but also Hayes's brothers Ned and Mike, sister Kathleen and aunt Bridie Fuller.

After less than an hour, Hayes admitted what had happened: 'I had the baby boy at home… The baby is dead, I buried it at home.' She delivered the premature baby by herself in a field on the farm, saw it die, left it on some hay, went back to bed and said nothing. As she explained, the family had been upset about her having Yvonne but had accepted her daughter and helped her. With the second pregnancy, she 'felt thoroughly and absolutely ashamed of myself and I tried to hide it'.[9] Next morning she got up and went out alone to find the body. She wrapped it in some turf bags and put it in a pool of water.

Over the course of the day, however, a new story began to take shape in the statements being extracted by the Gardaí. Ned Hayes allegedly confessed that Joanne's baby was in fact the one that had been stabbed, dumped off Slea Head and then washed up onto White Strand. Gardaí searched the Hayes farmhouse and came back with a Prestige carving knife, a bath brush and a turf bag. The lead interrogator, Detective Sergeant Gerry O'Carroll, confronted Hayes and 'shouted out that she was insane, a murderess, that she had stabbed the baby with the knife, that she had beaten it with the bath brush and that the baby was taken away in a turf bag'.[10] Shortly afterwards Hayes made a detailed statement to this effect. Kathleen Hayes and Mary Hayes then signed statements corroborating this story. Joanne was then charged with murdering her child; the other members of the family with helping to conceal the birth and to dispose of the body.

There was just one problem. The following evening, the body of Joanne's dead baby was found on the farm. It could not have been thrown into the sea off Slea Head and washed up across the bay on White Strand. It was there on the farm, exactly where Joanne said it was. But the Gardaí were undaunted. Their narrative inventiveness was more than equal to the task of elaborating the plot to take account of this unexpected twist. Joanne, they decided, had indeed, as she claimed, given birth in the field. She came back into the house and went to bed. But then she realized that she was in fact giving birth to twins. She was too tired and weak to go back outside. The second baby was the one that she beat with the bath brush and stabbed with the knife, the one her brothers then threw into the sea.

In its own way, this was a tribute to the persistence of the Irish tradition of storytelling. It seems apt that all of this was happening in Kerry, home of the great seanchaithe like Peig Sayers and the first person I had ever seen on television, Eamon Kelly. Slea Head, where the baby was supposedly thrown into the Atlantic, juts right out towards one of the last redoubts of traditional storytelling, Great Blasket Island. The three leading members of the murder squad – Detective Superintendent John Courtney, Detective Sergeant Gerry O'Carroll and Detective Garda P. J. Browne, were all Kerrymen, all products of a culture that valued the arts of elaboration and digression. What they became involved in was not so much an investigation of reality, more the amplification of sordid shards of real life into a lurid fable, a gripping yarn that could also be understood as a parable of the workings of evil in the world.

The plain and rather disappointing truth was that Joanne and the Hayes family had nothing to do with the baby found on White Strand. Simple blood group tests quickly established that Hayes could not have been the mother of the White Strand baby and that Locke could not have been the father. When all of this became public, the case led to a public tribunal of inquiry into the obvious question of how several people came to sign statements that could not have been true. In October 1985, the judge, Kevin Lynch, produced an eccentric report, full of speculations and shaped by a barely concealed rage at Hayes's sexual conduct. At its conclusion, he quoted James Thurber: 'We live, man and worm, in an age where almost everything can mean almost anything…'[11] It seemed that the judge, too, was overwhelmed by the task of extracting meaning from these events.

Those statements signed by the Hayes family are arguably the most impressive work of Irish fiction of the early 1980s. The ones ascribed, in particular, to Joanne and Kathleen have the vividness and immediacy of a horror movie: the white bath brush with which Joanne beat the infant on the head, the brown timber handle of the carving knife, Joanne stabbing the baby in the chest and then turning him over to repeat the operation on his back, the blood everywhere on the bed and on the floor, the afterbirth being thrown out into the hay, the white plastic bag into which the men put the baby before wrapping it in a turf bag, the sound of the car pulling away from the backyard, the way the bag with the baby in it 'was thrown in… sank and resurfaced and floated on the water', the silence in the house afterwards. Joanne even, apparently, had a name for the baby: Shane (perhaps coincidentally a near-homonym for shame.)

There is a kind of imaginative power here. It is not very different, after all, from the creativity of that little girl in Asdee church seeing the plaster Sacred Heart crook his finger and beckon her over to him. It is not so much invention as projection. The people who, after this Kerry Babies story became the biggest news story in Ireland, flocked to godforsaken fields and stared at statues, were seeing what they needed to see. In this, they were continuing the work begun by the police in Tralee station that day. The cops, too, were visionaries. They conjured an apparition that was equal and opposite to the one the pope had endorsed when he visited Knock. There – as at Ballinspittle later – it was of the ultimate in female goodness, the mother who conceived immaculately, without sex, the Blessed Virgin. The police conjured from the depths an equal and opposite force, the ultimate in female evil, the insatiable sexual creature who murders her baby with the implements of proper female domesticity, the kitchen knife and bath brush.

Years later, showing an unusual degree of insight, the interrogator who created this nightmarish vision, Gerry O'Carroll, described the story as 'a catharsis, it was symptomatic of a dead Ireland… It was a witch hunt'.[12] It was in fact a symptom not so much of a dead Ireland, as of an undead culture, one that was moribund but desperate to revive itself. The moving statue is an inanimate object that is eerily alive.

Catholic Ireland was still like that. It had, even in the pope's first sermon on Irish soil five years earlier, a sense of impending doom. But it was not going gentle into the night. Its dying body was galvanized by the papal visit and by the triumph of the abortion referendum. But it was losing its most potent weapon: the power of shame and sin.

Cops make up confessions in most societies, but the extravagant way the stories ramified in the Kerry Babies case was quite specific to this time and place. What the police did in their interrogation of the Hayes family was to move the story out of the secular world of crime and into the religious universe of sinfulness. Joanne was the embodied nightmare of uncontrolled female sexuality: she had in fact conceived three times by Locke (the first baby being miscarried before she brought Yvonne to term). Superintendent Courtney described her directly as a woman of 'loose morals'.[13] The formal apparatus of control that would have whisked her away from home and locked her up in an institution was no longer available. The informal pressure of shame was also waning – in her own (true) account, it was clear that she was not abashed by the birth of her daughter outside wedlock and that the feeling of having something to hide only arose with her next pregnancy. It was no coincidence that what was projected onto Joanne Hayes was the image so recently invoked during the abortion referendum: the sinful woman as baby killer. (What was not noticed was that, in having sex without protection, Hayes was, in the eyes of conservative Ireland, committing one sin but avoiding what was, for the church, the even greater one of using contraceptives.)

Grotesquely misogynistic as this was, this trope also stimulated a feverish creativity. How, in the face of the scientific evidence that Hayes was not the mother of the White Strand baby, could the police maintain the necessary belief that she was? They let loose the great 'what if'. What if Joanne had given birth to twins who had different blood groups because she had sex with two different men and became pregnant by both?

As this story ramified, it was not enough that Hayes had one lover, Jeremiah Locke. When the tribunal of inquiry into the events was established, it took a bizarre detour into a search for the identity of the suspected second father, a man called Tom Flynn. His name was found by a state forensic scientist written in blue biro on the frame of the mattress on Joanne Hayes's bed.

Who was this phantom lover? Men appeared in Tralee and other towns wearing T-shirts that said, 'I am Tom Flynn'.[14] Eventually, it was revealed that, in 1968 and 1969, a Tom Flynn had worked in the furniture shop in Castleisland where Bridie Fuller bought the mattress. It seemed apt that he had then emigrated to America and 'he had not been home since'.

The other 'what if' was even more imaginative. What if, the Gardaí asked, there was a third, phantom baby? The first baby was the one found in the field that was Joanne's. The second was the one found on White Strand that had nothing to do with her. But Joanne really did have twins and the second baby really was beaten, stabbed and then thrown in the sea off Slea Head. It just so happened that the exact same thing had been done to the baby found on White Strand. Joanne's murdered baby was still out there, floating, perhaps, somewhere between America and Ireland.

Back in Asdee, in the Jesse James Tavern, next door to St Mary's Church, where the statues were moving, the woman of the house kept a small hardcover notebook behind the bar. The tavern had a low, uneven ceiling, smoke-stained walls and a sign on the wall facing the back door: 'Please use the toilet'. Apart from the pool table, the juke box and the framed photographs of Jesse James that hung above the fireplace along with a Wanted Dead or Alive poster, it was an old-style village pub. The juke box was on and the air was filled with the nasal tones of Tony Stevens singing a country and western song, 'Send Me No Roses', the B-side of the local anthem, 'The Village Of Asdee'.

The notebook behind the bar was the legacy of the man who put Asdee on the map, the former parish priest, Father Liam Ferris. It contained in bold, clear handwriting, a romantic version of the life and death of the outlaw Jesse James, along with stories about his Asdee ancestors, collected by Father Ferris from old people around the village. Father Ferris dominated the village from the Second World War until the end of the sixties, and he always believed that Asdee was marked out for a special distinction.

A colourful and unorthodox man, he came to believe that the forebears of Jesse James had come from Asdee and, on 4 April every year, he would say a solemn Requiem Mass, in the same church where the children would see the moving statues, for the repose of the soul of the greatest desperado of them all. He spent many years researching the connection with the James family. He touched the village with the sense of the extraordinary, and at the same time tried to encourage a simple piety, organizing and encouraging devotion to Saint Eoin's holy well, half a mile from the village towards the estuary.

One of the tales in the notebook in the Jesse James Tavern concerns Saint Eoin's well. In April 1965 Father Ferris wrote a story he had collected under the heading Blindness: 'The Jameses were Protestants. A servant girl of theirs was going blind and she went to the local holy well. She made a "round" there and got her sight. At the same time her master had a horse gone blind. He took it to the holy well, and marched it around several times. The horse got its sight, but James, its owner got blind.'

Many people in Asdee still believed in the magical properties of Saint Eoin's well, particularly as a healer of the eyes. They told me that some years ago a woman called Ellen Welch was praying there when she saw two fish in the water. She was immediately cured of her illness. They said that when the fish appear again in the water whoever sees them will be cured.

The notebook in the Jesse James Tavern was not Father Ferris's only legacy. He invested Asdee with a sense of the otherworldly. Father Ferris's views were so unorthodox that in ecclesiastical circles the term 'feresy' was coined to cover his many sub-heretical opinions. He believed that all those who attended Mass should share in the mysteries of the priesthood and thus the communion should be given in the hand. He believed that Moses, Plato and Aristotle should be canonized. He wrote an unpublished history of the world, 'The Story of Man', which featured the French Revolution only as a footnote on page 72. He invented a new world, Pollantory, a place where souls went to have the good knocked out of them before they went to Hell, just as they went to Purgatory to have the bad knocked out of them before they went to Heaven. And once, in one of the sermons, in St Mary's Church, which he would deliver with alternate sentences in English and Irish, he told the people of Asdee, in relation to Jesus walking on water, that 'anyone could walk on water if they had enough ESB running through their bodies'. (ESB meaning the product of the Electricity Supply Board.)

I sat quietly for a while in the back of the church, wondering if the statues would move for me. The sacristan was filling the candle stalls at the back of the church with yet another box of votive candles, replenishing those lit and quenched by the continuing stream of pilgrims. Forty little flames were flickering around the statues, causing shadowy movements on their painted surfaces. In the three months since the statues moved, the people of the village had come to take the miracles in their stride. 'There have been so many miraculous movements in Asdee', the sacristan told me, 'the people don't remark on them much anymore. The only thing we haven't had yet is a cure, and I'm sure that will come. But we've had a lot more movements than Knock ever had.'

There were now almost as many adults as children who claimed to have seen movements in the statues – hands lifting, eyes moving, small spots appearing on the Blessed Virgin's neck. Some said they had smelled heavenly perfumes. 'It's like a reminder that there is another world', said a woman across the street from the church. 'And these things never happen except in poor little places like Asdee and Knock. Our Lady never appeared in Dublin.'

There was still, in Ireland, not one way of knowing. In their own place, the Asdee people were believers – in the face of rival claims, they were sceptics. Shortly after the movements were seen in Asdee, a group of children in Ballydesmond, a village on the far side of Kerry's border with Cork, saw the statues move in their local church. The people of Asdee were scornfully amused at the Ballydesmond stories. 'Do you know what happened in Ballydesmond a few weeks ago?' one local man asked me. 'Two young fellas were playing in the church one evening and the sacristan locked the door without checking if there was anyone inside. Well, a little later, weren't a few others walking down past the church and they heard these figures banging on the windows from the inside. Well, they ran like the clappers over to the priest's house shouting, "Come quick, Father, the statues are trying to get out of the window".'

Yet many villagers in Asdee still expected a revelation. Some thought it would surely come at Easter. When it didn't come, they simply carried on. 'There will surely be a message', said a man whose daughter had two visions. 'With all that is happening it wouldn't make sense if there was no message.' The pilgrims and petitioners were drawn not by miracles, but by the mundane mysteries of the everyday world of Ireland in 1985. From half past two on Sunday they bowed their heads and stepped humbly into the twilight zone around the statues, the light from outside refracted from the rain and strained through the coloured glass.

The older women covered their heads and mumbled Rosaries in unison. The younger women and most of the men stood stock still staring at the plaster images, their eyes not revealing whether they were daring or begging the statues to move. Red-haired, plump children played on the floor, their boredom and frustration held in check by occasional warnings. Sometimes the petitioners scribbled notes and left them at the foot of either statue, mostly that of the Blessed Virgin. A woman left a leaflet that proclaimed the power of Holy Water – 'the devil cannot long abide in a place or near a person that is often sprinkled with this blessed water'.

But mostly the petitions were more personal, more reflective of the daily troubles of this bleak time. 'Our Blessed Lady, please bless all of my family and help us sort out all our problems. Make Mam, Dad, better again and let us be one big family together forever.' 'Please, please, help Jim to stop drinking and give us peace in our home.' 'Sacred Heart of Jesus, grant all my intentions and help me pay my bills.' They fondled the hands of the statues continually, rubbing and stroking them. A woman took a small white child's vest from her bag and rubbed it to the statue of the Sacred Heart, then quickly replaced it and moved out through the door, as if she had stolen something and might be caught. Now and then another candle guttered out and sent a last exhalation of smoke towards the roof beams.

27

1987–1991: As Oil Is to Texas

In 2010, an unknown group of protestors was painting two slogans in big letters on the A5 motorway at Doogary, Co. Tyrone, and on the main Cookstown to Omagh road close to the turnoff for Mountfield. One sign demanded 'Status for Republican Prisoners'. The other asked 'Who Shot JR?'[1] I wondered if this was an anniversary tribute to the 1980s. Thirty years earlier, these had been the biggest questions on the minds of the nation. On 22 November 1980, for example, one page of the *Irish Press* juxtaposed a large ad for the National H-Block March in Dublin that day ('Don't let the prisoners die') with a picture of a grinning Larry Hagman, in character as the vicious oilman in the lurid American TV soap *Dallas*, wearing his J. R. Ewing Stetson and brandishing a fistful of dollars: 'Here's who shot JR'.[2] The answer was printed upside down to prolong the suspense.

That summer, a country singer who wore a Stetson, Tom Allen, rebranded himself as T. R. Dallas and released a hit single called 'Who Shot JR?' It was written by a Cork man who called himself Rocky Stone but credited on the label to Dallas's manager, Donie Cassidy. Allen/Dallas sang in a hybrid Westmeath/Texas accent about how JR was an oilman and thus

he knows an oilman's got to do
What an oilman's got to do.

At the end of the song, he cried plaintively: 'The world's got a right to know.' Both Allen and Cassidy were elected to office for Fianna Fáil, the singer as a member of Westmeath County Council, the manager as a TD, councillor and later leader of the Senate.

In 1984 and 1985, the Industrial Development Authority, the state body charged with attracting multinational investment to Ireland, began an international ad campaign with three related catchlines. One used the slogan 'We're the Young Europeans'. It was placed initially in the *Wall Street Journal*, *Business Week*, *The Economist*, *Handelsblatt* and *FAZ* in Germany and *Nikkei Business* in Japan. It also ran on outdoor billboards in the US and in major European airports.[3] A variant on the theme was displayed for arriving passengers at Dublin Airport: 'The Irish – Hire Them Before They Hire You'.[4] It showed a class of graduates from UCD.

The novelist Joseph O'Connor, who was then in his final year at UCD, encountered the photographer sent out by the IDA: 'He wanted images of handsome and clever looking students who would be willing to dress up in tweed jackets and Laura Ashley frocks, and peer into the lens of his Leica and smile and forget about the fact that they would never be able to get jobs in their own country... Payment was involved, I understand.'[5]

Less than a year after that big poster of the UCD graduating class went up at Dublin Airport, the newspaper I was working for, Vincent Browne's *Sunday Tribune*, tracked down all the students shown in the photograph. Almost all of them had emigrated. The rest were either unemployed or were working in jobs entirely unrelated to their degrees.[6] O'Connor had already gone through the photograph with one of his friends 'pointing out to me that this person was in America, that one was in Australia, several were in Spain, or France, or Italy, and, of course, many more were in England.' They were indeed smart and entrepreneurial. Passing by the US embassy in Ballsbridge, you became used to seeing the long queues, snaking for half a mile down the road, of well-mannered, patient young people, sometimes including couples with small children.

But the third part of the ad campaign used a photograph of five clean-cut, smiling young Irish people. Beneath it was an illustration of four oil rigs. The slogan between them said 'People Are To Ireland As Oil Is To Texas'.

These seemed to be mixed messages. The Young Europeans ad suggested to American corporations that they ought to set up in Ireland, that their capital should flow to where the labour was, and employ the new, enthusiastic highly educated workforce that was emerging from the late Irish baby boom of the 1960s and from the rapid expansion of secondary and university education. This had been the success story of Irish modernization. By 1984, 850 foreign companies were operating manufacturing facilities in Ireland. American investment alone over the previous twenty-five years had totalled $4.6 billion, and American companies now provided 18 per cent of all manufacturing jobs.

But the line about people being to Ireland what oil was to Texas suggested the flow would go the other way, that, as in the long history of Irish emigration, the labour should go to where the capital was, that these fine young people were a raw commodity for export. It called to mind JFK's speech in Cork in 1963, which also equated oil and people: 'Most countries send out oil or iron, steel or gold, or some other crop, but Ireland has had only one export and that is its people.'[7]

It also, though, called to mind *Dallas* and the sleazy, corrupt world of J. R. Ewing. If people were to Ireland as oil was to Texas, who might Ireland's JR be? In 1986, the leader of Fianna Fáil fronted a documentary film for Channel 4 in the UK called *Charles Haughey's Ireland*. He described himself in it as 'perhaps a little sentimental, even romantic, in my loyalties to people'. He displayed his great personal wealth, with sequences showing him with his family on his own private Blasket island, Inishvicillaun. 'According to folklore', he intoned, 'Inishvicillaun was the home of the fairies.' He recalled how he had bought the island from its last inhabitants, the Ó Dalaigh brothers, the wise old men who initiated him into the ancient lore of the Gael and 'taught us about island life'. This script runs over shots of Haughey at the wheel of his yacht. One of his sons touches the wheel. Haughey says, 'Don't touch my wheel. Don't you dare touch my wheel!'

A little later, we see Haughey at the races in Phoenix Park in September 1985. He talks of the pride of being able 'occasionally to see my black and blue colours go past the winning post'. There's a shot of a hand passing a £20 note to a bookie and then a close-up of a leather bag full of cash. Suddenly, out of nowhere, Haughey bumps into the actual J. R. Ewing, Larry Hagman in the flesh, who was at the races as a guest of the famous Irish trainer Vincent O'Brien. Haughey, rubbing his fingers with his thumb in the universal signal of the demand for a backhander, asks him: 'Have you any of those dollar bills?' Hagman says, 'I do.' He reaches into his inside jacket pocket, saying, 'I hate to bribe anyone.' He hands Haughey a note, saying, 'Spend it wisely.' Haughey holds it up in front of the camera. It is a joke thousand-dollar bill with a picture of J. R. Ewing where George Washington should be. 'Will I put it on the favourite this time?' 'Absolutely', says Hagman, 'And I hope you collect after that.'

I wrote about this at the time, but hardly anyone else seemed to find it remarkable. I remember watching the sequence on television and feeling dizzy from the semantic overload. The encounter, coming after Haughey's display of his island, his yacht and his racehorses, was obviously spontaneous. But Haughey had decided to leave it in the film. What did he intend it to mean? That a politician who was really on the take surely wouldn't act out this little burlesque of bribery – a double bluff in which a reality is made so obvious that it must not be true? Or was it a tease, a hint, a joke on the credulity of his own followers, a wink to the sophisticates, a sign of his own impunity?

By this time, Haughey, as well as receiving money from his business backers, was stealing directly from the public purse. Haughey had effective control of the Party Leader's Allowance, paid by the taxpayer and meant to fund his expenses as leader of the Opposition. His protégé and eventual successor Bertie Ahern was a co-signatory on the account, but he would 'sign blank cheques in advance', on at least one occasion 'pre-signing a full book of blank cheques'.[8] Between April and October 1986 alone, five sums were withdrawn from the account and lodged into the account in Guinness & Mahon bank used to pay Haughey's personal bills. Another withdrawal, of £25,000, was simply made out to cash.

While Ahern was signing these blank cheques, young Irish citizens were on their way to becoming the greatest form fillers in the world. In 1987, when Haughey was back in power, a bureaucratic act that most people dread became the centre of a unique form of social life. It was perhaps the first truly indigenous genre of indoor entertainment to be developed in Ireland since the days when *The Late Late Show* replaced the seanachaí. It was called the Donnelly Visa party. It was, in a way, a subgenre of gambling: the point was to win a lottery by improving your odds. The prize was a green card that would allow you to get the hell out of Ireland and settle legally in the United States.

The visa was named after an Irish-American Democratic Congressman, Brian Donnelly. He sponsored a programme to award 10,000 visas to randomly chosen applicants from round the world. The Donnelly scheme commenced in January 1987. There were 1.5 million applicants from thirty-six countries. Yet, of that first tranche of visas, 4,161 went to Irish applicants. How did one small country get 41 per cent of the prizes in a worldwide lottery?

Young people in Ireland realized that each application had to be filled and signed individually – no photocopies would be accepted. And there was a target date on which the first 10,000 applications would be processed. But nothing in the rules said that only one application was valid. Hence the Donnelly Visa party – get your friends together, supply some drink, give them a template and get them to work on your application forms. Some applicants were known to have sent as many as 500 forms.[9]

Also, there was an advantage to getting the forms in early. Small ads began to appear in provincial newspapers: 'We are travelling to the USA on January 18 [1987] and will post your application for a Donnelly Visa in Washington DC on January 20 to ensure its arrival at PO Box 96097 on the first post on January 21.'[10] Adrian Flannelly, the host of a popular radio show for Irish emigrants in Boston, personally delivered over 16,000 applications sent to his programme.[11]

By the beginning of 1990, 20,000 Donnelly visas had been issued to Irish people. But one strange thing noted on both sides of the Atlantic was that one in four visas awarded to Irish citizens remained unused.[12] Many people were applying for visas without having any actual plans to emigrate. It was just a thing you imagined you probably wanted to have if things got worse. Which they very well might.

For all of my life until about 1980, I had been told to think of myself as the end of something and the beginning of something else. It was a big thing: we were the first generation since the early nineteenth century that did not have to face the prospect of emigration. For all that was wrong with the place, it was our place. We would travel; we would not migrate. During the 1970s, more people came into Ireland (largely Irish families who had emigrated to Britain returning home) than left it. This hadn't happened for well over a century. This was what Fianna Fáil could point to. In 1967 Charles Haughey was able to announce that 'emigration is gone'.[13] Less than twenty years later, Haughey, in opposition, was wailing that emigration was again 'horrifying' and 'reaching catastrophic levels'.[14]

Haughey expressed quite well the sense of national déjà vu, the way the 1980s were becoming, in this crucial respect, the 1950s all over again: 'the country has been forced back to the situation of 30 years ago… most of us thought that this defeatist acceptance of emigration was something that had been banished from Irish life since the sixties.' Yet there was also in this bleak return a certain comfortable familiarity. Ending mass emigration had been a grand project even when his party had done nothing about it. Now, there could be a second bite at finality. The catastrophe that had been banished forever could be, rhetorically, banished forever again: 'To end [emigration] successfully was Fianna Fáil's great achievement in the sixties. To eliminate it again from Irish life will be our objective in the eighties.' The Fianna Fáil of 1988 is the same as the Fianna Fáil of 1958. In spite of all the upheavals, the party remains true to itself, its integrity of purpose is assured. National unity may be unattainable, the revival of Irish a bad joke, economic self-sufficiency jettisoned thirty years ago, but in emigration there was still one Great National Goal that had emotional and rhetorical power.

We were back to bodies in motion. The politics of the 1980s, with the hunger strikes and the abortion wars, were brutally biological. So was the underlying reality. The combination of economic growth and Catholicism had produced a baby boom in the 1960s and 1970s. The Irish really were the young Europeans. But foreign investment, however impressive, could not produce enough jobs for them. Fianna Fáil, in the late 1970s, tried to make up the deficit by expanding the public service. The proportion of workers who were on the government payroll rose to a third of the entire working population.[15]

This could not be sustained – state borrowing went out of control. The response was to try to shrink the state. Expenditure on social housing was cut by half; the number employed in the civil service was cut over the course of the 1980s from 30,800 to 25,000; spending on public hospitals was slashed. The number of registered unemployed rose from 61,000 in 1971 to 230,000 by 1993; the rate of unemployment tripled. But even these figures masked a much larger crisis, because much of the workforce was emigrating. In 1988–9 alone, an astounding 70,600 people left the country – 2 per cent of the entire population. Most of these were young – those aged between fifteen and twenty-four made up 69 per cent of the total.[16] The slow demographic recovery that validated the revolution of 1958 was going into reverse. By 1986, there were fewer people in the Republic than there had been in 1981. The birth rate was also dropping very rapidly: from 21.9 per thousand in 1980 to 16.6 per thousand in 1987.[17]

In many urban working-class areas, houses, normally in fierce demand, were being left on the local authorities' hands as families emigrated. In the sports pages of the provincial newspapers, a recurring phrase reflected the reality that local GAA games were being called off because too many young people had vanished: 'Hollymount were unable to field a team against Claremorris in the semi-final of the South Mayo minor football championship at Ballinrobe on Friday evening'; 'St. Brigid's were unable to field and we received a walk over'; 'On Sunday last Carrickedmona were unable to field a team against Clonguish in the Championship'; 'Ballyduff were unable to field a team and Kilmoyley were left without a game'.[18]

What struck me at the time, though, was how easily the society slipped back into emigration mode. Psychologically, it was now as if the period of my own life in Ireland had been an aberration. What I thought had been banished forever – the instinct to just get the hell out of Ireland when times were bad – had merely itself been in temporary exile. Irish young people, it seemed, were prepared to put up with any amount of personal disruption rather than contemplate a radically altered future in their own country. This was the great paradox: personal discontinuity was still the guarantor of political and social continuity.

In November 1988, the *Cork Evening Echo* published a study, conducted for it by the department of sociology at University College Cork, of the experiences of emigration of 648 students in eight secondary schools in the city. One in five had at least one brother or sister who had left Ireland to look for work abroad. Almost all of the young Corkonians saw their future as bleak: 49 per cent 'very bad' and 25 per cent 'poor' or 'bad'. Three-quarters said they had seriously considered emigration. Half said they thought they would actually have to emigrate.[19]

This fatalism was now creeping back into official thought. Alongside the traditional claim that Fianna Fáil would end emigration, there was a testing of the idea that maybe it was not a curse at all but a blessing. Joseph McCabe, chairman of the IDA, imagined emigration as a giant training scheme: 'Many of these "Young Europeans" have gained invaluable training experience with leading multinational companies at no cost to the State for their training. Therefore, it would be short-sighted and unduly pessimistic to view this development in purely negative terms.'[20]

Fianna Fáil's minister for foreign affairs, Brian Lenihan, gave a breezy account of what was happening to *Newsweek*: 'What we have now is a very literate emigrant who thinks nothing of coming to the United States and going back to Ireland and maybe on to Germany and back to Ireland again... After all we can't all live on a small island.'[21] Even Ken Whitaker, who had been so affected by mass emigration in the late 1950s, was quite blasé. 'Migration used to be a bad word here', he told the *New York Times*. 'Now, one might see emigration not as a sad and tearful thing, but as a migration within the European community.'[22]

The image of the new emigrant as a sophisticated, rootless cosmopolitan, hopping between New York, Dublin and Berlin, was false. In the study of Cork school-goers, 44 per cent said their siblings who had emigrated were working in manual jobs, as against only 14 per cent who were in higher professional or managerial occupations. Another study in Cork in 1990 found that only a third of emigrants from the city had a third-level qualification, and a majority even of these were not university graduates. As Jim McLaughlin, who conducted the survey, put it, 'The vast majority of Cork emigrants are not climbing social ladders abroad. Indeed many are simply climbing ladders because the construction industry alone accounts for almost 30 per cent of male emigrants from Cork.' He also found that a similar proportion of female emigrants were working in low-paid service employment in retail and hospitality. Fewer than one in ten, on the other hand, were in high-status jobs.[23] The evidence over time, moreover, strongly suggested that, given a choice, even most of well-educated young professional migrants would have preferred to stay in Ireland.

Most of this reality was rendered invisible in the gentrification of emigration. The element of compulsion was played down and the idea of cosmopolitanism and adventure-seeking played up. The 'Ryanair generation', named after the Irish airline that provided cheap flights, was all about mobility, young people hopping on and off planes in new cities. What was occluded was the immobility of many emigrants to the United States, who could not get on a flight to Ireland because they were illegal and might not get back into the place they now called home.

This mass exodus produced another great unknown: the undocumented. How many illegal Irish were there in the US? The figures used in 1987 ranged from 25,000 to 60,000 to 100,000 to 250,000.[24] Figures from the US Immigration and Naturalization Service in June 1987 showed that an astounding 500,000 Irish people had entered the US on tourist visas since 1981. Nobody was quite sure how many had left again. But few of those who overstayed their legal welcome were making it big. More than half of the undocumented Irish women in the US in 1988 were working in someone else's home and most of the rest were waitresses. Just 14 per cent were working in offices.[25] They were not very different from the generations of women who had gone before them.

There was a new variant in Irish fiction: the fake documents provided to immigrants to enable them to get US passports. In a case prosecuted by the New York district attorney Rudi Giuliani, eighteen Irish immigrants were provided with fake birth certificates from the state of Vermont.[26] They had been born again in the USA.

28

1986–1992: Internal Exiles

The culture of deliberate unknowing had shaped Ireland throughout my lifetime. It was, mostly, about survival, the things people did to get by, the ways a society held itself together by preserving the barriers between what it knew and what it wanted to know. But in the 1980s, these mechanisms became embedded in a very different domain: money. People who had it could be both inside and outside Ireland. They could take their leave from the obligations of home without ever actually leaving. They could occupy two worlds – the local and the global – in such a way that they owed nothing to either. Faced with this possibility, the Irish financial system, the nexus of bankers, regulators and tax authorities, adopted the mindsets that Ireland applied to, say, abortion or child abuse: don't ask, don't see, don't say.

It was rather apt that the Irish Central Bank literally could not spell the word 'ethical'. One of its inspection reports on a small Dublin merchant bank, Guinness & Mahon, which was running a huge tax scam for its elite clients, Charles Haughey among them, expressed the view that 'it is not, in our view, appropriate or ethitical [sic] for a bank to participate in, as distinct from advise on, tax avoidance schemes'.[1] For more than thirty years, before the Irish banking system eventually collapsed, it had been colluding, on a massive scale, with fraud, tax evasion and routine breaches of exchange control laws. Large sections of the Irish business class, from strong farmers to chairmen of blue-chip companies, were hiding money in offshore accounts or claiming to be living outside the country when they were in fact making that money in shops, pubs, property deals and companies within its borders. While Ireland was suffering from mass unemployment, mass emigration, a squeeze of vital services in health and education and a persistent crisis in its public finances, many of its most respectable citizens were simply going absent from society. The banks were helping them to do so, and the authorities in turn were scrupulously ignoring what was going on.

The scale of the scams can be judged from the amount of tax that was harvested after media investigations had prompted official inquiries. In all, the Revenue was eventually able to identify 34,000 people who had engaged in one or other of five major tax-dodging enterprises. By April 2009, it had recovered €2.5 billion from these individuals. To put this in perspective, €2.5 billion was almost a tenth of the entire Irish national debt in 1987. These people, of course, were merely those who were ultimately caught.

The important point about these rackets, however, is that they were not secret conspiracies, so wickedly brilliant that even the best minds in the public service could not penetrate their dark purposes. The Central Bank and its political master, the Department of Finance, had a very good idea of what was going on. The state authorities knew about widespread organized crime, committed by financial institutions and their customers and did essentially nothing to stop it. The desire of the wealthy to evade taxes was by no means unique to Ireland. What was distinctive was that the frauds were so open that it took a conscious effort on the part of the authorities to pretend not to see them. Not looking was more than an omission. When the crimes were so flagrant, the official eye must have been strained from constant aversion.

The popular side of this culture was, aptly, the hiding of a thing called DIRT. Deposit Interest Retention Tax (DIRT) was introduced in 1986. It obliged banks to withhold tax at source from the interest paid to borrowers and pass it directly on to the Revenue. Non-residents, however, could sign a form stating that they did not ordinarily live in Ireland and therefore requesting that DIRT not be taken from their interest payments. Almost immediately on the introduction of DIRT, the number of non-residents with Irish banking accounts increased threefold. By the end of 1998, an astonishing 17 per cent of all Irish-held deposits (amounting to IR£7.6 billion) was held by non-residents. The sheer number of non-residents was staggering: Allied Irish Bank alone had 88,000 of them in 217 branches – an average of over 400 per branch.

Given that the country had, at the time, almost no immigrant population, and that the figure excludes all of the financial institutions that actually dealt specifically or mainly with non-residents, it was patently obvious that most of this was bogus. It was not hard to figure out what was going on: very large numbers of people were simply walking into their local bank branch, signing the forms and fraudulently claiming to be resident outside the state. Often the bank staff knew them very well: they were the local farmers, publicans, shopkeepers or small business owners. But they literally pretended not to know them. They filed their plainly deceitful forms and exempted them from the tax.

This was bad Irish fiction run rampant. Every single one of these account holders committed an act of fraud by filling out a form claiming to be a non-resident. Yet, even though the forms were simple enough, many of them were not filled out correctly. As late as 1999, over a quarter of the relevant forms were not properly completed. As Mark Hely-Hutchinson of Bank of Ireland explained: 'Well, if he is a farmer, which means, by definition, he is a resident, part of his difficulty might be that he doesn't know quite which answers he ought to give to make sure that he evades the tax.'[2] The attitude of the banks was such, however, that most didn't even bother about incomplete, or incorrect forms. As the internal auditor of AIB Tony Spollen put it, the 'feeling was that once the declarations were complete or once the declarations were there, and in some instances even if they weren't, that once the depositor said: "I am a non-resident", then I think that was almost taken as good enough.' As frauds go, this one was remarkably easy – it wasn't even necessary to lie properly.

Or, in reality, even to lie at all. To call this lying would miss the point. Most of this scam was going on in rural towns, where everybody knows everybody. The scenario must have played out time and again. 'Good morning, Mary.' 'Good morning, John.'

'How's business?' 'Ah sure grand.' 'What can I do for you?' 'Well, you see, I'm not here at all.' 'Oh right.' 'I'm in Boston.' 'I get you. Can you sign a wee bit of a form?' 'Grand so.' 'Tell your husband I was asking for him.' 'I will, but sure you'll see him at the golf club on Saturday. I'll be there myself.' 'Lovely, see you then.'

When I heard the phrase first in the early 1990s, 'bogus non-resident' seemed almost excessively apt. It was a sort of dark mirror image of the other fleeting non-person of the 1980s, the 'undocumented' Irish migrant in the US, who was, I suppose, a kind of bogus resident. One was here but not here; the other there but not there. These two ghostly figures were, moreover, intimately related. People had to leave Ireland physically because so much of its own bourgeoisie had left it morally.

In the case of AIB, the internal auditor, Tony Spollen, estimated in 1991 that the amount of money in bogus accounts was of the order of £300–400 million – which would mean that the unpaid tax was around £100 million. This was, at the time, about the size of AIB's annual profits – the liability could in principle push the country's biggest bank into the red. This fraud was so obvious (simply from the figures for money in non-resident accounts) that even the authorities could not help noticing. The official files of the Department of Finance were seasoned with piquant statements like 'half the non-resident accounts are thought to be bogus' and 'at least £1 billion of non-resident deposits are thought to be held by Irish residents'. By 1993, the Department's own internal estimates were that the amount of money in bogus accounts was £2 billion. Yet it did nothing.

Deeply embedded within the state were two related beliefs. One, never openly articulated, but clearly assumed at the level of unconscious, and therefore especially potent, instinct, was that the rich in Ireland had no sense of social or patriotic responsibility whatsoever. Given any level of pressure, they would evade their taxes and salt their money away offshore. Second, the conclusion to be drawn from this was not the obvious one that the law would therefore have to be enforced with rigour and consistency. It was, rather, that the lawlessness of the rich would have to be indulged. The aim of enforcement would be to avoid anything that might scare them into hiding their money. Maurice O'Connell, then governor of the Central Bank, told the Comptroller and Auditor General that 'We were broadly aware of the fact that people were avoiding tax. And all this had to be corrected, this was wrong. Everybody agreed it was wrong. [But] for God's sake, whatever you do, don't rock the boat.'[3]

The telling phrase on official documents dealing with these scams in the Department of Finance was always 'in view of the sensitive nature of the issue...'[4] The sensitivity was both general and very, very specific. There was the broad anxiety that the rich would send their money abroad, that the Irish economy was so porous that its lifeblood could simply drain away overnight. But there was also a much more precise fear. The biggest bogus non-resident of them all was the man who, for long periods of the 1980s, was running the country, Charles Haughey himself.

The Ansbacher Cayman scam was a high-level, elite version of the non-resident fraud that the banks operated for publicans and farmers and builders. It was established in 1971 by the small Dublin merchant bank Guinness & Mahon (G&M) and initially run as Guinness Mahon Cayman Trust. After 1988, it became the responsibility of the Irish branch of the Ansbacher group, and was known as Ansbacher (Cayman) Limited. These changes in ownership had little impact – at all times, the operation was under the control of Des Traynor, even after he ceased to run the bank itself in 1984. Traynor was not just a highly regarded financier and businessman (from 1987 until his death in 1994, he was chairman of one of Ireland's most successful companies, Cement Roadstone), he was also widely known as a close friend of Charles Haughey. (Traynor and Haughey had met in the early 1950s at the accountancy firm Haughey Boland.) Most importantly, he handled Haughey's money.

Traynor's Ansbacher Cayman scam was simple in principle, if rather less so in practice. Essentially, members of Traynor's circle – the eventual Revenue investigation would take in 137 people – would give him money, which he would deposit, through front companies, in the bank's Cayman Island accounts (and to a lesser extent in similar accounts in the Channel Islands). These deposits would be unrecorded in Ireland except on secret coded files held by Traynor (Haughey himself, for example, was S8 and S9). The same clients would then 'borrow' money from G&M in Dublin. The security for these 'borrowings' (the offshore funds) was not listed on G&M's accounts. The 'loans' were merely described as 'suitably secured' or 'adequately secured'.

The money thus had a kind of magical double life. It was at home and abroad, onshore and offshore. The clients had immediate access in rainy Dublin to funds that were supposedly 7,300 kilometres away in the sunny Caribbean. They could make lodgements and withdrawals through Traynor even though the money was stowed in a tax haven. And because of the system of so-called 'back-to-back loans' (essentially clients borrowing their own money), an asset was recorded for tax purposes as a debt. Even while lodging large chunks of cash, the clients could pretend that they had in fact borrowed it. Herein lay the breathtaking brazenness of the scheme. Instead of merely hiding the money from the tax authorities, Traynor's clients could actually claim tax relief on their 'borrowings'. There was a certain magnificence to the effrontery. It evokes the same admiration as a gangster who robs a bank and then claims compensation because his own account had been emptied.

As a licensed bank, G&M was subject to regular inspections by the Central Bank. The 1976 inspection was carried out by three inspectors, one of whom, Adrian Byrne, subsequently became the Central Bank's Head of Banking Supervision, a position he still held in 2002. It was obvious to them that G&M's offshore subsidiary in the Caymans was involved in tax fraud. The deposits it held, noted Byrne, were 'part of a scheme which was surrounded by a unique level of secrecy and which appeared to involve tax evasion'.

Yet, in reporting on this obvious fraud, the inspectors adopted the tone of a maiden aunt who has peered through a neighbour's window and inadvertently seem him indulging in a private and intimate pleasure. Metaphorically, they made their excuses and left. 'The bank', they noted, 'is in effect offering a special service which assists persons to transfer funds, on which tax has been avoided, to offshore tax havens. The possibility of the bank abusing its position as an authorized dealer in providing this service cannot be ignored. In view of the delicate nature of these matters we did not pursue the matter further…'

With an admirable fastidiousness, the inspectors broached the subject with the directors of G&M. The directors 'were initially reluctant to give information about the activities of these companies to the Central Bank because it [sic] feared that the information might be conveyed to the Revenue authorities' – a concern that the inspectors clearly both understood and assuaged. They agreed that they would be shown documents relating to the deposits on condition that they would not note the names of the owners. Its inspectors having written that the bank's abuse of its licence 'cannot be ignored', the Central Bank proceeded effectively to do precisely that. Nothing flowed from the 1976 inspection beyond a desultory communication to the effect that the Central Bank was 'somewhat concerned'.

The Central Bank even doctored its own internal files to minimize the nature of the Ansbacher fraud. In the report of the 1976 inspection, the phrase 'tax evasion' was later altered, by Byrne's superiors, to 'tax avoidance'. This was done again in relation to a document drawn up by Byrne two years later. In evidence to the High Court inquiry into Ansbacher, Byrne referred to this complete change of meaning, in which unlawful evasion is redefined as lawful avoidance, as 'coding'.

It might more accurately be called a deliberate act of unknowing. If the Central Bank knew that Des Traynor was operating a sophisticated tax fraud, there would have to be consequences. Therefore, the Central Bank, 'knew' instead that Traynor was just a clever banker, lawfully working the system to suit his clients.

One reason for this tendency to call a crook a sheep-herding implement may have been the realization that one of the Central Bank's own directors was implicated in the Ansbacher fraud. At least by 1978, the Central Bank knew that one of those directors, Ken O'Reilly-Hyland, was one of Traynor's chosen few. At that stage, O'Reilly-Hyland, a Central Bank director from 1973 to 1983, had a 'loan' of £426,000 from Ansbacher (Cayman). This knowledge, confirmed in the Central Bank's 1978 inspection, remained entirely inert and unofficial: 'There appears', noted the High Court inspectors, 'to be no documentary record within the bank recording receipt or consideration of this information.' By 1988, O'Reilly-Hyland's Ansbacher 'loan' exceeded £1 million.

Since the early 1960s, Ken O'Reilly-Hyland had been a pivotal figure in the nexus of connections between business and politics in Ireland. He was one of the directors of Taca, the controversial Fianna Fáil fundraising organization, associated with the 'men in mohair suits', the young and ambitious new generation of politicians whose most prominent figures were Donogh O'Malley, Brian Lenihan and, of course, Haughey. At the time the Central Bank discovered his involvement in the Ansbacher Cayman scam, O'Reilly-Hyland was chairman of Taca's successor organization, Fianna Fáil's so-called 'general election fundraising committee'. This was a secret body, not under the control of the party leader and not given to publishing accounts. It operated, not from party headquarters, but from the discreet privacy of Room 547 in the Burlington Hotel in Dublin. As chairman of this committee, O'Reilly-Hyland was involved, not merely in obtaining large donations from wealthy business people, but in securing loans from some of the very banks the Central Bank was meant to supervise.

As well as being deeply embedded in Fianna Fáil's financial dealings, however, O'Reilly-Hyland was also part a network of business connections among fellow holders of Ansbacher (Cayman) accounts, including the architect Sam Stephenson, the solicitor who had acted for G&M in establishing its Cayman operations, Liam McGonigal (both fellow members of the Taca committee), and the auctioneer John Finnegan. Finnegan in turn was connected through the builders Brennan and McGowan to another powerful Fianna Fáil politician, Ray Burke. In 1984, Finnegan, jointly with Brennan and McGowan, made what a tribunal of inquiry subsequently found to be a 'corrupt payment' to Burke.

At the end of the 1970s and in the early 1980s, O'Reilly-Hyland was caught up in tensions between the secretary of his Fianna

Fáil fundraising committee, Des Hanafin, and the new party leader, Charles Haughey. Haughey wanted direct control over the committee, and Hanafin, suspecting his motives, resisted his advances. Haughey was particularly anxious to get hold of the committee's so-called Black Book, a top-secret list of donors. Infuriated by Hanafin's resistance, Haughey decided to disband the committee. A standoff ensued until, shortly after Haughey was re-elected as Taoiseach in 1982, he summoned the committee members to his Georgian mansion at Kinsealy and got them to sign a document ordering Hanafin to hand over the secret fundraising accounts into his own control.

O'Reilly-Hyland told a tribunal of inquiry that at the time of his appointment to the board of the Central Bank in 1973, he informed the then minister for finance, George Colley, that he had an offshore trust in the Cayman Islands. That this was no barrier to a role as guarantor of the integrity of the country's banking system was itself eloquent testimony to the prevailing standards in public life. O'Reilly-Hyland's position, however, cannot but have placed those in the bank who were trying to uphold higher standards in an excruciatingly difficult position.

There is no evidence that knowledge of O'Reilly-Hyland's involvement in the Ansbacher tax evasion scam had a direct bearing on the Central Bank's supine approach to this criminality. Those at the bank, however, knew two things. One was that one of their own directors was deeply involved in both the scam itself and in Fianna Fáil. The other was that Des Traynor, who was running the Ansbacher fraud, was close to the sometime Taoiseach, Haughey. In a supervisory culture that was already remarkably deferential, such knowledge was hardly likely to encourage bold scrutiny.

During 1979, before Haughey took over as party leader and Taoiseach in December, the Central Bank began to express more forceful concerns to Des Traynor, pointing out rather plaintively that the Ansbacher scheme was 'not in the national interest'. In theory, these apparent warning shots should have become louder after Haughey's election. The arrival of the Boss into power was the signal for a massive growth in the scale of the Ansbacher scam. In April 1979, the deposits stood at just under £5 million sterling.

Three years later, they had reached almost £27 million sterling. By then, the Cayman operation, initially a sideshow, had become larger than its parent company.

This happened in spite of the Central Bank's own weak-kneed compromise with Traynor. Instead of closing down his operation and calling in the police, it merely extracted from him an informal agreement that the Ansbacher racket would be kept at its current levels. Even when it discovered in 1982 that the Ansbacher deposits were in fact increasing significantly, however, the bank did nothing.

This may or may not have been connected to something else the Central Bank discovered in 1982. In December of that year its exchange controls division received a formal request from a man who wanted to take out a foreign currency loan to the tune of £350,000 sterling. The request, on behalf of Abbeville Stud, clearly stated that the lending bank would be 'Guinness Mahon Cayman Trust Ltd, PO box 887, Grand Cayman, British West Indies' and that, as security, the title deeds to the stud farm would be lodged with Guinness Mahon Cayman Trust Limited. The signature on the letter was that of Charles J. Haughey. It was delivered personally by Des Traynor to the general manager of the Central Bank. Approval was issued the following day, a response time that may say more about the source of the request than about the bank's efficiency.

It is striking that the Central Bank's scrutiny of G&M, never very acute, became far less inquisitive after Haughey came to power. At a review meeting in April 1981, there was, as a High Court inspectors' report puts it, 'some passing reference to particular loans with a Cayman connection' but 'no further discussion of the overall nature of this banking activity or of its taxation implications'. The Central Bank conducted further examinations of G&M in 1986, 1988 and 1992 and failed every time to blow the whistle on what was now a large-scale criminal conspiracy involving the country's most senior politician.

In 1988, however, a neophyte inspector, Terry Donovan, was sent to accompany two more senior colleagues on their visit to G&M. He came across references in the books to 'hypothecated loans' and 'hypothecated deposits' ('hypothecated' indicates an asset pledged against a debt). On asking what this meant, he was told directly by a G&M executive that the reference was to deposits in the Cayman Islands. Perhaps sensing Donovan's concern, the executive pressed him into meeting the bank's general manager, Michael Pender. At the meeting, Pender 'mentioned Mr Des Traynor, a name which had no particular significance for me at the time other than perhaps as chairman of Cement Roadstone, and said that Mr Traynor had already explained the back-to-back loan arrangement to Mr Adrian Byrne of the Central Bank'. Had Donovan not been a naive beginner (this was his first inspection) he would presumably have understood that the mention of Des Traynor's name was meant to convey more than a point of detail about the workings of the bank. For anyone in the know, Traynor was a cipher for Haughey.

Donovan continued to examine the G&M files, and to turn up worrying indications of the scale and nature of the fraud, but he was told by one of his superiors that there was no need to include details of what he discovered in his final report. She alluded, he said, to 'matters not being pursued further because of the sensitivity of the matter'. A subsequent offer by Donovan to provide a written memorandum of his findings and concerns was politely refused by his superiors and he was told that he should not have been 'placed in such a difficult situation, given the history of the matter'. He was later told, he recalled, that there would be no need to circulate the bank's completed report of its inspection of G&M, 'and it would be sent directly to the file, probably a box file'.

There is, in the Ansbacher case, an unmistakable correlation between political power (in effect, Fianna Fáil) and regulation, with the Central Bank's level of scrutiny rapidly diminishing after Charles Haughey came to power. What is important about this correlation is that it was entirely unspoken. There is absolutely no evidence of direct political interference in the workings of the Central Bank. There are no threatening phone calls and no Fianna Fáil moles on the bank's staff.

Everything was much subtler, and much more insidious, than that. In the very small and overlapping worlds of Irish banking, business, politics and public service, people knew who Des Traynor was and for whom he worked. They knew that there was a system of networks and connections, with the ruler of the country at its centre. Inchoate, instinctive and perhaps even unconscious, that awareness was all the more powerful because it did not require those who held it to do anything. On the contrary, it required them to do precisely nothing.

29

1989: Freaks

It was another of those phone calls that have become all too familiar by 1989, another contemporary of mine bailing out of Ireland, another set of farewell drinks in another Dublin hotel, another bout of frantic reminiscences to hide the fact that the one who's leaving feels like a traitor and the ones who are staying feel betrayed, more jokes to suppress the questions that they know are stupid but that won't go away. So we're not good enough for you anymore? What's wrong with us? Who do you think you are, anyway, off to the Continent?

This one, though, was that bit more puzzling. Seán, the guy who was leaving, was the most profoundly and unselfconsciously Irish person I knew. He wasn't a bigot or a Provo or a mountainy man with tweed knickerbockers and a little shamrock farm in the West. He was from Drimnagh, the Corporation estate next to Crumlin, and he grew up in a house identical to mine. He had a Dublin accent as thick as the EU butter mountain. He had grown up after Vatican II and *The Late Late Show* and The Rolling Stones, and he had most of the attitudes that went with that. He had fluent French and Breton and very good German. I once found him sitting on the bus studying Swahili for fun.

But he also spoke Irish as if the battle of Kinsale and Oliver Cromwell and the Famine had never happened, as if this were the most natural thing in the world for a Dublin working-class suburbanite to do. Neither of his parents had a word of the language, but somehow he imbibed it and shaped his thinking around it. He'd be nattering away in English to you – he had no hang-ups about which language you preferred to speak – and he'd suddenly stop and say, "Ah, Jaysus, what's the word for that in English?" and give you the Irish expression. He thought in Irish. He also played a mean tin whistle and had spent a part of his working life in a Gaeltacht. If a passing UFO had nabbed him and taken him off to study him as a representative Irishman, the aliens would have concluded that the famed wound in the Irish historical consciousness was all guff, that the Irish were perfectly at ease with both their past and their present.

It was a real shock to discover that he was leaving. He had a good job as a translator in the Dáil, one that he genuinely liked doing. He was not particularly well paid, but then he didn't have kids and a mortgage and all the impediments of us thirtysomethings. I watched him, so at ease in the flow of slagging and nudging in that hotel lounge, and wondered why. And then something struck me, something that seemed so obvious and natural to him, as natural certainly as his love of the Irish language, that I hadn't even thought of it. I waited until the hubbub of conversation had risen to become a seamless blanket of sound and then I asked him if he was leaving because he was gay. Was that it?

It was. This man, so at ease with all the contradictions of being Irish, so sure-footed in negotiating the divides between tradition and modernity, between country and city, between a Gaelic past and an Anglo-American present, had been trapped and ground down by something as simple and natural as a sexual preference. He had a boyfriend who was unemployed and from another working-class Dublin suburb. Neither of them belonged to the stereotyped world of the gay man; sophisticated, trendy, mercurial, glittering, creative. They didn't belong to a set, a clique, a scene, or any of the other things that heterosexual society imagined as going with being gay. Nor did they want to belong to any such thing. They wanted merely to be normal, to live in the same places, have the same friends, do the same things that they would do if they were straight. And it was this simplest of things that they found to be denied them. Alone and discreet, they could get by and be tolerated. Living together they would be a challenge to the Family, an affront to normality as the Black Mass is an affront to the Mass. They would cease to be two ordinary people and become a symbol. And that they couldn't take.

But what, I asked Seán, about his job, the one he liked so much? 'I would rather', he said to me, 'do a menial job in a foreign city and be normal than have a good job in Dublin and be a freak.' He was right. He was a freak – and a criminal. The operative law in Ireland was literally Victorian: the 1861 Offences Against the Person Act that made 'buggery' punishable by penal servitude for life; and the 1885 act outlawing 'gross indecency' under which Oscar Wilde had been imprisoned. These laws, repealed in England and Wales in 1967, would remain in place until 1993.

David Norris, a lecturer in English at Trinity College Dublin and one of the very few openly gay men in Ireland, had challenged the constitutionality of the anti-gay laws in a series of court cases from 1977 onwards. In April 1983, his appeal reached the Supreme Court. Just a month earlier, four boys aged between fourteen and nineteen were convicted in Dublin of beating and kicking to death a young man, Declan Flynn. They had been preying on men who used Fairview Park on the north side of the inner city, as a meeting point, and assumed that Declan Flynn was one of them. When they came to be sentenced, the judge, Seán Gannon, suspended their (already light) sentences for manslaughter and allowed them to walk free. There was cheering in the nearby flats where one of the boys lived.[1] A group of about twenty teenagers staged a jubilant demonstration that evening, marching behind a makeshift banner that read 'We are the champions'.[2]

Apart from the impunity for the killers, what struck me at the time was the silence of the other victims. According to one of the gang in his statement to the Gardaí, 'A few of us had been queer-bashing for about six weeks before and had battered 20 steamers.'[3] Yet, at the trial, the police told the judge that 'there had been no report of violence in the park before the fatal attack'.[4] The local parish priest had even warned from the pulpit that 'something dreadful' would happen in the park because of the gang. But none of the twenty or so men who had been 'battered' felt it possible even to report the assaults. This was something else that was known but not said.

There could hardly have been a more vivid demonstration of the way the laws that criminalized gay men stripped them of their most basic right of citizenship – protection against violence. But within weeks of the release of the Fairview Park killers, the Supreme Court dismissed David Norris's appeal against those laws. In the majority judgement, the chief justice, Tom O'Higgins, who, in his earlier life as a Fine Gael politician had almost defeated Eamon de Valera in the presidential election of 1966, spoke of 'how sad, lonely and harrowing the life of a person, who is or has become exclusively homosexual, is likely to be'. He claimed that homosexuals 'constitute a threat to public health' because they spread venereal diseases and that 'homosexual activity and its encouragement may not be consistent with respect and regard for marriage as an institution'. He ruled, as a matter of fact, that 'The homosexually orientated can be importuned into a homosexual lifestyle which can become habitual.' Most importantly, he pointed out that 'Homosexuality has always been condemned in Christian teaching as being morally wrong. It has equally been regarded by society for many centuries as an offence against nature and a very serious crime.' He rejected Norris's appeal 'On the ground of the Christian nature of our State and on the grounds that the deliberate practice of homosexuality is morally wrong, that it is damaging to the health both of individuals and the public and, finally, that it is potentially harmful to the institution of marriage.'[5]

O'Higgins's ruling was not just a collection of cheap and nasty prejudices. It was endorsed without demur or qualification by a majority of the court. It was also part of a wider reaction against the social drift towards liberalism and away from the Catholic state. It was delivered just five months before the abortion referendum and at a time when the PLAC campaign was in full swing. The unravelling of the project of economic modernization in mass unemployment and the resumption of emigration had produced a desire to reset the boundaries of social change. If Ireland could not be convincingly defined as a model of economic globalization, it would have to fall back on its previous self-definition as a model of Catholic morality.

In 1982, my then girlfriend Clare, with whom I was living in sin contrary to the laws of the Catholic Church, signed a contract of employment as a secondary school teacher. Like the vast majority of publicly funded secondary schools, hers was controlled by a religious order, in this case the Sisters of Charity, the order that ran Temple Hill and managed much of the traffic in adopted children. The contract specified that she could not be a member of any union or professional organization that did not conform 'in its aims, constitution and activities to the accepted doctrine and moral practice of the Catholic Church'. It also made clear that the nuns 'may at any time summarily' dismiss her 'on the grounds of misconduct'.

Such provisions probably seemed more theoretical than real when they were drawn up. But shortly after she signed up to them, the church decided to demonstrate its power to fire teachers and to test the state's willingness to uphold its rights to do so. In August 1982, Eileen Flynn was dismissed from her job as an English and history teacher at the Holy Faith Convent in JFK's ancestral home town, New Ross, Co. Wexford. She was unmarried with a baby son and was living with the baby's father, a separated man, Richie Roche. It was accepted by the nuns that she was a 'gifted teacher'. The letter of summary dismissal referred to complaints from parents about her lifestyle and her open rejection of the 'norms of behaviour' and the ideals the school existed to promote.

In March 1985, Declan Costello, another of the supposed Fine Gael liberals of the 1960s, now turned High Court judge, ruled on Flynn's claim that her dismissal was unlawful. He found that the nuns were fully 'entitled to conclude that the appellant's conduct was capable of damaging their efforts to foster in their pupils norms of behaviour and religious tenets which the school had been established to promote' and therefore to sack her. What had been implicit was now explicit: teachers, even though they were paid by the state, could be sacked if their 'lifestyle' was not in keeping with orthodox Catholic 'norms of behaviour'. This was not a whim of the nuns – it was now the law of the land.

In 1983, Clare and I got married. But we were married by the civil registrar in a solicitor's office in Dublin, and not in a church.

We were therefore, in the religious sense, not married at all. We were still living in sin and when we had children they were the product of that sin. They were also unbaptized. There was no doubt whatsoever that, in the eyes of the church and the state, the Sisters of Charity who employed Clare were perfectly entitled to summarily dismiss her. By transgressing the norms of behaviour laid down by the church, she was forfeiting her rights as a citizen and as a worker.

Because we were not getting married in church and could therefore not have the banns read, we had to put an ad in a national newspaper declaring our intention to wed. We put it in Irish on the assumption (correct as it turned out) that no one would read it in the language of the Gael. There was still the problem that Clare's head nun had to send her marriage certificate to the Department of Education so she could be issued with a new tax certificate. The school secretary put it in the post before the head nun could see it. Nothing was said verbally. Everything was communicated – and understood – through silent looks.

So Clare was not sacked, just as most gay men were not prosecuted or imprisoned. The point of this moment of repression was not to round up deviants or make Ireland an international pariah. It was neatly expressed by the Circuit Court judge who had originally dismissed Eileen Flynn's appeal against her sacking, Noel Ryan, who had recently stepped down as chairman of the Censorship of Publications Board. Ryan, in his ruling, expressed the view that the nuns had in fact been 'far too lenient' in not sacking Flynn before they did.[6] He explained that 'Times are changing and we must change with them, but they have not changed that much…' Ryan said of Flynn's behaviour that 'In other places women are being condemned to death for this sort of offence. They are not Christians in the Far East. I do not agree with this of course.'[7] Ryan told Flynn while she was giving her evidence that 'there has to be a limit somewhere… the question was where the boundaries should be drawn'.[8] To set a limit to how much times could change, it was important that deviant people felt grateful that they were not stoned to death.

The limit was not that an unmarried woman must not get

pregnant. That was undesirable and unfortunate, but there was a way of dealing with it. In her evidence in court, the principal of the school, Sister Pauline Leonard, said that when Flynn admitted she was pregnant, 'she had told Ms Flynn then that she had a brother in London who was a parish priest, and asked if she would like him to help her'.[9] This was what Flynn was supposed to do – leave the country and have the problem dealt with out of sight by a priest in England. Asked if Flynn had left to have her baby and then returned would she have been given her job back, Sister Pauline said: 'There is no reason why not, if she had given up her relationship with a married man.'

What mattered was the vindication of 'norms' and the reinforcement of the church's ultimate power to set them. That this was what the democratic majority wanted, however, was made completely clear in 1986. Garret FitzGerald, now back in office as Taoiseach, had long argued that the Constitution's ban on divorce – its most flagrant encoding of a specifically Catholic doctrine – was an obstacle to reconciliation with Ulster Protestants. He proposed a change to the Constitution to allow for the introduction of a very restrictive regime for the dissolution of marriage five years after it had broken up. The proposal was denounced by the Catholic hierarchy and by priests from the pulpit. Early polls showing a majority in favour of change were quickly reversed. Divorce was comprehensively rejected in the referendum, by a two-thirds majority similar to the one that had favoured the abortion ban three years earlier.

The scale of the defeat was, to me, shocking. The church was now at the peak of its moral power. The pope's anxiety in 1979 about the future of Ireland now seemed completely misplaced. It was not that there would be no gay men or lesbians, that teachers would not live in sin, or that marriages would not break down or that Irish women would not continue to travel to England for abortions. Nobody really thought that court rulings and referendums restating in such emphatic terms 'the Christian nature of our State' would actually change what the citizens of that holy state would do. But they would do it as freaks – and if they did not at least tacitly accept their abnormality, they could be placed outside the law.

In our own lives, myself and Clare respected these boundaries. She did not show wedding photographs to friends and colleagues at school. I did not write about being married in a civil ceremony or not having our sons baptized. The nuns, for their part did not ask about such things – just as they did not ask how all of their female teachers apparently controlled their fertility without using contraceptives. The courts had ruled, in effect, that all of those teachers could be summarily sacked for having a 'lifestyle… repugnant to the values which the nuns held'.[10] But applying this law would be catastrophic. It was there as a marker and a warning. We knew the rules – don't ask for trouble and we won't go looking for it.

This was the price of staying in Ireland. Many – especially young women and LGBTQ people – found they couldn't keep paying and just left. Exile, as always, had its double effect. It freed Ireland of the awkward ones and let them find freedom, albeit at the expense of personal and civic belonging. This, too, was power: the system could make its problems go away. And in those years, it seemed as if that power had reasserted itself triumphantly, that it had emerged from all the madness of the Kerry Babies and the moving statues with its authority not just intact but renewed.

It was not, though, quite like that. Nothing was really as solid as it seemed. Behind the great conservative victory of the divorce referendum, there were pale shadows and blotchy half-secrets.

Officially, Fianna Fáil had taken no position on the divorce referendum. On 20 May 1986, however, Charles Haughey had issued a statement that was, he emphasized, not a party political one, but a 'purely personal view': 'I approach this issue from the point of view of the family. I have an unshakeable belief in the importance of having the family as the basic unit of society. My experience tells me that this is the best way in which to organize a society.' He rejected the 'attraction of superficial freedom': 'the family is an anchor for the individual, a haven of security and support.'[11]

Over the course of the year in which he issued this statement, 1986, Haughey's bill-paying service for his casual expenditure was dishing out £177,000, or £3,400 a week. Some of this money was coming from the taxpayer-funded party Leader's Allowance. Some of it came from a £100,000 donation to Fianna Fáil (not intended for Haughey personally) from Irish Permanent Building Society.[12] A significant part of it was spent at a restaurant in Dublin, Le Coq Hardi, where Haughey entertained his mistress Terry Keane twice a week in the private dining room. The bill for their dinners was around £1,000 a week.[13] This was about five times the average weekly earnings of an industrial worker.

Frank Dunlop, who had been Haughey's press secretary, recalled that 'Everybody seemed to know what was going on and nobody wanted to admit to not being up to date with the latest piece of gossip about it.' The British satirical magazine *Private Eye* had begun to write regularly about Haughey and Keane's 'horizontal jogging'. One senior Fianna Fáil figure, Ray Burke, had a brother-in-law who worked for *Private Eye*. Burke was terrified that the Boss would think he was behind the articles. In fact, Haughey didn't care. At one point he summoned Dunlop into his presence, adding, 'And you can bring *Private Eye* with you'. Dunlop thought Haughey was going to instruct him to try to stop the stories. In fact he read the latest one as they walked along. 'He doubled up with laughter and said, "Jaysus, Frank, she'll go bananas when she reads this", and pointed out a reference to "the ageing Terry Keane".'[14]

Haughey could afford to laugh. When he made his statement on the sacredness of the family and emphasized its 'personal' nature, he was daring journalists and politicians to break their silence. If his personal 'experience' of the family was the basis, as he insisted, for his opposition to the removal of the ban on divorce, that experience was now in the public domain. But Haughey knew that no one would dare to expose his hypocrisy and the corruption and venality that surrounded it. He felt sure that there were two Irelands and that the one that wished to declare its exceptional holiness by holding on to a 1930s ban on divorce was not the one that lusted after the latest piece of gossip about what he was getting up to with Terry. Ireland, he knew, was still very good at compartmentalization.

Even while the Catholic Church was winning such huge public support for its insistence that marriages could never be dissolved, it was dissolving marriages. It had its own system for granting annulments, one that even Charles Haughey had admitted in 1982, constituted 'a certain anomaly'.[15] The couple seeking an annulment had to convince the diocesan Marriage Tribunal 'with moral certainty that a defect at the time of the ceremony prevented real marriage taking place'.[16] This was another exercise in fiction – the church, and only the church, could make a marriage go away by declaring that it had never been 'real' in the first place.

In Dublin, the priest you had to convince of this unreality was called Ivan Payne. He grew up close to Crumlin and, as we have seen, in 1968 he was appointed as chaplain to the Children's Hospital in succession to Father Paul McGennis, the priest who had been caught photographing the genitalia of little girls and was protected by John Charles McQuaid. From 1974 until 1995 Payne was on the church's Dublin Regional Marriage Tribunal and was promoted to the title of Vice-Officialis.

He had begun to abuse boys when he was chaplain at the Crumlin Children's Hospital, where he had sixteen known victims. There were concerns and suspicions about others. At least another fifteen children were abused by Payne after he left the hospital and joined the Marriage Tribunal.[17]

The church authorities knew that Payne was an active paedophile from 1981 onwards, when Andrew Madden made a formal complaint. Payne had begun to abuse him five years earlier when Andrew was twelve, in Payne's big red-brick house opposite the Botanic Gardens on the north side of the city. Payne described the abuse in 1993 as 'going as far as was necessary to get satisfied without unnecessary violation'. Andrew eventually told the guidance counsellor at his school, Mr Duggan, about what was happening. Duggan went to the chancellor of the diocese, Father Alec Stenson. Stenson was an old friend and classmate of Payne. He was also a fellow member of the Marriage Tribunal. Stenson in turn spoke to the head of the tribunal, Monsignor Gerard Sheehy. He advised him to inform the archbishop, who in turn instructed one of his bishops, Donal O'Mahony, to deal with it.

After some weeks, Andrew asked Duggan what was happening with his complaint. Duggan told him that he himself had had to contact O'Mahony, who had made no effort to come back to him. But 'They've spoken to Father Payne and he has accepted that what you have said is true… They say they're going to deal with him from here on.'[18] The bishop made no effort to contact Andrew or his family. Nor, of course, did he or anyone else go to the police to report Payne's crimes. Payne was merely moved from the parish where he had assaulted Andrew to a new one.

The Marriage Tribunal, of which he remained a member, was the church's testing ground for the sacred sacrament of wedlock. During all the period leading up to and beyond the divorce referendum, its members included a man who had admitted the sexual abuse of a child and two other priests who knew about that abuse. These men were the ones who questioned distressed couples in intimate details about their sex lives and who held in their own hands the power to make judgements about whether their marriages had been real or unreal.

In 1984, Sheehy, the head of the tribunal, asked Archbishop Dermot Ryan to promote Payne to Vice-Officialis, in effect his deputy. Ryan refused. But in June 1985, Ryan's successor Kevin McNamara agreed to the promotion.

I interviewed McNamara in May 1986, a few weeks before the divorce referendum, for *Magill* magazine, which I was then editing. He was stern and cerebral and utterly self-contained. He spoke a language of contagion and biological resistance. Divorce was 'a plague' and Ireland's Catholicism had not 'immunized' it from the 'modern culture' that was 'streaming incessantly into our society and our homes through television, radio, newspapers, magazines, etcetera'. He compared divorce to the greatest catastrophe then unfolding in the world: 'The Chernobyl disaster of recent weeks can be a useful reminder of how negative radiation can filter across and permeate society. Divorce legislation has had a somewhat similar effect in the way it has permeated western societies and undermined the stability of married life.'[19]

At the time, it seemed to me merely that I might have been speaking to John Charles McQuaid. The mindset was entirely unaltered: Ireland as a healthy body under constant assault from the diseases of the outside world, modern media as vectors of sickness and corruption. His Chernobyl comparison seemed like an even more extreme version of the same basic metaphor, the fallout from a foreign calamity drifting inexorably into Irish airspace. Only much later did it seem to me that his metaphor contained much more truth than he knew. Negative radiation was filtering out from his own archbishop's palace. The fallout was not yet detected but it was coming.

At the same time as Eileen Flynn was being sacked by the nuns in New Ross in 1982, the Ferns diocese in which the school was located had several active child rapists on its books, none of whom was sacked. In the diocesan school, St Peter's, Seán Fortune, who was then a seminarian, had violently raped or assaulted several boys. Stephen, a boy who was raped by Fortune in the late 1970s, when he thirteen, told the school principal what had happened. 'The school Principal reacted angrily to what Stephen said and refused to believe him, telling him that Seán Fortune was going to be a good priest and that if he persisted in saying those things about him, he would be thrown out of the college.'[20]

In and around the time of the Eileen Flynn case, when the nuns and the courts used the word 'repugnant' to describe her life in a consensual adult relationship, at least two boys in the county took their own lives as a result of violent abuse by Fortune. The parents of one of the boys recalled that they had heard that some of the boys in the village where Fortune was the curate were alleging that he was abusing them. 'However, they said that they thought that it was a terrible thing for the boys to be saying about a priest and did not understand it.'[21]

Yet almost immediately after Fortune's arrival in the parish, some of the parishioners were sufficiently alarmed by his behaviour towards children that they wrote both to the bishop and to the pope's representative in Ireland, the papal nuncio. They made 'an indirect reference to incidents of a sexual nature'. The papal nuncio acknowledged the letter and told the parishioners that 'the Holy See [i.e. the Vatican] had been apprised of their concerns'.[22] That was the last they heard from him.

In 1989, after Eileen Flynn's sacking for 'repugnant' behaviour had been thoroughly upheld by the Irish courts, and long after the diocese in which she had been so ruthlessly punished had overwhelming evidence of Fortune's depravity, the church quietly moved him to another parish in the county. One of his roles there was as chairman of the board of the local primary school. He continued to give classes in it until he was finally arrested by Gardaí in March 1995.[23]

All of this depended on the maintenance of the cognitive dissonance that was so deeply engrained in Irish society. The great reaction of the 1980s rested on the certainty that Irish realities were so perfectly compartmentalized that they would never bleed into each other. The one that contained Eileen Flynn could never overlap with the one in which Seán Fortune existed. The one whose politics was based on Haughey's personal reverence for the family could not contain Terry Keane. The one in which marriage was a sacrament could not be supervised and pried into by paedophiles and their enablers. But in 1987, the Catholic Bishop of Galway said, 'God does not work in little compartments.'[24] His name was Eamonn Casey and he was right.

30

1985–1992: Conduct Unbecoming

I was in the passenger seat of a low-slung Lancia sports car. We were pulling out onto the main Dublin road from Maynooth seminary, the headquarters of the Irish bishops who have been meeting there. The driver was a stocky, moon-faced, bald man in black clerical garb with a gold pectoral cross hanging from his neck. He had offered me a lift back to Dublin. I was glad to accept. He was good company – friendly, intelligent, loquacious in a lilting Kerry accent. I admired him because he had very publicly refused to meet Ronald Reagan when the American president visited Ireland the previous year, 1984. He had been present when the US-backed junta in El Salvador murdered the Archbishop of San Salvador, Oscar Romero, in 1980 and he fearlessly denounced the atrocities that continued in Latin America.

At the exit from Maynooth College, Eamonn Casey just hurled the car out onto the road without stopping or, as far as I could tell, even looking. As soon as we were in traffic, he swerved out and overtook two, three, four cars before veering back into his lane. He stayed behind a line of trucks for a few minutes, then pulled out again and pressed down on the accelerator. I looked at the speedometer: 120 and rising.

Over the brow of the hill a car was coming towards us. Casey accelerated again. The Lancia was surging like a rocket. The oncoming car was nearly on us and there was still one truck blocking our return to the inside lane. The approaching driver blared his horn. Casey darted left in front of the truck and sped on.

My skin was tingling with the fright. But all the time, the Bishop of Galway was chatting away in his mellifluous manner. I had no idea what he was saying because all I could hear was the blood pounding in my ears. But his cadence had never altered. He was completely unconcerned, so much so that he did the same thing again a few minutes later. When he dropped me off in the city and I climbed out of the Lancia, my knees were weak.

When I was composed enough to think about what had happened, I had only one thought: this man likes to take risks. Part of it was pure arrogance, a sense of entitlement so ingrained that he was no longer conscious of it. He was too important to follow the rules. But part of it seemed to be a real pleasure in dicing with danger. I supposed, if I had not been too terrified to ask him what he was doing, he would have said that he trusted the Lord to look after him and given me some bluster about Providence. But it was clearly more visceral than that. This was how he got his kicks – why, after all, did he buy an Italian sportscar?

Much later, his girlfriend, Annie Murphy, would recall him driving her through villages in Co. Kerry at 65 mph and joking about what would happen if he killed someone: 'And won't I do them the honour of giving them the last rites of holy Mother Church? Imagine being sent to heaven courtesy of a bishop.'[1]

Around the time of my hair-raising ride in his car, Casey was involved in a personal battle against female sterilizations and vasectomies. In August 1985, he had intervened to condemn the publicly owned Regional Hospital in Galway for performing sterilizations 'if they were for contraceptive purposes'.[2] He also wrote to all the general practitioners in the diocese reminding them of the church's teaching on the subject. In an address to nurses, he warned against 'any form of sterilisation whose direct and immediate effect is to render the sexual faculty incapable of procreation' and urging them to refuse to participate in any operation that 'sets out to make it impossible for the act of sex to be open to the gift of life'.[3] The following month Calvary Hospital in Galway was being sold by the nuns who had run it to a consortium of doctors in the city who were planning to take advantage of the decline of the public health service by establishing it as a private business. The contract was complete but, at the last minute, Casey personally intervened. There would have to be a covenant added to the conditions of the sale, he insisted, ensuring 'that no sterilisations be carried out' in the hospital, even by doctors who were already performing such operations. The consortium agreed to his demand. The women and men of Galway would, if Casey had anything to do with it, remain fertile.[4] It could be said, at least, that Casey had practised what he preached. At that time, his son Peter was ten years old.

There was a certain irony in the fact that one of the accusations made against the bishops by liberal critics was that they pronounced on sex without having experienced it. In April 1971, Noël Browne, then the Labour Party's spokesman on health, made a speech in which he suggested that 'The judgment of the Catholic clergy on matters of sex and heterosexual relationships could not be trusted… It was long overdue that they acknowledge the understandable ignorance of men living celibate lives; that they were not competent to advise the rest of them in the complex matters of marriage relations… It is also true to say that consciously, or otherwise, many of them have chosen their celibate lives because they find the whole subject of sex and heterosexual relationships threatening and embarrassing.'[5]

The Labour parliamentary party issued a long statement condemning Browne: 'Parts of the speech were insulting and belittling to the Roman Catholic clergy. To suggest that many of those who chose the religious life do so out of fear of sexual relations is an insult to men and women who regard their vocations as a service to God and humanity…'[6] No one in the parliamentary party – even the generally outspoken Conor Cruise O'Brien – supported Browne. What he had said was obviously true, but it was also unsayable. Priests, still less bishops, were not to be spoken about in that way. And if the subject of clerical celibacy was not up for discussion, that of non-celibate clergy was even less so.

It was, though, increasingly difficult to maintain this kind of absolute control on the limits of discussion. Just as the royal family in Britain had to modernize its image by letting the TV cameras into Buckingham Palace, its equivalent in Ireland – the Catholic hierarchy – needed a bishop who could go on *The Late Late Show* and sing a song, who could perform in the media circus on its terms. Eamonn Casey was that man. He represented a complementary model of authority, one that won the battle for attention by sheer force of personality. His exuberance, his energy, his attractiveness, his impulsiveness – the very qualities that led to his downfall – were the qualities the church so badly needed. They needed a bishop who could win exposure. They could not imagine what, eventually, that exposure would be like.

Gay Byrne adored Casey because he might have invented him. What Byrne called 'his ebullience, his extrovert nature, his generosity, his expansiveness'[7] embodied the same conservative modernity that he himself had perfected. When Casey was promoted from the bishopric of Kerry to the larger diocese of Galway in 1976, the local newspaper hailed the fact that he 'has proved himself on *The Late Late Show* to be quite a wit and adroit at handling press questions'.[8]

On the surface, this was all working very well. At the end of the 1980s, the church's position was extremely strong. In the decade before 1985, Sunday Mass attendance had fallen only very slightly, from 91 per cent of Catholics to 87 per cent. If anything, the intensity of devotion seemed to have increased. In 1974, 23 per cent of Catholics in Ireland attended Mass more than once a week. In 1984, 30 per cent did so. In 1974, 28 per cent received Holy Communion every week; in 1984 that was up to 38 per cent.[9]

This surge of devotion in the early 1980s, from the pope's visit in 1979 through to the divorce referendum of 1986, began to ebb slowly in the second half of the 1980s. But Ireland was still an anomaly in Catholic Europe. It was not just that the Irish were still Catholic. It was that Irish Catholics were more Catholic than their co-religionists in continental Europe. They held much more strongly to traditional orthodoxies. The 1990 European Values Survey showed that 80 per cent of Irish Catholics believed in life after death, compared to fewer than 50 per cent in West Germany, France or Spain. Fifty-four per cent believed in the Devil – just 21 per cent of German and 24 per cent of French Catholics did so. The faith of 72 per cent of Irish Catholics in the resurrection of the dead was shared by just 39 per cent in France, 42 per cent in Germany and 35 per cent in Spain.[10]

Ninety-seven per cent of the population of the Republic now identified themselves as Catholic. This homogeneity was reflected in continuing very high levels of church attendance. More than half of western Europeans almost never attended church in 1990. This was true of fewer than one in ten Irish people. Eighty-two per cent of Irish people said they 'drew comfort and strength from prayer'. Opposition to divorce and abortion remained far higher than in Europe as a whole. On a scale of one to ten, the average European score for agreeing that divorce could be sometimes justified was 8.3. For abortion it was seven. The equivalent figures in Ireland were 4.1 and 2.4. Ireland, in other words, was less than half as liberal as Europe was on these questions.[11] There was simply 'no evidence of a general process of secularisation operating throughout the 1980s'.[12]

The bishops had suffered a minor setback when, against their strongly expressed wishes, the laws on contraception were liberalized in 1985 to allow for their sale to anyone over eighteen through pharmacies, family planning clinics and health boards. It would no longer be necessary to get a doctor's prescription to buy condoms. The pretence that only married couples were allowed to buy them was dropped. The measure was more a recognition of reality than a profound change of policy: since the pope's visit in 1979, Ireland had officially imported 100 million condoms, 64,000 intra-uterine devices, 263,700 diaphragms, 960,000 contraceptive pessaries and 1.2 million spermicides.[13] Nobody really believed that all of these were being used in accordance with Haughey's highly restrictive law of 1979. Everybody knew that it was 'ignored, broken and flouted', and that the true conservative position was that 'Once our legislation doesn't show that unmarrieds or teenagers are using contraceptives, then it isn't happening.'[14]

This position was legally untenable: the state could not take the risk of large-scale prosecutions of those who were flouting the law. The bishops surely understood this. But what actually happened was not the point. As always, what mattered was the maintenance of the twin-track Irish mind. Reality could continue on its own sweet way, so long as it was not reflected in what the state said about itself. The façade was much more important than the building. What should be must always outweigh what was. This was the Irish way. And in its desire to maintain it, the church found in 1985 that it had an absolutely reliable partner: Charles Haughey. Haughey controlled Fianna Fáil, and Fianna Fáil was still the natural party of government, the only one that had the keys to the machinery of state.

In the testing of the boundaries in 1985, at the time when I was in Casey's Lancia and he was asserting his absolute right to interfere with the most intimate lives of the women and men of Galway, Haughey was not found wanting. A year earlier, he had pretty much admitted that the restrictions on contraceptives that he had introduced in 1979 were a nonsense. Asked by John Waters for *Hot Press* magazine 'isn't it true that the actual behaviour and practice of young people has long since made the question irrelevant?', he paused and said, 'Ah yeah, I think that's probably true enough'.[15]

Yet, when it came to actually reforming those laws, he held the old line: to recognize that young people were having sex outside marriage would be to encourage a promiscuity that was not only morally wrong but unIrish. The party's spokesman on agriculture, Michael Noonan, insisted that liberalizing the law was 'opening the sluice gates of widespread promiscuity' and 'threatening traditional Irish values'.[16] He expressed the party's sense of itself as the bulwark of real Irishness: 'As ever, we in Fianna Fáil represent the values and traditions that make us Irish, and we will continue to do so.' In the parliamentary debate on the legislation, not one woman from Fianna Fáil spoke a single word.[17] That same month, a Fianna Fáil women's conference in Athlone was overwhelmed by male members of the party who showed up uninvited. 'What the hell are you here for?' one was asked. 'A bit of skirt', he replied.[18] He and his colleagues were obviously hoping for some of the promiscuity they had warned the nation about.

Fianna Fáil, at Haughey's instigation, went so far as to expel one of its most prominent members, Desmond O'Malley, because he abstained on the vote on the Contraception Bill. This was deemed to be 'conduct unbecoming a party member'.[19] At the party's national executive, seventy-three delegates voted to expel him; just nine voted against. Emerging from the meeting, O'Malley kissed his wife in front of the cameras and told reporters: 'I wonder if this is conduct unbecoming a member of Fianna Fáil.'[20] The following morning, the tribunal of inquiry into the Kerry Babies case resumed its hearings in Dublin. A Garda, Liam Moloney, gave evidence about the 'common gossip in Abbeydorney that Joanne Hayes was pregnant again as far back as November/December 1983' and that he had called to her house to tell her 'to break up with Jeremiah Locke'. He added that 'gossip in the shops was fairly widespread'.[21]

After O'Malley's expulsion, Haughey's sidekick and press secretary P. J. Mara told political correspondents: 'There will be no more nibbling at my leader's bum.' He added the Italian fascist slogan: 'Uno duce, una voce.' In case they missed the point, Mara put his finger across his upper lip, in imitation of a moustache, and goose-stepped up and down the political correspondents' room. Only one of them, Geraldine Kennedy of the *Irish Times*, reported this, even though Mara had not said that his comments were off-the-record. When it emerged, Haughey summoned Mara, who explained that it had been a joke: 'for fuck sake, Mara, be careful in future, you must resist your base instincts. Put a button on your lip!'[22]

Haughey's own base instincts never wavered. Leering at young women was one of them. He returned to power in 1987 and held on until 1992. In 1989, he attended an EU summit in Athens. He dispatched Mara to ogle on his behalf Dimitra Liani, the new young girlfriend of the Greek prime minister Andreas Papandreou: 'what's she like? — tell me exactly how she looks.' When Mara reported back, he 'listened to every word with interest, took a deep breath, and softly declared: "Papandreou, my hero!"'[23]

Yet Haughey had decided that Fianna Fáil and the church would remain joined at the hip. There was a deep logic in this. Fianna Fáil had inherited from the church the ability to divide the country into us and them, the damned and the saved, the true Irishman and the faithless traitor, a turn of mind greatly assisted by the identification throughout history of Catholicism and Irish nationality. Eamon de Valera had dominated Irish politics by drawing its great dividing line around himself. In the modernizing era, the party had played down this polarization, with Lemass and Lynch functioning largely as soothing and unifying figures. But as the 1958 project ran out of steam, Haughey revived the older tribal style.

In this resurgent national-populism, 'Charlie' was the embodiment of the party and the party defined the people. Because it would never, on principle, enter a coalition government, Fianna Fáil was able to distinguish itself from all other parties put together. The advantages, in a multi-choice electoral system that practically invited voters to express their preferences for individuals across party lines, were electoral as well as ideological. Fianna Fáil voters had always been characterized by a very high degree of exclusivity and solidarity. The party managed to get its supporters to think of themselves as 'us' but also as 'not them'. Just as the church controlled the idea of what was legitimate and illegitimate in the moral sphere, Fianna Fáil did it in the political sphere.

Haughey made this analogy explicit again. His attempt to fuse religion and politics was made clear in his 1981 speech to the party's fiftieth annual conference, in which he defined the reason 'we adhere to Fianna Fáil' as the fact that 'it represents not this pressure group or that sectional interest this class or that Creed but because in the broad sweep of its membership and their faith and devotion to their country there resides what one can call the "Spirit of the Nation"'.[24] In this credo, social class, conflicting economic interests and the real divisions of society gave way to the religious virtues of faith, devotion and spirit. Politics ceased to be politics and became a secular version of religion. And just as there was one true church, there could only be one true party – 'the only party with a truly national vision'.[25] Just as the Holy Spirit spoke with one voice through the pope, so must the Spirit of the Nation speak through the Boss: una voce, uno duce.

Haughey was, in his own imagery, the embodiment of Ireland, the fulfilment of both time and space. He evoked 'a long cycle of history' that was coming to its desired end under his leadership – the Irish past as a long march towards Abbeville. What was true of time was true of space – a sundered Ireland was brought together in his own person. He cultivated the image of a man 'from' each of Ireland's four provinces, born in Connacht of Ulster parentage, living in Leinster and inhabiting his very own island in Munster. 'Look at the dilemma I'm in', he tells his family over breakfast discussing the All-Ireland football semi-finals in the television film *Charles Haughey's Ireland*. 'Of the four teams in it, three of them are Dublin, Kerry, Mayo. I was born in Mayo, I live in Dublin, then I have my holidays in Kerry.' Shortly afterwards we see him in Swatragh, Co. Derry, in the fourth province of Ulster: 'As a child, I used to spend my holidays here.' He thus evoked the image of the dismembered country made whole, of the divisions between country and city, West and East, North and South healed in the mystical body of Charlie.

This kind of stuff still worked. The appeal of nationality remained as strong as that of Catholicism. Even after the near-collapse of the modernizing project in the 1980s, amid the resumption of mass emigration and with the Troubles still grinding grimly onwards, Irish people remained weirdly delighted with their membership of this turbulent nation. In 1990, an average of 38 per cent of Europeans said they were 'very proud' of their country. More than twice that proportion – an astonishing 78 per cent – of Irish people were very proud to be Irish. Ninety-nine per cent were either very proud or 'quite proud'.[26] A grand total of zero per cent were 'not at all proud'.

Equally, Ireland remained a society in which authority was respected. Irish people were vastly more likely than western Europeans in general to assert that 'greater respect for authority is a good thing' (83 per cent); somewhat more likely to want 'absolutely clear guidelines about what is good and evil' (43 per cent); and significantly less likely to agree that 'protection of free speech is a priority' (42 per cent). This was the great paradox of the long 1980s, which ran, in effect, from 1979 to 1992. Things were falling apart, but they were also holding together.

In 1984, Haughey told *Hot Press* magazine that he was not at all worried about the prospect of a youth revolt: 'I wouldn't be all that worried about an explosion. Y'see, if you go back [to 1968], all the campuses in America were exploding and you had the French situation – well that's all suddenly changed. There's a big reversal, I think now, among young people. They've become much more cautious – not conservative. But much more committed to trying to find their own way in life, rather than trying to change society.'[27] He was not far wrong. Changing society was much harder than changing location. Finding your own way in life was a euphemism for finding your way to the airport.

The alliance of the church and Fianna Fáil was therefore still very much the dominant power. The focus of this dominance was still on the control of women's reproductive and sexual behaviour – or, rather, on the ways in which that behaviour could be acknowledged as reality. In 1988, the Supreme Court, acting on the basis of the 1983 abortion amendment to the Constitution, unanimously upheld an injunction granted to SPUC banning a pregnancy advisory service from giving information on abortion services in other countries to Irish women. It 'perpetually restrained' everyone in Ireland from helping women to make arrangements to travel for such purposes or to inform them 'of the identity and location of, and the method of communication with, a specified clinic or clinics'.[28]

Here, again, was the great unknowing. It was now a crime to tell a woman the name of an abortion service in London or Birmingham. Phone numbers that could be read in the English phonebook were contraband in Ireland. British-based magazines, like *Cosmopolitan*, were obliged to print special editions with advertisements for women's health clinics blacked out. In February 1990, *Company*, a British magazine for young women, pulled eight pages from the copies of an issue sent to Ireland. They merely laid out an explanation of what an abortion was, but, because there was a page dealing with the abortion pill, lawyers advised that the publishers risked prosecution.[29] The Censorship of Publications

Board continued to warn publishers not to carry any information that might help a woman who wanted an abortion.[30] Student union handbooks were forced to remove pregnancy advice that included details on terminations.

The point in all of this was not to change anything in the real world. It was to sustain the system of feigned ignorance. Fianna Fáil and the church had tied themselves firmly together in the maintenance of that system. Together, they made it strong. But that very togetherness created a shared vulnerability. They were mutually dependent on the confidence, so deeply engrained in both Eamonn Casey and Charles Haughey, that the aura of authority, maintained now by personal charisma and defiant insouciance, could always prevent covert things from becoming overt. It did not seem conceivable that this authority could unravel so suddenly.

31

1990–1992: Mature Recollection

In the first week of December 1991, unease about Charles Haughey and large sums of money was everywhere. It was emerging that he had effectively ordered UCD to buy the campus of a teacher training college, Carysfort, which had been owned by the Sisters of Mercy. They had sold it to a big supporter of Haughey's, Robert 'Pino' Harris. He in turn sold it on to UCD, making in a few months a profit of £1.5 million. At the same time, a public inquiry was hearing accounts of strange goings-on in the relationship between Haughey's government and one of Ireland's wealthiest men, the beef baron Larry Goodman. At the end of that week, on the south side of Dublin city, a fourteen-year-old girl was raped by a forty-two-year-old man in a car parked in an unlit alleyway behind a swimming pool. She became pregnant.

None of this was yet the problem. The immediate predicament began with Brian Lenihan's liver. Lenihan was Tánaiste (deputy prime minister) and minister for foreign affairs. One of Haughey's closest contemporaries in the generation of Fianna Fáil politicians that had surfed the wave of change in the 1960s, Lenihan was smart and cultured. He had liberalized the censorship laws when Haughey had refused to do so. Along with Haughey and Donogh O'Malley, Lenihan was part of the triumvirate of brash, hard-living, fast-moving politicians who were going to remake Ireland. But he was not, like them, abrasive. He played the likeable buffoon – the warm-up man, the blusterer, the man who would go on TV to defend the party when it was in such trouble that no one else would. As a result, he was indeed universally liked. His amiability was especially useful to Haughey. It could make everything sinister seem harmless.

In 1989, Lenihan's liver gave out. He needed a transplant, and it was decided that he should go to the Mayo Clinic in Minnesota. The Irish health service was not good enough for members of its own government. The board of the state-owned Voluntary Health Insurance company quietly decided that it would pay the full cost. Haughey knew this. He nonetheless asked a Fianna Fáil fundraiser, Paul Kavanagh, discreetly to request a number of sympathetic businessmen to stump up between them somewhere between £150,000 and £200,000 for Lenihan's new American liver. Eight individuals or companies answered the call – the largest single contribution being £25,000 from Goodman.

The people who raised and contributed what may have been as much as £265,000 for Lenihan's liver acted in good faith, believing that they were saving the life of a popular national figure. But the whole thing was essentially a scam perpetrated by Haughey. He knew that the full cost of Lenihan's direct treatment would be borne – as indeed it was – by the VHI. Other expenses amounted to around £70,000. So he helped himself to most of the money ostensibly raised for the operation: probably about £200,000.[1] He spent it on handmade shirts from Charvet in Paris, dinners with Terry Keane at Le Coq Hardi and the general upkeep of his extravagance. The cheques were signed, blank, by his acolyte Bertie Ahern.

Not that Haughey was not thinking of the Lenihan family. On the morning of her departure for the Mayo Clinic, he sent Lenihan's wife Ann a gift of £200 – 0.1 per cent of the money he had stolen from the fund he established for her husband's treatment. There was something magnificent in this depravity. Haughey had wept openly when told of Lenihan's plight.[2] But he quickly saw the opportunity. He would later claim that he knew nothing about the handling of his own finances, but this was hands-on, highly personal fraud. When one donor asked who to make a £20,000 cheque for Lenihan out to, Haughey replied simply: 'To myself.' Later, when the whole affair unravelled, he insisted that his efforts 'for the good and salvation of my friend Brian Lenihan' was 'the most compassionate thing I had ever done in my life'.[3]

The operatic villainy of the Lenihan swindle should itself have been a danger sign. It crossed a line into outright and intimate theft. Even while flaunting his wealth, Haughey had been careful to hide its sources in elaborate fictions like the Ansbacher Cayman operation, to maintain, perhaps even in his own mind, the idea that his bagman Des Traynor handled all the details so that he could get on with the real business of embodying the Spirit of the Nation. But now this compartmentalization was breaking down. He was exploiting the drama of his friend's imminent death, personally extracting money from donors, having their cheques cashed and the bundles of notes delivered to his office. None of this was public yet, but it was sitting there, radiating betrayal and cynicism and cold-eyed rapacity. Haughey must have known that, if it was discovered, he would be ruined, not just politically, but morally. That he did it anyway suggests a faith in the inviolability of the boundaries around what could be known in Ireland that had escalated itself to a sense of absolute invulnerability.

In April 1990, Lenihan returned from the Mayo Clinic, a new man. There was general relief at his resurrection. He was accorded the Irish equivalent of a Roman triumph: Gay Byrne devoted the entire *Late Late Show* to a back-slapping celebration of Brian Lenihan and everything he stood for in Irish life. I remember watching and being amazed at how unguarded it was, how, in this euphoria, it seemed okay to tell stories about the abuse of power when Lenihan was minister for justice as if they were not just funny, but essentially Irish, a charming part of who we were.

It made me wonder how the show would have looked to Seán Doherty. Doherty had been one of the key figures in the weird events of 1982, when Haughey's government had seemed on the brink of mere anarchy (see Chapter 25). He had been forced to resign from the party, and his shenanigans as minister for justice had made him the embodiment of the dark side of Fianna Fáil. But now, with Lenihan on *The Late Late Show*, the same kind of behaviour was being treated, not just as roguish and amusing, but as somehow quintessentially Irish. The line between national disgrace and national treasure seemed strangely thin.

It made me wonder when roguery stopped being roguery and became sleaze. When is a stroke a stroke and when is it an abuse of power? When is a politician 'colourful' and when is he a national scandal? I thought of Seán Doherty, looking at the show, and imagined him shaking his head ruefully: 'Why me?' Why was he pilloried for interfering with the Garda in the course of their duties, yet now the country was laughing at the story the Dubliners singer Ronnie Drew told about Brian Lenihan, Charles Haughey and a district justice being caught by a rookie Dublin guard after hours in Groomes Hotel? 'Would you like a large whiskey and a pint of stout', the guard in the story was asked, 'or would you like a posting on an island somewhere between here and America?'

There were other funny yarns. A former civil servant, Tony Ó Dalaigh, told a story about the minister drinking in Kilcock on Monday mornings instead of being at his desk. And the *Irish Times* columnist John Healy brought us back to Groomes Hotel in Dublin, to an evening where various favours were being organized for various people, and Brian Lenihan was making notes on little pieces of paper. Later that night, the pieces of paper were allowed to blow into the River Liffey.

But why was that funny and Seán Doherty's leaning on policemen to interfere with the course of justice scandalous? Was it because the guard who was being bullied was also offered a drink? Did that make it lovable? Was it because the stories referred to Groomes Hotel, which was no longer there and thus ripe for nostalgia? Because those smoky backrooms were our version of Kennedy's Camelot, the young princes in their first bloom of power, the sheen on their faces almost as bright as the sheen on their suits? Was Haughey Prince Hal in the tavern with Lenihan as his Falstaff, enjoying their days of carousal before emerging into the full responsibility of power? Was it because the comic punchline of the little bits of paper blowing into the Liffey softened the reality of the favours being sought with, presumably, the expectation that they be granted?

Because the context of the Lenihan stories was one of congratulation and admiration for a man who was genuinely liked and genuinely brave, these revelations became tributes. In other words, we were so ambivalent about our politicians that we took our cue from the way they were being presented. If certain incidents in their careers are presented as funny, warm, delightfully roguish, then that is what they are. If the same incidents are presented as scandalous and sulphurous, then that is what they are. Because we didn't know what to think, the message must lie in the medium. Gay Byrne, as only he could, gave permission for a culture of fixes and favours and drinking and debauchery, to be understood as colourful rather than as dark.

The crucial difference was rhetoric. Seán Doherty had become the nearest thing to a pariah in Irish politics because he came from a generation that had lost touch with and interest in the abstract, flowery, flowing, almost religious language of old Fianna Fáil. His strokes, deprived of the cloak of rhetoric, were left shivering and naked in the cold light of publicity. Brian Lenihan, on the other hand, had been rightly summed up by the historian Joe Lee as 'an amiable virtuoso of shadow language'.[4] The shadow language was shadowy because we were both amused by its verbal game-playing and, at some level, still touched by its emotions.

On the one hand, we could laugh at it, on the other it still conferred on those who use it a degree of sanctity that protects them from criticism. In his role as John the Baptist to Charles Haughey's Messiah, a role he repeated most years in his warm-up to the leader's speech at the party Árd Fheis, Lenihan would say things like 'This party represents the real Ireland. This great party of ours represents anything that is good in the Celtic attitude to life. We want to pass on the torch to a new generation. Fianna Fáil is out there in the vanguard like the Fenians of old … This man [Charles Haughey] epitomizes everything that is best in this great party of ours.'

At one level, the stuff was comic in its self-conscious bloviation, but at another its mixture of John F. Kennedy, Eamon de Valera and the Celtic Twilight was exactly right for the party faithful. And at both levels it worked: since the party was the real Ireland

and Haughey the epitome of the party, then the Taoiseach and his warmer-upper were the epitome of the epitome of the country. And this is why the stories on *The Late Late Show* were funny, warm and charming rather than shocking or sleazy. They were stories about the 'Celtic attitude to life', stories the effect of which is not 'Isn't this disgraceful?' but 'Aren't we a queer people altogether?'

Lenihan had managed to take our whimsicality, our resigned sense of ourselves as a race of chancers, and to make it into a political weapon. The ambivalence was in us and in our political culture, in our ability to be amused at our own follies, in the sense of ourselves as a nation of nod-and-winkers that made it by no means unreasonable to present Brian Lenihan as the epitome of Irishness. When you're winking, you have one eye open and one closed, and we hadn't yet decided whether we wanted to look at the country with both eyes open. Until we did, the wink would remain our most eloquent political gesture.[5]

There was already, at that time, strong speculation that Lenihan, riding on his post-operative popularity, would be the Fianna Fáil candidate for the presidential election of November 1990. The office had always been held by Fianna Fáil, and though the duties of the head of state were largely ceremonial, this fact validated the party's claim to permanent hegemony as the voice of the Irish people. Lenihan, duly nominated in September, was a racing certainty for the job. His main opponent would be the Labour Party's nominee, Mary Robinson, who had broken the consensus on contraception, challenged repressive laws and opposed the abortion referendum in 1983. I thought she would do very well, but as his campaign manager, Haughey's protégé Bertie Ahern, put it: 'There was so much affection for Brian, it was difficult to see how he could lose.'[6]

He found a way. It began with a very minor question: had Lenihan, along with Haughey and other Fianna Fáil figures, phoned a previous president, Patrick Hillery, in 1982 to urge him not to dissolve parliament but instead to allow Haughey, then in opposition, to try to form a government? Even if he had done this, it was quite an obscure issue and not one that most people really cared about. The problem was that Lenihan, asked about it on television, said he didn't do it. Then the *Irish Times* produced a tape of an interview with a postgraduate student, in which he said the opposite. Lenihan went on the television news, to say that, when he gave the taped interview his mind was 'not attuned', but that 'on mature recollection' he was now absolutely certain that he did not call Hillery.[7] In a gesture that even his campaign manager Ahern thought to be 'pathetic', he turned to stare straight into the camera, as if he could look everyone watching in the eye.[8]

Gay Byrne, perhaps thinking he was helping matters for Lenihan, told the listeners to his radio show that they should consider the possibility that Lenihan was just being nice to the student who made the tape, Jim Duffy: 'There's a possibility I know it's remote, I know, but knowing Brian for what he is there is a remote possibility that what he was doing with Duffy on the tape was giving him a splurge knowing that there wasn't a word of truth in it all and just trying to make it sound good for the young fella. I know, I know you find it hard to cope with that but it's just possible that he was making it up as he went along and now of course he regrets it.'[9] Under pressure from his coalition partner Des O'Malley, Haughey, sacrificing his friend to save his life, fired Lenihan as minister for foreign affairs 'with great sadness and great sorrow', but continued to back him for the presidency.[10]

I thought, as all of this was unfolding, of Ron Ziegler, Richard Nixon's press secretary, explaining that previous statements about Nixon's involvement in Watergate were untrue: 'This is an operative statement, the others are inoperative.' In such an epistemological nightmare, language becomes a hall of mirrors forever throwing back a distorted reflection on itself, its relationship to reality becoming weirder and weirder. The more Lenihan said 'my position is perfectly clear', the more you knew the opposite was the case. Once begun, a little lie takes on a life of its own, becoming a fast breeder reactor of radioactive language. You take a harmless turn off the road of reality and there you are in a maze of falsehoods. You get in so far that there is no going back.

Lenihan's lies had this quality of almost complete purity about them. Usually with political mendacity, there was a truth out there somewhere waiting to be discovered and the lie is merely the opposite of that truth. But here the lie was a free-floating entity, two opposite signifiers with no real signified. It was not an attempt to cover up something which was patently shameful. There was no accepted truth: the only real evidence that Lenihan had done what he now denied doing was his very own. It was quite possible that both versions of what did or did not happen were untrue.

The whole thing was entirely self-enclosed, Lenihan playing the role both of accuser and accused, his own disembodied voice on tape contradicting his own embodied voice on television. It was a story out of Kafka or Beckett, not one out of Agatha Christie or Raymond Chandler. All statements were inoperative.

It takes a lot of practice to achieve this kind of perfect purity: a lie that has no relationship at all to a truth. Lenihan had functioned for a long time as his party's great verbal escape artist. Now that he had been caught, how strange it seemed that the slipperiest of eels should have been enmeshed in a verbal net of his own devising. Before you can construct this sort of lie for its own sake, you have to already have constructed a sort of language for its own sake. You need free-floating words, words so completely divorced from reality that they form their own life-support system, entirely independent of facts.

This was where Fianna Fáil had come to: what begins as patriotic mysticism ends up as mere mystification. The little lies were the tip of an iceberg of frozen meanings, empty formulae, dead rhetoric, words designed to obscure rather than elucidate, to mislead rather than to point us in the right direction. All of them seemed, finally, to be unravelling in the surreal drama of Lenihan's meltdown. All he could do was double down on that old language of faith and nation. Addressing Mass goers in West Limerick he said, 'The good Lord has given me back my health and my energy. We will say a prayer or two. That is more important than anything else... The Lord is on our side – I feel it in my bones. It is a tangible thing... I share the national Christian Irish views and values that are inherent in our country, the values that give us our own identity as a people.' He worked himself up over 'the Irish Way' and 'the common ethos' that allowed him 'to relate to the people in every corner of Ireland'.[11]

Returning to the religious theme, Lenihan's director of elections, Bertie Ahern, told the final rally of his campaign, referring to the candidate's self-contradictory stories about what happened in 1982, that 'I have discussed this matter with a priest. He says Brian's little "bit of balderdash" is worth only three Hail Marys as a penance.'[12] I felt sure I know who this priest was: Michael Cleary. In his column in the *Dublin Tribune*, Cleary used the same line: 'whether this lie wrecks Brian Lenihan's career or not, I will offer him the consolation that he can walk into any confession box and his transgression will only merit him three Hail Marys...' He implicitly compared Lenihan's merely venial sin of lying to the electorate to the mortal sins of those like Robinson and her media supporters 'who have condoned and accepted promiscuity, adultery... information on abortion and who would put condoms freely into the hands of young people'.[13]

It could have been 1950, not 1990. A Fianna Fáil TD, John Browne, asked at a Lenihan rally in Wexford, if Robinson won the election, 'is she going to have an abortion referral clinic in [the presidential residence], Áras an Uachtaráin? That's what I'd like to know.'[14] To reinforce the contrast between the godly Lenihan and Robinson, Haughey accused her of being a front for a 'Marxist-Leninist Communist Party'.[15]

There was still a chance that this appeal to religion and identity might work. Ireland was still a deeply uncertain place, still subject to the old desire to assert values it knew to be hollow. But one leading Fianna Fáil minister, Pádraig Flynn, recently returned from a visit to the Crazy Horse cabaret in Paris ('the best nude show in the universe'), paid for by Haughey's former press handler Frank Dunlop, now a lobbyist, took a hand in the campaign.[16] Flynn went on the radio to accuse Robinson of faking her commitment to her own family, 'changing her image to suit the fashion of the time and having a new found interest in the family... none of us who knew Mary Robinson well in previous incarnations ever heard her claiming to be the great wife and mother.'[17]

I remember, listening to Flynn on the radio, thinking that there was no going back now. Something had been done and it would never be undone. It was not that Flynn was being

18. A demonstration in support of the IRA hunger strikers in Belfast, 1981.

19. Pilgrims waiting for the arrival of Pope John Paul II at Knock, Co. Mayo, 1979.

20. Bishop Eamonn Casey and Father Michael Cleary at the Pope's youth Mass in Galway, 1979.

21. Old and new at Westport Horse Fair, 1983.

22. The abortion referendum of 1983 seemed to copperfasten Catholic power.

23. Joanne Hayes leaving the Kerry Babies inquiry, 1985.

24. Crowds gather hoping to see the statue of the Blessed Virgin at Ballinspittle move, 1985.

25. Charles Haughey (right) with his most generous benefactor, Ben Dunne.

26. The picture of Annie Murphy with her son Peter that shattered the image of the Catholic Church.

27. President Bill Clinton in Belfast with UK prime minister Tony Blair and SDLP deputy leader Seamus Mallon.

30. Campaigners greet the announcement of the results of the referendum on same-sex marriage, May 2015.

28. An unoccupied 'ghost estate', 2011.

29. The Island of Ireland in Dubai encapsulated the follies of the Celtic Tiger.

misogynistic – there was nothing remarkable in that. It was that the misogyny was open, crude, unguarded. Whether his brain was still reeling from the best nude show in the universe or whether, as I was not alone in suspecting, he was merely brainless, he had broken something that could not be fixed. Misogyny was encoded in debates about 'morality' (abortion, contraception, divorce). It was played out in psychodramas like the Kerry Babies. It was embedded in structures, assumptions, above all in silences. It was not to be stated.

Lenihan or Haughey would never have said what Flynn said. They knew the shadow language of suggestion and circumlocution and grandiose bombast. I could hear, as I listened to Flynn that morning, the shadow language turning into a very Irish form of Macbeth's 'tale told by an idiot'. Instead of 'signifying nothing', as Fianna Fáil language was supposed to, Flynn was signifying far too much. It did what must not be done: revealed the reality obscured by the rhetoric, a deep contempt for women. It triggered a visceral rage that had been built up over generations. A few hours after Flynn spoke, Ahern, campaigning in Galway city and as yet unaware of what Flynn had said, was grabbed by the lapels by a furious woman who said 'she was Fianna Fáil through and through and that her father had supported de Valera'. She hissed at Ahern: 'Would you ever do something about that bastard Pádraig Flynn?'[18]

His party colleague Charlie McCreevy was canvassing votes for Lenihan in Co. Kildare. As they moved through a newly built housing estate 'the spontaneous hostility which Flynn's remarks had generated forced them to end their canvas in mid-afternoon'.[19] On election day, Lenihan's canvassers were dismayed to encounter, even in rural towns, stony-faced women who pushed past them as they went into the polling stations as if they were on a mission. They knew they were voting for Robinson.

Robinson's defeat of Lenihan shattered the illusion of hegemony, the feeling that the deep alliance of Fianna Fáil and the church had a permanent hold over Irish culture. It was clear, in the short term, that Haughey was now on borrowed time. The party membership was 'angry and confused'.[20] The aura of power evaporated. By the summer of 1991, his understudy Ahern was 'convinced Charlie had made his mind up to get out'.[21] The whiff of corruption was growing stronger with the Carysfort story, the forced sale of valuable convent land to a crony of Haughey's; another extraordinary property deal in which the state-owned telecommunications company Telecom Éireann bought for £9.4 million a building that had recently been sold for £4.4 million; the inquiry into misdeeds in the beef industry and simpler revelations, like the fact that Dublin County Council had laid sewerage pipes under Haughey's lands at Kinsealy, enhancing their commercial value. The fiercely ambitious Albert Reynolds was plotting to overthrow Haughey.

After one failed coup by Reynolds, the *coup de grâce* was administered by a figure from the past: Seán Doherty. I had wondered how Doherty must have viewed the indulgence of wild stories about the abuse of power by Lenihan on *The Late Late Show* in 1990 and the contrast to his own ostracization. He got his revenge in January 1992. He popped up to allege that, nine years earlier, Haughey had known all about his tapping of the phones of journalists – indeed that he had read the transcripts. This was yet another case of double vision: if Doherty was telling the truth now, he had lied in 1982 when he denied that Haughey knew anything and 'would have stopped it' if he did.[22] It was the Lenihan affair all over again: a Fianna Fáil politician accused of lying, not by a hostile critic, but by himself. As Bertie Ahern put it, 'We will never know whether Doherty was telling the truth on this occasion or in his initial account. What's certain is that only one version can be correct.'[23] Except, of course, that neither might be entirely true. We were again lost in a cognitive maze. Haughey, though he vehemently denied the allegations, realized that he was lost, too, and resigned, to be replaced by Reynolds.

Haughey's fall was the beginning of the end of one side – the political wing – of the alliance that was holding conservative Ireland together. The other side – the reasserted dominance of a Catholic ideology – began to unravel almost immediately and even more dramatically.

On Reynolds's first day of office, he discovered that his attorney general, Harry Whelehan, had gone to the High Court to seek an injunction to prevent a fourteen-year-old girl from travelling to Britain for an abortion. She was the child raped behind the swimming pool in Dublin in December 1991. The case was held in camera, but on 12 February the *Irish Times* reported laconically that an interim injunction had been granted, that the girl and her parents, who were already in England, had returned to Ireland as a consequence, and that a full judgement was expected within days. The paper also reported that Whelehan had been informed of the case because the girl's parents had gone to the police to ask whether DNA from the foetus might be useful in prosecuting the rapist. They, in turn, had contacted Whelehan's office for advice.[24] The story was accurate, though in fact the Garda had first gone to the Director of Public Prosecutions, who in turn contacted the attorney general.

Father Michael Cleary later used his radio show on 98FM to suggest that the whole story was a conspiracy, 'a model… planned deliberately to test the [anti-abortion constitutional] amendment'.[25] This was pernicious nonsense, but the idea was interesting. In the Irish way of doing things, there really ought to have been a conspiracy. The proper way to handle this unwanted knowledge was, as Reynolds's new government press secretary Seán Duignan noted privately at the time, that the attorney general should have passed it up the line to the minister for justice, Pádraig Flynn. The general view in political circles, according to Duignan, was that 'Harry and his people should have sought advice, i.e. deferred action until it was too late – "let the file fall behind a radiator" – or at least dawdled until the deed [the abortion] was done, so as to keep them out of the whole embarrassing mess while the young rape victim underwent an abortion somewhere outside the jurisdiction'.[26] Reynolds kept pleading with Whelehan: 'You've got to think political, Harry.'[27] In other words, what became notorious as the X case, should have been an unknown known.

Whelehan behaved entirely properly – the Constitution banned abortion and the courts had ruled that that included any facilitation of travel outside the country to have one. But he was, from the point of view of the system, the kind of literal-minded dolt 'that can cause all kinds of mayhem'.[28] He did not understand that the point of these laws was not to do things in the real world, not to actually stop Irish women – still less fourteen-year-old girls who had been raped – from having abortions in England. It was to maintain the fiction that Ireland was different, holier, more spiritual. The characters in that fiction were not supposed to become too lifelike.

As well as Whelehan, there were other characters who were behaving too literally: the girl's parents. They had voted in favour of putting the abortion ban into the Constitution in 1983. They were not looking for trouble. They did not want their daughter to be a test case. It would have suited everyone had they pretended that they did not know about the injunction. They had flown to London with their daughter. They had an appointment at an abortion clinic next day. It was only when the father phoned his son in Dublin that he was told that the police wanted to talk to him urgently. Informed of the temporary injunction, he decided to cancel the abortion and return. Asked why he had done this, he replied: 'I am a law-abiding citizen.'[29] But abiding by the law, as the family and Whelehan did, was not the proper response. What you were supposed to do was misunderstand the instructions, delay until there was nothing to be done, create a fait accompli that everyone could regret and deplore and forget.

Just as Flynn's attack on Robinson ripped the delicate fabric of half-truths, evasions and tacit understandings about the nature of official misogyny, Whelehan's failure to do the decent thing and lose the file down the back of a radiator created an excess of knowledge. It meant that Ireland really was going to act on its piously amended Constitution, keep a child from leaving the country and force her to have a baby. In the full High Court hearing, the judge, yet again Declan Costello, heard evidence from the child's psychiatrist that the girl, who had been abused by her rapist from the age of twelve, was suffering 'devastating' damage to her mental health and that there was a real danger she might 'commit suicide or decide to terminate it herself by throwing herself down the stairs or something like that.' Costello, in granting the full injunction, ruled that the risk to her life was 'of a lesser magnitude' than the certainty of the death of the foetus if the abortion went ahead.[30] This was not illogical: the amendment had specified that the right to life of a mother was merely equal to that of the foetus. If the two were of equal value, it was reasonable to conclude that a possibility that the mother might die was outweighed by the inevitability of a termination.

When the Dáil debated the ruling, no woman's voice was heard – all the speeches were made by middle-aged men.[31] Of course, the realization of what the amendment actually meant sparked outrage. It meant that every pregnant woman in Ireland could have her right to travel freely within the European Union suspended. Martyn Turner's cartoon in the *Irish Times*, showing a little girl in the middle of a map of Ireland surrounded by a barbed wire fence made an explicit connection to the most disastrous British policies in Northern Ireland: '17th February 1992. The introduction of internment in Ireland… for 14-year-old girls.'

What was especially striking was that even the anti-abortion campaigners I had interviewed ten years earlier claimed that none of this was supposed to happen. Bernadette Bonner actually insisted that the family should not have returned to Ireland when they heard of the injunction and suggested that the fact they did so pointed to a 'set-up'. She claimed that it was never the intention of the anti-abortion campaign to actually stop women from travelling to England for terminations.[32] This, at least, was some kind of truth: none of this had ever been about what happened, only about what happened officially and openly within Ireland.

Ireland could not bear too much reality. But nor could it bear too much shame. The case became a big international story, in which Ireland did not seem like all the things it wanted to be: modern, progressive, sophisticated. Nor did it even seem holy. It just seemed half-crazy, brutal, barbaric.

There was thus great relief when the Supreme Court solved the immediate problem of Miss X by overturning the injunction on the grounds that her life was, after all, equal in value to that of her foetus and that the risk of suicide justified an abortion. This left Irish law in an absurd state: the Constitutional amendment, it turned out, did not ban abortion entirely – it actually permitted it in some (albeit very limited) circumstances. But the criminal law continued to impose an actual ban. The state moved to restore the real status quo of winking at abortions in England, by holding referendums (comfortably passed) to allow for information on abortion services to be given and for women to travel to avail of them. Miss X travelled to Manchester for an abortion (accompanied this time by a policeman to take custody of DNA samples) but had a miscarriage instead. Her rapist was prosecuted and jailed.

But things were not just the same as before. The great gulf between what Ireland liked to say about itself in principle and how it wanted to be seen in the everyday world had been cruelly exposed. Very soon, it would be widened to an impossible abyss.

32

1992: Not So Bad Myself

I was awake but still in bed. Before I could turn on the radio, Clare burst in the door: 'Bishop Casey has resigned. He had a child. He's fled the country.' The *Irish Times* had the story but, even though I worked for the paper, it was news to me, too. Even in the gossipy world we inhabited, there had been no intimations of what was coming. Aside from the editor Conor Brady and the US correspondent Conor O'Clery, who did the reporting, only four other people knew about it before publication. It was handled like a cargo of nitroglycerine. As it appeared in the paper that morning of 7 May 1992, the story was delicately handled. It simply said that Eamonn Casey had paid money to a woman in Connecticut who had a child. As the paper was going to press, the Vatican issued a statement that Casey had resigned as Bishop of Galway.

It was significant that the *Irish Times* was anxious to frame the narrative primarily as being about money, not about sex. In the atmosphere of financial corruption that pervaded the country during and after the Haughey years, it was somehow easier to process pecuniary perversions than bodily transgressions. The initial reporting hinged on a final settlement that Casey had made with Annie Murphy and their son Peter. This $117,000 came from the funds of the Galway diocese and was transferred via an escrow account in New York to Murphy in Connecticut.[1] The negotiations were handled by a priest in Brooklyn, Monsignor James Kelly, who was also a lawyer. On the books of the Galway diocese, Casey had entered a transaction in the Reserve Fund over which he had personal control, a fictitious 'loan' to a person who had no involvement in the affair at all. Here was another case of the familiar practice of bogus accounting, another piece of funny paper. So this was not about private life, but about low standards in high places. We were comfortable with that.

It was also not wrong. As Murphy gradually told her story, it was indeed as much about money as about sex. The view from the bishop's bed, as she was able to recall it, was a new angle on the sumptuousness and luxury of life at the top of the clerical ladder. There was nothing shocking in the notion that some bishops lived in palaces, ate like kings and behaved like princes, that they were waited on, flattered and pampered. But this was seldom described because outsiders did not get close enough to do so. Murphy was one outsider who became privy to a world whose sensual delights were supposed to exclude sex but that legitimately included the best of food and drink, the finest places to live, the swankiest sports cars, the handmade shoes, the clothes brought straight from Harrods of London. Once, Murphy would recall, a police car passed by as she and Casey were making love in his car and she went to cover herself with his coat: 'No, Annie, that's from Harrods and it's got my name stitched into it.'[2]

Yet there was always the question – which was always unanswerable – about what the paper would have done if there was no funny money involved, if this were simply a matter of sexual hypocrisy. Haughey's double life had not yet been exposed. There was still the sense that one did not go there, even when Haughey himself had made his devotion both to his own family, and to family life as the centrepiece of social order, a political matter. Why should Casey be different? Because he was a powerful churchman and a supposed celibate? How was that qualitatively different from an even more powerful politician and supposed upholder of monogamy? The money granted permission. It made Casey's subterranean life fair game. But neither I nor I think anyone else in the country really believed that it was the thing that made this moment so epochal. That was a very different, much more epic, kind of false accounting, the rigging not of a ledger but of Irish reality.

On that first day when the story broke, it was all about absence. Casey had skulked out of Ireland unnoticed on an Aer Lingus flight to New York. (We afterwards learned that he then hid for six months in a convent in San Antonio, Texas, before going to remote rural Ecuador for the next six and a half years.) One of the most visible people in Irish life had vanished. But it was an eloquent and resonant emptiness. It was not just that the idea of a bishop being smuggled incognito out of the country had a quality of comeuppance. It replayed the flights of so many Irish women over so many decades, so many women who could not say their names or show their faces. It was also that this void was the blank space between the two Irish realities. That cavity was now active, alive, the centre of attention.

Casey's decision to resign had been precipitated by an angry phone call from Annie Murphy in which she threatened him with a video. That tape was also central in the decision by the *Irish Times* to pursue the story. It recorded the last meeting between the lovers, in the lobby of the Grand Hyatt Hotel in New York in August 1991, when they discussed a final settlement for their son Peter's college fees. It was secretly videotaped on a camcorder by a friend of Murphy's. It consisted mostly of shots of the back of Casey's bald head. It did, though, include one shot of Casey kissing Murphy.[3] And at one point, the camera was jolted and captured for a moment Peter hiding behind a pillar.[4] It was never released. It presumably has some kind of ghostly existence. 'My son will keep this videotape for his grandchildren', said Murphy at the time,[5] but I have always imagined someone finding it in an attic in 2050 and not knowing what to do with it, since the technology used to record it will itself have vanished. It is like a key to a moment when Irish history changed, but a key that has rusted beyond use.

I think, too, that on this unplayable camcorder tape, there is that accidental frame, when the hand holding the camera was jogged or jostled and the lens picked out what was not supposed to be seen: that boy hiding behind the pillar. He stands, in his furtive stance and unintended discovery, for all the invisible children, carried to England in their mothers' wombs, secreted in Mother and Baby Homes, adopted, their names changed, their identities concealed, their origins known only to a silent woman and to God.

When Murphy was pregnant, Casey had urged her to attach herself to God, not to the baby she was carrying. Giving the child up for adoption, he urged, would be 'an unselfish act' that 'would cast from me all evils'. After Peter was born in the Rotunda Hospital in Dublin in July 1974, Casey was disturbed to find that she kept him in a cradle at the foot of her bed. He spoke to her in a voice 'low and stern', warning her again about the dangers of 'attachment'. He told her that Peter was not her child, but 'a child of God's'.[6] Murphy and Peter were placed in a home run by nuns where Casey 'cajoled, laughed and finally started to bully me, waving adoption papers in my face, slapping his hands down on the table. He called one of the head nuns in – then they started on me. "What right had I to keep this child I had borne out of wedlock in sin?"'

It was the same line that Michael Cleary had used on Phyllis Hamilton four years earlier, when their son Michael Ivor was born. Cleary and Hamilton had often stayed with Casey in his country house in Kerry and, according to Hamilton, the bishop 'was the first cleric to know our secret'.[7] These men knew things about each other. They also knew that there were ways of dealing with the consequences of what they knew, that disappearances could be arranged. Problems could vanish. There were systems to turn their offspring into God's children. All that was necessary was to avoid 'attachment'.

Before he fled Ireland in May 1992, Casey called Cleary's home. The priest was away golfing in Spain and instead Casey spoke to Hamilton, the mother of his children. His voice was 'full of panic'. He was 'breathing fast and sounded like he was in a hurry'. He left a message for Cleary: 'I am rushing… I am going away. Tell Michael I won't be back for a long time. Thank him very much for everything he has done for me.'[8] Hamilton felt the same panic. She emptied a drawer full of lingerie that the priest had bought her, as if it bore the mark of incrimination. She got all the poems, love letters and cards that Cleary had written her and burned them. Along with the camcorder tape, they form a part of a vaporous trail of evidence, an unreadable testament to the power of hidden intimacies.

It would not be until January 1994, after his death, that Cleary's own story became public. But he undoubtedly knew that it was only a matter of time, that a code of silence had been broken forever. When Cleary arrived home the weekend after Casey's flight, he seemed to Hamilton a 'broken man'. He was afraid that the church might now, as it had done to Casey, 'pack him off to South America'. But, he reassured Hamilton, 'you are no Annie Murphy'.[9] This was true. A big part of the difference was America.

Ireland had been living the American Dream for decades, but Murphy was, for Catholic Ireland, a very specifically American nightmare. On the second day of its revelations, the *Irish Times* published a big photograph of her on its front page and there was a sharp intake of collective breath. She looked like trouble. She was beautiful. She had bold lipstick and glinting earrings and lush dark hair. But the shock was in her gaze. She had huge dark eyes and they were fixed on the viewer with unblinking assurance. There was in them neither repentance nor supplication. She wasn't mortified and she wasn't looking for sympathy. In that gaze there was something looking fiercely back at us – not just the history of shame but also a history of exile. She was the return of everything that had been repressed in the intertwined experiences of mass emigration and holy Ireland.

Murphy's family could have been invented by Eugene O'Neill, such was its archetypal drama of lace-curtain Irish respectability riddled with alcoholism, subdued violence and the hard bitterness of exile. John Steinbeck looked at the Irish-Americans and wrote in *East of Eden* that they 'do have a despairing quality of gaiety, but they have also a dour and brooding ghost that rides on their shoulders and peers in on their thoughts'.[10] Annie Murphy embodied both the despairing gaiety and the brooding ghost, with a view of the world that was often wildly comic and often haunted by nameless forebodings. Her love for Eamonn Casey seemed inextricable from her love for Ireland, the exile's love of the dream homeland.

She was in love with the place as much as with the man, the landscape he drove so wildly through when he collected her from the airport in 1973, having promised her father, a surgeon in

Connecticut, that he would look after her while she recovered from a bad and broken marriage. The sea, the mountains, the flowers were characters in her love affair. She brought to her passion for Casey both the illusory longing and the driven ambition of Irish-America, both the rosy view of Ireland and the all-American drive to make the world correspond to her views of it. That second part was the big problem.

In many ways Casey was as typically Irish as Murphy was Irish-American: energetic, garrulous, at home with the world, but also full of evasions and denials. The trouble was that, although he was older and much more powerful, she was, in a sense, much more ambitious than he was. For she wanted the world to change, wanted a clerical potentate to come down off his throne and take charge of her messy life, while he wanted things to be the same only more so. He wanted everything he already had and something else as well: the joy of sex, maybe the comfort of being loved rather than merely venerated and obeyed.

He just had to make room in the busy whirl of his life for yet another pleasure. She had to try to reinvent the whole world of Catholic Ireland, make it conform to her desires. It was a clash of mother country and restless exile as much it was the collision of Mother Church and restless desire. As in a Greek play, the conflict of these incompatible but ineluctable forces could produce only tragedy. The directness which the Irish learned in America could not communicate with the evasions of life at home. The elaborate cathedral of self-justifications Casey undoubtedly built on the shifting foundations of his desire was demolished by her impatience. The scale of her American yearning, the vision of a future in which she and Eamonn and Peter would live happily ever after, was thwarted by his very Irish ability to live with all the contradictions in a never-ending present rather than have to face the hard choices that such a future would demand.

In the few days after Casey's exposure, the Irish Catholic bishops began to say something that most Irish people had been saying to themselves all along, as they did their best to negotiate the incompatible demands of exemplary piety and actual life: that we must try not to judge others, that what happened to Casey was a matter for his conscience, that none of us know the secret suffering of human beings. They were recognizing, for the first time perhaps, that morality was not about a set of rules but about the dark and difficult choices that face real people in their own hearts.

They were in this applying a very different standard to their brother bishop than they had applied to say, Eileen Flynn, but there was not necessarily anything contemptible in that. All over the country there were hundreds of thousands of lay Catholics who had been forced to learn to do the same thing, to come, when faced with the suffering of those close to them, to conclusions different from the ones they knew they were supposed to arrive at. They had to say 'sex outside marriage is wrong' but 'of course I will help Mary with the baby' or 'divorce is wrong' but 'my Johnny should be allowed to remarry' or 'I hate abortion' but 'Sharon just can't go through with this pregnancy'. Mothers like my own had learned that their sons who stopped going to Mass weren't necessarily on the road to perdition. Fathers had learned that the daughter who was living with that fellow wasn't a tramp and that the child they had together was a joy, not a shame. They had all learned that their children who loved others of the same sex as themselves were not perverts but ordinary people.

These were the true moralists of modern Ireland and it was no easier for them than it was now for the bishops. They had borne the pain and made the choices. Finally, and in the most traumatic of circumstances, their leaders had begun to follow them. Faced with the suffering of someone close to them, they had begun to learn what their faithful had learned a long time ago. Not that they did not have a long way to go. I had yet to hear a senior churchmen say that a man faced with the choice between his church and his child must choose the child, or that if Casey was guilty, his guilt lay not in loving the mother but in abandoning the son. To say this would have been no more difficult than the choices thousands and thousands of Irish Catholic parents had made by going – as my mother did to mine – to the registry office weddings of their children or by loving their grandchildren who were brought up in a different faith, or by welcoming their son's boyfriend to the Sunday dinner table.

This, I think, was what really changed: ordinary Catholics realized that, when it came to lived morality, they were way ahead of their teachers. The flock was much more sophisticated than the pastors. In the days after the revelations about him, a Mercy sister, Mairéad Ní Chonaola, confirmed that she had written a poem in Irish in honour of Bishop Casey. It 'welcomed him to our world'.[11] That seemed entirely right as a description of what was happening. There was not much bitterness or outrage, merely the jokes about the Irish condom called the Just In-Casey that I heard at a football match that Sunday. But those little words – 'our world' – were momentous. It was now the world of the ordinary, decent people, doing their best to do the right thing in a confusing universe. The bishops – and by extension the power structure of which they had been part – would have to learn to live in it, and if they could not it would have no time for them.

There was a great moment that formed a resonant coda to this chronicle of a death foretold. In April 1993, almost a year after the *Irish Times* reports, Annie Murphy went on *The Late Late Show* to promote a book she had published about the affair. The set-up was startlingly hostile. It seemed to me as I watched it that Byrne, too, had sensed the waning of his own power. He liked and admired Casey, but there was more to his quiet anger than that. Murphy had destroyed the world in which Byrne had thrived, his uncanny ability to move between the unsaid and the outspoken. There was a sense that *The Late Late Show* would itself never be the same again because it was now so much less necessary. Byrne was like a poet who wrote best within the bounds of strict meters and rhyme schemes, delighting in the paradoxical freedom that comes with being able to play with them. Murphy had inaugurated a whole new form of free verse.

Whatever the reasons, the show was conducted as a trial of Murphy. The audience was packed with Casey's friends and his episcopal secretary, who called Murphy a fallen woman and a liar and tried to insist that she had made it all up for money. They suggested that the bishop was not even the father of the child – even though he had admitted that he was. They asked her to answer crazy questions: what colour was Casey's dog? Was a certain night moonlit or not – the questioner claimed to have checked the meteorological records and found Murphy out.

Byrne himself was scarcely less antagonistic. He told Murphy, 'I can see how coquettish you can be on occasions'. When she denied having seduced the bishop, he asked, 'what woman doesn't pursue a man?' Byrne intimated that he knew Casey had asked Murphy to have their son adopted because he did not feel she would be able to bring him up properly. (She replied, 'but I have brought that child up well'.)[12] It was the Kerry Babies all over again, the woman to blame, even though Casey held all the power when their relationship started. She was, throughout, calm, dignified, unabashed. At the end, Byrne said to Murphy that her son Peter would be 'not be doing too badly' if he turned out to be half the man his father was. Murphy said, 'I'm not so bad, Mr Byrne, not so bad myself as you'd like to think', stood up and walked off the floor. That was it exactly. We were not so bad ourselves and we never would be again. It was an exit line, not just for her, but for the entire era in which Irish people were made to feel that not so bad could never be good enough.

33

1992–1994: Meanwhile Back at the Ranch

In June 1992, Albert Reynolds, who had succeeded Haughey as Taoiseach and leader of Fianna Fáil, was continually 'flying off the handle' and becoming 'obsessed'. He was, as his press secretary Seán Duignan wrote in his diary, 'convinced that O'Toole is out to bring him down, he probably would if he could, but I dread it when he picks up on something we can't do anything about. It's so shagging complicated.'[1] It was indeed. I was not particularly out to get Reynolds – not, in any case, beyond the imperative of all journalism to be constantly trying to bring down the government. But I was trying to understand how political power had been working in Ireland, to grasp at the fleeting shadows that money cast on the walls as it passed through the inner rooms of the state. Trying and, ultimately, failing. There was something I felt I knew but could never prove.

I spent a lot of the early 1990s in cowboy country. This was the other Ireland, the one that was not shaped by modernity and multinationals, the one that had survived intact through the massive changes in land ownership at the end of the nineteenth century, through revolution, civil war and the establishment of an independent state, through the transformations initiated by Whitaker and Lemass. The US consultancy firm Stacy May had opened its report on the Irish economy in 1952 with that line: 'In the Irish economy, cattle is king'.[2] There was still an economy – and a politics – in which this was true. And within this kingdom there was one uncontested monarch: Larry Goodman.

Even in 1978, the leading Irish journal *Hibernia* was still describing Larry Goodman as 'Ireland's least known beef baron'. At that time his privately owned meat business was turning over £60 million annually, but he nonetheless seemed a remote figure. He did not give interviews or seek publicity. Where other leading personalities in the trade tended to be ebullient and colourful, he was quiet, soft-spoken and apparently shy. He had risen virtually without trace through a slow and steady series of acquisitions. By the time he began to be noticed, he was already a real power in the land.

Like many of the beef barons, he came from the Borderlands between the Republic and Northern Ireland. He was born in 1940 into the meat trade in Co. Louth and left school without qualifications at the age of sixteen. His family had been cattle dealers for five generations and his father Laurence, as well as shipping live cattle to the British market, also had a small abattoir in Dundalk. When Larry left school, he took to buying up sheep intestines, cleaning them and selling them to butchers as sausage casings. By 1961 he was exporting meat to England. At the age of twenty-six, he bought, for just £31,000, a heavily mortgaged plant, Anglo-Irish Meats in Ravensdale, close to the border with Northern Ireland.

The Borderlands were not an easy place for a young man trying to build a business. The Border itself was a lawless zone of smuggling and small-scale banditry, often linked to the then dormant, but still potent, paramilitarism of the IRA and its allies. The smuggling of cattle and pigs to avoid import levies, or to take advantage of government grants, gave the meat business a shifting, shadowy side. For a serious and ambitious young businessman like Larry Goodman, it was a tough world in which to survive.

But Goodman was a kind of fulfilment of the Whitaker dream. He took a basic economic activity and built it into an international empire, gradually using his dominance of the Irish beef trade to create a group of companies, Goodman International, that could sell on global markets. As his counsel boasted at the tribunal of inquiry established to investigate the beef industry and its political entanglements, he was 'dragged up from nowhere over the last 30 years from a primitive killing line in one part of the country to an international operation that competes with Brazil from this small island'. Yet even as he expanded his global operation, he kept tight personal control over his companies. The main one, Anglo-Irish Beef Processors, was 98 per cent owned by Larry Goodman with the other 2 per cent of the shares held by his brother Peter.

His rise had an innately political element. A large part of the programme for change in Ireland in the late 1960s depended on a successful transition from primary agricultural production to food processing: from bulk milk to Kerrygold butter and from cattle on the hoof to a Sunday roast on a British supermarket shelf. This was economically, but also politically, critical. Unless a link between farmers and industrial workers could be forged through the creation of food industries in which the two were interdependent, the 'classless' appeal of Fianna Fáil's nationalism could be threatened by serious conflicts of interest. The high consumer prices for food within the EU, which would bring large benefits to farmers at the expense of urban workers, would be a real source of tension unless agricultural production itself were seen to create industrial jobs.

The paradox of Larry Goodman's emergence is that while on the political level his success was understood as vital to social and political stability, the business he came out of was one with an outlaw image closer to the Wild West than to the brave new Europe. As Goodman's counsel told the beef tribunal, 'anyone who thinks that the meat industry is conducted according to the same principles as the activities of Mother Teresa of Calcutta would be mistaken'.

It was a rough, frantic and sometimes brutal business, a world of blood and bone and knives and stench. One contractor who worked extensively for Goodman, said to me, 'you need to be half savage to do it. It's not women's knickers we're making, or ladies' perfume.'[3] It was not unlike a war or, in its more refined moments, a contact sport. When a big contract was on, men worked long hours at a ferocious pace, earning big money, taking big physical risks. Teams of boners moved from factory to factory, and between Northern Ireland and the Republic, peripatetic mercenaries, selling their skills to the highest bidder, paying no tax, working for cash.

In the midst of this mayhem, Goodman stood out for his sobriety, steadiness and efficiency. The companies he took over – seventy-four of them by 1986 – were stabilized, often after histories of bankruptcy and uncertainty. He neither drank nor smoke and cultivated an almost Spartan image, once telling a trade union negotiator who asked him 'how would you like to live on £96 a week?' 'but I do live on £96 a week'. This was not the case, since the trappings of his wealth included a mansion in Castlebellingham, a private jet and a helicopter. But the claim was in keeping with his single-minded, almost monkish devotion to the work of building his empire. Where other Irish self-made men tended to see wealth as a means to luxury and self-indulgence, he saw it as an end in itself. He was willing to travel anywhere, to suffer any privation, even to forgo his Christmas dinner, in order to make more money.

The serious money came after Ireland joined the EU in 1973, leading to an immediate boom in the meat industry. Whereas before 1973 Irish prices were essentially those of the open competitive British market, they were now determined by a whole range of protective interventions under the Common Agricultural Policy: import levies, intervention buying, export subsidies. In a sense, the basic product of Goodman's empire was no longer beef. It was documents. In spite of his status as a hero of rugged private enterprise, he devoured public money in the form of EU subsidies that flowed from paperwork. For all the truth of the story of a man who had worked his way up from the bottom of a dirty trade, the managers he typically hired were not men like himself but young, very bright chartered accountants who could work their way through the complexities of intervention and export refunds.

This was why Goodman was such a crucial figure. He was a processor – not just of beef but of modes of power. He fed in at one end the raw, rough Ireland that had never settled down into the law or the state or proper European modernity. He produced, at the other end, a business empire that was truly indigenous, one of the very few Irish companies that was not a branch of an American multinational but that could still be a big force in a global trade.

Goodman became the largest beef processor in Europe and personally controlled about 4 per cent of the entire GDP of 1980s Ireland, while still operating in a world of pre-modern values, where rules and taxes and laws were to be avoided. He brought these systems together with extraordinary success. But in doing so he created a political fault line that ran right through the heart of the Fianna Fáil system. On one side was the state, with all its aspirations to respectable modernity. On the other was a kind of anarchy that had its own claims on the loyalties of those at the top of the party.

Goodman's companies (though not Goodman personally) engaged in a series of systematic frauds: attaching bogus EU stamps to meat, stealing vast quantities of beef that the EU had purchased from farmers to keep prices high and selling it to its own commercial customers in Britain, paying its workers large parts of their wages off the books and in cash so as to avoid tax. In 1987, one of the most senior figures in the group, Nobby Quinn, was found guilty of uttering forged documents. He was given a two-year jail sentence, but it was suspended. Around the same time, customs authorities uncovered a very large-scale fraud at two of the group's plants, in Waterford and Ballymun. And also in 1987, a young trainee accountant working on a routine audit of the Goodman plant in Cahir stumbled on large payments to hauliers whose names were not evident on any of the trucks visiting the plant. He traced the cheques and realized that they had all been cashed at the local branch of Allied Irish Bank. He had stumbled on another form of routine local corruption, in which banks pretended not to know that the manager of the local meat plant was cashing bogus cheques and using the money to pay the workers under the counter.

Even while this criminality in the ranks of his organization was being discovered, Fianna Fáil retained strong links to Larry Goodman. A £50,000 payment from Larry Goodman to Fianna Fáil in 1989 was recorded by the party financial controller as 'anonymous' on Haughey's personal instructions. Another payment – of £25,000 – from Larry Goodman to Fianna Fáil around the same time was made out to 'Fianna Fáil (Party Leadership Fund)', which was under Haughey's direct control. Larry Goodman also advanced about £600,000 to the then-influential Fianna Fáil politician Liam Lawlor and his companies in the late 1980s, of which only £350,000 was subsequently repaid. These transactions, which related to the purchase of lands in west Dublin, went through offshore companies.

Meanwhile, Albert Reynolds, who was Haughey's minister for industry and commerce, had sought to have his own business relationship with Goodman. The two men had known each other since the 1960s, and were close enough for Reynolds to invite Goodman to his daughter's wedding in October 1990. For much of 1987, Reynolds's company, C&D Pet Foods, was seeking funding from a venture capital fund Food Venture Fund (FVF), jointly established and owned by Goodman. Paul Dempsey, chief executive of C&D, in which Reynolds had a 'controlling and beneficial interest', approached the chief executive of FVF and asked it to invest in a project to develop new aluminium and plastic trays for pet food. FVF approached Goodman's right-hand man Brian Britton, and in May 1987 two FVF directors visited the C&D plant and were 'quite keen on the project'.[4] Nothing actually came of the proposal, but it was still a live prospect while Britton and Goodman were engaged in important negotiations with Reynolds in his role as government minister.

All of this was very interesting to me. It hinted at the ways in which private and public interests overlapped in Ireland and at the utter indifference of Fianna Fáil to criminality in companies to which it was close. But the aspect of what unfolded that really intrigued me was the part that remained out of reach: the one that involved Saddam Hussein and his monstrous regime in Iraq. What became clear to me was what would always remain unclear – the way these tawdry events in Ireland were somehow related to a brutal dictatorship 4,500 kilometres away.

At one level, the connection was obvious enough. In September 1987, Reynolds, with Haughey's full backing, decided to use Irish taxpayers' money to underwrite a huge contract that Goodman had signed to supply beef to the Iraqi regime, worth an initial $134 million. Saddam Hussein was the very definition of a dodgy customer. Not only was his regime fantastically corrupt, but he was locked in an existential war with Iran. No sane business person would take the risk of selling him goods on that scale – which is why Goodman didn't. He got Reynolds and Haughey to assume the risk instead. At a time when the Irish exchequer was in a terrible state and basic state services were being savagely cut back, Reynolds and Haughey staked Goodman's wild gamble.

But this was a gamble the state could not win. The justification for guaranteeing Goodman full payment even if Saddam defaulted was that the exports were good for Irish beef farmers, still an important political constituency. But this was entirely untrue. Like so much else, Goodman's contract with Iraq was essentially fraudulent. It specified that the beef to be shipped out from Ireland was fresh and slaughtered in accordance with the Islamic laws of Halal. In fact, almost all the beef was old stuff taken from EU cold stores and there was no way of knowing whether it was Halal or not. This was not a secret – it was fully known to Reynolds at the time. It meant that there was no economic benefit to Irish farmers at all.

It seemed that it was also not a secret to the Iraqis. Larry Goodman would later claim under oath that the nature of the beef he was sending to Iraq was 'very well known by the [Iraqi] authorities and by all concerned'.[5] Why did the Iraqis not object? Almost certainly because they had no intention of ever paying anyway. It was the Irish public that would be stuck with the bill. But why on earth did two successive leaders of the Irish state go along with this? I could never really answer that question. All I could say for sure was that both Haughey and Reynolds had financial connections to the Iraqi regime.

In October 1979, shortly before he replaced Jack Lynch as Taoiseach, Charles Haughey offered his bankers, Allied Irish Bank, a deposit of £10 million from the Iraqi Rafidain Bank. Rafidain was a commercial bank wholly owned by the Republic of Iraq. The Central Bank of Iraq controlled all its transactions and it, in turn, was controlled by Saddam Hussein and his cronies.

Haughey's only subsequent explanation of this staggering offer was one that actually deepened the mystery: 'He did recall something in relation to his having mentioned a large deposit from an Iraqi bank: Ireland was then in dire financial straits, and this was one of many instances in which persons came from places like the Middle East, and offered money at lower rates than were current in Ireland. He had offered to pass this possibility on to Allied Irish Banks, and they had shown no interest in it.'[6]

The other thing I knew is that when Goodman was doing his deal with the Iraqis and made threats to the Irish embassy in Baghdad because he felt that they were not giving him the exclusive attention he deserved, these threats were passed on to Haughey himself. A note marked 'highly confidential' and 'Baghdad – NB not recommended for use in Cabinet. For direct conversation with Taoiseach if considered suitable' was given to the minister for foreign affairs, Brian Lenihan. Asked about this at the beef tribunal, John Swift, assistant secretary of the department, explained that 'it was my understanding that the Taoiseach had a particular interest in the matters relating to economic relations with Iraq in the broader sense. I know that because the matter came up more than once that he had a particular interest in Iraq since the time as minister for health that he had visited Iraq [in 1979].'[7]

Albert Reynolds, after he left office, made no effort to conceal his business interests in Iraq. When Reynolds became chairman of an Irish-based oil exploration company, Bula Resources, in 1999, the company pointed out that the ex-Taoiseach's contacts in Libya and Iraq would significantly enhance Bula's position. The extraordinary general meeting of Bula which approved Reynolds's appointment as chairman was told that he was receiving 87.5 million penny shares under a once-off option scheme granted because of these Libyan and Iraqi contacts.

It is clear, moreover, that Reynolds had a personal stake in Iraqi oil even before he took up this Bula position. A subsequent Bula AGM was told that Reynolds would receive a 3.75 per cent share in an oil development in the western desert of Iraq if Bula was granted a licence to drill by the Saddam Hussein regime.[8] According to Reynolds, this stake arose from an agreement with a consultant, Bill Griffin, which predated his appointment as chairman of Bula. Griffin, a petroleum specialist who described himself as Bula's 'main negotiator with the Arab countries', said he had given Reynolds this personal stake in the oilfield concession because Reynolds had called for UN sanctions against Iraq to be lifted. Reynolds also explained to the Bula AGM in 1999 that the oilfield in question, Block 4, was 'much sought after, a very good, highly-prospective block', but that its full development depended on a lifting of sanctions. He also stressed that he was not claiming any 'extreme influence' with the Saddam regime.[9]

In Haughey's case, the mystery deepened even further as the nature of his rapacity was revealed. It became possible to see, broadly, where the money to feed his lavishness was coming from – for every year except the year when Goodman's deal with Saddam's regime was in operation; 1988 turned out to be a blank. He kept spending money at the usual rapid rate, but none of it was coming from the Guinness & Mahon accounts that otherwise always paid his bills. The tribunal of inquiry later hunted through all other bank accounts associated with Haughey's bagman Des Traynor 'but none of these accounts appeared to have been the source of funding in 1988'.[10]

There was some hinterland that always remained unmapped, some set of connections between Dublin and Baghdad that would shed light on the weird way Irish politics was functioning – if only it could be established. But this was another story that could never quite cohere. Reynolds feared its revelation even more than he feared the other mysteries of the Irish system, even more than abortion. Before his boss's appearance at the beef tribunal, Seán Duignan attended a briefing by a barrister who was acting for the state. As he left, he remarked to Reynolds's adviser Tom Savage that 'it's a hundred times more complicated than abortion'. Another adviser, Bart Cronin, had already warned Duignan: 'If you think the X case thing gets Albert wound up, wait until the Beef Tribunal starts motoring. That's what really gets to him.'[11]

For Reynolds the probing of his relations with Goodman was 'a constantly tormenting affront'.[12] He was so obsessed by it that he drove himself out of power over it – twice. His first government was a coalition with the Progressive Democrats, formed by Des O'Malley after he was expelled from Fianna Fáil for conduct unbecoming. In Opposition, O'Malley had been one of the people who had done most to raise in the Dáil the scandal of the Iraq deal. When Reynolds came to give his own evidence to the tribunal, he went out of his way to accuse O'Malley of being 'reckless, irresponsible and dishonest' in his own previous sworn evidence – essentially of perjury. It was astonishing to watch this, to see a Taoiseach sabotaging his own government in real time. In the subsequent general election, Reynolds brought Fianna Fáil to a new low, with the loss of ten seats. He then formed a new coalition with another fierce critic of his relationship with Goodman, Dick Spring of the Labour Party. But, in July 1994, he again destroyed his own government over the beef issue. So fixated was he on what the tribunal report would say about him that, when it was sent to government, he seized it and refused to allow Labour ministers or advisers to see it.

When Spring's press secretary Fergus Finlay went to government buildings to collect a copy, he 'went down to the Taoiseach's office which is at the end of a long corridor on the first floor. I'd often been there before and was astonished to find halfway down the corridor a set of double doors that I had never noticed before – and certainly never saw locked before. They were locked tonight and my knocking on them produced no result.'[13] Spring, when he phoned Reynolds's office, was told (falsely) that he was not in the building and could not be contacted. Even though there had been an agreement in cabinet that the only statement on the report would be a joint one by both leaders, Reynolds then put out a statement with a few highly selective and equally misleading quotes from the report and claimed that he had been 'fully vindicated' by the judge.

This behaviour was demented. That the government did not collapse immediately was because there was a real possibility of dramatic developments in Northern Ireland. But Reynolds had shattered the trust that his administration needed and it was only a matter of time before it would fall apart. There was something about this whole story that drove him to self-destruction, even on the brink of one of the great achievements of modern Irish politics. I never managed to understand exactly what it was. If the truth was out there, it was out there somewhere in Baghdad.

34

1993: True Confessions

I got my first job in the summer of 1972, working as a boy assistant for Dunnes Stores in George's Street in the centre of the city. I remember the year because it has a soundtrack. My immediate boss John – really just a nineteen-year-old trainee manager in a cheap pinstripe suit – lived three stops further up the 81 bus route from Crumlin into town. I had no choice but to sit beside him for the journey. He was a nice guy but he liked to sing on the bus. At the top of his voice. And he had one song, the one that had been playing over and over for months on Irish radio, Shel Silverstein's 'Sylvia's Mother'. John would start low, as we went down Clogher Road. But by the time we got to Leonard's Corner, he'd be sobbing in a Texas-Crumlin drawl: 'Pulleeese Mississ Ay Vurry, I've just godda talk to err / Ah'll owny keep errr a why-ill.' He would do it every morning and every morning I would sit rigid with mortification. It was not just that people would think I was part of this shameless act. It was that this histrionic mishmash of Ireland and America was hideously uncool.

It is not quite as decorous as Proust's madeleine, but John's renditions of 'Sylvia's Mother' came into my head twenty years later in February 1992 when the news broke that Ben Dunne, scion of the retail dynasty that owned and developed the Dunnes Stores chain of clothes and food shops that were a cornerstone of Irish modernity, had been arrested in Florida, charged with trafficking in cocaine. He had gone crazy in the Grand Cypress hotel in Orlando. There was something apt about this other mishmash of Irish history and expensive American hotels. Just as Annie Murphy's last encounter with Eamonn Casey in the Grand Hyatt the previous summer had opened an aperture into one kind of Irish reality, Ben Dunne's freak-out in the Grand Cypress lifted the lid on another.

My own traumatic memory of the trainee manager who sang on the bus brought to mind a day that summer that I spent with Ben Dunne, or Young Ben, as he was called then to distinguish him from his father, who had founded the empire in Cork during the Second World War. In 1972, Dunnes had just bought a rival shop on George's Street, Cassidy's. I was ordered to help Young Ben move stock from Cassidy's down to Dunnes. We spent hours, just the two of us, wheeling rails loaded with dresses down the busy street, dodging pedestrians and traffic. It seemed completely mad – there was easily a truck load of stock to be shifted. Why had they not bothered to do it the obvious way? It also seemed very menial for the boss's son. He was twenty-two and heir to a dynasty. I was fourteen and being paid fifteen pence an hour. The task placed us both on the same level.

He was not surly, just taciturn and a little gruff. We were constantly at the far ends of a rail from each other, so we were not able to talk much, and even if we could we had nothing in common. I just wondered what was going on. They could have sent my travelling companion John to do the job and he could have serenaded the traffic we were holding up as we forced the swaying garments across its path. Was Young Ben being humiliated, taught a lesson, kept in his place? I would see Old Ben around the store sometimes and he seemed stern and dour and quietly menacing. Once, trying to impress a girl who worked on the shop floor, I did a crude impression of Old Ben for her. She laughed and told me that, yes, that was just like her grandfather. So maybe this was just the ritual of the family business, that the prince would have to do the grunt work before he could inherit the throne. In a very rare interview, given to the *Irish Times*, Old Ben said that it was his intention that 'the whole six [members of the] Dunne family would kill themselves working'.[1]

It seemed that, even though he was the youngest of five siblings, Young Ben was always the chosen one. He was given his father's name and when the paterfamilias duly died in 1983, the leadership of the company did indeed pass to him, along with sixty-four branches and 3,500 employees. What he had not been given was much of a formal education – his father disapproved of it and Young Ben left school at sixteen. It was presumably important that he had earned it by working at all levels of the company, even if that meant pushing dresses down the street with a skinny fourteen-year-old kid from Crumlin.

What he inherited was not just a retail empire. It was a part of the story of Irish modernization. His accession was given the personal blessing of the primary author of that story, T. K. Whitaker, who assured the nation that 'the enterprise and management skills of the parents have been inherited by their children and the future of Dunnes Stores is in capable hands'. Old Ben Dunne was from the same village, Rostrevor in Co. Down, as Whitaker. He was planning to emigrate to the United States, but Whitaker's father persuaded him that he had a future in retail and helped him get a job south of the Border in a drapery shop in Drogheda. When he died in 1983, a discreet appreciation appeared in the *Irish Times*, signed TKW – Whitaker's own initials. He rather wistfully noted that his own father's intervention in Ben Dunne's life 'probably diverted him from achieving even bigger success on a bigger stage', suggesting that he would have been a big shot even in the US, and that Ireland's gain was America's loss.[2] But this was also what made Dunne an ideal figure of the Lemass–Whitaker project – an American-style self-made man pouring his energies into the new Ireland.

What made Dunne even more perfect as an exemplar was that, along with American business culture, his other model was the Catholic Church: 'I run my place like the Catholic Church. The Catholic Church is a very successful organization. I said "you can have the parish priests the bishops and the curates but you've got to get the Cardinals and the Pope before you get Dunnes Stores". When you tell me the Pope is infallible, certainly he's bloody well infallible. You know why? Because the Catholic Church runs the Pope not the Pope runs the Catholic Church. If he didn't do the job they'd fire him… and it's the same thing in Dunnes Stores. I've always made it that Dunnes Stores is the boss, not me.'[3]

In 1966, Old Ben had opened the first American-style mall in Ireland, on a fifteen-acre site in south Dublin called Cornelscourt. He promised a 'fully integrated modern centre of superstores, shops, motel, steak house and filling station'.[4] It was officially opened by Seán Lemass's wife, a mark of approval for the kind of prosperity it augured, an American life at home.[5] Even that term 'filling station' was American – Irish people said 'petrol station'. Old Ben attended the conventions and seminars of the US National Retail Merchants Association and was even elected to its board of directors in 1970.[6]

But, in fact, Old Ben's great insight was that Ireland had no version of the British retail giant, Marks & Spencer. M&S was too expensive. Dunnes created its own brand, St Bernard, an imitation of M&S's St Michael. Most of its clothes were made in Ireland and produced more cheaply. Gradually, the company became brilliantly adept at imitation. It had affordable versions of the latest fashions in its shops apparently within weeks of them appearing in Britain. It was telling that Dunnes eventually opened a branch in Fuengirola on the Spanish Costa del Sol, so that the new generation of Irish people who could afford foreign holidays could still feel at home.

This mattered. Dunnes grew alongside the new working and lower middle classes. It gave us confidence. I remember my sisters, as they came into their teenage years, always looking great when they were going out because there was enough money to buy them stuff that looked new, up to date. There was a world of difference between a knock-off and a hand-me-down. Young Irish people quite liked the idea that what they were wearing was a native imitation. That, after all, was the mix we were going for – our own brand of what was out there in the modern world. If you were wearing something nice and someone asked where you got it, you would say 'Dunnéz' in a mock French accent, the joke both deflecting shame and claiming pride. It spoke of a certain confidence.

The Irish labour movement recognized that Dunnes had an even better feel for the rise of this more self-confident working class than it did itself. In 1990, the general secretary of the Irish

Congress of Trade Unions, Peter Cassels, told me of the years when he had travelled the country building up union organizations: 'If you were giving an intelligence report back to headquarters as to the position in a particular town where you'd been, one of your rules of thumb was: Is there a Dunnes Stores there? That gave you an indication that there was a sufficient number of working people in that town with an income that Dunnes felt it worthwhile to put a shop there. In a sense, they were doing the market research for us. That would be a sign that that was a town that should be serviced by us as well, in terms of running shop stewards' courses or establishing a trades council. And, as a rule of thumb, it has certainly worked for us.'[7]

Charles Haughey did not understand this. In March 1968, he flew to New York to open a new office for the Irish tourist board, Bord Fáilte, and to launch an Irish Trade Fair in a hotel in Manhattan. One of the most prominent stands was Ben Dunne's display of drip-dry Bri-nylon shirts. Haughey, whose own shirts were handmade in Paris, was furious. He confronted Dunne, referring to a flea market in Dublin: 'What do you think this is, the fucking Iveagh Market?'[8] He instructed officials from the Irish Trade Board to dismantle Dunne's stand. It was an act of open humiliation and contempt, and also an indication of his own insecurity. Perhaps, having grown up at a time when the Irish were the descaminados of Europe, he felt that the shirtless ones could clothe their nakedness only in the Charvet chemises he himself favoured, and certainly not in drip-dry nylon.

Yet that insecurity eventually worked the other way. In 1987, when Haughey was back as Taoiseach, he was again anxious to parlay power into large payments from rich supporters. Young Ben was now in charge of the family empire. Haughey knew Noel Fox, an accountant who was the closest financial adviser to Young Ben, as he had been to his father. He had been intimately involved in the payment of a ransom to the IRA after it kidnapped Young Ben and demanded £500,000 for his release. His six days in captivity were undoubtedly traumatic, but, in keeping with the family virtues, he had no counselling and returned to work immediately on his release.

Old Ben was publicity shy. 'If there is one thing I hate, it's publicity. No one's allowed to write about Ben Dunne, for anyone could have done what I did but they didn't do it. That's the only difference. The two people I don't like are people who talk about what they are doing and the people who talk about what they're going to do.'[9] But in that rare interview, Old Ben mentioned how impressed he was when he was walking down a street in Florida and 'I saw an advertisement for an undertaker that said "Willie Snuffit, the man who makes dying a pleasure". He did big business.'

It was in Florida over twenty years later that his son's pleasure also became a time of dying. Young Ben had developed a cocaine habit that made him feel grandiose. He had also developed a Charlie habit of a different nature, but with similar effects. In May 1987, shortly after Haughey had come back into power, the manager of Dunnes Stores in Bangor, Co. Down, wrote out a sterling cheque for £285,000. The payee was a shell company called Tripleplan, whose directors, John Furze and John Collins, were the Cayman Islands bankers who ran that end of the Ansbacher scheme. The cheque was transferred to Des Traynor's Guinness & Mahon in Dublin and used to pay a debt owed by Charlie Haughey.[10]

Sometime earlier, probably after Haughey became Taoiseach again in February 1987, Ben Dunne had asked Noel Fox to arrange an introduction. Fox spoke to Haughey's bagman Des Traynor who told him that the Boss had a money problem and that he was asking six business people to each contribute £150,000 to clear his debts. When Fox told Dunne about this, his response was to imagine Haughey as Jesus: 'I think Haughey is making a huge mistake trying to get six or seven people together… Christ picked twelve apostles and one of them crucified him.'[11] Dunne said he would pay the whole £900,000 from a slush fund in the Far East but that he needed to do it in stages.

In November, Traynor asked urgently for another £205,000 for the Boss. Another cheque to Furze was sent from the manager of Dunnes in Bangor and then on to the Ansbacher deposits in Dublin. Within a month, Haughey had spent it all, some clearing debts but much of it to pay for his lordly lifestyle. In July 1988, Traynor asked for £471,000, which was sent from a Swiss bank account owned by Dunne to Furze's account in Knightsbridge. In October 1988, Dunne gave a cheque, made out to cash, to Haughey's son Ciarán for 'consultancy services' that involved advising him on what kind of helicopter he might buy. In spring of 1989, there was another £150,000 sterling from the Swiss account; and in February 1990 £200,000 sterling from an Isle of Man account controlled by Dunne. This took the total paid directly to Haughey to more than £1 million sterling – much more than the £900,000 Dunne had actually promised. He seemed not to notice. In November 1990, he had another £200,000 sterling transferred from his Far East stash to Haughey's Ansbacher account.

In November 1991, when Haughey was at bay politically, Dunne was playing golf in north Dublin and arranged to call in on the Boss for a cup of tea in Abbeville. Dunne found Haughey depressed and decided to cheer him up. As he was about to leave, he took from his pocket three bank drafts, each for £70,000 sterling. They were made out to 'fictitious persons' – more ghosts.[12] On impulse, he handed them to Haughey: 'look, that's something for yourself.' Haughey replied: 'Thank you, big fella.' He gave them to Traynor, who had them lodged in the usual Ansbacher Cayman accounts.[13] They were not the last payments: after Haughey's fall, he got another three cheques totalling £180,000 from Dunne.[14]

In all, between 1987 and 1992 Young Ben gave the Boss at least £1.8 million. Why did he do it? Haughey had humiliated his father. Dunne did not need him – his own empire was a real power base in Ireland. Dunne could control his own politicians if he wanted to. The rising star in the other main party, Fine Gael, was Michael Lowry. Lowry set up a refrigeration company to work exclusively for Dunnes. He was paid hundreds of thousands of pounds through offshore bank accounts in order to evade tax. Lowry rose to be chairman of the party and then a senior and influential government minister. As a tribunal of inquiry concluded, 'By evading tax in this way, Mr Michael Lowry made himself vulnerable to all kinds of pressures from Dunnes Stores had they chosen to apply these pressures. The threat to disclose the payments and the offshore accounts could have been used by

Dunnes Stores to obtain favours, as indeed could a threat to cut off this source of income to Mr Michael Lowry.'[15]

There is no real sense that Dunne sought to control Haughey in this way. It seems much more like a kind of addiction – the repeated buzz of knowing that he was important to the man who embodied the state. Being called Big Fella by the biggest fella was the main reward. Perhaps the sense of being in on a secret of his own devising also satisfied some need to be on the inside.

Yet the idea of Haughey's secret life was itself becoming ever more surreal. His mistress Terry Keane was writing a gossip column every week in the *Sunday Independent*. The bits that everyone learned to look for were about her lover, usually called Sweetie but sometimes referred to directly as Charlie. In 1990, when he was still in office, she described Lord Henry Mountcharles telling her not to be 'seduced by those in power' to general laughter at the table. After he resigned, the striptease had become ever less coy. 'The international media (CNN et al.) are constantly on to my office to inquire as to how Taoiseach-in-exile Charlie is spending his retirement', she wrote in November 1992. 'With Terry, of course, is the nonchalant reply and to those who need to put their fingers in the side, and there are not many, the laughing couple were to be seen having a cozy few drinks (Montrachet and Scotch on the rocks) in the pub in Abbeville last Tuesday.'[16] Abbeville, it is worth remembering, was the family home that Haughey shared with his wife.

On his golf trip to Florida in February 1992, the same month that Miss X was prevented from leaving Ireland to have an abortion, Ben Dunne ordered a huge bag of cocaine, containing at least forty grammes. Under its influence, he talked incessantly to the sex workers he also ordered to his room about his business in Ireland but also about 'the Catholic Church and Confession'.[17] When he moved to the $1,200-a-night suite 1708 in the Grand Cypress, he took the cocaine with him. At 1.30 in the morning, he was joined by another sex worker, Denise Wojcik. They shared the cocaine, doing between twenty and twenty-five lines, and emptied the minibar.[18] By around eight in the morning, Dunne had become psychotically paranoid. He picked up a piece of wood and became, as Wojcik recalled, 'like some crazed King Kong, jumping up and down and swinging this object over his head'. Wojcik made her way to the lobby and told the security manager that 'a man from Ireland had gone mad'.

In a weird coincidence, the same seventeenth floor of the Grand Cypress was occupied at the same time by the great icons of a new form of global Irishness, the rock band U2. They were about to launch in Florida what would come to be regarded as the most spectacular stadium rock show ever staged, the Zoo TV tour. Even weirder is that one of the daring innovations of the show was a video confession booth where fans could look into the camera and tell it their most intimate secrets. Some of these would then be streamed during the concert. While Ben Dunne was raving to escorts about the Catholic Church and Confession, his compatriots a few doors away were about to launch a parody of the same sacrament.

When the hotel security staff heard that an Irishman was going mad on the seventeenth floor, they assumed that this must be typical rock star behaviour. They contacted U2's security staff, and they all made their way up there. In fact, the band members were down in the lobby, preparing to go for rehearsals. When another sex worker that Dunne had called arrived, she was surprised to see three police cars and an ambulance outside the hotel, but even more freaked out when Bono walked out past her. 'I've always been a fan', she recalled, 'but it hardly seemed the time to introduce myself.'[19] There was another odd echo of the past – when Bono told U2's manager that a guy named Dunne had been arrested at the hotel with cocaine, they both assumed that he must one of the Dunnes who had introduced heroin to Dublin.

The police found Dunne on the balcony outside his room, still in a state of extreme agitation. He was hog-tied, cuffed at the wrists and ankles and carried out of the room on a pole held over the shoulders of two officers, like a big beast being brought home from the hunt. The police also found the bag that still had 32.5 grammes of cocaine in it – enough for Dunne to be charged with trafficking rather than mere possession. (The search had been screwed up legally, so the charge later had to be downgraded.)

The story was sensational, but not immediately of any great political significance. And yet suite 1708 in the Grand Cypress in Orlando, conveniently close to Disneyland, was another site of modern Irish revelation. Because of his meltdown, three of his siblings, led by the formidable Margaret Heffernan, moved against Dunne in February 1993 and succeeded in having him removed as chairman of the company and from all executive functions. Ben sued and the struggle for control of the company went to the courts. Haughey was collateral damage in this boardroom dynastic war.

At some point, Ben had taunted Margaret, telling her that he had made payments of £1 million to Haughey. (It seems apt that he had forgotten that he had in fact handed over almost twice as much.) Margaret, who carried her father's resentment of Haughey from the 1968 humiliation over Bri-nylon shirts, visited Abbeville and asked Haughey if this was true. He told her he couldn't be responsible for what her 'unstable' brother said or for 'wild rumours' that were going around. She then visited Des Traynor, who also denied knowing anything. But in pleadings in a legal action to try to break up the family trust, Ben Dunne himself claimed that he had paid Haughey (as he thought) £1.1 million. This information leaked out on 3 December 1996, when Cliff Taylor reported in the *Irish Times* that 'A prominent Fianna Fáil figure is believed to have received more than £1 million from Dunnes Stores in the early 1990s.'[20] The figures came from a report commissioned by Margaret Heffernan from the accountants Price Waterhouse. Everyone knew who the prominent figure must be. So, of course, did Haughey, who made seventeen calls to, and had several meetings with, Ben Dunne's lawyer and fixer, Noel Smyth, between December 1996 and February 1997.

But by March 1997, Dunne had admitted the payments that he remembered to a tribunal of inquiry established to look into the relationship between Dunnes Stores and both Haughey and Lowry. Haughey made a written statement to the tribunal: 'I never had to concern myself about my personal finances as Desmond Traynor took over control of my personal financial affairs from about 1960 onwards. He saw to it as his personal responsibility to ensure that I would be free to devote my time and ability to public life and that I would not be distracted from my political work by financial concerns.'[21] He admitted getting £1.3 million from Dunne, but flatly denied that he had accepted the three bank drafts made out to fictitious persons totalling £210,000. It was easy to see why: they blew his story about having no knowledge of his own finances. (So, of course, did the scam he had pulled with Brian Lenihan's medical expenses, but that was as yet unknown.)

I was in Dublin Castle in July 1997 when Haughey finally appeared before the tribunal of inquiry. Less than five years previously, I had watched how he had answered questions in the same place and before many of the same lawyers, when he gave evidence over three days to the beef tribunal. He had retired by then, but he was still patently the Boss. He swept into Dublin Castle like a potentate, surrounded by his minions, and he made no real effort to disguise the disdain he felt for the petty people who imagined in their folly that they could hold him to account under cross-examination.

He was, back then, by turns languidly contemptuous and thunderously indignant. He dismissed some central and accurate allegations as not amounting 'to a row of beans'. 'I wonder', he sneered, 'what we're all doing here.' He described other questions about his conduct of public policy as mere 'details' that it would be absurd to expect a man of his stature to be concerned with. In response to one mildly critical question from a barrister, his eyes withdrew behind their hooded lids like a weasel watching for the kill and he spat out the words: 'I won't have it. I won't listen to it.'

Watching him then it was clear that this was not a mere performance. It sprang from a profound assurance of his own invulnerability. The authority of the Catholic Church may have been dealt a paralyzing blow a few months earlier with the revelation of Eamonn Casey's relationship with Annie Murphy. The mystique of Fianna Fáil itself may have been fatally undermined by Mary Robinson's victory over Brian Lenihan in the 1990 presidential election. Stray pieces of his own past (most notably his involvement with Seán Doherty in the tapping of journalists' phones) may have already returned to haunt him. But over those few days on which he gave evidence to the beef tribunal every word, every gesture of his, marked him as the last of the untouchables.

It was not hard to guess at the sources of his bitter impatience of being called to account and his supreme confidence that he would emerge untouched. Had he not leapt over every grave dug for him in the previous thirty years? He had come out of the arms trial with a declaration of innocence. He had, with astonishing resilience, returned from the political wilderness to lead his party. He had headed off all internal challenges, forcing his enemies into retirement or exile from Fianna Fáil. He pulled off the most astonishing strokes, hammered out the most unlikely deals, evaded responsibility for the most outrageous scandals.

As his political epitaph he had chosen, on his last day as Taoiseach, a line from *Othello*: 'I have done the state some service.' I thought he might more appropriately have chosen one from another Shakespearean tragedy, *Antony and Cleopatra*: 'Comest thou smiling from the world's great snare uncaught?' He had passed through a forest of snares, if not quite smiling, then certainly uncaught.

Five years later, watching him again in the same place, facing lawyers' questions, he was a hollow man. Now that he had been snared, he seemed to shrink into the vast gap between his image and his reality. A man whose love of abstract grandiloquence did not preclude petty, self-serving and barefaced lies. A man who almost wept when talking of his devotion to the institutions of the state and then thought little of treating a tribunal of inquiry established by parliament with contempt by attempting to flatly deny the truth. A man of infinite pride without sufficient self-respect to keep him from becoming a kept man. A self-proclaimed patriot whose spiritual home was in the Cayman Islands. A lover of his country who could treat it as a Banana Republic. A leader who called for sacrifices from the people but was not prepared to sacrifice a tittle of the trimmings of wealth and luxury to the cause of preserving the dignity of the state he professed to serve. A man who, in his Channel Four film had declared himself 'perhaps a little sentimental, even romantic in my loyalties to people' yet was happy to sneer at one 'unstable' friend who had given him a small fortune and to steal from another's medical fund.

In the end, it was his own evidence at the inquiry in 1997 that achieved the impossible: who else could, in the course of two hours, so completely demolish the myths that had been forty years in the making? Time and again politicians and journalists had tried and failed to cut him down to size. By presenting himself as a hapless victim of circumstance, he did the job himself with devastating efficiency. Rather than hand his image of command over to his enemies, he chose to scuttle it himself. He had been the man of extraordinary shrewdness and perspicacity, his eye on the ball, his fingers pulling the strings, the man who knew all the secrets, who had a long memory and a formidable grasp of detail. An essential aspect of this appeal was that all of this terrifying craftiness was being used on our behalf.

But now, in the witness box, he chose to present himself very differently. He was an extraordinarily passive creature. Far from having a mind of legendary sharpness, he could not even remember Ben Dunne coming to his house and giving him bank drafts totalling £210,000 pounds. His memory of such events was, in his own words, 'increasingly remote and confused'. Asked what he did when he 'discovered' the apparent truth that Traynor, the bagman to whom he had entrusted everything, had raised huge sums for him while he was in office he said meekly, 'I accepted it.'

This very diminishment undercut the sense of revelation, the hoped-for feeling of long-hidden truths being divulged at last. There was nothing much, after all, to reveal. It had really been not much of a con job – anyone who wanted to know, knew all along the essence, if not the detail, of the truth. It had all been a case of the Tinkerbell effect. Haughey had been kept in existence by the belief of his audience. That drug of wilful self-delusion had simply worn off and the Haughey of myth vanished.

35

1993–1994: Angel Paper

On a Saturday afternoon in October 1993, a shy, polite young man, Thomas Begley, went into Frizzell's fish shop on the Shankill Road, the heartland of the Protestant side of West Belfast. He played the flute and drums in the Carrick Hill Martyrs Band and graduated from there to membership of the IRA. It seems likely that, less than a year earlier, he had shot a young Protestant man, Stephen Waller, who was home on leave from his posting with the British army in Cyprus.[1] Now, Begley and another IRA member, Seán Kelly, went into the fish shop wearing white coats to give the impression that they were making a delivery.

The bomb they were carrying went off prematurely and Begley was blown to bits. Nine innocent civilians were killed, and fifty-seven people were injured, including a seventy-nine-year-old woman and two two-year-old baby boys. The dead included a married couple, George and Gillian Williamson, a seven-year-old girl, Michelle Baird, who died along with both her parents, and Leanne Murray, who was thirteen and who had gone into the shop to buy a tub of whelks.

The IRA justified the massacre on the basis that its target was the West Belfast brigade of the Loyalist paramilitary organization, the Ulster Defence Association, which had been terrorizing the Catholic community under the flag of its murder squad, the Ulster Freedom Fighters (UFF). It had held meetings in an office above the shop. In fact, the UFF was no longer using the office, which was empty. But in any case, the possibility of detonating a bomb in a shop on a busy Saturday afternoon without killing innocent civilians was so remote as to be practically non-existent. The whole operation had, alongside its horror, a purposeless malignity. There was, at that time, a feeling in the air that the IRA might well be edging towards a ceasefire, and perhaps to a winding down of its armed campaign. The Shankill massacre made this hope seem futile. It felt as if no one was really directing the carnage anymore, as if the violence was an independent, unstoppable force.

In the days leading up to the massacre, I was standing on the street in the Catholic enclave of New Lodge, just north of the Shankill Road, at the heart of the area that had borne the worst of the violence for twenty-five years. Joe Austin, a Sinn Féin councillor and a senior member of his party's leadership, was at the site of yet another Loyalist assassination attempt, being interviewed by the BBC. It was the middle of the morning and the women, having left their children to school, were doing their day's shopping. Normal life was proceeding but it was a strange kind of normality, overshadowed by fear and anger. As the women emerged from the shops, they noticed Austin being interviewed and they started to gather around him. Within twenty minutes there were about twenty of them, ordinary women in ordinary clothes, their shopping baskets full of the ordinary staples of the poor. And as he talked, they started to shout at him, to badger him. Why isn't the IRA doing something? Why aren't these bastards being taken out? When are they going into the Shankill to punish them?

Austin pleaded and reasoned. He knew they were angry. He knew they were scared but, he said to them 'it's the fear that's talking'. Just imagine, he asked them, how they would feel if the IRA went up the Shankill Road and killed a load of innocent Protestants. They may say they want it, but wouldn't they feel ashamed and shocked? Wouldn't they realize that it was just adding to the suffering and achieving nothing else?

Eventually, the women dispersed. It was hard to know whether they were convinced or not, since what was happening had little to do with abstract conviction and everything to do with the drip-by-drip terror of the UFF's murder campaign. As I followed him around New Lodge and Ardoyne that morning on his rounds of council work, Austin provided a focus for the complex set of emotions that surrounded politics and violence in a nationalist enclave of Belfast. In neat, houseproud rooms where the wallpaper always looked new and ornaments cluttered the mantlepieces, the terrible question still hung in the air. Nice, decent people wanted to know when the IRA was going to 'do something', just as they wanted to know when the Housing Executive was going to fix their tiles. The mundane and the terrible mingled even in the way this rapid man, full of wit and suppressed energy, moved around the housing estates, now kicking a football with the kids on the road, now changing cars in a cul de sac, in case the UFF was following him.

He gave the same response every time the awful question of revenge arose: that it would be very wrong, that the people who wanted it now because they were in a panic would hang their heads in shame and sorrow if it really happened. One middle-aged woman stood up to him. It worked before, she said: tit-for-tat killing worked in the 1970s. It was the only thing that ever stopped them. She did not seem a bloodthirsty woman and it was clear that she believed that such an act of terrible violence would stop the killing around her, would end the torment of regular awfulness, would in the end save lives.

All through those weeks before the Shankill fish shop massacre, in different parts of nationalist Belfast, Sinn Féiners would say the same thing when I asked about the rising panic that the slow torture of the UFF assassinations was causing. Thank God, they would say that the IPLO wasn't around anymore. The Irish People's Liberation Organisation was a particularly vicious breakaway faction that had engaged in naked sectarian attacks on Protestants before it broke up in 1992. Sinn Féin activists seemed convinced that they themselves, and the IRA they supported, were morally different.

Can you imagine, they would ask me, what those lunatics would do in an atmosphere like this? It wouldn't be beyond them to go into the Shankill and wipe out a load of innocent people. The unmistakable feeling was that the IRA wasn't like that anymore, that those crude days were over, that violence was a small and increasingly irrelevant part of a sophisticated self-confident political movement. There was quiet pride in the way they spoke, a conviction that, without people like themselves, the ordinary Protestant people of the Shankill would be in the hands of madmen who would kill them indiscriminately.

In those weeks of moving around those areas, it was possible to observe something of the mechanism that created the harsh terror of those women who wanted blood. To be in the company of a group of West Belfast nationalists when the word came over the radio that another person had been shot was to witness a complex process of response. When a name was mentioned, the first reaction was an exhalation of relief: it isn't a friend or family member. Then there was a process of consultation and recollection. Who do I know of that name? Would that be so and so's brother? The mind was searched for links, for details, for a way of making a connection with the victim so that he becomes real. And in this intimate society, very often some connection was indeed found. And then followed a mixture of shame and anger. Shame at the first reaction of relief, anger that someone has made you go through all this terrible calculation. Even at this small level of private reaction, almost everyone was made in some way complicit with violence.

If a place goes through this process time and again over twenty-five years then these mixed and ambivalent reactions to violence become ingrained. And added to them was a deep suspicion that can look paranoid from the outside, but that looks like common sense from the inside. A few days before the Shankill massacre, I arrived at the corner of Whiterock Road and Springfield Road, the edge of nationalist Ballymurphy, shortly after an attempt had been made to kill the driver of a black taxi waiting on the rank. A car had driven down from the direction of Loyalist Springmartin, across the other side of the peace line, and from it a man had opened up with four shots. The car had driven past, turned back up the road and the gunman had let off another five shots.

In the catalogue of violence, the incident was unimportant. Incredibly, no one was killed or wounded. It didn't make the evening news or the next day's papers. The taxi man who had been the target was back in his taxi a few hours after. But it twisted the rope of terror another bit tighter and in the longer term it reinforced basic political beliefs. That corner was overlooked by one large army fort, the car would have driven past another. There was no objective evidence of any collusion between the would-be killers and the army. But to the people there, used to being watched, used to the idea that the British army sees everything, the obvious question was how come the army hadn't seen the car? How come the would-be killers felt confident enough to turn and come back for a second go before escaping? People see and interpret what is around them, not what people tell them. The very intensity of the presence of the army and the RUC led people to the conclusion that anything terrible that happened was their fault, either because they colluded in it or because they failed to stop it.

And because, over twenty-five years, Catholic West Belfast had learned to distrust media images of itself, information from the outside was seldom allowed to disrupt this basic understanding of its own world. Sinn Féin, in this climate, moved around inside a protective cocoon, as Joe Austin acknowledged to me. The very simplistic image of Sinn Féin and its supporters as mere bloodthirsty thugs actually protected it from the scrutiny it deserved. 'The media image of Sinn Féin which is put across, which is a hard-nosed terrorist entrepreneur, is fine for the media', he said. 'But the reality as seen by people in these areas is almost cocooned. We're almost immune from whatever the media says, which has a good side and a bad side.'

The good side, from his point of view, was that people learned to disbelieve what they heard from the outside and to trust the alternative versions generated by the Republican movement's own propaganda. 'That's the positive side of the cocoonism within the nationalist community. The other side is more dangerous. Probably the best example of it would be in the immediate aftermath of the Enniskillen bomb [in 1987, when the IRA massacred eleven Protestants attending a war memorial service] where any Republican who had any sense of right and wrong felt ashamed and had their heads down as far as their knees, but people were saying "but what about Bloody Sunday?" This whataboutism, I think you can end up pandering to that and you can become a victim of that.'

And yet, even knowing that, even understanding how wrong it is to pander to the blind desire for revenge, Joe Austin ended up in the days after the fish shop massacre at the home of his constituent Thomas Begley, who had died planting the bomb, trying to cope with the disaster that he had told his people should not be allowed to happen. The women who had been warned by him that they would feel grief and shame if what they called for actually happened were now left to bear precisely those emotions. Having constructed a political and electoral identity for itself, Sinn Féin could not escape the violence that it had done so much to sustain.

And the woman who said tit-for-tat killing worked, who felt that one good assault on the Shankill would end the murders of Catholics, was, of course, wrong. On the day of the massacre, Jackie Hewitt, chairman of the Shankill Community Council, was driving back to Belfast from Millisle on the Antrim coast where he had been at a war memorial ceremony. He had the radio on in the car and the news came in that there had been a bomb, that three people were dead. He told me that, blinded by anger, he thought to himself, 'That's it, we need a bomb on the Falls [Road]', the centre of Catholic West Belfast. As he neared the city, he heard another news flash on the radio: seven people were now thought to be dead, and he thought to himself: 'we need two bombs'. But when he got to the scene and stood there amid the grief and anger of his community, his own thoughts haunted him: 'Whenever I heard other people saying what I was thinking', he told me, 'then it frightened me.'

Two weeks later I went with Hewitt, who was now the chairman of the appeal committee for the victims of the atrocity, back to the site of Frizzell's fish shop to organize the removal of the flowers that had covered its emptiness for a fortnight. The gap in the street where the shop had been was eerily neat, just a small hole in an otherwise unaltered façade that seemed to reduce and nullify the scale of the grief it must contain. Its sad sense of absence seemed for many in the Protestant working-class community to symbolize the fate of the world they had once known. Loss, grief, decline

– these were words that cropped up again and again as I spoke to Protestants in West or North Belfast. Or the words on the wall further up the Shankill Road, protesting at the imminent closure of an old people's home, another in a series of abandonments and retreats that had affected this side of the peace line: 'Deprivation Alienation Humiliation Now Evacuation'. The traumatic loss of people in the massacre was for the wider community a dramatic expression of a process of loss that had been slower but no less devastating, the slow erosion of the world of industrial might and Protestant power. That dark absence lent itself to a kind of nihilism that expressed itself in murderous violence against Catholics.

In spite of the wishes of people like Jackie Hewitt, the UFF used the Shankill fish shop massacre as the excuse to step up its campaign of sectarian killings. There were individual murders and then, a week after Shankill, a counter-massacre. Two UFF gunmen entered the packed Rising Sun lounge in the mostly Catholic village of Greysteel, wearing boiler suits and balaclavas. One of them called out 'trick or treat'. A woman, thinking this was a Halloween stunt, turned and said, 'That's not funny'. The gunmen shot nineteen people, killing eight of them, including James Moore, who was eighty-one.[2] He was a friend of the father of one of his killers.

Hewitt told me that most people on the Shankill were sickened by Greysteel but added, 'although when you probed that bit deeper they looked upon Greysteel as something that was inevitable after what happened on the Shankill'. That was the dynamic of violence on both sides – the belief that it was inevitable made it inevitable. Violence, that was supposed to be an expression of power, had actually become an expression of powerlessness.

The IRA's armed struggle, meanwhile, was regarded on the Catholic side of the divide as a static element in a fluid situation, as having reached a state of equilibrium where 'we're not going to drive the British army into the sea and they're not going to drive the IRA into the hills'. It was seen as a constant, a kind of permanent standoff in which neither victory nor defeat was possible. The Sinn Féin voting community was neither sufficiently appalled by it to force it to stop, nor sufficiently enamoured of it to demand that it continue. It was seen as merely a fact of life. It was no longer really about a United Ireland. It was about itself. It was a closed loop of action and reaction – and of self-justification. The big reason not to stop was that doing so would render the last twenty-five years of suffering meaningless. The killing continued in order to validate the killing.

Yet even in the middle of this mayhem there was a sense of the mundane slowly asserting itself. I could see then that the political need for the IRA and Sinn Féin to play down the cost of the armed campaign, to assert the community's infinite capacity for endurance, was being increasingly undermined by two important changes in Republican culture. One was that the Sinn Féin leadership was getting older. In almost every Republican household I visited there were young children. To sit, for example, in Sinn Féin councillor Anne Anderson's home in Twinbrook and see the bullet holes on the sitting-room wall after a UFF attack, was to witness a personal vulnerability at odds with the battle-hardened image. The bright young schoolgirls sitting on the sofa told me they were afraid to come downstairs after dark, afraid to let their mother out of their sight.

Even for those who had not suffered attack, the sense of vulnerability and of the preciousness of life involved in having children was an important source of change. Mairtín Ó Muilleoir, one of the party's younger councillors, who became involved at the age of twenty-one during the 1981 hunger strike, recognized the process: 'I think your attitude to everything changes as you get older. I think that I'm not as young as I was when I first got involved in politics and I'm not as naive. That colours your attitude to everything in life. I think when you have children of your own, you realize how dreadfully wounding it is for children to get hurt. I think when you experience loss, then you move on to another plateau of understanding other people's losses. When you're sixteen, you might have a comic book idea of what a war is about, what a conflict is about. As you get older, you lose that… I think now I will take a much more sober and sombre attitude to killings, to people getting killed, whether it's those people shot by the Loyalists or someone shot in South Armagh by the IRA.'

The other important change was that the shift to community activism had itself made it increasingly difficult for Republicans to ignore the daily cost of the armed struggle for their own communities. Being on the streets, knocking on doors, attending meetings – all of this wins votes but it also makes it impossible to avoid the rough realities of everyday life. Shortly before the Shankill bombing, I went around the streets of Ballymurphy with the former hunger striker Pat McGeown, now a Sinn Féin councillor. It was like seeing a legend brought to earth. Here was a man who was part of a mythic event, who endured forty-two days of the 1981 hunger strike, before he lapsed into a coma and his family took him off it. Now, twelve years later, he was making his way around ordinary houses to talk to harassed people about cracked walls and uneven pavements, disability cheques and electricity bills. He was so nearly a martyr, so nearly a face on a mural, so nearly sanctified. There was a deep incongruity in this quiet, modest man knocking on doors and listening to the everyday miseries of people, the miseries of poverty made much worse by the IRA's endless war.

At the same time as Joe Austin was being berated on the streets because the IRA hadn't yet attacked the Shankill, his constituency manager told him to call to an old lady's house where there was a problem. The cat from next door wouldn't stop spraying the flowers in her garden. She made it clear that she wanted the IRA to do something about it. Austin called next door, where an unshaven man in a vest looked up from his newspaper and said, 'Hello, Joe, I suppose it's about the cat.' 'It is.' 'Look, I'll tell you what. It's not my cat at all. I'm just minding it for a friend. I'll leave it back and you can get that oul' wan off my back.' 'Good man.' Austin went back to the old lady's door: 'That's okay about the cat. You'll have no more trouble.' The woman was awestruck: 'Did you get it shot? Did the IRA shoot it? Is it dead?'

In order to expand as a political force, the IRA and Sinn Féin had to reduce themselves, to come down from the commanding heights of martyrdom and deal with the humdrum, the banal, the unheroic. This created a momentum towards politics, a logic of pragmatism. In itself, this would not have been enough to generate the willpower needed to stop the armed struggle. But there were also those generational forces of exhaustion and fear. A crucial cohort of activists was simply tired – their 'long war' had gone on too long. They were afraid, not so much for themselves, as for their kids. Paradoxically, one of the great pressures towards making it all stop was that it did not need to stop. It had settled down into a background noise of obscenities punctuated by occasional atrocities. It was infinitely sustainable. What I sensed on the ground was a knowledge among the generation now in control of the IRA that, if this did not end now, it would replenish itself. It would consume the lives of their children just as it had consumed their own.

There was a window of time before the new wave of kids with their comic-book view of war took over. People knew this. John Hume, leader of the majority nationalist party the SDLP, had been talking to Gerry Adams since 1991. The British government was talking to the IRA. Albert Reynolds, the Fianna Fáil Taoiseach with his gambler's instincts and pure pragmatism, was pushing for a deal. Formulae of words were being written down by officials on what the Irish referred to as non-paper and the British called angel paper – documents that had no status, that could be disowned or made to disappear but that occupied the liminal zone where possibilities might germinate.[3]

Hume was the moral and intellectual driving force. In the early 1990s, it was easy to lose sight of this fact. I met him from time to time during this period. He was often edgy, depressed, exhausted, a man living on his nerves. He had kept going throughout the Troubles, seeking to keep open a space that was consistently critical of unionism and of British policy but also implacable in its opposition to the IRA's violence. He had taken on the burden of trying to get the IRA to stop the killing. This meant that he had to wade into the moral quagmire. The IRA regarded him with contempt – Sinn Féin mocked that SDLP stood for Stoop Down Low Party. But equally those who hated the IRA lambasted him for allegedly going soft on terrorism, for being a useful idiot who was ushering unrepentant terrorists into the fold of democratic politics.

I was talking to him privately one day in 1993, asking him about some details of the talks, when he suddenly stopped dead, as if overcome by a terrible sense of futility. His face seemed to shrink into itself. 'I'm not well', he said. 'I get very depressed. I'm not able for this anymore. I'm not fit for it.' His voice was full of anguish. We were not friends, merely acquaintances. It felt like he shouldn't be telling me this. But his politician's façade had crumbled, making visible the accumulated distress of the bloody decades, the accrued agony of so many funerals, the unbearable strain of being the one who had to pretend that there was hope while feeling only despair.

It was imposible not to feel for him, but also not to worry about the fragility of a process that depended so heavily on this fragile man. Yet he did go on. He repeated himself. The dismissive joke about Hume was that he had a 'single transferable speech'. It was true. But it was also true that, like an old-fashioned teacher, he said things over and over until he could hear other people saying them back to him. He changed the language. A United Ireland became an 'agreed Ireland'. There was no 'solution', just a 'process'. It was people that must be united, not territory. These were still essentially nationalist ideas but they radically altered the meaning of Irish nationalism, shifting its centre of gravity towards the need to persuade and reconcile with those who did not share its assumptions.

On 15 December 1993, just two months after the Shankill and Greysteel massacres, Reynolds and the British prime minister John Major signed the Downing Street Declaration, a sweetly crafted 'agreed framework for peace'. It made clear that the British government had no 'selfish, strategic or economic interest' in holding onto Northern Ireland, that it would uphold the wishes of the majority there on whether to support continued membership of the Union or a United Ireland and that this self-determination was a matter for agreement between the two parts of Ireland to be reached on the basis of consent. It was the angel paper, so exquisitely balanced between the competing demands and rights that it could hover in the air and never have to land on either side.

But Reynolds was also, in the manoeuvring that followed,

admirably sharp. He wanted the IRA to declare a ceasefire. It was becoming obvious that the IRA would offer a temporary cessation of violence. Reynolds had an instinct for time, for the now-or-never that was this moment in history. He would have no truck with the temporary. He wanted a permanent ceasefire and he wanted it declared in 'language that an eleven-year-old can understand. No messing – there's to be no messing.'[4] This roughness was essential. The complex language of ambiguities in the frameworks and agreements had to be underpinned by a simple bluntness of intent. The creative 'messing' that was required to arrive at formulations of intricate nuance could not be messed up by ambiguities about killing. Death, as so many had found, is not temporary or uncertain. The IRA was either going to stop inflicting it or it was not.

This clarity was coercive. The doubleness that had sustained the IRA and Sinn Féin since the hunger strikes – electoral politics and mass killing, political party and private army, victim and perpetrator – was of a piece with the larger Irish capacity for being in two minds simultaneously. In other areas of Irish life, that capacity was radically diminishing. And so, too, with the IRA's campaign. When it declared its ceasefire on 31 August 1994, no one really thought that the rest would be easy, that there was not a long way to go to get a settlement. But the habit had been broken. The violence that fed on itself was gradually running out of sustenance.

36

1998: The Uses of Uncertainty

In the last week of October 1995, US president Bill Clinton was locked in battle with the Mighty Morphin Power Rangers, a group of California high school students who themselves were engaged in an existential struggle against the alien sorceress Rita Repulsa. The arena for the conflict between Clinton and the Power Rangers was Belfast City Council. At stake was the crucial question of which of them would have the honour of turning on the lights for the Christmas tree at City Hall. The council had agreed to pay £7,000 to have the Power Rangers flick the switch on 16 November. But the Northern Ireland Office, the British government's local administration in Belfast, had a different idea: Clinton would do it on 1 December.[1]

Opinions on the council broke down on tribal lines, Sinn Féin favouring Clinton but most Unionists sticking by the Power Rangers. Yet, for once, an agreement was hammered out – Clinton could turn on the Christmas tree lights but the Power Rangers would host a 'family fun night'. As Alliance Party councillor Steve McBride put it, 'we will be the centre of attraction around the world for having the president switch on our lights and the whole of the province will be delighted to see one of the most popular TV programme characters for a night'.[2] To seal the deal, the US government had a bigger and better Tennessee pine tree flown to Belfast from Nashville for the president to illuminate while Catholics and Protestants came together to wave plastic American flags and blow-up baseball bats decorated with the Stars and Stripes.

Canvassed for his opinion, while the issue was still doubtful, one Belfast primary school pupil, Michael Courtney, suggested a compromise: 'Why don't we put Mr Clinton in a Power Rangers suit so he can look like one of them?' This was not an entirely far-fetched idea. It felt at the time that, in search of a deal that might end the Troubles, the president of the United States might well dress up as a Power Ranger. Or as a Teenage Mutant Ninja Turtle, or as Dracula or as Madonna. Northern Ireland's politicians would, and did, try the patience of a saint, but in coaxing them into making a comprehensive peace deal, even the most powerful man on earth would put up with a lot.

Objectively, Clinton's great interest in what was now being called the peace process made no sense. Weighed against, for example, the horrific wars triggered by the breakup of Yugoslavia in the early 1990s, the Troubles were not, even within Europe, all that substantial. After the extreme violence of the early 1970s, when civil war did seem imminent, there was what the British home secretary Reginald Maudling had called, in 1971, an acceptable level of violence. Between 1976 and the Loyalist ceasefire in October 1994, there had been an annual average of eighty-six deaths. This was dreadful, and, if you were Irish, it was a slow burn of anguish and shame. But it was not enough to prevent the feeling that a certain equilibrium of terror had settled in. The murder rate in those years in Northern Ireland was 6 per 100,000 people. In Miami, the mean homicide rate between 1985 and 1994 was 34 per 100,000; in New York it was 25; in Chicago 27. In Washington DC, where Bill Clinton lived, it was 60 – ten times a bad as in Northern Ireland.[3] A cynic might have wondered why Clinton was pouring his energies into ending the violence in a small, sad corner of Europe, when it was flourishing at much greater heights far closer to home.

One obvious answer was that there was a very active Irish-American lobby and that it was important to Clinton. A consequence of two centuries of migration was that Ireland had an outsized presence in the US and thus in the global media. It was also true that the Troubles had the peculiar fascination of white, European Christians killing each other and the epic resonance of a conflict that could be construed as the tragic working out of immemorial history. But the most important truth about the Northern Ireland question was that it was, in fact, answerable. For Clinton, and for Tony Blair who came to power in the UK in 1997, there was something to be won. The Troubles could be ended because they were deeply anomalous.

The elements of a settlement had been clear since 1973, when the British and Irish governments had signed the Sunningdale Agreement, with the support of what were then the main unionist and nationalist parties and the cross-community Alliance Party. That settlement had been wrecked in 1974 by the crippling Ulster Workers' Council strike, supported by hardline Unionists and enforced by the Loyalist paramilitaries. But its broad outlines were always going to be the basis for any possible settlement: the sharing of power in a devolved administration in Belfast between Unionists and nationalists; cross-Border bodies on the island that would deal with relatively noncontentious issues of co-operation but nonetheless establish an 'Irish dimension' to appease nationalist aspirations to unity; and a mutual commitment by the two governments to recognize the principle of consent. Britain would acknowledge that Northern Ireland would stay in the United Kingdom only so long as a majority of its citizens wished it to do so; the Republic of Ireland would accept that a United Ireland could come about only with the consent of that same majority.

The real question was thus not about the rough shape of a deal. It was about who was at the table. Both the IRA and the Loyalist paramilitaries (allied to a wider constituency of militant Unionism led by Ian Paisley) had shown that they could wreck any settlement, not by winning elections, but by the power of violence to feed off itself. In a deeply polarized society, it was all too easy to unleash anarchy, to keep generating the fear and loathing that undermined the mandate of any new regime. Democratic determination – the clear majorities in Britain, Ireland and Northern Ireland that craved a decent compromise – could not assert itself against the undemocratic authority of terror. The real dilemma was not about the construction of a settlement. It was about the inclusion of the second form of authority within the first. How do democracies recognize, through negotiations, the legitimacy of those forces without simultaneously destroying their own?

The key to unlocking this sealed chamber of possibilities was the way the IRA and Sinn Féin had, after the hunger strikes, gradually developed a twin-track strategy, the Armalite and the ballot box, murder plus electoral politics. In its way, this was another typically Irish form of doubleness, a system of compartmentalization that kept two contradictory realities alive by keeping them ostensibly apart. It was hugely successful, but that very success made it unsustainable. It began to fail at the same time as all the other Irish systems of double-mindedness were running into deep trouble.

Part of the problem was that the twin-track strategy had a very limited reach in the Republic. The vast majority of the Republic's population was not ambivalent about one big thing: the basic legitimacy of its democracy. It did not buy the proposition that Sinn Féin had to sell – that one could simultaneously recognize that legitimacy by seeking an electoral mandate and seek to undermine it by claiming that elections didn't really matter because the only true state was the Republic established in 1916 to which the IRA and the IRA alone could claim to be the rightful successor. But for obvious reasons, Catholics in Northern Ireland were much more ambivalent about the democratic legitimacy of the state. Within Northern Ireland, where Sinn Féin under Gerry Adams developed a formidable political machine, the twin-track strategy was much more successful, with the party taking up to 15 per cent of the vote.

Yet, even there, the contradictions between politics and violence became obvious and even ludicrous. While the IRA was bombing the factories, shops and warehouses that provided work, Sinn Féin politicians were demanding jobs for Catholics. While Sinn Féin politicians were denouncing breaches of human and civil rights by the authorities, the IRA was torturing alleged informers, shooting what they called 'anti-social elements' (petty criminals) in the kneecaps for crimes like car theft, and inflicting capital punishment in cruel and unusual ways. (Between 1973 and 1997, Republicans maimed 1,228 people in Catholic communities through 'punishment' shootings for alleged petty crimes. Between 1982 and 1997, they also severely beat 755 such people.[4]) While Sinn Féin was horrified that the British Special Forces were operating a 'shoot to kill' policy against the IRA, the IRA shooting, say, retired policemen, in order to kill them, was perfectly fine. Republicans who denied the legitimacy of the state were, as the local politicians they had become, helping their constituents to claim welfare benefits and public housing made possible by large subventions from the British taxpayer. While the IRA disdained any notion that it needed a democratic mandate for its armed campaign, Sinn Féin placed more and more emphasis on its own democratic mandate as the primary reason why it should be at the negotiating table.

Something had to give, and the Republican leadership knew it. Danny Morrison, who formulated, in a speech to the Sinn Féin Árd Fheis in 1981, the promise that 'with a ballot paper in this hand, and an Armalite in this hand, we [will] take power in Ireland', later admitted to Richard English that 'deep down I knew there were contradictions. I knew there was a ceiling to how far you could go.'[5] But in the perpetually embattled, psychologically fraught world of the conflict, this knowing was very hard to put into fixed thoughts. The most difficult and delicate part of the painfully slow process of reconsideration was the realization, at least by some of its leaders, that there was a fundamental misunderstanding at the very heart of the IRA's campaign. Central to the IRA strategy had been the belief that Protestant allegiance to Britain and refusal to join a United Ireland was just a bluff. In the IRA's narrative of the near future, Britain would declare its intent to withdraw from Northern Ireland. The Protestants would realize that the game was up, accept their fate, and work out a deal with the victorious Republicans, ushering in an era of peace and prosperity. A 'Scenario for Peace' that Adams produced in 1987 set out this fantasy as serious political analysis, though a first draft gave the game away by suggesting that Protestants who did not appreciate the peace and equality they were to be offered would be given grants to resettle on the British mainland.

John Hume, who began a series of private dialogues with Adams in 1988, forced the Republican leadership to confront the hopelessly unreal nature of this scenario. At least some of those at the top of Sinn Féin began to acknowledge that, if a United Ireland was ever to come, the real British presence in Northern Ireland – a million Protestants who regard themselves as British – would have to be persuaded of its virtues. Though the IRA continued to define Protestant consent merely as the right to be consulted about the terms on which the Protestants would enter an all-Ireland state, some voices at the top of the movement began to concede that Republicans, so insistent on their own right to a political and cultural identity, had failed to accord the same right to Protestants.

In 1995, in a speech to the Sinn Féin Árd Fheis, Tom Hartley, an important member of the group around Gerry Adams, suggested that the idea that the British must agree to withdraw before the rights of Protestants could be considered was a political dead end that had turned the Protestants into a 'non-people'. A settlement, he added, would have to ensure 'a place for those who consider themselves British and *those who wish to stay British*' (my italics), a phrase that implied, at the very least, that the Britishness of a minority would have to remain as a legitimate part of the Irish future. Such conciliatory words were meaningless to Protestants while the IRA, as an armed conspiracy to force them into a political arrangement they did not want, remained in existence. But, at the conceptual level, they completely undercut the case for the armed struggle. Once Protestant and British identity in Northern Ireland was accepted as a genuine reality, and not a mere figment of false consciousness, it became increasingly obvious that violence would serve merely to harden that identity.

Another cornerstone of the IRA's ideology that began to crumble was the idea of self-determination. In a brilliant act of appropriation, the two governments turned Republican rhetoric back on itself by accepting 'the right of self-determination' of the Irish people and re-emphasizing that, if a majority in each part of the island voted for a United Ireland, Britain would accept the result and withdraw. The question facing the IRA and Sinn Féin was no longer 'How do we force the British to give us a United Ireland?' but 'How do we get the Protestants to agree to it?' Killing

Protestants was never a good answer to that question. Now it became not just an obscene answer but an absurd one as well.

Faced with this logic and with the fundamental truth that a United Ireland was no nearer than it was in 1970 when they began their campaign, Gerry Adams and his colleagues committed the IRA to the ceasefire of 1994. It lasted for eighteen months, but broke down in the face of internal opposition from hard-line Republicans and poor political management by John Major's weak government. It was reinstated in July 1997, allowing Sinn Féin to enter into peace talks with the other Northern Irish parties, including the largest Unionist party, the small parties that spoke for the Loyalist paramilitaries, the Women's Coalition and Alliance parties and the British and Irish governments.

What, though, did any of this have to do with the United States? Essentially, America's role was to supply the drama. Clinton instinctively understood that his own charisma, his willingness to pay attention, lifted local deal-making into a stratosphere of global importance. It addressed one of the big problems of peace – how do you come down from the high of violence? All those years ago, in 1972, when Stormont fell and it seemed for a moment as if the IRA's war must surely be over, the mother of the then IRA commander Martin McGuinness, now Sinn Féin's chief negotiator, had asked plaintively, 'what will become of Martin?' Now there was an answer: Martin will be drinking tea in the White House.

The dreary awfulness of the conflict had also conferred on those who lived inside it a deep sense of their own importance, a feeling that they were characters in an epic. An IRA member explained to the English journalist Toby Harnden: 'We didn't really think of killing or being killed; in later years you might think about it but at the time it was all a high. There was a feeling of great exhilaration after an operation.'[6] On the other side of the paramilitary divide, the journalist John Lyttle, whose father Tommy 'Tucker' Lyttle was a big noise in the murderous Ulster Defence Association, evoked this brilliantly in 1996: 'we were living inside the reports we saw on the television news, which had the odd, almost Brechtian effect of distancing you from things you might have actually participated in: a riot, for example. The result was a kind of documentary unreality. That, and a sort of vicious glamour which would increasingly loosen moral constraints and permit previously unimaginable behaviour. Men who traditionally read only thrillers, spy novels, war books and James Bond – like my father – and whose cinematic tastes ran to gangster flicks... and the rough justice of the Western, now had a chance to star in their own home-grown, patriotic versions of heroic fantasies.'[7]

The paradox of the peace process was that, in order to de-glamorize violence, it was necessary first to re-glamorize it. I had watched someone like Pat McGeown go from being an iconic hunger striker to spending his days asking council officials to fix a hole in a constituent's driveway. That, writ large, was the fate even of those who led the IRA and Sinn Féin. The best they could aspire to was to be ministers in a devolved administration in a tiny province of a vanished empire. They could not go cold turkey, sweating out overnight the vicious glamour of running private armies. They had to be afforded the transitional allure of a glamour that was no longer vicious but virtuous. Clinton, who knew all about allure, was willing to share some of his own, to allow it to reflect off the faces of men who had until recently been pariahs. It was not accidental that a crucial moment in the process was the granting of a special visa in January 1994 to allow Adams to visit the US. What mattered was not just the act itself, but the fact that Clinton had personally intervened, over the objections of his State Department and of the British government, to grant the visa. Merely by being seen to concern himself personally with such details, Clinton framed the often tedious manoeuvring in Belfast, London and Dublin as a grand matter. At a time when the US was the world's only superpower, some of those superpowers were being invested in the minutiae of this Irish affair.

A crucial part of this process was the exploitation of Adams's own talent for ambiguity. To spend time with him, as I occasionally did, was to be more deeply baffled by him, to understand less than before what he really thought or felt. He had grown up with a father who was a serial paedophile, and he had the traumatized child's ability to compartmentalize experience. This had allowed him both to participate in violence and to seem coldly aloof from it. But just as this ability had helped to sustain the armed struggle, it was equally crucial to ending it. The very ambiguity of his position, after all, was one of the great assets of the peace process. If Adams were not accepted as a democratic politician, he could not be brought into negotiations. If, on the other hand, he did not have at least a significant degree of control over those who killed people, he could not deliver what the governments and most of the Irish people wanted: an end to the IRA's sordid campaign.

Thus Gerry Adams the godfather of terrorism was replaced by Gerry Adams the tree-loving, wine-drinking celebrity politician. In 1996, he published an autobiography, *Before the Dawn*, which almost entirely glossed over his career in the IRA. In promotional interviews for the book, he went even further and claimed that he had never been a member of the organization and had never engaged in any act of violence. Since most of the international press and all of the relevant governments were anxious not to damage the peace process, these incredible assertions were allowed to pass with no more than mild expressions of scepticism. As a result, Adams generated so much fascination that, at a Sinn Féin fundraising dinner in New York in early November 2002, he was introduced with the suggestion that if Ian Fleming were alive and looking for a new James Bond, 'he wouldn't need a script and he wouldn't need to do anything other than read about the life of Gerry Adams'.[8] Surreal as the analogy with a British spy undoubtedly was, it also captured the knowing contradictions: licensed to kill but supremely suave, stirred by circumstance into support for violence but never shaken by its consequences.

It was imperative to play along with this cognitive game and to allow paramilitaries on both sides to become heroic peacemakers. American prestige, then at its height in the wake of victory in the Cold War, cast a glamour over this necessary fiction. It was not just that the US was neither Britain nor Ireland, that it had historic affinities with both islands. It was that the idea of America contained, for both sides in Northern Ireland, a deep history of aspiration – not least the aspiration to escape the nightmare of Irish history. While Clinton's envoy, the saintly George Mitchell, did the hard, patience-sapping work of chairing the negotiations, the knowledge that the president's gamey eye was always watching created for the participants the idea that they were not just making history but transcending it.

Although the rough shape of a deal was well known, the negotiations that resulted in the Belfast (Good Friday) Agreement of 10 April 1998 nonetheless produced three critical innovations. One was the idea that 'national self-determination' would not be just a concept – it would be an act. There were simultaneous referendums (on 22 May 1998) on both sides of the Border. This mattered, not just for democratic legitimacy but because it was the first such vote on the whole island since the Westminster general election of 1918. In the theology of the IRA, that election, which Sinn Féin won, was the only one that mattered – every subsequent vote was in one or the other of the 'illegitimate' entities created by Partition. Now, all the voters on the island could express their collective will – which was to accept the Belfast Agreement. In Northern Ireland, 71 per cent, including a majority of both Catholics and Protestants, voted in favour. In the Republic, 94 per cent of all voters did so. Overall, 85 per cent of voters on the island as a whole supported the Agreement. There could be no doubt that anyone seeking to undermine it was defying the will, not of one majority but of four: in Northern Ireland, in the Republic and within both Protestant and Catholic communities.

The second set of innovations lay in the mechanisms for ending the armed conflict. They were complex and finely balanced. On the one side, all prisoners from paramilitary organizations that signed up to the Agreement would be released within a maximum period of two years. This inevitably included prisoners who had committed horrendous crimes. It also, incidentally, constituted an implicit acceptance by the British that Republican prisoners were political detainees after all – and therefore that the whole H-Block saga and the suffering it unleashed had been avoidable. This was a decisive factor in securing the support of the IRA. The offer of a two-year timeframe for release had been made to the IRA prisoners at Long Kesh and immediately accepted by them. The opening of a way out of the Troubles was not just political – for the prisoners it was literal. The emotional drama of their pending release swept through the Sinn Féin Árd Fheis that endorsed the Agreement by 331 delegate votes to 19.[9]

On the other side, the signatories restated their commitment to 'the total disarmament of all paramilitary organisations' and to work in good faith with an Independent Commission on Decommissioning to achieve this within two years. This was much less clear-cut than it seemed because the paramilitaries were not themselves signatories to the Agreement – they were represented by their political wings, which could claim to have influence with them but not to make absolute commitments on their behalf. The very word 'decommissioning' was oddly grandiose. It was usually used about naval vessels or nuclear power stations, not about Semtex or AK-47s. And the form that was eventually agreed and implemented was all about the creation of an unknown known. Nobody except the three members of the Independent Commission on Decommissioning, headed by the retired Canadian general John de Chastelain, would be allowed to see the paramilitaries' weapons being destroyed. The physical evidence would represent surrender. It would have to exist in public consciousness as a signifier without a signified – an assurance that actions that could not be shown had most definitely taken place. Weapons would become non-weapons in an event that was a non-event.

The third innovation was that, unlike previous attempts at an agreement, the deal pushed its way into the difficult terrain of culture and identity. More than any other previous international treaty, it explicitly recognized sovereignty and citizenship as contingent, multiple and a matter, not of destiny or of law, but of free choice. It asserted that the signatories 'recognise the birthright of all the people of Northern Ireland to identify themselves and be accepted as Irish or British, or both, as they may so choose, and accordingly confirm that their right to hold both British and Irish citizenship is accepted by both Governments and would not be affected by any future change in the status of Northern Ireland'. That 'or both' had its own grave beauty. The change in the Irish Constitution agreed in the deal and subsequently endorsed overwhelmingly in the referendum went even further: 'It is the firm will of the Irish nation, in harmony and friendship, to unite all the people who share the territory of the island of Ireland, in all the diversity of their identities and traditions'. This acknowledged that there were not in fact just two identities, Protestant/British and Catholic/Irish. The number, as it had to be in a Republic that was becoming radically more diverse, had to be open-ended. Pluralism was now literally constitutive of the Irish polity. One of the most monolithic political identities in the western world was now embracing its own multiplicity.

There were still deliberate ambivalences. The biggest problem was that the key concession that Sinn Féin had to be able to claim had in fact been conceded a long time ago. To end the IRA's campaign without implicitly acknowledging its futility, it was necessary for Adams and McGuinness to be able to say: the armed struggle forced the Brits to concede that Northern Ireland is not an integral part of the United Kingdom, that it could leave at any time if a majority of its people voted in favour of such a change. But this had been explicit British policy – and indeed law – since 1973. The Northern Ireland Constitution Act of that year already defined Northern Ireland as an entity that could determine its own sovereignty. It would not cease to be part of 'Her Majesty's dominions and of the United Kingdom without the consent of the majority of the people of Northern Ireland voting in a poll held for the purposes of this section'.[10] Which, of course, could be put the other way: Northern Ireland would no longer be part of Her Majesty's dominions if a simple majority voted to leave. This was made even more explicit in the Sunningdale Agreement the same year: 'If in future the majority of the people of Northern Ireland should indicate a wish to become part of united Ireland the British government would support that wish.'[11]

Essentially, then, there was no new concession from the British on the constitutional issue. But it was vital that Sinn Féin be allowed to pretend not to know this. At the crucial party Árd Fheis after the signing of the Agreement, Martin McGuinness told the delegates that the Good Friday Agreement had weakened the Union because of a clause limiting its life to the will of a majority in the Six Counties. Britain's role in the Union was now 'a bit like one partner saying the relationship was over but that he or she was willing to wait until the children have grown up'. There was now 'no absolute commitment [to maintaining the Union], no raft of parliamentary acts to back up an absolute claim, but only an agreement to stay until the majority decides otherwise'.[12] This was broadly true – but it had been true for twenty-five years.

That fact needed to be un-known. If the armed struggle was an attempt to bring about a United Ireland by force, it had failed completely. The constitutional situation, from a British point of view, was unchanged by a quarter of a century of suffering and death. In fact, from the IRA's point of view, it was now appreciably worse because the Irish state, as part of the deal, had given up its territorial claim to Northern Ireland and replaced it with an aspiration to unite 'in friendship and harmony', the people who share the island. The veteran nationalist politician Seamus Mallon called the 1998 peace talks 'Sunningdale for slow learners'[13] but it was best for everyone else to avoid such blunt truth-telling.

As the senior IRA member Tommy McKearney put it, 'it was difficult for the IRA high command to admit frankly to its volunteers that they, the leadership, had decided finally to abandon armed struggle in favour of a strategy that the IRA had decried for decades. They were unwilling to acknowledge that a new era had arrived that would involve an acceptance of Partition and the Union and an irreversible break with armed insurrection.'[14] Not just unwilling, however – unable. How do you tell your members they've killed 1,700 people in pursuit of a strategy that was now being abandoned?

Within the IRA itself there were other fictions. In Co. Fermanagh the local commander attempted to spread the entirely false story that the decommissioning of its weapons had never actually taken place. He told his members that de Chastelain, the head of the International Commission that was supervising the process, had been compromised by IRA intelligence and forced to make a bogus report confirming the destruction of the materiel.[15] This was utter nonsense, not least because, as we subsequently learned, British intelligence had so deeply penetrated the IRA that it had no need of outside commissioners to confirm that the weapons had been destroyed. Its own agents at the heart of the

IRA and Sinn Féin (Freddie Scappaticci, the head of IRA internal security, and Denis Donaldson, an important member of Gerry Adams's kitchen cabinet with access to all documentation) could tell it that.

For once, though, fictions, ambiguities, the capacity to believe opposite things at the same time, had played a benign part in Irish history. Peace was about accepting uncertainty, blurring hard definitions, allowing a fruitful double-mindedness to take the place of a murderous single-mindedness. The basic gesture of the Belfast Agreement was to accept that Northern Ireland's future was unknown, that it could not be fixed in advance – and that this was, for most people, okay. Certitude was what you killed and died for. Doubt was what you could live with. The vast majority of Irish people had made it clear which option they preferred.

37

1990–2015: America at Home

When my mother-in-law was happy, she used a phrase she had learned in her childhood in rural Ireland in the 1930s. If you served her a nice dinner, for example, and asked her how everything was she would sigh contentedly and say, 'Ah sure, it's America at home.' It was the Irish ideal of perfection: to have the pleasures and promises of America without having to emigrate. There was a soupy sentimental ballad for the Irish abroad to weep along to into their beer: 'If We Only Had Old Ireland Over Here'. But the authentic anthem of the Irish in Ireland was 'If We Only Had America Over Here'. And then we had.

In all the misery of 1980s Ireland, with its falling population, mass unemployment and large-scale emigration, it was not too easy to grasp that something astonishing was starting. The continuing flow of young Irish people to the States masked the slow tide that was coming in from the Atlantic, the drift, at first a steady current and then a surge, of American multinational investment. The flow was beginning to be reversed: America was coming home to us.

In 1982, Charles Haughey boasted that 'on an earth made smaller every year by advancing communications we have become a stepping-stone between the Old World and the New, a bridgehead in Europe for America'.[1] The metaphors were apt but implicitly odd. A stepping-stone is a rock on which you barely set foot, a mere point on a line. It is also the metaphor that W. B. Yeats used in one of the most famous meditations on the violence that gave birth to the Irish state, Easter 1916:

Hearts with one purpose alone
Through summer and winter seem
Enchanted to a stone
To trouble the living stream.

Yeats was imagining the stone as the implacable force of nationalist zeal, refusing to yield or change as the stream of life flowed around it. Sean O'Casey had taken up the image at the end of *Juno and the Paycock*, when two mothers are mourning the sons who have died in the civil war: 'Sacred heart o' Jesus, take away our hearts o' stone, and give us hearts o' flesh.' Now, the stone in the stream was no longer the nationalist faith, but Ireland itself, a rock in the Atlantic, a foothold for American capital to steady itself as it moved towards the further shore of the European Union.

Haughey's image of Ireland as bridgehead was even stranger – a bridgehead is an advanced position seized and held by an army in hostile territory. It was as if Ireland were Omaha Beach on D-Day, a landing site for the forces of American commerce as they invaded EU markets. Ireland was a safe zone on the far side of the Atlantic, familiar, English-speaking, friendly, from which US capital could gather itself for the push into the more foreign and awkward terrain of the Continent.

The oddness of Haughey's images betrayed, perhaps, the difficulty of aligning this new idea of Ireland with the old Catholic and nationalist self-definitions. Over time, the metaphor was simplified. Ireland was to be understood as what the American Chamber of Commerce Ireland called 'the Transatlantic Bridge'. Yet this, too, spoke a curious kind of truth. Ireland was indeed being reshaped, in economic (and thus in social and cultural) terms, as the bridge between the US and the EU. But a bridge is not a place – it is a line between two places. It hangs between two pieces of solid ground, but over an aqueous, ever-changing flow. It is perpetually suspended, always liminal, always up in the air. I came to think of Ireland as being like one of those medieval bridges where there were houses and workshops and people selling their wares from stalls, and jugglers and ballad singers and itinerant preachers, all dangling permanently over the rushing waters of the river. To live on the bridge was to be always in flux, or, as Seamus Heaney evoked the condition in 'Postscript':

> ... You are neither here nor there,
> A hurry through which known and strange things pass.[2]

It was towards the end of 1989 when a glossy leaflet came in the front door of our house on the north side of Dublin. There was almost no junk mail in those days and there had certainly never been anything like this. It was a message from Intel. They were looking for 'talented people' who would be 'attracted to Intel, drawn by the dynamic, achievement orientated work environment which values hard work and innovation'. It announced that 'We are now ready to start building the Intel Ireland Team' and mentioned specific jobs: manufacturing engineers, business system managers, test engineering managers and, not incidentally, a capital tax accountant.[3] None of them matched my highly limited skills. But the very idea that they were canvassing so aggressively for recruits to the Intel Ireland Team was a kind of wonder.

Intel moved into the space occupied by the Catholic hierarchy – its new plant in Leixlip, built on a former stud farm, was down the road in Co. Kildare from the church's headquarters in Maynooth. At first, its plant was not all that different from the kind of foreign investment that had come into Ireland since the 1958 revolution. It was essentially an assembly line, albeit for Intel's basic but highly successful 486 processor. But the success of the operation encouraged Intel to take a quantum leap. It added on the world's first high-volume 200-millimetre semiconductor wafer plant, Fab 10.

In 1994, when Intel launched the Pentium processor that was central to the emergence of the personal computer as an everyday consumer product, more than half of worldwide processor production was based in Leixlip. In one vertiginous leap, Ireland had gone from backwater to leading edge. Over the next decade the

Irish plant produced one billion Pentium chips. Intel went on to invest over €6 billion at the site, making it the most technologically advanced industrial location in Europe. Over thirty years, Intel alone would invest €15 billion in Ireland.

The strategy of depending on foreign direct investment (FDI) for development had, of course, been operating for more than thirty years. In the 1960s, foreign companies set up 350 new enterprises in Ireland. They were British and European as well as American. Among the early arrivals were pharmaceutical plants like Denmark's Leo Laboratories (1959), Warner-Lambert (1960) and Pfizer (1969). In the 1960s, FDI delivered 70 per cent of new employment and 90 per cent of increased exports in transportable goods. This steady inflow of pharma companies continued in the 1970s and early 1980s: Smith Kline & French (1974), Merck, Sharp & Dohme (1976), Allergan (1977) and Eli Lilly (1981).

Electronics had also been important. By the early 1980s, many of the world's leading electronics companies had established basic assembly and test facilities, including Digital Equipment Corporation (1971), Measurex (1973), Northern Telecom (1973), Ericsson (1974), Data 100 (1975), NEC (1975), Nixdorf Computer (1977), Westinghouse Electric Corporation (1978), Analog Devices (1977), Amdahl (1979), Wang (1979), Apple (1980) and Fujitsu (1980). The third important stream of investment was in the manufacture of medical devices: Baxter Travenol (1971), Abbott Laboratories (1974) and Bausch & Lomb (1980).

All of this was important and, in the dreary 1980s, it helped to keep the Irish economy afloat. But from the mid-1980s, the Industrial Development Authority developed a more sophisticated strategy of trying, not so much to attract this or that company, as to build clusters of world-leading companies, most of them American, in these three fields: information technology, pharmaceuticals and medical devices. This was the new Holy Trinity that would replace the old ones, the religious triad of father, son and Holy Ghost and the ideological troika of land, nationality and religion. In the 1990s, as these old systems were imploding in Ireland, the new one arrived just in time to take their place.

The clusters formed. In IT, along came Lotus (1984), Microsoft

(1985), Intel (1989), Motorola (1989), Dell (1990), HP (1995), IBM (1996), Oracle (1996), Xerox (1998) and Cisco (2007). In pharma, each of the world's top ten pharmaceutical companies established operations in Ireland. In medical devices, Boston Scientific arrived in 1994 and was soon exporting 10 million medical devices worldwide annually, including stents, balloons, platinum coils, catheters, inflation devices, pacemakers and implantable cardioverter-defibrillators. It was followed by other huge American companies in the field, including Cook Medical (1994) and Medtronic (1999).

The scale of this inflow was staggering. In the twenty-five years after 1990, US companies would invest roughly $277 billion in Ireland; the comparable figure for Brazil is $92 billion; for Russia $10 billion; for India $32 billion; and for China $51 billion.[4] By 2012, Ireland, which was 1 per cent of the EU economy, accounted for 11.5 per cent of sales by US affiliate companies in Europe. By 2017, US direct investment stock in Ireland totalled $457 billion, a greater investment stake than in Germany, France, Italy, Spain, Belgium, Denmark and Sweden combined.[5]

There was nothing quite like this in world history. Some poor countries had experienced very rapid development in the late twentieth century, but they had done so primarily by reordering their own societies and developing indigenous industries that could trade on world markets. There was no Irish equivalent of, for example, South Korea's Samsung and no imaginable native political and industrial culture from which such an enterprise might emerge. The Irish Great Leap Forward was powered almost entirely from without. The template of Ireland's development was not organic expansion – it was seduction. The Irish gaze on globalization was a come-hither look. In 2019, when the Industrial Development Authority published a glossy book to mark the highlights of its seventy years in existence, it was called *The Art of Attraction*. It also commissioned five Irish artists to produce works on the theme of Attraction.

One of the artworks, a totemic sculpture by Ruth Lyons, used beeswax on stone: 'While the stones speak of legacy, sugar has more bodily and sensual connotations bringing desire and attraction into the equation.' Desire, the force that had been suppressed in Irish society for so long, was now at the centre of the national project – Ireland had to be desirable. Its art of attraction was based on its people, the young and well-educated workforce it could provide, and on its politics: the Republic, for all the dramas of the 1980s, had a strong cross-party consensus on the importance of keeping the multinationals happy. But the honey coating was the corporate tax rate that settled, in the mid-1990s, at 12.5 per cent. This was low but it was also manipulable. And in the way this worked, it was crucial that, as Gertrude Stein said about the vanished California of her childhood, 'there is no there there'.

It was not that there was no physical reality to what was happening. Apple, for example, opened a manufacturing facility in Cork in 1980, employing 700 people. By 1990, there were 1,000 jobs; by 2019, there were 6,000. This was very real. But there was another side to Apple's benevolence. In 1990, when the company was in trouble, it met with the Irish government, conveying a polite but unmistakable threat: 'the company is at present reviewing its worldwide operations and wishes to establish a profit margin on its Irish operations.' The problem was that Apple was making too much money in those Irish operations. It was declaring a net profit of $270 million on a turnover of $751 million. But, it argued to the Irish Revenue, most of this was related to its technological patents and its global brand, not to the manufacturing in Ireland.

Apple proposed a deal – it would 'be prepared to accept a profit of $30–$40m' – provided the Irish authorities helped to make the other $230 million go away. Asked what the basis for the $30–$40 million profit might be, Apple's negotiator 'confessed that there was no scientific basis for the figure. However, the figure was of such magnitude that he hoped it would be seen to be a bona-fide proposal.'[6] In other words, we'll say that the profit we make in Ireland is $30–$40 million, you will agree to collect the tax on that amount, and we will both be happy. All you need to do is to accept that the rest of the money exists in that place that has always been so central to the Irish imagination: elsewhere.

The acceptable solution for both the corporation and the state was that Apple established two Irish incorporated companies of the Apple group, Apple Sales International and Apple Operations Europe. With these entities, there would be no there there. Almost all sales profits recorded by these two companies were internally attributed to a 'head office'. These 'head offices' existed only on paper and could not have generated such profits. They had no premises, no staff, no directors who were not full-time executives of other Apple entities. Thus, the profits allocated to these 'head offices' were not subject to tax in any country. As a token gesture, they paid tiny amounts of tax in Ireland, at an effective rate that dropped as low as 0.005 per cent by 2014.

And so we had a whole new kind of unknown known. The Irish state knew very well what Apple was doing but it decided not to absorb that awareness into its active consciousness. It would look the other way. This was the irony of Ireland's Great Leap Forward. It was emerging, in its ways of thinking about itself, from that old culture of wink-and-nod, of having a real, lived self on the one hand and an official, fictional self on the other. But that culture returned in a whole new form, as part of the package of turbocharged economic development. Fictions reverted to the centre of Irish life, but now they were not stories about holiness and purity. They were tall tales about profit rates and companies that were not companies and magical money that could be everywhere and nowhere. We could not, it seemed, escape our need for fables and fabrications. They were the hidden clauses in the rules of attraction.

As part of its series of artworks on that theme, the IDA commissioned from Paul Hallahan a set of paintings 'inspired by the mythical island of Hy-Brasil, thought to have lain off the west coast of Ireland, and only visible once every seven years. They create the idea of a place that comes in and out of focus, existing mostly in the imagination.' This, too, seemed apt, for the offshore island that Ireland now was came in and out of focus, appeared and disappeared. Basic facts became impossibly slippery.

One thing that it became impossible to know about this new Ireland was how rich it really was. Other countries could get some rough idea of their wealth by dividing their gross domestic product (GDP) by their population numbers. But Irish GDP, or even its gross national income (GNI), were unmoored from Irish reality. The low corporate tax rates gave multinational companies an incentive to declare as much of their global profit in Ireland as possible. This could be done by having an Irish-based entity 'purchase' components from branches in other countries at artificially low prices, so as to make the Irish operation more lucrative. Over time, as Ireland became the location of more sophisticated processes, most of this was no longer about physical components, but about intangible assets like patents and intellectual property. The movement of these vast intangible assets into a small economy could create astonishing spikes in GDP, most spectacularly in 2015, when Irish GDP grew by 26 per cent, a miracle that was also mostly a mirage.

In most countries, GDP, representing all the activity recorded in the economy and GNI, representing the activity that really took place, are more or less the same. In Ireland, from the 1990s onwards, the two diverged ever more widely. In 1995, real GNI[7] was 8 per cent lower than GDP. In 2019, it was 40 per cent below. We were back, in other words, with double realities – the way things seemed to be and the way they were – and the gap between them was getting steadily larger.

This was more than a headache for statisticians. Because GDP is so widely used across the world to measure prosperity, it made Ireland look incredibly rich. By the beginning of the twenty-first century, Ireland generally had the highest GDP per head of population of any EU country apart from Luxembourg. By 2017, Ireland was ranked third in the world (among countries with populations of more than half a million) behind only Qatar and Singapore.[8]

The descaminados of the 1950s had become richer than the Americans they had envied or the Europeans they were too poor to join. But this was fiction. In reality, measured by actual individual consumption per capita, Ireland was not in the top quarter of EU countries – it was in twelfth place, still behind all of the original six EU member states. Indeed, in 2019, actual consumption in Ireland was about 95 per cent of the EU average. Nor was Ireland really catching up with America. In 1950, consumption per person in Ireland was 47 per cent of that in the US. By 1981, it had risen to 50 per cent. By 2007, it had reached 68 per cent. It then fell again to 60 per cent. When it came to the simple reality of what Irish people could actually afford to buy with their incomes, we never actually had America at home.

This is not to say that becoming an average western European country was not fabulous. To be normal was a wonder that deserved celebration. The problem was that its achievement was drowned out by a constant drumbeat of hype. It is apt that, by the late 1990s, Ireland's chief exports included Viagra, made by Pfizer in Ringaskiddy, Prozac, whose active ingredients were made by Eli Lilly nearby, and Botox, whose world supply came from Allergan in Carrowmore, outside Westport, Co. Mayo. Artificial highs and cosmetic enhancements were products of Ireland's magical form of development. Satisfaction all too easily shaded into euphoria.

Along with the recreation of fictional ways of thinking, the vast influx of American capital also made for a new form of compartmentalization. As of 2013, multinationals were responsible for the direct and indirect employment of 260,000 people in Ireland – 15 per cent of the workforce. This was a very good thing, but it meant, of course, that 85 per cent of jobs were in indigenous businesses, most of them small or medium-sized. There was not an Irish economy – there were two of them. And each had its own way of doing things. There was an understanding that the multinationals were not to be messed with, that their power had to be respected. But since they were the engine of growth, the rest of the economy could, it seemed, afford a lot of messing. The outsourcing of development let the established native nexus of cronyism and low standards off the hook. There was no need for the culture that Fianna Fáil epitomized, and that encompassed critical institutions like the Irish banks, to clean up its act. The globalized economy would do its thing. Therefore the still unreconstructed local system could continue to do its thing. That, too, was, for those in power, highly attractive.

38

1990–2000: Unsuitables from a Distance

The state of Irish culture as the country completed its transformation from basket case to poster child of hyper-globalized modernity can be summed up in three dances.

In April 1990, I went to the opening night of a new play at the Abbey Theatre, Brian Friel's *Dancing at Lughnasa*. It is set in August 1936 in (as almost all Friel's plays were) the fictional village of Ballybeg in Co. Donegal. It explores the constrained lives of the five Mundy sisters who live together in the same household. It is full of beautifully crafted, precisely calibrated dialogue. But at its centre is a wordless sequence, a mad dance. The radio has been broken, and, when it is fixed, we hear the strains of an Irish and Scottish traditional tune, 'The Mason's Apron': 'Very fast; very heavy beat; a raucous sound'.[1]

One of the sisters, Maggie, seems to absorb the sound into herself, to be possessed by it, as if by a devil. She 'emits a wild, raucous "Yaaaah!" – and immediately begins to dance, arms, legs, hair, long bootlaces flying'. Gradually, each of the other sisters joins in this unconstrained physical outburst. 'With this too loud music, this pounding beat, this shouting – calling – singing, this parodic reel, there is a sense of order being consciously subverted, of the women consciously and crudely caricaturing themselves, indeed of near-hysteria being induced.' There was something mesmerizing about this scene in 1990, about the way it hung between exuberance and insanity, joy and pain. It seemed to contain both the grimness of the way Ireland had been for so long and the desperate yearning for release from that oppressive condition.

Five years later I was at the opening in Dublin of another wordless spectacle. It was much anticipated because it was a development of a routine, based on traditional Irish dancing, that had been put together for the previous year's Eurovision Song Contest, a cheesy bauble of international esteem that Ireland, back then, seemed to win every year. Everybody had loved the act and wanted to see what the producers would now do with it. But there was also an anxiety that, this being Ireland, the full-length show, called *Riverdance*, would fail.

What I remember most about that night was that you could hear, even above the pounding feet and the swirling music, the audience gasping for breath. And then an explosion of shouts and whoops as all that air burst out again in a wave of wonderment. It was, of course, the sheer force and energy of the dancing, the rapture of the music, the fantastic sight of so many bodies in motion. But there was something else as well, some long-submerged emotion breaking the surface and gulping in the oxygen. It was like a great exhalation of relief and release.

I had been forced, when I was at primary school, to attend Irish dancing classes. The Christian Brothers approved of this form of highly controlled motion, all feet and no hips, everything happening from the knees down, the back rigid, the arms held so tightly against the sides that they might as well not exist. There was no gyration, no expression, and no girls. If you were really good at it, you would be forced into competition, for which you would have to wear a kilt which felt, in our world, like being desexed. I had no interest in being good at it.

The social form of this torment was the céilí. In his 1996 book *Last Night's Fun* the great Belfast poet and traditional musician Ciaran Carson defined the céilí of his teens, and mine, as 'a social event imprimatured by the Catholic Church where boys and girls met each other under close sacerdotal supervision and practised minimal contact dancing'. In that sense all Irish dancing as we knew it in the cities was liturgical. It was an act of piety, a homage to the Holy Trinity of Catholicism, Irish nationalism and sexual continence.

But here in *Riverdance* it was sex and energy and a swirling, pounding intoxication, the intimate and secret madness of that scene in *Dancing at Lughnasa* making a shameless show of itself. Only Irish-Americans could do this. The lead male dancer and choreographer, Michael Flatley, was raised on the South Side of Chicago, the son of immigrants from Sligo and Carlow. Jean Butler was from Mineola, New York, the daughter of a Mayo woman. Both had learned Irish music and dance in America. They embodied a notion of return. Just as JFK's visit in 1963 had contained the promise of a payback for all the pain of emigration, a restitution in a new and glamourous form of all that had been lost, Flatley and Butler did the same for the new Ireland that was emerging from the waves of American capital that were flowing over it. They were benign revenants. Usually in Irish culture, the past came back in the dark shape of the return of the repressed. *Riverdance* was the return of the flagrantly unrepressed.

In *Riverdance*'s 'too loud music and too fast beat' there was, as in *Dancing at Lughnasa*, an element of hysteria and self-caricature. The shadow both of Catholic puritanism at home and of Stage Irish display abroad both were present, not on stage but in the wings, as alternative possibilities of failure, the monster and the whirlpool between which *Riverdance* had to trip the light fantastic. Its grace was that of an elegant swerve away from dangerous traps.

The pleasure of *Riverdance* was unimaginable without the pain of mass emigration. Not only were its choreographer and original principal dancers children of the Irish diaspora but its narrative was about migration itself: a dance developed on a small misty island having to find its feet on the streets of New York among a plethora of competing cultures. And its cultural form – Irish traditional music and dance refigured as a big Broadway show – had the tangled relationship between Ireland and America embedded within it. Its raptures could not be entirely careless.

There is in Ireland a deep connection between dancing and displacement. In most cultures, dancing is an expression of the community, a ritual of togetherness. To go to a dance is to participate in a place. Through dancing the private – sexual desire, courtship, family relationships – is played out as a public display. The gap between the personal and the social is narrowed. But in Ireland, for most of the twentieth century at least, dancing was often about avoiding the community, even avoiding communication. It became a private activity, an act not of self-expression, but of escape. In his Limerick Rural Survey of 1962, the most detailed and brilliant description of the Irish countryside before the radical changes brought by multinational industry and membership of the European Union, Patrick McNabb notes that even those young people who stayed at home preferred to dance away from their own townland or parish.

McNabb found that there was a habit of actively avoiding the dancehall in one's own place. When he asked dancers why they did so, he got evasive answers: 'A better band, floor, better dancers, greater selection of partners, were mentioned as reasons for going further afield to dance.' But he realised that this made no sense because young people from outside the area travelled to the very hall that these dancers were avoiding. The real point was 'simply escaping the observation of the home community… Dancing is as anonymous in rural areas as it is in cities. Conversation is pared down to laconic statements about the floor, the band or the weather.'[2]

It was precisely this connection between mobility and dancing that most alarmed the Catholic Church in the early years of the Irish state. In a pastoral letter issued in 1931, Cardinal Joseph MacRory pointed out the moral danger posed by the willingness of young people to travel long distances to dances: 'Even the present travelling facilities make a difference. By bicycle, motor car and bus, boys and girls can now travel great distances to dances, with the result that a dance may now be attended by unsuitables from a distance.'

One of the very first pieces of social legislation introduced by Fianna Fáil when it came to power was the Public Dance Halls Act of 1935, requiring all dancers to be licensed and to operate under strict supervision. The priests and the police used the legislation to break up dances at crossroads and in houses, the places where living, non-commercial, traditional dancing survived. The great Co. Clare fiddle player and composer Junior Crehan told an RTÉ radio documentary in the 1980s that 'We were forbidden to have a dance. The guards were sent out. I was at a couple of them where the guards came out and took names and the owner of the house was brought to court and fined and the poor man was only trying to make a few pounds to pay the rent or the rates... The dance halls started then.'

According to Crehan, there was an intimate connection between the death of dancing and emigration: 'The country house dance was gone and the countryman didn't fit in with the jazz and the foxtrot, so it died away. And a world of fellas left for England. They had no social activity at all, nothing here for them and they got fed up so they went off. There was no country house dance after that then. Except you'd have a small party if Americans came and friends would be invited. It wouldn't be like the old times at all.'

And yet there was also an intimate connection between emigration and the survival of Irish dancing as an element of American popular culture. Watching Jimmy Cagney play George M. Cohan in *Yankee Doodle Dandy*, I always assumed that the original Broadway song and dance man was a Jewish hoofer called Cohen. The knowledge that he was actually a Mick called Keohane given to proclaiming that

> Proud of all the Irish blood that's in me,
> Divil a man can say a word agin me

brought with it the delightful but slightly disturbing realization that there was a real connection between 'The Mason's Apron' and the soft shoe shuffle. Keohane's father Jerry, himself the son of famine immigrants, was a famous traditional Irish dancer who developed new versions of jigs and reels for the travelling variety show in which his son first appeared on stage, dancing to Irish tunes played by the great uilleann piper Patsy Touhey.

Somehow, this was all coming back home. The idea that there might be a link between céilís and chorus lines was hard to get your head around, but *Riverdance* took that odd connection and reworked it into the most unlikely reconciliation of Irish piety and American pizazz since Annie Murphy fell in love with Eamonn Casey – except that *Riverdance* went on to live happily ever after.

It became customary to talk of *Riverdance* as an act of reclamation, a taking back for popular entertainment of a form that had been prettified and stultified. Such talk was accurate enough as far as it went. But what was most significant was that what was being reclaimed was not just Irish folk dancing but also the Irish contribution to the Broadway musical. The tradition that was being revived was that, not of de Valera's comely maidens dancing at the crossroads, but of George M. Cohan's fusion of an Irish past with an American future. 'Yankee Doodle Dandy' was taking its place with 'The Walls Of Limerick' or 'The Mason's Apron' as an authentic antecedent for contemporary Irish culture.

In that sense *Riverdance* was as much a redefinition as a reclamation of Irish tradition. What made it so exhilarating was the sense, not so much of invention, as of recognition. The slickness, the confidence, the professionalism may have been a far cry from the Irish immigrant dance halls of the 1950s in New York or Boston where céilí bands alternated with swing orchestras, and jigs and reels were thrown in with rumbas, waltzes, cha-chas and tangos. But the cultural mix was the same. Ireland and America, folk art and Tin Pan Alley, the pure and the hybrid, never had been, for most Irish people most of the time, distinct entities. What *Riverdance* was saying was not only that this was okay, but that it was sort of splendid. Cultural promiscuity was a lot more fun than cultural purity.

It was not supposed to be like that. For many Irish artists, from Seán Ó Riada onwards, the process of modernization could only be one of loss. The idea that Ireland was becoming a provincial outpost of the US was, for them, a return of the same fear that haunted Irish writers in the late nineteenth century, when Ireland seemed destined to be a provincial outpost of England. Brian Friel put it succinctly in 1972: 'I am uneasy about the future of the writer in Ireland. Ireland is becoming a shabby imitation of a third-rate American state... We are rapidly losing our identity as a people and because of this, that special quality an Irish writer should have will be lost... We are no longer even West Britons; we are East Americans.'[3] Tom Murphy's brilliantly dark *Conversations on a Homecoming*, premiered in 1985, had the Irish exile returning from America as a lost soul, doomed to be neither here nor there. It also had a hilarious denunciation of the 'country-and-western system' that was taking over Ireland: 'Unyielding, uncompromising, in its drive for total sentimentality... that would have us all an unholy herd of Sierra Sues, sad-eyed inquisitors, sentimental Nazis... with spurs a -jinglin', all ridin' down the trail to Oranmore.'[4]

And yet, Friel and Murphy were themselves glorious evidence that nothing was being lost. One of the great joys of Irish life for me in the 1970s, 1980s and 1990s was the prospect that, in any given year, one or other of them would produce a new play of breathtaking accomplishment. You could go to the theatre and see the stuff of Ireland, both in its past and its present tenses, being played out on stage with a sophistication and intensity and artistry that made you aware that you were living through a golden age at least as exciting as that of the early twentieth century when W. B. Yeats and Augusta Gregory and John Synge were trying not to be West Britons. The determination to be more than East Americans was no less productive. The 'special quality an Irish writer should have', whatever it might be, was blazingly alive. In the theatre, in the novel, in poetry, in music (both popular and traditional), in film, in visual art and architecture, Irish artists were producing work of great depth and vibrancy and daring. They were doing so, not by being paranoid or seeking protection from the big bad world, but by getting on with the business of exploring the tensions and possibilities of Irish life and Irish identities.

Those possibilities came from the endless potential of uncertainty. The habits of mind that created so many problems for politics and public discourse – the slipperiness, the ambivalences, the not-knowing – are also conducive to creativity in art. Irish artists could have everything (at least) both ways. They could be at once realists and fabulists, social critics and mythmakers. They could draw, from the Troubles and from the slow implosion of Catholic Ireland, a sense of the epic, a feeling that even the mundane and the awful were steeped in the grandeur of history. They could at once rail against Catholicism and raid its vast storehouse of imagery, knowing that their audience could still be touched by the power of its iconography. They could be both sacrilegious and sacramental.

What, after all, was the 'special quality' that had made Irish culture so rich? It was never a sacred hoard of precious inheritances that must be guarded from the depredations of change. It was, as far back as one could trace it, a constant set of negotiations, in which whatever was valued had to be recast and reimagined in the light of new challenges – literacy arriving into an oral culture, Christianity embedding itself within paganism, Vikings bringing both threats and new ideas like cities and money, English imposing itself on a Gaelic linguistic landscape, emigrants having to create hybrid identities in foreign cities. There was no Irish culture outside of this constant process of translation and fusion, of preserving things by remaking them. Just as emigration had become Ireland's paradoxical marker of continuity, Irish culture was always a shapeshifter. In order to stay the same, it changed. It never had a steady state. It was always Heaney's 'hurry through which known and strange things pass', an endless argument between the familiar and the outlandish. That conformation is not a threat to tradition – it *is* the tradition.

This is not to say that the fears of an East American crassness were entirely misplaced. In 2005, Michael Flatley's own dance show, *The Celtic Tiger*, taking its name from the equally tacky label that had become a synonym for the new Ireland, replayed the narrative of *Riverdance*, from the Celtic mists of time to American emigration to cultural fusion to triumphant transatlantic return. But it did so in a form that had lost all the inner complexities of its progenitor.

Flatley created a high-kitsch presentation of Irish history as a pure pastiche in which whole eras melted into each other. Devout monks dervish-danced with lurid temptresses. Horny-headed Vikings danced chastely with Irish maidens. An Irish Garden of Eden blossomed until invaded by a chorus line of Brits, identifiable by their red coats and powdered wigs, goose-stepping and robotic, like clockwork Nazis. They burned a thatched cottage. (The Irish maidens barely escaped the fire, but, distressingly, the bottom three-quarters of their skirts had been consumed by the flames.) There was much writhing around to indicate the Famine. Father Michael Flatley enters in a nineteenth-century soutane intoning the Lord's Prayer. The Brits surround him and shoot him dead with their fingers. A man sings 'The Four Green Fields' (a traditional nineteenth-century ballad written in the late 1960s). A boy playing soccer is blown up by a British tank (presumably one of the little-known nineteenth-century prototypes exclusively used for oppressing the Irish). Then Michael Flatley leads the 1916 Rising. It is not surprising that he wins, since the Brits are still in their redcoats and powdered wigs and are still using their fingers for guns. Everybody sings 'A Nation Once Again'. Ireland is free and triumphant.

But there's not much to do in Ireland now that it's free, so everyone goes to New York. But what of Ireland back home? It's struggling to become modern – here's Kathleen Ní Houlihan as an Aer Lingus stewardess in a green uniform, dancing a jig in high heels – modernity and tradition. Then Michael and his crew of sun-glassed beefcake boys in Pan Am uniforms fly her over New York. She sees Ireland's destiny. She does a striptease act, peeling off her green Irish uniform to reveal underneath a bra and panties imprinted with the Stars and Stripes. Ireland was really America all along and now the Celtic Tiger has allowed itself to reveal its true identity. All that suffering – the Famine, the evictions, the murder of Saint Michael Flatley by the redcoat Brit bastards – has been repaid at last. Flatley leads the chorus line in a big, rapturous tap-along to 'Yankee Doodle Dandy'. Ireland's destiny as the fifty-first state of the Union is now complete. None of this was meant to be funny.

The best way to imagine Irish culture in this era is to think of these three dances going on, not in sequence, but simultaneously on the same stage. There was still the anguish of the past expressed in that hysterical reel in *Dancing at Lughnasa*. There was, on the far end of the spectrum, the idiot jive of *The Celtic Tiger*, the capering foolishness that would embrace uncritically the notion of Ireland as a creature of the American Dream, its history caricatured to the point of obliteration. And in the middle, there was the fancy footwork of *Riverdance*, the making of a new national myth from available materials: traditional music, mass emigration, liberation from repression, the ways in which American capital was altering Ireland's possibilities.

The necessity for a new myth was two-sided. The dominant structure of thought and feeling, the fusion of nationalism and religion that gained hegemony through the alliance of Fianna Fáil and the Catholic Church, was falling down. It was a centre that could no longer hold. But on the other side, it could not merely be replaced by a new monolith. This impossibility was rooted in two processes that changed Ireland radically in the late 1990s. Living through them, it was hard to say which of them was more unimaginable.

One of them was the reversal of the thing I had always known, the thing that had loomed so large at the time I was born that it had forced change on a brutally conservative system: mass emigration. It had been the pulse of my lifetime: waning in the 1960s and 1970s, waxing again in the 1980s and early 1990s. The simplest thing about it is that it was something we did to other places – we landed ourselves on top of them. But quite suddenly in the late 1990s they began to land themselves on top of us. Ireland, unthinkably, became a place that people came to, not to retreat from the world, but for the same reason the Irish had gone to America or Britain or Australia: to get a job, perhaps to make a life.

No one knew better than us that labour follows capital – we'd been doing it for centuries. But it did not much occur to us that this law applied to the American capital that was flooding into Ireland – labour would follow it. The art of attraction worked on people as well as on money and technology. Between 1995 and 2000, a quarter of a million people arrived in Ireland, about 7 per cent of the entire population at the time (3.6 million in 1996). Around half of these were Irish migrants returning from their exile of the 1980s. But there were also people from a wide variety of nationalities and ethnicities. Between 1991 and 2002, the share of foreign-born people living in Ireland rose from 6 per cent to 10 per cent (though about 1.3 per cent were born in Northern Ireland). In 1992, a grand total of thirty-nine people sought asylum in Ireland; in 2000, the total was 10,938.[5] After 2004, when citizens of the new EU states in central and eastern Europe were allowed free movement into Ireland, people from Romania, Poland, Latvia, Lithuania and Estonia also began to arrive in large numbers. In 2004–5 alone, 94,000 workers from these states registered in Ireland, about three-quarters of the total arriving in the UK, whose population is fifteen times greater. This process continued – by 2016, 17 per cent of people living in the Republic of Ireland were born elsewhere.

Ireland was already becoming far more diverse in religious and ethical belief – by 2016, 10 per cent of the population was non-religious. But this influx meant that, even if the old orthodoxy had not become untenable, the pretence that there was one way of being Irish could not have held. Immigrants came from 180 countries. Polish passed out Irish as the second most spoken language in the home in Ireland. In 1981, 93 per cent of the population was Catholic. By 2016, that was down to 78 per cent. The fastest growing faiths were Orthodox Christianity, Pentecostalism, atheism and Islam. In a very short time, Ireland became a multicultural society.

The other imperative driving the need for a new kind of identity was the possibility of a solution to the Troubles. It had always been the case that a republic that defined itself primarily through its synthesis of Catholicism and nationalism could never be a credible political partner for those who defined themselves as Protestant and Unionist. Any conceivable settlement, even one far short of the nationalist goal of a United Ireland, would have to involve a recognition by the Republic of the legitimacy of other identities on the island. It would have to accept pluralism, not as a grudging resignation to the impossibility of the purist ideal, but as a value in itself.

This was why, even if it was only seen as an entertainment, a phenomenon like *Riverdance* was important. It existed alongside the success of the Irish international soccer team in these years, managed by an archetypal Englishman, Jack Charlton, and featuring players born in British cities of Irish descent; the songs of Shane MacGowan and The Pogues; the plays of Martin McDonagh; the fictions of the (rediscovered) Maeve Brennan and Alice McDermott. They opened a place in Irishness for the diasporas that were, in many ways, the truest products of its history. It brought home the reality that had been obscured in the idea of emigration as tragedy and shame: we are a hyphenated people. The new immigrants to Ireland, with their attachments to different homeplaces reminded us in the most vivid way that the hyphens in their identities had long punctuated the many personalities of Irishness. Perhaps this is why the wave of Americanization was, for all the follies it could bring, not experienced as a threat of annihilation. It was not just that it was associated with rising prosperity and with liberation from repression. It was that it was not alien. It had those elements of homecoming that made it as much about reconciliation with the Irish past as about the creation of an Irish future.

39

1999: The Cruelty Man

In the early 1980s, my father was working on a bus when it crashed on the long road south from the city to Bray. He was thrown violently to the floor. An ambulance came and took him to Loughlinstown hospital. The doctor was worried that he had hit his head and ordered an X-ray. It showed a hairline fracture running along the top of his skull. But the bone was mostly knitted. The fracture could not have been a result of the bus crash. It had been there, the doctor thought, for a very long time.

I remembered my father telling me a slightly odd story some years before. I had asked him why he gave up boxing after becoming the Irish juvenile champion. He said he had fractured his skull. In the ring? No. He had been climbing a set of steps on the side of a building when one of them gave way and he fell through from a height onto the ground. The odd thing was that it was hard to imagine how your whole body could drop through a hole the width of a stair. I knew he was lithe and slender in his boxing days, but even so it was a puzzle. And if you did plummet down like that, would you not break your leg rather than your skull? It was not that I imagined for a moment that he was not telling the truth, just that I struggled to picture it – the step giving way underfoot, his slim, adolescent frame slotting through the hole, his head cracking on the ground.

Now, he told a different story. His mother had given birth to twins. His stepfather, James Hanlon, came home roaring drunk. There was water boiling on the stove. Hanlon lifted the pot and made to throw the boiling water over the infants. My father picked up a brush handle and hit him. Hanlon was small in height but strong as a bull from years of lifting and shovelling on the docks. In the fight, my father, taking advantage of Hanlon's surprise and his intoxication, managed to wrangle him outside the flat onto the balcony. But Hanlon gathered his strength and threw my father down a flight of concrete steps. That's how he broke his skull.

In April 1953, James Hanlon was unloading timber from a ship when a big stack of wood fell over and crushed him. Someone ran from the dock up to the flat and gave my father the news. He went over to see the body. He knelt down beside him and quietly and discreetly spat in his stepfather's face. The death notice in the *Irish Press* said that James Hanlon, who had died 'suddenly' was 'deeply regretted by his sorrowing wife, children, brothers, relatives and friends'. Well, not all of them. The official history was not quite the same as the real story.

That story was about the industrial school system. James Hanlon was in my father's life because of it. He was two when his own father, Patrick, died of tuberculosis at the age of thirty-four. All that he ever seemed to know about my grandfather was that he had worked in the Paul and Vincent animal feed mill on the Liffey quay; that he had left school long before he was fourteen and had not attended regularly, yet that he was thought to be 'an avid reader and great wit'. When he died, his wife Maggie was left with Kevin, Rita, Eileen, Paddy and my father. She was thirty-two.

The matriarch of the clan was Maggie's formidable mother Ellen. We just knew her as Great Granny Winders. She was in her eighties when I was old enough to remember her, but she was still beautiful with iron-grey hair and big dark brown eyes. Everyone was still afraid of her. She had kept things together by working as a cleaner and she had Maggie and the kids under her command, too, doing whatever cleaning jobs she told them to do. When my grandfather died, Great Granny Winders issued her decree: Maggie could not look after all of those kids and some of them would have to go into the industrial schools.

Maggie was determined that this would not happen. Even then, and even in the conditions of poverty and precariousness she was used to, she must have known that there was something worse, that the system of care run by the very church she was so faithful to was cruel beyond the bounds of acceptability. But what choice did she have? The only salvation for my father and his siblings was for her to marry quickly. Who would take on a widow with five kids aged between two and eleven? Only a bad prospect: James Hanlon. He was a casual docker, part of the brutal system where men turned up every day for the 'read' by a stevedore who might or might not hire them to unload or load a ship. If he got work, he was paid in the pub (with an obligation to buy drink for the stevedore). If he didn't, he went to the pub to drink off the humiliation. He was known for a famous feat, which was to drink twenty pints of stout, jump in the Liffey, swim over and back, and go back to the pub. Maggie married him surely knowing exactly what he was like. She did it to keep my father and his brothers and sisters out of the industrial schools.

This was a story about my father's most private self, the marks on his skull and inside his head. But it was also a story about something much bigger, a darkness that Ireland would have to delve into in the 1990s, with immense consequences. It was about what happened to working-class children when a parent died, when poverty or alcoholism wrecked their home lives or when they themselves got into minor trouble with the law. The legal regime of the Edwardian Children Act of 1908 was not changed in Ireland until 1991, and even then the changes were not fully in operation until 1996.

The ironically named 'cruelty man' from one of the organizations supposedly established to prevent cruelty to children would report their condition to the authorities, who in turn would hand them over to the industrial schools that were part of the vast system of coercive confinement that also included the Magdalene Laundries, the Mother and Baby Homes and the mental hospitals. Between 1930 and 1970, a minimum of 42,000 children were incarcerated in them, but the fear they generated hung over almost all working-class families. Micheál Martin, the Fianna Fáil leader who became Taoiseach in 2020, recalled how, after his grandfather died in working-class Cork, his father and younger siblings lived in fear of the 'cruelty man' and could well have ended up in an industrial school but for his grandmother Maura. 'She's the real hero in all of this. She kept it together.'[1]

I don't remember a time when I did not know certain words: Artane, Letterfrack, Daingean – the names of the places where the biggest industrial schools were. They formed a hinterland of dread. When I was eight, Georgie, a boy who lived just across from me on Aughavannagh Road, a boy I was at school with, disappeared. The word that emerged from the street was: Artane. He was a good kid, a little bit wild but sweet-natured. It was said he had stolen a bike.

Yet like everything else, Artane hid in plain sight. Anytime I went with my father to a GAA match at Croke Park, the Artane Boys Band, kitted out in their neat blue uniforms with red piping, played the national anthem before the game and performed at half-time. The band was the front for the system. In May 1962, it toured to Boston and New York. There is a big photograph of some of the members in the *Irish Independent* from that month. Each one of them is smiling and holding up for the camera a few dollar bills.[2] They were to stay with Irish-American families. Each boy carried some Waterford glass and Irish linen for his hosts, as if they themselves were part of the package of typically Irish exports. In Boston, they were received by the mayor and by Cardinal Cushing, who gave the director of the band, Brother Joseph O'Connor, $500 and every boy a signed colour photograph of himself.[3]

The then minister for education, Brian Lenihan, visited Artane in 1967. When he was about to leave, a number of the boys had assembled on the school steps behind the brothers. One of them, Anthony Burke, stepped forward. He said to Lenihan: 'They beat us every day. Stop them beating us.' Lenihan turned to his chauffeur and said: 'Get me out of this fucking place.' It became a catchphrase among the boys: 'Get me out of this fucking place.'[4] Lenihan's successor, Pádraig Faulkner, visited one of the other hell holes, Daingean. He asked the boys in a workshop which they preferred, woodwork or metalwork. Most favoured metalwork. When Faulkner asked why, the school manager replied, 'Keys are made from metal.'[5] Faulkner later wrote that 'It was to be quite some time after I left the Department of Education that I first heard the word “paedophile”. During my time as minister I hadn’t an inkling that child sex abuse existed.’

And yet, the phrase ‘child slavery’ was used about the Irish industrial school system as early as 1947, and by probably the most famous of Irish Catholic priests, Monsignor Edward Flanagan, founder of the Boys Town residential care centre in Nebraska. Flanagan was a huge celebrity because he had been played by Spencer Tracy in *Boys Town*. When Tracy won the best actor Oscar for the role, a special Oscar was struck for Flanagan. There could hardly have been a more perfect fusion of Hollywood glamour and Irish Catholic piety.

In 1946, Flanagan, who came from Co. Galway, made a triumphal homecoming tour of Ireland. But he also visited industrial schools, and called them ‘a disgrace to the nation’. Addressing a packed meeting in Cork, he urged his audience to do what my grandmother did when she sacrificed herself by marrying James Hanlon: ‘You can do something about it first by keeping your children away from these institutions’.[6] He warned that ‘punishment administered with the rod, the cat o’ nine tails and the fist is horrifying to most people. They see it for what it really is, an expression of physical revenge carried over from the early stages of primitive society.’ Flanagan called for an inquiry: ‘avoiding facts and appealing to cliches and individual prejudices is as futile as trying to settle a dispute by seeing who can shout the loudest. Little is gained unless argument leads to inquiry… My prayer is that the Christian people of Ireland will see conditions as they are and that they will take such action as they themselves may choose in attacking this problem.’[7]

Flanagan went on in 1947 to compare the system both to slavery and Nazism, describing the industrial schools as places ‘where little children become a great army of child slavery in workshops, making money for the institutions that give them a little food, a little clothing, very little recreation and a doubtful education’. He wrote: ‘We have punished the Nazis for their sins against society… I wonder what God’s judgment will be with reference to those who hold the deposit of faith and who fail in their God-given stewardship of little children?’[8]

For his pains, he was roundly denounced in the Dáil by the then minister for justice, Gerry Boland, by James Dillon, leader of Fine Gael and by an editorial in the *Irish Press*. Boland accused him of using 'offensive and intemperate language' about conditions of 'which he has no first-hand knowledge'.[9] There was a deep determination not to know. Flanagan did not allege that sexual abuse was endemic in the industrial schools (though it was) but the extreme physical violence he alluded to was the context in which every kind of depravity was possible.

Not knowing was part of the regime. As in many systems of institutionalized terror, the randomness of violence was used to generate a sense of utter powerlessness. The official Ryan report later summarized this reign of terror as 'a daily existence that involved the possibility of being hit by a staff member at any time, for any reason or for no reason'. The existential condition for the children was the cruel absurdity of 'generally not knowing why they were being beaten'.[10]

The forms of violence were unpredictable, but 'included punching, flogging, assault and bodily attacks, hitting with the hand, kicking, ear pulling, hair pulling, head shaving, beating on the soles of the feet, burning, scalding, stabbing, severe beatings with or without clothes, being made to kneel and stand in fixed positions for lengthy periods, made to sleep outside overnight, being forced into cold or excessively hot baths and showers, hosed down with cold water before being beaten, beaten while hanging from hooks on the wall, being set upon by dogs, being restrained in order to be beaten, physical assaults by more than one person, and having objects thrown at them'.

The implements used to beat children included 'canes, ash plants, blackthorn sticks, hurleys, broom handles, hand brushes, wooden spoons, pointers, batons, chair rungs, yard brushes, hoes, hay forks, pikes and pieces of wood with leather thongs attached… bunches of keys, belt buckles, drain rods, rubber pram tyres, golf clubs, tyre rims, electric flexes, fan belts, horse tackle, hammers, metal rulers, butts of rifles, t-squares, gun pellets and hay ropes'.[11]

I did not, as a child and a young man, know all of this detail. But there was never the slightest doubt that the whole point of these institutions was to be terrifying. The enslavement and torture of children was not accidental. If Artane and Letterfrack and Daingean had been like Flanagan's Boys Town, they would have failed in their primary purpose, which was to sustain a culture of fear. They had their secrets – the endemic sexual abuse of children was not meant to be known. But they were not themselves secret – Artane, for example, was a vast and very public complex with up to 830 children in it at any given time. And the violence within them radiated a dark energy of horror, a constant, invisible pulse of anxiety. If your family was not 'good', if your father died or lost his job or took to drink, you could be transported at any time into this parallel universe of absolute powerlessness.

I remember when I first read James Joyce's *Ulysses* as a student, being startled to find Artane right there as a sinister shadow, already imprinted on the imaginary life of the city. Leopold Bloom goes to the funeral of Paddy Dignam and the men discuss the fate of his young son: 'Martin is trying to get the youngster into Artane.' The Jesuit priest, Father Conmee, walks out to the industrial school to make the arrangements. The kid walks through the streets, unaware of what is being planned for him. Later on, in the night-town dream world, 'Artane orphans, joining hands, caper round' Bloom. The place flits in and out of consciousness, never quite coming into focus but always there as a portent, a sequel, the unseen fate that awaits the innocent boy. Reading the book, this made complete sense to me. It wasn't literary modernism. It was social realism.

Artane and the wider system of child slavery would break the surface of the known Irish world every now and then. Neil Jordan and the Sheridan brothers, Jim and Peter, presented a play about Artane at the Project Arts Centre in Dublin in 1971. On one of the evenings of the run, 'before the performance had quite ended a protest was made from among the audience by a [Christian] Brother who claimed it as an honour to have himself taught at one of the establishments in question. He spoke in the grip of evident passion to be answered in a like collective passion by the cast and by a considerable part of the audience and in no uncertain terms.'[12] The same year, RTÉ aired Brian MacLochlainn's innovative TV drama, *A Week in the Life of Martin Cluxton*, following a young man who has returned to Dublin after two and a half years in Letterfrack.

Yet, in 1972, the *Irish Times* could report in passing that there were more than thirty-five boys aged under twelve in Letterfrack and that 'they also have one six and a half year old boy from a broken home'.[13] There were no headlines about this, no sense that the imprisonment of a tiny child in a bleak place that the report itself described as 'bare and grim like the desolate waste of a prison yard', in the care of men who were mostly in their thirties and forties, was remarkable, still less sensational. The reporter, Mary Cummins, was told by the Brother in charge that unfortunately the keys to many parts of the complex had just gone missing, so the doors couldn't be opened. The head Brother also remarked casually that many of the boys had worked as slaves (though he did not use the term) for local farmers: 'the boys used to have to work without pay very often from seven in the morning until late at night.' There was no whiff of scandal from any of this.

Stories accumulated. Bernard MacLaverty's novel *Lamb*, published in 1980 and filmed in 1985, was clearly based on a real case in which a young Christian Brother had kidnapped a boy from an industrial school in order to try to rescue him and had ended up killing him. But when Gerard Mannix Flynn's *Nothing to Say* came out in 1983, the title was not accidental. Flynn's was the first account from inside the system (soon followed by Paddy Doyle's *The God Squad*) based on his own incarceration in Letterfrack when he was eleven. But that experience was unspeakable. He did not tell it all. 'I wasn't brave', he would write twenty years later. 'I wasn't brave enough. I was too frightened.' He told 'as much truth as I dared'. But Flynn also felt that everyone was already, at some level, aware of his story: 'they all knew that children were being sexually abused by those in authority; the government knew, the police knew, the clergy and religious knew, yet nobody could name it. They were afraid of their own shame, and conspired to deny and hide it.'[14]

Nobody could name it – or at least not fully – until my friend Mary Raftery did in 1999 in her documentary series *States of*

Fear. Three years earlier, Louis Lentin made a powerful film, *Dear Daughter,* centred on the experiences of Christine Buckley, Bernadette Fahy and a few other survivors of the industrial school for girls in Dublin, Goldenbridge, run by the Sisters of Mercy. Buckley had given an interview in 1992 to Gay Byrne for his morning radio show that generated a great deal of short-term media coverage. The nuns commissioned their own internal report from a childcare expert, who noted of Goldenbridge that 'Very powerless people had enormous and immediate power over troubled and troublesome children. The abuse of the power and powerlessness was almost inevitable. Almost any kind of abusive incidents could have occurred.'[15] But the order continued in public to flatly deny that 'the regime was cruel, abusive or neglectful'.

This was still the fundamental problem of knowing. The church, after the Casey affair, had lost the ability to define Irish reality, but it could still contest that reality. It could not stop individual stories from being told. But it could deny their authenticity, make them at best untypical aberrations, at worst outright lies. There was still a great divide of respectability. The perpetrators, even if they were losing their grip, had been in power for well over a century. They counted. The victims had never had any power. They were the refuse of Irish society. Their very trauma told against them. They were assumed to be broken people with broken narratives.

What Mary Raftery set out to do in 1998 was to tell the whole story of a system that incorporated fifty-two institutions and incarcerated something close to 50,000 children. She understood that the only way to do this was to listen in depth to hundreds of survivors. She and her researcher Sheila Ahern did what no official body had ever done in the history of the state, which was to treat the evidence of those who had been locked up and abused under its watch as valid. It was a two-woman tribunal of inquiry that required both women simultaneously to go down into the deepest dark of Irish experience and to stand back from it, to go in very close and to maintain a steady wide shot of the structural, institutional, political and cultural forces that made all of this pain, not just possible, but in a sense necessary.

I would meet her often during 1998 and 1999 and I got a sense of this burden. It was not just that the work was grim and terrifying. It was also ethically dangerous. She knew that she was intervening in people's lives, asking them to excavate layer after layer of buried trauma, without being able to offer them any formal psychological support. She knew, too, from the response to *Dear Daughter*, that there would be a wall of denial, that any mistake would be punished relentlessly and used to discredit every other claim. There was a risk for the survivors who went on camera that this could be the worst of both worlds, that they would lay bare their lives only to have them mocked yet again as delusions or shams.

When Mary's *States of Fear* series began on RTÉ on 27 April 1999, the first episode went out at 9.30 p.m., immediately after the nine o'clock news. RTÉ didn't want to do this. It, too, was afraid of what it had. In the TV listings published in the papers on April, the first film is advertised for 10.10 p.m. The timing was not a minor detail. It was a crucial signifier and Mary understood this. Coming straight after the news made the programme a national event. Mary had to take the master tapes home and threaten not to come back until the prime slot was agreed.

It was obvious from the end of the first film that a revolution was happening. Even from the day after the screening, the state was discussing a formal apology to the victims and survivors of institutional abuse. The wall of denial was definitively breached – though the Christian Brothers issued a statement about allegedly inadequate funding and claiming that '20,000 boys went through institutions run by the Brothers but only 145 complaints of mistreatment had been made'.[16]

In a sense, *States of Fear* was not quite revelation – something so deeply woven into the fabric of a society cannot be revealed because it is already known. It was an exposure certainly, a placing of certain truths in a very public place where they could not be ignored. But the real transformation was in the definition of knowledge itself – what it is, who owns it, how it is deployed. What Mary did in listening to the survivors and in giving them a way to tell their own stories was to remap the landscape of fact. The facts about this system – and therefore about the society that sustained it – had been contained within certain fields. They were in the state's official records and in the records of the religious orders. They were, more obliquely, in novels and plays. But the actual lived experiences of tens of thousands of children were not facts. They did not constitute the basis for an act of recognition.

States of Fear changed that. It used official files and historiography and the techniques of investigative journalism. But they existed to support and validate the witnesses. It started from the assumption that those who knew most and who knew best were those who had lived through and with and under the system. They were the travellers who had entered into, and ultimately emerged from, this parallel universe. For the first time in Irish public life, first-hand experience, the direct encounter with power and powerlessness in their rawest Irish forms, was put forward as primary fact. The unspeakable was not merely spoken – it was heard as evidence of the nature of the place we inhabited.

This was what was so shattering. There was no shortage of denial and obfuscation from the religious orders. Fianna Fáil, even though Bertie Ahern did issue a formal state apology, would ensure that the orders were protected from the financial consequences of their depredations. But this new order of knowledge – this is what happened to me – could not be undone. The consignment of lived experience to the margins of official reality had been crucial to the culture. From now on, at least in relation to sex and sin and shame, it would be at the centre.

40

1997–2008: The Makeover

At the beginning of March 2002, I was walking home up the Drumcondra Road on the north side of Dublin. All along the far side of the road was the outer wall of the grounds of the palace of the Archbishop of Dublin. I was thinking of how John Charles McQuaid had once ruled so much of our lives from there, how the place had exuded an inscrutable and implacable power. And that got me thinking of its current occupant, my old philosophy teacher from UCD, now Cardinal Desmond Connell.

I felt a pang of sympathy for him. He was so far out of his depth that the waters were lapping against his dog collar and all that was visible was his stern face whose expressionless impassivity was that, not of a stoic, but of a martyr about to be burned at the stake. He was even a bad liar. In May 1995, asked on television if he had paid money to victims of abuse by priests, he said: 'I have compensated nobody. I have paid out nothing whatever in compensation.' He insisted that the finances of the diocese 'are not used in any way' to make settlements in civil actions concerning clerical child abuse.[1]

In fact, in 1993 he had given £30,000 from diocesan funds to settle a case taken by Andrew Madden. He had been abused by Ivan Payne, the priest McQuaid, just after I served Mass for him in 1968, appointed as chaplain of the Children's Hospital in Crumlin. Connell had not just helped to protect Payne by paying the money, he refused even to remove him from parish work, in the course of which he continued to abuse children. The lie had been exposed in 1995 when Madden spoke out. Yet, instead of being sanctioned by the church, Connell was promoted to cardinal – an honour that had eluded even McQuaid.

As Connell himself saw it, though, there was a crucial difference between an untruth and a lie. He practised, as he told an official investigation into abuse in his diocese, the art of 'mental reservation', a form of cognitive gymnastics that demanded supreme conceptual agility: 'Well, the general teaching about mental reservation is that you are not permitted to tell a lie. On the other hand, you may be put in a position where you have to answer, and there may be circumstances in which you can use an ambiguous expression realising that the person who you are talking to will accept an untrue version of whatever it may be – permitting that to happen, not willing that it happened, that would be lying. It really is a matter of trying to deal with extraordinarily difficult matters that may arise in social relations where people may ask questions that you simply cannot answer. Everybody knows that this kind of thing is liable to happen. So, mental reservation is, in a sense, a way of answering without lying.'[2]

Connell later explained to Andrew Madden that he had not lied when he said that diocesan funds 'are not used' to compensate victims: 'He had responded that diocesan funds *are* not used for such a purpose; that he had not said that diocesan funds *were* not used for such a purpose. By using the present tense, he had not excluded the possibility that diocesan funds had been used for such purpose in the past.'[3]

It was foolish of me to be feeling sorry for Connell that morning in March 2002. He had covered up and facilitated terrible crimes. But what evoked sympathy was the handsome commercial building directly opposite the entrance to his palace. It struck me that he would have to see it every time he drove out of the gate, that the salon on the ground floor was directly in his eyeline. The elegant sign said 'Beauty at Blue Door' and, just a little less prominently, 'Prop Celia Larkin'. Engraved into the frosted glass was a slogan: 'Relax the mind, nourish the soul'.

On offer inside was a full range of adornments for the temple of the holy spirit: bikini wax €15, Brazilian wax €40, St Tropez full body tan €50.79, and reiki ('a simple, natural healing method using the laying-on of hands to transmit energy') €57.14.

The problem for the cardinal was not just this evidence of an alternative laying on of hands, a rival bid to 'nourish the soul of Ireland', a country that was now adoring – and hoping to be adored by – new gods. It was not even the perplexing nature of a Brazilian wax to a lifelong celibate. It was that 'Prop Celia Larkin'. Celia Larkin was the partner of the Taoiseach, Bertie Ahern, who was himself still married to his wife Miriam. His constituency headquarters and sometime residence, St Luke's, was just up the road, so that church and state were in extremely close physical proximity. But this part of the state, this first lady in all but name, had planted her temple of Aphrodite right opposite the cardinal's power base.

In June 1999, I was, by some mistake, invited to a state dinner in Dublin Castle in honour of the visiting prime minister of Canada, Jean Chrétien. The invitation came from Bertie Ahern and 'Ms Celia Larkin'. Celia greeted us guests as we arrived, making it clear that she represented Ireland on an equal par with her boyfriend. This was just the way it was now. But in 2001, Connell let it be known that he was 'distressed and embarrassed' by the official invitation to a state reception to honour his elevation as cardinal.[4] It, too, came from 'The Taoiseach, Mr Bertie Ahern TD and Ms Celia Larkin'.

The church had heretofore applied mental reservation to this tricky subject. Men who were in relationships with women who were not their wives were not allowed to receive Holy Communion in church, but no attempt had been made to apply this ruling to Ahern, who was a regular Mass-goer. The explanation from the church was 'We do not know the nature of their relationship'.[5] It could be an unknown known. But including Larkin on an official state invitation to a reception to mark Connell's own promotion as a prince of Holy Mother Church was pushing it too far. Things were rearranged: Larkin was not on the receiving line and Connell made a coded speech about 'marriage and family as the deep centre of human intimacy, on which the whole future of our society depends'.[6] Territory had been marked.

And yet, though Connell could never have the flexibility of mind to understand it, all of this was not quite what it appeared to be. It was not a standoff between an old Catholic Ireland and a new, more morally relaxed one, in which most people didn't really mind that the Taoiseach was making a public matter of his unorthodox private life. What was really going on was something that Beauty at Blue Door could manage much more professionally than the Archbishop's palace: the makeover. For what Ahern's long period in power, from 1997 to 2008, represented was the last throw of the dice for the old system – a cosmetic restyling and beautification of the alliance of Fianna Fáil and the church. Ahern had an instinctive feeling for a basic truth of power in Ireland – that these two pillars must stand or fall together and that it was in the party's interests to maintain the substance, if not the form, of the grand alliance.

Thus, on the one side, Ahern's foregrounding of his partnership with Larkin was a way of saying, as he put it, 'My conscience was my own business'.[7] This was, increasingly, what most Irish people felt, and it therefore did him no harm to be seen to be on their side. But, on the other hand, what made me think about the cardinal and the cosmetic salon that day in 2002 was that it was just before the vote in a referendum on abortion that Ahern himself had put forward. Its intent was not to liberalize the laws, still less to remove the absolutist amendment inserted in 1983. It was to roll back the effects of the Supreme Court judgement in the X case, by making it explicit that the threat that a girl or woman might be at risk of suicide was not grounds for abortion. This was exactly what the church and the militant lay Catholic groups wanted – to make it as if the X case had never happened. It would also reinforce the reality that, where women and girls were concerned, their conscience was emphatically not their own business. Conscience, in this renovated Ireland, was still to be an exclusive property.

Grotesquely, the man at the centre of the X case was convicted just before the new abortion referendum, of again kidnapping and sexually assaulting a girl, this time a fifteen-year-old. Ahern was proposing that if that girl, like his previous victim, had become pregnant as a result of the assault, she would be forced to give birth – or quietly flee to England. In 1995, the same man had appealed his sentence of fourteen years in prison for the X case assault. The Court of Criminal Appeal reduced the sentence to four years because, as Mr Justice Hugh O'Flaherty put it, he was a 'hard-working family man' who had not committed 'out and out rape'. O'Flaherty added that 'The court is convinced that it is not dealing with a man who is likely to re-offend.'[8]

In the event, Ahern's proposal was defeated in the referendum, albeit by a tiny margin of less than 1 per cent. But the effort to restate Ireland's position as a beacon of Catholic morality, even in face of the social change of which he himself was a beneficiary, was telling. Perhaps even more importantly, Ahern ensured, also in 2002, that the religious orders who had run the industrial schools would be effectively indemnified from the cost of claims by their victims. He made an agreement with eighteen religious congregations that, in return for some token payments, the state would pay all those costs. By 2015, the state had paid out €1.5 billion to settle claims. The religious orders had stumped up €192 million.[9]

Why did he go to such lengths to try to restore the church's authority and to save it from the consequences of its decades of misrule? Objectively, the clerical church was dying. Between 1966 and 1996, vocations to all forms of Catholic religious life fell from 1,409 to 111, a decline of 92 per cent. In 1984, the number of new diocesan clergy ordained was 171; in 2006 it was 22 and in 2012 it was 12. During the 1990s the once-great seminaries in Dublin, Thurles, Kilkenny, Waterford and Carlow all closed, leaving only Maynooth.[10]

But there were, for Ahern, reasons beyond his own Catholic instincts to make sure that the church's seawalls were shored up. He had come to power on the back of a scandal that showed how intertwined Fianna Fáil was with the church and how their fates could not be separated. In November 1994, his predecessor, Albert Reynolds, resigned as Taoiseach and party leader. It was an astonishing turnaround. He had just delivered the IRA's 'complete cessation' of its armed campaign, which was followed by a similar declaration by the Loyalist paramilitaries. His abilities as a poker player had been triumphantly vindicated. But, as his press secretary Seán Duignan put it ruefully, 'the priest was the wild card'.[11]

The priest was called Brendan Smyth, and his leering face had become creepily familiar to most Irish people from an investigative documentary made by Chris Moore for Ulster Television and broadcast on 6 October 1994. The hour-long programme used a slow-motion black-and-white sequence of Smyth in clerical garb walking towards the camera into a schoolyard, a real-life horror movie that radiated pure evil. The documentary followed Smyth's trail of destruction over four decades as he attacked children in the Republic, Northern Ireland, Scotland and the United States and, just as damningly, the repeated willingness of the church to cover up and facilitate his crimes. Those involved in the cover-up included the most senior figure in the church, Cardinal Cahal Daly, who wrote to the parents of one of Smyth's victims after they sought his intervention: 'There have been complaints about this priest before, and once I had to speak to the Superior [of Smyth's order] about him. It would seem that there has been no improvement. I shall speak with the Superior again.'[12]

This was another grim saga in which the church's waning moral authority was further undermined. But it did not seem to threaten the state – until it jumped species. It emerged that the British authorities had sought Smyth's extradition to face charges in Northern Ireland in April 1993. The warrant had lain dormant for seven months in the office of the attorney general, Harry Whelehan – the same man who had initiated legal action in the X case. This became a political problem when Reynolds unilaterally, and without seeking the consent of his Labour Party coalition partners, decided to appoint Whelehan as president of the High Court. Labour, blaming Whelehan for the X case, wanted to block the appointment, but Reynolds, in his most bullish mode, pushed it through. But then the story of Smyth and the extradition warrant ran wild. After various dramatic convolutions, Reynolds had to resign, Fianna Fáil was out of office and Bertie Ahern was its new leader.

This was, of course, Ahern's good fortune. Reynolds had fallen at a moment when, with the peace process and the beginnings of an economic boom discernibly under way, he might have transcended his earlier scandals and gone on to dominate Irish politics for another decade. But Ahern's good luck was also his warning: if the church was imploding, it could bring Fianna Fáil down with it. It would be necessary for the two sides of the national consensus to hang together lest they be hanged separately.

From her beauty business, Celia Larkin would develop a career as a 'highly regarded image consultant and personal branding consultant', preaching the new gospel that 'A strong personal brand is of vital importance – it takes control of the process of how others perceive you. It is much better to take control, as it places you in a strong leadership position and helps you increase your earning potential.'[13] There was no doubt that her first makeover project was Bertie Ahern himself, who she managed to get out of the anoraks he favoured and into serious politician suits. But when it came to controlling the process of how others see you, nobody had had much to teach him.

He had learned from his master, the man he always called Boss and would hail in death as 'a patriot to his fingertips': Charles Haughey. But what he learned from Haughey's fall was to do everything the other way round. He was the Boss inverted. While Haughey flaunted the money he got from wealthy fans, Ahern hid it. While Haughey could barely conceal his sense of superiority, Ahern was ever humble. While the Boss played the squire on his high horse, Bertie shambled around at ground level, a spectacularly ordinary man, making a splendid show of his mundanity.

I was coming home one day when he was Taoiseach and, as I was turning into the side street where I lived, I could see two police cars just across the road from my house. I was alarmed and ran up to see what was wrong. But there was no alarm. Joan, a woman who ran a little hairdressing salon in the block of shops facing my house, had had it redecorated – a new lick of paint, some new chairs and mirrors. Bertie was performing the formal opening of the redecorations. The prime minister was presiding over the grand state occasion. Our road was just outside his constituency, but some of Joan's customers naturally came from the other side of the boundary. It was important that they should see him in their daily lives.

Not that this was hard. If you went for a pint on a Saturday night, he was usually there, up at the counter, drinking the ostentatiously bland Bass beer with his cronies, always male. If you went for a walk in the Botanic Gardens, he was usually out for a stroll with his daughters. He was, it struck me, exactly like a ward boss from the great days of Tammany Hall, a nineteenth-century machine politician who made sure not to be seen to get above himself even when he was pocketing some of the proceeds of power.

He had two great gifts. He genuinely loved retail politics and he was extraordinarily good at it, moving about the streets, knocking on doors, chatting to people, making jokes, talking about football, promising to look into their little problems. A Latin American ambassador who had to accompany him for several days on a state visit to his own country told me that the great difficulty was that Ahern was not even vaguely interested in the sights and treasures that are shown off to visiting dignitaries. The ambassador realized that Ahern could talk about only two things – sport and politics in the very narrow sense of party organizations and electoral tactics. The diplomat had no interest in sport but found that Ahern would become utterly fascinated by any discussion of the minutiae of political life in some distant province he had barely heard of before. The process mesmerized him.

His other great gift was as a fixer. Because his ego was so completely under control and because he had an endless appetite for negotiations, he had long been the man who averted strikes or arranged pacts between unions and employers. As Taoiseach, these skills would be invaluable to the peace process and to the creation of the Belfast Agreement of 1998. The aptitudes of the deal-maker turned out to be a universal currency, applicable to international treaties as much as to committee meetings in dingy backrooms.

These skills led him, though, to understand that the makeover he could manage best was not dressing up, but dressing down. His instinct was to save Fianna Fáil by making it nothing and everything, not heroic or romantic but just there, just what it had long been in reality but not in image: the embodiment of the way power worked in Ireland. The very diminutive by which he was universally known, Bertie, suggested an unthreatening amiability, a man who wasn't going to have a fight with anybody because he was everybody's friend. Where Haughey was a centrifugal force, Bertie was centripetal. Where Haughey carried a knife to cut the unfaithful away from the faithful, his protégé carried a magnet. His favourite politician was Bill Clinton. Clinton's craving for love was extravagant and extraordinary. Bertie's was quiet and ordinary. But the impulse was the same: the desire to pull everything towards himself. His political method was to establish himself as the nucleus of pragmatic good sense and attract disparate elements towards that centre. Planet Bertie spun serenely on its own axis, exercising its own silent gravity. Approaching objects, even those that once looked like potentially destructive meteors, fell into its orbit and took up their positions as compliant satellites.

Money flowed towards him, too. A tribunal investigating corruption in the planning system (its star inside informant was the former government press secretary turned 'lobbyist' Frank Dunlop) began looking into an allegation that Ahern had accepted money from the Cork-based property developer Owen O'Callaghan (a claim both men vigorously denied). It found itself examining bank lodgements and other transactions totalling IR£452,800 – the equivalent in 2008 of €886,830. These lodgements – some of them in sterling and therefore almost certainly not from his salary – were made to Ahern's accounts in the period between 1988 and 1997. On his own evidence, he didn't have a bank account for the years between 1987 and 1993 – including the period when he was minister for finance – and kept his money in cash. As he later complained – suggesting that this was the reason why he could not fully exonerate himself – 'Cash has no earmark. Cash does not identify its source.'[14] It was also the case, he claimed, that he was very lucky with bets on horses: 'As is well-known publicly I am interested in horse racing and over the years I have placed bets on horse races. Over the years I have won various sums of money. Some of these would have been paid in sterling.'[15]

In explaining why he gave Bertie Ahern money even though he barely knew him, one businessman, Barry English, encapsulated the connection between Ahern's amiability and his attraction of money: 'I work in the construction industry and my clients are developers and the like and I don't think it does me any harm to be known as a friend of Bertie Ahern's.' On the other side of this exchange, Ahern's expression of gratitude to English was equally telling: 'He said "Thanks very much and I'll sort you out".'

The evil twin of this warm glow of inclusion was the fear of exclusion. If membership of the circle gave you the sense that you were being 'sorted out' by the minister for finance (as Ahern was at the time), not being one of the lads made you wonder whether a rival was being sorted out ahead of you. In the RTÉ documentary *Bertie*, Ahern's money man Des Richardson explained, of an exercise in December 1993, when he raised IR£22,500 for his pal, that 'If I wanted to raise IR£100,000 for Bertie Ahern, I could have done that in one week.' He subsequently explained to me what he meant by this statement. Richardson referred to a payment of IR£5,000 from Pádraic O'Connor of National City Brokers (a payment O'Connor maintained he intended for the party, not for Ahern personally): 'I could have raised IR£100,000 for Bertie in one week, and let me explain how. Pádraic O'Connor from NCB had given me £5,000 for Bertie. If I had gone to every stockbroker in Ireland and said "Pádraic O'Connor/NCB has given me £5,000 for Bertie Ahern, who was minister for finance at that time, so I would like you to do likewise", in my view, they would have been falling over themselves to do so, just to maintain a "perceived" level playing pitch for their company. It's all about perception.'

In the minds of those who were raising money for Fianna Fáil (and Richardson was the party's chief fundraiser), business people were not giving money because they wanted to support democracy but because they 'perceived' that otherwise their company would be playing on a pitch that was slanted against them. In many ways, it barely matters whether that perception was accurate or not. It served in itself to create both the fear of not being on the inside and the promise of being 'sorted out' if you were. It tilted the operation of relations between money and politics, business and the state away from the general public interest and towards a search for mutual benefits in which politicians got access to the money and business people got access to the politicians.

The beauty of this dependence on 'perception' is that it is unquantifiable, unaccountable and therefore limitless – not that different from the spiritual power of the church. A system in which everyone knows that bribes have to be paid in return for favourable treatment from the authorities is disastrous. But one in which everyone is trying to size up who's in and who's out, who is in a state of grace and who is risking damnation, is more insidious and even more corrosive. It generates, on the one hand, a feeling, for those who see themselves as insiders, of being untouchable. It creates, on the other, an unnameable dread among those who see themselves as outsiders. They never feel they quite know what's going on. They believe there is a power that could, if it wished, do them harm. They learn to be cautious, watchful and discreet. They are slow to challenge bad behaviour. These germs would prove to be fatal.

Ahern was as lucky in politics as he had been in betting on horses. He became Taoiseach in 1997, just in time to inherit a boom that was, as he would later famously put it, 'getting even more boomer'. As the economy went into overdrive, it became possible for him to be, indeed, everybody's friend, simultaneously cutting taxes and increasing public spending, spreading money around to keep almost everybody at least a little bit happy. This was the great cosmetic for the deep crisis of authority. Ireland had entered, it seemed, a post-historical time when enmities and divisions and competing interests could all be managed painlessly and Fianna Fáil would just keep the system going. The new Ireland was a machine and Bertie would stroll around in his overalls, keeping it well oiled.

The success of this makeover meant that, in the first period in its history when Ireland had real and widespread prosperity, there would be no change in its political culture, no reflection on its values, no thought given to anything but the sustaining of the system itself. It may have been dying inside but it glowed with the fake tan of success.

41

2000–2008: Tropical Ireland

'The "Island of Ireland" is strategically located at the centre of "The World".' As a statement of the self-absorption and grandiose delusions of Celtic Tiger Ireland, this one would take some beating. But it was intended literally. The 'Island of Ireland' is not the island of Ireland. 'The World' is not the world. The island is part of a man-made archipelago off the coast of Dubai, 300 artificial platforms in the Arabian Gulf, surrounded by an oval breakwater, shaped to form the map of the world. 'The World', as the sales pitch had it, 'reinvents the earth', which was pretty much what Irish elites thought they were doing in the first decade of the twenty-first century.[1] 'The expected completion date of The World', it added, 'is 2008.' This was also, as it happened, true of the Celtic Tiger. Except that completion, in this case, meant that it really was finished.

The 225,000-square-foot Island of Ireland was bought in 2006 for €20 million by a consortium of Irish business people led by the Galway-based property developer John O'Dolan.[2] They intended to build a range of apartments, with basic suites to be sold for €750,000 and penthouses for €2.8 million. There would be a full-sized authentic recreation of the Giant's Causeway,[3] and a hint of 'the architecture of Ireland through the ages'. In case potential investors might be put off by the thought of damp thatched cottages festering in the rain or mock-adobe bungalows on windswept hills, the promotional brochure stressed that this would mostly consist of a 'landscaped courtyard area, evoking the wide Georgian squares of Dublin'. For older property developers, there would presumably be a warm glow of nostalgia for the Georgian squares that they and their political allies had done their best to obliterate in the 1960s and 1970s.

One of the attractions of this new Ireland was that, unlike the artificial mounds to its east where European countries were crowded together, it had the wide Atlantic between itself and the next landfall. 'Ireland's position is great', explained one of the developers, Ray Norton. 'Because America is quite far away, there are fantastic sea views and few waves so it's ideal for swimming.'[4] At the same time, though, you could travel by water taxi from Ireland to New York in ten minutes – the best of both worlds.

The plan, aptly enough, was endorsed on the scheme's website by the serving Taoiseach Bertie Ahern who evoked 'substantial Irish achievement across a wide range of human endeavours' and expressed the hope that the 'Island of Ireland' would be 'seen as symbolic of the best of those achievements and reflect the confidence and vision of Irish people in the new millennium'.[5] Those achievements, the brochure made clear, were those of the millionaires who had made Ireland what it was and who now deserved a literal place in the sun: 'We had a vision… to bring a little piece of Ireland to the sun. To create a luxury hotel resort to which those who have shaped our modern, thriving nation can escape as a little reward once in a while, without ever losing touch with home.'

These potential buyers were told that they would be honoured with the title 'the founder members of Ireland'.[6] It would be as if they were the revolutionary heroes of the 1916 Rising or the war of independence, the more cosmopolitan equivalents of Patrick Pearse or Michael Collins or Constance Markievicz. Irish history, that tangled mess of pain and darkness, was now beginning again and they were the Adam and Eve in its Garden of Eden. If history, as Joyce's Stephen Dedalus had complained, was a nightmare from which he was trying to awake, where better to open one's eyes on the new day than on a simulacrum of Ireland dredged up from the bottom of the Persian Gulf?

Even before the scheme was advertised, word spread among the rich in Ireland and there were 125 expressions of interest in buying a piece of this dream within a few days. The pitch was perfectly tuned. The great men who 'shaped our modern thriving nation' could feel their Irish pride in villas with 'more than just a hint of Irishness to them', but they would not actually have to be in Ireland – a particular advantage for those among them who were tax fugitives. This would be the perfect Ireland, with a vague sense of 'history' in its mock-Georgian square but no politics, with a simulacrum of Irish conviviality ('bars that will remind you of home') without the bother of an unruly plebeian populace (this is 'the most exclusive real-estate development on the planet'). It would also be the perfect form of globalization – a world with Ireland at its centre, like Jerusalem in medieval maps. The multi-millionaire's solipsism and self-regard would mesh seamlessly with the fantasy of a Hibernocentric universe: 'The World can actually revolve around you!!'

In fact, the Island of Ireland in Dubai was the fulfilment and incarnation of a fantasy that had hovered around the collective imagination of Ireland's elite for a long time. In the late 1980s and early 1990s, Irish intellectuals revived the idea of the Fifth Province (Mary Robinson evoked it in her inaugural speech as president in 1990). They meant a place of art, ideas and ideals. But the real fifth province of the Irish imagination was a sunny Ireland, washed by a bluer, warmer ocean, where there were no taxes, no history and no social obligations.

In Charles Haughey's era, this fifth province was Grand Cayman Island, where money frolicked under palm trees, free from the predations of the taxman and the prying eyes of those who wondered about its origins. In Bertie Ahern's era, it was Bermuda, whose tax-haven status Ireland hoped to emulate. It was not for nothing that while English critics referred to the Irish Financial Services Centre in Dublin as 'Lichtenstein on the Liffey', the Industrial Development Authority preferred the aspiration to be 'the Bermuda of Europe'.[7] The Island of Ireland in Dubai brought these two notions together – a sunny island that was far away but still, somehow, 'home'.

Even when this fantasy had to be brought home to the real process of making money from property development in dark, rainy Ireland, it retained its grip. The great satirist of the boom, Paul Howard, speaking through his alter ego Ross O'Carroll-Kelly, noted that the Southside of Dublin had 'a hot humid climate not unlike that of the Cayman Islands with whom southsiders share a natural affinity'.[8] In the Celtic Tiger era of property development, Ireland was always sub-tropical. As the property editor of the *Irish Times*, Orna Mulcahy, noted of one of the iconic (doubly iconic in being, in the end, unbuilt) developments of the boom years, Sean Dunne's would-be 'new Knightsbridge' in the swanky Dublin district of Ballsbridge: 'I dug out the architects' drawings from the bottom of a heap under my desk and yes, there it was: sunshine, flooding the imagined plazas and courtyards and bouncing off the glass of towering apartment blocks. Pert-breasted women strolling around in T-shirts and sunglasses.' Even the underground shopping mall was filled with palms, orchids and cacti. The sense of direction was madly askew. As Mulcahy noted, 'On the property developer's compass, you see, there is no north... the vast majority of balconies built during the boom faced south – even the many that actually looked due north and enjoyed direct sunlight about once a year.'[9]

In other countries, global warming was a threat. In Ireland it was a fantasy. The sun-drenched country of the developers' plans became the place in which much of the population took up mental residence. During the boom years, people under forty stopped wearing overcoats, even in the dismal winter. The Atlantic wind that stabbed through a flimsy jacket and T-shirt or turned the bare legs of short-skirted girls blue was really a gentle zephyr. Cafés and restaurants began to colonize the footpaths outside their doors for the alfresco dining appropriate to the rain-free, sunlit climate.

There was, moreover, a physical extrusion of Ireland to the world's sunspots as Irish people invested vast sums in property abroad. Of the €50-plus billion of Irish money spent on buying foreign property, much of the large-scale commercial investment was in the UK or the US. But a substantial amount was spent on acquiring either second homes or investment properties in the Mediterranean, the Adriatic or even further afield. Nowhere was too exotic, especially if it was an island and sunny. At the height of the boom a not untypical report in the property pages of the *Irish Times* stated that 'Cape Verde Development, a company started by Tom Sheehy, a Clonakilty-based property fit-out specialist and backed mainly by Cork and Limerick business people, sold 200 units of its 449-unit scheme off plans when it launched a few weeks ago, most of them to Irish buyers'. Sheehy's company was planning to spend €2 billion on the scheme. To put that in context, it was the same as the pre-tax profit of the most profitable company registered in the state, Microsoft Ireland.

Cape Verde is off the coast of Senegal. I was chatting to a Dublin taxi driver in 2007 and he mentioned, almost in passing, that he had just bought an apartment there. I asked him where it was (I was genuinely quite hazy about the location). He said he didn't know, though he reckoned it was quite close to Tenerife. Had he ever been there? No. Why did he buy the apartment? Because it was a sound investment for his savings – it would certainly rise in value over the years. In the Ireland of this time, security for your old age could be imagined as a punt on a place you could not locate on a map of the world. A year later, when the Irish property market collapsed, developers were offering to throw in a free Cape Verde apartment if you bought a house in Co. Cork.[10]

Foreign property replaced emigration as the Elsewhere that had long been part of the Irish imagination. The little Irelands of Brixton or Boston were now the little islands in the sun. This imaginative displacement was part of the larger confusion of space that came with Ireland's experience of extreme and rapid globalization. The question of whether Ireland was a balmy sub-tropical paradise or a wet, wind-lashed rock on the eastern Atlantic was a subset of a larger question – what continent was Ireland in anyway? That, in turn was part of a wider problem – the uncertainties of both space and time that made it hard for Irish people to be quite sure where they were living, and when. The fixed co-ordinates of geography and history ceased to be especially useful.

The question of which continent Ireland belonged in was posed by Mary Harney, Tánaiste and minister for enterprise, trade and employment, when she told the American Bar Association in 2000 that 'History and geography have placed Ireland in a very special position between America and Europe… Geographically we are closer to Berlin than Boston. Spiritually we are probably a lot closer to Boston than Berlin.' This idea of Ireland as a liminal space, between one continent and another, its proximity to continental Europe a mere detail, was, of course, highly political. It was intended to identify Ireland as an outpost of American values at the physical and political margin of European ideals. Ireland was to be seen as a part of an 'Anglo-Saxon' sphere, sharing the thirst of the US and the UK for frantic consumption, property bubbles, free-range banking and the elevation of the private sector above all public purposes. A less flattering way of putting this was deployed in the *New York Times* in 2005, reporting that 'Dublin has become known in the insurance industry as something of the Wild West of European finance'.[11] All that cowboy imagery that had done so much to shape our imaginations as we strove for modernity could now be turned back on us.

In this headlong plunge into a euphoric embrace of hyper-globalized postmodernity, the whole idea of place was submerged. Ever-rising house prices in the cities forced would-be homeowners out into new commuter belts. Astonishingly, just 4 per cent of the growth in the Irish population between 2002 and 2006 took place in the five main cities combined. The result, especially in relation to Dublin, was a vast expansion of the effective area of the city. Large swathes of Wicklow, Wexford, Meath, Louth, Westmeath, Carlow, Offaly, even Cavan and Monaghan, became parts of outer Dublin. The very concept of Dublin became extraordinarily diffuse. As early as 2001, the president of the Royal Institute of Architects in Ireland, Tony Reddy, pointed out that Greater Dublin 'could occupy an area the size of Los Angeles by 2010', even though it would have just a quarter of the American city's population.[12]

The bewildering of our sense of space was matched by a disorientation of time. There was a specifically Irish 'end of history'. Two of the great continuities of Ireland since the eighteenth century – mass emigration and political violence – seemed, by the late 1990s, to be definitively over. The church, the great guarantor of continuity over the centuries, was coming apart at the seams.

The old was imploding but the new was not yet fully born. The familiar religious code of values, the language in which right and wrong could be discussed, lost its meaning before Irish society had fully learned to speak any other tongue. The institutional Catholic Church had dominated both the public identity and the personal values of a majority of the population from the middle of the nineteenth century. The gradual rise of urban, secular and Anglo-American cultural norms on the one side and the horrific crimes of child abuse on the other broke that dominance. The real effect of the loss of church authority was that there was no deeply rooted civic morality to take its place. The Irish had been taught for generations to identify morality with religion, and a very narrow kind of religion at that. Morality was about what happened in bedrooms, not in boardrooms. Now, instead of moving from one sphere to the other, it seemed to be lost somewhere in between.

The landmarks of historical time were crumbling. This helped to feed a feeling that the past had little relevance to the new era and that it should be, quite literally, obliterated. On a visit to Shanghai, Bertie Ahern sighed with envy at the power of the city's mayor to bulldoze everything in his way: 'Naturally enough I would like to have the power of the mayor that when he decides he wants to do a highway and, if he wants to bypass an area, he just goes straight up and over.' Paradoxically, this obliteration of a sense of historic time also suggested that the future would be pretty much like the present. The operative tense in the grammar of Ireland's boom was the present continuous. The idea of the future as a different time, with its own imperatives, was largely absent from the Tiger mentality. Sustainability – a concept that incorporates a sense of the future into the present – was the great unthinkable.

The non-existence of the future meant that it was okay to build huge numbers of one-off houses in the countryside where the inhabitants were assumed to be ageless – otherwise it might have seemed wise to think about issues like isolation and immobility that might arise when they got old. It also underpinned the extraordinary decision, in the age of global warming, to create an almost completely car-dependent society. With very limited fossil fuel resources of its own, and a share of energy from renewable sources that was less than half the OECD average, Ireland became one of the highest per capita carbon emitters in the world. Ireland's total energy consumption increased by 83 per cent from 1990 to 2007 – a bad enough record. But transport energy use increased by 181 per cent. The future that Ireland was imagining was an American motopia of the 1950s in which petrol was dirt cheap, guilt-free and infinitely available.

There was an abiding irony in this. The whole revolution of the 1950s had been necessitated by the sense that there was no Irish future. This was then a terrible thing. But fifty years on, this absence of futurity was a good thing. Property prices would keep rising. All assets would continue to inflate. All lives would get better. The boomer would get boomer. The consequences of this inability to imagine the future were not at all abstract. Since the present was one in which property prices were constantly rising and the historic experiences of boom and bust had been rendered irrelevant, there was no point in listening to those who droned on about what had happened before. To insist that all known property bubbles had always burst was to miss the point that this was a new time with its own new laws of perpetual motion.

The other paradox, though, was that this apparent reassurance that the vicissitudes of history had been disarmed generated, not reassuring calm, but hysteria. Time speeded up to a frenzy. In their book *The Builders*, Kathy Sheridan and Frank McDonald quoted one property industry insider on the shift in the idea of a 'phase' in relation to construction and sale of housing estates: 'Before the boom, it used to be Phase 1 this year and Phase 2 the next; now there was a day between them if that.' Builders would set a price, sell a lot of houses quickly and then decide that the price was too cheap. 'What happens then is that you call the next bunch of exact same houses "Phase 2", and the price is hiked maybe 15 per cent. And that could all happen in a few days or in an afternoon.' In the property bubble, the clock was always ticking loudly – time really was money as prices rose by the day and the pressure to buy something – anything – right now became irresistible.

The greatest befuddlement of all lay in the upending of Ireland's relationship with the rest of the world. The project of modernization had been an attempt to become like other countries. But between the late 1990s and 2008, other countries were told they must strive to be like Ireland. Our already hyped-up vision of ourselves was magnified by being reflected back at us in the admiring gaze of foreigners. This, ironically, was particularly true in the years when the Irish economy was most like Humpty Dumpty – bloated, fragile, sitting smugly at a great height and headed for a fall. In 2005, the official government publication *Lithuania in the World* announced that 'Lithuania is keen to repeat the economic growth story of Ireland, the Celtic Tiger'. In 2006, two centre-right Latvian parties, Latvia's Way and Latvia First, promised the electorate that they would follow the Irish path and raise living standards to Irish levels within a decade. In January 2007, the government of Trinidad hosted a seminar on 'The Irish Model of Economic Development – Lessons For Trinidad and Tobago'. The following August, the Americas Society and the US/Uruguay chamber of commerce heard a presentation on Ireland, concluding that the 'Irish model is a strategy that can work for other countries, irrespective of time and place'. Even as late as February 2008, the first minister of Scotland, Alex Salmond, was pledging that 'we will create a Celtic Lion economy to rival the Celtic Tiger across the Irish Sea'.[13]

We were truly trapped in the hall of mirrors, though, when Republican politicians in the US started to suggest that America itself should follow the Irish path. In April 2008, Phil Gramm, the former Republican senator and economics adviser to presidential candidate John McCain, told *U.S. News & World Report* that 'The only place socialism is seriously debated in the world is in Washington, D.C… Ireland is a perfect example. Senator McCain's people immigrated from Ireland along with millions of others because they were hungry. Today, Ireland has among the lowest tax rates in the world, one of the best business climates in the world, and as a result they have overtaken Americans in per capita income.'

In September, McCain himself picked up the theme in one of his televised presidential campaign debates with Barack Obama: 'Right now, the United States of American business pays the second-highest business taxes in the world, 35 percent. Ireland pays

11 percent. Now, if you're a business person, and you can locate any place in the world, then, obviously, if you go to the country where it's 11 percent tax versus 35 percent, you're going to be able to create jobs, increase your business, make more investment, et cetera.'[14]

McCain got the figures wrong (the corporation tax rate in Ireland was 12.5 per cent) and his timing was rotten: even as he spoke the Irish banking system was frantically trying to hide the scale of the bad loans to property developers that rendered it effectively insolvent. The whole argument was based on the same delusion that had gripped Ireland itself – those fabulous GDP figures that showed the Irish as having 'overtaken Americans in per capita income' were essentially fictional. But in citing Ireland as the model that his putative presidency would follow, McCain was putting the final seal on the idea that this previously benighted island was now the star that must be followed. The Irish formula was the new universal truth of economics, society and development. It transcended history and geography and, as the Uruguayans had been told, it worked 'irrespective of time and place'. Even sceptical Europeans began to believe this: in May 2008, an extensive article in *Le Monde* hailed Ireland as 'un "american dream" à l'européenne'. But what was much, much stranger if you were Irish was the notion that the US might seek to create 'un Irish dream à l'Amérique', that the tribute band was now more popular than the original hitmakers.

The problem with this idea was not just that it was factually wrong or that it was believed by politicians and policymakers around the world. It was that the Irish themselves came to believe in it. They managed, collectively, to misunderstand why they become prosperous and in doing so to waste and eventually to destroy that prosperity. The rise and fall of the Celtic Tiger was indeed a kind of moral tale, but the lesson is not that free-market globalization is a panacea for the world's ills. It is, on the contrary, that politics, society, morality and collective institutions matter.

There is no doubt that Ireland's economic performance in the late 1990s was genuinely remarkable. The rate of unemployment in the fifteen European Union countries as a whole remained more or less static throughout the 1990s. In Ireland, it was cut in half, from a desperately high 15.6 per cent to 7.4 per cent (and shortly afterward to less than 5 per cent). The level of consistent poverty fell from 15 per cent of the population to 5 per cent. The overall value of Irish exports more than doubled between 1995 and 2000. The number of people at work in Ireland also doubled, from just over a million in 1988 to 2.1 million in 2007. In the country that had dreaded total depopulation, the population rose at a phenomenal rate. While the rest of the EU added one person to every 1,000 between 1998 and 2008, Ireland added ten.

All of this was wonderful to live through, and it was also a lot of fun. Coinciding with the gradual establishment of peace in Northern Ireland, it made Irish people feel a lot better about themselves. Ireland shook off much of its authoritarian religiosity and became a more open and tolerant society. The pall of failure that had hung over the Irish state for most of its independent existence seemed to have been blown away forever. Ireland was young, buoyant and energetic, and to those who complained that older spiritual values were being lost, the ready answer was that having a job and a house and a choice about staying in your own country can be pretty spiritually uplifting, too. Even the undertone of hysteria in the increasingly frantic consumer spending could, for the first few years, be forgiven – Irish people had been relatively deprived for a long time and were now working at least as hard as they played.

But a simplistic narrative took hold. The power of free-market globalization had been unleashed by low taxes and light regulation. Ireland became a large-scale version of a TV makeover show, with the 'before' pictures showing a slovenly, depressed wretch and the 'after' images a smiling, bling-bedecked beauty, who went on to start her own self-improvement course for similarly abject little countries.

This story required the forgetting, not of the dim, dark past, but of very recent history, the history that most people in Ireland had actually experienced. For a start, one of the reasons the Irish economy grew so fast after 1995 is that it had grown so slowly before that. As the historian Joe Lee noted in 1989, 'No other European country, east or west, north or south, for which remotely reliable evidence exists, had recorded so slow a rate of growth of national income in the twentieth century.'[15] Much of what happened in the 1990s was simply that Ireland, integrated into the European single market, caught up with the living standards of the region it belongs to – western Europe – and got to where it should have been all along. The energy unleashed by this process, combined with the advantages of not being weighed down by an old heavy industrial base, allowed Ireland (temporarily) to outperform those European neighbours. But, in a longer perspective, all that was happening was a regional levelling-out.

There was also amnesia about why Ireland had changed. Feminism, for example – the long struggle against the control of female sexuality and reproduction by the Catholic Church and Fianna Fáil – was a *sine qua non* for the miraculous doubling of the workforce. Paradoxically, the Ireland of the late 1990s and early 2000s reaped enormous economic benefits both from the repression of women before the 1970s and from their subsequent relative liberation. The old culture produced a demographic boom – Irish fertility had been startlingly high well into the 1980s, with the result that there were a lot of youngsters around in the 1990s. At the same time, however, those fertility rates dropped dramatically as women gained more freedom, allowing ever larger numbers of mothers to join or stay in the paid workforce. Rather grotesquely, Ireland was also reaping the economic benefits of mass emigration in the 1950s, which meant that many of the elderly people who should have been in Ireland were actually in the UK and elsewhere.

Nor was it easy to recall that Irish governments themselves did things to make the boom possible, the very mention of which would have caused the average Republican senator in the US to call for an exorcism. One was to invest heavily in the expansion of state-funded third-level education. A rare reason to be cheerful after the bursting of the Irish bubble was that 42.3 per cent of the population aged twenty-five to thirty-four had completed third-level education, the second highest rate in the EU and a crucial factor in attracting multinational investment.

But instead of trying to understand itself and the complex social, historical and political processes – and sheer good fortune

– that had created the Celtic Tiger, the ruling elites encouraged the belief that Ireland had captured a genie whose golden lamp need only be stroked to ensure success. The formula was ultimately simple – be nice to the rich. Give capital its head, don't stand in its way, and it will work its magic. This self-delusion became stronger as the boom was actually petering out. In essence, the real boom lasted from 1995 until 2001. What made it real were two tangible forces: sharp rises in output per worker (productivity) and in manufacturing exports. Both of these forces began to wind down in the new millennium. Productivity growth between 2000 and 2006 slowed to its lowest level since 1980. It was half what it had been in the classic boom years and actually slipped below the average for the developed (OECD) economies. By 2008, Irish productivity levels were below the OECD average.

So was the level of growth in Irish exports. Ireland's total share of the world's trade in goods, which had risen steadily since the mid-1990s, peaked in 2002 and then started to decline every year. While there was a steady rise in the export of services (especially of financial services), it was more than offset by the fall in the share of trade in tangible merchandise. Between 2000 and 2006, the number of manufacturing jobs in Ireland actually declined by about 20,000 – a fall masked by large rises in the numbers at work in construction and the public services.

None of this was disastrous in itself. The boom had given Ireland a historic opportunity. There was money in the government coffers. There were more and more people at work. The demographics were uniquely favourable. The air of depression and inferiority had been banished. What made the real end of the Celtic Tiger after 2001 disastrous, however, was the decision of the Fianna Fáil-led government to replace one kind of growth with another. Ireland had become prosperous because its workers were unusually productive and because its economy was exporting stuff that people wanted to buy. The government decided that it would stay prosperous by going for what the National Competitiveness Council would later summarize as 'growth derived from asset price inflation, fuelled by a combination of low interest rates, reckless lending and speculation'. Being prosperous would be replaced by feeling rich. Consumption would replace production. Building would replace manufacturing as the engine of growth. The nation was to think of itself as a lottery winner, the blessed recipient of a staggering windfall. It was to spend, spend, spend. Understanding why Ireland had become prosperous and how prosperity could be sustained was much less important than the manic need to keep growing, and spending, at all costs.

This was a very odd time to be writing about Ireland. To state the obvious was to be a heretic. I wrote in July 2005, for example, that 'Life in Ireland now is surrounded by a constant, low-level awareness that things don't quite add up. There is a gap between the upbeat, boom-time atmosphere and the nagging feeling that the frantic, almost hysterical insistence on how rich we all are is a case of protesting too much. We see the evidence before our eyes – the houses, the cars, the Prada handbags, the designer clothes. But the great unspoken question of contemporary Ireland is "how can they afford that?" How can people with relatively ordinary jobs afford €1.5 million houses and two cars and creches and two foreign holidays and private schools? And the answer, the thing that fills the gap between appearance and reality, is a four-letter word: debt. We stuff the breach between the way we think we ought to be – cool, fabulous, on top of the world – and the way we really are, with borrowed bank notes. Why are we behaving like this? The basic reason, surely, is because we believe the hype about ourselves. We have delusions of grandeur, created by the constant stream of assurances about how rich we are and fed by the insecurity of a consumer society that measures wealth by expensive display. We forget that our incomes are... somewhat illusory'.[16]

It took no skill or insight to think or say this kind of stuff. But to do so was, in a phrase that became more current as the boom became more self-evidently absurd, 'talking down the economy'. In 2007, Bertie Ahern complained in a speech about those of us who were full of gloom: 'Sitting on the sidelines, cribbing and moaning is a lost opportunity. I don't know how people who engage in that don't commit suicide.'[17] The chief executive of the largest bank, Allied Irish Banks, Eugene Sheehy, who was steering it towards the rocks full steam ahead, warned that 'perception can become reality'.[18] What he meant was that those who saw what was happening and spoke of it were in fact creating the very problems they perceived.

It struck me at the time that this was all very churchlike. The church had always covered things up because to expose them would be to commit the sin of 'giving scandal'. Scandal was not the appalling behaviour of churchmen. Rather, the revelation of that behaviour was much worse because it damaged the faith of the flock and therefore endangered their immortal souls. In the post-Catholic culture that was emerging at this time, this notion had simply migrated from religion to economics. To say what one saw was to damage the faith in the Irish miracle that was needed to sustain it.

As early as August 2000, the International Monetary Fund put the Irish bubble in the context of all known modern property booms and concluded that 'there has not been a single experience of price inflation on the scale of Ireland's which did not end in prices falling'.[19] Given that prices actually doubled in the six years after that warning, the scale of the coming crash was utterly predictable. Yet the overwhelming majority of Irish economists either contented themselves with timid and carefully couched murmurs of unease or, especially in the case of most of those who worked for stockbrokers, banks and building societies and who dominated media discussions of the issue, joined in the reassurances about 'soft landings'.

I must admit that my own faith in what I was writing was becoming quite shaky. Reality defied reason. It was like watching an acrobat perform increasingly outlandish tricks on a high tightrope with no safety net. Every time you gasp in fright and wait for the terrible fall, she steadies herself and does another pirouette. And each time, you feel more like a fool. You come to doubt your own eyes. The boom carried on for a good five years after its reality had disappeared. It was a giant machine for sucking in borrowed money that the Irish used mostly for buying bits of the country from each other at ever more inflated prices and, when they ran out of bits of Ireland, doing the same with bits of other, sunnier islands.

It began to feel as though, in the hyped-up world that Ireland inhabited, there was no difference between illusion and reality, substance and spirit. Maybe we had created an economy of pure imagination, in which things were true because we believed them to be so. All that it needed to keep going was regular injections of belief – and outsiders provided that by confirming that, yes, they, too, could see the miracle. Maybe this time, the statues really were moving.

42

2009–2013: Jesus Fucking Hell and God

Towards the end of 2008, debt brokers in the City of London started to use a mocking acronym: PIIGS. American investment banks like Citigroup and JPMorgan Chase began to use it even in their research reports. It stood for the new descaminados, the shirtless ones of an imploding Europe: Portugal, Italy, Ireland, Greece and Spain. PIGS had been around for decades as shorthand for the Mediterranean economies; now the second 'I' placed Ireland among them. Just as it had been fifty years earlier, Ireland was in bad company, consigned again to the exterior darkness of failure. And, as in 1958, there was a yearning to ascend from this Purgatory into the Heaven of European respectability. By January 2010, the government's economic adviser expressed the hope that Ireland might 'be in a strong enough position within two years to be no longer associated with the 'PIIGS' group of European countries'.[1]

We no longer wanted to be in balmy climes. The perpetual sunshine of the boom years, with southern light illuminating our spotless lives, was switched off and we came home to the grey skies and the slanting rain and the Atlantic winds. We did not wish to be numbered with the other little PIIGS, whose houses, like ours had been blown down by the big bad wolf of the great banking crash. All of them were Mediterranean countries. Sure, Ireland was practically polar.

The minister for finance, Michael Noonan, insisted that Ireland must be thought of as a 'northern European country' – not, in other words, like those chaotic, irresponsible southerners.[2] Noonan also mocked Greece in an interview with Bloomberg: 'If you go into the shops here [in Ireland], apart from feta cheese, how many Greek items do you put in your basket?' Defending the dismissive tone of these remarks, he insisted: 'I just wanted to make it important to an international audience that Ireland does not have strong links with Greece… I'm trying to stop contagion.'[3]

This was, in its own odd way, familiar ground. Fear of contagion had been the dominant anxiety of the Irish State for its first five decades. Back then, the contamination to be kept at bay was moral and spiritual: modernity was a plague and Catholic purity was the vaccine. Now, the idea of infection was economic: Ireland had to protect itself from the imputation that it was one of those hot countries with feckless attitudes and dodgy morals. This was a case of protesting too much – Ireland's crisis really was exacerbated by decades of political corruption and regulatory indifference. But the more truth there was in the feeling that Ireland's own public culture had helped to create the disaster, the greater the imperative to prove that we were good northern Europeans. We could immunize ourselves from contagion by being ostentatiously righteous – a gesture deeply encoded in our muscle memory.

Just as this imprinted impulse was stirring itself anew, a related instinct also asserted itself: the old comforts of sin and shame. This was a paradox. The disintegration of the Celtic Tiger coincided with the final collapse of the Catholic Ireland. In 2009, the Ryan report into the hideous abuse of children in the industrial school system was published. It was followed, that same year, by the Murphy report into clerical abuse and cover-up in the Dublin Catholic archdiocese. Two worlds were dying together. The sudden and dramatic end of the great delusion of infinite Irish progress towards the nirvana of endless abundance converged with the long, agonized death throes of Mother Church. Ireland found itself at once post-boom and post-Catholic. The time zone it inhabited lay between two bitter aftermaths.

These afterlives were encoded in two kinds of haunted, empty spaces. In 2014, my mother died. I went back to Saint Bernadette's, the church where I had served Mass for John Charles McQuaid, to help arrange the funeral. It was a cold spring. The priest, who was looking after the parish on his own, explained apologetically that he could no longer afford to turn on the heating in the church. His congregations were, in any case, too small to justify the expense. Emptied of its throngs, the place now seemed eerily cavernous. You could see your breath in the chilly air. Voices echoed off the soaring vaults. The permanent place that had replaced the temporary shed-like structure where my mother had married my father was now itself overtaken by time, stranded in a future that was, when I served Mass there, unimaginable. It was a factory of faith that had now become part of Ireland's religious rustbelt, a temple of a lost culture whose meaning was, to those who inhabited its hinterland, increasingly obscure.

Side by side with these imaginative ruins were the ruins that Ireland has spent much of the early twenty-first century so frantically constructing: uninhabitable houses. In 2006, when the boom was apparently still at its height, David McWilliams had coined the term 'ghost estate' to describe empty or unfinished housing developments in out-of-the way places. They, too, like Saint Bernadette's, had been built on pure faith. They were acts of devotion – shrines dedicated to the fervent belief that anything you constructed anywhere would repay the true believer through the magic of ever-rising property values. Between 1991 and 2006, the number of households in Ireland had increased by 440,000. The number of housing units had increased by 763,000. The 2011 census showed that 230,000 housing units were empty (not including holiday homes).[4]

This double emptiness had to be filled, and here, too, there could be a strange solace in a resurgence of old habits of mind. How to understand the plain and terrible fact that, in the global banking crash of 2008, Ireland was not suffering just like everybody else? Its fall was more vertiginous. Its collapse was more dramatic. Its reversal of fortune was more extreme. There was a cold but effective consolation in the return of the barely repressed – this was a drama that could be shaped as a medieval morality play. That drama had three acts – sin, punishment and redemption. We would confess that we had transgressed. We would take our penance. And we would, by enduring the pain without complaint, redeem our reputation and be welcomed, chastened but purified, back into the communion of northern European saints. This religious approach made Ireland's real problems infinitely worse in reality. But it provided a dramatic arc that was curiously satisfying. Ireland had lost the plot but, in this ancient narrative, it could find it again.

To grasp what was happening in Ireland between 2008 and 2013, it was necessary to confront that most tormenting of questions: how could we not have known? There had not been any great mystery about what was coming. The basic figures told the story: a breathtaking three-quarters of the total lending of the Irish banks – €420 billion, or about two and a half times the size of the economy in 2008 – was lent for property, construction and land speculation.[5] Catastrophe was preordained – once property prices stopped rising, the banking system was doomed. But the last years of the boom had been a crazed, defiant howling against the incoming tide of inevitabilities, a tragicomic rage against the dying of the light. It was as if a sheer act of willpower could prevent the future. If we refused to acknowledge it by doing yet more of what we had been doing, it would not arrive.

Such was the determination not to know, that the response of the system to warnings of its imminent demise was to carry on defiantly – out of spite if nothing else. Seán Fitzpatrick, whose Anglo Irish Bank was the core of the meltdown, later came close to blaming the economist Morgan Kelly, who had publicly predicted a collapse in property prices and hence deep trouble for banks like Anglo, for this: 'In some ways, actually, the Morgan Kellys who were predicting the [bust] actually prolonged [the bubble] because people were, you know, really determined to prove him wrong – [to] say, Ah no, that is a whole load of shit, that is not going to happen.'[6] This belief was not abstract. There was a frantic, deranged insistence that if you just keep constructing, those buildings will form a dyke to keep the floods at bay. From the beginning of 2006, when all the signs of the coming crash were glaringly present, to December 2009, when the property market was in freefall, almost a quarter of a million new housing units were built.

Another thing that carried on regardless was the shopping trip to New York or Philadelphia or Boston. Through the boom years, it had become normal to fly across the Atlantic once or twice a year and spend a long weekend in the megastores, malls and outlets. Woodbury Common in New Jersey, Franklin Mills near Philadelphia and Wrentham Village outside Boston were suburbs of middle Ireland. I remember in Macy's in New York, when you went to get your discount card as a foreign visitor, they didn't even ask for your passport anymore. They just asked: 'You Irish?' and you nodded 'of course'. This craze did not slow down as the portents of doom were gathering – it accelerated. In 2007, New York City alone received 291,000 visitors from Ireland. In 2008, 520,000 Irish residents flew across the Atlantic. That was more than twice as many as in 2000. It was also close to one in eight of the entire population. There was a sense in all of this of a final fling and perhaps also of one more rub of the American relic, a last prayer in the air-conditioned temples of consumerism. But last before what?

When the fall did come, the Fianna Fáil-led government, headed by Ahern's chosen successor Brian Cowen, simply could not grasp what was happening. Its entire reaction was based on incomprehension. It was cognitively impaired. Since the 1960s, Fianna Fáil had linked itself, financially and morally, to the property developers who epitomized the native resurgence. This co-dependency had embraced the bankers who funded those developers, especially Fitzpatrick's brash, upstart Anglo Irish Bank. It could not believe that these gods were failing. It chose instead, with dreadful consequences for the Irish public, to believe that they were merely experiencing some temporary troubles. What the gods needed were more sacrifices.

The specific conceptual error was to confuse liquidity with insolvency. The only way for Irish officialdom to understand the crisis was to think of the banks as having a liquidity problem – the flow of cash through the system had dried up because of the global credit crunch that had started with the subprime mortgage crisis in the US. In fact, the Irish banks were insolvent. They were not financially embarrassed; they were broke. Two of them in particular – Anglo Irish and Irish Nationwide – had no real functions in the economy. They did nothing but provide the chips for the gamblers in the great Irish property casino. And those chips were now worthless. The game was up. These banks were dead – but the state insisted on believing that they were sleeping beauties, waiting to be revived by timely infusions of public money.

The government behaved like a general who has lost 10,000 men on a failed attack, but, in order not to have sacrificed them in vain, loses 100,000 on the next assault. Figures ceased to mean anything. Numbers – the hard currency of policy and power – were treated as if they were pure fiction. They had already been untethered from reality by the untrustworthiness of Irish GDP, subject as it was to accountancy as creative as any Irish literary genius. The irony now was that they were actual – the vast sums being poured into the banks truly did represent the collective wealth of the Irish people. But the bigger they got, the more fantastical they seemed and the more free-floating, as if they referred to nothing but themselves.

When Anglo Irish Bank's chief executive, David Drumm, demanded that the Central Bank put €7 billion into its coffers (a figure, as he was recorded saying on internal tapes, he 'picked... out of my arse'), the hapless financial regulator, Patrick Neary, responded with panic: 'Jesus, that's a lot of dosh... Jesus fucking hell and God... well you do know the Central Bank only has €14 billion of investments'. But as Anglo's director of capital markets, John Bowe, explained to his colleagues at the time, even €7 billion was mere bait on the hook: 'the reality is that actually we need more than that. But you know the strategy here is that you pull them in, you get them to write a big cheque... and they have to support their money.'[7] The strategy worked because the state was primed by its necessary delusions to take the bait.

The scale of the public money put into the banks was – and remains – scarcely comprehensible. By the end of 2018, the state had spent €66.8 billion directly on the banks and a further €22 billion to service the debts it entered into in borrowing much of this money.[8] That's €100 billion taken from a working population of 2.2 million. For this, the people got assets and income worth about €48 billion. Around €42 billion, in other words, was sucked into a black hole. This, moreover, was money Ireland did not have. After the national savings had been drained, Ireland went out and borrowed money to put into its failed banks: €40 billion or so in additional net debt was taken on for this purpose.[9]

Ireland's meltdown was undeniably part of the wider crisis of the global banking system and of the Eurozone's near-death experience. But it was not a normal part. The scale of its bank bailout was vastly, grotesquely inflated in comparison with other countries in Europe. Between 2008 and 2015, Ireland injected €62.8 billion into its banks. Germany, which had a very serious banking problem of its own, put €64.2 billion into its troubled financial institutions. Germany issued €135 billion in guarantees for bank liabilities. Ireland issued €284 billion.[10] Proportional to the size of their economies, in other words, the Irish poured more than ten times as much of their money into failing banks than the Germans did. In 2013, it was calculated that Ireland, with less than 1 per cent of the EU population, had paid 42 per cent of the total cost of the European banking crisis.[11]

This was another kind of disappearing Ireland. The money – €42 billion of it – just went. Asked plaintively by the chairman of a (very belated) parliamentary inquiry into the disaster, 'So where did it go to?', the governor of the Central Bank, Patrick Honohan, said, 'It went on buildings that nobody wants to live in, that is part of it. It went on paying wages for the builders of those buildings. Some of the money, I would say a much bigger sum, went from borrowers... to the sellers of property and good times... Where did the money go up in smoke? It went up in smoke on property that was not worth anything and is no use to anybody.'[12]

This new Vanishing Ireland, was, as the narrator of Anne Enright's 2007 novel *The Gathering* puts it, 'a whole fucking country – drowning in shame'.[13] But shame and sin were our familiars. In the haze generated by all this money going up in smoke, we could make out these unforgotten landmarks. So long as we could see them, we were not entirely lost.

A religious narrative of Ireland's fall suited a lot of different interests. It was good for those most directly responsible. As Brian

Lenihan, the minister for finance who implemented the enormous bank bailout (and the son of his namesake who had been a senior Fianna Fáil figure for so long before him), put it in November 2010, 'let's be fair about it, we all partied'. Everybody was to blame – and because it was true that so many people had been in some way complicit with the delusions of the boom, much of the population was highly susceptible to this imputation of collective guilt. But it was also good for the international political and financial establishment. The disaster had two sides – stupid borrowing by Irish people and stupid lending by international bankers. The Irish willingness to accept the burden of sin made the second part of this equation go away. Blame was collectivized – but only up to a point. All Irish people were responsible for the debts of a few Irish casino banks; no international agencies were responsible for pumping money recklessly into those banks.

The wages of sin was a kind of political death. In December 2010, Ireland's existence as a sovereign state was effectively suspended. In return for a €67.5 billion package of loans, a Troika of international institutions – the International Monetary Fund, the European Central Bank and the European Commission – took over the direction of Irish fiscal and therefore of political and social policy. The local administration operated under strict supervision. It was obliged to implement a savage programme of what one influential figure in devising it, the German government adviser Professor Hans Kastrop, later called 'overblown austerity measures'.[14] In an economy that had shrunk by 10 per cent in 2009 alone, this was insane. Unemployment had already shot up from 4.5 per cent in 2007 to 13.5 per cent in 2010, and was evidently still rising. The rate of child poverty was doubling. Nevertheless, under the Troika programme Ireland continued to put money into its banks – €17 billion was injected after the international consortium took charge. But wages, pensions and jobs were cut in the public sector and there were savage cuts to welfare benefits, healthcare and education. There were sharp tax rises, including for low-paid workers. Even among those now in charge, there was an acceptance that much of this went too far, too fast. Ajai Chopra, the IMF's member of the Troika, later suggested that the cut of €6 billion implemented in

2011 'was more aggressive than warranted by the weak state of the economy'.[15]

But rationality was not the point. The operative ideas were punishment and purgation. The approach was no more scientific than the premodern practice of bleeding a sick patient. Yet not only did Irish governments meekly accept and implement the Troika programme, but most of the public did so, too. There were sporadic protests, most of them eventually cohering around resistance to charges for domestic water use. But the main reaction to the whole disaster was conventionally electoral. It was both radical and highly limited.

In the general election of February 2011, Fianna Fáil was destroyed. It suffered by far the biggest defeat for any outgoing government since the formation of the state. It lost more than half its vote and its number of seats dropped from seventy-one to twenty-one. This was a big moment. One half of the alliance that had dominated Ireland since the 1930s, the institutional Catholic Church, was already on its knees. Now the other half was brought to the same level. And it was clear that neither of them would ever return to their old positions of dominance, either jointly or individually. The system had been broken. Or, more accurately, it had broken itself by mocking the faith that its adherents had placed in it. The church corrupted its own holiness. The nationalist party could not even maintain the sovereignty of the nation. These were breaches that could never be repaired.

But even with Fianna Fáil's collapse, there was no real political challenge to the Troika's punishment programme. Fianna Fail's votes went largely to the traditional, and entirely likeminded, opposition party, Fine Gael, and to the Labour Party which promised to challenge the new regime but, when it took office under Fine Gael's cheery and palliative leader Enda Kenny, contented itself with implementing it. It was obvious that Sinn Féin, which won 10 per cent of the vote in the Republic in that 2011 election, would now become the main political alternative, with predicatable long-term consequences for politics on the island as a whole. But for the moment, it was able to do no more than articulate dissent along with an array of smaller leftist parties.

There was, of course, the old alternative of voting with one's feet. Emigration started up again: 420,000 people left Ireland in the five years between 2011 and 2015. Most of them were young. Those who were not among the recent European migrants who now returned to their home countries headed off mainly to Australia, Canada and the UK. But, as in the 1950s and 1980s, this was not just physical migration. It was also mental withdrawal. The dormant gene of exile switched itself on again with remarkable speed. Even those who did not go, thought about it. Though raised amidst an unprecedented Irish prosperity, young Irish people still found it natural to accept that change was locational, not political. A poll conducted in October 2012 found that 51 per cent of those between 18 and 24, and 42 per cent of those between 25 and 34, said they considered emigration as an option. This was not wanderlust – only 10 per cent said they would emigrate 'to experience living abroad'.[16] The rest were bailing out as a result of the conditions created by the bailout.

But even the quick reopening of this old escape hatch did not fully explain the widespread sense of resignation to collective punishment. There was plenty of grief and despair – suicide rates rose sharply between 2007 and 2011. There was huge financial distress – by 2014, 12 per cent of all residential mortgages in Ireland were in arrears. Unemployment and poverty caused deep anguish. But most of this was kept behind closed doors. Other than kicking out Fianna Fáil, there was neither a very coherent campaign of protest nor an effective demand for a fundamental reordering of the political system that had first created the disaster and then, by its deluded response, magnified it by turning a banking crisis into a sovereign debt crisis.

This implied, deep down, a low level of expectation. It was as if Ireland had not been prosperous enough for long enough to consider that condition as the norm. It was something to be enjoyed while it lasted – with the fatalistic implication that of course it would not persist. The journey to modernity had been a roller-coaster ride, shooting up in the 1960s and 1970s, plunging down in the long 1980s, soaring to dizzying heights in the great boom, plummeting nauseously in the great bust. The collective experience was one of shifting between extremes, and this had created a mentality in which the self-delusions of the Celtic Tiger had been haunted by unspoken expectations of comeuppance. The frantic, hyped-up feeling of boomtime had been driven in part by an underlying belief that this time was finite and probably short, that Ireland would soon revert to a very mean mean. If we were going to have to endure the hangover, we might as well enjoy the prelude. 'We all partied' was, on the large scale, a big lie, but it worked as a small and intimate psychological truth.

And it sustained an acceptance of the PIIGS story. Irish culture was not sufficiently post-Catholic not to be drawn into a narrative that combined the old appeal of Confession and penance with a new, celebrity drama: rehab. The Troika years were Ireland's stay in Purgatory reimagined as the Betty Ford or Priory Clinic. In order to be rehabilitated, Ireland had to show itself to the world as willing to undergo a regime of discipline and deprivation. In return, it would be accepted again as a northern European country. It would even be used as an example again. Just as, in the delusions of boomtime, the 'Irish model' of development was one to be followed, now the Irish model of redemption through suffering was an example, especially to the recalcitrant Greeks. The reward was that the Irish 'I' could be deleted from PIIGS. A new self, formed by expiation and exoneration, could be restored to respectability.

43

2018– : Negative Capability

On 26 May 2018, I was sitting in a pub across the road from Dublin Castle with a Fianna Fáil TD from the West of Ireland. We had both been in the castle for the official declaration of the results of a referendum to remove the ban on abortion that had been placed in the Constitution in 1983. The result was stunning: the Eighth Amendment was repealed by the same majority – two to one – that had passed it thirty-five years earlier. The choice to repeal was endorsed, moreover, in almost every part of Ireland – there was no great difference between the cities and the country, no epic cleavage anymore between the new and the old, the traditional and the modern. Whatever side of the debate you were on, it was undeniable that Ireland's sense of itself had been turned upside down.

The Fianna Fáil TD I was having a drink with was both happy and sad. He had, against the grain of most of his party, supported repeal and he was pleased that it had passed so emphatically. He was sad because he had not spoken to his elderly parents, who were in their eighties, for a few weeks. They lived on a small farm. They were devout Catholics. They belonged to the old world that was now vanquished. Since he had come out in favour of repeal, he had felt uneasy with them. He avoided talking in particular to his father about the subject, certain that it would lead only to awkwardness and upset.

While we were chatting, his phone rang and he answered it. It was his sister at home on the farm. I couldn't help overhearing the conversation. She was very happy with the result, too, and they talked about that. Then he asked her how their father and mother were taking it all. Delighted, she said – sure both of the parents had voted for repeal. 'Daddy said he couldn't bear thinking of all those women coming back from England and not being able to tell anyone what they were going through.' There had been, all along in the old man's mind, another history, a history of migrants and absentees, of secrets and silences. He was, it seemed, glad to let it out at last.

The pub was packed and getting noisier by the minute as ecstatic campaigners came across the road from the castle. They were all young, more women than men. They were lit up by the still-dawning realization of what they had achieved, not just that they had won but that they had done so more comprehensively than anyone had imagined possible. Three years earlier, I'd seen many of the same faces in the same places, when they had fought and won a brilliant campaign to make Ireland the first country in the world to introduce by direct popular vote equal marriage for any 'two persons without distinction as to their sex'.

That was an epochal moment, too. I had been in the United States while most of that campaign was going on and arrived home a few days before the vote. I went to see my father. I asked him about the referendum: what did he reckon? He was always an open-minded man, unprejudiced and humane. But I wasn't quite sure how he felt about marriage and the family – things that had been so much at the centre of his life – being redefined so radically. He looked at me with deep puzzlement, as if in the months I had been away I had completely lost the plot and become a stranger to Ireland. 'Sure of course it will pass', he said. 'Everybody knows somebody who's gay.'

Everybody knows – words of liberation. That campaign for same-sex marriage was the best I had ever seen because that's really all it said. It was not about revelation. It was all about recognition: you know us, you are us, we are you. But what was being recognized was not just the wonderful and ordinary variousness of Irish lives and desires, it was Irish society's other secret self – not the one that contained all the darkness and in-turned violence, but the great secret of intimate grace. Ours had been a place in which the quiet kindness of human acceptance, of loving and liking people even when their lives were not as they were supposed to be, had been consigned to the private realm, even while, paradoxically, we presented to the world a face of intolerance that was never really our own. On the morning of that referendum result in 2015, it had struck me that 'We had a furtive, anxious hidden self of optimism and decency, a self long clouded by hypocrisy and abstraction and held in check by fear. This Ireland [has] stopped being afraid of itself. Paranoia and pessimism lost out big time to the confident, hopeful, self-belief that Irish people have hidden from themselves for too long.'[1]

But, three years later, pretty much everyone thought that the abortion referendum debate would be more harrowing and more divisive, and the outcome much closer. Abortion had been symbolic in a way that LGBTQ rights had never been. All the psychic energy of change and resistance, all the fierce desire to control and define the future as a predictable extension of the past, had been invested in it. It was the great boundary line, the limit beyond which Ireland would never go, the border that gave shape to the whole territory. So long as it was there, there was a safety net of Irish exceptionalism, an encoded memory of holiness. If it was gone, the high-wire act of Ireland's modernity would be seen for what it really was – openly precarious. It was easy to understand why, for many people, the loss of this illusion of comfort might be too much to bear.

In fact, the result of the abortion referendum in 2018 was even more emphatic than that on same-sex marriage in 2015 and, devastating though it was for the losing side, it did not really feel like a civil war. The big reason for this was the one I was overhearing on the phone as the Fianna Fáil TD talked to his sister about why their elderly, rural, Catholic parents had voted for repeal. The really startling fact was not that the young had voted for change. It was that, in absolute terms, a greater number of people aged sixty-five and over had voted to repeal the anti-abortion amendment than those aged twenty-five and under.[2] The obvious way to understand what was happening was to think about how young Ireland was, how many of its people were cosmopolitan, highly educated, shaped by the experience of growing up in one of the most globalized economies in the world, repelled by the double standards of a society that expected women to deal discreetly with the messy parts of their lives in order to preserve the vestiges of tattered illusions.

All of that was true and, to me, exhilarating. But it missed this more remarkable fact that fully 40 per cent of the over-sixty-fives voted for repeal and, because they actually turned out in bigger numbers than the young, that meant that they outnumbered the young in the ranks of the supposedly new, liberal Ireland. As I sat there listening to the Fianna Fáil TD's phone call, I was much more intrigued by the news of how his parents had voted than by the buzz of excitement around us. There was, within it, a double recoil. There was his surprise at the realization that he did not quite understand his parents. And there was their rebound from what they themselves had almost certainly done thirty-five years earlier, which was to vote to make a statement about Ireland's perpetually exemplary place as the great beacon of the Catholic world.

In that vote to undo what had been done in 1983, Ireland was not just going back to revisit a moment in its recent past. It was being taken aback – by itself, by its own subtleties and complexities, by the ambiguities that had been there all along but that could only now be fully acknowledged. For that older generation, this was not really a change of mind. It was an acceptance that it was always in two minds. One of them craved certainty, fixity, the ability to declare an imaginary future that would conform to an imaginary past. The other knew that the real lived history of the place and the people who inhabit it was one of being utterly unfixed, of dealing with radical uncertainty through evasions, silences and fictions. It was time to allow that second, submerged consciousness to come up for air.

Did it surface because the great monoliths of the church and Fianna Fáil had fallen, or were they themselves undermined by its upward pressure? Both, of course. The great gamble of 1958 – that economic transformation would sustain rather than destroy the existing system – had seemed, over the subsequent decades, a winning bet. The hegemony formed by the fusion of nationalism with Catholicism had not merely weathered the great shift from rural to urban, agricultural to industrial, protected space to hectic corridor of global capital. It had not merely withstood the challenge of the Troubles. It had seemed to thrive. It did so because it successfully imported development. It found a way to keep economic transformation separate from the process of indigenous, organic change. Two things – the great wave of investment and technology coming from America and the functioning of politics and power within Ireland – could, it appeared, coexist without disturbing each other.

If anything, for a long time this idea of economic development as a separate sphere, a force to be attracted from outside rather than one generated from within, had allowed the native system to indulge itself. Religious obscurantism was okay because the place in which Pfizer was making all the Viagra was another Ireland. Not knowing was okay because the high-tech, knowledge-based economy was a parallel universe. High-level corruption in banking and politics were okay because they did not threaten the multinationals, who had their own sacrosanct relationships to money and power.

It had also been okay to set aside the people who were left behind in the great transformation. They were not necessary to the process of development. Those who could not do as I had done and acquire the educational capital that was the currency of the new society – the children and grandchildren of the rural dispossessed and of the urban labourers – were surplus to requirements. Ireland did not, it seemed, need to do the things that other European societies had done as part of the modernizing process: create robust systems of public provision of housing, healthcare and education. These systems could be left perpetually half-built, stranded like ghost estates somewhere between nineteenth-century ideas of religious-based charity (the education and health systems remain largely under church control) and a twentieth-century welfare state. There was no imperative to be fully serious about laying social and institutional foundations. The massive edifice of the globalized economy would not be built on top of them. It would land on them from above.

It is just about imaginable that this separation could have gone on indefinitely. Yet that would have required three things not to happen. The church would have needed not to destroy itself from within by unleashing and facilitating so much viciousness against women and children. The system of patronage and power perfected by Fianna Fáil would have needed not to tip over into outright kleptocracy, with such devastating consequences for the indigenous economy and the lives of citizens. And Irish nationalism would have had to sustain its romance of martyrdom purely as a matter of sentiment and aspiration, to not become so brutally real that it had to be faced and painfully rethought.

But all of these things did happen. Ireland had its own continuing history. It was not merely thrust into a twilight zone where it went from the premodern to the postmodern at warp speed. Its own stories were also unfolding in their own forms and at their own pace. They were interacting with the grand narrative of modernization in ways that made it impossible for the 1958 revolution to save the old order without ultimately destroying it.

The first person I ever saw on television, the storyteller Eamonn Kelly, remembered a Christmas in his childhood in Killarney when the postman brought a parcel. The label said: If undelivered please return to Mrs Mary Rudden, 35–36 Ditmar's Boulevard, Queens, Long Island, New York, USA. Inside was some article of clothing for everyone in the house, including 'a very bright looking tie for my father – he'd nearly want to be under chloroform before he'd wear it'. For himself, there was a suit. 'When the coat was finally buttoned up on me and the trousers, a bit like a plus-fours, strapped below the knees over long stockings and buttoned shoes with patent leather that you could nearly see yourself in, then I was told to parade up and down the floor. And this show-off was great until I began to realize that more of the family were laughing than were giving vent to admiration. So, I demanded a looking-glass to see what was the cause of all the merriment.'

When he saw in the mirror, he realized that 'what might be the height of fashion in Ditmar's Boulevard would only reduce me to ridiculosity in… Killarney'. His mother was 'prevailed upon to go to work on it with the scissors… and by taking it in a bit here and letting it out there, by shortening it where it was too long and by lengthening it where it was too short, she ended up with a suit of clothes more in keeping with the hand-me-downs and the home-made outfits' of the town.[3]

This is what happened in Ireland in my lifetime. A huge parcel of modernity was delivered. We tried it on, paraded around in it and eventually caught sight of ourselves in the looking glass. We got to work with the scissors and refitted it around ourselves, shaping it to the hand-me-downs of our own collective experiences: to the pre-existing conditions of national and religious identity, to the realities of our geography as part both of an archipelago with its own very specific historic entanglements and of a wider Europe, and to the common search for belonging in a globalized world. We ended up with something more in keeping with the homemade experience of mass migration, belated economic development, brutal conflict and the competing desires to be both distinctively ourselves and the same as everybody else.

In the years after the great crash of 2008, I realized that I had been quite wrong about stability in Ireland, or at least that what I had been right about had now changed beyond recognition. For most of my life, Irish society was, in spite of the fierce tensions of modernization and of the Troubles, remarkably stable. The thing that seemed innately and radically unstable was the foreign direct investment, the flow of American money. It was by definition mobile capital. Increasingly, too, much of it was intangible, vested not in plant and production but in patents and brands and intellectual property. It came, so it could go. It was dangerously unstable.

This was still true. But it obscured another truth: however unmoored American capital was, it was actually less so than Ireland itself. This was not an abstract idea. In those years after the crash, there was one overwhelming reason why Ireland did not go under. The multinational sector of the economy carried on as if nothing was happening. On paper, the amount of US investment in Ireland actually more than doubled between 2010 and 2015. Some of this at least was real and it helped to balance out the effects of the punitive austerity programme. It kept the show on the road. It was not that Ireland's dependency on this kind of inward investment had become fundamentally less dangerous. But, in relative terms, that hazard was now less unpredictable than our own homemade volatilities.

We had come to take American investment more or less for granted. We could no longer do the same for the country it was being invested in. What we knew about ourselves now was mostly what we were not. Different modes and models – some complementary, some competing – had, over the course of sixty years, been adopted. Each had had its triumphs. None had endured.

We were not holy. The idea of Ireland as an exemplar of faithfulness to immemorial religious orthodoxies is now dead. It had its great revival in the 1980s, but it proved to be almost all performance. It could not get a grip on reality. It could not change behaviour. It could not stop women and LGBTQ people and the children of the industrial schools asserting themselves and infiltrating their truths into the collective consciousness. It could not withstand the revelation of its own betrayals. In particular, it could not endure against the most shocking realization of all: the recognition by most of the faithful that they were in fact much holier than their preachers, that they had a clearer sense of right and wrong, a more honest and intimate sense of love and compassion and decency.

We were not violent revolutionaries. The pull of an irredentist nationalism had been very strong. Its ideological and emotional sources were still flowing in my childhood and they formed a powerful confluence with the Catholic uprising in Northern Ireland. They were fed by Loyalist reaction and by British misrule. But violent nationalism did not match the contours of our reality either. The vast majority of us didn't have the stomach for it – the killing was too brutal, too nauseating, too futile and too apparently unending. It did not offer a plausible future. A United Ireland imposed without consent, with the Brits driven into the sea and the Protestants subdued, was not any kind of possible endpoint. It could only be the beginning of another conflict.

But Ireland was also not, sixty years into this process of change, East America – any more than it had been, after spending the nineteenth century in the United Kingdom, West Britain. The fear that stalked so many Irish artists and intellectuals in the 1960s and 1970s – that Ireland would disappear as a distinctive cultural space – was misplaced. It was true, of course, that an urbanized culture was not the same as a rural one, that (as happened everywhere else) new technologies and social forms stripped away the intimate, infinitely nuanced local meanings inherent in an older sense of place. But it was also true that that older sense of place had always competed with an equally old sense of displacement, that there was no simple indigenous culture to be lost. Irish culture was perfectly fine with transformations and translations, with negotiating between contexts. That was, in fact, where it was most at home. Ireland did not feel any less Irish for knowing and accepting the fluid, contrary, conflicted nature of what that term, home, must contain in a migrant culture. It felt more so.

The last thing Ireland was not, though, was settled. There had been a long and sometimes desperate struggle to belong, to be accepted as one of those advanced countries that has achieved the proper, privileged stage of being fully developed. This, too, had its great moment in the Celtic Tiger boom, when it seemed that Ireland could not merely hold its head high but could look down on others – even its partners in the European Union with their old-fashioned vestiges of social democracy and institutional restraint. This, too, had been another illusion – the illusion of arrival. Ireland had not in fact arrived. The boomtime years were not, as they appeared, the happy ending to a tragic history, the just reward for suffering and endurance. They were merely another failed attempt to hold a slippery and fluctuating existence in place, to pretend that it had assumed, once and for all, its rightful form, that the future would be an infinite extension of the fabulous now.

In not being all these things there is, at least, a sense of possibility. What is possible now, and was entirely impossible when I was born, is this: to accept the unknown without being so terrified of it that you have to take refuge in fabrications of absolute conviction.

In 1958, and for many decades afterwards, there was this sense that, if it did not pretend to know itself thoroughly and absolutely,

Ireland would not exist at all. It was so unbearably fragile that, without a hyper-exaggerated self-image, it would vanish. The fear that it might be nothing meant that it must be everything. So many of its real stories were hidden, occluded in shame and secrecy, that it had to have vast official fictions: the beacon of spiritual values, the oppressed nation moving inexorably towards its destiny of unity and freedom, the poster child of economic globalization. Ireland was not to be expressed. It was to be asserted – in political rhetoric, in public piety, in cruel violence. Because the complexities were unendurable, reassurance could be found only in such grand and hollow simplicities.

This same logic applied north of the Border. Northern Ireland, too, was a polity built as a rampart against an undesired future, a redoubt of Protestant hegemony that would keep at bay forever the threat of annexation by a Catholic state. But this, too, required a culture of pure assertion. Because its sense of itself was embattled, it had to be constantly embellished. It demanded an excess of definition, an inflated identity that could not include its minorities, its dissidents, its actual complexities. If it did not constantly proclaim itself, it too would vanish. That exaggerated and exclusive self-image mirrored the one on the other side of the Border. But it also solidified, within its own borders, a minority counterimage with the same fear of annihilation and thus the same need for overstatement, the same craving for sharp-edged definition.

Perhaps we are learning to live without being so defined. Over sixty years of change, and through periods of despair, delusion and derangement, we have arrived at what the poet John Keats called negative capability: 'capable of being in uncertainties, Mysteries, doubts, without any irritable reaching after fact & reason'.[4] Or, in Ireland's case, an island capable of living with uncertainties, mysteries and doubts without reaching after fictional certitudes. Keats suggested that there is a problem with 'being incapable of remaining with half-knowledge'. Maybe Ireland has reached the point of accepting that half-knowledge – the ability to see clearly what is, while also acknowledging what remains dark – is better than the swinging between the pretence of knowing everything and the denial of what you really do know.

When I was born, there was no future and now there is no future again. Back then, it was a distressing thought, an alarm bell that awakened energies of change. Now, it is a more positive idea: there need not be a single, knowable future. The Belfast Agreement of 1998 suggested that it is possible to live and thrive without knowing what some imagined final state might be – and even, implicitly, that there need not be a final state at all. In the Republic, the ambiguities and reverses of the modernizing process, the swings between euphoria and desolation, have at least banished daydreams of inevitable progress and the illusions of arrival. Almost anything seems possible and, where once that was a thought too terrifying to be entertained, it is now, at least, two-sided: a warning but also a promise.

The change that was unleashed in 1958 went far beyond the intentions of those who created it. But for all its tensions and disruptions, it worked because it was not just a transformation. Ireland did not start as one fixed thing and end up as another. It moved between different kinds of unfixity. In the hurry through which known and strange things pass, the strange things were sometimes very well known and the known things were often deeply strange. Ireland came to accept that its familiar self had hidden a deep estrangement – of exile, of reality, of ordinary experience. It did not start out as isolated and become globalized. It brought its global history back home and, in the process, came to be, if not quite at home with itself, then more so than it had been before. It grew – in wealth, in population, in economic and political standing – but it also allowed itself, gradually, painfully, and with relief, to contract, to shrink away from the stories that were too big to match the scale of its intimate decencies. We ended up, not great, maybe not even especially good, but better than either – not so bad ourselves.

Acknowledgements

My life is too boring for a memoir and there is no shortage of modern Irish history. But it happens that my life does in some ways both span and mirror a time of transformation. I am of the generation that all the change was meant to be for. And it also happens that, for almost all of my adult life, I have been privileged to be able to write in public about that process of change while it has been unfolding. This book builds on these two things – the particular perspective of a particular family background and the decades of trying to articulate something about the place that might make some sense to my contemporaries.

In relation to the first of these, I owe everything to my parents, Mary and Samuel, to my siblings Kieran, Mary, Valerie and Patrick and to the love of my life, my wife Clare Connell. For the second, I have drawn on work made possible by the support and indulgence of many great editors: John Doyle and David McKenna at *In Dublin*; Vincent Browne at *Magill* and the *Sunday Tribune*; Dermot Bolger at Raven Arts Press and New Island; Conor Brady, Geraldine Kennedy, Kevin O'Sullivan, Paul O'Neill and a great range of colleagues at my homeland in the *Irish Times*, one of the world's most civilized newspapers; and Robert Silvers, Ian Buruma and Jana Prikryl at the *New York Review of Books*.

Throughout almost all of this period, I have worked, as with this book, with my editor Neil Belton, whose insights and inspiration have been valuable beyond measure. I have also had great help from my agent Natasha Fairweather. I would also like to thank Colm Tóibín, Catriona Crowe, Leonard and Ellen Milberg, Eamon Duffy, Padraic MacMathúna, Liam Glynn and the people of Ballyvaughan who made lockdown endurable and, I hope, productive.

Notes

Prelude. The Loneliest Boy in the World

1 Mícheál de Mórdha (trans. Gabriel Fitzmaurice), *An Island Community* (Dublin: Liberties Press, 2015), p. 566.
2 Ibid., p. 509.
3 *Irish Press*, Saturday, 25 December 1948, p. 6.
4 de Mórdha, *An Island Community*, p. 506.
5 Ibid., pp. 442–6.
6 Fred Hoyle, *Ossian's Ride* (London: William Heinemann, 1973, reprint), p. 9.
7 Ibid., p. 10.
8 *Irish Independent*, 2 January 2004.

Chapter 1. 1958: On Noah's Ark

1 *Irish Press 1931–1995*, Monday, 16 December 1957, p. 4.
2 Reproduced in Tom Garvin, *News from a New Republic: Ireland in the 1950s* (Dublin: Gill & Macmillan, 2010), opposite p. 119.
3 *Irish Times*, Thursday, 16 August 1951, p. 5.
4 *Irish Times*, Wednesday, 29 April 1953, p. 8.
5 *Irish Times*, Monday, 3 January 1955, p. 1.
6 John F. McCarthy (ed.), *Planning Ireland's Future: The Legacy of T. K. Whitaker* (Dublin: Glendale, 1990), p. 46.
7 *Irish Times*, Saturday, 15 February 1958, p. 1.
8 *Irish Times*, Wednesday, 19 February 1958, p. 1.
9 Des Hickey and Gus Smith, *A Paler Shade of Green* (London: Leslie Frewin, 1972), p. 138.
10 *Irish Times*, Monday, 17 February 1958, p. 1.
11 *Irish Times*, Tuesday, 18 February 1958, p. 1; *Hansard*, 17 February 1958, vol. 582, col. 861.
12 *Irish Times*, Tuesday, 18 February 1958, p. 1.
13 *Irish Examiner*, Tuesday, 18 February 1958, p. 7.
14 *Irish Independent*, Wednesday, 19 February 1958; p. 3.
15 *Evening Echo*, Wednesday, 11 March 1959, p. 2.
16 *Evening Herald*, Monday, 12 May 1958, p. 9.
17 *Irish Independent*, Wednesday, 19 February 1958, p. 3.
18 *Irish Times*, Wednesday, 14 May 1958, p. 1.
19 *Irish Examiner*, Saturday, 1 April 1961, p. 8.
20 Gearóid Ó hAllmhuráin, *Flowing Tides: History and Memory in an Irish Soundscape* (Oxford: Oxford University Press, 2016), p. 172.
21 *Irish Times*, 17 February 1958, p. 10.
22 Patrick Fitzgerald and Brian Lambkin, *Migration in Irish*

History, 1607–2007 (Basingstoke: Palgrave Macmillan, 2008), p. 244.

23 Mary E. Daly, *The Slow Failure: Population Decline and Independent Ireland 1920–1973* (Madison: University of Wisconsin Press, 2006), p. 184.

24 John McGahern, *Memoir* (London: Faber & Faber, 2005), p. 211.

25 *Irish Times*, 'G.B.S. answers four questions', 19 April 1949, p. 6.

26 Heinrich Böll, *Irish Journal* (New York: McGraw-Hill, 1967), p. 83.

27 Quoted in John A. O'Brien (ed.), *The Vanishing Irish* (London: W. H. Allen, 1954), p. 44.

28 Eric Bentley, *In Search of Theater* (New York: Knopf, 1953), p. 328.

29 *Irish Times*, Thursday, 4 March 1954, p. 6, Friday 5 March 1954, p.6

30 O'Brien (ed.), *The Vanishing Irish*, p. 7.

31 *Irish Times*, Saturday, 9 March 1957, p. 9.

32 *Irish Times*, Thursday, 6 September 1956, p. 8.

33 Böll, *Irish Journal*, p. 78.

34 *Irish Times*, Saturday, 20 November 1954, p. 1.

35 Dominic Behan, *My Brother Brendan* (London: Leslie Frewin, 1965), p. 57.

36 John Cooney, *John Charles McQuaid: Ruler of Catholic Ireland* (Dublin: O'Brien Press, 1999), p. 328.

37 Ibid., p. 329.

38 *Irish Times*, Wednesday, 19 February 1958, p. 6.

39 Cooney, *John Charles McQuaid*, p. 282.

40 Richard English, *Armed Struggle: A History of the IRA* (London: Macmillan, 2003), p. 73.

41 *Limerick Leader*, Monday, 24 January 1949, p. 2.

42 Brian Hanley and Scott Millar, *The Unfinished Revolution: The Story of the Official IRA and The Workers' Party* (Dublin; Penguin Ireland, 2009), p. 6.

43 Seamus Heaney, *Electric Light* (London: Faber & Faber, 2001), p. 18.

44 Diarmaid Ferriter, *The Border* (London: Profile, 2019), p. 61; *Irish Independent*, Saturday, 5 January 1957, p. 10.

45 *Limerick Leader*, Saturday, 5 January 1957, p. 1.

46 *Limerick Leader*, Saturday, 5 January 1957, p. 1.

47 Hanley and Millar, *The Unfinished Revolution*, p. 16.

48 Donnacha Ó Beacháin, *Destiny of the Soldiers: Fianna Fáil, Irish Republicanism and the IRA 1926–1973* (Dublin: Gill & Macmillan, 2010), p. 239.

49 See for example *Anglo-Celt*, Saturday, 2 February 1957, p. 11.

50 Hanley and Millar, *The Unfinished Revolution*, p. 18.

51 Ó Beacháin, *Destiny of the Soldiers*, p. 250.

52 *Irish Times*, Wednesday, 12 February 1958, p. 8; *Irish Independent*, Wednesday 12 February 1958, p. 10.

53 *Irish Times*, Thursday, 13 February 1958, p. 7; *Irish Independent*, Thursday, 13 February 1958, p. 8; *Irish Examiner*, Thursday, 13 February 1958, p. 7.

54 *Irish Press*, Tuesday, 18 February 1958, p. 7.

55 D. J. Maher, *The Tortuous Path: The Course of Ireland's Entry in the EEC 1948-73* (Dublin: Institute of Public Administration, 1986), p. 82.
56 Dáil Éireann debates, 2 July 1959.
57 Frank Barry and Mícheál Ó Fathartaigh, 'An Irish industrial revolution: the creation of the Industrial Development Authority (IDA), 1949–59', *History Ireland*, May–June 2013, Vol. 21.
58 T. K. Whitaker, *Economic Development* (Dublin: Stationary Office, 1958), p. 69.
59 Ciaran Buckley and Chris Ward (eds), *Strong Farmer: The Memoirs of Joe Ward* (Dublin: Liberties Press, 2007), p. 113, p. 114.
60 Buckley and Ward (eds), *Strong Farmer*, p. 139.
61 *Irish Times*, Monday, 17 February 1958, p. 4.
62 Whitaker, *Economic Development*, p. 86.
63 Ibid., p. 170.
64 Ibid., p. 240.
65 Paul Rouse, 'The Farmers since 1950', in Eugenio Biagini and Mary Daly (eds), *The Cambridge Social History of Modern Ireland* (Cambridge: Cambridge University Press, 2017), p. 141.
66 *Irish Times*, Friday, 3 September 1954, p. 1.
67 Garvin, *News from a New Republic*, p. 175.
68 *Irish Times*, Saturday, 10 May 1958, p. 9.
69 Buckley and Ward (eds), *Strong Farmer*, p. 141, p. 145.
70 *Irish Times*, Monday, 17 February 1958, p. 4.
71 Daly, *The Slow Failure*, p. 183.
72 Tom Garvin, *Judging Lemass* (Dublin: Royal Irish Academy, 2009), p. 127.
73 Gerard McCann, *Ireland's Economic History: Crisis and Development in the North and South* (London: Pluto Press, 2011), pp. 89–90.
74 Garvin, *Judging Lemass*, p. 130.
75 Daly, *The Slow Failure*, p. 171.
76 Ibid.
77 Ibid., p. 172.
78 Donall MacAmhlaigh (trans. Valentin Iremonger), *An Irish Navvy/ Dialann Deoraí* (London: Routledge and Kegan Paul, 1964), pp. 5–6.
79 McCarthy, *Planning Ireland's Future*, p. 18.
80 Maher, *The Tortuous Path*, p. 26.
81 McCann, *Ireland's Economic History*, p. 117.
82 Garvin, *News from a New Republic*, p. 30.
83 Maher, *The Tortuous Path*, p. 31.
84 Dáil Éireann debates, 2 April 1952.
85 Quoted in Miriam Hederman, *The Road to Europe: Irish Attitudes 1948–1961* (Dublin: Institute of Public Administration, 1983), p. 35.
86 Hederman, *The Road to Europe*, p. 133.
87 Dáil Éireann debates, 2 July 1957.
88 Maher, *The Tortuous Path*, p. 64.
89 Ibid., p. 63, italics in original.
90 Ibid., p. 68.
91 Dan Laurence (ed.), *Bernard Shaw, Collected Letters*, Vol. 3 (New York: Viking, 1985), pp. 276–7.
92 Maher, *The Tortuous Path*, p. 80.
93 Ibid., p. 91.
94 McCann, *Ireland's Economic History*, p. 126.

95 *Irish Times*, Monday, 31 March 1958, p. 8.
96 Frank Barry and Clare O'Mahony, 'Regime Change in 1950s Ireland: The New Export-Oriented Foreign Investment Strategy', *Irish Economic and Social History*, 44:1 (2017), 46–65. doi.org/10.21427/mb3p-jm68
97 Michael Mulreany (ed.), *Economic Development – 50 Years On 1958–2008* (Dublin: Institute of Public Administration, 2009), p. 7.
98 T. K. Whitaker, 'Looking Back to 1958', in Mulreany (ed.), *Economic Development*, p. 21.
99 Mulreany (ed.), *Economic Development*, p. 7.
100 Alan Bestic, *The Importance of Being Irish* (London: Cassell, 1969), p. 17.
101 Whitaker, *Economic Development*, p. 9.
102 Ibid., p. 160.
103 *Irish Times*, Saturday, 23 February 1957, p. 9.
104 McCarthy, *Planning Ireland's Future*, p. 51.
105 Ibid.
106 *Irish Press*, Tuesday, 25 November 1958, p. 6.
107 Whitaker, *Economic Development*, p. 9.
108 Garret FitzGerald, *All in a Life: An Autobiography* (Dublin: Gill & Macmillan, 1991), p. 44.

Chapter 2. 1959: Modern Family

1 *Limerick Leader*, Wednesday, 18 March 1959, p. 1.
2 John B. Keane, *Self-Portrait* (Cork: Mercier Press, 1964), p. 66.
3 Ibid., p. 88.
4 Paul McMahon, *British Spies and Irish Rebels: British Intelligence and Ireland, 1916–1945* (Woodbridge: Boydell Press, 2008), p. 358; https://www.historyireland.com/20th-century-contemporary-history/ailtiri-na-haiseirghe-irelands-fascist-new-order/
5 *Irish Times*, Saturday, 2 May 1959, p. 8.
6 *Evening Herald*, Tuesday, 28 April 1959; p. 5.
7 Quoted in *Irish Times*, Saturday, 12 September 2015, p. 45.
8 John B. Keane, *Sive* (Cork: Mercier Press, 1986), p. 50.
9 Joanna Keane O'Flynn, introduction to Keane, *Sive*, p. 7.
10 *Sunday Independent*, Sunday, 30 June 1957, p. 5.
11 Finola Kennedy, *Cottage to Creche: Family Change in Ireland* (Dublin: Institute of Public Administration, 2001), p. 8.
12 Ibid., pp. 9–10.
13 Finola Kennedy, *Family, Economy and Government in Ireland* (Dublin: Economic and Social Research Institute, 1989), p. 9.
14 Keane, *Sive*, p. 89.
15 Tom Murphy, *On the Outside* in *A Whistle in the Dark and Other Plays* (London: Methuen, 1989), p. 190.
16 Ibid., pp. 185–9.
17 *Irish Press*, Thursday, 15 January 1959, p. 1.
18 Garvin, *Judging Lemass*, p. 207.

Chapter 3. 1960: Comanche Country

1 Kathleen Behan and Brian Behan, *Mother of All the Behans* (Dublin: Poolbeg, 1994), p. 91.
2 E. H. Mikhail (ed.), *Brendan Behan*, Vol. 1: *Interviews and Recollections* (London: Palgrave Macmillan, 1982), p. 126.
3 english.nsms.ox.ac.uk/holinshed/texts.php?text1=1587_0295
4 Patrick Abercrombie, *Dublin of the Future: The New Town Plan* (Liverpool: University of Liverpool, 1922).
5 Ellen Rowley, *Housing, Architecture and the Edge Condition: Dublin Is Building, 1935–1975* (London: Routledge, 2019), p. 101.
6 David Dickson, *Dublin: The Making of a Capital City* (London: Profile, 2014), p. 481.
7 Rowley, *Housing, Architecture and the Edge Condition*, p. 102.
8 T. W. Dillon, 'Slum Clearance: Past and Future', in *Studies* (No. 34, March 1945), p. 19.
9 Quoted in Sheppard, 'Infectious piousness' – Advertising and the Eucharistic Congress, 1932, https://www.theirishstory.com/2017/08/30/infectious-piousness-advertising-and-the-eucharistic-congress-1932/#_ednref15
10 Alice Curtayne, 'The Story of the Eucharistic Congress', Capuchin Annual (1933), p. 75.
11 Quoted in Sheppard, 'Infectious piousness', op. cit.
12 Reproduced in Rowley, *Housing, Architecture and the Edge Condition*, p. 100.
13 Anthony Cronin, *Dead as Doornails: A Chronicle of Life* (Dublin: Dolmen Press, 1976), p. 8.
14 John M. Synge, *Collected Works*, II: *Prose* (Gerrards Cross: Colin Smythe, 1982), p. 216.
15 Rowley, *Housing, Architecture and the Edge Condition*, p. 105.
16 Dominic Behan, *My Brother Brendan*, p. 21.
17 Brian Behan, *The Brothers Behan* (Dublin: Ashfield Press, 1998), p. 7.
18 Evidence of Thomas Bourke, Allocations Officer, Dublin Housing Inquiry 1939.
19 Evidence of James Larkin, Dublin Housing Inquiry 1939.
20 Alexander J. Humphreys, *New Dubliners: Urbanisation and the Irish Family* (London: Routledge and Kegan Paul, 1966), p. 187.
21 Ibid.
22 http://www.clarelibrary.ie/eolas/coclare/songs/cmc/the_shannon_scheme_nlynch.hm
23 https://esbarchives.ie/2017/04/04/modernising-the-farm-kitchen/
24 Vona Groarke, *Other People's Houses* (Dublin: The Gallery Press, 1999), Kindle edition.
25 https://www.herald.ie/news/three-toilets-for-90-people-peter-relives-city-tenement-life-36060122.html
26 https://www.cso.ie/en/media/csoie/census/census1961results/volume6/C_1961_VOL_6_T28a.pdf
27 https://www.cso.ie/en/media/csoie/census/census1961results/volume6/C_1961_VOL_6_T25c.pdf
28 For example, *Irish Press*, Tuesday, 3 October 1961, p. 3.

29 Bestic, *The Importance of Being Irish*, p. 41.
30 https://esbarchives.ie/wp-content/uploads/2017/03/re-pr-29.pdf
31 *Irish Press*, Saturday, 12 November 1960, p. 7.
32 *Irish Examiner*, Thursday, 25 April 1963, p.16; *Irish Independent*, Wednesday, 8 May 1963, p. 2.
33 *Evening Herald*, Thursday, 11 April 1968, p. 4.

Chapter 4. 1961: Balubaland

1 Declan Power, *Siege at Jadotville: The Irish Army's Forgotten Battle* (Dublin: Maverick House, 2005), Kindle edition, p. 14.
2 Máire Cruise O'Brien, *The Same Age as the State* (Dublin: O'Brien Press, 2003), p. 233.
3 Ibid., p. 234
4 theguardian.com/world/2013/apr/02/mi6-patrice-lumumba-assassination
5 Power, *Siege at Jadotville*, p. 29.
6 Ibid., p. 30.
7 http://www.militaryarchives.ie/fileadmin/user_upload/Documents_2/Congo_Unit_Histories/35_Inf_Bn_Congo.pdf
8 *Irish Independent*, Tuesday, 26 September 1961; p. 9.
9 *Evening Herald*, Saturday, 12 November 1960, p. 1.
10 *Irish Press*, Monday, 21 November 1960, p. 1.
11 *Irish Times*, Wednesday, 23 November 1960, p. 4.
12 *Irish Times*, Wednesday, 23 November, 1960, p. 4.
13 *Irish Times*, Tuesday, 15 November 1960, p. 4.
14 *Irish Examiner*, Saturday, 19 November 1960, p. 10.
15 *Irish Press 1931–1995*, Friday, 18 November 1960, p. 1.
16 *Irish Examiner 1841–current*, Tuesday, 22 August 1961, front page.
17 *Irish Times*, Friday, 1 December 1961, p. 9.
18 *Evening Echo 1896–current*, Monday, 16 January 1961, p. 8.
19 https://www.irishtimes.com/opinion/gone-west-we-are-too-hard-on-the-balubas-1.333386
20 *Nationalist and Leinster Times 1883–current*, Saturday, 8 July 1961, p. 36.
21 *Connacht Tribune*, Saturday, 1 July 1961, p. 22.
22 *Irish Farmers Journal*, Saturday, 14 October 1961, p. 24.
23 Graeme Thomson, *Cowboy Song: The Authorised Biography of Philip Lynott* (London: Little, Brown, 2016), Kindle edition.
24 Terence Patrick Dolan, *A Dictionary of Hiberno-English*, 3rd edition (Dublin: Gill & Macmillan, 2012), p. 15.
25 *Irish Independent 1905–current*, Thursday, 27 February 1986, p. 10.
26 *Southern Star*, Saturday, 25 May 1968, p. 16.
27 *Irish Times*, Tuesday, 12 December 1961, p. 9.
28 *Irish Examiner*, Saturday, 18 November 1961, p. 13.
29 *Western People*, Saturday, 17 April 1965, p. 13.
30 *Irish Times*, Monday, 15 March 1965, p. 1.
31 *Western People*, Saturday, 22 February 1969, p. 12.

32 *The Nationalist* (Tipperary), Saturday, 19 October 1968, p. 13.
33 *Mayo News*, Saturday, 4 January 1969, p. 3.
34 *Nationalist and Leinster Times*, Friday, 25 October 1963, p. 21.
35 *Sunday Independent*, Sunday, 4 February 1968, p. 24.
36 Conor Cruise O'Brien, *To Katanga and Back* (London: Hutchinson, 1962), p. 42.
37 Ibid., p. 41.
38 Ibid., p. 35.
39 Rose Doyle, *Heroes of Jadotville* (Dublin: New Island Books, 2006), Kindle edition.
40 Conor Cruise O'Brien, *To Katanga and Back*, p. 251.
41 Power, *Siege at Jadotville*, p. 90.
42 *Evening Herald*, Friday, 14 September 1962, p. 3.
43 *Irish Times*, Saturday, 16 September 1961, p. 1.
44 *Evening Herald*, Saturday, 16 September 1961, p. 1.
45 Máire Cruise O'Brien, *The Same Age as the State*, p. 247.
46 Ibid., p. 248.
47 Ibid.
48 *Evening Herald*, Friday, 15 September 1961, p. 1.
49 Doyle, *Heroes of Jadotville*, Kindle edition.
50 *Irish Independent*, Thursday, 21 September 21, 1961, p. 1.
51 Dáil Debates, 5 February 2019, col. 978, no. 8.
52 Conor Cruise O'Brien, *To Katanga and Back*, p. 283.
53 Declan Power, *Siege at Jadotville*, p. 143.
54 Doyle, *Heroes of Jadotville*, Kindle edition.
55 *Irish Times*, 28 October 1961, p. 4.
56 Maher, *The Tortuous Path*, p. 138.

Chapter 5. 1962: Cathode Ní Houlihan

1 Reproduced in John Bowman, *Window and Mirror: RTÉ Television 1961–2011* (Cork: Collins Press, 2011), p. 11.
2 Bestic, *The Importance of Being Irish*, p. 5.
3 Dáil Éireann debate, Tuesday, 3 April 1962, Vol. 194, No. 7.
4 Dáil Éireann debate, Tuesday, 3 April 1962, Vol. 194, No. 7.
5 *Irish Press*, Monday, 1 January 1962, p. 1.
6 Quoted in Martin McLoone and John MacMahon (eds), *Television and Irish Society: 21 Years of Irish Television* (RTÉ, 1984), p. 21.
7 Dáil Éireann debate, Tuesday, 3 April 1962, Vol. 194, No. 7.
8 Cooney, *John Charles McQuaid*, p. 347.
9 Ibid., pp. 347–8.
10 *Irish Press*, Monday, 1 January 1962, p. 5.
11 *Irish Times*, Thursday, 23 June 1960, p. 11.
12 Cooney, *John Charles McQuaid*, p. 348.
13 *Irish Times*, Monday, 14 May 1962, p. 7.
14 Dáil Éireann debate, Tuesday, 3 April 1962, Vol. 194, No. 7.
15 Dáil Éireann debate, Tuesday, 3 April 1962, Vol. 194, No. 7.
16 León Ó Broin, *Just Like Yesterday: An Autobiography* (Dublin: Gill & Macmillan, 1986), p. 210.
17 Dáil Éireann debate, Tuesday, 3 April 1962, Vol. 194, No. 7.
18 *Irish Examiner*, Friday, 16 June 1961, p. 7.

19 Bowman, *Window and Mirror*, p. 26.
20 Ibid., p. 27.
21 Dáil Éireann debate, Tuesday, 3 April 1962, Vol. 194, No. 7.
22 *Irish Times*, Friday, 13 October 1967, p. 13.
23 *Irish Times*, Tuesday, 17 October 1967, p. 14.

Chapter 6. 1963: The Dreamy Movement of the Stairs

1 *Irish Times*, Tuesday, 26 March 1963, p. 1.
2 *Evening Herald*, Tuesday, 26 March 1963, p. 9.
3 *Irish Press*, Wednesday, 27 March 1963, p. 8.
4 *Irish Times*, Friday, 3 May 1963, p. 1.
5 Carl Sferrazza Anthony, *The Kennedy White House: Family Life and Pictures, 1961–1963* (New York: Touchstone, 2002), pp. 23–5.
6 Ryan Tubridy, *JFK in Ireland: Four Days that Changed a President* (London: HarperCollins, 2010), Kindle edition.
7 *Irish Times*, Thursday, 27 June 1963, p. 1.
8 *Irish Times*, Thursday, 27 June 1963, p. 1.
9 https://www.oireachtas.ie/en/debates/debate/dail/1963-06-28/2/
10 *Munster Express*, Friday, 28 June 1963, p. 7.
11 https://www.jfklibrary.org/asset-viewer/archives/JFKPOF/045/JFKPOF-045-033
12 Kevin C. Kearns, *Ireland 1963* (Dublin: Gill Books, 2018), Kindle edition.
13 Ibid.
14 Tubridy, *JFK in Ireland.*
15 *Irish Times*, Wednesday, 26 June 1963, p. 4.
16 *Irish Times*, Friday, 28 June 1963, p. 8.
17 *Irish Times*, Friday, 28 June 1963, p. 8.
18 *Irish Times*, Friday, 28 June 1963, p. 8.
19 *Sligo Champion*, Saturday, 6 July 1963, p. 4.
20 Tubridy, *JFK in Ireland.*

Chapter 7. 1962–1999: Silence and Smoothness

1 Bowman, *Window and Mirror*, p. 46.
2 *Irish Times*, Saturday, 9 September 1989, p. 21.
3 Maurice Earls, '*The Late Late Show* – Controversy and Context', in Martin McLoone and John MacMahon (eds), *Television and Irish Society* (Dublin, RTÉ-IFI, 1984), p. 111.
4 Levine, *Sisters*, Kindle edition, loc. 4083.
5 McLoone and MacMahon (eds), *Television and Irish Society*, p. 117.

Chapter 8. 1965: Our Boys

1 Barry Coldrey, *Faith and Fatherland: The Christian Brothers and the Development of Irish Nationalism 1838–1921* (Dublin: Gill & Macmillan, 1988), p. 125.
2 Ibid., p. 127.

3 Ibid., p. 258.
4 Ibid., p. 122.
5 Lars Mjøset, *The Irish Economy in a Comparative Institutional Perspective* (Dublin: National Economic and Social Council, 1992), p. 282.
6 *Irish Times*, Friday, 25 September 2020, p. 14.
7 *Irish Examiner*, Saturday, 5 December 1987, p. 33.
8 Donald Harman Akenson, *A Mirror to Kathleen's Face: Education in Ireland 1922–1960* (Montreal: McGill-Queen's University Press, 1975), pp. 87–8.
9 Garvin, *News from a New Republic*, p. 177.
10 Eileen Randles, *Post-Primary Education in Ireland 1957–1970* (Dublin: Veritas, 1975), p. 27.
11 Garvin, *News from a New Republic*, p. 192.
12 Harman Akenson, *A Mirror to Kathleen's Face*, p. 98.
13 Randles, *Post-Primary Education in Ireland 1957–1970*, p. 22.
14 Dáil Éireann debates, 8 April 1959, col. 55.
15 Garvin, *News from a New Republic*, p. 187.
16 McCarthy (ed.), *Planning Ireland's Future*, p. 105.
17 Garvin, *News from a New Republic*, p. 185.
18 Harman Akenson, *A Mirror to Kathleen's Face*, p. 76.
19 Garvin, *News from a New Republic*, p. 184.
20 Bestic, *The Importance of Being Irish*, p. 91.
21 Áine Hyland, The Investment in Education Report – recollections and reminiscences, *Irish Educational Studies*, Vol. 33, 2014, pp. 123–39.
22 Fergal Tobin, *The Best of Decades: Ireland in the 1960s* (Dublin: Gill & Macmillan, 1984), p. 175.
23 Randles, *Post-Primary Education in Ireland 1957–1970*, p. 216.
24 *Sunday Independent*, Sunday, 24 February 1974, p. 13.
25 Gay Byrne, *The Time of My Life: An Autobiography* (Dublin: Gill & Macmillan, 1989), p. 60.
26 *Evening Herald*, Monday, 30 November 1987, p. 3.
27 For these quotes and those from *Our Boys*, see Fintan O'Toole, *The Ex-Isle of Erin* (Dublin: New Island Books, 1997), pp. 73–89.

Chapter 9. 1966: The GPO Trouser Suit

1 *Evening Herald*, Friday, 6 December 1963, p. 8.
2 *Evening Herald*, Wednesday, 23 March 1966, p. 6.
3 OECD Economic Surveys: Ireland 1966, Paris, p. 19.
4 *Irish Examiner, Tuesday*, 8 March 1966, front page.
5 Diarmaid Fleming, The man who blew up Nelson, 12 March 2016, https://www.bbc.com/news/magazine-35787116
6 Ibid.
7 *Irish Independent*, Thursday, 21 April 1966, p. 13.
8 *Irish Press*, Monday, 18 April 1966, p. 5.
9 Bowman, *Window and Mirror*, p. 82.
10 Mary E. Daly and Margaret O'Callaghan (eds), *1916 in 1966: Commemorating the Easter Rising* (Dublin: Royal Irish Academy, 2007), p. 12, p. 19.

11 Roisín Higgins, 'Pageant and Drama in the 1966 commemoration's', in Daly and O'Callaghan (eds), *1916 in 1966*, p. 158.
12 Louis Lentin, *The Making of Insurrection*, RTV Guide, 8 April 1966.
13 *Irish Times*, Thursday, 18 April 1968, p.1 o.
14 RTÉ Archives, https://www.rte.ie/archives/2016/0323/776859-critique-of-insurrection/
15 Daly and O'Callaghan (eds), *1916 in 1966*, p. 6, p. 275.
16 *Evening Herald*, Saturday, 28 May 1966, p. 11.
17 Daly and O'Callaghan (eds), *1916 in 1966*, p. 46.
18 Daly and O'Callaghan (eds), *1916 in 1966*, p. 20.
19 *Irish Examiner*, Monday, 18 April 1966, p. 6.
20 *Evening Herald*, Wednesday, 13 April 1966, p. 10.
21 Daly and O'Callaghan (eds), *1916 in 1966*, p. 32.
22 *Irish Press 1931–1995*, Saturday, 16 April 1966, front page.
23 Ferdia MacAnna, in Dermot Bolger (ed.), *Letters from the New Island* (Dublin: Raven Arts Press, 1991), p. 219.
24 Daly and O'Callaghan (eds), *1916 in 1966*, p. 24.
25 *Irish Independent*, Thursday, 14 April 1966 p. 3.
26 *Irish Press 1931–1995*, Thursday, 14 April 1966, p. 5.
27 Daly and O'Callaghan (eds), *1916 in 1966*, p. 29.
28 Ibid., p. 54.
29 *Irish Examiner*, Monday, 18 April 1966, p. 6.
30
Thomas Kinsella, Selected Poems (Manchester: Carcanet, 2007), Kindle edition, loc 452.
31 Presidential Elections 1938–2011, https://www.housing.gov.ie/sites/default/files/migrated-files/en/Publications/LocalGovernment/Voting/FileDownLoad,661,en.pdf
32 *Irish Independent*, Friday, 2 December 1966, p. 4.
33 *Irish Press*, Friday, 2 April 1965, p. 13.
34 *Irish Independent*, Thursday, 1 April 1965, p. 15.
35 *Irish Times*, Friday, 18 October 1963, p. 8.
36 *Irish Press*, Friday, 2 April 1965, p. 13.
37 *Irish Times*, Monday, 8 February 1965, p. 10.
38 David Dickson, *Dublin: The Making of a Capital City* (London: Profile, 2014), p. 528.

Chapter 10. 1967: The Burial of Leopold Bloom

1 *Irish Times*, 4 January 1941.
2 Asher Cohen, 'Jewish Genealogy in Ireland', in *Aspects of Irish Genealogy*: Proceedings of the 1st Irish Genealogical Congress, 1991, p. 26.
3 Cohen, 'Jewish Genealogy in Ireland', pp. 26–7. See also Dermot Keogh, *Jews in Twentieth-Century Ireland* (Cork: Cork University Press, 1998), p. 258.
4 Keogh, *Jews in Twentieth-Century Ireland*, p. 9.
5 Cohen, 'Jewish Genealogy in Ireland', p. 19.

Chapter 11. 1968: Requiem

1 Cooney, *John Charles McQuaid*, p. 371.
2 Ibid., p. 123.
3 Report of the Murphy Commission of Inquiry into the Catholic Archdiocese of Dublin, Part 2, p. 189.
4 Report of the Murphy Commission, part 2, p. 363.
5 Report of the Murphy Commission, part 2, p. 178.
6 Report of the Murphy Commission, part 2, p. 179.
7 Report of the Murphy Commission, part 2, p. 296.
8 Cooney, *John Charles McQuaid*, p. 393.
9 *Irish Times*, Saturday, 8 October 2005, p. 122.
10 Bestic, *The Importance of Being Irish*, pp. 114–15.
11 Ibid., p. 115
12 *Irish Times*, Saturday, 2 May 1981, p. 9.
13 Anne Enright, *The Gathering* (London, Vintage, 2007), p.96.
14 *Irish Times*, Wednesday, 13 October 1976, p. 1.
15 *Irish Times*, Monday, 3 April 1978, p. 11.
16 John McGahern, *Love of the World: Essays* (London: Faber & Faber, 2009), p. 147.

Chapter 12. 1969: Frozen Violence

1 *Irish Independent*, Thursday, 24 July 1969, p. 9.
2 *Irish Independent*, Tuesday, 16 December 1969, p. 12.
3 *Evening Herald*, Saturday, 19 July 1969, p. 3.
4 Stephen Hopkins, *The Politics of Memoir and the Northern Ireland Conflict* (Liverpool: Liverpool University Press, 2013), p. 22.
5 *Irish Times*, Saturday, 4 March 2017.
6 Michael Farrell, *The Orange State* (London: Pluto Press, 1976), p. 249.
7 Fionnbarra Ó Dochartaigh, *Ulster's White Negroes: From Civil Rights to Insurrection* (Edinburgh: AK Press, 1994), p. 14.
8 Coldrey, *Faith and Fatherland*, p. 122.
9 *The Listener*, 24 October 1968.
10 Valerie Morgan, Marie Smyth, Gillian Robinson and Grace Fraser, *Mixed Marriages in Northern Ireland Institutional Responses* (Centre for the Study of Conflict, University of Ulster, 1996), https://cain.ulster.ac.uk/csc/reports/mixed.htm
11 Brian Hanley, *The IRA: A Documentary History* (Dublin: Gill &Macmillan, 2010), pp. 150–51.
12 Reproduced in Hanley, *The IRA*, p. 155.

Chapter 13. 1970: The Killer Chord

1 Tomás Ó Cannain, *Seán Ó Riada* (Dublin: Gill Books, 2003), Kindle edition.
2 *Irish Times*, Tuesday, 20 November 1962.
3 Ó Cannain, *Seán Ó Riada*.

4 Ibid.
5 *Sunday Independent*, Sunday, 9 December 1962, p. 4.
6 *Irish Independent*, Thursday, 24 September 1970, p. 2.
7 *Evening Herald*, Monday, 8 May 1972, p. 9.
8 *Irish Times*, Thursday, 7 October 1971, p. 8.

Chapter 14. 1971: Little Plum

1 Augustine Martin (ed.), *Exploring English 1: Anthology of Short Stories* (Dublin: Gill & Macmillan, 1969), p. 90.
2 Dáil Éireann debate,Tuesday, 14 November 1967, Vol. 231, No. 1.
3 *Evening Herald*, Monday, 29 March 1971, p. 4.
4 *Irish Press 1931–1995*, Monday, 15 March 1971, p. 6.
5 Bowman, *Window and Mirror*, p. 221.
6 *Irish Examiner*, Thursday, 11 March 1971, p. 12.
7 Dáil Éireann debate, Wednesday, 21 July 1971, Vol. 255, No. 12.
8 Dáil Éireann debate, Tuesday, 3 April 1962, Vol. 194, No. 7.
9 Dáil Éireann debate, Wednesday, 30 May 1962, Vol. 195, No. 13.
10 Kevin Rockett, *Irish Film Censorship* (Dublin: Four Courts Press, 2004), p. 192.
11 J. J. Lee, *Ireland 1912–1985* (Cambridge: Cambridge University Press, 1989), p. 360.
12 Humphreys, *New Dubliners*, p. 141.
13 Ibid., p. 140.
14 *Irish Times*, Saturday, 12 March 1966, p. 7.
15 *Irish Times*, Saturday, 5 June 1971, p. 10.
16 *Irish Times*, Saturday, 5 November 1966, p. 7.
17 *Irish Times*, Thursday, 6 May 1971, p. 12.
18 Anton Trant, *Curriculum Matters in Ireland* (Dublin: Blackhall, 2007), p. 41.
19 Bestic, *The Importance of Being Irish*, p. 118.
20 https://www.bbc.co.uk/news/resources/idt-sh/the_girls_of_bessborough
21 Bestic, *The Importance of Being Irish*, p. 118.
22 Ibid.
23 Aileen O'Hare, Margaret Dromey et al., *Mothers Alone? A study of women who gave birth outside marriage, Ireland 1983* (Dublin: Federation of Services for Unmarried Parents and their Children, Dublin, 1989), p. 3.
24 *Irish Times*, Tuesday, 15 September 1964, p. 8.
25 *Irish Mail on Sunday*, 1 February 2015, p. 5.
26 Mike Milotte, *Banished Babies: The Secret History of Ireland's Baby Export Business* (Dublin: New Island Books, 1997), p. 16.
27 Ibid., p. 77.
28 Ibid., pp. 47–9.
29 Ibid., p. 114.
30 Dáil Éireann debate, Tuesday, 28 June 1960, Vol. 183, No. 4.
31 June Levine, *Sisters* (Cork: Cork University Press, 2009), Kindle edition.
32 Anna Bryson, *No Coward Soul: A Biography of Thekla Beere* (Dublin: Institute of Public Administration, 2009), p. 144.

33 Ibid., pp. 144–5.
34 Ivana Bacik and Mary Rogan (eds), *Legal Cases that Changed Ireland* (Dublin: Clarus Press, 2016), p. 18.
35 Louise Fuller, *Irish Catholicism Since 1950* (Dublin: Gill & Macmillan, 2002, p. 207.
36 Ibid.
37 Mary Robinson, *Everybody Matters: A Memoir* (London: Hodder & Stoughton, 2013), Kindle Edition, p. 73.
38 Ibid., p. 74.
39 Ibid., p. 61.
40 Levine, *Sisters*.
41 Ibid.
42 Nell McCafferty, foreword to Levine, *Sisters*.

Chapter 15. 1972: Death of a Nationalist

1 https://www.hotpress.com/culture/the-charlie-haughey-hot-press-interview-2869326
2 *Irish Times*, Monday, 27 March 1972, p. 7.
3 David McKittrick, Seamus Kelters, Brain Feeney, Chris Thornton and David McVea, *Lost Lives* (Edinburgh and London: Mainstream, 2004), p. 146.
4 https://www.oireachtas.ie/en/debates/debate/dail/1972-02-04/2/#spk
5 *Irish Times*, Tuesday, 1 February 1972, p. 1, p. 6.
6 *Irish Times*, Tuesday, 1 February 1972, p. 7.
7 *Irish Times*, Wednesday, 2 February 1972, p. 1.
8 Frank Dunlop, *Yes, Taoiseach* (Dublin: Penguin Ireland, 2004), p. 2.
9 *Irish Times*, Thursday, 3 February 1972, p. 7.
10 *Irish Times*, Friday, 11 February 1972, p. 8.
11 *Irish Times*, Friday, 18 February 1972, p. 7; McKittrick et al., *Lost Lives*, p. 153; *Irish Independent*, Thursday, 17 February 1972, p. 22; *Irish Examiner*, Tuesday, 15 February 1972, p. 1.
12 Hanley, *The IRA*, p. 171.
13 Paul Bew and Gordon Gillespie, *Northern Ireland: A Chronology of the Troubles 1968–1999* (Dublin: Gill & Macmillan, 1999), p. 50.
14 *Irish Times*, Monday, 27 March 1972, p. 1.
15 Elgy Gillespie (ed.), *Nell: The Nell McCafferty Reader* (Dublin: Lilliput Press, 2005), p. 52.
16 Malachi O'Doherty, *The Telling Year: Belfast 1972* (Dublin: Gill & Macmillan, 2007), p. 118.
17 Hanley, *The IRA*, pp. 171–2.
18 O'Doherty, *The Telling Year*, p. 163.
19 Ed Moloney, *Voices from the Grave* (London: Faber & Faber, 2010), pp. 105–6.
20 McKittrick, *Lost Lives*, pp. 217–18.
21 Ibid., pp. 297–8.
22 Moloney, *Voices from the Grave*, p.118 ff.
23 Henry Glassie, *Passing the Time in Ballymenone* (Bloomington: Indiana University Press, 1995), pp. 247–51.
24 Report of the Police Ombudsman of Northern Ireland, Belfast, 2010, p. 8.

Chapter 16. 1973: Into Europe

1 *Irish Press*, Tuesday, 25 July 1972, p. 15.
2 *Irish Press*, Friday, 14 July 1972, p. 3.
3 David Hannigan, *The Big Fight* (London: Random House, 2012), Kindle edition.
4 *Limerick Leader*, Saturday, 8 July 1972, p. 37.
5 Hannigan, *The Big Fight*.
6 Maher, *The Tortuous Path*, p. 259.
7 *Irish Times*, Friday, 20 June 1969, p. 13.
8 *Irish Times*, Thursday, 13 June 2019, p. 5.
9 Maher, *The Tortuous Path*, p. 375.
10 *Irish Times*, Monday, 30 October 1961, p. 6.
11 Bestic, *The Importance of Being Irish*, p. 34.
12 *Irish Times*, Wednesday, 11 January 2017, p. 33.
13 Michael J. Gear y, *An Inconvenient Wait: Ireland's Quest for Membership of the EEC 1957–73* (Dublin: Institute of Public Administration, 2009), p. 157.
14 Maher, *The Tortuous Path*, p. 247.
15 Geary, *An Inconvenient Wait*, p. 165.
16 Böll, *Irish Journal*, p. 122, p. 124.
17 Ferriter, *Ambiguous Republic*, p. 387.
18 https://www.cso.ie/en/media/csoie/releasespublications/documents/statisticalyearbook/2004/ireland&theeu.pdf
19 Maher, *The Tortuous Path*, p. 304.
20 T. Ryle Dwyer, *Fallen Idol: Haughey's Controversial Career* (Cork: Mercier Press, 1997), p. 54.
21 Quoted in Barry Desmond, *Finally and In Conclusion: A Political Memoir* (Dublin: New Island Books, 2000), p. 76.
22 *Irish Times*, Monday, 24 January 1972, p. 7.
23 Maher, *The Tortuous Path*, p. 392.
24 Ferriter, *Ambiguous Republic*, pp. 398–9.
25 Ibid., p. 390.
26 S. J. Sheehy, 'The Common Agricultural Policy and Ireland', in P. J. Drudy and Dermot McAleese (eds), *Ireland and the European Community* (Cambridge: Cambridge University Press, 1984), p. 80.
27 John Blackburn and Eoin O'Malley, 'EEC Membership and Irish Industry', in P. J. Drudy and Dermot McAleese (eds), *Ireland and the European Community*.
28 Ferriter, *Ambiguous Republic*, p. 394.
29 Desmond, *Finally and In Conclusion*, p. 78; Dermot Keogh, *Ireland and Europe 1919–1989* (Cork and Dublin: Hibernian University Press, 1989), p. 248.
30 *Irish Examiner*, Monday, 9 April 1973, p. 10.
31 Quoted in Eamonn Sweeney, *Down Down Deeper and Down: Ireland in the 70s & 80s* (Dublin: Gill & Macmillan, 2010), p. 23.
32 *Irish Times*, Tuesday, 10 April 1973, p. 20.
33 *Irish Times*, Wednesday, 11 April 1973, p. 13.
34 *Irish Times*, Thursday, 12 April 1973, p. 6.

Chapter 17. 1976: The Walking Dead

1 FitzGerald, *All in a Life*, p. 280.
2 Ibid., pp. 280–82.
3 McKittrick et al., *Lost Lives*, p. 626.
4 *Western People*, Saturday, 7 February 1976, p. 1.
5 *Irish Press*, Friday, 20 February 1976, p. 4.
6 FitzGerald, *All in a Life*, p. 280.
7 *Irish Times*, Saturday, 28 February 1976, p. 10.
8 *Irish Times*, Friday, 27 February 1976, p. 12.
9 *Irish Press*, Monday, 7 November 1977, p. 1.
10 *Connaught Telegraph*, Wednesday, 25 February 1976, p. 12.
11 *Connaught Telegraph*, Wednesday, 25 February 1976, p. 12.
12 *Mayo News*, Saturday, 28 February 1976, p. 1.
13 *Irish Times*, Tuesday, 11 May 1976, p. 5.
14 *Irish Times*, Friday, 13 August 1976, p. 11.
15 FitzGerald, *All in a Life*, p. 280.
16 *Irish Press*, Monday, 7 November 1977, p. 1.
17 *Irish Press*, Monday, 7 November 1977, p. 4.

Chapter 18. 1975–1980: Class Acts

1 *Irish Times*, Monday, 2 April 1990, p. 17.
2 *Irish Times*, Monday, 18 January 1965, p. 8.
3 Philip J. O'Connell, 'Sick Man or Tigress?: The Labour Market in the Republic of Ireland', in Anthony Heath et al. (eds), *Ireland North and South: Perspectives from Social Science* (Oxford: Oxford University Press, 1999), pp. 219–21.
4 Richard Breen, Damian F. Hannan, David B. Rottman and Christopher Whelan, *Understanding Contemporary Ireland: State, Class and Development in the Republic of Ireland* (Dublin: Gill & Macmillan, 1990), pp. 16–17.

Chapter 19. 1971–1983: Bungalow Bliss

1 Jack Fitzsimons, *Bungalow Bliss* (Kells, 1981), p. 50.
2 Jack Fitzsimons, *Bungalow Bashing* (Kells, 1990), p. 2.
3 Fitzsimons, *Bungalow Bliss*, p. 7.
4 Ibid., p. 53.
5 Maurice Moynihan (ed.), *The Speeches and Statements of Eamon de Valera 1917–1973* (Dublin: Gill & Macmillan, 1980), p. 466.
6 Fitzsimons, *Bungalow Bliss*, p. 53.
7 *Evening Herald*, Thursday, 4 May 1972, p. 7.
8 Tim Ryan, *Albert Reynolds: The Longford Leader* (Dublin: Blackwater Press, 1994), p. 24.
9 Fitzsimons, *Bungalow Bashing*, p. 5.

Chapter 20. 1979: Bona Fides

1 Siobhán Kilfeather (2002), 'Oliver Plunkett's head', *Textual Practice*, 16:2, 229–48.
2 *Irish Times*, Monday, 1 October 1979, p. 15; *Drogheda Independent*, Friday, 5 October 1979, p. 3; *Sunday Independent*, Sunday, 30 September 1979, p. 14.
3 *Irish Times*, Monday, 1 October 1979, p. 11.
4 Ferriter, *Ambiguous Republic*, p. 674.
5 Brian Girvin (2018), 'An Irish Solution to an Irish Problem: Catholicism, Contraception and Change, 1922–1979', *Contemporary European History*, 27(1), 1–22. doi:10.1017/S0960777317000443
6 Girvin, 'An Irish Solution to an Irish Problem'.
7 Dáil Éireann debate, Wednesday, 28 February 1979, Vol. 312, No. 3.
8 John Caden (2006,) RTÉ's coverage of the campaign on the eighth amendment, DCU Master's thesis.
9 Brian Friel, *Collected Plays*, Vol. 2 (Oldcastle and London: Gallery Press/Faber & Faber, 2016), p. 491.
10 *Irish Times*, Thursday, 28 December 1978, p. 13.
11 *Sunday Independent*, Sunday, 30 September 1979, p. 14.
12 http://www.vatican.va/content/john-paul-ii/en/homilies/1979/documents/hf_jp-ii_hom_19790929_irlanda-dublino-drogheda.html
13 *Irish Times*, Monday, 1 October 1979, p. 19.
14 *Irish Times*, Tuesday, 2 October 1979, p. 1.
15 *Irish Times*, Wednesday, 3 October 1979, p. 5.
16 Tommy McKearney, *The Provisional IRA: From Insurrection to Parliament* (London: Pluto Press, 2011), p. 143.
17 Ibid., pp. 146–7, p. 151.
18 Ibid., p. 151.
19 Dunlop, *Yes, Taoiseach*, p. 210.
20 Martin Mansergh (ed.), *The Spirit of the Nation: The Speeches of Charles J. Haughey* (Cork: Mercier Press, 1986), p. 312.
21 Dunlop, *Yes, Taoiseach*, p. 120.
22 *Connacht Tribune*, Friday, 5 October 1979, p. 12.

Chapter 21. 1980–1981: No Blue Hills

1 *Evening Herald*, Thursday, 12 May 1960, p. 1.
2 *Irish Times*, Friday, 13 May 1960, p. 1; *Irish Press*, Friday, 13 May 1960, p. 1.
3 Jason O'Toole, 'Was He the Godfather?', *Hot Press*, 25 July 2012.
4 Mary Raftery, 'The Dunnes – the inside story of a criminal family', *Magill*, 31 October 1983.
5 Jason O'Toole, 'Was He the Godfather?'.
6 *Irish Press*, Saturday, 26 February 1983, p. 3; Paul Williams, *Badfellas* (Dublin: Penguin Ireland, 2011), p. 71.
7 Williams, *Badfellas*, p. 71.
8 Raftery, *The Dunnes*.
9 Dáil Éireann debate, Tuesday, 19 November 1968, Vol. 237, No. 4.

10 *Irish Times*, Wednesday, 27 February 1985, p. 5.
11 Kieran Kennedy, 'The Context of Economic Development', in J. H. Goldthorpe and C. T. Whelan (eds), *The Development of Industrial Society in Ireland* (Oxford: Oxford University Press, 1992), p. 8.
12 Eoin O'Malley, 'Problems of Industrialisation', in *The Development of Industrial Society in Ireland*, p. 41.
13 O'Malley, *Problems of Industrialisation*, p. 35.
14 Ibid., p. 36.
15 *Irish Independent*, Thursday, 29 March 1973, p. 8.
16 *Irish Independent*, Wednesday, 16 February 1983, p. 8.
17 *Irish Independent*, Wednesday, 16 February 1983, p. 8.
18 O'Malley, *Problems of Industrialisation*, p. 34.
19 John S. Bradshaw, Drug Misuse in Ireland 1982–83, Medico-Social Research Board, Dublin, 18 April 1983, p. 1.
20 André Lyder, *Pushers Out: The Inside Story of Dublin's anti-drugs movement* (Bloomington: Trafford Publishing, 2003), p. 27.
21 Barry Desmond, Minister for Health, Dáil Éireann debate, Wednesday, 27 March 1985, Vol. 357, No. 4.
22 Bradshaw, Drug Misuse in Ireland 1982–83, p. 41.
23 Ibid., p. 39.
24 Raftery, *The Dunnes*.

Chapter 22. 1980–1981: A Beggar on Horseback

1 Dunlop, *Yes, Taoiseach*, p. 181.
2 Tony Farmar, *Ordinary Lives: Three Generations of Irish Middle-Class Experience* (Dublin: Gill & Macmillan, 1991), p. 182, p. 187.
3 *Irish Press*, Wednesday, 21 March 1962, p. 4.
4 *Sunday Independent*, Sunday, 1 September 1963, p. 3.
5 *Kilkenny People*, Friday, 26 June 1964, p. 15.
6 Breandán Ó hEithir, *The Begrudger's Guide to Irish Politics* (Dublin: Poolbeg, 1986), pp. 2–3.
7 Colm Keena, *Haughey's Millions: Charlie's Money Trail* (Dublin: Gill & Macmillan, 2001), p. 23.
8 Mansergh (ed.), *The Spirit of the Nation*, p. xxxi.
9 https://www.businesspost.ie/legacy/man-whose-midas-touch-wore-out-597c89e0; Keena, *Haughey's Millions*, p. 29.
10 Keena, *Haughey's Millions*, p. 39.
11 *Evening Herald*, Wednesday, 22 April 1970, p. 1.
12 Bruce Arnold, *Haughey: His Life and Unlucky Deeds* (London: Harper Collins, 1993), p. 90.
13 *Irish Press*, Thursday, 23 April 1970, p. 3.
14 Kevin Rockett, *Irish Film Censorship* (Dublin: Four Courts Press, 2004), pp. 125–6.
15 Ibid., p. 194.
16 Joe Joyce and Peter Murtagh, *The Boss: Charles J. Haughey in Government* (Dublin: Poolbeg, 1983), p. 102.
17 *Irish Times*, Saturday, 22 May 1999.
18 Kevin O'Connor, *Sweetie* (Dublin: KO Publications, 1999), p. 93.
19 Keena, *Haughey's Millions*, p. 61.
20 Mansergh (ed.), *The Spirit of the Nation*, p. 325.

Chapter 23. 1979–1982: The Body Politic

1 David Beresford, *Ten Men Dead* (London: Grafton, 1987), pp. 24–5.
2 Moloney, *Voices from the Grave*, p. 218.
3 Ibid., p. 224.
4 Ibid., p. 223.
5 Beresford, *Ten Men Dead*, p. 31.
6 Moloney, *Voices from the Grave*, p. 221, p. 219.
7 Ibid., p. 228, p. 235.
8 *Irish Times*, Wednesday, 2 August 1978, p. 5.
9 *Irish Times*, Wednesday, 2 August 1978, p. 5.
10 https://www.tate.org.uk/art/artists/richard-hamilton-1244/former-hunger-striker-on-hamiltons-ira-painting-citizen
11 http://www.vatican.va/content/john-paul-ii/en/homilies/1979/documents/hf_jp-ii_hom_19790929_irlanda-dublino-drogheda.html
12 Richard English, *Armed Struggle: A History of the IRA* (London: Macmillan, 2003), pp. 213–14.
13 McKittrick et al., *Lost Lives*, p. 849.
14 Eileen Fairweather, Roisin MacDonough and Melanie McFadyean, *Only the Rivers Run Free: Northern Ireland – The Women's War* (London: Pluto Press, 1984), p. 221.
15 Ibid., p. 222.
16 *Donegal Democrat*, Friday, 1 May 1981, p. 16.
17 *Irish Times*, Friday, 5 September 1980, p. 10.
18 Fairweather, *Only the Rivers Run Free*, p. 185.
19 Ibid., p. 226.
20 Moloney, *Voices from the Grave*, p. 239.
21 Ibid., p. 238.
22 Beresford, *Ten Men Dead*, p. 46.
23 Moloney, *Voices from the Grave*, p. 241.
24 Beresford, *Ten Men Dead*, p. 54.
25 Ibid., p. 56.
26 Ibid., p. 77.
27 Moloney, *Voices from the Grave*, p. 243.
28 Bew and Gillespie, *Northern Ireland: A Chronology of the Troubles*, p. 149.
29 https://irishstudies.sunygeneseoenglish.org/1981-hunger-strike/history/1981-2/murals-of-1981/
30 FitzGerald, *All in a Life*, p. 371.
31 McKearney, *The Provisional IRA*, p. 152.
32 *Irish Times*, Saturday, 13 June 1981, p. 1.
33 McKearney, *The Provisional IRA*, p. 147.

Chapter 24. 1981–1983: Foetal Attractions

1 *Irish Times*, Monday, 4 May 1981, p. 6.
2 Sweeney, *Down Down Deeper and Down*, p. 243.
3 Beresford, *Ten Men Dead*, p. 30.
4 Dáil Éireann debate, Thursday, 11 July 1974, Vol. 274, No. 6.
5 Brendan Behan, *After the Wake* (Dublin: O'Brien Press, 1981), p. 57.
6 Christopher T. Whelan, *Values and Social Change in Ireland* (Dublin: Gill & Macmillan, 1994), p. 23.

7 Michael Fogarty et al., *Irish Values and Attitudes* (Dublin: Dominican Publications, 1984), p. 125.
8 Ibid., p. 126.
9 Ibid., p. 139.
10 Ibid., p. 158.
11 Tom Hesketh, *The Second Partitioning of Ireland: The Abortion Referendum of 1983* (Dublin: Brandsma Books, 1990), p. 4.
12 *Evening Herald*, Tuesday, 6 November 1973, p. 1.
13 *Irish Independent*, Friday, 26 January 1973, p. 8.
14 *Sunday Independent*, Sunday, 4 February 1973, p. 15.
15 Rockett, *Irish Film Censorship*, p. 222.
16 *Irish Press*, Wednesday, 6 October 1976, p. 6.
17 *Evening Herald*, Tuesday, 6 November 1973, p. 1.
18 *Irish Press*, Wednesday, 6 October 1976, p. 6.
19 Dáil Éireann debate, Wednesday, 9 February 1983, Vol. 339, No. 10.
20 Phyllis Hamilton, *Secret Love: My Life with Father Michael Cleary* (London and Edinburgh: Mainstream, 1995), pp. 58–9.
21 Caelainn Hogan, *Republic of Shame* (Dublin: Penguin Ireland, 2019), Kindle edition, p. 20.
22 Fifth Interim Report of the Commission, https://assets.gov.ie/26901/6de0eb1f8c4647bda67985e2a4428e37.pdf
23 FitzGerald, *All in a Life*, p. 416.
24 Hesketh, *The Second Partitioning of Ireland*, pp. 16–17.

Chapter 25. 1982: Wonders Taken For Signs

1 Hesketh, *The Second Partitioning of Ireland*, pp. 102–3.
2 Ibid., p. 148.
3 Joyce and Murtagh, *The Boss*, p. 224.
4 Ibid., p. 225.
5 Dunlop, *Yes, Taoiseach*, p. 269.
6 *Irish Press*, Tuesday, 17 August 1982, p. 1.
7 *Irish Examiner*, Wednesday, 18 August 1982, p. 1.
8 Bruce Arnold, *Haughey: His Life and Unlucky Deeds* (London: HarperCollins, 1993), p. 210.
9 Pádraig Faulkner, *As I Saw It* (Dublin: Wolfhound Press, 2005), p. 174.
10 Joyce and Murtagh, *The Boss*, p. 283.

Chapter 26. 1984–1985: Dead Babies and Living Statues

1 *Irish Independent*, Friday, 15 February 1985, p. 11.
2 *Irish Examiner*, Friday, 15 February 1985, p. 8.
3 *Kerryman*, Friday, 1 March 1985, p. 1.
4 *Irish Press*, Tuesday, 27 August 1985, p. 9.
5 *Irish Times*, Saturday, 17 August 1985, p. 5.
6 *Irish Times*, Saturday, 17 August 1985, p. 5.
7 *Irish Times*, Tuesday, 4 October 1988, p. 8.
8 *Irish Times*, Saturday, 17 August 1985, p. 5.

9 Tom Inglis, *Truth, Power and Lies: Irish Society and the Case of the Kerry Babies* (Dublin: University College Dublin Press, 2003), p. 31.
10 Ibid., p. 29.
11 Report of the Tribunal of Inquiry into the 'Kerry Babies' Case, 1985, p. 158.
12 Inglis, *Truth, Power and Lies*, p. 19.
13 Report of the Tribunal of Inquiry into the 'Kerry Babies' Case, 1985, p. 151.
14 *Irish Independent*, Friday, 22 February 1985, p. 1.

Chapter 27. 1987–1991: As Oil Is to Texas

1 *Tyrone Herald*, Monday, 13 September 2010, p. 4.
2 *Irish Press*, Saturday, 22 November 1980, p. 4.
3 *Irish Examiner*, Tuesday, 25 June 1985, p. 26.
4 *Evening Herald*, Wednesday, 10 September 1986, p. 25.
5 *Sunday Independent*, Sunday, 19 September 1993, p. 27.
6 *Irish Times*, Friday, 24 April 1998, p. 79.
7 https://www.jfklibrary.org/asset-viewer/archives/JFKWHA/1963/JFKWHA-201-002/JFKWHA-201-002
8 Moriarty Tribunal report, p. 110, https://moriarty-tribunal.ie/wp-content/uploads/2016/09/SITECONTENT_26.pdf
9 *New York Times*, Friday, 17 March 1989, Section B, p. 1.
10 *Irish Examiner*, Saturday, 10 January 1987, p. 7.
11 *Irish Times*, Tuesday, 14 June 1988, p. 13.
12 https://www.rte.ie/archives/2018/1214/1017139-united-states-visas/
13 Mansergh (ed.), *The Spirit of the Nation*, p. 79.
14 Ibid., p. 1135, p. 1140.
15 McCann, *Ireland's Economic History*, p. 161.
16 Fitzgerald and Lambkin, *Migration in Irish History, 1607–2007*, pp. 246–7.
17 *Irish Times*, Saturday, 23 July 1988, p. 1.
18 *Western Journal*, Friday, 31 July 1981, p. 16; *Westmeath Examiner*, Saturday, 2 July 1988, p. 10; *Longford Leader*, Friday, 3 November 1989, p. 17; *Kerryman*, Friday, 21 June 1985, p. 6.
19 *Evening Echo*, Monday, 14 November 1988, p. 1, p. 7.
20 *Irish Independent*, Friday, 28 November 1986, p. 4.
21 Fitzgerald and Lambkin, *Migration in Irish History, 1607–2007*, p. 246.
22 *New York Times*, Monday, 4 June 1984, Section D, p. 8.
23 *Evening Echo*, Tuesday, 5 June 1990, p. 2.
24 *Irish Press 1931–1995*, Monday, 29 June 1987, p. 4; *Irish Times*, Tuesday, 14 June 1988, p. 13.
25 *Irish Times*, Thursday, 16 June 1988, p. 15.
26 *Irish Times*, Friday, 4 December 1987, p. 1.

Chapter 28. 1986–1992: Internal Exiles

1 Fintan O'Toole, *Ship of Fools* (London: Faber & Faber, 2009), p. 48.
2 Ibid., p. 51.
3 Ibid., p. 55.
4 Comptroller and Auditor General, Report of investigation into the administration of DIRT, 1999, p. 92.

Chapter 29. 1989: Freaks

1 *Irish Times*, Thursday, 10 March 1983, p. 4.
2 *Irish Independent*, Saturday, 12 March 1983, p. 1.
3 *Irish Times*, Wednesday, 9 March 1983, p. 9.
4 *Irish Press*, Friday, 15 April 1983, p. 1.
5 http://www.bailii.org/ie/cases/IESC/1983/3.html
6 *Irish Times*, Thursday, 5 July 1984, p. 1.
7 *Irish Times*, Friday, 6 July 1984, p. 8.
8 *Irish Times*, Wednesday, 4 July 1984, p. 8.
9 *Irish Times*, Tuesday, 3 July 1984, p. 8.
10 *Irish Times*, Thursday, 5 July 1984, p. 1.
11 *Irish Times*, Wednesday, 21 May 1986, p. 4.
12 Moriarty Tribunal report, pp. 123–4.
13 O'Connor, *Sweetie*, p. 44.
14 Dunlop, *Yes, Taoiseach*, p. 183.
15 *Irish Times*, Monday, 8 February 1982, p. 7.
16 *Irish Times*, Thursday, 11 March 1982, p. 7.
17 http://www.inis.gov.ie/en/JELR/DACOI%20Part%202.pdf/Files/DACOI%20Part%202.pdf
18 Andrew Madden, *Altar Boy: A Story of Life After Abuse* (Dublin: Penguin Ireland, 2003), p. 49.
19 *Magill*, June 1986, p. 22.
20 The Ferns Report, October 2005, p. 86.
21 Ibid., p. 96.
22 Ibid., p. 156.
23 Ibid., p. 165.
24 *Irish Independent*, Tuesday, 3 November 1987, p. 8.

Chapter 30. 1985–1992: Conduct Unbecoming

1 Peter de Rosa and Annie Murphy, *Forbidden Fruit* (London: Little, Brown, 1993), Kindle edition, loc. 123.
2 *Connacht Tribune*, Friday, 16 August 1985, p. 1.
3 *Connacht Sentinel*, Tuesday, 20 August 1985, p. 1.
4 *Irish Press*, Thursday, 19 September 1985, p. 5.
5 *Irish Independent*, Saturday, 24 April 1971, p. 3.
6 *Irish Times*, Friday, 30 April 1971, p. 1.
7 Finola Doyle O'Neill, *The Gaybo Revolution* (Dublin: Orpen Press, 2015), p. 153.
8 *Connacht Sentinel*, Tuesday, 27 July 1976, p. 6.
9 *Irish Times*, Friday, 29 September 1989, p. 13.
10 Christopher T. Whelan (ed.), *Values and Social Change*

in *Ireland* (Dublin: Gill & Macmillan, 1994), p. 39.
11 Ibid., p. 35.
12 Ibid., p. 42.
13 *Connacht Tribune*, Friday, 15 February 1985, p. 10.
14 *Connacht Tribune*, Friday, 15 February 1985, p. 10.
15 https://www.hotpress.com/culture/the-charlie-haughey-hot-press-interview-2869326
16 *Irish Times*, Saturday, 9 February 1985, p. 7.
17 *Irish Times*, Monday, 25 February 1985, p. 8.
18 *Irish Times*, Monday, 25 February 1985, p. 8.
19 *Irish Times*, Friday, 22 February 1985, p. 1.
20 *Irish Press*, Wednesday, 27 February 1985, p. 1.
21 *Irish Times*, Thursday, 28 February 1985, p. 6.
22 Tim Ryan, *Mara, PJ* (Dublin: Folens, 1992), Kindle edition, loc. 850.
23 Ryan, *Mara, PJ*, loc. 2084.
24 Mansergh (ed.), *The Spirit of the Nation*, p. 480.
25 Ibid., p. 481.
26 Whelan (ed.), *Values and Social Change in Ireland*, p. 131.
27 https://www.hotpress.com/culture/the-charlie-haughey-hot-press-interview-2869326
28 Case of Open Door and Dublin Well Woman v. Ireland, European Court of Human Rights, 1992 https://hudoc.echr.coe.int/fre#{%22itemid%22:[%22001-57789%22]}
29 *Irish Times*, Tuesday, 6 February 1990, p. 8.
30 *Irish Times*, Tuesday, 6 February 1990, p. 6.

Chapter 31. 1990–1992: Mature Recollection

1 Moriarty Tribunal report, https://moriarty-tribunal.ie/wp-content/uploads/2016/09/SITECONTENT_26.pdf
2 Keena, *Haughey's Millions*, p. 182.
3 Ibid., pp. 190–91.
4 Joe Lee, *Ireland 1912–1985, Politics and Society* (Cambridge: Cambridge University Press, 1989), p. 480.
5 *Irish Times*, 5 April 1990.
6 Bertie Ahern, *The Autobiography* (London: Hutchinson, 2009), p. 113.
7 *Irish Times*, Friday, 26 October 1990, p. 1.
8 Ahern, *The Autobiography*, p. 116.
9 *Irish Times*, Monday, 29 October 1990, p.10.
10 Ryle Dwyer, *Fallen Idol*, p. 150.
11 *Irish Times*, Thursday, 8 November 1990, p. 12; *Irish Independent*, Monday, 5 November 1990, p. 11.
12 *Sunday Independent*, Sunday, 11 November 1990, p. 12.
13 *Irish Times*, Saturday, 3 November 1990, p. 10.
14 *Irish Times*, Saturday, 3 November 1990, p. 10.
15 *Irish Independent*, Monday, 5 November 1990, p. 1.
16 Dunlop, *Yes, Taoiseach*, p. 315; *Observer*, 31 March 1985.
17 *Irish Times*, Monday, 5 November 1990, p. 4.
18 Ahern, *The Autobiography*, p. 120.
19 Ruairi Quinn, *Straight Left: A Journey in Politics* (Dublin:

Hodder Headline Ireland, 2002), p. 275.
20 Ahern, *The Autobiography*, p. 117.
21 Ibid., p. 129.
22 Ryle Dwyer, *Fallen Idol*, p. 178.
23 Ahern, *The Autobiography*, p. 131.
24 *Irish Times*, Wednesday, 12 February 1992, p. 1.
25 Wendy Holden, *Unlawful Carnal Knowledge: The True Story of the Irish X Case* (London: HarperCollins, 1994), p. 114.
26 Sean Duignan, *One Spin on the Merry-Go-Round* (Dublin: Blackwater Press, 1995), p. 20.
27 Ibid., p. 1.
28 Ibid., p. 20.
29 Holden, *Unlawful Carnal Knowledge*, p. 22.
30 Ibid., p. 73.
31 *Irish Times*, Wednesday, 19 February 1992, p. 4.
32 *Irish Times*, Wednesday, 19 February 1992, p. 5.

Chapter 32. 1992: Not So Bad Myself

1 *Irish Times*, Wednesday, 13 May 1992, p. 1.
2 de Rosa and Murphy, *Forbidden Fruit*, Kindle edition, loc. 3069.
3 Ibid., loc. 6108.
4 *Irish Times*, Monday, 11 May 1992, p. 4.
5 *Irish Times*, Wednesday, 13 May 1992, p. 5.
6 *Irish Times*, Saturday, 9 May 1992, p. 5.
7 Hamilton, *Secret Love*, p. 65.
8 Hamilton, *Secret Love*, p. 139.
9 Ibid., p. 141.
10 John Steinbeck, *East of Eden* (London: Penguin Modern Classics), Kindle edition, pp. 39–40.
11 *Irish Times*, Wednesday, 13 May 1992, p. 5.
12 *Irish Times*, Monday, 5 April 1993, p. 4; *Irish Press*, Saturday, 3 April, p. 3.

Chapter 33. 1992–1994: Meanwhile Back at the Ranch

1 Duignan, *One Spin on the Merry-Go-Round*, p. 34.
2 Frank Barry and Mícheál Ó Fathartaigh, 'An Irish industrial revolution: the creation of the Industrial Development Authority (IDA), 1949–59', *History Ireland*, May–June 2013, Vol. 21.
3 Fintan O'Toole, *Meanwhile Back at the Ranch* (London: Vintage, 1995), p. 25.
4 Ibid., pp. 74–5.
5 Ibid., p. 179.
6 Moriarty tribunal report, part 1, p. 36.
7 O'Toole, *Meanwhile Back at the Ranch*, p. 111.
8 *Irish Times*, Friday, 10 September 1999.
9 *Irish Times*, Tuesday, 16 January 2001.
10 Moriarty tribunal report, part 1, p. 172.
11 Duignan, *One Spin on the Merry-Go-Round*, p. 33.
12 Ibid.
13 Fergus Finlay, *Snakes & Ladders* (Dublin: New Island Books, 1998), pp. 232–3.

Chapter 34. 1993: True Confessions

1 *Irish Times*, Friday, 13 August 1971, p. 14.
2 *Irish Times*, Tuesday, 19 April 1983, p. 14.
3 *Irish Times*, Friday, 13 August 1971, p. 14.
4 *Evening Herald 1891–current*, Thursday, 15 December 1966, p. 12.
5 *Irish Independent*, Saturday, 29 October 1966, p. 4.
6 Sam Smyth, *Thanks a Million, Big Fella* (Dublin: Blackwater Press, 1997), p. 19.
7 *Irish Times*, Wednesday, 4 April 1990, p. 13.
8 Smyth, *Thanks a Million, Big Fella*, pp. 19–20.
9 *Irish Times*, Friday, 13 August 1971, p. 14.
10 Keena, *Haughey's Millions*, p. 143.
11 Ibid., p. 151.
12 Report of the Tribunal of Inquiry (Dunnes Payments), Dublin, 1997, p. 21.
13 Report of the Dunnes Payments tribunal, p. 54.
14 Keena, *Haughey's Millions*, p. 160.
15 Report of the Dunnes Payments tribunal, p. 39.
16 *Sunday Independent*, Sunday, 25 January 2015, p. 19.
17 Smyth, *Thanks a Million, Big Fella*, p. 93.
18 *Irish Independent*, Wednesday, 20 May 1992, p. 9.
19 Smyth, *Thanks a Million, Big Fella*, p. 97.
20 *Irish Times*, Tuesday, 3 December 1996, p. 1.
21 Keena, *Haughey's Millions*, pp. 275–6.

Chapter 35. 1993–1994: Angel Paper

1 McKittrick et al., *Lost Lives*, p. 1305.
2 Ibid., p. 1335.
3 Finlay, *Snakes and Ladders*, p. 190.
4 Ibid., p. 237.

Chapter 36. 1998: The Uses of Uncertainty

1 *Belfast Telegraph* 1976, Friday, 27 October 1995, p. 43.
2 *Belfast Telegraph*, Monday, 30 October 1995, p. 26.
3 https://www.ojp.gov/sites/g/files/xyckuh241/files/media/document/homicide_trends.pdf
4 English, *Armed Struggle*, p. 275.
5 Ibid., p. 225
6 Toby Harnden, *Bandit Country: The IRA and South Armagh* (London: Hodder, 1999), p. 47.
7 *The Independent Magazine*, Saturday, 30 March 1996, p. 28.
8 As reported by Marion McKeone in the *Sunday Tribune*, Sunday, 10 November 2002.
9 Thomas Hennessy, *The Northern Ireland Peace Process* (Dublin: Gill & Macmillan, 2000), p. 189.
10 Ibid., p. 11.
11 Ibid., p. 15.
12 *Irish Times*, Monday, 20 April 1998, p. 10.
13 *Irish Times*, Wednesday, 11 March 1998, p. 14.
14 McKearney, *The Provisional IRA*, p. 179.
15 Ibid., p. 181.

Chapter 37. 1990–2015: America at Home

1 Mansergh (ed.), *The Spirit of the Nation*, p. 682.
2 Seamus Heaney, *100 Poems* (London: Faber & Faber, 2018), p. 135.
3 *Sunday Independent*, Sunday, 5 November 1989, p. 23.
4 Joseph p. Quinlan, *The Irish–US Economic Relationship* (American Chamber of Commerce Ireland, 2015), pp. 11–12.
5 https://www.bea.gov/sites/default/files/2020-07/dici0720_0.pdf
6 *Financial Times*, Tuesday, 30 September 2014.
7 Ireland had to introduce a special measure called GNI*.
8 Patrick Honohan, 'Is Ireland really the most prosperous country in Europe?', Central Bank of Ireland, Economic Letters, Vol. 2021, No. 1, February 2021.

Chapter 38. 1990–2000: Unsuitables from a Distance

1 Brian Friel, *Dancing at Lughnasa* (London: Faber & Faber, 1990), Kindle edition, p. 21.
2 Fintan O'Toole, *The Ex-Isle of Erin* (Dublin: New Island Books, 1997).
3 Hickey and Smith, *A Paler Shade of Green*, p. 224.
4 Tom Murphy, *Conversations on a Homecoming* (Dublin: Gallery Press, 1986), p. 58.
5 Fitzgerald and Lambkin, *Migration in Irish History 1607–2007*, pp. 227–8.

Chapter 39. 1999: The Cruelty Man

1 *Irish Times*, Monday, 26 January 2015, p. 2.
2 *Irish Independent*, Thursday, 17 May 1962, p. 10.
3 *Evening Herald*, Friday, 1 June 1962, p. 5.
4 *Irish Times*, Saturday, 25 September 1999, p. 10.
5 Faulkner, *As I Saw It*, p. 68.
6 Mary Raftery and Eoin O'Sullivan, *Suffer the Little Children: The Inside Story of Ireland's Industrial Schools* (Dublin: New Island Books, 1999), p. 190.
7 *Tuam Herald*, Saturday, 19 October 1946, p. 4.
8 Raftery and O'Sullivan, *Suffer the Little Children*, p. 193.
9 *Irish Independent*, Wednesday, 24 July 1946, p. 6.
10 Ryan Report, 7.15 http://www.childabusecommission.ie/rpt/03-07.php
11 Ryan Report, 7.16; 7.23.
12 *Irish Times*, Friday, 10 September 1971, p. 8.
13 *Irish Times*, Saturday, 22 July 1972, p. 6.
14 Gerard Mannix Flynn, *Nothing to Say* (Dublin: Lilliput Press, 2003), p. 6.
15 Ryan Report, 7.70.
16 *Irish Times*, Wednesday, 28 April 1999, p. 3.

Chapter 40. 1997–2008: The Makeover

1 *Irish Times*, Wednesday, 16 December 2009, p. 2.
2 Murphy report, Chapter 11, pp. 643–4.
3 Murphy report, Chapter 11, p. 644.
4 *Irish Times*, Monday, 14 May 2001. p. 6.
5 *Irish Times*, Saturday, 12 May 2001, p. 1.
6 *Irish Independent*, Tuesday, 15 May 2001, p. 7.
7 Ahern, *The Autobiography*, p. 247.
8 *Irish Times*, Wednesday, 6 March 2002, p. 5.
9 *Irish Times*, Thursday, 9 March 2017, p. 1.
10 Thomas Bartlett (ed.), *The Cambridge History of Ireland*, Vol. 4 (Cambridge University Press, 2018), p. 84.
11 Duignan, *One Spin on the Merry-Go-Round*, p. 163.
12 Chris Moore, *Betrayal of Trust* (Dublin: Marino Books, 1995), p. 147.
13 *Irish Times*, 29 February 2008.
14 Ahern, *The Autobiography*, p. 305.
15 *Irish Times*, 5 June 2008.

Chapter 41. 2000–2008: Tropical Ireland

1 https://www.privateislandsonline.com/asia/united-arab-emirates/the-world-islands-dubai
2 *Irish Times*, Tuesday, 8 August 2006.
3 http://news.bbc.co.uk/2/hi/uk_news/northern_ireland/6918900.stm
4 *Irish Times*, Tuesday, 8 August 2006.
5 O'Toole, *Ship of Fools*, pp. 168–9.
6 *Irish Independent*, Friday, March 2007.
7 https://www.businessinsurance.com/article/19990411/STORY/1000788
8 *Irish Times*, Friday, 7 February 2009, p. 15.
9 *Irish Times*, Friday, 7 February 2009, p. 15.
10 *Irish Times*, Thursday, 6 November 2008, p. 38.
11 *New York Times*, Friday, 1 April 2005.
12 *Irish Times*, Wednesday, 26 September 2001, p. 9.
13 O'Toole, *Ship of Fools*, pp. 12–13.
14 Ibid.
15 Lee, *Ireland 1912–1985*, pp. 514–15.
16 *Irish Times*, Tuesday, 19 July 2005, p. 12.
17 *Irish Times*, Thursday, 5 July 2007, p. 1.
18 *Irish Independent*, Saturday, 3 November 2007, p. 1.
19 https://www.elibrary.imf.org/view/IMF002/03832-9781451818789/03832-9781451818789/03832-9781451818789_A001.xml?language=en

Chapter 42. 2009–2013: Jesus Fucking Hell and God

1 *Irish Times*, Tuesday, 26 January 2010.
2 https://www.rte.ie/news/business/2011/0721/304012-ntma/

3 *This Week*, RTÉ radio, 20 May 2012.
4 Rob Kitchin, 'Ghost Estates', in Brian Lucey, Eamon Maher and Eugene O'Brien (eds), *Recalling the Celtic Tiger* (London: Peter Lang, 2019), pp. 143–4.
5 Stephen Kinsella, 'Banking Culture', in *Recalling the Celtic Tiger*, p. 40.
6 Tom Lyons and Brian Carey, *The Fitzpatrick Tapes* (Dublin: Penguin Ireland, 2011), p. 261.
7 *Irish Independent*, Monday, 24 June 2013, p. 1.
8 audit.gov.ie/en/find-report/publications/2019/2018-annual-report-chapter-2-cost-of-bank-stabilisation-2018.pdf
9 https://inquiries.oireachtas.ie/banking/hearings/patrick-honohan-clarification-of-evidence-previously-given-to-the-committee/
10 https://www.bde.es/f/webbde/SES/Secciones/Publicaciones/InformesBoletinesRevistas/ArticulosAnaliticos/2017/T2/files/beaa1702-art10e.pdf
11 Michael Taft, https://notesonthefront.typepad.com/politicaleconomy/2013/01/with-considerable-speculation-about-an-impending-deal-on-bank-debt-with-the-taoiseach-and-the-german-chancellor-jointly-sta.html
12 https://inquiries.oireachtas.ie/banking/wp-content/uploads/2015/01/15012015_Honohan_vol11.pdf
13 Anne Enright, *The Gathering* (London: Jonathan Cape, 2007), p. 168.
14 *Irish Times*, Tuesday, 26 November 2019.
15 inquiries.oireachtas.ie/banking/wp-content/uploads/2015/09/Ajay-Chopra-Opening-Statement.pdf
16 https://www.youth.ie/documents/nyci-youth-emigration-report/

Chapter 43. 2018– : Negative Capability

1 *Irish Times*, Saturday, 23 May 2015.
2 *Irish Times*, Friday, 25 May 2018.
3 Archive recording broadcast on *Bowman: Sunday: 8.30*, RTÉ radio, 3 January 2021.
4 *The Poetical Works and Other Writings of John Keats* (London, 1883), Vol. 3, p. 99.

Credits

Text Permissions

I am very grateful to the following for permission to quote from poems and lyrics:

Extract from 'The Lighthouse' by Vona Groarke from *Selected Poems* (2016) reproduced by kind permission of the author and The Gallery Press. www.gallerypress.com.

Extract from 'Claudy' by James Simmons from *Poems 1956-1986* (1986) reproduced by kind permission of the author's Estate and The Gallery Press. www.gallerypress.com.

Extracts from 'The Border Campaign' and 'Postscript' by Seamus Heaney reproduced by kind permission of Faber & Faber, Farrar Strauss and Giroux and the estate of Seamus Heaney.

Extract from 'The Men Behind the Wire' by Patrick McGuigan reproduced by kind permission of the author and Waltons Music.

Image Permissions

1. "Crumlin housing area section no. 6, as on block plan 7," held by G. & T. Crampton © Unknown. Digital content by Dr. Joseph Brady, published by UCD Library, University College Dublin http://digital.ucd.ie/view/ucdlib:47016.
2. Reproduced courtesy of the National Library of Ireland.
3. Author's own.
4. © University College Dublin, National University of Ireland, Dublin. Reproduced by kind permission of UCD-OFM Partnership.
5. Courtesy of the Irish Military Archives.
6. Abbie Rowe. White House Photographs. John F. Kennedy Presidential Library and Museum, Boston.
7. Author's own.
8. Independent News and Media/ Getty Images.
9. Courtesy of The Commission to Inquire into Child Abuse.
10. Keystone/Getty Images.
11. Lensman/Irish Photo Archive.
12. Independent News and Media/ Getty Images.
13. SKP & Associates Ltd/Lensmen Photographic Archive/Irish Photo Archive.
14. SKP & Associates Ltd/Lensmen Photographic Archive/Irish Photo Archive.
15. © Irish Times.
16. PL Gould/Images/Getty Images.
17. © Limerick Leader, Part of Iconic Newspapers Ltd.
18. Jacob SUTTON/Gamma-Rapho via Getty Images.
19. © Martin Parr/Magnum Photos.
20. Independent News And Media/ Getty Images.
21. © Martin Parr/Magnum Photos.
22. © Irish Times.
23. © Irish Times.
24. Liam White / Alamy.
25. © Eamon Farrell, Photocall Ireland.
26. © Irish Times.
27. © Irish Times.
28. Charles McQuillan/Getty Images.
29. © Anthony Haughey 2011.
30. Model constructed and presented by Crowley Modelmakers, www.crowleymodelmakers.com.

Index

50th anniversary commemorations (1966) 138–49
1916 Rising (Easter Rising) 3, 20, 22, 77, 104, 117, 132, 133, 138, 139–42, 145–9, 309, 327, 332, 491

Abbeville mansion 310, 312, 413, 457, 458, 460
Abbeville Stud 312–13, 389
Abbey Theatre, Dublin 16–17, 47, 48, 138–9, 145, 188, 192, 278, 499
Abercorn restaurant, Belfast 225–6
Abercrombie, Patrick 53–4
abortion 282, 338–50, 364, 376, 398, 409, 414, 425, 427–30, 436–7, 458, 525, 560–3
Abortion (radio documentary) 282
Action Committee for the United States of Europe 242
Adams, Gerry 182, 229–30, 473, 479, 480, 481, 482, 483–4, 487, 489
Before the Dawn 484
Admiral Nelson public house, Kilburn 138
adoption 205–6, 344–5, 396, 433–4
Aer Lingus 43, 147, 336, 337, 432–3, 507
Agate, Jeffrey 324
Agnew, Paddy 334
agriculture 27–9, 183–4, 247, 248, 442
Ahern, Bertie 152, 373–4, 417, 421, 422, 424, 426, 521, 524, 525–32, 534, 535, 539, 546
Ahern, Noel 152
AIB *see* Allied Irish Bank
Aiken, Frank 65
Ainsworth, Joe 356
Albatross Company 97
Aldershot bombing (22 February 1972) 225
Alexandra College, Dublin 210
Ali, Muhammad 235, 236–8, 246, 312
All-Ireland Amateur Drama Festival, Athlone 47–8
Allen, Tom (aka T.R. Dallas) 370–1
Alliance Party 476, 478, 482
Allied Irish Bank (AIB) 382, 383, 444, 446, 546
altar boys 159–64, 172, 176
American Bar Association 537–8
American business investment 37–8, 296–8, 372, 453, 454, 490–8, 537, 564, 566–7
American Chamber of Commerce Ireland 491
American Dream 435–6, 507–8, 542
American Fortnight 92
American popular culture 88, 89–91, 124–5, 138, 140–1, 142, 266–74, 503
An Naisiún Gaelach (the Gaelic Nation) 187
Anderson, Anne 471
Anderson, Mary 208, 210, 211
Andrews, Eamonn 84, 88, 118, 119
Andrews, Todd 116, 118
Anglo Irish Bank 552, 554
Anglo-Irish Beef Processors 442
Anglo-Irish Meats 441
Anna Livia Boutique, Dublin 146–7
Ansbacher (Cayman) Limited 384, 386–7, 457
Ansbacher Cayman scam 384–90, 418, 456
anti-Semitism 31, 47
Apple group 493, 495–6
Áras an Uachtaráin, Phoenix Park 102–3
Arbour Hill, Dublin 104
Architects of the Resurrection (Ailtirí na hAiséirgh) 47
Ardoyne 465–6
Aristocracy (racehorse) 310
Arlington Cemetery, Virginia 104
Armagh jail 326
Arms Trial (1970) 244–5, 313
Arnold, Bruce 355–6
Arnotts department store, Dublin 92
Artane Boys Band 514
Artane industrial school 291, 514, 517
Arthurs, Francis 230
Ascendancy 307–8, 310, 311, 312
Asdee, Co. Kerry 358–60, 365–9
Asmal, Kadar 245
Austin, Joe 465–6, 468, 472

Baile Mhúirne, Co. Cork 183
Baird, Michelle 464
Baldonnel aerodrome, Co. Dublin 68
Baldoyle racecourse, Dublin 193
'The Ballad Of Claudy' (song) 233

Ballina, Co. Mayo 212, 250
Ballinspittle, Co. Cork 359, 360, 363
ballrooms 270–2
Ballydesmond, Co. Cork 359
Ballyfermot Boys' Band 135
Ballymun 150–1
Ballymurphy 467–8
Baluba people 67–72, 180
Bank of Ireland 382
banks, banking 380–91, 552, 553–6, 564
BBC 75, 82, 87, 91, 107, 193, 465
Beano 115, 175, 196
Beckett, Samuel
  All That Fall 11, 17, 18
  Waiting for Godot 20
beef trade 441–50
Beef Tribunal 448, 461, 462
Beere, Thekla 210
Begley, Philomena 268
Begley, Thomas 464, 469
Behan, Brendan 17, 56
  The Catacombs 338
  'Moving Out' 57–8
  The Quare Fellow 47
Behan, Dominic 221
Behan, John, *St Francis and the Birds* (sculpture) 278
Belfast bombings 219–20, 225, 228–33, 284, 464–8
Belfast City Council 476–7
Belfast (Good Friday) Agreement (19 April 1998) 485–6, 489, 529
Belfast-Derry march (1969) 180–1
Belfast-Dublin March (1971) 214–15
Belvedere College, Dublin 117
Benstead, Patrick 230
Bereen, Janet 225–6
Berkeley, George 19
Bernard Shaw, George 15, 36, 294
Bertie (documentary, 2008) 531
Bessborough, Cork 345–6
Best, William 229
Bestic, Alan 82, 169, 203
Bewley's café, Westmoreland Street (Dublin) 208
The Big 8 (country & western group) 266–7, 271
Big Tom (singer) 268
Binchy, William 342
Blácam, Aodh de 31
black magic 357–8
'The Black and Tan Gun' (rebel song) 141–2, 142–3, 221
Black and Tans 142, 143–5
Blackrock, Dublin 344, 351–2
Blair, Tony 478
Blandford army camp, Dorset 12, 21, 22, 24
Blaney, Neil 150, 151, 220, 244
Blasket Islands 1, 3, 5, 317, 372
Bleeding Horse pub, Camden Street (Dublin) 155, 156
Bloody Friday (21 July 1972) 228, 229–30, 233
Bloody Sunday (30 January 1972) 219–20, 225, 284, 468
Bloom, Leopold 155–7
'Blue' Lewis 235
Blythe, Ernest 47
Boland, Eavan 208, 278
Boland, Frederick Henry 64–5, 73
Boland, Gerry 516
Boland, Harry 117
Boland, Kevin 244
Böll, Heinrich 15, 16, 92, 242
  Irish Journal 242
bombs, bombing 132–8, 221, 222, 225–6, 228, 229, 230–1, 233, 234, 284, 325, 464–5, 469, 472
  see also the Troubles; violence
Bonner, John 169
Bono (singer) 459
boom years 536–48, 551, 552, 553, 559
Bord Fáilte (Irish tourist board) 455
Bórd na Mona (turf company) 118
Border Campaign 21, 24, 91, 135, 179
Border country 231–2, 441
Bosley, Thelma 225
Bourke, Thomas 58
Bowe, John 554
Bowman, Emer Philbin 208
Bowman, John 304–5
Bowyer, Brendan 266, 267
boy scouts 161, 182, 275
Boys Town (film, 1938) 515
Bradley, Gerry 179
Bradshaw, George 234
Bradshaw, John 299–302
Brady, Conor 431
Branigan, Sergeant Lugs 71
Brennan, Canon 279
Brennan and McGown (builders) 387
Brennan, Maeve 510
British Army 219–20, 221, 224, 229, 284, 468
British Embassy, Merrion Square (Dublin) 222–3
Britton, Brian 445
Brother Cahill 197
Brother Cyprian 135
Brown, Christy 48
'Brown Sugar' (song) 191
Browne, John 424
Browne, Loretto 347–9
Browne, Michael, Bishop of Galway 240
Browne, Noël 85, 91, 407
Browne, Detective Garda P.J. 362
Browne, Vincent 304, 355, 371
Brugha, Cathal 117
Buckley, Christine 519
Budin, Burt 108
Bula Resources 447–8

bungalows *see* houses, housing
Bunratty folk park 14
Burke, Anthony 514
Burke, Dick 70–1
Burke, Ray 387, 400
Burlington Hotel, Dublin 387
Burntollet Bridge 180
Business Week 371
Butler, Hubert 245
Butler, Jean 501
Byrne, Adrian 385, 386, 390
Byrne, Gay 105–13, 129–30, 200, 316, 408, 418, 420, 422, 439, 519
Byrne, John 311
Byrne, Linda 101
Byrne, T.J. 271

C&D Pet Foods 445
Cagney, Jimmy 503
Caherciveen, Co. Kerry 357–8
Cahill, Joe 252–3
Calvary Hospital, Galway 406–7
Cape Verde Development company 537
The Capitol (showband) 268, 270
Carey, Johnny 116
Carrick Hill Martyrs Band 464
Carriglea, Dún Laoghaire 291
Carson, Ciaran, *Last Night's Fun* 500
Carson, Johnny 108
Carter, Frank 200
Carty, Ciaran 342
Carysfort teacher training college 416
Casablanca (film, 1942) 315
Casey, Eamonn, Bishop of Galway 287, 404, 405–8, 410, 415, 431–9, 461
Cassels, Peter 455
Cassidy, Donie 370, 371
Castleblayney, Co. Monaghan 267–8
Cathode Ní Houlihan *see* television
Catholic Church 3, 7, 10, 40, 56, 122, 159–73, 203, 248, 257, 258, 279, 302, 396, 400–4, 407, 453, 461, 526, 538–9, 557
Catholic clergy 407–8, 409–10, 526
see also named individuals
Catholic seminaries 526
Catholics, Catholicism 21, 22, 23, 24, 42–3, 54–5, 87–8, 115, 180–2, 213, 223, 239, 241, 246, 284, 287–9, 340–1, 402, 408–9
see also sectarianism
The Cattle Raid of Cooley (*Táin Bó Cúalinge*) 193
Cavan 86
Cayman Islands 384, 388, 390, 456, 462, 535
CBS *see* Christian Brothers Schools
Ceannt, Éamonn 152
ceasefire declaration (31 August 1994) 475, 482, 526
céilí 500–1, 503
Celtic Revival 192–5, 568
Celtic Tiger 507, 533, 536, 541, 542, 545, 550, 559
The Celtic Tiger (dance show) 506, 507
Cement Roadstone 384, 390
censorship 201, 342, 343, 416
Censorship of Publications Board 86, 397, 414–15
Central Bank 381, 384, 385, 386, 387, 388, 389, 390, 554, 555
Central Bank of Iraq 446
Chains or Change manifesto (1971) 209
Charles Haughey's Ireland (documentary) 372, 413, 462
Charlton, Jack 509
Chastelain, John de 486, 488
Chesney, James 233
Chicago Tribune 15
The Chieftains (Ceoltóirí Cualann) (folk group) 186
child sexual abuse 165–8, 196–8, 208, 401–4, 515, 515–16, 522–3, 550
see also paedophiles
child slavery 515–22
Childers, Erskine 28
Children Act (1908) 513
Children of Mary 161
Chopra, Ajai 556–7
Chrétien, Jean 524
Christian Brothers 109–10, 114–19, 123–31, 141, 159–73, 191–2, 196–8, 500, 518, 520
Christian Brothers Schools (CBS) 114–15, 118, 119, 123–31, 159–61, 171, 191–2, 309
Christie's auction house 138
Christle brothers (Mick & Joe) 135
Chubb, Basil 119
Cisco Kid (TV series, 1950-56) 89
Citigroup 549
citizenship 180, 207, 239, 486
Civics 114–15
civil rights march (Derry, 1972) 219
civil rights movement (Northern Ireland) 180, 237, 298, 333
civil rights movement (US) 94, 180, 211
civil service 118–19, 121
The Clancy Brothers (folk group) 137
Clarke, Austin 245

Clarke, Harry, 'The Last Hour of the Night' 54
Clarke, Thomas 152
Clary, Michel de 74
class *see* social revolution
Claudy, Co. Derry 233
Cleary, Father Michael 216, 218, 287, 288, 344–5, 424, 427, 434–5
Clinton, Bill 476–8, 482, 483, 484–5, 530
Clonmel, Co. Tipperary 71
Coláiste Caoimhín (secondary school), Crumlin 196–7, 202
Cold War 33, 34, 65, 484
Cole, Paddy 266, 269, 270, 271
Colley, George 287, 388
Collins, Hugh 232
Collins, John 456
Collins, Michael 68
Collins, Pan 112
'Come Back To Stay' (Eurovision song) 134, 135
'Come Out Ye Black and Tans' (song) 217
Comerford, Máire 245
Comhaltas Ceoltóiri Éireann gatherings 268
comics 115, 124–5
Commission on Emigration 31
Commission on the Status of Women (1970) 209–10
Common Market Defence Campaign 245–6, 248
Company magazine 414
Comptroller and Auditor General 384
Condell, Frances 99–100
Confederation of Irish Industry 249
Conference of Major Religious Superiors 342
Congo 64–78, 182
Congregation of the Sacred Hearts of Jesus and Mary 346
Connell, Cardinal Desmond 256, 522, 524–5
Connie Dodgers (biscuits) 169
Connolly, Frank 311
Connolly, James 132, 147, 152
Connolly, Patrick 352–5
contraception 168–71, 202, 209, 211–15, 242–3, 279–81, 348, 364, 406–7, 409–10, 411, 425
Coogan, Fintan 83, 86–7
Cooney, Patrick 293
Corish, Brendan 201
Cork Evening Echo 69, 377
Cork Opera House 360
Corpus Christi procession 161
Cosgrave, Liam 251, 292
Cosmopolitan magazine 414
Costello, Declan 280, 293, 396, 428
Costello, John A. 34
Costigan, Daniel 103
Council of Education 120–1
Council of Europe 34
Country and Western Alliance 274
country and western music 266–74, 365–6, 370–1
Courtesy for Boys and Girls 114
Courtney, Detective Superintendent John 362
Courtney, Michael 477
Courtney, Corporal William 12
Cowen, Brian 553
Cox, Tom 18
Craven, Brother Canice 115
Creation (women's magazine) 305–7
Crehan, Junior 503
Criminal Justice Bill (1960) 206–7
Criminal Law (Amendment) Act (1935) 211
Croke Park, Dublin 145, 147, 216, 226, 235, 344, 353, 514
Cronin, Anthony 56
Cronin, Bart 448
Cronkite, Walter 140
Cross, Dr Raymond 169
Crowe, David 196
Crumlin 53–63, 70, 94, 136, 150, 151, 291, 293, 299
  Armagh Road 70
  Aughavannagh Road 8, 9, 44, 45–6, 54, 56–7, 64, 126, 156, 196, 218–19, 234, 290, 514
  Leighlin Road 55, 56, 70
  Rutland Avenue 290, 293
'Crumlin from the Air' (photograph, 1939) 55–6
Cúchulain 147
Cúil Aodha, Co. Cork 183–7, 189, 192, 194–5
The Cure of Patty Switl (German film) 342
Curtayne, Alice 55
Curtis, Robert 213
Cushing, Cardinal 514

Dáil 34, 91, 117, 121, 201, 217, 220, 223, 293, 338, 429, 516
Daingean industrial school 291–2, 514–15, 517
Dallas (TV series) 370, 372
D'Alton, Cardinal John, Primate of All-Ireland 85
Daly, Cardinal Cahal 527
Daly, Father Edward 219
dancing 86–7, 500–4, 504, 507
Dandy 115, 175
Darkest Africa 68, 71, 75, 76–7, 125
Daunt, William J. O'Neill, *Catechism of the History of Ireland* 117
Davis, Jimmie 142

de Burca, Máirín 208, 210, 211, 326
de Gaulle, Charles 79, 238–9, 242, 246, 249
de Valera, Eamon 2, 3, 20, 23, 37, 40–1, 51–2, 84, 85, 95–6, 99–100, 102–3, 104, 108, 112, 116, 117, 137, 148–9, 186, 249, 309, 310, 395, 412
de Valera, Professor Éamon (gynaecologist) 205
de Valera, Síle 287
de Valera, Vivion 20
Dean, James 62
Deane, Seamus 256
Dear Daughter (film, 1996) 519
Delap, Kathleen 210
Dempsey, Paul 445
Department of Education 397
Department of External Affairs 34
Department of Finance 34, 121, 381, 383, 384
Department of Foreign Affairs 242
Department of Industry 35
Department of Posts and Telegraphs 119
Deposit Interest Retention Tax (DIRT) 381–2
Derry massacre (Bloody Sunday, 30 January 1972) 219–20
d'Estaing, Valéry Giscard 242
Devenney, Samuel 178–9
Devine, Michael 335
Devlin McAliskey, Bernadette 179, 221, 223, 237, 329, 332
Dickie Rock and The Miami Showband 216
Dickson, David 151
Digital Equipment Corporation (DEC) 297
Dillon, James 26–7, 30, 301, 516
Dillon, John 207, 208
DIRT *see* Deposit Interest Retention Tax
disappearances 231
divorce 209, 398, 399, 400–1, 402, 409, 425, 436–7
The Dixies 270
Doherty, Kieran 334
Doherty, Seán 355, 418, 419, 420, 426, 461
Dolan, Seamus 86
Dolan, Terence, *Dictionary of Hiberno-English* 70
Dolphin's Barn Jewish Cemetery, Dublin 153–7
Donaldson, Denis 489
Donegal Democrat 326
Donegall Street bomb (20 March 1972) 228
Donnelly, Brian 374
Donnelly Visa party 374
Donnelly visas 374–5
Donoghue, Denis 255
Donovan, Brother S.B. 191
Donovan, Terry 389–90
Doogary, Co. Tyrone 370
Douglas, James, *The Savages* 71–2
Down and Conor diocese 182
Downey, Brian 216
Downey, Lawrence James 336–7
  The Christian Manifesto 337
Downing Street Declaration (15 December 1993) 474
Doyle, Paddy, *The God Squad* 518
Doyle, Rose 78
Doyle, Thomas 133
Drew, Ronnie 419
Drimnagh, Dublin 392
Drogheda 284, 286
Drogheda Corporation 275
drugs 293, 294–5, 298–303, 451–2, 456, 458–9
Drumm, David 554
Drumm, Máire 251
Drumshanbo, Co. Leitrim 182
Dublin 8, 22, 53–5, 67, 68, 70–1, 92, 101, 117, 139, 150, 298–9, 306, 312
  O'Connell Street 77, 133, 140, 207, 234, 360
  Sackville Place 234
  Seán MacDermott Street 207, 279
  see also Crumlin
Dublin Airport 95, 134, 135, 279, 342, 371
Dublin Castle 461, 524, 560
Dublin Corporation 93, 101
Dublin County Council 426
Dublin Opinion 8, 9–10, 81
Dublin Rape Crisis Centre 349
Dublin Regional Marriage Tribunal 401, 402
Dublin Shakespeare Society 110
Dublin Theatre Festival 10–11, 14, 17–19
Dublin Tribune 424
The Dubliners (folk group) 137, 245, 419
Duddy, Jackie 219
Duffy, Jim 422
Duffy, Thomas 234
Duggan, Mr (school guidance counsellor) 401–2
Duignan, Seán 427, 440, 448, 527
Dún Laoghaire College of Art 278
Dunlop, Frank 287, 400, 424, 530
Dunn, Father Joe 85, 249
Dunne, Ben 'Old Ben' 452, 453–4, 455, 456
Dunne, Ben 'Young Ben' 451–3, 455–63, 463
Dunne, Christy Jr, *Wildfire* 292
Dunne, Donal 351
Dunne family 290–3, 294, 298, 299, 302–3
Dunne, Sean 119, 536
Dunnes Stores 451, 452–3, 454–5, 456, 457–8, 460

Dunphy, Sean 142
Dunphy, Tom 266

Eakin, Kathryn 233
Easter Rising (1916) *see* 1916 Rising
Economic Development ('Grey Book') (1958) 39, 41, 42, 119
The Economist 371
economy 27–43, 100–1, 134, 242–3, 247–9, 283–4, 295–8, 305, 336, 376, 492–8, 528, 532, 541–8, 564
education 114–31, 202–3, 255–7, 291–2, 339, 342, 513–21, 544
Edwards, Hilton 11
EEC *see* European Economic Community
EFTA *see* European Free Trade Area
Eighth Amendment to the Constitution, repeal of 560–3
Elbaum, Don 235
Electricity Supply Board 62
electronics companies 492–4
elite 102–4
Elizabethville, Congo 67, 72, 73, 74, 76
Ellis, Dr Havelock 348
English, Barry 530–1
English, Richard 480
Enniskillen bomb (1987) 468
Enright, Anne, *The Gathering* 170, 555
EU *see* European Union
Eucharistic Congress (1932) 54–5
European Central Bank 556
European Commission 556
European Common Market 13, 37, 78–9
European Economic Community (EEC) 78–9, 209, 237–8, 239–49, 263, 295
European Free Trade Area (EFTA) 13, 26, 34, 36–7
European Monetary System 283
European Union (EU) 442, 443, 497, 509, 542
Eurovision Song Contest 134, 500
Evening Herald 47, 75, 77, 93, 133, 145, 193–4, 290, 315, 342
Evening Press 137

Fagan (schoolboy) 160–1
Fahy, Bernadette 519
Fairview Park killers 395
Falls Road, West Belfast 469
family 94–5, 98
Farrell, Michael 180
Father Malachy 198–9
Faul, Father Denis 330
Faulkner, Brian 213
Faulkner, Pádraig 83, 356, 514–15
Fay, W.P. 35
FAZ 371
Fean, Johnny 193
Feeney, John 315
female prisoners 325–7, 337
female rights 204–12
female sexuality 363–5, 414, 435, 544
feminism 208, 544
Fennell, Nuala 208
Ferris, Father Liam 366–7
Fianna Éireann 182
Fianna Fáil 3, 23, 30, 37, 41, 86, 94, 112, 122, 149, 150, 200, 206, 209, 217, 220, 222, 245, 257, 287, 306, 309, 343, 356, 371, 372, 375, 376–8, 400, 410–12, 416, 420–1, 444–5, 449, 461, 502, 521, 529, 545, 553, 557
Fianna Fáil Árd Fheis (annual conference) 201, 420
'fifth province' 535
financial crash 549–59, 566
financial irregularities 384–90, 417–18, 431–2, 444–9, 530–1, 542, 564
Fine Gael 3, 26–7, 70, 93, 109, 207, 217, 222, 245, 251, 280, 292, 347, 395, 516, 557
Finlay, Fergus 449
Finnegan, John 387
Finucane, Marian 282
First Programme for Economic Expansion 100, 305
Fitt, Gerry 285–6
FitzGerald, Garret 43, 251, 294, 333, 347, 398
Fitzgerald, Martin 359
Fitzgerald, Patrick 2
Fitzpatrick, Jim 192
Fitzpatrick, Seán 552
Fitzsimons, Jack. *Bungalow Bliss* 262, 264, 265, 273
Flanagan, Monsignor Edward 515–16
Flanagan, Oliver J. 109–10
Flannelly, Adrian 374
Flatley, Michael 501, 506–7
Flynn, Declan 394
Flynn, Eileen 396, 397–8, 403–4, 437
Flynn, Elizabeth 358–9
Flynn, Gerard Mannix, *Nothing to Say* 518
Flynn, Pádraig 424–5, 427
Flynn, Tom 365
Foley, Des 220, 223
Food Venture Fund (FVF) 445
football 217–18, 226
foreign direct investment (FDI) 493–4
Forristal, Desmond 85
Fortune, Seán 403–4
'Forty Shades of Green' (song) 176
Fox, Eileen 109

Fox, Noel 455, 456
Franciscans 197–8
free trade 13, 26, 30, 32, 34–6
Freeman, Merritt E. 92
Friel, Brian 504–5
Dancing at Lughnasa 499–500, 501, 507
The Mundy Scheme 188
Translations 282
Frizzell's fish shop (West Belfast) bomb (23 October 1993) 464–5, 466, 469, 469–70, 474
Fuller, Bridie 361, 365
Furze, John 456–7
FVF *see* Food Venture Fund

G&M *see* Guinness & Mahon
GAA *see* Gaelic Athletic Association
Gaelic Athletic Association (GAA) 24, 145, 147, 216, 258, 376, 514
Gaj, Margaret 208
Gallagher, Matt 311
Gallagher, Patrick 311, 317
Galway County Council 346
Gandon, James 312
Gannon, Seán 394
Garda, Gardaí 161, 167, 280, 285, 300, 351–2, 355, 356, 360–1, 365, 404, 419, 427
Gargan, Bridie 351–2
Gate Theatre, Dublin 11
The Gathering (An Tóstal) 13–14, 15
Gaughan, Michael 250, 252
General Agreement on Tariffs and Trade (GATT) 34
General Post Office, Dublin 77, 133–4, 141, 147
Gibbon, Monk 245
Gibson, Chloe 85
Girl Guides 275
Giuliani, Rudi 379
Glackin, Brendan 69
Glasnevin Cemetery, Dublin 68
Glassie, Henry 231
Goldenbridge industrial school 519
Goldin, Paul 190
Good, Father James 168, 248–9
Goodman International 441
Goodman, Larry 416, 417, 440–6, 448–9
Gopaleen, Myles na 38, 258
Grady, Abe 236, 237
Granada TV 86, 107
Grand Cypress hotel, Orlando 451–2, 458–60
Grand Hyatt Hotel, New York 433
Grant, Margaret 225
Great Blasket Island 362
Great Famine (1840s) 35
Greendoor coffee shop, Patrick Street (Cork) 169
Greenville Hall *see* United Hebrew Congregation synagogue, South Circular Road (Dublin)
Gregory, Augusta 505
Cuchulain of Muirthemne 192–3
Grehan, Ida 102
Gresham Hotel, Dublin 147–8
Grey, Bennie 137–8
Grey, Ken 140
Greysteel massacre (30 October 1993) 470, 474
Griffin, Bill 448
Griffin, John 357
Griffith, Arthur 117
Groarke, Vona, 'The Lighthouse' 60
Groomes Hotel, Dublin 419
Guéguinou, Jean 238
Guinness & Mahon (G&M) bank 374, 380, 384, 385–7, 389–90, 448, 456
Guinness Mahon Cayman Trust 384, 389

Hagman, Larry 370, 373
Hall, Tammany 529
Hall, Tom T. 269
Hallahan, Paul 496
Hamilton, Phyllis 344, 434, 435
Hammarskjöld, Dag 72
Hanafin, Des 388
Handelsblatt 371
Hanlon, James 511–12, 513, 515
Harnden, Toby 482
Harney, Mary 537–8
Harris, Robert 'Pino' 416
Hartnett, Michael 189, 194
Haughey Boland (accountancy firm) 384
Haughey, Charles 86, 107, 129, 149, 193, 194, 217, 245, 249, 258, 273, 279, 280, 281, 287, 302, 347, 352, 354–5, 356, 375, 409, 490, 491
finance and lifestyle 304–7, 308–17, 372–4, 380, 384, 387, 388, 389, 399–400, 416, 417–18, 444–50, 455–8, 460–3, 528, 535
resignation 244, 425–6, 458
sexual morality 315, 316, 400, 404, 409, 410–15, 417, 458
tribunal of inquiry 460–3
The Spirit of the Nation 311
Haughey, Ciarán 457
Haughey, Maureen 306, 309, 314, 316
Have Gun – Will Travel (TV series, 1957–63) 90–1

Hayes Code 88
Hayes, Joanne 360–3, 364, 365, 411
Hayes, Kathleen 361–2
Hayes, Mary 361–2
Hayes, Ned 361
Health (Family Planning) Bill (1979) 411
Healy, John 71, 169–70, 419
Heaney, Denis 268
Heaney, Seamus 21–2, 278, 506
Heath, Edward 226
Heffernan, Margaret 460
Heffernan, Willy 64, 66–7, 72, 73, 74, 75, 76–7, 78
Helga (documentary, 1968) 342
Hely-Hutchinson, Mark 382
Hendrix, Jimmi 193
Hennessy, Brother Patrick 130
Henry, Dr Mary 171
Herman's Klipjoint (unisex hair salon), Crumlin 191
Hewitt, Jackie 469, 470
Hewitt, John 278
Hibernia journal 441
Higgins, Michael D. 245
The High Chaparral (TV series) 266
Hilditch, Stanley 328, 329
Hillery, Patrick 421
hippies 190–1
Ho-Ga-Na-She 92
Hoedown (TV show) 142
Hoerhammer, Joe 240
Hogan, Caelainn 345
Holford, Sir William 150
Holinshed, Raphael, *Chronicles* 53
Holland, Mary 203
Holocaust 157
Holy Faith Convent, New Ross (Co. Wexford) 396, 403
homecoming 501, 503–10, 515
homosexuals, homosexuality 348–9, 393–5, 398
Honohan, Patrick 555
Hoppy (Christian Brothers teacher) 127–9, 130
Horgan, John 211
Horslips (Celtic rock band) 193, 194
Hot Press magazine 410, 414
houses, housing 53–63, 150–2, 162–6, 311, 551
see also property development
Howard, Paul (aka Ross O'Carroll-Kelly) 536
Hoyle, Fred, *Ossian's Ride* 3–5
Hughes, Brendan 229, 327, 329, 331
Hughes, Francis 330
Humanae Vitae (1968) 168, 171
Hume, John 332, 473–4, 480–1
Humperdinck, Engelbert 266
Humphreys, Alexander 58–9, 202
hunger strikes 147–8, 250–4, 321, 324, 327, 329–35, 336, 376, 483
see also political prisoners
Hussein, Saddam 445–6, 448
Hutchinson, Pearse 278
Hyde Park, London 176, 191
Hydson, Gary 5

IDA *see* Industrial Development Authority
'If We Only Had Old Ireland Over Here' (song) 490
IMF *see* International Monetary Fund
In Dublin 304
independence 2–3, 26, 39, 116–18, 124
Independent International Commission on Decommissioning (1997) 486, 488
Industrial Development Authority (IDA) 4, 38, 371, 377, 494
The Art of Attraction 494–5, 496
industrial schools 291–2, 512–21, 526, 550, 567
Inishnabro 5
Inishvicillaun 354, 372
INLA *see* Irish National Liberation Army
Institute for Industrial Research and Standards 29–30, 31
Insurrection (TV series, 1966) 138, 139, 140, 147
Intel Ireland 492–3
International Monetary Fund (IMF) 34, 547, 556
International Planned Parenthood organization 348
internment 213, 217, 219
Into Europe (TV series) 239
IPLO *see* Irish People's Liberation Organisation
IRA *see* Irish Republican Army
Iraq 445–50
Ireland at Home (proposed festival) 14
Ireland is Building (1950) 54
Irish Air Corps 251–2, 354
Irish army 66–9, 72–8, 275
Irish Brigade 182
Irish Catholic 23, 111
Irish Central Bank 380
Irish Collie Club 324–5
Irish Congress of Trade Unions 454–5
Irish Constitution 49–50
Irish Countrywomen's Association 61–2

Irish culture (musical, oral, artistic) 186–95, 499–510, 521, 550
see also named individuals; songs, singers
Irish Examiner 358
Irish Export Board (Córas Tráchtála) 37
Irish Farmers Journal 70, 247
Irish Financial Services Centre, Dublin 535
Irish Free State 2–3
Irish Great Leap Forward 494
Irish identity 25, 146, 150, 248, 251, 284, 423–4, 481, 486–7, 504–10, 560, 567–70
Irish Independent 77, 248, 297, 298, 337, 514
Irish Medical Association 171, 280–1
Irish National Liberation Army (INLA) 327, 328
Irish Nationwide 554
Irish People's Liberation Organisation (IPLO) 466
Irish Permanent Building Society 400
Irish Pharmaceutical Union 170
Irish Press 2, 20, 41, 42, 62, 93, 137, 150, 200, 208, 256, 314, 370, 512, 516
Irish Red Cross 161
Irish Republican Army (IRA) 11–12, 13, 20–6, 91, 116, 117, 133–4, 142, 179, 182, 213, 223, 224–9, 250–3, 284–5, 286, 324–5, 328, 329, 331–5, 441, 455, 464–75, 478, 479–89, 526
see also hunger strikes; political prisoners
Irish Supreme Court 341–2, 394, 395, 414, 429, 525
Irish Times 9, 14, 15, 16–17, 29, 38, 68, 75, 78, 79, 92, 102, 140, 150, 170, 187, 204, 205, 208, 238, 279, 283, 336, 351, 411, 419, 427, 429, 431, 433, 435, 438, 452, 460, 518, 536, 537
Irish tourist board (Bord Fáilte) 200
Irish Trade Fair, Manhattan (1968) 455
Irish Transport System (Córas Iompair Éireann, CIE) 8
Irish Union of School Students 130
Irish Women's Liberation Movement (IWLM) 208–9, 210, 211, 212, 213
Irish-Americans 14, 19, 38, 87–8, 142–3, 435–6, 501
Island of Ireland, Dubai 533–6
IWLM *see* Irish Women's Liberation Movement

Jadotville, siege of (1961) 64–5, 67, 72–8
Jaeger House Ballroom, New York 142
Jagger, Mick 176
Jesse James Tavern, Asdee 365–7
Jesuits 17–18, 117, 202, 307
Jetland ballroom, Limerick 270Barrowland ballroom, New Ross 270
Jewish Cemetery *see* Dolphin's Barn Jewish Cemetery, Dublin
Jewish Holy Burial Society 156
JFK *see* Kennedy, John Fitzgerald
John Paul II, Pope 276–9, 283, 284–6, 287–8, 344
John XXII, Pope 104
Johnston, Máirín 208
Jones, Brian 176
Jordan, John 278
Jordan, Neil 517
Jorgensen, Ib 102
Joyce, James 17, 19
Finnegans Wake 352
Ulysses 10–11, 137, 155, 517, 534
Joyce, Joe, *The Boss* (with P. Murtagh) 315
JPMorgan Chase 549
Just In-Casey (condom jokes) 438

Kastrop, Hans 556
Katanga, Katanganese 64–5, 73, 74–8
Kavanagh, Paul 417
Keane, John B. 245
Sive 46–9, 50–1, 85
Keane, Ronan 315
Keane, Terry 315, 316, 400, 404, 417, 458
Keating, Justin 239, 245
Keats, John 569
Kelly, Eamonn 81–2, 89, 565
Kelly, Grace 87–8, 308
Kelly, James 244
Kelly, John (IRA activist) 244
Kelly, John V. (auctioneer) 97
Kelly, Luke 245
Kelly, Monsignor James 431
Kelly, Morgan 552
Kennedy, Geraldine 355, 411
Kennedy, Jackie 100, 104
Kennedy, Joe 94–5
Kennedy, John Fitzgerald (JFK) 94–101, 132–3, 237, 278, 292, 309, 310, 312, 372, 396
Kennedy, Robert 211
Kennelly, Brendan 278
Kenny, Mary 200, 208
Kerr, Adrian 180
Kerry Babies (1984) 357–8, 359, 360–5, 411, 425, 439
Kevin Barry (song) 232

Kielty, Brendan 182
Kilcock 419
Kilkenny Social Services Conference (1970) 204
King, Martin Luther 211
Kinsella, Thomas 148, 194
'A Country Walk' 148
Kinvara, Co. Galway 70
Knights of Columbanus 275, 279
Knock, Co. Mayo 43
known unknowns 168–70, 229–30, 305, 524–5
Koster, Herman 191

La Mon hotel bombing (1978) 325
Labour Party 201, 245, 338, 407, 449, 527, 557
LacLochlainn, Brian, *A Week in the Life of Martin Cluxton* 517–18
Lamb (film, 1985) 518
Lampedusa, Giuseppe Tomasi di, *The Leopard* 41–2
Laredo, Texas 142
Larkin, Celia 523–4, 528
Larkin, James 58
Larkin, Jim 360
Las Vegas 266, 267
The Last Temptation of Christ (film, 1988) 360
The Late Late Show (TV series) 105–13, 130, 200, 279, 374, 408, 418, 421, 426, 438
see also television
Lawlor, Liam 445
le Brocquy, Louis 194
Le Coq Hardi restaurant, Dublin 400, 417
Le Monde 542
Leader's Allowance 373, 399–400
Lee, Joe 420, 543–4
Legion of Mary 161
Leixlip, Co. Kildare 492–3
Lemass, Seán 13, 14, 26, 30, 33, 39, 52, 73, 85, 87, 107, 117, 139, 149, 179, 188, 201, 239–40, 249, 261, 306, 309, 312, 412, 454
Leneghan, Joseph 87
Lenihan, Brian 377, 387, 416–26, 447, 514, 555–6
Lennon, Monsignor James 275
Lentin, Louis 139, 519
Leonard, Hugh 138
Leonard, Sister Pauline 398
Letterfrack industrial school 291, 514, 517, 518
Levine, June 208, 211, 214
Lewis, Diane 235–6
LGBTQ 399, 562, 567
Liani, Dmitra 411
Liberty Hall, Dublin 234
Limerack Rural Survey (1962) 502
Limerick District Court 71
Limerick Leader 236
Listowel Drama Group 46
Lithuania in the World (government publication, 2005) 541
Little Plum (Christian Brother) 196–7
Littleton, Michael 282
The Live Mike (TV series) 273–4
Locke, Jeremiah 361, 365, 411
Lockhart, Jim 193
Long Kesh 326, 337, 485
Longley, Michael 278
Loughman, Tony 267–8, 271, 272
Loughrea, Co. Galway 109
Lourdes 43
Lowe, General 139
Lowry, Michael 457–8, 460
Loyalists 213, 226, 230–1, 233, 329, 464, 467, 478, 482, 526, 567
Lucey, Cornelius, Bishop of Cork 169
Lumumba, Patrice 64, 65
Lunn, Joan 225
Luykx, Albert 244
Lynch, Jack 122, 216, 218, 226, 242, 243–5, 287, 309, 314, 317, 344, 412, 446
Lynch, Kevin 363
Lynch, Liam 117
Lynott, Phil 193, 216
Lyttle, John 482
Lyttle, Tommy 'Tucker' 482

Mac an tSaoi, Máire 65, 76, 147
Mac Stiofáin, Seán 232
MacAmlaigh, Dónall 31–2
McAnally, Ray 139, 192
MacAnna, Tomás 145
MacAonghusa, Prionsias 85, 309, 311
Macarthur, Malcolm 353–5
McAuley, Muriel 152
McAuley, Oscar 152
McBride, Steve 476
McBrien, Owney 232
McCabe, Joseph 377
McCafferty, Nell 202, 208, 215, 226–7, 326
McCaig brothers (Joseph & John) 213
McCain, John 541–2
McCann, Daniel 224
McCann, Eamonn 227
McCann, Susan 268–9, 272–3
McCann, Tommy 224, 226
McCartan, Patrick 238
McCarthy, John 41
McCartney, Rose 231
McCaughren, Tom 103
McClean, Revd Lucius 199
MacClelland, Alan 17
Bloomsday (adaptation of *Ulysses*) 10–11, 19
McClenaghan, David 230
McClosky, Francis 178, 179
McConville, Jean 231
McCreesh, Raymond 330
McCreevy, Charlie 424–5
MacCurtain, Tomás 117
McCutchan, Mary 208
McDermott, Alice 510

McDermott, Seán 147, 152
McDonagh, Martin 510
MacDonagh, Thomas 152
McDonald, Frank, *The Builders* (with K. Sheridan) 540
McDonnell, Thomas, Bishop of Killala 211–12
McEntee, Seán 33
McGahern, John 15, 172
McGee, Mary 279, 342
McGennis, Father Paul 165–6, 401
McGeown, Pat 335, 483
McGonigal, Liam 387
MacGowan, Shane 510
McGrath, Tom 108
McGuinness, Martin 227, 229, 482, 487–8
MacIntyre, Tom, 'An Aspect of the Rising' 148
McKearney, Tommy 286–7, 334, 488
McKenna, Seán 327
McKenna, Siobhán 245
McKeown, Seán 65, 73
McLaughlin, Patrick 302–3
MacLaverty, Bernard, *Lamb* 518
MacLiammóir, Micheál (aka Michael Wilmore) 145–6
McLoughlin, Jim 378
McManus, Noel 170–1
McNab, Patrick 502
McNamara, Kevin, Archbishop of Dublin 113
McNamara, Ryan 402
McNamee, Father James ('Father Smack My Gee') 166–8
McNulty, Sister Hildegarde 206
McPhillips, Séamus 101
McQuaid, John Charles, Archbishop of Dublin 10, 17–21, 30, 68, 77, 85, 86, 107, 113, 145, 158, 162–7, 168, 205, 211, 240, 249, 315, 401, 522, 550–1
MacRory, Cardinal Joseph 502
MacSherry, Ray 356
MacSwiney, Terence 250, 251, 332
McWilliams, David 551
Madden, Andrew 401–2, 522–3
Magdalene Laundries 206–8, 279, 302, 361, 513
Magherafelt courthouse 21–2
Magill magazine 280, 304, 402
The Magnificent Seven (film, 1960) 141
Maguire, Frank 332
Maher, Mary 208
Maidstone, Kent 176–8
Major, John 474
Mallon, Seamus 488
The Man's House pub, Leonard's Corner, Dublin 209
Mansfield, Jill 225
Mara, P.J. 411
Marchal, Georges 66
Markievicz, Constance 138
Marks & Spencer (M&S) 454
marriage 8–10, 49–50, 62, 182, 198, 199, 201–2, 209, 279–81, 395, 396–9, 399, 401–2, 436–7, 524, 561
Marrinan, John 129
Marshall Plan (1948) 29, 33, 37
Martin, Micheál 513
martyrs 68, 104, 117, 141, 142–3, 143–4, 148, 179, 181, 232–3, 245, 251, 331, 334, 472, 522
Marx, Father Paul 342, 343, 345
Masonic-Jewish-Communists 21, 23
Mathers, Joanne 333
Maudling, Reginald 221, 263, 477
Mayflower Hotel, Washington 94–5
Maynooth College 106, 405, 492, 526
Mayo Clinic, Minnesota 417, 418
Mayo News 252
Meath VEC 109
medical devices companies 493
Mellowes, Liam 117
'The Men Behind the Wire' (song) 217
Mi-Tsi-Ga 92
Mighty Morphin Power Rangers 476–7
migrants, migration 1, 10, 14–15, 17, 25–6, 28, 31–2, 36, 95, 97, 134, 142–3, 251, 268–9, 296, 336, 371–2, 374–9, 392–3, 399, 490, 501, 503, 508–9, 538, 544, 558, 566
Millisle, Co. Down 469
Mise Éire (documentary film, 1959) 147, 186
Miss Cossie (racehorse) 308
Mitchell, George 484
modernization 102, 243, 295, 372, 395, 453, 504–5, 540–1, 565, 566
monetary policy 32–3
money, class & ascendancy 304–17
Monkstown, Eaton Place 44–5
Monnet, Jean 242
Monroe, Marilyn 97
Montague, John 278
Montrose House, Dublin 105
Moore, Chris 527
Moore, James 470
Moore, Seán 94
Moriarty, Eileen 358
Morrison, Danny 480
Mother and Baby Homes 204–8, 302, 344–6, 433, 513
Mountbatten, Lord Louis 284, 324

Mountcharles, Lord Henry 458
Mountjoy Jail, Dublin 12–13
Moy, Co. Tyrone 12
Mulcahy, Orna 536
Mulcahy, Richard 121
Mulholland, Revd Charles 25
Mullaghmore 284
Munich air disaster (1958) 25
Munongo, Godefroid 65, 74, 75
Munton, Cherie 225
murder 351–6, 359, 360–5, 394, 470, 477
see also bombs, bombing; violence
Murphy, Annie 406, 431–2, 433, 434, 435, 438–9, 461
Murphy, Lenny 230
Murphy, Mike 360
Murphy Report into clerical abuse (2009) 550
Murphy, Richard 278
Murphy, Tom
Conversations on a Homecoming 505
On the Outside 51, 85
Murray, Leanne 464
Murtagh, Paddy 92
Murtagh, Peter, *The Boss* (with Joe Joyce) 315
music, musicians *see* songs, singers
myths and legends 184, 189–90, 192–3, 194

Nangle, Tom 355
'A Nation Once Again' (song) 217, 222
National City Brokers 531
National Competitiveness Council 545
National Coordinating Committee on Drug Abuse (1985) 300–1
National Farmers' Association 29
National Organisation of Ex-Servicemen 145
nationalists, nationalism 1, 3, 10, 20, 22, 23–7, 117–18, 138, 181, 187, 219, 413, 442, 467, 474, 508, 564, 565, 567
Nazis 154–5, 174, 241, 244, 323, 505, 515
Nelson, Horatio 132–4, 135–8, 253
New Lodge, West Belfast 465–6
New Ross 96, 97
New York Post 354
New York Times 378, 538
Newman, Angela 192
Newman, Jeremiah, Bishop of Limerick 122
Newman, John Henry 256
Newman, W.A. 150
Newsweek 377
Newtownbutler, Co. Fermanagh 224
NFFC *see* Nottingham Forest Football Club
Ní Chonaola, Mairéad 438
NICRA *see* Northern Ireland Civil Rights Association
Niemba massacre, Katanga (1960) 67–70, 72
Nikkei Business 371
Nixon, Richard 422
Nolan, Sean 70
Noonan, Michael 410, 549–50
Norris, David 394, 395
North Atlantic Treaty Organization (NATO) 33, 34, 99
Northern Ireland 20, 22, 135, 179, 180–1, 187, 226, 231–2, 284, 287, 478, 479, 480, 481, 485, 486–9, 569
Northern Ireland Civil Rights Association (NICRA) 180, 181
Northern Ireland Constitution Act (1973) 487
Norton, Ray 534
Nottingham Forest Football Club (NFFC) 116
Nowlan, Professor Kevin B. 140

Ó Broin, León 87
Ó Cannain, Tomás 187
Ó Catháin, Gearóid 1, 2–3
Ó Catháin, Revd Sean 202
Ó Ciobhain, Blaithín 88–9
Ó Conaill, Dáithí 334
Ó Criomhthain, Tomás 1
Ó Dalaigh brothers 372
Ó Dálaigh, Cearbhall 118
Ó Dalaigh, Tony 419
Ó Faolúns, Seán, 'The Trout' 109–10
Ó Faracháin, Roibéard 18
Ó Fiaich, Tomás 327
Ó hEithir, Breandán, *Begrudger's Guide to Irish Politics* 310
Ó hEithir, Micheál 129
O. Henry, 'The Caballero's Way' 89
Ó Móráin, Micheál 71, 293
Ó Muilleoir, Mairtín 471
Ó Riada, Seán (aka John Reidy) 185–9, 193, 194–5, 249
Ó Súileabháin, Muiris 1
O'Brien, Conor Cruise 65, 72–3, 74, 76, 78, 147, 181–2, 354, 407
O'Brien, Edna 203
The Country Girls 85–6, 214
The Lonely Girl 86
The Wedding Dress 86
O'Brien, Flann (aka Myles na Gopaleen) 14, 17, 19, 150
O'Brien, John 16–17
O'Brien, Kate 203
O'Brien, Vincent 373
Observer 95
O'Byrne, Father Simon 345
O'Callaghan, Owen 530

O'Carroll, Detective Sergeant Gerry 361, 362
O'Casey, Sean 17, 18, 19, 59
Juno and the Paycock 491
The Drums of Father Ned 11
The Plough and the Stars 46, 138–9
O'Clery, Conor 431
O'Connell, Daniel 360
O'Connell, Maurice 384
O'Connell Schools 117
O'Connor, Father Joseph 162, 514
O'Connor, Joseph (photographer) 371
O'Connor, Pádraic 531
O'Doherty, Malachi 227
O'Dolan, John 533
O'Donnell, Pat 69
O'Donnell, Peadar 245
O'Donoghue, Martin 356
O'Donoghue, Noel 51
O'Donovan, Fred 112
O'Duffy, Eoín 182
OECD *see* Organisation for Economic Co-operation and Development
OEEC *see* Organisation for European Economic Co-operation
Offences Against the Person Act (1861) 394
Office of Public Works 120, 121
O'Flaherty, Mr Justice Hugh 526
O'Grady, Abe 236
O'Grady, Desmond 236
O'Grady, Pat 263–4
O'Grady, Sean 236
O'Grady, Stanislaus 236
O'Hanlon, Fergal 21, 24, 91, 221
O'Hara, Patsy 330
O'Hara, Philomena 238
O'Higgins, Kevin 117
O'Higgins, Tom 292, 395
oil crisis (1979) 283–4, 295
oilfield concession 447–8
Oireachtas 96
O'Keefe, Jim 93–4, 292
O'Kelly, Seán T. 34
Olympia Theatre, Dublin 188, 190
O'Mahony, Donal 401–2
O'Malley, Desmond 411, 422, 449
O'Malley, Donogh 23, 122–3, 387, 416
O'Malley, Ernie 117
O'Neill, Terence 179
Operation Morthor (1961) 74
O'Reilly-Hyland, Ken 386–8
Organisation for Economic Co-operation and Development (OECD) 134, 336, 540, 545
Organisation for European Economic Co-operation (OEEC) 33, 35
O'Shannon, Cathal 78, 237
O'Sullivan, T.J. 222
O'Toole, Peter 47
Our Boys (comic) 115, 124–6
Our Lady of Sorrows, Ballina 251–2
Our Lady's Children's Hospital, Crumlin 165, 166, 401, 522
Owens, Ann 225–6

paedophiles 165–8, 196–8, 401–4, 515
see also child sexual abuse
Paisley, Ian 478
Pan American Airlines 14, 15
Papandreou, Andreas 411
Parachute Regiment 219, 225
Parker, Stephen 231
Parnell, Charles Stewart 56
Parr, Jack 108
'The Patriot Game' (song) 233
Paul, Michael 263–4
Paul VI, Pope 168, 249
Payne, Father Ivan 166, 401–2, 522–3
peace process 478–89
Peacock Theatre, Dublin 72, 189
Pearse, Patrick 115, 132, 141, 147, 152, 187, 251, 287
'The Mother' 141
Pender, Aidan 248
Pender, Michael 390
People's Democracy group 180–1
pharmaceuticals companies 493
Philbin, William, bishop of Clonfert 42
Phoenix Park 279, 373
PIIGS acronym 549, 559
the Pillar, Dublin 132–4, 135–7, 152
Pilot View, Dalkey 353–4
Pius XI, Pope 203
PLAC *see* Pro-Life Amendment Campaign
Playhouse Theatre, Limerick 46
Plunkett, Saint Oliver 275–6
The Pogues 510
political prisoners 318–35, 337, 370, 485–6
see also hunger strikes
Pompidou, Georges 242
Porter, Cole, 'Always True To You' 18
Portumna Carnival 142
Pound, Ezra 294
Lustra 186
Power, Declan 66
Presbyterian Church 145
pregnancy 203–8
Prendergast, Peter 360
Price sisters (Marian & Dolours) 325
Price Waterhouse (accountants) 460
priests, priesthood 159–65

Prisonniers de la brousse (*Prisoners of the Congo*) (film, 1960) 66, 69
Private Eye 400
Pro-Life Amendment Campaign (PLAC) 338, 342, 346–7, 349, 395
Proclamation of the Irish Republic 141, 332
Programme for Economic Expansion (White Paper, 1958) 39
Project Arts Centre, Dublin 517
property development 533–40, 551, 552
see also houses, housing
protectionism 30–1, 33, 35, 38–43
Protestants 23, 115, 175, 180, 182, 187, 223, 324–5, 398, 480, 481, 567
see also sectarianism
Provisional Army Council 213
Provisional IRA ('Provos') 222, 225, 226, 228–9, 244, 251, 285, 328, 334
Public Dance Halls Act (1935) 502–3
punishment shootings 479–80
'Put our Sweet Lips A Little Closer To The Phone' (song) 274
Pye, Patrick 278

Quane, Blanaid 359
Quigley, Senator J.B. 110
Quinlan, Patrick 64, 67, 73–4, 75, 77
Quinn, Bob 2
Quinn, Nobby 444

racism 70–2, 103–4, 180
Radio Éireann 18, 118, 119
Rafidain Bank 446
Raftery, Mary 518–21
rape 167, 209, 340, 349, 357, 403, 416, 427–8, 430
Rasquin, Françoise 66
RDF (French radio station) 186
Reagan, Ronald 405
Reddy, Tony 538
Redmond, Owen 121
Reeves, Jim 176, 268, 269, 274
Reidy, Sergeant Patrick 357–8
Reilly, Private Terence 275
religion-politics fusion 411–15, 423–4, 508, 509, 525–32
religious beliefs 408–9
religious certainty, sexuality and hypocrisy 159–74, 196–9
Republic of Ireland 15, 135, 182, 231–2, 286, 337–8, 478, 485
Republican News 228
Republicans 20–1, 213, 247, 252–3, 468, 471, 479–80, 480
Responsible Society 349
Resurrection: the Easter Pageant (Aiséiri: Glóir Réim na Cásca) 145, 146
Reynolds, Albert 270, 426–7, 440, 445–6, 447–50, 473, 474–5, 526, 527
Rice, Edmund Ignatius 116, 117, 119, 130
Richards, Shelagh 85
Richardson, Des 531
riddles 115–16
right to life *see* abortion; contraception; Mother and Baby Homes
Riordan, Moyra 169
The Riordans (TV soap opera) 189
Rippon, Geoffrey 242
Riverdance 500, 501, 506, 508, 509
Robinson, Liam 2
Robinson, Mary 211–12, 421, 424, 424–5, 461, 535
Roche, Brother 118
Roche, Richie 396
Roches Stores, Dublin 93–4, 102
Rock, Dickie 134, 135
Roe v. Wade (1973) 342
'Róisín Dubh'(song) 186
The Rolling Stones 176, 191
The Rose of Tralee festival 14
Rostrevor, Co. Down 453
Roth, Edward J. 88, 90
Rotunda Hospital, Dublin 434
Rowley, Ellen 57
Royal College of Surgeons 346
Royal Institute of Architects 538
Royal Irish Rangers 229
Royal Ulster Constabulary (RUC) 178–9, 180, 355, 468
Rozier, Willy 66
RTÉ Authority 112
RTÉ broadcaster 138–9, 141, 186, 189, 219–20, 237, 239, 273, 282, 503, 517, 531
RUC *see* Royal Ulster Constabulary
Rush, Kevin 242
Russell, Jane 206
Ryan, Dermot, Archbishop of Dublin 167, 402
Ryan, Elizabeth 359
Ryan, Noel 397
Ryan Report on Industrial Schools (2009) 516, 550
Ryan, Richie 292–3
Ryanair generation 378–9

Sadurski, Jennifer 345
Saint Agnes's, Crumlin 166
Saint Bernadette's Church, Clogher Road (Crumlin) 93, 158–65, 172–3, 292, 550–1
St Bricin's Military Hospital, Dublin 13

St Catherine of Alexandria 42
Saint Eoin's Well, Co. Kerry 366
St Gallen 241
Saint Gobnait's, Cúil Aodha 184–6
St Joseph's CBS, Marino 191
St Joseph's Rehabilitation Centre, Dublin 238
Saint Margaret's convent, Canning Town (London) 175–6
St Mary Magdalen's Asylum, Dublin 207
St Mary's Church, Asdee 358–60, 367
St Nicholas Collegiate Church, Galway 100
St Peter's diocesan school, Wexford 403
saints 240, 241
Salinger, Pierre 101
Salmond, Alec 541
Salzburg 241
same-sex marriage 561–2
San Antonio, Rexas 433
Sands, Bobby 328–34, 335, 336, 337, 346
Sanger, Margaret 348
Savile, Jimmy 193–4
Sayers, Peig 1, 362
Scappaticci, Freddie 489
Scenario for Peace (1987) 480
Schlesinger, Arthur 99
Scoil Íosagáin (primary school), Crumlin 119, 122, 123, 126–7, 141
Scorses, Martin 360
Sean Dunphy and The Hoedowners 142
Sean Ross Abbey, Co. Tipperary 206
'Seán South of Garryowen' (song) 23, 217, 232
Seán South (song) 232
Second World War 3, 32, 60, 145, 150, 154–5, 174, 177, 240
sectarianism 178–82, 213, 225, 464–75
see also Catholics; Protestants
Seery, Father 172–3
Selma-Montgomery march (1966) 180
'Send Me No Roses' (song) 366
Sevcik, Sonia 240–1
Seven Men, Seven Days (*Seachtar Fear, Seacht Lá*) pageant 147
sex education 202–3
sex, sexuality 169–71, 173, 199–209, 211–12, 213–15, 271, 272–3, 348, 359, 406–7
see also child sexual abuse
sexual morality 204–8, 211–12, 313–14, 315–16, 396–9, 425, 436–8, 526, 539
Shakespeare, William
Antony and Cleopatra 462
Macbeth 192
Othello 462
Shankill Butchers 230
Shankill Community Council 469
Shankill Road, West Belfast 464–7, 469–70, 472, 474
Shanley, Lily 192
Shattenhemel, Dr 240
Shaw, George Bernard *see* Bernard Shaw, George
Sheehy, Eugene 546–7
Sheehy, Monsignor Gerard 401, 402
Sheridan brothers (Jim & Peter) 517
Sheridan, Kathy, *The Builders* (with F. McDonald) 540
Sherwin, Frank 91–2, 201
Shields, Corporal James 275
Shinwell, 'Manny' 12
Shipquay Street (Derry) bomb (23 March 1972) 228
Siemens 59–60
Silverstein, Shel (singer) 451
Simmons, James 233
Sinatra, Frank 97
Sinn Féin 213, 224–5, 245, 327, 332, 334, 465, 466, 468, 470–1, 473, 476, 479–89
Sinn Féin Árd Fheis 480, 481, 486, 487
Sister Frances 344
Sisters of Charity 344, 396, 397
Sisters of Mercy 519
Skuse, Corporal Frank (aka Paul Murphy) 12–13, 22
slaves, slavery 180, 207
see also child slavery
Sligo Champion 103
Smith, George Ivan 76
The Smokey Mountain Ramblers 269–70
Smyth, Brendan 527
Smyth, Noel 460
Sneem, Co. Kerry 238
Sniffer Cohen 155–7
Snow, Hank 269
Soames, Christopher 12
Social Democratic and Labour Party (SDLP) 285, 332, 473
social mobility 117–18, 119
social revolution 255–61
Society for the Protection of Unborn Children (SPUC) 347–8, 414
songs, singers 134, 135, 141–5, 176, 180, 186, 191, 193, 216–17, 218, 221, 222, 231–2, 233, 266–74, 365–6, 370–1, 490, 510
see also Irish culture (musical & oral)
The Soul of Our Vocation (Christian Brothers internal guidebook) 130–1

South (or Sabhat), Seán 21, 22–3, 24, 91, 221, 251
Southern Star 71
Spaak, Paul-Henri 34
Special Branch 244
Special Forces 480
Special Government Task Force on Drug Abuse (1983) 300
Spirit of the Nation 412, 418
Spring, Dick 449
Springfield, Massachusetts 1
SPUC *see* Society for the Protection of Unborn Children
Stack, Austin 117
Stacy May consultancy 27, 38, 440
Stagg, Frank 250–4, 331
States of Fear (documentary, 1999) 518–21
Stein, Gertrude 495
Steinbeck, John, *East of Eden* 435
Steinbock of Moosburg 240–1
Stella Maris soccer club 166
Stenson, Father Alec 401
Stevens, Tony 365–6
Stillorgan Shopping Centre, Dublin 149
stories, story-telling 80, 81–2, 89, 124–6, 362, 363, 364, 366, 565
Stormont 226, 482
The Storytellers (backing group) 268
Stradbally, Co. Laois 70
Stronge, Sir Norman 324
Sugrue, Butty 138, 235
Sullivan, John 357
Sunday Independent 16, 49, 129, 199, 458
Sunday News 227
Sunday Press 315
Sunday Times Magazine 308–9
Sunday Tribune 371
Sunningdale Agreement (9 December 1973) 478, 487
supernatural 358–60, 363, 365–9
Sutcliffe, Liam 135
Swadlinbar, Cavan 231–2
Swatragh, Co. Kerry 413
Sweetman, Father Michael 292
Sweetman sisters (Rosita & Inez) 208
'Sylvia's Mother' (song) 451
'Sympathy For The Devil' (song) 176
Synge, John M. 56–7, 505
  The Playboy of the Western World 46, 233, 253
Synge Street CBS 118, 119, 122, 129, 191, 198

Taca 387
Taheny, Jimmy 67
tax, taxation 380–91, 541–2, 543
Taylor, Cliff 460
Telecom Éireann 426
Telefís Éireann (TÉ) 82, 83, 84, 85, 86–92, 111, 200
television 80–92, 82, 119, 138–9, 140, 142, 372, 507
Temple Hill, Dublin 344–5, 396
terrorists, terrorism 137, 319, 468, 473, 484
Thatcher, Margaret 333, 335
theatrical performances 10–11, 46–9, 50–1, 71–2
Thin Lizzy (rock band) 216
  Vagabonds of the Western World 193
Thornley, David 338
Thurber, James 363
Tidy, Fred 143–4, 145
tit-for-tat killings 464–75
The Tonight Show (US TV series) 108
Toomevara Carnival 142
Top Rank organisation 267–8
Touhey, Patsy 503
town planning 150–2
Tracy, Honor 1
Tracy, Spencer 515
tradition 149–50, 187–90, 192–5, 197–8, 506
Tralee 357, 361
Transatlantic Bridge 490–8
Traynor, Desmond 317, 384–6, 388, 390, 418, 448, 456, 457, 460–1
Traynor, Oscar 206
Treacy, Seán 71, 117
Trevaskis, Brian 109
Trinity College Dublin 211, 346, 348, 394
Tripleplan (shell company) 456
Troika programme 556–9
the Troubles 143, 178–82, 212–13, 219–34, 242–3, 244–5, 284–5, 318, 332, 335, 413, 464–75, 477–8, 485, 564
Trudden, Bernadine 146
Truman, Harry 33–4
Tshombe, Moïse 74, 76
Tuam Children's Home, Co. Galway 346
Tuam, Co. Galway 51
Turner, Martyn 429
twin-track strategy (Armalite & ballot box) 479–80
Twink (aka Adele King) 266, 267, 269, 271
Twomey, Michael 170

U2 (rock band) 459
UCD *see* University College Dublin
UDA *see* Ulster Defence Association
UFF *see* Ulster Freedom Fighters
Uí Shúilleabháin, Bean 183
Ulster Defence Association (UDA) 230, 329, 464, 482

Ulster Freedom Fighters (UFF) 464–6, 470, 471
Ulster Television 527
Ulster Volunteer Force (UVF) 230, 286
Ulster Workers' Council strike (1974) 478
Ulster Youth Orchestra 231
UN *see* United Nations
unemployment 100, 123, 134, 174, 283, 295–6, 301, 336, 376, 490, 542–3, 556, 558
Union Minière du Haut-Katanga 73
Unionists 22, 179–80, 181, 213, 217, 223, 226, 476, 478, 482
United Hebrew Congregation synagogue, South Circular Road (Dublin) 154–5
United Ireland 41, 181, 217, 225, 471, 474, 478, 480, 481–2, 488, 509, 567
United Nations (UN) 34, 64–5, 66–7, 72–3, 74, 74–8
United Press International 285
University College Cork 377
University College Dublin (UCD) 222, 255–7, 309, 339, 346, 371, 416, 522
Unknowns (IRA unit) 231
US Chamber of Commerce 92
US Immigration and Naturalization Service 378–9
US National Retail Merchants Association 454
U.S. News & World Report 541
US Supreme Court 342
UVF *see* Ulster Volunteer Force
'The Vanishing Irish' 16
Vardy, Marie 101
Vaughan, Dr Julia 347
Vesey, Arthur 15
VHI *see* Voluntary Health Insurance
Vietnam War 99, 211, 237
Villa des Roches, Elizabethville 76
'The Village Of Asdee' (song) 366
Viney, Michael 204
violence 91–2, 117, 126–31, 135, 137, 141, 178–9, 180–1, 212–13, 219–20, 221, 284, 285, 324, 394, 464–75, 477, 478, 479–80, 515–16
see also bombs, bombing; the Troubles
Voluntary Health Insurance company (VHI) 417

Waldorf Astoria, New York 146–7
Walker, Robin 150
Wall Street Journal 360, 371
Wandsworth prison, London 250
Ward, Joe 27, 29
Warrenpoint (1979) 284
Was-Be-Was-Ska-Ka 92
Waterford 116
Watergate 422
Waters, John 410
Watts riots, Los Angeles (1965) 222
'We Shall Overcome' (song) 180
West, Trevor 211
Westerns 88, 89–92, 125, 138, 140–1, 180, 266, 483
Westland Row CBS 115
Westmeath County Council 371
Wexford town 99
Whelan, Liam 25
Whelehan, Harry 427–8, 527
'When It's Round-Up Time In Heaven' (song) 142
Whitaker, T.K. 'Ken' 10, 38–40, 41, 42, 119, 121, 179, 188, 241, 242–3, 249, 261, 377–8, 453
White House, Washington DC 94, 97–8, 292
White, Jack 85
White Strand, Co. Kerry 357, 361–3, 365
Whitelaw, William 229
'Who Shot JR?' (song) 370–1
Widgery, Lord 220
Widow Mulchrone 88
Williams, Hank 269
Williamson, George & Gillian 464
Wilson, Harold 229
Wojcik, Denise 458–9
The Wolf Tones (ballad group) 216–17
Women's Coalition 482
Women's Right to Choose campaign 348
Woodfield, P.J. 229
Woods, Máire 208
Woods, Michael 343
Woolfe Robe, Chief 92
World Bank 34
Wuthering Heights (film, 1970) 342

X case (1992) 427–30, 448, 458, 525–6, 527
The X-Men (comic-book heroes) 115

Yankee Doodle Dandy (film, 1942) 503, 504, 507
Yeats, W.B. 147, 491, 505
You Are There (US TV series) 140

Zeppelin, Led, 'Stairway to Heaven' 193
Ziegler, Ron 422